D0787052

MONKS ELEIGH MANORIAL RECORDS,

1210–1683

SUFFOLK RECORDS SOCIETY

President
†David Dymond

Vice-Presidents
Robert Malster
Clive Paine

Chairman
†Victor Gray

Treasurer
Clive Mees

Co-ordinating Editor
David Sherlock

Membership Secretary
Tanya Christian

Secretary
Claire Barker
Westhorpe Lodge, Westhorpe,
Stowmarket, Suffolk IP14 4TA

Website: www.suffolkrecordssociety.com
Email: info@suffolkrecordssociety.com

Monks Eleigh Manorial Records, 1210–1683

Edited by
VIVIENNE ALDOUS

General Editor
NICHOLAS AMOR

The Boydell Press

Suffolk Records Society
VOLUME LXV

© The Trustees of the Suffolk Records Society 2022

All Rights Reserved. Except as permitted under current legislation
no part of this work may be photocopied, stored in a retrieval system,
published, performed in public, adapted, broadcast,
transmitted, recorded or reproduced in any form or by any means,
without the prior permission of the copyright owner

A Suffolk Records Society publication
First published 2022
The Boydell Press, Woodbridge

ISBN 978-1-78327-679-0
ISBN 978-1-73980-960-7 (members)

Issued to subscribing members for the year 2022

The Boydell Press is an imprint of Boydell & Brewer Ltd
PO Box 9, Woodbridge, Suffolk IP12 3DF, UK
and of Boydell & Brewer Inc.
668 Mt Hope Avenue, Rochester, NY 14620–2731, USA
website: www.boydellandbrewer.com

The publisher has no responsibility for the continued existence or accuracy of
URLs for external or third-party internet websites referred to in this book, and
does not guarantee that any content on such websites is, or will remain, accurate
or appropriate

A catalogue record for this book is available
from the British Library

This publication is printed on acid-free paper

Printed and bound in Great Britain by TJ Books Limited, Padstow, Cornwall

CONTENTS

ILLUSTRATIONS AND TABLES

DAVID DYMOND, MA, PhD, Hon. D.Litt., FSA, FRHistS, President 2012–21, an Appreciation

David Dymond was a passionate advocate for the work of record societies. He joined the Council of the Suffolk Records Society in 1966 and was president from 2012 until his death in 2021 at the age of eighty-eight. He was general editor of volumes XXXIV to L (1992–2007). During his tenure, volumes were published on documents from the fourteenth to nineteenth centuries, demonstrating his competence over a broad span of history. In 2007, he inveigled me into completing *Wills from the Register 'Baldwyne', Part II: 1461–1474* (volume LIII), commenced by Peter Northeast, and compiling the indexes to it. He was also a diligent editor of several texts: not only *The County of Suffolk Surveyed by Joseph Hodskinson, Published in 1783* (volume XV, 1972) in our main series and *The Charters of Stanton, Suffolk, c. 1215–1678* (Charters volume 18, 2009) in our charters series, but also *The Register of Thetford Priory* (2 volumes, jointly Norfolk Record Society and the British Academy, 1995 and 1996) and *The Churchwardens' Book of Bassingbourn 1496–c.1540* (Cambridgeshire Record Society 17, 2004).

David began his professional life as an investigator in the Royal Commission on Historical Monuments (RCHM), initially based in York. His work ranged way back in time: subjects of his early articles (published outside the RCHM) include bridges in Roman Britain, hillforts and prehistoric implements. His extensive knowledge of buildings and building work comes across in many of his other publications. Tucked away amongst them are two short edited texts giving details of medieval building craftsmanship: 'A Fifteenth-Century Building Contract from Suffolk' (*Vernacular Architecture* 9, 1978) and 'Five Building Contracts from Fifteenth-Century Suffolk' (*Antiquaries Journal* 78, 1998).

David was a vice-president of the Suffolk Institute of Archaeology and History. He wrote six articles in its *Proceedings* and indeed his last book was published by the institute. *The Business of the Suffolk Parish 1558–1625* (2018) outlines the wide variety of activities that occurred in early modern parishes. The discussion of the changing role of the parish and its officers is based on his own research in original parish records and some published transcripts, and also his knowledge of church buildings. It is a model publication that sold out almost immediately. He explained to me that he had forbidden a long print run; perhaps, for once, he was wrong.

David was also well known as a local historian outside his adopted county of Suffolk partly due to his various roles in the British Association for Local History

(BALH), including council member, chairman and vice-president. He edited *The Local Historian* from February 1976 to November 1982 and had several articles published in it, including his last ever article, 'The Game of Camping in Eastern England' (*TLH* 51, January 2021). (Camping, a notoriously rough East Anglian game, was a cross between football and rugby.) His own style of writing was clear, concise and informative, and he provided sage advice to others on how to write, principally through his book *Writing Local History: A Practical Guide*, first published by BALH in 1981 and revised and expanded in 1999 and 2009 as *Researching and Writing History: A Guide for Local Historians*. That this guide has been reissued twice is testament both to its popularity and to its enduring usefulness. My favourite section is that on how *not* to write: David's gentle yet probing digs at various historians (from all academic levels) who were too verbose, used obscure jargon or wrote what was, in effect, nonsense, highlight the need for clarity when writing. Two particular pieces of his advice are always worth remembering: the little word 'the' is overused and can often be deleted without changing the sense of what is being said; inanimate objects or abstract concepts cannot express emotions or move in any way.

David was known to many more through his role as staff tutor in Local and Regional History for the University of Cambridge's Board (now Institute) of Continuing Education (UCICE) from about 1993 to 2007. I first met him on a fieldtrip to Ashwell (Herts.) in the summer of 1994 and then again in November 1994 as one of the tutors on a weekend school entitled 'Unrest, Riots and Rebellions', organised by Mark Bailey. Unbeknown to me, this weekend was to shape my own development and interests as a local historian. I still have my notes on his session 'Leisure and Social Control', which covered, amongst other things, camping. These notes conclude 'games of camping in fenlands spread over the area, [they were] cover for breaking drainage mechanisms etc – "political protests"'. Some years later, a study of early modern riots against fenland drainage formed part of my PhD. David was one of the tutors who ran the UCICE Master of Studies in Local History. It is not too dramatic to claim that his informative and authoritative teaching changed the lives of many Master of Studies students. One told me 'he certainly helped mould the course of my life over the past two decades and has left a valuable and lasting legacy of local history and historians'. Both while a tutor and afterwards, he was often to be seen beavering away in the University Library and would engage in lengthy conversation during breaks in the tea room. He was a good listener who, despite his own vast experience and knowledge, was happy to seek information and advice from others, particularly on how to access sources newly available online, and he was always interested in others' research projects. I remember talking with him about local historians in terms of the 'professional' *versus* 'amateur' debate: some of that discussion reappeared (with due acknowledgement) in his arguments in 'Does Local History Have a Split Personality?', in *New Directions in Local History since Hoskins* (University of Hertfordshire Press, 2011).

David was always willing to give talks to historical societies. In April 2005, he spoke at the Eighth Triennial Conference of the Richard III Society, 'Richard III and East Anglia: Magnates, Gilds and Learned Men'. As many (but not all) attendees were only interested in a certain monarch and his immediate circle, David's talk on ordinary folk and their involvement in 'Socio-Religious Gilds of the Middle Ages' was quite an eye-opener. This new light on late-medieval life was, nevertheless, much appreciated and was subsequently published in the *Proceedings* of that conference.

The esteem in which David was held was manifested practically in 2020 when he was honoured with a Festschrift entitled *Shaping the Past: Theme, Time and Place in Local History* (University of Hertfordshire Press, Studies in Regional and Local History, volume 18). Some contributors were colleagues in various organisations, many were his former students. The subjects of their chapters, ranging in time from the early thirteenth to the early twentieth century, reflect the depth and breadth of David's own scholarship. The appendix listing his publications has no fewer than twenty-three books and fifty-eight articles. (Two articles were published subsequently.) The planned launch in St Edmundsbury cathedral was cancelled due to Covid-19 restrictions, but several contributors were able to join David and Mary in their lovely garden, where he was given a presentation copy. Although it had not been possible to keep the book a secret, David was genuinely pleased to receive it and spoke of his delight and pride in being so honoured. The University of Hertfordshire Press's representative commented that 'it was a real privilege to come along to the launch of the book and meet him in person, such a lovely man with an obviously brilliant sense of humour. I'm so pleased he got to see the book in published form.'

Given all of the above, it is not surprising that David had numerous professional and academic qualifications and awards. As early as 1964, he was elected a fellow of the Society of Antiquaries of London. He was also a fellow of the Royal Historical Society, and in 2017 the High Sheriff of Suffolk awarded him a Certificate of Recognition for his hard work and service to the county. In 2000, he received a PhD from the University of Cambridge by submission of published works (principally his *Register of Thetford Priory*) and also an Honorary Litt.D. from the University of East Anglia for services to history and education in the region. It is entirely fitting and deserved that he was Dr David Dymond twice over. More than that, he will be remembered as a gentle man and gentleman.

Heather Falvey

VICTOR GRAY, MBE, MA, FSA, Chairman 2014–21,
an Appreciation

Victor (Vic) Gray, our chairman from 2014 to 2021, died at Halesworth on 30 September 2021 after a short illness, aged seventy-four. A man of many parts and many talents, if he had a fault it was excessive modesty. Anyone who spent more than a moment with Vic soon became aware that although characteristically unaffected and self-effacing, he possessed a razor-sharp intellect combined with extraordinary shrewdness and panoptic vision. He was fond of the past but also wise and often remarkably prescient about what challenges lay ahead for the historical organisations with which he was involved, invariably in a leadership role.

These were abilities and insights honed across a long and lustrous professional and academic career. Vic graduated from King's College, Cambridge, with first-class honours in English in 1968 and then trained as a professional archivist at University College London. He gathered experience in the archives of Devon and Suffolk before becoming head of the Essex Record Office in 1978, then recognised as the most prestigious county archive in Britain. After thirteen years at Essex, Vic took up the challenge of developing the internationally renowned Rothschild Archive. Under his stewardship, the Rothschild collection's reputation as one of the world's great business archives was fortified. Vic once reflected that the job had its perks, beyond the obvious. Most organisations that employ archivists do not possess French vineyards that oblige the keepers of records to occasionally visit. He published *The Life and Times of N.M. Rothschild 1777–1836* jointly with Melanie Aspey in 1998 and contributed four articles on members of the Rothschild family for the *Oxford Dictionary of National Biography*.

The esteem with which Vic was held within his profession was reflected in his part in other senior offices and consultancies. He was chairman in turn of the Association of County Archivists, the Society of Archivists and the National Council on Archives. He held the presidency of the Society of Archivists from 2005 to 2008 and was also a board member of the Council for Museums, Libraries and Archives, acting as vice-chairman of its Archives Task Force, which reported on the state and future of British archives in 2004. He served on the Historical Manuscripts Commission and on archive advisory committees for the Lord Chancellor, the Master of the Rolls and the Church of England. After retiring from the Rothschild Archive in 2004, Vic continued to devote himself to consulting, writing and lecturing on archive matters. A keen interest in oral history led him to develop the Oral History Archive for Essex, and he was the founder chairman of the Community Archives Development Group, which supports the development of community archives across the UK. He also undertook archive development work for Faber & Faber and for the T.S. Eliot Estate.

Vic's career achievements and services to academic history were recognised through the award of an honorary degree by the University of Essex in 1993 for contributions to the study and publication of Essex history. In 2007, he was elected a fellow of the Society of Antiquaries of London. Even more celebrated recognition followed in 2010 when Vic was awarded an M.B.E. for services to British archives.

His return to Suffolk in 2011 coincided with the publication of his second monograph. *Bookmen: London; 250 Years of Sotheran Bookselling* (2011), a history of Henry Sotheran, the oldest-surviving antiquarian book dealers in Britain, reflected his long-standing interest in historic libraries, publishing and bookselling. This was a passion partly stimulated by Vic's work as a trustee of the seventeenth-century Thomas Plume Library in Maldon, Essex. His other main research interest, the history of utopian communities, was reflected in a more recent publication *A New World in Essex: The Rise and Fall of the Purleigh Brotherhood Colony, 1896–1903* (2019).

Retirement in Suffolk also provided further opportunities for Vic to put his experience and talents to greater use on behalf of the county's history community. He served on the committees of the Friends of Suffolk Record Office and the Suffolk Heritage Forum, as well as acting as trustee of the Halesworth and District Museum and Honorary Archivist at Helmingham Hall. Vic's association with the Tollemache family library was also reflected in his role as general editor for the Suffolk Record Society's volume 61, *The Household Inventories of Helmingham Hall, 1597–1741*, edited by Moira Coleman. In 2014, he was appointed to the role of Honorary Research Fellow in History at the University of Suffolk. In the same year, following three years as a committee member, he also became chairman of the SRS.

It was possibly in his role as chairman of our society that many members reading this appreciation will have mainly encountered Vic, although some will have been fortunate enough to have benefitted from his expertise and friendship in other contexts too. Like other chairmen of the SRS, Vic found himself following in the wake of another stalwart of the Suffolk history scene and with big shoes to fill. However, it came as no surprise, especially perhaps to the former incumbent who had recommended him for the role, that Vic's personal qualities and experience not only made him the consummate chairman, but also the right man to refocus the society's activities during a period of rapid technological and cultural change. It is largely thanks to him that many of our volumes are now digitised and available to all to read online.

Putting even these qualities and achievements aside, most of us will long remember Vic as a person of great integrity and warmth, with an understated but extraordinary gift with people. He possessed a serious intellect but never took *himself* too seriously and rarely let an opportunity for humour slip by. He was a lovely man whom one always looked forward to seeing again.

Harvey Osborne

PREFACE AND ACKNOWLEDGEMENTS

Monks Eleigh is one of a number of manors in East Anglia that have belonged to Christ Church, Canterbury, since before the Norman Conquest. Most of its records survived because they were stored centrally in Canterbury, where they remain to this day in the care of the Cathedral Archives. The distance of these primary sources from Suffolk probably explains the relative lack of research by local historians into a very rich collection, which not only throws light on the lives of those who lived and worked in the manor over the centuries, but also illustrates more general trends in the history of English manorial administration. This volume, prompted by over twenty years' research by the late John Brian Weller, aims to make a selection of these records more accessible for researchers.

Many people have helped with its production. I would like to thank Michael Stansfield for originally making his transcripts for Weller, generously sharing them with me and giving his permission for them to be edited for this volume. Secondly, I thank Marion Allen for her permission to use and edit her translations of five charters at Suffolk Archives (formerly Suffolk Record Office), which she made for Weller in the 1990s. I am grateful to Nicholas Amor, my general editor, for his advice and practical help. I would like to thank Cressida Williams, archives and library manager and Canterbury Cathedral archivist, for permission to reproduce images of the Monks Eleigh archives in her custody; my thanks also to her staff, especially Toby Huitson and Daniel Korachi-Alaoui, for assisting me with access and for photography. In addition to my visit to the archives, attending evensong in Canterbury Cathedral and hearing the celebrant offer prayers for the work of the archive staff there was a particular delight. Likewise, thanks are due to Kate Chantry for permission to reproduce documents held by Suffolk Archives; to Edward Martin for sharing his research on Loose Hall, Hitcham; to Mark Bailey; and to Bridget Kerr at the Leverhulme Trust and James Parker of the Church Commissioners for their help on particular points. I am grateful to Keith Briggs and David Mills, who have helped with particular place and personal naming queries. I have received support and encouragement from my colleagues in the history department at the University of Suffolk, Louise Carter, Max Drephal, John Greenacre, Edward Packard and most especially Harvey Osborne and Lisa Wade. The last two, with Vic Gray and other members of the Weller Bequest Committee, have made available to me Weller's archive and funded me from his bequest to the university, enabling me to produce this volume. I thank them for their unfailing support over a long project. I am grateful to my fellow members of the late John Ridgard's two palaeography groups, who have enthusiastically helped me over several years to untangle the knottier palaeographical problems in some of the original documents: my thanks to them all. Any errors that remain are mine alone. I thank my good friend Tig Lang for cheerfully and helpfully discussing all manner of Latin, palaeographical and historical issues that came up during the work. Our conversations invariably added to my knowledge and clarified my thoughts. Special thanks go to my husband Paul and son Ian, who have given much-appreciated practical and moral support throughout the project: I could not have done it without them. Finally, the volume could not have been produced at all without the research of J.B. Weller, who commissioned the translations originally and devoted so many of his later years to the study of Monks Eleigh. His generosity in bequeathing to the University of Suffolk his archive and funding to further his work has been the impetus behind this volume.

The Suffolk Records Society is grateful to the University of Suffolk and to Monks Eleigh Parish Council for financial assistance towards the cost of publishing the volume.

Vivienne Aldous
Ipswich, July 2021

JOHN BRIAN WELLER: AN APPRECIATION
by Vivienne Aldous *and* Harvey Osborne

The origins of this volume lie in the personal research of the late John Brian Weller, a professional architect whose increasing passion for the history of the Suffolk village of Monks Eleigh took up much of the final two decades of his life. Sadly, he did not live to complete his research, but this volume represents the University of Suffolk's commitment to honouring his last wishes expressed in his will to continue and publish his studies on the history of Monks Eleigh. It is hoped that in publishing the selected translations and transcripts of records for the manor of Monks Eleigh that he commissioned, sufficient source material will become more widely available to stimulate further research, not only on Monks Eleigh itself, or the local history of Suffolk, but also as a contribution to the corpus of source materials for the wider study of medieval history.

Weller's professional and family background was soundly architectural. In order to practise independently, in 1964 he moved to Suffolk from the family architectural firm at 15 King Street, Wolverhampton, where he had practised as the latest (John Weller IV) of a long line of distinguished architects beginning with John Weller I (1798–1869). The long-standing Weller Architectural Partnership there is commemorated by a blue plaque, installed in 2008, sponsored by the Wolverhampton Civic Society and Wolverhampton Society of Architects.[1]

Even before moving to Bildeston, Weller developed a particular expertise in historic farm buildings, particularly tithe barns. He was the National Farmers' Union Research Fellow (farm buildings) 1958–60 at the Department of Agricultural Economy, Cambridge University, and specialised from 1960 onwards 'in farm and rural buildings and in land-use conservation'.[2] Whilst running his own architectural practice in Suffolk, he also published on farm buildings, modern architecture and rural planning and the history of the farmstead. He took on part-time and seasonal work for the Open University as a teacher in design and technology and served on the European Community Farm Building Committee and other national, regional and local bodies on related subjects up to 1992. Between 1982 and 1985, he was a Leverhulme Research Fellow (tithe barns), and he co-authored an article on Glastonbury Abbey's tithe barns in Somerset in 1991. He published privately and in local historical publications on medieval barns during the 1980s, including *Grangia and Orreum: The Medieval Barn; A Nomenclature* (1986) and *Tithe Barns and Their Tithes* (1986).[3]

---

[1] The family and business archive of the Weller architectural practice are held by Wolverhampton Archives and Local Studies Service. Weller's own archive on Monks Eleigh he bequeathed to the University of Suffolk (UoS), files from which are hereafter cited as Weller Archive, file, …

[2] Weller Archive, file, 'Monks Eleigh Secondary Sources', application form for funding under the Architecture Grants Scheme from the Arts Council of Great Britain, 30 September 1992.

[3] We are indebted to Bridget Kerr at the Leverhulme Trust for these two references. Weller's research notes and drafts are in Weller Archive, file, 'Tithe Management: Collection and Storage Evidence and Tithe History'.

In 1991, the village of Monks Eleigh celebrated the millennium of its association with Canterbury Cathedral, the village being part of the estate bequeathed to the monks of Canterbury by Ealdorman Byrhtnoth in 991. Weller's expertise on medieval buildings and outstanding draughtsmanship inevitably led to a request that he undertake architecturally based historical studies of two houses, Hobarts and the Manor Farm, in Monks Eleigh for the commemoration booklet. In his own words, Weller was 'sucked into helping Monks Eleigh ... celebrate 1000 years since it was given to Canterbury Cathedral'.[4] This, in turn, pulled Weller into 'a more ambitious programme ... to relate its medieval buildings to both documentary and drawn evidence'.

From then until his death in 2009, Weller continued his research, commissioning the translation and transcription of many of Monks Eleigh's manorial documents held at Canterbury Cathedral Archives (CCA), chiefly during the early to mid-1990s and mentored for part of that time by the late David Dymond, director of studies in local and regional history at the Institute of Continuing Education, Cambridge University.

In addition to the three cited in the bibliography in this volume, Weller's other publications include:

The Yard and Parlour: Capital Costs and Work Requirements (Cambridge University School of Agriculture, Farm Economics Branch, Report no. 58 (1962), with John S. Nix, Deryke Gerald Rosten Belshaw and Andrew Hay Scott

Farm Buildings: Structural Techniques and Materials, Volume 1; Techniques, Design, Profit (Lincoln, 1965)

Modern Agriculture and Rural Planning (Lincoln, 1968)

Farm Buildings: Structural Techniques and Materials, Volume 2; Foundations and Floors (Lincoln, 1972)

Farm Wastes Management (London, 1977), with Stephen Willetts

History of the Farmstead: The Development of Energy Sources (London, 1982)

Grangia and Orreum: The Medieval Barn; A Nomenclature (published privately, 1986)

Tithe Barns and Their Tithes (Bildeston Booklets, 1986)

'The Somerset Barns of Glastonbury Abbey', with C.J. Bond, in Lesley Abrams and James P. Carley (eds), *The Archaeology and History of Glastonbury Abbey: Essays in Honour of the Ninetieth Birthday of C.A. Ralegh Radford* (Woodbridge, 1991), pp. 57–87

Lindsey Castle, Suffolk: A Preliminary Re-Appraisal for Comment following a short visit 2 February 2000, with Christopher Hawkins (Weller Archive, file 'Castles')

'A Fifteenth Century Inclosure: The Little Highfield in Monks Eleigh of 1540', *Suffolk Review*, New Series no. 40 (Spring 2003)

This volume is dedicated to the memory of
John Brian Weller, 1930–2009.

---

4   Weller Archive, file, 'Monks Eleigh: Secondary Sources', letter from Weller to Professor Peter Carolin, Department of Architecture, Cambridge University, 24 June 1991. In May 1991, sponsored by the *East Anglian Daily Times*, 1,000 copies of the commemorative booklet went on sale in aid of the £80,000 appeal fund for St Peter's Church ('Village's 1,000 Years Go into Print', *East Anglian Daily Times*, Thursday, 23 May 1991, p. 11).

ABBREVIATIONS

AALT	Anglo-American Legal Tradition
AgHR	*Agricultural History Review*
BL	British Library
CCA	Canterbury Cathedral Archives
DEEDS	Documents of Early England Data Set (University of Toronto)
DMLBS	*Dictionary of Medieval Latin from British Sources*
EcHR	*Economic History Review*
EHR	*English Historical Review*
HMC	Historical Manuscripts Commission
MED	*Middle English Dictionary*
ODNB	*Oxford Dictionary of National Biography*
OED	*Oxford English Dictionary*
PCC	Prerogative Court of Canterbury
PSIAH	*Proceedings of the Suffolk Institute of Archaeology and History*
SA(B)	Suffolk Archives (Bury St Edmunds)
SA(I)	Suffolk Archives (The Hold, Ipswich)
SRS	Suffolk Records Society
TNA	The National Archives, Kew
UoS	University of Suffolk, Ipswich
VCH Kent 2	W. Page (ed.), *Victoria History of the County of Kent: Volume 2* (London, 1926)
VCH Suffolk 2	W. Page (ed.), *Victoria History of the County of Suffolk: Volume 2* (London, 1907, reprinted 1975)

Many of the publications above are also available online. See Bibliography.

INTRODUCTION

The ownership of the manor of Monks Eleigh: A bequest from Byrhtnoth, A.D. 991

The estate that became the manor of Monks Eleigh was bequeathed to the monks of the priory of Christ Church, Canterbury, by its last secular lord, Byrhtnoth, ealdorman of Essex, who was killed at the battle of Maldon in 991.[1] Monks Eleigh had belonged to Byrhtnoth's father-in-law, Ælfgar, the previous ealdorman of Essex, who bequeathed it in *c.* 958 to his younger daughter, Ælflæd, with reversion to her husband Byrhtnoth and any children they might have. If they had no children (as was indeed the case), the estate was to revert, under Byrhtnoth's will, to the convent of Christ Church, Canterbury.

Byrhtnoth was one of the most powerful ealdormen of his day and achieved lasting fame as the hero of an ill-fated conflict against Viking raiders that led to a major change in royal policy to deal with such raiders.[2] According to the commemorative heroic Old English poem 'The Battle of Maldon', Byrhtnoth, at the head of an English army, allowed a band of Viking raiders, which had already plundered Ipswich, to advance across a causeway near Maldon in order to have room to fight. The English lost the ensuing battle and Byrhtnoth was killed, but his retainers fought on, choosing to die in battle avenging their lord, rather than to survive him. The poem celebrates their loyalty and sacrifice and Byrhtnoth's inspiring leadership as ideals of Anglo-Saxon warrior heroism. Although the poem acknowledges that Byrhtnoth's decision to allow the Vikings to cross the causeway to engage in battle was controversial, it is now generally accepted that it was a strategic necessity, as it prevented the enemy from leaving and raiding elsewhere, where there might not have been armed men to counter them. Even though the Vikings won the battle, their forces were so depleted, according to the poem, that they could barely crew their ships to sail home after it. Their victory was pyrrhic, whereas Byrhtnoth's memory remains evergreen in Maldon, where a statue of him was erected in 2006, as well as in Monks Eleigh, which commemorated 1,000 years of association with Canterbury as a result of his gift in 1991.

Monks Eleigh was one of many estates held by Byrhtnoth, who was probably in his early sixties at the time of Maldon, a strong, wealthy, well-connected and greatly respected ealdorman. Although he was the ealdorman of Essex and had considerable estates there, he also held extensive lands in Suffolk, Cambridgeshire and elsewhere, and the range of his authority was extensive. He and his ally, Ealdorman Æthelwine of East Anglia, who died the year after Maldon, were the two most senior English ealdormen of their day under King Æthelred II (better-known to history as famously 'unready'), and their deaths came to be seen as a watershed in the government of the period. After Maldon, Æthelred changed his policy towards the Viking raiders,

---

[1] Byrhtnoth's original will does not survive, but later copies do exist. An image and translation are reproduced in Margaret Woods, *Medieval Hadleigh: The Chief Manor and the Town* (Layham, 2018), pp. 23–24.

[2] Richard Abels, 'Byrhtnoth [Brihtnoth] (d. 991)', *ODNB* (2004).

choosing to buy them off with large sums of money (the infamous Danegeld) rather than fight them, a policy that led to a reputation for poor judgement and thus to his famous nickname.[3]

Byrhtnoth's bequest to a monastic house was characteristic, for he was a notably religious man. Byrhtnoth and Æthelwine were strong supporters of the tenth-century monastic reforms promoted by Bishop Æthelwold of Winchester and Archbishops Dunstan of Canterbury and Oswald of York. These two senior ealdormen defended the monks at Ely and Ramsey against the attempted depredations by various laymen of monastic estates in the early part of Æthelred's reign. It is not surprising to find, therefore, that Byrhtnoth was generous in his bequests to religious houses: he left extensive property in Cambridgeshire, Huntingdonshire, Norfolk and Suffolk to Ely Abbey, and other properties to the abbeys of Abingdon, Ramsey, Mersea and Christ Church, Canterbury. The properties left to Canterbury were the estates of Lawling (with Latchingdon), Essex and Hadleigh and Monks Eleigh in Suffolk. Hadleigh was left to Byrhtnoth's wife, Ælflæd, for her lifetime, with reversion to the monks of Canterbury after her death, which occurred in 1002.[4]

The lordship of what came to be known as the manor of Monks Eleigh was vested in the prior of Christ Church, Canterbury, from 991 until the monastery was dissolved by Henry VIII in March 1540. Most of the priory's properties, including the manor of Monks Eleigh, and its administrative documents, were transferred to the dean and chapter of the new Canterbury Cathedral when it was constituted in April 1540.[5] The manor was sold by Parliament during the interregnum but restored to Canterbury Cathedral following the restoration of 1660.[6] The dean and chapter retained lordship of the manor until 1863, when it was transferred to the Ecclesiastical Commissioners.[7] In 1948, the Ecclesiastical Commissioners became the Church Commissioners, the body that still holds the lordship of the manor today.[8] For more than 1,000 years, therefore, Monks Eleigh has been held by influential and powerful absentee landlords with influence at the royal court and substantial estates over much of southern England. As part of a much larger estate, it benefitted from the continuity of a consistent and usually well-organised centralised administration. At the same time, its outlying position and absentee lords may have given its tenants more scope for independent thought and action.

Canterbury's management of its East Anglian estates

The food-farm

Byrhtnoth's gift of Monks Eleigh was one of many bequests to Christ Church Cathedral Priory for the feeding and maintenance of the religious community. The archbishop of Canterbury was the titular abbot of the priory, but for most of the period

---

[3]   The epithet is a pun on his name *Æpelræd* (Old English: *æpel* = noble, *ræd* = counsel), so *Æpelræd unræd* translates as 'noble counsel, no counsel'; in short, an unwise man (Simon Keynes, 'Æthelred II [Ethelred; Known as Ethelred the Unready (*c.* 966x8–1016)', *ODNB* (2004)).

[4]   J.F. Nichols, '*Custodia Essexae*: A Study of the Conventual Property Held by the Priory of Christ Church, Canterbury in the Counties of Essex, Suffolk and Norfolk' (London University PhD Thesis, 1930), pp. 13–14, 22.

[5]   *VCH Kent* 2, pp. 113–21.

[6]   W.A. Copinger, *The Manors of Suffolk* 1 (London, 1905), pp. 162–63.

[7]   A.F. Northcote, *Notes on the History of Monks Eleigh* (Ipswich, 1930), p. 17.

[8]   Personal communication from James Parker of the Church Commissioners.

covered by the documents in this volume, it was ruled by the prior. Little is known about the early organisation of the provision of food for the monks and clerks of the priory from their estates. This would have taken a good deal of logistical organisation in co-ordinating supplies from different estates to arrive evenly throughout the year. Like every other large monastery of the period, therefore, the priory developed a complex administrative machinery, both central and local, to maintain the flow of money and supplies from its estates to Canterbury.[9]

The estates in the priory's custody of Essex (comprising manors in Essex, Suffolk and Norfolk) were made up of agriculturally rich land, the produce from which either fed the monks of the priory directly or was sold to produce money that could be used to do so. R.A.L. Smith states that the priory's agricultural development was determined by two chief factors, both based on geography. Firstly, most of its manors were in south-east England, which was prime grain-growing country, and secondly, most were within easy reach of markets and sea-ports, through which produce might be transported to Canterbury, sold locally or exported.[10] The priory principally concentrated on cereal farming, therefore, which was closely linked to its system of food-farms, whereby certain estates were allocated the function of feeding the monks at Canterbury for a certain period each year. There was always a tension between farming to feed the priory directly and making the most of high prices to sell grain in the market and use the money to buy produce local to Canterbury to feed the monks.

Archbishop Lanfranc (1070–92) re-organised the existing food-farm system to provide food for Canterbury's monks throughout the year, with certain estates chosen to supply food and supplies for a specified number of weeks each year. This became the standard for subsequent calculations and was known as the *ebdomada* or weekly system. In Lanfranc's day, seventeen manors were classed as food manors, five of which were in the Essex custody yielding fourteen weeks' food-farms in kind each year – Lawling (two weeks), Monks Eleigh (four), Hadleigh (three), Bocking (four) and Milton (one).[11] Table 1 gives the produce of a four-week food-farm (such as Monks Eleigh's) as cited by John Nichols.

Table 1: Four-week food-farm under Archbishop Lanfranc's ebdomada system, c. 1070–92

Wheat	8 hoppas
Barley	2½ hoppas
Oats	3 hoppas
Oat malt	13 hoppas, 5 ferthings
Barley malt	6½ hoppas, 5 ferthings
Pigs	35, worth 2s. each

---

9   For fuller details, see especially R.A.L. Smith, *Canterbury Cathedral Priory: A Study in Monastic Administration* (Cambridge, 1943) and Nichols, '*Custodia Essexae*' (1930), the latter concentrating on the Essex custody.

10   See Smith, *Canterbury Cathedral Priory* (1943), pp. 129–34, who states (p. 130) that the priory was in the habit of locally marketing and even exporting abroad its grain from the early thirteenth century at the latest.

11   Nichols, '*Custodia Essexae*' (1930), pp. 199–202.

Table 1 continued

Cows	4, worth 3s. each
Cheese	4 weys
Honey	1½ sestaries
Wood and salt	Sufficient for the needs of brew-house and kitchen
Peas and beans	Sufficient for the needs of the monks and their servants
Tallow	For the six cressets in the dormitory
Plus	1s. 2d. for the master brewer's wages and 2s. for his three assistants

This list (which was probably an idealised standard) is a good example of the difficulty in interpreting medieval documents with obsolete terminology. All of the measurements cited are now obscure: a hoppa (Latin *hoppa*, probably from Middle English *hep* or *hop*) is related to the word heap and was a dry measure, known to have been used for grain and salt, but the actual quantity is now lost to us. Ferthings represent some kind of sub-division of a hoppa (but almost certainly not the expected fourth part as there are five in the list), whilst sestaries (or sextaries, from the Latin liquid measure *sextarius*) had local variations in the Middle Ages of between 4 and 6 gallons, according to the *OED*. Even a wey of cheese had variant measures: 256 lb in Suffolk and 336 lb in Essex, but which one of these weights (if either) would have been used by Canterbury is unknown. It is probably best treated as an indication of the proportions of typical crops and goods supplied – the quantities of malt (more than the unmalted crop itself) and the brewers' wages suggest an emphasis on beer-making rather than food crops, perhaps, and it must have been adjusted according to the particular agricultural specialisation of each manor, or the weather conditions in a particular year.

Lanfranc's system was overhauled *c.* 1285, coinciding with the beginning of Prior Henry of Eastry's reforming term of office, when a list was made of manors that supplied food-farms in kind and those that paid cash instead.[12] The manors in this list differ slightly from those providing food in Lanfranc's time, with more emphasis on local Kent manors, which would have been more practical in terms of transportation. However, four of the earlier five Essex custody manors still provided food in kind in this later list. Monks Eleigh and Hadleigh jointly accounted for three weeks' food-farms, valued at £93 16s. 8¼d. (a single week's being valued at £31 5s. 6¾d., which suggests, as Nichols again states, that this was an idealised standard, subject to variation on each manor in any given year). Lawling and Milton jointly accounted for three weeks' food-farms with the same valuation. By this date, the model of a food-farm for one week (rather than four weeks as given in Lanfranc's time) was set at the levels in Table 2.

---

[12] Nichols, '*Custodia Essexae*' (1930), pp. 202–5; Smith, *Canterbury Cathedral Priory* (1943), pp. 131–32, the latter citing Lambeth MS 1212, fol. 363, *Adhuc de maneriis monachorum que firmant, non firmant* ('Again, concerning the manors of the monks, which [*provide food-*]farm, [*and which*] do not [*provide food-*]farm').

Table 2: One-week food-farm (c. 1285). Taken from Nichols, Custodia Essexae
(1930), pp. 202–5

Wheat	30 seams (1 seam = 1 quarter, comprising 8 bushels)
White peas	3½ seams
Barley for bread[13]	13½ seams
Fodder	15 seams
Barley for malt	46 seams, 6 bushels
Oats for malt	47 seams, 2 bushels
Cheese	1 wey
Honey	3 stoups (= 9 gallons)

This gives a more comprehensible list of the produce that Monks Eleigh was expected to furnish to the priory at that time.[14] Margaret Woods tried to ascertain when the manor of Hadleigh ceased to supply food to Canterbury and went over to purely cash rents but could not find unequivocal evidence.[15] Evidence for Monks Eleigh sending its produce to Canterbury, or ceasing to do so, is likewise difficult to discern from the records reproduced here. However, for Monks Eleigh and the other Essex custody manors it might well have been very shortly after the 1285 list above, for Smith states that in '1288 the senior monks at the exchequer issued an ordinance which revised the statutes of Lanfranc and limited the render of food-farm to certain large Kentish manors'.[16] It looks therefore as if the system revised *c.* 1285 was further revised within the first three years of its operation. Monks Eleigh, together with the rest of the custody of Essex manors, ceased to send produce in kind to Canterbury between 1285 and 1288, and from then on, they paid their rents to the priory in cash, with which food and other produce could be bought in markets more local to Canterbury. This might explain why the Monks Eleigh tenants owed a labour service of transportation to Ipswich (from where supplies might be easily shipped to Canterbury) *c.* 1260–*c.* 1270 (see Extent 5, p. 33), but this does not appear in the 1285–86 accounts (Accounts 1, below, p. 43) or subsequent extents or accounts.

---

[13] Nichols, '*Custodia Essexae*' (1930), p. 204, has 'barley for cakes', but the *DMLBS* gives *torta* as meaning 'a round loaf of bread' and cites as an example a Canterbury source (CCA-DCc-Register/J, fol. 282), so bread is probably a better translation.

[14] To calculate the total amounts of produce of Monks Eleigh's food-farm for the year, the amounts in this list need to be divided by two (to allow for the joint responsibility of Hadleigh) and then multiplied by three (for three weeks). Whether or not Monks Eleigh met its food-farm obligations year-on-year should appear in CCA's series of annual *assisa scaccarii* (not included in this volume), which record details of the delivery of each manor's food-farms and note whether each manor had supplied its quota or not.

[15] Woods, *Medieval Hadleigh* (2018), pp. 235–40.

[16] Smith, *Canterbury Cathedral Priory* (1943), pp. 119, 132 and Appendix I, the last including a transcript of the ordinance, *Ordinacio facta ad scaccarium in die quatuor Coronatorum de blado mittendo domi anno regni Edwardi xvi* (16 Edw. I, 8 November 1288) [cited by Smith as 'Cant. MS R.E. II, No 99'; modern reference: CCA-DCc/RE/99], which does not mention Monks Eleigh or any Essex custody manors as supplying food-farms.

Demesne management

The nature of the administration of the priory's manors changed over time. At the time of Domesday and for much of the twelfth century, most manors in England were leased out by their lords as was common throughout north-western Europe at that time. Then, during a period of transition from the late-twelfth century onwards until the mid- to late-thirteenth century or thereabouts, most manors in England (although not in continental Europe) changed their method of management to what is known as direct demesne management.[17] The steady rise in the English population in the centuries that followed the Conquest meant that the prices of agricultural produce became relatively high and the cost of agricultural labour relatively low. In turn, this made demesne management of estates highly profitable. Manors were managed in-house by their lords (or ladies, to be understood) through their own officials with a variety of titles depending on local usage (discussed below). Of course, even in times of demesne management, the greater part of most manors was let out to tenants, free and unfree, who paid cash rents and, in the case of the unfree, spent time working on the lord's land. Mavis Mate suggests that maintaining discipline within a monastic establishment might also have been pertinent in the adoption of demesne management by Canterbury (see below), which she dates to 1282 or thereabouts.[18]

Following the Black Death of 1348–49, the population fell dramatically. The same economic forces that had pushed up prices and forced down wages now worked in reverse, so that demesne management was no longer profitable. Most English manors gradually reverted to being leased out again. For Canterbury manors, the priory briefly experimented with leasing some of its manors in the 1350s before taking them back into demesne management again. Mate suggests this brief period of experimentation might have been due to the loss of a large number of long-serving experienced manorial officials in the Black Death and a prolonged drought, causing the priory to pass on the risks of running their manors to lessees for that short period.[19] Monks Eleigh may have been one of these temporarily leased manors because the 1358–59 accounts note that almost all the corn and stock at the beginning of the accounting period were received from Richard Forester, some of them by tally. This implies that he had been lessee of the demesne for the previous year at least. Although that experiment was brief and demesne management resumed, the priory's manors were gradually and permanently put out to lease again between the 1370s and the end of the century, reflecting the general retreat from demesne administration elsewhere at that time. Monks Eleigh was probably leased from 1380 and certainly from 1400.

These trends in management systems had obvious effects on the kind of records produced by manors. Demesne management produced far more detailed records, since the manorial official, the reeve, bailiff or serjeant, had to answer in detail for

---

[17] See P.D.A. Harvey, *Manorial Records of Cuxham, Oxfordshire, A.D. 1200–1359* (London, 1976), pp. 12–15; P.D.A. Harvey, *Manorial Records*, British Records Association Archives and the User no. 5 (London, 1984, revised 1999), pp. 3–7; Harvey, 'Manorial Records', in Margaret Faull, P.D.A. Harvey and Sylvia Thomas (eds), *Medieval Manorial Records* (Leeds, 1983), pp. 4–6; Mark Bailey, *The English Manor c.1200–c.1500* (Manchester, 2002), pp. 98–116. Bailey (p. 98, n. 2) gives a useful list of introductory reading on the subject.

[18] Mavis Mate, 'The Farming Out of Manors: A New Look at the Evidence from Canterbury Cathedral Priory', *Journal of Medieval History* 9 (1983), pp. 331–43.

[19] Mate, 'The Farming Out of Manors' (1983), p. 337.

his custodianship before the lord's auditors, and the lord had a vested interest in how his manor was being run and in making sure his officials were not cheating him. The lord was also keen to maximise his return from each manor in order to meet the increasing demands for tax imposed by the crown. When a manor was leased, however, the lessee needed only to pay the contracted rent and claim any allowances (such as building repairs, for example, as reproduced in this volume) specified by the particular lease. So long as the rent was paid and there was no civil unrest in the manor (as there was in 1481)[20] to occasion interference in manorial affairs, the lord need pay little attention to how the manor was being run. Lessees' (or farmers') accounts from leased manors therefore tend to be much less detailed. Survival rates of records can be worse for leased manors too, since lessees changed periodically, and once their lease had ended, they did not have the long-term interest in retaining records that a lord who was managing his own manorial demesne would have had.

Monks Eleigh reflects these developments in management as well as having its own idiosyncrasies. It should be remembered that every manor was unique, whilst fitting within broader national or regional trends, and one of the purposes of this volume is to show how the manor of Monks Eleigh contrasts or is similar to manors elsewhere to shed light on how local particularities fitted in with larger trends.

Custodies, monk-wardens and manorial officials

Most of the priory's property was in southern England, where for administrative purposes it organised four geographical groupings called custodies: East Kent, West Kent, Surrey and Essex. The custody of Essex (*custodia Essexiae*) comprised the priory's East Anglian estates, most of them being in Essex, but also including Deopham in Norfolk and Hadleigh and Monks Eleigh in Suffolk.

From the late-twelfth century at least, each of the four custodies was under the supervision of its own particular monk-warden from the priory.[21] The role of the monk-wardens in the twelfth and early thirteenth centuries was principally administrative rather than financial. Their duties at this point might have been sufficiently vaguely defined to have caused a number of monks to disobey the rule of their order and by the later thirteenth century to live partly or semi-permanently on the priory's manors as *de facto* bailiffs or as monk-farmers leasing manors from the priory.[22] The practice of leasing monastic manors to monk-farmers was not unique to the priory of Christ Church and was frowned upon by church authorities as it detracted from the monk-farmers' concentration on their monastic lives, but it continued at Canterbury and elsewhere for a considerable time. Reforms in 1280–82 by Archbishop John Pecham (1279–92) and Prior Thomas Ringmer (1274–85) recalled these monks to their monastery at Canterbury and decreed that in future only laymen could hold office as manorial bailiffs. In 1281, Pecham confirmed the duties and system of the four monk-wardens. In 1289, Prior Henry of Eastry strengthened the monk-wardens' powers by making them responsible for bringing the revenues of all the manors in their custodies to the treasury in Canterbury, which before then had been the personal

---

[20] See the petition and legal papers on the 1481 riot in Section VII, below, p. 295.

[21] For fuller details of the duties of the monk-wardens and the development of their role, see Smith, *Canterbury Cathedral Priory* (1943), pp. 99–112 and Nichols, '*Custodia Essexae*' (1930), pp. 133–41.

[22] Smith, *Canterbury Cathedral Priory* (1943), pp. 102–3; Mate, 'The Farming Out of Manors' (1983), p. 332.

responsibility of each manor's reeve or bailiff.[23] Giving the monk-wardens financial, as well as supervisory, responsibility helped to tighten up the priory's administration of its manors and balance the decentralising tendencies of the previous century. In effect, the monk-wardens were now to act as senior managers of the custodies as discrete departments within the larger administration of the priory. Central decisions concerning such matters as how much and from where food was required to feed the monks, how many acres were to be sown with which crops, and stock levels were devolved on the monk-wardens to execute at custody level, making the necessary adjustments for each manor according to local conditions and circumstances.[24] Together with the adoption of demesne management and revisions of the food-farm system, these reforms made the 1280s a key period of change in the development of the prior's manorial administration. Cumulatively, they gave rise to the exceptionally efficient system of administration introduced and maintained by the long-serving and very effective Prior Henry of Eastry (1285–1331), which established a long period of financial stability and administrative continuity for the priory.

The monk-wardens themselves were usually senior members of the monastic community with administrative experience. At around Easter and Michaelmas every year, the monk-warden, accompanied by a small party including at least a clerk and grooms, would go on progress to visit each manor in his custody.[25] The accounts in this volume record the expenses for food, drink and farriery on these visitations, which usually lasted for one or two nights in each manor, although occasionally a little longer, as in the 1329–30 accounts, where the harvest-time expenses were more than usual because of a long harvest (six weeks) and the long stay (five days) of the warden and his party.[26] The Michaelmas visit always involved the presentation and auditing of each manor's accounts, the revenues of which had to be deposited in the treasury at Canterbury before 1 November. A warden's visit might also coincide with the holding of a manorial court, although in Monks Eleigh these appear to have been held at other times of the year as well as Easter and Michaelmas (see the section on court rolls below for details). If the warden was not present for a manorial court, his place was taken by the steward, an officer who assisted each monk-warden in his duties within the custody, and who was probably one of the colleagues who accompanied him on his progresses through the manors of the Essex custody.

The steward was usually a layman (often a gentleman) experienced in legal matters, including holding the manorial courts. In this, he was assisted by the clerk who might hold the courts in the absence of both monk-warden and steward.[27] The steward was also the official responsible for organising inquests of inquiry and drawing up extents, rentals and surveys. The title of the steward (usually *senescallus*) could cause confusion when he was sometimes referred to as the bailiff (more usually the term for the manorial official, sometimes alternatively called a reeve, bailiff or serjeant, who ran the manor day-to-day, as discussed below).[28] This

---

[23] Smith, *Canterbury Cathedral Priory* (1943), pp. 101–3; Nichols, '*Custodia Essexae*' (1930), pp. 133–35.

[24] Smith, *Canterbury Cathedral Priory* (1943), p. 107; Nichols, '*Custodia Essexae*' (1930), pp. 134–35.

[25] Smith, *Canterbury Cathedral Priory* (1943), pp. 104–5; Nichols, '*Custodia Essexae*' (1930), pp. 136–40.

[26] Accounts 3 (1329–30), see p. 61.

[27] For the detailed duties of the steward, see Nichols, '*Custodia Essexae*' (1930), pp. 141–46; Bailey, *The English Manor* (2002), p. 100.

[28] Nichols, '*Custodia Essexae*' (1930), p. 142; J.F. Nichols, 'Milton Hall, Essex: The Extent of 1309', *Transactions of the Southend-on-Sea and District Antiquarian and Historical Society* 2, part 1 (1929), p. 31.

confusion goes back to an early period of manorial demesne management as defined in the mid-thirteenth-century manual called the *Seneschausy*, which advised that a hierarchy of officers should usually supervise the reeve/bailiff/serjeant on the ideal manor: the first official above the reeve/bailiff/serjeant was (confusingly) also termed a bailiff (*ballivus*, one in charge of several manors), above whom was the steward, above whom were the auditors (the equivalent of the Canterbury monk-wardens of the custodies).[29] As the system of demesne farming grew more established across the country, these multiple layers of supervision were gradually removed from most manors, although the timing and degree of this varied according to different estates and times. This system of oversight adapted by Canterbury to its own hierarchy of administration probably accounts for the fact that the title of bailiff hung on and could also be used as alternative term for the steward on its manors.[30] Context and footnotes should clarify any confusion in the texts in this volume.

During the priorate of Henry of Eastry, the monk-wardens of the Essex custody were ably assisted by the even longer serving and equally efficient steward, John le Doo (1274–1326), who, after his retirement from office in 1326, held leases himself of some of the priory's estates in the custody until at least 1334.[31] As steward, he drew up a series of extremely detailed extents for the Essex custody manors of Bocking, Borley, Hadleigh, Lawling and Milton in the first decade of the fourteenth century.[32] Alas, Monks Eleigh was not included in this informative series of extents, and John le Doo himself appears in the Monks Eleigh records only twice in passing references.[33] Nichols speculates that after Prior Henry of Eastry's and John le Doo's period of efficient administration, the Essex custody experienced a period of comparative administrative neglect, although this is difficult to ascertain from the selection of Monks Eleigh documents presented here.[34]

As noted above, lesser manorial officials worked locally on the ground to administer the manor under demesne management. On many estates, the title (reeve, bailiff or serjeant) of the official who oversaw the day-to-day management of the manor could vary between manors and confuse the unwary scholar today. If he was called a reeve (*praepositus*), he was an unfree tenant of the manor.[35] On many manors, a reeve was usually given a reduced rent on his holdings in lieu of wages and was excused his customary works.[36] If called a bailiff, he was a freeman, or even an

---

[29] Bailey, *The English Manor* (2002), p. 100; Harvey, *Manorial Records (1999)*, pp. 5–6.

[30] Nichols, '*Custodia Essexae*' (1930), p. 142; Nichols, 'Milton Hall' (1929), p. 31.

[31] Nichols, '*Custodia Essexae*' (1930), p. 144, n. 2; J.F. Nichols, 'An Early Fourteenth-Century Petition', *EcHR* 2, no. 2 (January 1930), p. 301, n. 2; p. 303, n. 1. Leases of estates did continue, even during the period when demesne management was the norm. Nichols suggests that John le Doo was the prototype of 'John Doe', the fictional name for a man of straw in legal cases or an unknown person, a legal term that crossed the Atlantic with English settlers and is familiar to many today from American crime detection television programmes (Nichols, 'Milton Hall' (1929), p. 30).

[32] Versions survive in CCA Registers B, J and K, as well as BL Harleian MS 1006; for details, see Nichols, '*Custodia Essexae*' (1930), pp. 78, 178–85; Woods, *Medieval Hadleigh* (2018), pp. 8–10, 74–75. For the Hadleigh extent, see H. Pigot 'Extenta Manerij de Hadleghe', *PSIAH* 3 (1863), pp. 229–52 translated in Lord J. Hervey, 'Extent of Hadleigh Manor', *PSIAH* 11, no. 2 (1902), pp. 152–72). The Milton Hall extent is translated in Nichols, 'Milton Hall' (1929).

[33] Accounts 2 (1310–11) and Court Roll 1 (1305/6), see pp. 51, 97.

[34] Nichols, '*Custodia Essexae*' (1930), p. 144, n. 2.

[35] Harvey, *Manorial Records* (1999), pp. 5–6.

[36] J.S. Drew, 'Manorial Accounts of St Swithun's Priory, Winchester', *EHR* 62 (January 1947), p. 20, n. 2. This was certainly the case in nearby Hadleigh, where the reeve was selected from the manor's mondayland tenants (Woods, *Medieval Hadleigh* (2018), pp. 120–21 and Appendix A.

outsider brought in to work for a wage (usually a mixture of cash and kind). If termed a serjeant (*serviens*), he could be either a reeve or a bailiff (*serviens* can also mean servant, official or unfree tenant, a villein). Context or a footnote in this volume should indicate which official is intended.

Mark Bailey points out that the annual election of the reeve, who could not refuse to serve the office, could lead to inconsistent management of the estate if different people were elected each year, as well as to reluctant, possibly even resentful office-holders, because the post was onerous.[37] As a result, it was not uncommon in some manors for lord and tenants to contrive that one person serve as reeve continuously, thus building up considerable experience besides perhaps allowing more opportunity for the reeve to benefit himself as well as the lord. We see this in Monks Eleigh, where several of the reeves, bailiffs or serjeants held office for long periods (see Table 3).

Table 3: Reeves, bailiffs or serjeants of Monks Eleigh, 1258–1380 (with gaps)

Gilbert, reeve	1258–59*
Solomon de Hygel	1284–85*
'J', serjeant	1285–86
John de Bosco	1286–87*
Andrew le Forester, serjeant	1310–12*
William de Higg'/de Higgelegh, reeve	1317–46*
Robert Framesden, bailiff/serjeant	1358–73*
William atte Hel, bailiff/serjeant	1375–80*

Based on a list supplied to Weller by Michael Stansfield in the 1990s. Dates asterisked are from existing accounts, but it is possible that their terms of office might have begun earlier and ended later than the dates cited.

Whatever his title, reeve, serjeant or bailiff, the man in day-to-day charge of the manor had a team behind him, called collectively in the documents the *famuli*. The Latin word has been retained here as it is a technical word with a particular meaning in a manorial context: the *famuli* were servants, assistants or staff or, in lay manors, a resident lord's household with particular roles in manorial administration such as at Monks Eleigh hayward/reap-reeve (*messor*), ploughmen, carter, shepherd cow- and swine-herd and maid (housemaid or possibly dairymaid). The visiting monk-warden's entourage of colleagues, clerk and grooms were also termed his *famuli*. Smith notes that on Canterbury's Kent manors, there were large numbers of *famuli*, who did a considerable proportion of the work on the manor as wage-labourers.[38] In Monks Eleigh, there were fewer members of the *famuli* than on the Kent manors, but they were also paid wages, partly in cash, partly in kind, as detailed in the annual accounts in this volume.

---

[37] Bailey, *The English Manor* (2002), pp. 98–99.
[38] Smith, *Canterbury Cathedral Priory* (1943), pp. 124–27.

Tenants, rents and labour services

The conditions under which land was held by tenants from the lord of any given manor were many and various, usually determined by the custom of that particular manor, within an overarching system of hierarchical feudal tenures. Monks Eleigh fitted into this general context, so it is worth describing in general terms. Tenants, and tenures, were either free or non-free. Personal freedom (or non-freedom) was inherited through the male line, although the waters could be muddied by marriage and illegitimacy: in a mixed marriage, a woman took her husband's status during her marriage, as did their children, but an illegitimate child was judged to be free by default since its father was unknown and possible disparagement of its status by judging the child unfree was considered unjust. Free tenants usually held land from the lord of a manor for a money rent, although there might also be light services owed in addition to swearing fealty and paying a relief, or entry fine, to the lord on admission to his tenancy. Freeholders also owed suit of court, which meant they had to attend the manorial court when summoned, although they also had the right to defend their title to their holding in a royal court. A free tenant might transfer his or her freehold land (for which would be title deeds) to another tenant without the permission of the lord of the manor. Generally speaking, a free tenant might hold bond, or customary, land by an unfree tenure without sacrificing his personal free status, but a non-free tenant could not, in theory, hold free land.[39] The free land in the centre of Monks Eleigh in 1380 is illustrated in Weller's map at Plate 11.

Unfree tenants (known as serfs, villeins, customary tenants, bondmen or neifs) had no recourse to royal courts in respect of disputes with their lord, or about their holding of manorial land, but had to depend on the manorial court of their lord to defend title to their holdings. Unfree holdings were usually subject to much heavier labour services on the lord's demesne instead of, or in addition to, any cash rents. A villein tenant (usually termed a customary tenant in the Monks Eleigh documents) could not assign his holding to anyone else without the lord's permission, nor could he bequeath it except by the prevailing custom of the manor, which might involve, for example, descent to the eldest son, youngest son or division between all sons. At Monks Eleigh, the custom relating to inheritance was certainly to one son by default, but whether the eldest or youngest is not stated in the records in this volume. However, the custom of the manor constrained the lord too, and he seldom refused permission to assign customary land: effectively, therefore, villeins could buy and sell land, subject to surrendering it into the lord's hands for re-granting to the purchaser. If an unfree tenant wished to bequeath his or her manorial holding to a particular person, the procedure of surrendering a holding to the uses of a tenant's will gradually evolved in the early modern period: again, the tenant formally surrendered his or her holding back to the lord at a manorial court, and the lord re-granted it to the uses of the tenant's last will and testament. During the fifteenth century and into the sixteenth, a copy of the record of a villein's admission to a customary tenancy, as written in the manorial court rolls on his or her admission, also came to be legal proof and title to his or her tenancy, evolving into what became copyhold tenure, which remained as a legal title to land until 1925. In Monks Eleigh, we see copyhold land specifically appearing first in Rental 2 (*c.* 1503–*c.* 1513).

Besides being obliged to undertake labour works, which in Monks Eleigh included ploughing, sowing, reaping, carting, dung-spreading, roofing on the manorial build-

---

[39] Bailey, *The English Manor* (2002), pp. 26–28.

ings and other manual labour, on the lord's demesne, other feudal incidents, or dues, were also generally heavier on an unfree tenant. The rather limited number of Monks Eleigh court rolls contain no references to leyrwite (a fine payable to the lord by a woman who fornicated) or childwite (a fine for a woman giving birth to an illegitimate child), but they do contain references to merchet, the fine payable to the lord for permission for a villein's daughter to marry. This fine was generally heavier in most manors if she married outwith the manor or married a freeman. In Monks Eleigh in about 1349–50, for example, Agnes, daughter of Thomas Sparwe, married outwith the vill, and her marriage cost her father 2s. 6d. At the same court, John Gauge paid 2s. for his daughter Roisia to marry within the vill (see p. 101 for both examples). Even dying did not remove a villein's obligations to the lord: after an unfree tenant's death, his or her best beast was forfeit to the lord as a heriot, although sometimes it could be bought back by a widow or heirs if the lord allowed. There were safeguards, however. A widow's dower, as well as her joint tenancy with her husband, was honoured as dictated by the custom of the manor. And, as elsewhere, when a tenancy became vacant through the death of a tenant, the heirs according to the custom of the manor were sought, in order to take over the holding in their turn: custom therefore effectively supported the idea of the inheritability of customary tenancies, in fact, if not in theory.

There were also some allowances made for the customary tenants who undertook labour services, or works, for the lord, including the provision of food that accompanied or followed the performance of some of the most onerous works. In 1310–11, for example, those helping to clear out the dung from the outer courtyard of the manor were supplied with herrings and cheese worth 1s. 5d. by custom as well as 1½qr of wheat (presumably baked into bread). Those who helped with the wheat harvest were given beef worth 4s. 10d. and 3qr of wheat; at the oats harvest, herrings worth 1s. 3d. and 3qr of rye, and at both, cheese worth 4s. 2d. The communal consumption of such foodstuffs, whether taken on the job or at a specific feast afterwards, was no doubt appreciated and socially cohesive.

The Monks Eleigh records show several processes of change over time relating to tenants, rents and labour services. Firstly, the extents and accounts show the gradual increase in number, from at least the late-thirteenth century, of tenancies for fixed cash rents, not just for labour works and services. There was always a number of fixed, or as the records call them, assize rents paid in cash and fixed by agreement, which are recorded in extents of the manor as well as in the annual accounts and some of the charters.[40] In Extent 3 (probably c. 1250), these assize rents added up to £8 9s. By c. 1260–70, they had grown slightly to £8 13s. 5d. and by 1285–86, to £8 13s. 7¾d., but none of the particular rents were specified separately.[41] By 1310–11 and continuing in the accounts thereafter, these old assize rents remain totalled but unspecified, but to them are added increasingly longer lists of 'new rents', naming tenant and rent: the number of these new fixed rents increases over time (which co-incidentally helps to date the undated extents, by comparison with the dated accounts). In 1310–11, these new rents comprise 2s. from John ate Fen, 2s. from Simon Tollone, 1d. for a forge at Gedford, 8d. for a plot demised to John ate Tye

---

[40] Nichols, 'Milton Hall ...' (1929), p. 27, n. 2, citing Nellie Neilson, 'Customary Rents', no. IV in Paul Vinogradoff (ed.), *Oxford Studies in Social and Legal History*, II (Oxford, 1910), pp. 6–7. In the current volume, Charter 3 (1191–1213) in particular shows the priory directly leasing, for cash rents, various properties to several of its 'men [*and women*] of Eleigh'.

[41] See Extent 5 (c. 1260–1270); Accounts 1 (1285–86).

and 8d. for a headland demised to the said John at Ravenscroft. In 1329–30, the new rents comprise the old unspecified rents as a total only, plus the 1310–11 list of 'new rents', plus another tranche of new rents: 6d. from Margery le Forester for one rood of alder-carr, 6d. from William de Higglegh for a headland demised to him and 16s. 8d. from Richard de Broktone for 20 acres of land in Ravenscroft demised to him. Each successive set of accounts adds to the list of new rents, and many of them seem to be described specifically as rents for property 'demised' (that is, leased). Even at a time when the manor itself was being demesne managed, therefore, the tenants were increasingly leasing plots for fixed cash rents rather than undertaking labour works or services in lieu of rent. It is possible that at least some of these 'new rents' might have been for recently assarted land that had not previously been in cultivation.[42]

A second change relates to labour services (such as ploughing, harrowing, reaping, carting and spreading dung) performed by unfree manorial tenants for the lord on his demesne in lieu of money rents. These were very much the norm in most manors as they were in Monks Eleigh until 1379–80. But again, the accounts show a growing incidence of labour services being commuted for cash by the tenants. In 1285–86, the tenants paid 7s. 4½d. to commute or buy out a labour service of ploughing 14 acres 3 roods of land as a labour service for the lord, as well as 6s. for 143 unspecified works.[43] By 1310–11, the number and variety of labour works commuted to cash payments had increased and their cash value totalled £1 10s. ½d. By 1329–30, this had doubled to £3 18s. 10½d., and although the total value of commuted works dropped to £3 8s. 8¼d. in 1358–59 (after the crisis of the Black Death a decade before), a tipping point must have been reached by 1379–80, when, the accounts tell us, all labour services were commuted to cash payments for the first time.

The period between 1379 and 1380 seems to have been another key point of change in the management of the manor of Monks Eleigh. The same year saw the production of the first surviving rental, made over a period of ninety-four days by several men, probably an inquest jury made up of the chief pledges or the oldest inhabitants of the manor, whose memories were the staple evidence of such investigations (see also pp. xlvii–xlviii). The value of their time and trouble was given in the accounts as £3 7d., whilst the fee for the clerk writing up the rental itself, Thomas Rydle, amounted to 10s. These sums were not inconsiderable[44] and point to preparations for leasing the whole manor to a farmer, or lessee, which was almost certainly done around this time even though the first surviving lease (which does, however, refer to an earlier one) dates only from 1400. Weller typically put it into a modern if not academic idiom when he wrote to a correspondent about the leasing of the manor and commutation of labour services at this time being comparable to de-nationalisation:

---

[42] My thanks to Dr Nick Amor for this suggestion.

[43] 143 works sold for 6s. works out at a valuation of about ½d. per work, which is the usual valuation for works in the accounts between 1285/86 and 1358/59 in this volume. Using the same valuation of ½d. per work implies about 177 works for the 14 acres 3 roods of ploughing. The total number of works commuted to cash in 1285–86 was therefore about 320, compared with the works account total for that year of 1,812½ (cited by the clerk, but actually 1,803 by the editor's calculation) works. It looks therefore as if about 15 per cent of the total number of works owed before 1285–86 was commuted in that year.

[44] To put these costs into a relative contemporary context, compare, in the same set of accounts, the record of a forty-year lease of 18 acres of land to John Clerk atte Tye at a rent of 9s. a year.

Canterbury softened up the market, made the manor more attractive to bidders. It got rid of all restrictive practices. It made it money oriented. Tenants = £ rent. Court = £ income. Demesne = £ rent + x acres. There were no messy problems about managing labour within old trading practices.[45]

By 1379–80, then, Canterbury found it preferable to lease the manor of Monks Eleigh as part of a wider policy of monetarising its estates. As a result, the detailed series of serjeants' and reeves' accounts that commenced in the mid-thirteenth century ceased, and all that exists in the way of manorial records for Monks Eleigh for the fifteenth century are briefer and more limited farmers' accounts, a few court rolls for the early part of the century, and some draft and copy legal papers relating to a mass brawl in the village in 1481.

Monks Eleigh and the Peasants' Revolt of 1381

In Monks Eleigh, the changeover from labour services to cash rents and from demesne management to leasing was on the eve of the Peasants' Revolt. Was this timing merely co-incidence? How badly had the manor suffered in the Black Death and subsequently, economically and socially? Unfortunately, there are few complete court rolls surviving for Monks Eleigh to show how many might have died *c.* 1348–50 and in later outbreaks of plague, and how the manor coped with the sudden loss of labour and its longer-term consequences. Neither do we know what relationships between tenant and lord (or, more pertinently, lord's official) were like immediately prior to the revolt.

What is interesting, however, is the involvement in the Peasants' Revolt in the summer of 1381 of William atte Hel (or atte Hill), who was the serjeant or bailiff of Monks Eleigh in 1379–80 when a rental was made and the labour rents were all commuted to cash for the first time. John Ridgard wrote to Weller in 1994 with the names of five known Suffolk rebels he had found during his research who may have come from Monks Eleigh: 'William atte Hill of Essex alias William atte Hill formerly bailiff of the township of Illege in the county of Suffolk, Simon Bullock de Ely, Simon Bole wryghte, de Ele, John Clerke, Andrew le Kyng and John Font [*Fant?*].'[46] Ridgard also identified a tenant of the nearby manor of Hadleigh named Walter Tyler with the famous leader of the revolt, Wat Tyler.[47] Was there something about the conditions on these two priory manors that triggered these tenants in particular to revolt? Whether the reforms to labour services and manorial adminis-tration during William atte Hel's term as serjeant had anything to do with either the causes or the effects of the Peasants' Revolt cannot be determined. It seems counter-motivational for William to have experienced the cure of a grievance traditionally thought to be one cause of the Peasants' Revolt in his own bailiwick and yet to have

---

[45] Letter from Weller to Dr John Ridgard, 14 January 1994 (Weller Archive, file 'Monks Eleigh: Correspondence; Miscellaneous'). For a visual example of Weller's typical work practices, see Plate 1.

[46] Weller Archive, file, 'Monks Eleigh: Correspondence; Miscellaneous': Letter, 11 January 1994, Ridgard to Weller. In his typically enthusiastic style, Weller wrote to another correspondent shortly afterwards, expressing his excitement at the possibility that William atte Hel, the serjeant of Monks Eleigh in 1379–80, 'had a Monks Eleigh cell of five and got rid of labour as a form of rent before they joined the 1381 revolt – which may be why Monks Eleigh was spared being sacked'.

[47] See Woods, *Medieval Hadleigh* (2018), p. 104 for a summary of Ridgard's unpublished evidence.

DEMESNE - GARDEN : ORCHARD : MEADOW : BURTON
Development of Church Street and Town Street

9.1   The Hall and its grounds were in the lee of the church-
      yard where, in ancient times, the rector had kept his   *Chirograph 1213-1222*
      barns. A roofed gateway had divided the inner court to
      the Hall from its service buildings in the outer court
      and its entrance from Le Chirchstrett: beyond, to the
      west, was the large arable field of Byfeld stretching
      the demesne to where the curve of the land broke to the
      sky. Alongside the eastern boundary of the churchyard
      and the Hall was the Burton, the home field of the
      demesne, across which to the southeast clustered some
      of the villeins' dwellings. Here, at an island within   *See p.oo*
      the crossroads, the blacksmith had his forge nearby
      which, on freeland, he had his mansion overlooking the
      ford to the lord's river. Fanning out from the courts,
      down the south-facing slope to the king's highway, the
      Hall commanded its garden. Across the highway from
      Lavenham to Bildeston, stretching some 300m from Le
      Mellelane at the west to the ancient freelands of the
      villeins to the east, were the demesne orchards and
      meadows dipping southwards to the flood pastures and
      the fens with their several waterways and the deep
      stream of the lord's river and his mill. On the far bank
      were osier beds and small meadows held by the villeins
      and reached from Fennestrett above which, some 500m
      across the river valley from the Hall, rose the tree'd
      escarpment of the downs.

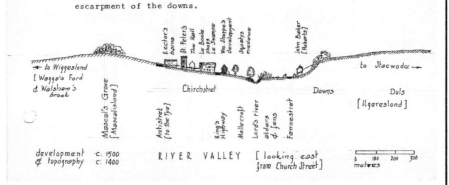

Plate 1. Example of Weller's draft work with a north–south section through the village of Monks Eleigh across the main street of Monks Eleigh and the River Brett (the lord's river). It is typical of Weller, always the architect, to word his thoughts in modern-day planning parlance and to draft his work in this format, with marginal references. It is also typical of him to adorn his notes with drawings, plans and sections of the manor, as here. (Weller Archive, file 'Monks Eleigh, 1475–1525'). For his sketch of the manorial hall and surroundings, as described above, see Plate 2.

joined in with the wider revolt with some of his fellow tenants.[48] In Monks Eleigh, one can only assume that the local changes of 1379–80 were either unpopular to the point of revolt or not connected with the causes of the revolt at all. Perhaps Monks Eleigh, under the local management of William atte Hel, and Hadleigh, were simply too far from seigneurial oversight from Canterbury and that this allowed plotters to flourish?

There were certainly incidents of revolt in 1381 on some other Essex custody manors, some of the evidence of which indicates what might have happened at Monks Eleigh. Nichols identifies three manors for which evidence survives in subsequent court rolls.[49] At Milton, court rolls were burnt and sufficient action taken by the rebels to warrant the loss of their holdings, for which they were fined heavily to be re-admitted. Nichols also points to various acts indicating unrest in the aftermath of the disorder, such as incidents of hue and cry in the court rolls, as well as outright resistance in December 1381 by an 'unusually large number [*fourteen*] of trespasses, with cattle, on the lord's pasture and growing crops, amounting apparently to a systematic defiance of the lord's rights'.[50] At neighbouring Southchurch and at Bocking, court rolls were again burnt, and tenants fined for re-admission to their holdings. There is no evidence from its court rolls of what happened at Monks Eleigh, as the rolls are missing between 1373/74 and 1413. If any were burnt here in 1381, therefore, they are likely to have been the most recent ones, as a majority of those that survive are from the 1360s and early 1370s.[51]

What Ridgard's list of Monks Eleigh rebels does however highlight is their social status as probably amongst the better off amongst those tenants: William atte Hel was serjeant/bailiff, and of the rest, John Clerke and Andrew le Kyng appear on numerous occasions in court rolls and other manorial records as tenants, acquiring and disposing of land, paying for the right to settle legal suits themselves and serving manorial offices. They were probably members of the emerging class of men who came to be known as yeomen by the fifteenth century, who were increasingly prosperous and locally influential middling farmers. An Andrew Kyng (possibly the same man, or a close family member) was also joint lessee of the manor in 1400.[52] John Fant was probably a relation of the wider family of Fants that was well established in the manor: one of his earlier relations might have been the William Fant who committed suicide in the mid-thirteenth century.[53] Bullock and Bole do not appear as tenants in the Monks Eleigh records, although there are references to a land called Boleslond in Court Roll 14 (1366/67–67), which might be the same as the land called Bolesquarter in Court Roll 17 (1373/74), but they could have been sub-tenants occupying property in the village, who would not necessarily appear in

---

[48] For a discussion of the causes and effects of the Peasants' Revolt, see M. Bailey, *After the Black Death: Economy, Society and the Law in Fourteenth-Century England* (Oxford, 2021).

[49] Nichols, '*Custodia Essexae*' (1930), pp. 85–90.

[50] Nichols, '*Custodia Essexae*' (1930), p. 87. Whether the number of trespasses was unduly large at fourteen, and therefore represents deliberate acts of resistance is debateable, however (see p. xlvii).

[51] From the poor condition of the few surviving rolls, historic neglect and bad storage conditions in the past are more of a factor in their lack of survival than deliberate destruction.

[52] For details of his lease, see Weller, 'The Manor of Eleigh Monachorum (Monks Eleigh, Suffolk): Lease of Demesne 21 November 1400', *Suffolk Review*, New Series no. 45 (Autumn 2005); transcript of the 1400 lease of the manor in Weller, 'Appendix A: Lease of Manor, 21 November 1400', *Suffolk Review*, New Series no. 46 (Spring 2006).

[53] See Charter 18 (*?c.* 1260s–1270s). For Weller's sketch of his possible burial place, see Plate 5.

manorial records. Alternatively, Bullock and Bole might have come from a different 'Ely' (perhaps the nearby Brent Eleigh) altogether.

The selection of documents in this volume

The documents reproduced in this volume are a selection from a larger whole that it is hoped will give access to primary sources for the scholar, as well as the non-specialist reader, to discover more about the lives of medieval and early modern people in Monks Eleigh.

The rationale behind the choice of items for inclusion was a pragmatic one: the items are chiefly those that Weller had had transcribed and translated by Michael Stansfield and Marion Allen in order to further his research in the 1990s. Weller's files make reference to a few other series of records translated by other people too, but these have not been found in the archive he bequeathed to the University of Suffolk. Weller was not a professional historian, and his research developed organically, sometimes in fits and starts. Despite his lack of historical training, he had some original insights. Sometimes, however, his choice of source documents and the way he interpreted them might seem arbitrary. Be that as it may, the existence of the transcripts Weller commissioned and their checking, editing and occasional augmentation by the present editor is the basis behind the choice. Each type of document is separately introduced below.

Charters

The thirty-six charters comprise all thirty-one of those known to exist relating to Monks Eleigh held by Canterbury Cathedral Archives, plus the five held by Suffolk Archives.[54] Of the thirty-one CCA charters, Stansfield translated thirty, principally from the enrolled versions of the charters in CCA-DCc/Register/E compared with the original charters (some of which were, and are, in very poor condition). The remaining CCA charter, Charter 2 (1152–1161), was translated by the current editor from its enrolment in both CCA-DCc/Registers B and E in order to complement Charter 1 (1152–1161), to which it relates in subject matter. Charters 5, 10, 11, 12 and 13 comprise the five original charters from the Iveagh Collection held at SA(I), which were translated for Weller in the 1990s by Marion Allen.[55]

The Suffolk Archives charters have been checked against the originals, an example of which is shown in Plate 4. The Canterbury charters have been checked and edited using photographs of the enrolled copies in CCA-DCc/Register/B (twenty-seven charters) checked against CCA's online gallery images of CCA-DCc/Register/E (nineteen charters, all also included in CCA-DCc/Register/B, in the same order), but they have not been compared here to the original CCA charters for editorial purposes. There are several reasons for this. Firstly, fourteen of the thirty-one Canterbury charters exist only as enrolled copies, so there are no originals to check for those. Secondly, many of the extant original charters are damaged owing to the passage of time and ancient storage problems, which has left some too fragile to handle. To these factors must be added the current editor's logistical and financial constraints (including the covid-19 pandemic restrictions of 2020–21),

---

[54] For details of all documents covered in this volume, see Bibliography: Manuscript Sources.

[55] Her typescripts of SA(I), HD 1538/307/1–5 (five charters formerly part of the Iveagh collection) are in Weller Archive, file, 'Monks Eleigh MS: Extents and Rentals; Charters'.

which prevented her from seeing them in Canterbury or obtaining photographs. However, because Michael Stansfield checked those original charters that were fit to be handled in the 1990s against CCA-DCc/Register/E, which has been checked by the current editor, a reasonable degree of confidence exists that the register copies and ensuing translations of the charters are accurate. Finally, the original charters have been calendared in the CCA online catalogue and reproduced in The National Archives' online Discovery catalogue, although in some cases, the current editor has suggested different dates from those in the catalogue as evidenced in the notes to each particular charter.

The dating of medieval charters bearing no explicit dates can be notoriously difficult.[56] In this volume, some have been placed within covering dates according to identifiable archbishops or priors, although this process is complicated by the fact that several priors had the same Christian name and no surname. Comparisons of witnesses and other people mentioned in particular charters can be used to establish a rough date or chronological 'pecking order' of items that probably pre- or post-date others within a framework of dated documents. Sometimes, individuals mentioned in charters can be identified from other Monks Eleigh manorial documents, or from documents held elsewhere and secondary sources. The editor's footnotes to individual charter transcriptions aim to clarify the most likely dates or covering dates, but there is no guarantee that the editor's imposed chronological order of the charters in this volume is absolutely correct.

Some of the early charters provide evidence for the longevity of names of land-holdings, as well as aspects of landscape and land use. Charter 3 (1191–1213), for example, lists a number of tenants to whom the prior and convent demised a variety of properties or rights over property for fixed annual cash rents. Some of these tenants gave their names to lands they rented (whether the lands demised in the particular charter or other property) and some of these names persisted for a long time. In Charter 3, William Tollune, Wlmar [sic] the carpenter, Sygar and Ilger were remembered nearly two centuries later in Rental 1 (1379–80) by the lands presumably named after them (Tollelones, Tollonesmundaylond, Wolmerys mundaylond, Sygaryscroft, Ilgereslond and possibly Ilidereslond). Skyppesmedewe, which is regularly referred to in many of the documents in this volume, may well have been named after Wybert Scip, who was also granted '1 perch and a certain way' in Charter 3. It was still called Scips Medowe in the rental of 1580, and its site was near to what is still known as Scripscross [sic] Bridge near Swingleton Green.

Apart from Wybert Scip's 'certain way', several other demises in Charter 3 were of ways or lanes that were probably more than mere access roads or rights of way. Charters 14 and 15 (mid-thirteenth century) record a grant and quitclaim to the prior and convent by the sons and widow of Richard Sygar of all their pasture 'which lies in the common roadway towards Sudbury', implying that road-side verges were broad enough to be worth grazing (perhaps they were also drove-ways) and were normal areas of pasturage for feeding animals. Charter 31 (1296) refers to a long, thin strip of land off Fen Street (*Fenstret*) measuring 40½ perches by 9 feet. This might at first be taken to imply that it was a strip of arable land in a common field, except for the fact that the charter also confers the right of free lopping of the trees

---

[56] Even with such modern online dating tools as the University of Toronto's 'Documents of Early England Data Set (DEEDS)'. See Bibliography: Websites.

growing on both sides of the plot: again, this must have been a lane-way or green lane, but in this case it is also described as an asset for the supply of wood.

A number of the charters relate to the granting of woodland, reflecting the value of woods as a resource for fuel, building, tool-making, staking and fencing. The main manorial woodland in Monks Eleigh was Manhey Wood, but in the 1220s, it seems that the prior and convent were seeking to consolidate and confirm their ownership of areas of woodland bordering Manhey, which appear to have been previously owned by or leased to other people: at some time between 1222 and 1238, Hugh the hayward quitclaimed a wood between Manhey and Turkilleslond that he had previously held as a tenant to the priory (Charter 7). At around the same time in Charter 9, in quitclaiming a nearby grove called Catteswode, 'formerly mine', John son of Adam confirmed that the prior and convent had the sole rights to it, and that it formed part of Manhey (*Maneiham*). In 1276, Nicholas, Henry and Thomas, the three sons of Anselm de Lellesey, each quitclaimed to the priory their interests in 2½ acres of wood bordering Manhey for 10s. each (Charters 21–23). A decade later, Thomas Forster made a grant in alms to the priory of a further half-acre of wood close by, also bordering Manhey (Charter 26).

In wetter areas, alder was grown as coppice-wood. The right to coppice seven acres of alder-holt was granted to Robert the clerk and his son Anselm between 1191 and 1213 (Charter 3). This might have been part of the alder-holt called Shortfen on the north bank of the lord's river just south of Byfold mentioned in Charters 14 and 15 (mid-thirteenth century). The comparative value of alder coppice to meadow is demonstrated in Charter 32 (1298), which records that Stephen Smith exchanged a strip of alder-holt measuring 10 perches by 12 feet for a piece of the priory's pasture measuring 7½ perches by 28 feet.

Extents

As part of manorial administration, landlords commissioned periodic surveys of one kind or another to enumerate the manor's assets. Monks Eleigh was no exception, and its extents and surveys fit into this wider context of developing documentation (an example is shown in Plate 7). A survey that detailed customs of a manor was known as a custumal, and often set out an idealised list of each tenant's obliga-tions, including labour services, to the lord. But, as P.D.A. Harvey noted, 'custumals are a very unsafe guide to the prevalence of labour services': such services could be commuted for cash, or provided by deputies, whilst renders in kind might be replaced by money, or another commodity of the same value.[57] The kind of survey known as an extent could comprise varying kinds of surveys including custumals but always included a valuation (equivalent to its yearly rental income). For private estates, extents became common from about the 1240s and became rare after the mid-fourteenth century, when demesne management began to decline and leasing of manors resumed. The trend to commute labour services for cash rents also helped to make the custumal, and aspects of the custumal within extents, obsolete.[58] From the fourteenth and into the fifteenth centuries and beyond, terriers, arranged topographi-cally, and rentals, arranged by tenant, were the kinds of surveys that replaced extents and custumals (see the Rentals section below). Some of the Monks Eleigh extents transcribed in this volume include custumals, but all have valuations.

---

[57] Harvey, *Manorial Records* (1999), p. 19.
[58] Harvey, *Manorial Records* (1999), pp. 19, 20–21.

Extents vary greatly in content, length and detail. A classic extent might cover the manorial hall and environs, mills, the demesne arable (strip by strip),[59] meadow, pasture and woods, as well as the tenants' rents and services, all valued and totalled. John le Doo's surveys of five of the Essex custody manors (see above p. xxv) made in 1305–10 were extents of this kind. Nichols, in writing about them, discerned what he termed a 'family likeness' in John le Doo's extents in terms of the works and organisation of land tenure.[60] He identified three kinds of services, which he termed week works, gafols and boons, and identified them as being due from the tenement rather than the tenant. He also argued (like Harvey) that the list of services due was 'an "ideal" arrangement in which the work required by the lord was levied as one imposition to be borne by a fixed number of holdings – virgates or lands (*terrae*)'. One therefore has to check the corresponding accounts to see what labour services were actually done on the ground in any given year. Nichols also recognised that although it was 'possible to reconstruct this ideal arrangement by regrouping the various holdings in accordance with the labour units of the custumals, … in many cases, especially on the more "progressive" manors, there has been so much sub-division and regrouping that the original plan can no longer be retraced'.

The Monks Eleigh extents in this volume are not as comprehensive as le Doo's extents of the five Essex custody manors, but some aspects of Nichols' family like-ness in some of their contents is apparent. The Monks Eleigh extents make refer-ence to separate, standardised holdings called lands, some divided into half-lands or quarter-lands. In Hadleigh, according to le Doo's 1306 extent, each full customary (unfree) land comprised 30 acres,[61] which fits with the common standard pattern of villein holdings elsewhere in the country described by Bailey:

> Landholdings in villeinage were often more standardised than freeholdings, commonly appearing as thirty-acre holdings called 'full-lands' or virgates; as fifteen-acre 'half-lands' or 'half-virgates'; or as small-holding 'cotlands'. These uniform, customary, holdings principally comprised arable land, although they could also include small quantities of meadow and perhaps woodland, and invariably came with a messuage. In some parts of the country the whole 'package' of land and messuage was described as a '*tenementum*'.[62]

As we shall see in the rentals section below, Monks Eleigh's twenty-one and a half full lands comprised various acreages and are complicated by variations in what we call an acre, but the concept behind the division of villein lands is similar to le Doo's and manorial sub-divisions elsewhere.

Both Monks Eleigh and Hadleigh had a differentiated class of customary lands called mondaylands, presumably because the works owed for them were customarily done on Mondays. These appear to have been a particularly East Anglian phenom-enon. Hadleigh had eight mondaylands, which were half-lands of 15 acres each.[63] Monks Eleigh had nine of varying acreages: two of them were half-lands, two more were of 13 acres, but the others varied between 1 and 10 acres. The number of works also varied on the Monks Eleigh mondaylands: five of them together accounted for

---

[59] For Weller's map of demesne arable in the northern half of Monks Eleigh, see Plate 9.

[60] Nichols, '*Custodia Essexae*' (1930), pp. 240–41.

[61] Woods, *Medieval Hadleigh* (2018), p. 109 and Appendix A, although a standard 'land' in Lawling was apparently 60 acres. See Nichols, '*Custodia Essexae*' (1930), p. 255. The difference may be between measured or customary acres and fiscal acres (see pp. xlviii–l).

[62] Bailey, *The English Manor* (2002), p. 28.

[63] Woods, *Medieval Hadleigh* (2018), p. 119; Nichols, '*Custodia Essexae*' (1930), p. 251.

400 works (eighty each), two more jointly owed ninety-six works, whilst the two remaining (both half-lands) owed forty-eight and thirty-seven works respectively. This difference might be due to the size of holding, quality of land, conditions at the time at which the services were laid down or what could be negotiated, but we simply do not know. In Hadleigh, besides specified labour services, mondayland tenants were obliged to guard prisoners at the mill before their delivery for trial and, more onerously, serve as reeves for the manor.[64] The records reproduced here are silent on whether these obligations were also owed at Monks Eleigh by its mondaylanders. As in Hadleigh, the only differentiation of tenants in Monks Eleigh is between free tenants and unfree customary tenants (*custumarii*).[65] There is no overtly derogatory terminology for unfree tenants such as serf by blood (*nativus de sanguine*), although the term offspring or brood (*sequela*), also used of animals, is ambiguous in Court Roll 15 (1368–69) (see p. 144).

Of Nichols' family likeness of labour services, ordinary week-works (just called works in the records), boons and *gafols* were all due from some land-holdings in Monks Eleigh. Boon-works were theoretically voluntary works, given willingly by the tenants to the lord as a response to his request or prayer. They appear in the records as the Middle English word *benerthes* (sometimes *bene* or the abbreviated *ben'*) or the Latin *precarius*. Whether boon-works were really given willingly by the tenants or were done in response to 'an offer they could not refuse' is a moot point. However, they are always differentiated in the Monks Eleigh records from labour services performed as *gavelearthes*, also recorded as the Middle English words *gafol*, *gavel*, *gable* or the Latin *gabulum*. Nichols follows Nellie Neilson in stating that *gafol* was a very early form of tribute or land tax, as the word *gafol* had time to form so many compound words in Old and Middle English, *landgavel* (by then a cash payment) being the one that survives in Monks Eleigh up to the 1379–80 rental.[66] They were considered obligatory rather than voluntary and part of the custom of the manor but could be commuted to cash.

The extents detail the kinds of works due on the Monks Eleigh lands and include ploughing, harrowing, sowing, reaping, carting and spreading dung, gathering straw for thatching the lord's barns and carriage services.[67] The manor's produce, whether food rents being sent to Canterbury or for sale more generally, might well have been transported by sea via Ipswich. Extent 5 (*c.* 1260–1270) refers to the customary tenants owing the service of carriage to Ipswich, which was both a market town and convenient sea-port, although Woods considers that produce from nearby Hadleigh was probably shipped through Cattawade, at the head of the Stour estuary, to Canterbury.[68] Other extents and the Monks Eleigh manorial accounts in this volume do not mention specific carriage services to Ipswich or elsewhere specifically, although such services could merely have been commuted to the tenants for cash, silently subsumed within more generalised transportation services, or even have disappeared after the late 1280s, when Monks Eleigh ceased to be a food-farm (as discussed above).

---

[64] Woods, *Medieval Hadleigh* (2018), pp. 120–21 and Appendix A.

[65] Woods, *Medieval Hadleigh* (2018), p. 107; Bailey, *The English Manor* (2002), p. 26.

[66] Nichols, 'Milton Hall ...' (1929), p. 27; Neilson, 'Customary Rents' (1910), pp. 42–47.

[67] Nichols, '*Custodia Essexae*' (1930), pp. 257–58.

[68] CCA-DCc-Register/P, fols 119r–120r; CCA-DCc-Register/H, fol. 160v; Woods, *Medieval Hadleigh* (2018), p. 235.

Dating the extents in this volume has been problematic because few are explicitly dated and most exist in later copies, so handwriting is no guide. Comparison with similarities such as assize rents in the dated series of accounts has been useful in dating the extents, however (see pp. xxviii–xxix above). The footnotes detail dating criteria for individual extents.

Accounts

The Monks Eleigh manorial accounts follow a common format after *c.* 1270, when manorial records of all kinds suddenly became much more numerous across the country (for an illustration, see Plate 8). The increase in accounts was partly due to the training given to a new and gradually expanding class of professional clerks to assist the local manorial officials, without whom the written accounts could not have been made. Their common format was drawn from late-thirteenth-century written guidance on estate management and agricultural practice, such as Walter of Henley's *Husbandry* and similar works.[69] The development of detailed accounts themselves can also be attributed to the change to demesne management explained above. The changes to and from demesne management were gradual over a period of time and piecemeal in terms of location, but the large ecclesiastical estates with their widely spread manors, educated ownership and more continuous centralised administrations tended to lead the way. Clearly, demesne management demanded checks on the local officials to avoid fraud, and a hands-on management style needed more data to allow the lord to see what was happening on his estates and to make informed management decisions. These led to the kinds of detailed manorial accounts such as are included in this volume.[70]

In the account (*compotus*), the bailiff, reeve or serjeant had to answer to the lord's auditors for the obligations with which he was charged during his term of office, usually an annual term from Michaelmas (29 September) each year. When the annual accounts were made up, the harvests would have been mostly gathered in and stock could be taken of crops and livestock on the manor. Most of the Monks Eleigh reeves and serjeants served for a number of years and so left several sets of such annual accounts (see Table 3, above). The accounts, in the form in which we have them, are not just the accounts as dictated by the manorial bailiff or reeve to a clerk; they are also the result of a dialogue between the bailiff and the auditor (the monk-warden or steward), who might amend them. For example, in the 1329–30 accounts, the auditors struck out the reeve's claim for allowance for 2s. for the expenses of lodging Hugh the clerk because the cost had been included in the warden's tally.

The first section of a typical account commences with cash received (the charge) and cash disbursed (the discharge) by the local official. This usually begins with any debt still owing to the lord by the reeve or bailiff from the previous year. None of the Monks Eleigh accounts in this volume has any such initial outstanding debt. Next come receipts from fixed or assize rents (see above), which were payable at five terms of the year (see Table 4).

---

[69] Elizabeth Lamond (ed.), *Walter of Henley's Husbandry, Together with an Anonymous Husbandry, Seneschaucie and Robert Grosseteste's Rules* (London, 1890).

[70] For the fullest details of how manorial accounts developed and were compiled, see Harvey, *Manorial Records of Cuxham* (1976), pp. 12–57. See also Harvey, *Manorial Records* (1999), pp. 25–40 and Bailey, *The English Manor* (2002), pp. 97–116.

Table 4: Assize rents and terms payable, 1285–86

Term date	Rent payable	% of total annual rent
St Andrew (*30 November*)	14s. 7d.	8.4
Palm Sunday (*Sunday before Easter*)	17s. 4d.	10.2
SS Peter and Paul (*29 June*)	£1 18s. 6¼d.	22.1
St Peter in Chains (*1 August*)	£1 9s. 2¾d.	16.8
Michaelmas (*29 September*)	£3 13s. 11¾d.	42.5
Total of annual assize rents	£8 13s. 7¾d.	100

These terms are not equally spaced through the year, nor are the rents the same each term, but they reflect the payment of most rents after a particular harvest or yield of receipts. Rents were probably paid in advance and the date of payment was probably the beginning of the term. Unsurprisingly, the term yielding the highest rents – Michaelmas – followed the main grain harvest. St Peter in Chains may reflect the yield from the hay harvest. That of SS Peter and Paul may follow the sale of the wool-clip after sheep-shearing. In successive accounts, the assize rents are repeated more or less as in 1285–86 (with occasional differences of not more than a fraction of a penny) but with the addition of increasing numbers of new rents added on to the assize rents, which can help to date the undated extents, as discussed above (see p. xxviii). In the account for 1379–80, when all the customary works were commuted into cash rents for the first time, the account merely gives a total sum of £29 7s. 4½d. for all assize rents and works, and then goes on to list all those previously 'new rents' formerly appended to assize rents in the earlier accounts as cottagers' rents and a separate section for larger holdings of leases. It is clear from these assize rents that even during the period of demesne management, certain lands were leased or rented for purely cash rents, and that these increased over time until all rents on the manor were converted to money in 1379–80.

Assize rents are followed in the first cash section of the account by other items of income, typically from sales of corn and livestock, other receipts and the perquisites (or profits) of the manorial court. In Monks Eleigh, these streams of income also included customary works commuted for cash, herbage (rights of pasture, or the produce of pasture or meadow), firewood, apples, hides, dairy and wool sold.

Cash expenditure, the discharge, follows next, listing the allowable expenses of the manorial reeve or serjeant submitting the account to set against the charge. These typically include expenses relating to ploughs and carts, new buildings or repairs, harvest expenses, threshing and winnowing, seed for the next year's sowing and livestock and wages of the manorial servants or staff (*famuli*). In Monks Eleigh, they also contain paragraphs on expenses for the visits of the warden and his party twice a year (once to audit the accounts), foreign or external expenses, various officials' expenses, costs of fencing, mowing, ditching and enclosing, weeding, making faggots and various petty expenses, including the maintenance and propagation of vines in the vineyard. The income and expenditure were totalled and balanced, and the difference stated. If the two balanced exactly, as they most often do in these accounts, then the equal balance is noted. Otherwise the balance shows whether the official owed the lord any sum, or vice versa.

In Monks Eleigh, it appears that despite a limited number of annual accounts from which to take the figures, both income and expenditure rose after 1285–86, reaching a consistently higher level in 1310–11, 1329–30 and 1379–80, but with a temporary dip back to 1285–86 levels in 1358–59. The rise after 1285–86 might well have been due to the changes in administration made by Prior Henry of Eastry. The dip in 1358–59 might reflect long-standing economic damage a decade after the Black Death or it might reflect more local, short-term changes at that time, such as the period immediately before 1358–59 when Richard Forester leased the manor. Without a larger sample of accounts, it is difficult to tell.

The second section of the account, usually on the dorse of the roll, covers the corn and livestock accounts, noting in detail charge and discharge. The corn account goes through each crop, usually wheat, rye, barley, beans, peas and oats in that order. Vetch appears solely in the 1310–11 accounts, where it is specifically stated to have been separated from the oats, so either it was a weed, or the seed of the two crops had been sown together, by accident or design. Maslin and dredge, mixed grains, often used to pay the *famuli*, are also specified in those for 1379–80. Wheat and oats were the leading crops for most of the fourteenth century, peaking in the 1358–59 accounts and dropping thereafter, although remaining amongst the top three crops in quantity accounted for. Rye and peas show less variation across time. Barley increased steadily until 1329–30, dipped in 1359–60 and then increased significantly from 8qr to 14qr in 1379–80, then being the most substantial crop grown.

The livestock account details all the stock of the manor in a specific order, beginning with the larger animals and going through each, starting with male then female adult animals, then the young, and gradually reducing in size or importance. Cart-horses appear from 1329 to 1330 but are not specified in 1285–86 or 1310–11, then stots (a type of horse), oxen, bulls, cows, bullocks, heifers, calves, wethers, ewes, hoggets, lambs, boars, sows, pigs, piglets, peacocks and peahens (1310–11 only), ganders and geese, capons, cockerels and hens, ducks, eggs and doves. In terms of livestock, it is the nature of the accounts that each bailiff merely had to show that he had maintained the required number of animals forming the stock of the manor. If an animal died or was sold, it had to be replaced either from recruitments from younger animals, births or purchases, ensuring that the stock of animals on the manor remained fairly static over time. For each of the corn and stock accounts, totals of charge and discharge were made and any debt or surplus calculated. The auditors took no notice of any surplus, which the bailiff probably considered his recompense for carrying out an onerous office, although any deficit would be carried over to the next accounting period as a debt owing to the lord by the bailiff.

Oxen and horses both feature as draught animals in this section of the accounts and were the most valuable animals on the manor.[71] Oxen were cheaper to maintain than horses, stronger for ploughing on heavy land, and kept their value, their meat and hide being useful as well as their draught capabilities after their working lives were over. Horses had less strength in ploughing and were more expensive to feed, but were more flexible, being more able to plough smaller and awkwardly shaped

---

[71] It should be noted that the accounts usually refer to draught horses as stots (*stotti*), which can also be translated, confusingly, as oxen (see *OED*, *MED* and *DMLBS*). The habit of hierarchical listing by medieval manorial accountants strongly suggests that horses are meant as horses are always listed first, above oxen, and oxen are listed immediately below stots in the stock account section.

pieces of land and to do jobs such as carting and harrowing.[72] Between 1285 and 1380 in Monks Eleigh, the number of oxen dropped from twelve to six, although these numbers are outliers and for most of the century represented in the selection here there was a manorial standard stock of eight. Between the same dates, the number of horses varied less in number, but altered in kind: nine stots in 1285–86, eight stots in 1310–11, two cart-horses and eight stots in 1329–30 and 1358–59 and four cart-horses and four stots in 1379–80. When the manor was leased in 1400, the manorial livestock included four cart-horses valued at £1 each, three stots at 9s. each and six oxen at various values between 16s. and 13s. 4d. each, showing their comparative monetary value.[73] The figures show an increase in the number of horses as draught animals on the demesne up to the middle of the fourteenth century and then a drop back to earlier levels, which coincided with a drop in the number of oxen. There does not appear to be a large-scale switch from oxen to horses on the demesne before 1400. It is possible that the tenants might have owned more horses than the demesne (see the Court rolls section, pp. xlvi–xlvii).

Horses were proverbial eaters, and more expensive than oxen to feed – so much so that at least one historian has referred to them as 'oat guzzlers'.[74] The accounts show in great detail how the horses on the demesne were fed oats during the autumn, winter and early spring, when they could not be pastured on grass. The rates of feeding at different periods of those seasons presumably reflect the periods during which they were ploughing or otherwise working more intensely. Between 6 October and 20 November 1329, eight stots consumed 5qr 5b. of oats at a rate of a bushel a night between them, at a period when they were probably autumn ploughing. The feeding rate dropped to ½b. a night between 20 November 1329 and 25 January 1329/30 when they were presumably working less, but then increased again to 1 bushel a night from then until 6 May during the period of spring ploughing. The total quantity of oats consumed by these eight stots over that period was 22qr 3b. Over the same period, two cart-horses consumed only 6qr 6b. of oats at the rate of 1 peck per night, half the quantity of a resting stot and a quarter of the quantity of one working. The 1358–59 accounts show a further contrast: between 6 October 1358 and 3 May 1359, eight stots ate 18qr of oats, two carthorses ate 6qr, whilst eight oxen ate 6qr. Horses were clearly used on the demesne, perhaps for specific purposes, but oxen were more economical to feed and remained at the heart of plough-teams throughout the fourteenth century.

There is just a hint that horses might have been one of Prior Henry of Eastry's innovations on the demesne in 1285–86, although too much emphasis should not be put on this as there are not enough sets of accounts in this volume from which to draw a conclusion. The hint comes from the fact that in that year the amount of oats produced on the manor of Monks Eleigh (49qr) was insufficient to cover even the manor's own seed requirements (54qr) let alone the fodder (19qr 3b. between 5 October and 1 May) for the nine stots. Yet after this, for most of the fourteenth

---

[72] J. Langdon, 'The Economics of Horses and Oxen in Medieval England', *AgHR* 30, no. 1 (1982), pp. 39–40. On horses more generally, see also J. Langdon, *Horses, Oxen and Technological Innovation: The Use of Draught Animals in English Farming from 1066 to 1500* (New York and Cambridge, 1986).

[73] Weller, 'The Manor of Illegh Monachorum' (2005), p. 8 and 'Appendix' (2006), p. 1.

[74] Kathleen Biddick, 'Review of John Langdon, *Horses, Oxen and Technological Innovation: The Use of Draught Animals in English Farming from 1066 to 1500* (New York and Cambridge, 1986)', *American Historical Review* 93, no. 2 (April 1988), p. 402.

century, the manor grew virtually all of its requirements for oats, which increased significantly to 100qr in 1310–11 and 132qr 1b. in 1329–30, when 41qr 4b. worth £6 3s. 5¾d. were sold, indicating that by then it was very much a cash crop too. Might it have been the case that horses were such a fresh innovation in 1285–86 that the manor had not yet caught up with the need to grow more oats to feed them? It has to be acknowledged that linking a possible increase in the use of horses and the increased growth of oats could be a chicken and egg question, and that the increase in the growth of oats across the fourteenth century could have been due to other factors.

The third section, the works account, comprises the labour services on the manor, giving details of the various services of ploughing, harrowing, harvesting and other customary services due from the unfree tenants to the lord. For Monks Eleigh, there are no accounts of labour services for 1285–86 (the membrane might have simply not survived following the stock account) or 1379–80 (when all labour services had been converted to cash).

The farmers' accounts, which take over from the detailed reeves' and bailiffs' accounts of the demesne management system, are much less detailed. They naturally record the payment (or not) of the farmer's rent to Canterbury, together with any approved expenditure that he might claim, usually for repairs, especially for buildings such as the manor's mill or granaries, as specified in the terms of the lease.[75] Two full transcripts of farmers' accounts are included here to give a flavour of the series and the known farmers 1400–1536 are listed in Table 5.

Table 5: Farmers (lessees) of the manor of Monks Eleigh, 1400–1536

John North	1400–1
William Bacoun	1406–7
Thomas Malcher	1419–38
Andrew Shopp	1449–50
Thomas Tornour	1454–56
Adam Turnour	1460–81
Andrew Vyncent	1481–97
John Warde	1504–14
Adam Goodeale	1519–36

All the dates in the table are from existing accounts, but it is possible that their terms of office might have begun earlier and ended later than the dates cited. This list is based on one supplied to Weller by Michael Stansfield in the 1990s and on the farmers listed in the extracted building accounts in Section IV.

This volume includes a separate section of building accounts (*custus domorum*), extracted from both the reeves' and farmers' accounts. They have been included because, in many ways, this was the starting point of Weller's research and the topic

---

[75] For the terms of one of these leases for Monks Eleigh, see Weller, 'The Manor of Illegh Monachorum' (2005) and his 'Appendix' (2006).

upon which he was most expert. Had he not been interested in the records of farm buildings of other Canterbury estates, he would never have been asked to provide architectural details of selected historic buildings in Monks Eleigh for the 1991 millennium commemoration and he would never have been drawn into researching the history of the manor. The records supply a wealth of detail on building materials, costs and techniques as well as subject-specific terminology. Buildings mentioned here and in the main accounts are a hall, chamber, wardrobe, kitchen, buttery, pantry, grange, granary, oats grange, ox shed, stable, sheep cote, neat house, well, dairy, dovecote, gateways, water mill (which needed the most amount of work), bridge, churchyard wall, cottage and a 'small house facing the street'. For Weller's plan of the manorial hall and associated buildings *c.* 1400, see Plate 2.

Court rolls

The dates and frequency of Monks Eleigh's manorial courts are hard to determine because relatively few court rolls survive, and those that do are often fragile or damaged. It might be supposed that the twice-yearly visits of the warden of the Essex custody would be an appropriate time for a court, but there is no evidence for or against this supposition. In his edition of the Walsham le Willows court rolls, Ray Lock suggested that only larger manors held courts every three weeks, with courts at Walsham averaging at about three each year.[76] At Monks Eleigh, the frequency of courts appears to have been similar. Its rolls of proceedings survive for only forty-one or forty-two courts between 1305 and 1590, although these terminal dates are outliers, with half (twenty-six) falling within the central period of *c.* 1349–74, six for the entire fifteenth century and six more for the sixteenth. Out of the surviving courts, specific dates cannot be ascertained for eight, and the dates for the remaining ones are fairly evenly scattered through the year, except for November and December, for which there are no surviving court records in any year. There seem to be periods when particular dates were favoured. The six fifteenth-century courts, covering 1413–22, by which time the manor was leased, were held on 1 August (four courts), 2 August (one), 2 September (one) and 21 October (one). By the late-sixteenth century, of the five courts the records of which survive between 1586 and 1590 (some of which records are estreats only, so they might be incomplete), four were held in May and one in late April. Most of the proceedings are on single membranes comprising records of one or two courts only. Most of those containing two fall into the undatable category, although a few runs of courts do occur: Court Rolls 7 and 8 contain successive courts dated 12 April, 9 August, 24 September 1361 and 17 January 1361/62. Some of the rolls contain three successive courts: Court Roll 14 for 14 January 1366/67, 29 July and 30 September 1367, and Court Roll 15 for 24 July, 2 October 1368 and 17 September 1369. For the fourteenth century, when the manor was being demesne managed rather than leased, the pattern of courts seems to have been two or three courts a year, usually one in January/February, another in late July/early August around Lammas Day (1 August) when the hay harvest was in and one around Michaelmas (29 September), after the main grain harvest had been gathered in.

Manorial courts had both administrative (called the general court or court baron) and judicial (leet) jurisdictions, through which the lord of a manor could exert a strong measure of legal, financial and social control over the work and behaviour of

---

[76] R. Lock (ed.), *The Court Rolls of Walsham Le Willows, 1351–1399*, SRS 45, 2002, p. 7.

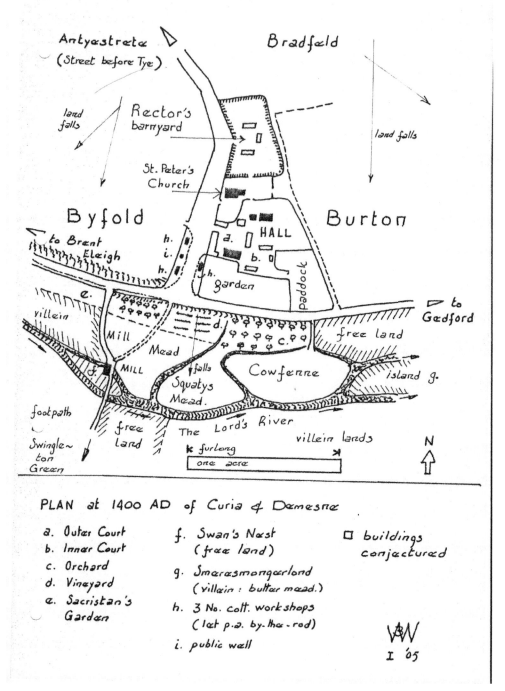

Plate 2. Weller's map showing the manorial hall, associated buildings and nearby demesne property at Monks Eleigh, c. 1400 (Weller Archive, file 'Maps')

his tenants. A manorial court was also a source of income for the lord.[77] All tenants were required to attend the manorial court (they were said to owe suit of court or common suit) but could excuse (essoin) themselves (with sureties) for up to three courts without being fined for default. The general court rolls usually open with a list of those essoining themselves from the common suit of attendance at the court, together with those standing surety for them: sometimes a number appears to the right of an entry, indicating the number of times a person had excused himself in this way.

The court served to regulate tenancies, and a considerable proportion of its rolls dealt with tenurial business. The market in land (free or customary) always seems to have been busy enough for every court to have dealt with changes in tenancies, or orders for new occupiers of manorial tenancies to prove how they had entered into occupation of particular holdings, including entries of freeholders who showed their charters or deeds granting their title to the land. Unfree tenants had no title deeds as such, although copyhold tenure developed from the fifteenth century as discussed above (p. xxvii). A new tenant, whether being admitted to land purchased or inherited, would have to attend the court to do fealty and pay an entry fine to the lord. This was recorded in the court rolls, although the rent or customary works due on the holding are rarely mentioned. When unfree land changed hands by sale, this occurred by the mechanism of the seller surrendering it back into the hands of the lord through the steward and the buyer being admitted as the new tenant.

The court rolls also recorded the payment of various manorial incidents payable by unfree tenants such as merchet and heriot, as described above: the custom of the manor defined these and was key to how tenancies descended to which heirs including to a widow by virtue of her right to free bench or joint tenancy (see pp. xxvii–xxviii).

Civil litigation was dealt with by the manor court.[78] Free tenants had the right to take disputes over title to their lands and other matters to higher courts, but for unfree tenants, the manorial court was their only option to settle such matters. If a dispute between two parties was brought, then pledges, or guarantors, might be required to provide surety so that the case was actually pursued to a conclusion through the court. The lord took a cut, whatever the result, as can be seen frequently in the Monks Eleigh court rolls: tenants in dispute with each other would pay the lord a fine for permission to come to their own mutual agreements in disputes, known as licence to settle. They could be distrained (threatened with, or actually made to forfeit goods) to respond in pleas of debt or trespass against other tenants, for which purpose they were often 'given a day' to attend court to settle the matter.

Cases might be brought to court by individuals, but many matters were brought to the court's notice by a jury (the homage), which would make presentments of faults, particularly those of community concern, such as leaving dung on the roadway, or obstructing water-courses or trespasses with animals. Specific inquest juries might be appointed to look into matters that required further investigation, and there would have been a special jury chosen to confer with the surveyor if a survey were made, as detailed in the 1379–80 rental accounts, discussed elsewhere in this introduction (see pp. xxix, xlvii–xlviii). Juries might also settle disputes. Jurors were usually the senior men of the vill, and at the view of frankpledge, the leet jury

---

[77] Bailey, *The English Manor* (2002), p. 168.
[78] Bailey, *The English Manor* (2002), pp. 172–75.

that made presentments was made up of the chief pledges, or heads of each tithing. The tithingmen, through their chief pledges, also paid to the lord the common fine, which in Monks Eleigh amounted to 4s. a year paid as of ancient custom at the view of frankpledge.[79] This 4s. common fine remained the same from c. 1260 to 1270 (Extent 5) until at least 1590 (Court Roll 24).

More serious offences known as felonies were tried by justices of the peace or by justices of gaol delivery at the periodic county assizes at Bury St Edmunds, but minor local criminal matters in Monks Eleigh were dealt with in the manorial court under its leet jurisdiction at the view of frankpledge.[80] Petty crimes and infractions were usually punished by fines (amercements), the offender either acknowledging the offence by putting him or herself in the mercy or grace of the lord or being judged to be in mercy by the court. The amounts of fines were set by two affeerors chosen by the court to assess how much should be paid. The commonest transgressions punished by such amercements in the Monks Eleigh courts were trespasses with animals, usually in the lord's crops, pasture or woods, assaults, illegal recoveries of impounded animals, theft, aggravated housebreaking (*hamsoken*), raising the hue and cry, justly or unjustly, to chase and take a transgressor, obstructing ways or water-courses, failing to do required works or services, forestalling the market, failing to undertake manorial offices, such as that of constable or ale-taster or doing them badly, brewing or baking against the assize of bread and ale, making illicit ways across fields, and not scouring ditches and water-courses.

Court rolls can therefore be used to investigate many aspects of rural life, such as what types of animals the tenants possessed compared with those of the manorial demesne stock detailed in the accounts. Court rolls for Monks Eleigh are relatively few in number and coverage of dates, and most are seriously incomplete, which hampers any kind of complete picture, but we can still gain impressions from the incidents of heriots and trespasses with animals. Out of the twenty-three references in the court rolls and accounts to heriots between 1305 and 1374, for example, five were to horses, four to oxen, five to cows, two to pigs, one to a sheep, one to a calf, five to unspecified animals and one to an unspecified heriot where the deceased had no animals. Taking horses and oxen as examples (as above under Accounts), heriots of these animals are fairly evenly spread across that period, so there is no pattern of change that can be ascertained. Using heriots as evidence, therefore, all that can be concluded from these figures is that nine tenants who happened to die at times covered by the surviving court rolls were sufficiently wealthy to have a best beast comprising a horse or ox: there is no way to tell from heriots what the spread of these animals was throughout the whole community of tenants over time.

Court rolls contain evidence other than heriots for ownership of particular animals, however. Taking horses as an example once more, records of trespasses with animals in the surviving court rolls show that a number of tenants of the manor of Monks Eleigh had horses, despite the relatively high cost of feeding them. John Langdon has suggested that tenants did not feed their horses solely on expensive oats, as manorial lords tended to do, but tended to use cheaper fodder, such as vetches, hay and straw, which sufficed for tenants' horses as they had less intensive work to do than the draught animals on the demesne (which required oats in quan-

---

[79] The common fine had its origins in the hundredpenny originally paid to the sheriff, but later paid to the lord holding leet jurisdiction by the members of each tithing at the view of frankpledge. See Bailey, *The English Manor* (2002), pp. 181, 244.

[80] See Bailey, *The English Manor* (2002), pp. 178–89.

tity, as discussed above on pp. xl–xlii). He also suggests that 'as a source of pasture, trespasses on the demesne must have ranked alongside the commons' in helping to feed them.[81] At Monks Eleigh, trespasses with animals were common entries in the fourteenth- and especially the early fifteenth-century court rolls and a large proportion of these being with horses and oxen, implying reasonable numbers of these animals in tenants' hands.[82] Nicholas Hygele was prosecuted in February 1351/52 for trespassing in the lord's rye with three horses and three bullocks on four occasions. In April 1361, he went further still, trespassing in the lord's pasture with his oxen, as well as his horses, beasts and sixty sheep, and for trespassing in the lord's wheat and peas with his household. At the same court in 1361, Walter Heyward trespassed in the lord's pasture with his horses, and John Farthing trespassed in the lord's oats with his horse and his ox. Either these were effectively licences to graze (the sixty sheep suggest on a large scale), or these tenants were making major inroads into the demesne grazing resources to feed their own animals by design, whether opportunistically or criminally, rather than by accident. It is possible that, as Nichols suggested was the case in other Essex custody manors at the time of the Peasants' Revolt of 1381 (see above, p. xxxii), these might even have been acts of resistance against the manorial authorities.

Rentals

Strictly speaking, in terms of type of document, rentals belong with extents and surveys, but at Monks Eleigh they take a very different form and are separated from the extents chronologically, so they have been given a separate section here. The first rental, for 1379–80 (illustrated at Plate 10), has already been mentioned as marking an important turning point in the administration of the manor of Monks Eleigh: it marks the year in which all labour works and services were commuted to cash for the first time, and probably the changeover to the leasing of the manorial demesne, rather than managing it in-hand. Of all the rentals in this volume, it is the one that gives an idea of how such rentals and surveys were made. Typically, in making a survey, a group of the oldest and most respected men of the manor would be assembled as an inquest jury (see also pp. xxix and xlv). The surveyor or other person making the rental would rely on these men's memories and knowledge of the land and people of the vill to put together a snapshot of the manor, showing who held which and how much land and how much rent they owed for it. Very often (although this is not apparent with the 1379–80 rental here), an old rental would be used as a pattern-book for the new one: rentals tended to be made every generation or so unless there were substantial changes (in land-holding, tenants or a change of lord, for example), so an old rental would be seen as authoritative proof of the *status quo* at a fixed past point in time, to add to the memories of the elder tenants. Rentals were frequently annotated with updates (such as changes of tenant) after they had been made, sometimes for many years, until it was felt that a new rental was warranted. The costs of the 1379–80 rental (£3 7d., plus 10s. for the clerk to write it) show that this was an expensive exercise, and therefore only to be undertaken when deemed absolutely necessary.

---

[81] Langdon, 'The Economics of Horses and Oxen in Medieval England' (1982), pp. 38–39.
[82] There were at least twenty-nine instances of trespasses with horses in twelve of the manorial courts between 1351/52 and 1422. There were also many more trespasses recorded with other animals.

Once assembled, over a period of days or weeks (ninety-four days in 1379–80) the surveyor and the jurors would perambulate the manor, successively discussing and listing for the clerk to note each holding and tenant and any details of the holding that were deemed worthy of remembrance. Land-holdings would frequently be recorded as having been 'formerly of [*an ex-tenant*]', or even 'formerly of [*ex-tenant*] and before that of [*another ex-tenant*]', and these genealogies of tenancies, evidenced by old rentals and jurors' memories, can cover a substantial period of time. Memory was a strong feature of law and custom, and medieval and early modern surveys and rentals not only established who held what and what rent was due to the lord, but also reinforced the place of the tenants in the landscape and placed a premium on established antiquity.

Custom was also paramount in marking the boundaries and areas of land-holdings. Measurement was not usually undertaken in the way we would understand it today, with our reliance on purely physical measurement to standard measures such as acres or hectares, yards or metres. Medieval acres were not simple, or absolute, measurements, and several different types are apparent in the Monks Eleigh records. Harvey identifies three kinds of acres: the customary acre, the measured acre and the fiscal acre.[83] The customary acre, also termed the acre as it lies (*acra ut iacet*) or field acre (*acra campestris*), was based on the selion, the ridged, ploughed strip in an arable field, whatever its size: customary acres carried no connotation of actual size. Harvey quotes F.W. Maitland to show how customary acres carried no connotation of actual size: 'To tell a man that one of these acre-strips was not an acre because it was too small would at one time have been like telling him his foot was not a foot because it fell short of twelve inches.'[84]

The measured acre (*acra mensurata*) was also based on the selion, often defined as 4 perches (22 yards) wide and 40 perches (220 yards) long, or 160 square perches. Where the perch was equivalent to the still-used standard of 16½ feet, it was 'exactly the size of our modern statute acre … a cricket pitch wide and a furlong long … [*and*] might be of any shape, as today'.[85] But there were local variations in the size of the perch, and even within a single survey, woodland in particular might be measured by a longer perch than 16½ feet. One tell-tale indicator of the use of the measured acre in a document is its sub-division into square perches (though all kinds of acre can refer to half- or quarter-acres otherwise known as roods).

The third kind of acre, the fiscal acre, is particularly pertinent to Monks Eleigh's Rental 1 (1379–80). This again did not indicate the physical size of the land in question but was a unit of tax assessment. Before the Norman Conquest, tax was assessed on units called the carucate (usually used in northern and eastern England) or hide (elsewhere), divisible into 120 fiscal acres. These remained the basis of tax assessment after 1066. Hides and carucates could also be sub-divided respectively into virgates (also called yardlands, there being 4 virgates/yardlands to the hide, so 1 virgate equalled 30 fiscal acres) or bovates (also called oxgangs) of which there were 8 to the carucate (so 1 bovate/oxgang equalled 15 fiscal acres). The most important complicating factor about fiscal acres is that they do not carry any corre-

[83] Harvey, *Manorial Records* (1999), pp. 16–17; Bailey, *The English Manor* (2002), pp. 23–24.

[84] Harvey, 'Manorial Records' (1983), p. 7, citing F.W. Maitland, *Domesday Book and Beyond: Three Essays in the Early History of England* (Cambridge, 1907), p. 442.

[85] Harvey, 'Manorial Records' (1983), pp. 7–8; Harvey, *Manorial Records* (1999), pp. 16–18; Bailey, *The English Manor* (2002), pp. 23–24.

spondence with the size of a holding, even on the same manor: all they reflect is the taxable assessment of that land.

In Rental 1 (1379/80), the fiscal acre as a unit of tax assessment is called *akyrwar*. In his own notes, Weller used the phrase 'the ware acre', apparently following the usage of R.H.C. Davis for this term.[86] Bailey calls them defence acres (*acreware*).[87] The word comes from the Old English verb *werian* (to defend), and warland was said to defend itself (*se defendit*) or account for itself or be assessed for tax.[88] Warland is known to have existed on some twelfth- and thirteenth-century ecclesiastical estates, including those of the abbeys of Bury St Edmunds, Ely and Westminster, so its existence at Monks Eleigh is not in itself surprising as it was an ecclesiastical manor. It was part of a system of tenure that divided estates, from pre-Conquest times, into inland and warland.[89] Rosamond Faith's view is that warland was land that once bore public obligations to the state: in the earliest times, this was manifested by providing food to the king or major lord, service in the army, undertaking certain labour services and above all paying tax (*geld*). The fulfilment of these public obligations gave rise to the understanding over time that the peasants who worked on warland were free, despite their obligations to provide certain labour services, which 'were limited, and, most importantly were fiercely defended as limited … later called boonworks with the implication that they were freely given – although we shouldn't be naïve about this'.[90] The corresponding inland parts of estates were 'serviced by a class of very dependant tenants and workers', whose works were more onerous and whose status was definitely lower and unfree.[91] This is not quite the end of the debate, however. David Pratt, taking the view that the system of 'inland' and 'warland' was more likely to have been a post-Conquest innovation, could still say, in 2013, that, 'The concept of warland is deeply problematic.' He gives a short definition of 'warland', however, saying that 'in all likelihood it represents a post-Conquest coinage, denoting land assessed to the geld which also retained associations, whether real or notional, with military service'.[92] Although over time population pressure on land forced many tenants who were free before the Norman Conquest to enter into servile tenancies, the idea of the connection of warland and personal freedom may have persisted, especially in East Anglia, where the proportion of freemen to serfs was higher than elsewhere.[93] The payment of geld (like that of *gafol*) was gradually privatised away from the king through his sheriffs to manorial lords and became a rent, payable on the standardised units of full, half- and quarter-lands, which were gradually broken up into smaller holdings.[94]

---

[86] R.H.C. Davis (ed.), *Kalendar of Abbot Samson of Bury St. Edmunds* (London, 1954), pp. xxxiii, xxxvii, 71.

[87] Bailey, *The English Manor* (2002), p. 24.

[88] David Pratt, 'Demesne Exemption from Royal Taxation in Anglo-Saxon and Anglo-Norman England', *EHR* 128, no. 530 (February 2013), p. 10; Rosamond Faith, 'Social Theory and Agrarian Practice in Early Medieval England: The Land without *Polyptyques*', *Revue belge de philologie et d'histoire* 90, issue 2 (2012), p. 305.

[89] Rosamond Faith, *The English Peasantry and the Growth of Lordship* (London and Washington, 1997), p. 91.

[90] Faith, 'Social Theory and Agrarian Practice in Early Medieval England' (2012), p. 305.

[91] Faith, 'Social Theory and Agrarian Practice in Early Medieval England' (2012), Abstract.

[92] Pratt, 'Demesne Exemption from Royal Taxation' (2013), p. 28.

[93] M. Bailey, 'Villeinage in England: A Regional Case Study, *c.*1250–*c.*1349', *EcHR*, New Series 62, no. 2 (May 2009), pp. 433, 443.

[94] Pratt, 'Demesne Exemption from Royal Taxation' (2013), pp. 4–5, 8.

In Monks Eleigh, warland appears only rarely, always in a fourteenth-century context. It is referred to most often throughout Rental 1 (1379–80). There are also two references in Court Roll 2 (*c.* 1349–50), one reference in Court Roll 4 (*c.* 1350–51), and two references in Court Roll 7 (1361). The taxable liability of warland (termed *le war* or *akyrwar* in Rental 1) is often also expressed in terms of the liability of non-fiscal acreage (although whether this is customary or measured acreage is not clear). What seems to be clear, however, is that *le war* was a multiple of the number of acres, based on the productivity of the land in the given holding, which itself was based on the system of standard 'lands' mentioned in the extents (above). For example, in the first entry in Rental 1, for the two quarter-lands called Goodyngesquarter and Gaywodequarter, we are told that this unit of land comprised 'half a land and contains 30½ acres of land and accounts for 15 *akyrwar* of custumary land, that is, two acres of land equals *le War*'. This example seems to imply that the standard land of 30 acres (referred to above) is based on the fiscal *akyrwar* acre, since the two quarter-lands comprised a half-land of 15 *akyrwar*, a ratio of 2:1. The half-land of Gokyslond, however, contained '15 acres and accounts for 15 *akyrwar* of land', a ratio of 1:1 between taxable and customary or measured acres, though still at the rate of 30 *akyrwar* to the land. Presumably, Gokyslond was twice as fertile, and therefore more able to pay *le war*, than Goodyngesquarter and Gaywodequarter.

Interpretation of land-holdings in later rentals in Monks Eleigh is less complex as the arrangement changes to being tenant-oriented around the payment of rent, once all labour services had been removed in 1379–80. The differential persists between freehold land (*libere*) and unfree land, held by either native or customary tenure (*native*), some of which developed into copyhold land as discussed above (p. xxvii).[95]

However, some of the rentals after 1379–80 can be difficult to date exactly. As mentioned above, rentals generally were made periodically (perhaps once a generation) and updated with annotations as tenants changed over time (through death, inheritance or sale). But being working documents, subject to constant use and annotation, they became worn and damaged, so were also sometimes re-copied, sometimes in a fair hand incorporating old annotations into the fair copy without comment, making the original annotations much less obvious. And those re-copyings might be very out-of-date by the time they were re-copied, including some tenants who were by then dead, or had moved away. Even though most of the post-1379–80 rentals are dated, some of those dates are incorrect (and were possibly indistinct to the copyist at the time), and it is sometimes unclear as to which date the 'snapshot' refers – was it the date the rental was first made, or the date of the last annotation or re-copying before the next rental was made? Rentals 2–4 are particularly problematic, so their dating is discussed in detail in notes under the heading of each.

One of Weller's claims was that he could put together genealogies of tenancies of most holdings from at least Rental 2 (*c.* 1503–*c.* 1513) onwards (see Plate 13 for an example relating to Rushbrooks), and he clearly found fascinating the various aspects of continuity and change in the naming and identifying of properties, as well as individuals and families, from the documents. It is certainly relatively straightforward to compile a concordance of holdings and their tenants from Rental 2 and most of the later rentals, which allows many of the holdings to be matched with

---

95 See Bailey, *The English Manor* (2002), p. 36. For Weller's map of free land in the manor, see Plate 11.

those on John Miller's large-scale map of 1725.[96] As an exercise in the continuity of land-holdings, this is a project that the reader could attempt from the records in this volume.

It is more difficult if not impossible to trace particular tenements back from Rental 2 to Rental 1 (1379/80) because of the way Rental 1 is arranged, which is by the early system of lands discussed above. Clearly, the lands were frequently sub-divided, but in such cases, particular field or tenement names are not noted in the rental, so unless the tenant is identifiable from Rental 1 in later records, any continuity of properties cannot be traced. Sometimes, however, the habit of naming more than one previous tenant can just bridge the gap. For example, in Rental 2 (see p. 210), Thomas Sprynge held 'one tenement lying at Stakwod formerly of John Tyler and before that of William Prior, chaplain, with various lands, meadows, feedings, pastures, a grove (*virgult*') belonging to the same tenement' at a rent of £1 14s. 2d. William Prior, priest, appears as one of the updated tenants in Rental 1 (1379/80) (p. 185), his name being annotated above the names of the original 1379/80 tenants whom he succeeded in several holdings, including 21 acres of land that were part of the half-land called Palmereslond at Stacwode, which he took over after the tenancy of John Abot. We cannot be absolutely sure that it was the same land – Rental 2 has no acreage, and Rental 1 no rent, to compare – but the location of the land at Stackwood, and the name of William Prior, priest, suggest it was.

Petition and legal documents relating to a riot in 1481

This group of papers relates to a dispute leading to an affray that took place in Monks Eleigh in August 1481, the final year of Adam Turnour's lease of the manor. He was lessee, or farmer, of the manor between 1460/61 (at the latest) and 1479/80. Indeed, his lease might even have been terminated as a result of the case, although this remains conjectural. Depending on which version of events one believes (the papers reflect the contradictory views of the opposing parties in the case), Turnour might, or might not have failed to repay a debt to a tenant of the manor, William Hobart (eldest brother of Sir James Hobart (d. 1517), judge and attorney general to Henry VII). Hobart, his sons and servants therefore confiscated or stole the manorial livestock and impounded them in his own farmyard, possibly for several days during which time they might not have been sufficiently fed and watered. Turnour himself was detained or kidnapped at Hobart's house for half a day. Tension between the two factions within the manor grew, resulting in men going armed to evensong one Sunday and coming to blows after leaving the service, several being wounded in the ensuing riot, as the documents term the affray. Turnour, as farmer of the manor, appealed to the prior as his landlord, and they jointly began legal proceedings in one of the royal courts, although it is not clear which. The documents suggest it went to court as an equity case: the records transcribed here comprise the petition (with draft) of the plaintiffs, the prior of Canterbury and the manor's lessee, Adam Turnour, which formed the bill of complaint to open the case, then the answer of the defendants, William Hobart, his sons and servants, and the plaintiffs' response. The result is unknown, although it is notable that Andrew Vyncent not Adam Turnour was the lessee of the manor in the farmer's accounts for 1481–82.[97] The documents

[96] SA(B), FL 607/1/3, map of the town and parish of Monks Eleigh, 1724, by John Miller. See cover picture.
[97] CCA-DCc/MA/6, fol. 138v, not included in this volume.

li

are all in English, and the original orthography has been retained more strictly in line with the original documents in this section, to reflect contemporary linguistic usage.

Manorial documents can be difficult to understand and interpret, but they reward the effort made to do so by giving us an insight into the lives and actions of our fore-bears. We can see something of the way they settled disputes, whether by peaceful means or occasional fisticuffs. We can learn something of the way they earned a living on the land, what animals they kept, the crops they harvested for the lord and the work they were obliged to do for him before the normalisation of cash rents. We can imagine their buildings from the records of repairs made to them. We can trace the development of forms of land tenure and the gradual decline of serfdom. We can glimpse aspects of their relationship with their lord, whether by the insulting references to 'churlish monks' by William Hobart and his men in 1481 or the earlier trespasses on the lord's crops and pasture with animals. The medieval world was very different from our own, but the records in this volume will hopefully show that in essence the people who inhabited it were not so very different from us.

EDITORIAL CONVENTIONS

As many of the original documents as possible have been checked against the transcriptions in editing the translations, but in a few cases, the original translations could not be checked and have been reproduced as received, edited only for formatting. Occurrences and reasons are given in footnotes in particular cases. Where a Latin word is considered noteworthy, it is given italicised in brackets after the translation.

Punctuation, capitalisation and the use of the letters 'i/j' and 'u/v' have generally been modernised in the translations from Latin and transcriptions of English documents. Middle English letters thorn (þ) and eth (đ) have been transliterated as 'th'; wynn (p) as 'w' and yogh (ʒ) usually as 'g' or 'y', with footnotes where different usage applies. English words used within otherwise Latin text have been left as such in italics. Place-names have generally been modernised, but with the original spelling in italics in brackets afterwards. Monks Eleigh was almost invariably called Illeigh (variously spelt) in the records, so has been transcribed as Eleigh unless the epithet 'monks' is specified. The spelling of personal names (including those based on place-names) has been retained as in the original, with variants drawn together in the index. Occupational surnames can be problematic in the period when surnames were still developing as a norm. Should, for example, *Adamus Faber* be translated as Adam Faber, Adam Smith or Adam the smith? In the main, surnames have been translated as English surnames (unless they are very obviously occupations), with the original form in brackets following, so that readers may make their own judgement.

Dates between 1 January and 24 March (inclusive) have been given split dating (e.g. 24 February 1316/17) for precision, the year change before 1752 having been on 25 March.

Where a single saint's day or other term is used for dating, the text has not been annotated on each occurrence. Instead, the saints' days and other terms used are listed in the glossary. For covering dates or those with the addition of another day of the week, for example 'the Friday before the feast of St Faith ...', then the full date is given.

The following editorial conventions have been used:

\text/	for insertions above the text
\\text//	for insertions above the text of insertions
/text\	for insertions below the text
<text>	for deletions that are legible in the original
[*sic*]	for all editorial insertions
[*illeg.*]	illegible words or sections
[*blank*]	empty spaces in the text
[*deleted*]	for deleted and unreadable sections

[*damaged*]	for damaged and unreadable sections
[?]	for a reading that is not certain
"text"	text within double quotation marks is taken from Michael Stansfield's translation where the original document is now illegible and could not be checked by the current editor.
fol., fols	folio, folios
m.	membrane
R	recto (the right-hand page of a folio)
V	verso (the left-hand page of a folio)

In translations, numbers have been converted from Roman to Arabic and money has been standardised (e.g. 63s. is transcribed as £3 3s. and 40d. as 3s. 4d.).

Money

£	= pound (money) (Latin, *libra*), comprising 20s. or 240d.
s.	= shilling (*solidus*), comprising 12d. 20s. = £1
d.	= penny (plural, pence) (*denarius*). 12d. = 1s. 240d. = £1
½d.	= halfpenny (*obolus* abbreviated to *ob.*)
¼d.	= farthing (*quadrans* abbreviated to *qa*)
½ ¼d.	= three farthings, ¾d. (*ob.qa*)
1 mark	= 13s. 4d. or two thirds of a pound
½ mark	= 6s. 8d. or one third of a pound

Weights and measures

Grain and dry goods (volume)

1 quarter (qr)	= 8 bushels
1 seam (*summa*)	= 8 bushels
1 bushel (b.)	= 4 pecks
1 peck	= 2 gallons

Area

1 acre (a.)	= 4 roods (1 a. = 0.4 hectares)
1 rood (r.)	= 40 perches or ¼ acre
1 perch (p.)	= 30¼ square yards
1 square yard	= 9 square feet
1 square foot	= 144 square inches

Length

1 furlong	= 40 poles (also known as perches or rods)
1 perch/pole/rod	= 5½ yards or 16½ feet
1 yard	= 3 feet
1 foot	= 12 inches (1 inch = approx. 2.5 cm; 1 foot = approx. 30.5 cm)

Weight

1 stone	= 14 pounds (lbs)
1 pound (lb)	= 16 ounces (oz.) (1 lb = 0.45 kg)

MONKS ELEIGH MANORIAL RECORDS, 1210–1683

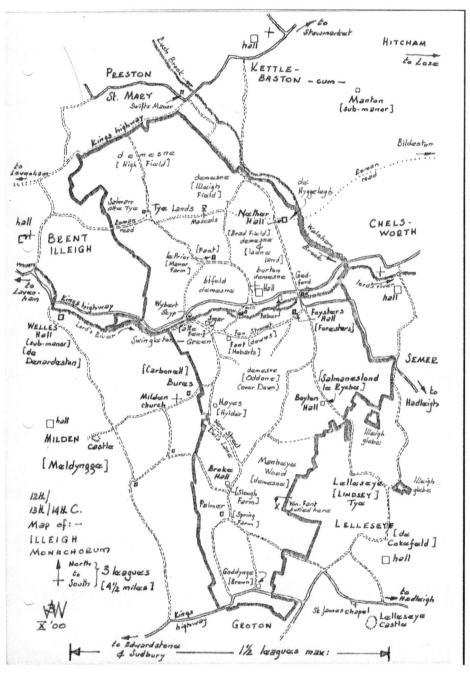

Plate 3. Weller's map of the whole of the manor of Monks Eleigh with features from the twelfth to the fourteenth centuries. The south-eastern boundary of the manor is also the boundary between the hundreds of Cosford and Babergh. Parcels of Monks Eleigh glebe land lay on both sides of the manor and hundred boundary (Weller Archive, file 'Maps')

I

CHARTERS

Mid-twelfth century to 1360[1]

Charter 1.[2] Letter from Theobald, archbishop of Canterbury to the prior and convent requesting the grant of the tithes of Monks Eleigh for Peter the scribe (1152–1161)[3]

T[*heobald*],[4] by the grace of God archbishop of Canterbury, primate of England and legate of the apostolic see, to his beloved sons in Christ, Wibert the prior and W[*?illiam*[5]] the sub-prior and all the convent of the church of Christ, Canterbury, greetings. For our dear son Peter, our devoted scribe, we extend our prayers universally, asking whether, for our said love and his devoted affection which we know he has towards us, you will grant the tithes of our lordship (*dominii*) of Eleigh[6] to be paid to his person whilst he lives. And lest this gift by us should cause prejudice or damage, after his decease, the tithes there shall be yielded to our use once more. And as witness against every malicious deed [*or*] usurpations, this little charter will remain and be valid forever with us.

---

[1] See Introduction, p. xxxiii.
[2] CCA-DCc-ChAnt/H/122; enrolled as 'Charter of Archbishop T. about the tithes of our lordship of Illegh' in CCA-DCc/Register/B, fol. 146r (twenty-sixth charter of twenty-seven enrolled); not enrolled in CCA-DCc/Register/E. CCA online catalogue states that this charter is transcribed in A. Saltman, *Theobald, Archbishop of Canterbury* (London, 1956), pp. 267–68, no. 40; noted in HMC, *Fifth Report of the Royal Commission on Historical Manuscripts* (London, 1876), Appendix, p. 461; and in T.A.M. Bishop, *Scriptores Regis* (Oxford, 1961), p. 75, no. S10.
[3] Dated by the overlap of Theobald's archiepiscopate (1139–1161) and Wibert's priorate (1152–1167).
[4] Theobald of Bec-Hellouin, archbishop of Canterbury 1139–1161, who is named explicitly in Charter 2 on the same subject. See D.E. Greenway (ed.), 'Canterbury: Archbishops', in *Fasti Ecclesiae Anglicanae 1066–1300*, 2 (London, 1971), pp. 3–8.
[5] Probably William Brito or Le Breton, sub-prior during, and perhaps before, the exile of Archbishop Thomas Becket (1164–1170). See J.C. Robertson, *Materials for the Life of Thomas Becket* (1875), 1, p. xxix.
[6] *Illega* in B, fol. 146r, although the original charter is filed in folder CCA-DCc-ChAnt/H, because Monks Eleigh is there written as *Hellega* as it is in Charter 2.

Charter 2.[7] Grant by the prior and convent of the tithes of Monks Eleigh to Peter the scribe (1152–1161)[8]

Wibert, prior of the church of Christ, Canterbury, and the whole convent, to his chief servants (*prepositis ministris suis*), both present and future, and to all his men, French and English, of Eleigh (*Hellega*), greetings. Know us to have granted and given, with common assent and kind affection, for the love of God and the prayers of our lord archbishop Theobald of Canterbury, to Peter the scribe, clerk of the archbishop and of us personally, the tithes of our whole lordship of Eleigh both in crops and in all other things accustomed to be tithed, to be possessed [*by him*] fully, for as long as he shall live or remain in the world. And when he shall die or renounce the world, the same tithes shall revert to our use and their original state, so that no-one who is habitually of the faithful is able to reclaim the tithes of that said church, nor shall any right be sold to them, that is to say, thereafter the church shall have the grain from four acres each year at harvest as of old, as it was accustomed to have. Witnessed by William the sub-prior, Thomas the third prior, Honorius the precentor, Florence, Ernulf the cellarer, Robert the sacrist, Laurence the almoner, Atso master of the sick (*magistro infirmorum*), Felix, Ailric the chamberlain, Richard de Whytstapla [*Whitstable*], Vivian de Sancto Albano [*St Albans*], monks of Canterbury and Hamo the reeve of Canterbury and Osbert the clerk of (*Horslega*) [*?Horsley, Surrey*] and William the chamberlain of the prior at Canterbury in chapter in the presence of the monks.

Charter 3.[9] Demises by the prior and convent of properties in Monks Eleigh (1191–1213)[10]

[*B, fol. 145v*] Know all to whom this writing shall come that G[*eoffrey*] the prior and the convent of the church of Christ, Canterbury, have demised certain lands, which are recognised to be part of our commonalty and estate, to our men of Eleigh (*Illegh*) to hold of us, saving all those customs which are customarily done first, with the rent noted below, and the number of acres, that is to say, to Hamo son of Ilger 1½ acres for 6d.; Warin de Lose, 2 acres for 2s.; Eilid the widow, 1½ acres for 2d.; William Tollune, 10 acres for 1s. 6d.; Wlmar [*sic*] the carpenter, 3 acres for 2s.; Godvin de Lose, 1 perch for 6d.; Hugh and Adam, half a perch for 2d.;

---

7   CCA-DCc-ChAnt/H/123; enrolled as 'In relation to Peter the scribe concerning the tithes of Illegh' in CCA-DCc/Register/B, fols 146r (title only)–146v (text) (twenty-seventh charter of twenty-seven enrolled); not enrolled in Reg CCA-DCc/Register/E. Translated and transcribed by the current editor to complement Charter 1. CCA online catalogue states that this charter is transcribed in Saltman, *Theobald, Archbishop of Canterbury* (1956), pp. 267–68, as note to no. 40; noted in HMC, *Fifth Report* (1876), Appendix, p. 461; noted in Bishop, *Scriptores Regis* (1961), p. 75, no. S11.

8   Dated as for Charter 1.

9   No original charter extant; enrolled as 'Chirograph' in CCA-DCc/Register/B, fols 145v–146r (twenty-third charter of twenty-seven enrolled); not enrolled in CCA-DCc/Register/E.

10 The date must be in the priorate of Geoffrey I (1125–1128) or Geoffrey II (1191–1213) (see D.E. Greenway (ed.), 'Priors of Canterbury', in *Fasti Ecclesiae Anglicanae 1066–1300*, 2 (London, 1971), pp. 8–12). The latter is more likely, based on some of the names mentioned in this charter: Hugh son of Thomas the reeve appears in Charter 9 (*c.* 1220s–1230s, bef. 1234/35); Robert the clerk is parson of Eleigh in Charter 4 (1191–1213), whilst Robert's son Anselm (de Ylleg') died between 13 October 1231 and 14 January 1234/35 (Suffolk feet of fines, TNA, CP 25/1/213/8, no. 23, CP 25/1/213/12, no. 142: digital images online at AALT, see Bibliography). William de Tenet is also mentioned as a former tenant of land in Charter 5 (*c.* 1210/11–1234/35), which suggests that the priorate of Geoffrey II (1191–1213) is a more likely period for this charter.

S[*?awen*] widow of Hugh, half an acre and half a perch for 1s. 2¼d. Also [*?to the same*] Sawen, 10 acres [*B, fol. 146r*] for 2s. 6d.; William de Helesee [*?*], 1 acre of marsh for 4d.; Burgnin, 3 acres for 2s.; Wybert Scip, 1 perch and a certain way for 1s.; [*?Umtren, ?Vintren*], 1 acre for 1s. 1d.; Sigar son of Turgod, 1 perch of marsh for 3d. and a certain way for 2 capons; Anselm Edith his master, 3 perches for 2s.; Warin Bucke, 2 acres, 1 perch for 2s. 6d.; William de Tenet [*?Thanet*], 1½ perches of Bruce for 2¼d; Godvin Hert, a certain way for 1d.; Robert and Simon, a certain way for 1d.; Hugh son of Thomas the reeve, half an acre for 2½d; the same Hugh, half an acre of marsh for 3d.; to eight fullers, 10½ acres for 6s.; Robert the clerk (*Roberto clerico*) and Anselm his son, the herbage[11] on 7 acres of alder-holt for 6d. and 1 acre of meadow for 1s.; Hugh son of Austin, 13 acres and 3 perches for 6s. and 8d. We wish that our aforesaid men and their successors aforesaid will hold the said lands well and in peace by the constituted payments and customs in perpetuity. And so that no other prior or monk or any other bailiff nor the aforesaid men should seize the aforesaid lands or increase their rents, let them be prevented. And so that this in future shall be corroborated firmly and ratified, we have appended our seal to this present writing.

Charter 4.[12] Grant by the prior and convent of the priory's land of Lose (in Hitcham) to William, nephew of Robert, parson of Monks Eleigh (1191–1213)[13]

To all to whom this present charter shall come, Geoffrey the prior and the convent of the church of Christ, Canterbury, [*sends*] greetings. Know us to have conceded to William, nephew of Robert the parson of Eleigh (*Illeg'*) and his heirs, our land of Lose, that is to say, 34 acres with the buildings constructed on the same land, which Ilger de Lose holds of us, for which land the aforesaid William and his heirs after him will render to us annually in our court of Eleigh (*Illege*), 6s. 8d. in rent at 2 terms, that is, at Easter, 3s. 4d. and at the feast of Saint Michael likewise 3s. 4d. for all services and customs except reasonable aids and scutages. Now for this grant he has given to us £2. So that this our grant may be firmly upheld to him and his heirs, we have corroborated it by appending our seal.

---

[11] The right to take the growth of the alder-holt for coppicing.
[12] CCA-DCc-ChAnt/I/218; enrolled as 'Also concerning the same' in CCA-DCc/Register/B, fol. 146r (twenty-fifth of twenty-seven enrolled); not enrolled in CCA-DCc/Register/E. In B, fol. 146r, this charter follows immediately after Charter 6 (1213–1222) (also not enrolled in E, and for which no original charter exists), which is also a grant to another rector of Monks Eleigh. Presumably the enrolling clerk put the two charters together because both concerned an incumbent of Monks Eleigh.
[13] Like Charter 3, Charter 4 must date from the priorate of Geoffrey I (1125–1128) or Geoffrey II (1191–1213). For Charter 4 too, the latter priorate is preferred on the assumption that Robert the parson of Monks Eleigh in 4 is the same man as Charter 3's Robert the clerk (whose son Anselm died before 14 January 1234/35).

Charter 5.[14] Feoffment by Adam Herth of Monks Eleigh to William the priest, son of Anselm de Ylleg', of 2½ acres of arable land in Monks Eleigh (c. 1210/11–1234/35)[15]

Know, both present and future, that I, Adam Herth[16] of Eleigh (*Ylleg'*), have given and granted and by this my present charter have confirmed to William the priest son of Anselm de Ylleg' for his homage and service and for 6s. of silver which he has given to me as a gersum fine (*in gersumiam*) and for one blue furred surcoat which he has given to me, 2½ acres of arable land with appurtenances which Hugh the reeve sometime held of me for a term, whether it be more or less, and lying between the land of John Ylger and the land of Adam Tele and of which one head abuts upon the land which was sometime of William de Teneth [*?Thanet*],[17] and the other, upper, head upon the land which was Thurkill's (*Turekylli*).[18] To hold and to have of me and my heirs to him and his heirs or to whom they shall wish to give or assign, and to the heirs of the assignees, freely, quietly, peacefully, honourably and in inheritance. He and his heirs or assigns paying annually in respect whereof to me and my heirs one halfpenny and to the court of Eleigh (*Ylleg'*) three pence halfpenny, to wit, at the term of the apostles Peter and Paul for all services, customs and secular exactions and demands. And I the aforesaid Adam and my heirs will warrant to the aforesaid William and his heirs or to whom they shall wish to give or assign and to the heirs of the assignees, all the aforesaid land with appurtenances for the aforesaid services against all men and against all women. With these being witnesses: Anselm de Ylleg',[19] Salomon de Ylleg', Hugh, Salomon, William, brothers; Hamo; Roger Prior (*Priore*);[20] Adam and Hugh de Marescall', brothers; Richard, Thomas, Walter, the sons of Hugh the reeve; John de Leleseye [*Lindsey*]; William, Roger, Saher, Hugh, the sons of Urcal and many others.

---

[14] Original charter SA(I), HD 1538/307/5 (one of five relating to Monks Eleigh formerly Phillipps MS 33,359).

[15] Dated by a comparison of some of the people mentioned in this document with others in this volume (as footnoted for each person).

[16] Adam Herth is also mentioned as Adam le Hert, in Charter 9 (c. 1220s–1230s, before 1234/35).

[17] William de Teneth appears as a living tenant in Charter 3 (1191–1213), but his description here and in Charter 10 (?c. 1220s–1230s) as a former tenant implies he was dead by the time of those documents.

[18] The land 'which was Thurkill's (*Turekylli*)' might be Turkilleslond mentioned in Charter 7 (see p. 7), a quitclaim by Hugh le Heyward, possibly the same as Hugh the reeve mentioned in this charter as the grantor's former tenant, and/or the mondayland called Turkyl in Extent 6 (c. 1285/86–1310/11, see p. 36).

[19] Anselm de Ylleg' had died by January 1234/35 at the latest (see p. 4, footnote 10).

[20] Roger Prior/le Priur/le Pryur appears as a witness to several charters in this volume, as does his son, Richard. If he were actually a prior of a religious foundation (rather than merely a servant of one, or someone nicknamed for having airs and graces, perhaps), then he might have been a prior of Kersey Priory nearby, a house of Augustinian canons established by the Cokefield family by 1184 (W.A. Copinger, *Manors of Suffolk* 3 (1909), p. 183; *VCH Suffolk* 2, pp. 107–8). Salomon de Ylleg' and Roger Prior both also appear as jurors in Extent 1 (1210–11, see p. 31).

Charter 6.[21] Grant by the prior and convent to Alexander de Rephham, rector of Monks Eleigh of 1 acre, 1 perch of land and the ditch around it next to Monks Eleigh churchyard (1213–1222)[22]

To all the faithful in Christ to whom this present writing shall come, Walter the prior and the convent of the church of Christ, Canterbury, [*sends*] greeting in the Lord. Know, all of you, that we have given and granted to Alexander de Rephham [?*Reepham, Norfolk*], parson of Eleigh (*Illegh*) and his successors 1 acre and 1 perch of our land and a certain ditch dug around the aforesaid land there, that ditch containing 7 feet in breadth, in our manor of Eleigh (*Illeg'*), next to the churchyard towards the north. To have and to hold to him and his successors in perpetuity freely and quietly and peacefully rendering in respect thereof annually 1s. sterling at our court of Eleigh (*Illeg'*) for all the services, customs and exactions at 2 terms each year, that is, at Easter, 6d. and at the feast of Saint Michael, 6d. Also that the said Alexander and his successors are not to build any building in any place in the churchyard there except where his barns have always been and there, they are not to build any building except barns and a granary. So that this our gift and grant may endure firmly and securely in perpetuity, we have appended our seal to this present writing.

Charter 7.[23] Grant and quitclaim by Hugh de Ylleg' the hayward of a wood between Manhey Wood and Turkilleslond, Monks Eleigh (1222–1238)[24]

Know all, present and future, that I, Hugh de Ylleg'[25] [*Eleigh*] the hayward (*le Heyward*), have granted and given and in respect of everything have quitclaimed for me and my heirs to John the prior and the convent of the church of Christ, Canterbury, one wood in Eleigh (*Ylleg'*), lying between the wood which is called Manheye[26] and Turkilleslond,[27] which once I held of the previously-named prior and convent. To have and to hold freely and quietly without any claim or contradiction from me or my heirs in perpetuity. Moreover, I, Hugh, and my heirs will defend and acquit the aforesaid wood with its appurtenances from all services, customs, aids and demands annually owed in respect thereof at the chief court of Eleigh (*Yllege*). However, for this grant and gift and quitclaim the said prior and convent have given to Hugh, by the hand of John de Hertford, monk of the aforesaid church, at that

---

21 No original charter extant; enrolled, as 'Chirograph between us and the rector of Illegh' in CCA-DCc/Register/B, fol. 146r (twenty-fourth charter of twenty-seven enrolled); not enrolled in CCA-DCc/Register/E.

22 This charter dates from the priorate of one of three medieval priors called Walter: Walter Durdent (1143–1149), Walter de Meri (or Moyri, otherwise Parvus) (1149–1152) or Walter (1213–1222) (see Greenway, 'Priors of Canterbury' (1971), pp. 8–12). There is no evidence in the charter to identify which one granted it, not even the handwriting, because this charter exists only in a later enrolment. On diplomatic evidence provided by DEEDS, however, the latest Walter's priorate (1213–1222) is suggested as the most likely.

23 CCA-DCc-ChAnt/I/217; enrolled, as 'Charter of Hugh le Heyward concerning a certain wood next to Manheye', in CCA-DCc/Register/B, fol. 143r (fourth charter of twenty-seven enrolled) and CCA-DCc/Register/E, fol. 385r (fourth charter of nineteen enrolled, no. '1911').

24 Dates based on priorates of John de Sittingbourne I (1222–1235 or 1236) and John de Chetham (before 1237–38) in Greenway, 'Priors of Canterbury' (1971), pp. 8–12.

25 *Ylleg'* in B, fol. 143r, *Yllege* in E, fol. 385r, both throughout.

26 *Manheie* in CCA-DCc-ChAnt/I/217.

27 Probably named after the tenant Thurkill in Charter 5 (*c.* 1210/11–1234/35). It might also be the whole, or part of, the mondayland called *Turkyl* in Extent 6 (*c.* 1285/86–1310/11).

time warden of the manor of Eleigh (*Ylleg'*), £1 sterling. And so that this my grant and gift and quitclaim may have authority in perpetuity, I have appended my seal to this present charter. These being witnesses: Roger de Aldham, John de Glovernia [*Gloucester*], Richard de Ylleg', Hugh Marshall (*Hugone Marscallo*), Adam his brother, Roger Prior (*Priore*), Richard Forester (*Forestar'*), Salomon de Yllege, Salomon the red (*rufo*), and many others.

Charter 8.[28] Demise and quitclaim by Peter Bigge of Milden of his right to 30[29] acres of land in Monks Eleigh (1222–1238)[30]

Know, present and future, that I, Peter Bigge[31] of Milden (*Melding*), have demised and in respect of everything, have quitclaimed, for me and for my heirs, to lord John the prior and to the convent of the church of Christ, Canterbury, all right and claim which ever I had or could have in 30 acres of land with appurtenances lying in the vill of Eleigh (*Ylleya*) in respect of which there was a legal suit between me, the claimant, and the lord prior, the defendant, by a writ of right of the lord king. To have and to hold to the said prior and convent and to whomsoever they might wish to give the same otherwise, without any claim from me or my heirs in perpetuity. Now, for this demise and quitclaim, the aforesaid prior and convent have given me 3 marks sterling. And so that this demise and quitclaim may be kept without harm and firmly established, without deceit, in good faith and irreproachably, I have appended my seal to this my charter of quitclaim for myself and my heirs. These being witnesses: Thomas del Paund, John de Glovernia [*Gloucester*], Ralph de la Cressuner, Roger de Audham [*Aldham*], Ralph de Burgo, Roger[32] le Priur, Salomon de Ylleya, Richard le Forester, Adam le Paumer, and many others.

Charter 9.[33] Acknowledgement and quitclaim by John son of Adam concerning Catteswode, a grove next to Manhey Wood, Monks Eleigh (*c.* 1220s–1230s, before 1234/35)[34]

[*B, fol. 143r; E, fol. 385r*] To all the faithful in Christ to whom the present charter shall come, John son of Adam greets [*you*] in the lord. Know, all of you, that I have made formal acknowledgement that a grove, formerly mine, which is near to Maneyham [*Manhey Wood, Monks Eleigh*] which [*E, fol. 385v*] is called Catteswode

---

28 No original charter extant; enrolled, as 'Charter of Peter Bigge of Meldinge concerning his right to 30 acres of land' in CCA-DCc/Register/B, fol. 143r (first charter of twenty-seven enrolled) and CCA-DCc/Register/E, fol. 385r (first charter of nineteen enrolled, no. '1908').

29 In Roman numerals in B, fol. 143r; in words in E, fol. 385r.

30 Dated as for Charter 7 (1222–1238).

31 *Bigge* throughout in B, fol. 143r; *Bygge* throughout in E, fol. 385r.

32 Roger in B, fol. 143r; Richard in E, fol. 385r. Roger is more likely to be correct here at this date: Richard, the son of Roger Prior, was active *c.* 1260s–1280s as evidenced in Charters 19, 21, 22 (all undated, but *c.* 1260s–1270s), 23 and 24 (both dated 1286–87).

33 CCA-DCc-ChAnt/I/216; enrolled, as 'Charter of John son of Adam concerning a certain grove next to Manheye' in CCA-DCc/Register/B, fol. 143r (fifth charter of twenty-seven enrolled) and CCA-DCc/Register/E, fols 385r–v (fifth charter of nineteen enrolled, no. '1912').

34 The date must be around the 1220s–1230s according to the witnesses: Thomas del Pant is probably the Thomas del Paund who witnessed Charter 8 (1222–1238). Salomon de Ylleg' and Roger Prior also witnessed Charter 8. The inclusion of Anselm de Ylleg' puts the date before January 1234/35 (by when he is known to have died: see p. 4, footnote 10 above). See also footnote 37 below on Richard de Berkesore.

and lies between the land of Hugh son of Thomas and the land of Adam le Hert to be the right of my lords the prior and convent of the church of Christ, Canterbury, and pertain to the aforesaid wood of Maneiham[35] and that I have now quitclaimed the same grove to the said prior and convent for me and my heirs in perpetuity \and[36]/ and that I have resigned the aforesaid grove into the hands of Richard de Berkesore[37] in the court of Eleigh (*Ylleg'*) before the full hall-mote (*coram pleno halimoto*), and now in the said hall-mote, I have abjured any right that I have or my heirs could have. And know that the said prior and convent have released me and my heirs from the rent of 5d. which I was held to pay to them each year, that is, to be rendered at the term of the apostles Peter and Paul. And since I, John, have recognised and resigned the right of the aforesaid prior and convent, the said prior and convent have given to me 2 marks of silver. And so that neither I nor my heirs shall be able to put aside this my recognition and resignation, I have corroborated this my present charter by appending my seal. These being witnesses: John de Wate-feld [*Whatfield*], Anselm de Ylleg', Thomas del Pant,[38] Salomon de Ylleg', Roger Prior (*Priore*), Walter son of Eadric, Adam his brother, John del Pant, William son of Robert, Roger de Lafham,[39] Hugh de Yllege, and many others.

Charter 10.[40] Feoffment by Adam, son of Huneman de Illeya to Robert, parson of Lindsey church, respecting ½ acre, 1 rood of land (?*c*. 1220s–1230s)[41]

Know, present and future, that I, Adam, son of Huneman de Illeya, have granted and given, and by this my present charter have confirmed to Robert, parson of the church of Lindsey (*Leles'*), for his homage and service, and for 4s. of silver which he has given to me for a gersum fine, half an acre with appurtenances, of which one rood lies lengthways (*de longo in longum*) next to the land which was William

---

35 *Manieham* here in B, fol. 143r; *Maneyham* in E, fol. 385v.
36 Insertion in B, fol. 143r.
37 Richard de Berkesore was a priory monk at the time of the monks' exile (1207–1214) under King John, and was one of the four custody monk-wardens in 1225 according to the first *assisa scaccarii* account of that year (Smith, *Canterbury Cathedral Priory* (1943), p. 101; W.G. Searle (ed.), *Christ Church Canterbury: I. The Chronicle of John Stone; II Lists of the Deans, Priors and Monks of Christ Church, Canterbury* (Cambridge, 1902), p. 172). Berkesore was a sub-manor in the parish of Halstow, near Upchurch, Kent, another Canterbury manor.
38 *del Pant* in B, fol. 143r; *del Pand* in E, fol. 385v. See following footnote on the origin of the surname.
39 Lafham here might be Layham, Lavenham, or a lost hamlet of Hadleigh of that name (P.H. Reaney, 'Lafham', *PSIAH* 28, no. 1 (1958), p. 101). The last of these is most probable because Hadleigh was a fellow manor of Christ Church, Canterbury, and the hamlet of Lafham was the origin of the manor of Pond Hall, giving rise to surnames in the twelfth century of de Lafham and del Pond (seen as del Pant/Pand/Paund in this volume). See S. Andrews and R. Hoppitt, 'Helming Leget, Royal Servant and a Possible Designed Landscape at Pond Hall, Hadleigh', *PSIAH* 42, no. 3 (2011), p. 302 and notes 16 and 21.
40 Original charter, SA(I), HD 1538/307/2 (one of five charters formerly comprising Phillipps MS 33,359). For a later grant of the same property (described slightly differently), see Charter 12 (mid-thirteenth century) and note there.
41 Dated by analogy with other witness lists: Adam Palmere is probably the Adam le Paumer who witnessed Charter 8 (1222–1238). Salomon de Illeya, Richard Forester and Roger Prior all also witnessed Charters 7 and 8 (both 1222–1238), whilst Salomon and Roger also witnessed Charter 9 (*c*. 1220s–1230s), before 1234/35. Roger Priur was head of a Monks Eleigh tithing that was fined 6s. 8d. for the flight of William Fant, a member of the same tithing who was suspected of and outlawed for theft in 1240 (see E. Gallagher (ed.), rev. H. Summerson, *The Crown Pleas of the Suffolk Eyre of 1240*, SRS 64 (2021), p. 61, entry 1485, p. 104). Hugh de Montechenesy also appears in entry 1403 and see also see next footnote.

Thenet's. And the other rood lies between the lands of Simon Smith (*Simonis ffabri*). To hold and to have to the said Robert and his assigns, of me and my heirs, freely and quietly, lawfully and in inheritance. Paying annually in respect of which to me and my heirs 1d., to wit on the feast of the apostles Peter and Paul for all service and custom and exaction. And I the aforesaid Adam and my heirs will warrant the said tenement to the said Robert and his assigns, against all men for the aforesaid service, forever. With these being witnesses: Hugh de Montechanesy,[42] John son of Adam, Anselm his brother, Salomon de Ylleya, Richard Forester (*fforestario*), Roger Prior (*Priore*), William son of Adam, Salomon son of Thomas, William son of Thomas, Adam Palmere, William Hylder and many others.

Charter 11.[43] Feoffment from Adam the chaplain, son of William, son of Adam de Illeg' to Sir Matthew, son of William de Melding, of 1 acre, ½ rood of arable land in Monks Eleigh (mid-thirteenth century)[44]

Know, present and future, that I, Adam[45] the chaplain, son of William son of Adam de Illeg' [*Eleigh*], have granted and given, and by this my present charter have confirmed to Sir Matthew, son of William de Melding' [*Milden*], for his homage and service, and for twenty shillings of silver which he has given to me for a gersum fine, one acre and half a rood of arable land with all its appurtenances lying in the field which is called Hauecheffeld, lengthways next to the land of Thomas, son of Hugh, of which the upper head abuts upon Hauecheffeldstrete and the lower head upon the land which is called Fynneslond. To have and to hold to the aforesaid Matthew and his heirs, to give, sell or assign the same as they will, and to their heirs, from me and my heirs, freely and quietly, well and peacefully, in fee and inheritance. Paying annually in respect thereof to me and my heirs one clove gillyflower,[46] to wit, at Easter for all services, aids, customs and demands. And I the aforesaid Adam and my heirs will warrant to the aforesaid Matthew and his heirs and assigns

---

42 Hugh de Montechanesy was a member of a relatively obscure branch of his family originating in Monte Canisio, Normandy, which settled in and around Edwardstone and Holton St Mary in the late-twelfth and early thirteenth centuries. The many varied spellings of their surname, and the fact that Hugh and his relative Hubert were also known as 'de Holeton' (Holton St Mary), makes them difficult to research. Hugh (active during the 1230s) is not noted in any of the limited secondary literature on the family, but from evidence in the Suffolk feet of fines (see p. 4, footnote 10 above) he married Alice, a daughter of Anselm de Ylleg', who died before January 1234/35. See also previous footnote.

43 Original charter, SA(I), HD 1538/307/1 (one of five charters formerly Phillipps MS 33,359). See Plate 4.

44 Exact dating is difficult, but if the identification of two of the witnesses, Sir Peter de Melding and Sir Henry de Shelton, is correct (see footnotes 47 and 48 below), then that would date this charter to a period before 1272, when Sir Peter de Melding died and before 1271, when Sir Henry de Shelton died. This charter is placed in this chronological position amongst the charters on the hypothesis that Sir Matthew de Melding in being described here as the son of William de Melding (see footnote 47 below on his family) had not yet established himself, and therefore had to be made known in this charter by reference to his father, indicating that Sir Matthew (who appears in several other later charters in this volume) was still relatively young.

45 Probably the same man as Adam de Ylleg', who was rector of Bocking, Essex (another Canterbury manor and a Camterbury peculiar) in Charter 23 (11 October 1276). He was still in office in 1285 and died in 1289 (see P.H. Reaney, 'Early Essex Clergy', *Essex Review* 49 (1940), p. 79). Here, being merely 'clerk', he might have been at the beginning of his clerical career.

46 The clove-pink flower, *Dianthus caryophyllus* (see Glossary). The original document has *clauu*[*m*] *g*[*ar*]*yco* at the end of one line followed by *frier* at the beginning of the next, probably a conflation of the French *clou de girofle*, *girofre* or *gilofre*.

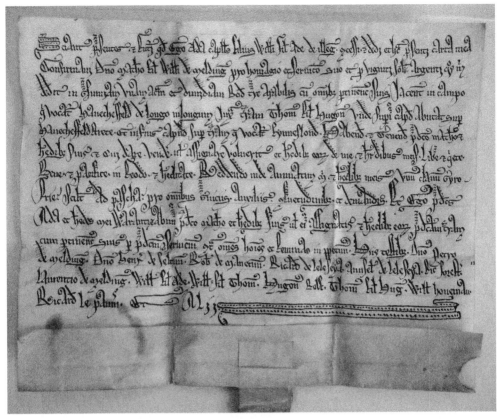

Plate 4. Charter 11 (mid-thirteenth century): feoffment from Adam the chaplain, son of William, son of Adam of Illeg' to Sir Matthew, son of William de Melding of 1 acre, ½ rood of arable land in Monks Eleigh. (SA(I), HD 1538/307/1) Photo: Vivienne Aldous. Reproduced courtesy of Suffolk Archives

and their heirs the aforesaid land with its appurtenances for the aforesaid service, against all men and women, forever. With these being witnesses: Sir Peter de Melding'[47] [*Milden*], Sir Henry de Seltun',[48] Robert de Manetun', Richard de Leleseya

---

[47] There were a number of related individuals called Sir Peter de Melding (variously spelt, including de Mewling, de Melding, de Meandlingg) in this area in the twelfth and thirteenth centuries. The most likely here is the Sir Peter who died in 1272, whose widow Alice made an agreement in 1274 with Remigius, Sir Peter's brother, that she would retain the manor of Meaudlingg [*Milden*] for her lifetime, it having been enfeoffed to her by a Laurence de Meaudlingg (perhaps another brother), who may well be the Laurence de Melding witnessing this charter (see Copinger, *Manors of Suffolk* 1 (1905), p. 158); H.C. Maxwell Lyte (ed.), *Calendar of Close Rolls, Edward I: Volume 1, 1272–9* (1900), pp. 120–23).

[48] Probably *Seltun'* or possibly *Feltun'*, the initial letter depending on which exemplars are chosen from elsewhere in the text, which is written in an eccentric and elaborate style (see Plate 4). Assuming that this man is Sir Henry de Shelton, there are two local candidates. The first was Henry (the son and heir of Ralph de Shelton and his wife Catherine, daughter of Henry de Illegh), who held the manor of Brent Eleigh, which came to him through his mother after his father's death in 1244. The second (probably the more likely) was Henry (grandson of Ralph and Catherine and possibly the

[*Lindsey*], Anusel[49] de Leleseya, Richard Forester, Laurence de Melding', William son of Adam, William son of Thomas, Hugh Rolf, Thomas son of Hugh, William Honeman, Richard le Paumer and others.

Charter 12.[50] Feoffment from Adam, son of Huneman of Monks Eleigh to Sir Matthew de Melding, knight, of ½ acre of land in Monks Eleigh (mid-thirteenth century)[51]

Know, present and future, that I, Adam, son of Huneman de Yllegh monachorum [*Monks Eleigh*] have given and granted, and by this my present charter have confirmed to Sir Matthew de Melding' [*Milden*], knight, for his homage and service, and for 3s. of silver and 6d. which he has given to me for a gersum fine, 1d. rent which Robert, parson of Lindsey (*Leles'*) was accustomed to pay to me annually, to wit, at the feast of St John the Baptist,[52] for half an acre of land lying in the vill of Eleigh (*Ylleg'*) in the field which is called Oddunelond[53] and one rood of land with appurtenances, lying lengthways between the lands of Simon Smith (*Simonis fabri*) in the vill of Eleigh (*Ylleg'*) aforesaid, of which one head abuts upon the way which is called Gilbertesgate and the other head upon the land which is called Tuderingewrthe. To hold and to have to the aforesaid Matthew and his heirs or assigns and their heirs, of me and my heirs, freely, quietly, well and in peace, in fee and inheritance, paying annually in respect thereof to me and my heirs one pair of white [*?gloves*] (*arrocetarum*) or ½d., to wit, at Christmas for all services and aids, customs and exactions. And I the said Adam and my heirs or assigns will warrant to the said Matthew and his heirs or assigns the said rent and the said land with appurtenances against all men and women for the aforesaid service forever. With these being witnesses: Richard de Leles' [*Lindsey*], Anselm de Leles' Richard Forester

---

son of Nicholas de Shelton who was lord of that and other manors in 1257), who died in 1271 (see Copinger, *Manors of Suffolk* 1 (1905), p. 37).

49 Clearly written as Anusel. Possibly intended to be Anselm, but perhaps more likely to be Ansel or Aunsel, since there was still a holding called Auncelislond in Rental 1 (1379–80). I thank Dr Tig Lang for discussion of this name.

50 Original charter, SA(I), HD 1538/307/3 (one of five charters formerly Phillipps MS 33359). For an earlier grant of the same property, see Charter 10 (*c.* 1220s–1230s). There is ostensibly a more detailed description of the land in question here than in Charter 10, although the grant is for half an acre *and* 1 rood of land, rather than half an acre, *comprising* 2 roods, as in Charter 10. Perhaps the 1d. rent was more important to the clerk drafting this document than the exact measurement of the land it was for.

51 Dated by a comparison of some of the people mentioned in the document with other witness lists in this volume: the grantor, Adam son of Huneman, is in Charter 10 (*c.* 1220s–1230s), so this document must date to within his lifetime. It must be later than Charter 10, however, as Robert the parson of Lindsey is referred to in Charter 10 in the present tense, but here in the past tense. Richard Forester could be either of the two (or even more) men of that name witnessing charters at the beginning and end of the thirteenth century. Thomas son of Hugh appears in other charters dated to the mid-thirteenth century (Charters 11, 14, 15), as do Emma, Thomas and William, the widow and sons of Richard Sygar (Charters 14–15). The sons of Anselm de Leles'/Lellesey, Nicholas, Henry and Thomas, flourished in 1276 (Charters 21–23). Other witnesses to this charter appear to have been active in both the mid- and late-thirteenth century: Richard de Leles'/Lellesey, in Charters 11, 13–15 (all mid-thirteenth century) and Charters 16, 17 and 18 (all *c.* 1260s–70s); Hugh son of Ralph (also Hugh Rolf or Radulph) in Charters 11 and 14 (mid-thirteenth century), and Charters 16–20 (all *c.* 1260s–70s). On balance, a mid-thirteenth-century date seems most likely.

52 More likely to be the feast of the nativity of St John, 24 June, a quarter day when rents were customarily paid, than his beheading on 29 August.

53 Probably later known as Oddon(e): see Accounts 4 (1358–59) and Rental 1 (1379–80).

(*Forestar* '), Richard de Higgeleg',[54] Symon son of Huneman, Thomas son of Hugh, Walter his brother, Hugh son of Ralph, Salom' de Stakwde,[55] Richard Sygar, Roger son of John Ylger, Richard his brother and others.

Charter 13.[56] Quitclaim by Richard de Lelseya to Sir Matthew de Mewling and Alice his wife of his interest in 16 acres of land in Milden (mid-thirteenth century)[57]

Know, present and future, that I, Richard de Lelseya [*Lindsey*], have remised and quitclaimed for me and my heirs, all right and claim which I had or could have in sixteen acres of land with appurtenances in the vill of Milden (*Mewling*) to Sir Matthew de Mewling[58] and Alice his wife and their heirs or their assigns, that is to say, those 16 acres which Robert, formerly rector of the church of Lindsey (*Lelseya*), gave to the aforesaid Matthew in marriage with Alice his daughter and which land I exacted from the aforesaid Matthew and Alice his wife by writ of novel disseisin. For this remise and quitclaim however the said Matthew gave to me 5 acres of land in the vill of Monks Eleigh (*Yllega monachorum*). And so that this remise and quitclaim may be acknowledged and established forever, I have set my seal to this present writing. With these being witnesses: Sir William de Mewling, John Waylond, Thomas his brother, Master Laurence de Denbardestun'[59] [*Denston*], Laurence de Mewling, Robert de Waldingfeld, Alan de Padebrok', Gervays de Mewling, William Hog and others.

---

[54] Higgeleigh (variously spelt) later Higlens, now Highlands Farm, was a small farm in Monks Eleigh on the road running north from the village towards Kettlebaston. As a surname, de Higgelegh was common in the village during the medieval period, and William de Higgelegh was reeve 1317–46 (see Introduction, p. xxvi, Table 3 and Accounts 3 (1329–30) for example).

[55] Stackwood was a wood in the south of the parish of Monks Eleigh, somewhere near Stackwood (now Stackyard) Green (see Plates 6 and 9).

[56] Original charter, SA(I), HD 1538/307/4 (one of five charters formerly Phillipps MS 33359).

[57] Dated by a comparison of some of the people mentioned in the document with other lists in this volume: Sir William de Mewling is referred to as Sir Matthew's father in Charter 11 (mid-thirteenth century), and Laurence de Mewling, probably another relative, also witnessed Charter 11, linking together Charters 11 and 13 in date and personnel. The possibly recent death of Sir Matthew de Mewling or Melding's father-in-law, Robert, parson of Lindsey, implied in both Charters 12 and 13, also link them. Master Lawrence de Denston (whose title is a mystery) appears in a document dated 24 June 1251 in the Stoke-by-Clare cartulary (C. Harper-Bill and R. Mortimer (eds), *Stoke-by-Clare Cartulary*, SRS Charters Series 5, part 2 (1983), pp. 210–11, entry 295). A Laurence de Denardiston was also involved in legal proceedings against Isabella, widow of William de Meuling, over property in Milden in 'Calendar of Patent Rolls for 2 Edw. I (1273–74)' in William Hardy (ed.), *Forty-Third Annual Report of the Deputy Keeper of the Public Records* (London, 1882), Appendix I, no. 4, p. 494. These references support the dating of this charter as mid-thirteenth century.

[58] One of a number of variants of the surname 'de Melding'.

[59] See footnote 57 above.

Charter 14.[60] Grant by Thomas and William, sons of Richard Sygar, of their pasture in Monks Eleigh (mid-thirteenth century)[61]

Know all, present and future, that I [*sic*] Thomas and William sons of Richard Sygar[62] of Monks Eleigh (*Ylleg'*[63] *Monachorum*) have given and granted and by this present charter have confirmed to the prior and convent of the church of Christ, Canterbury, in pure and perpetual alms, all that our pasture which lies in the common roadway towards Sudbury (*Subire*) in their manor of Monks Eleigh and lies between the field of the aforesaid prior which is called Bivolde [*Byfold*] towards the north[64] and the alder-holt of the said prior which is called Schortfen[65] towards the south and abutts in length upon the garden of William Sacrist (*Sacriste*) towards the west and the pasture of Sir Matthew de Melding [*Milden*] towards the east in the said roadway. To hold and to have of us and our heirs to the aforesaid prior and convent and their successors in perpetuity as of their pure and perpetual alms. In testimony of which thing we have appended our seals to this writing. These being witnesses: Sir Matthew de Melding, Richard de Leleseye [*Lindsey*], Richard Forester (*Forestario*), Simon de Stakwde, Hugh Rolf, Thomas son of Hugh, Thomas de la Lane, and others.

Charter 15.[66] Quitclaim by Emma widow of Richard Sygar of her right in pasture in Monks Eleigh (mid-thirteenth century)[67]

Know all, present and future, that I, Emma, formerly wife of Richard Sygar of Monks Eleigh (*Ylleg'*[68] *Monachorum*) have quitclaimed for me and for my heirs to the prior and convent of the Church of Christ, Canterbury, all the right which I had or could have in that pasture which lies in the common roadway which leads towards Sudbury (*Subire*) in their manor of Eleigh (*Ylleg'*) and lies next to the field of the said prior which is called Bivold [*Byfold*] towards the north[69] and the alder-holt which is called Schortfen[70] towards the south and abuts in length upon

---

[60] No original charter extant; enrolled as 'Charter of Thomas and William sons of Richard Sigar concerning a certain pasture' in CCA-DCc/Register/B, fol. 143r (second charter of twenty-seven enrolled) and CCA-DCc/Register/ E, fol. 385r (second charter of nineteen enrolled, no. '1909'). For the grantors' mother's quitclaim of the same property, see next charter.

[61] Dated by a comparison of some of the people mentioned in the document to other witness lists in this volume (see p. 12, footnote 51 to Charter 12, mid-thirteenth century).

[62] In the heading, *Sigar* in B, fol. 143r; *Sygar* in E, fol. 385r. Presumably this is the Richard Sygar who also witnessed Charter 12 (mid-thirteenth century).

[63] *Illeg'* in B, fol. 143r, *Illege* in E, fol. 385r, both throughout, the added *Monachorum* only here in both.

[64] The scribes of both B, fol. 143r and E, fol. 385r use English words for the compass points in this item: *north*, *suth*, *west* and *est* in B, fol. 143r; the same, but with *east* in E, fol. 385r.

[65] *Schortfen* in B, fol. 143r; *Shortfen* in B, fol. 385r.

[66] No original charter extant; enrolled as 'Charter of Emma widow of Richard Sygar concerning her right in the said pasture' immediately following Charter 14 (mid-thirteenth century), in CCA-DCc/ Register/B, fol. 143r (third charter of twenty-seven enrolled) and CCA-DCc/Register/E, fol. 385r (third charter of nineteen enrolled, no. '1910'). For the grant by the grantor's sons, see previous charter.

[67] Dated by a comparison of some of the people mentioned in the document with other witness lists in this volume (see p. 12, footnote 51 to Charter 12, mid-thirteenth century).

[68] *Ylleg'* in B, fols 143r, *Illege* in E, fol. 385r, both throughout, the added *Monachorum* only here in this charter.

[69] The scribes of both B, fols 143r and E, fol. 385r use English words for the four compass points in this item.

[70] *Schortfen* in B, fols 143r; *Sortfen* in E, fol. 385r.

the garden of William Sacrist [*Sacriste*] towards the west and the pasture of Sir Matthew de Melding [*Milden*] towards the east. To have and to hold of me and my heirs to them and their successors freely and quietly and in peace, as of their pure and perpetual alms in perpetuity. In testimony of which thing I have appended my seal to this writing. These being witnesses: Sir Matthew de Meldinge [*Milden*], Richard de Leleseye [*Lindsey*], Richard Forester (*Forestar'*), Gilbert de la Tie, Walter de Finchuile, Thomas son of Hugh, Simon of Stackwood, and others.

Charter 16.[71] Grant by Richard de Alneto and Claricia his wife of the homage, service and rent of Richard de Lelleseye (?*c.* 1260s–1270s)[72]

Know, present and future, that I, Richard de Alneto, and Claricia my wife of Monks Eleigh (*Yllege Monachorum*), have given, granted and by this our present charter have confirmed to God and the blessed Mary and the church of Christ, Canterbury, and the monks there, the servants of God, for the health of our souls and those of our ancestors in free, \pure[73]/ and perpetual alms all the homage and service which we had or could have in 1s. 3d. annual rent together with 3s. \and three half-pennies[74]/ of arrears, that is to say, wholly taking the aforesaid 1s. 3d. annual rent at 2 terms in the year, namely at the feast of [*St*] Michael, 7½d. and at Easter, 7½d., which Richard de Lelleseye [*Lindsey*] is accustomed to pay us for 3 roods of land which Seman son of Austin sometime held lying in the vill of Monks Eleigh, that is, between my land and the king's way which leads towards the bridge of Gedeford. To have and to hold to the aforesaid monks in perpetuity without any hindrance by ourselves or our heirs. And [*so that*] neither I, the said Richard, nor the said Claricia my wife, nor our heirs, shall be able to exact any right or claim in the aforesaid homage, service and rent, as it is aforesaid, we have corroborated this present charter with our seal. With these witnesses: Sir Matthew de Meldinge [*Milden*], knight, John de Haliberg' [*?Hallingbury, Essex*], then steward, Richard de Leleseye, Richard son of Roger Prior (*Rogeri Prioris*), Symon de Grotene [*Groton*], Walter de Fynchesleye, Gilbert son of William, Anselm son of Salomon, Hugh Radulfo and William son of Thomas, and others.

---

71 No original charter extant; enrolled, as 'Charter of Richard de Alneto and Claricia his wife concerning the homage of Richard de Lelleseye with 1s. 3d. rent', in CCA-DCc/Register/B, fol. 144v (fifteenth charter of twenty-seven enrolled, no. 'xv') and CCA-DCc/Register/E, fol. 387r (fifteenth charter of nineteen enrolled, no. '1922'). This charter is repeated immediately afterwards in B and E, with minor variations in phrasing, under the heading 'Charter of the same about the same': see Charter 17 (?*c.* 1260s–1270s).

72 Dated to *c.* 1260s–1270s by the presence of John de Haliberg', the priory steward, who also witnesses Charters 17, 19–20 and other grants to the priory of Christ Church, Canterbury, relating to Chartham (dated to 1275–76) and Monkton, Kent (dated January 1261). See CCA online catalogue for CCA-DCc-ChAnt/C/480 (also enrolled at CCA-DCc-Register/C, fol. 172r, and CCA-DCc-Register/E, fol. 245r) and CCA-DCc-ChAnt/M/136 (also enrolled at CCA-DCc-Register/C, fol. 131v, and CCA-DCc-Register/E, fol. 204r).

73 Insertion in B, fol. 144v only.

74 Insertion in B, fol. 144v.

Charter 17.[75] Grant by Richard de Alneto and Claricia his wife of the homage, service and rent of Richard de Leleseye (copy, ?c. 1260s–1270s)[76]

[*B, fol. 144v; E, fol. 387r*] Know, present and future, that I, Richard de Alneto, and Claricia my wife of Monks Eleigh (*Ylleye Monachorum*), have given, granted and by this our present charter have confirmed to God and the blessed Mary and the church of Christ, Canterbury, and the monks there, the servants of God, for the health of our souls and those of our ancestors in free, pure and perpetual alms all the homage and service which we had or could have in 1s. 3d. annual rent which Richard de Leleseye [*Lindsey*] is accustomed to pay us for 3 roods of land which Seman son of Austin sometime held of us in the vill of Monks Eleigh, lying between my land and the king's way which leads towards the bridge of Gedeford wholly taking the aforesaid 1s. 3d. at 2 terms in the year, namely at Easter, 7½d. and at the feast of St Michael, 7½d. To have and to hold of us and our heirs to him and his heirs in perpetuity without any hindrance. And [*so that*] neither I, the said [*B, fol. 145r*], Richard, nor Claricia my wife, nor our heirs, shall be able to exact any right or claim in the aforesaid homage, service and rent, as it is aforesaid, we have corroborated this present charter with our seal. With these witnesses: Sir Matthew de Melding', knight, John de Halibergh', then steward, Richard de Leleseye, Richard son of Roger Prior (*Rogeri Prioris*), Symon de Grotene [*Groton*], Walter de Fynchesleg', Gilbert son of William, Anselm son of Salomon, Hugh Radulfo and William son of Thomas, and others.

Charter 18.[77] Inquest into the locations of the burial of those considered damned and any gallows in Monks Eleigh (?c. 1260s–1270s, possibly 1261 or shortly thereafter)[78]

[*B, fol. 145r; E, fol. 387r*] Inquest made by order of the lord prior [*as to*] where the certain and accustomed place in the vill of Eleigh (*Ylleghe*) is, where the damned[79]

---

[75] No original charter extant; enrolled, as 'Charter of the same about the same', immediately following Charter 16 (*?c.* 1260s–1270s), in CCA-DCc/Register/B, fols. 144v–145r (sixteenth charter of twenty-seven enrolled, no. 'xvj') and CCA-DCc/Register/E, fol. 387r (sixteenth charter of nineteen enrolled, no. '1923'). This charter is a copy of the one immediately preceding it in B and E, with minor variations in phrasing: see Charter 16.

[76] Dating as for Charter 16 (*?c.* 1260s–1270s).

[77] CCA-DCc-ChAnt/I/226; enrolled as 'Inquest made for the burial of the damned', in CCA-DCc/Register/B, fol. 145r (seventeenth charter of twenty-seven enrolled) and as 'Inquest made by order of the lord prior into where the damned were accustomed to be buried and where gallows were accustomed to be in the same vill', in CCA-DCc/Register/E, fols 387r–v (seventeenth charter of nineteen enrolled, no. '1924'). It is discussed and translated in Nichols, '*Custodia Essexae*' (1930), pp. 109–10. He mentions an abbreviated, late-seventeenth-century transcription in BL Add. MS 6037, fol. 170, which the BL catalogue dates to the early eighteenth century. This has not been checked for this edition. For Weller's sketch and map of the site, see Plate 5.

[78] Dated by a comparison of some of the people mentioned in the document with other witness lists, especially those to Charters 16–17, 19–20 (all *?c.* 1260s–1270s) and the dated Charters 21–23 (all 1276). Walter de Finchesleg', Symon de Grotene and Matthew Marscallo all witness Charters 21–23, which are all dated precisely to 1276. The presence here of Sir Matthew de Melding pushes back the potential date bracket to the mid-thirteenth century (see Charters 11–15), so c.1261 seems likely.

[79] The word translated here as 'damned' (*dampnati*) can also be translated as 'condemned', as translated by Nichols, '*Custodia Essexae*' (1930), pp. 109–10, which would fit with the inquest jurors' statement respecting a gallows for the execution of criminals. However, their statement about the burial of William Fant, a suicide, implies that the inquest was held to discover more about the burial place of those whose souls were considered damned rather than just those executed for secular crimes. For

are accustomed to be buried and where gallows were accustomed to be in the same vill, taken by Sir Matthew de Meldinge [*Milden*], knight, Richard le Priur, Hugh son of Ralph, Symon de Grotene [*Groton*], Richard Palmer,[80] [*E, fol. 387v*] Walter ate Mere, Robert Godhyne,[81] Walter de Fynchesll',[82] Stephen de Venell', Richard Marescallu', Richard ate Fen, and Matthew le Marescal who all upon oath say that where a certain William Fant, who killed himself in the vill of Eleigh (*Ylleya*), was buried is Richard de Lelesie's own tenement and his severalty and by a fixed service he and his ancestors have defended that tenement in the court of Eleigh (*Ylleye*). Indeed, moreover, they say that in a certain place near the said tenement of the said Richard, that is to say, in the demesne of the lord prior, in a certain ditch, a certain woman was burned and a cow was interred[83] for a trespass and that at no time had any other judgement been made in the same place, nor had gallows ever been raised there. Indeed, they say that at another time gallows were raised in a certain place in the same vill which is called Fulsclo, in the demesne of the lord prior, and by a certain powerful man named Fyn le Lord the aforesaid gallows were thrown down and by Fyn himself the aforesaid judgement in the aforesaid place near the said tenement of the said Richard, was made and completed.

Charter 19.[84] Grant by Hugh son of Ralph of the homage, service and rents due from Anselm Abot, Adam son of Hugh and Walter de le Mere (*?c.* 1260s–1270s)[85]

[*B, fol. 144v; E, fol. 386v*] Know, present and future, that I, Hugh, son of Ralph de Ylleya Monachorum [*Monks Eleigh*], have given, granted and by this my present charter have confirmed to the prior and convent of the church of Christ, Canterbury, for the health of my soul, in free, pure and perpetual alms, the homage and service of Anselm Abot [*and*] 7d. annual rent which he is accustomed to pay to me for 3 acres of land which he holds of me in the vill of Monks Eleigh lying in the field which is called Swdaynesland [*sic*], the homage and service of Adam son of Hugh [*and*] 4d. annual rent which he is accustomed to pay to me for a certain messuage which he holds of me in the aforesaid vill lying between the royal road and the land of Walter de le Mere,[86] the homage and service of Walter de le Mere [*and*] 5d. annual rent which he is accustomed to pay to me for 1 acre of land which he holds of me in the said town lying in the field which is called Havedland with all the escheats, wards and reliefs and all their appurtenances. [*E, fol. 387r*] To have and to hold to the said prior and convent and their successors freely, quietly, well

---

Weller's sketch and maps of the site and the boundaries of the parishes of Monks Eleigh and Lindsey and the hundreds of Cosford and Babergh, see Plates 5 and 6.

80 *Palmer* in B, fol. 145r; *Paulmer* in E, fol. 387r.

81 *Godhyne* in B, fol. 145r; *Godhune* in E, fol. 387v. Possibly the tenant after whom the tenement Godhynesquarter was named. See also Court Rolls 7 (*c.* 1361) and 8 (1361–1361/62) and Rental 1 (1379–80).

82 *de Fynchesll'* in B, fol. 145r; *de Fynchesleghe* in Reg E.

83 *in quoda[m] fossato q[ua]dam femi[n]a [com]busta fuit et una vacca pro t[ra]nsgressione infossata.*

84 No original charter extant; enrolled, as 'Charter of Hugh son of Ralph concerning the homage of Anselm Abot, Adam son of Hugh and Walter de le Mere with 6d. [*sic*] rent', in CCA-DCc/Register/B, fol. 144v (fourteenth charter of twenty-seven enrolled, no. 'xiiij') and CCA-DCc/Register/E, fols 386v–387r (fourteenth charter of nineteen enrolled, no. '1921').

85 Dated as Charter 16 (*?c.* 1260s–1270s). The three tenants whose homage, service and rents were granted to the prior by this charter are listed as paying their rents to the treasury at Canterbury in Extent 7 (late-fourteenth-century copies of earlier documents dating from between *c.* 1260 and 1330).

86 *de le* [*sic*] *Mere* in B, fol. 144v; *del Mere* here only in E, fol. 386v.

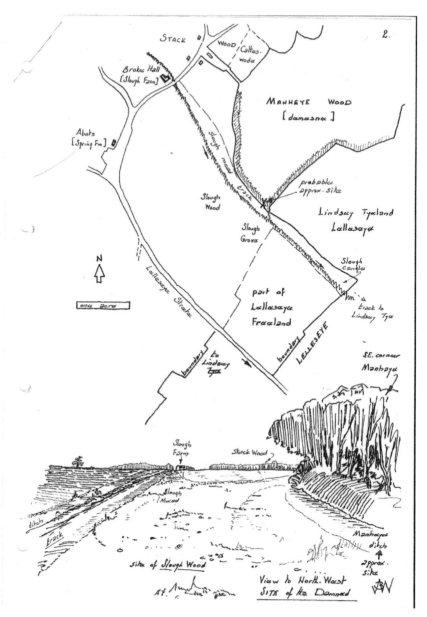

Plate 5. Weller's map and sketch of the site of 'where the damned were accustomed to be buried' in Monks Eleigh. The prior instigated an inquiry into the location of the place, at some time after the suicide of William Fant who was buried there (see Charter 18, c.1260s – 1270s). The inquest jury reported that in earlier times, in a ditch near to Fant's burial site, 'a woman was burned and a cow was interred for a trespass'. The burial site is on the Monks Eleigh parish and manorial boundaries as well as the boundary between the hundreds of Babergh and Cosford. The burial of criminals and social outcasts on such boundaries was not uncommon in the medieval period and was a marker of social exclusion even after death (Weller Archive, file 'Maps'). For a larger map of the southern half of the manor, giving the wider context of the hundred, parish and manorial boundaries, see Plate 6.

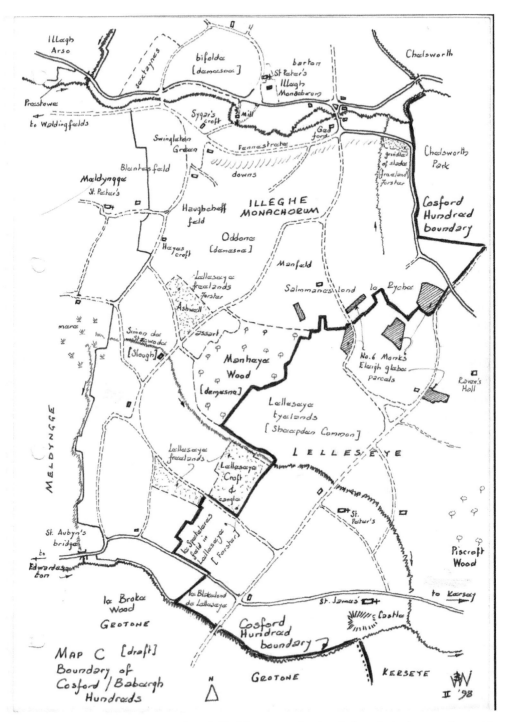

Plate 6. *Weller's draft map of the southern half of the manor, showing the boundaries between the parish, manor and hundreds of Cosford and Babergh (Weller Archive, file 'Maps')*

and in peace in perpetuity. And I, the said Hugh, and my heirs will warrant, acquit and defend the aforesaid homages, services and rents with all their appurtenances as aforesaid to the aforesaid prior and convent and their successors against all people in perpetuity. Now for this gift, grant and, by this charter, confirmation, the said prior and convent have received me in their prayers. And so that this gift, grant and, by this charter, confirmation, may endure firmly and stably we have appended our seal to this present writing. These being witnesses: Sir Matthew de Melding [*Milden*], knight, John de Haliberg', Richard Pryor,[87] Adam de Ylleya [*Eleigh*], clerk, Gilbert son of William, Anselm son of Salomon, Matthew Marescall',[88] Salomon Marescall', Symon de Stacwode, Richard le Paumer, William Huneman, Robert Auty, Stephen de Venell', Richard Marescall', and others.

Charter 20.[89] Grant by Anselm Abot of the homage, service and rent of Hubert de Montecanisio (?*c.* 1260s–1270s)[90]

[*B, fol. 144r; E, fol. 386v*] Know, present and future, that I, Anselm Abbot, and Agnes my wife of Monks Eleigh (*Ylleya Monachorum*) have given, granted and by this our present charter have confirmed to the prior and convent of the church of Christ, Canterbury, for the health of our souls in free, pure and perpetual alms, the homage and service of Hubert de Montecanisyo [*and*] 6d. annual rent which he is accustomed to pay to us concerning 3 acres of land which he holds of us in the vill of Monks Eleigh lying in a certain hamlet which is called Stacwode with all the escheats, wards and reliefs and all its appurtenances. To have and to hold to the \aforesaid[91]/ prior and convent and their successors freely, quietly, well and in peace in perpetuity. And I the aforesaid Anselm and Agnes my wife and our heirs will warrant, acquit and defend the aforesaid homage, service and rent with all their appurtenances as is aforesaid to the aforesaid [*B, fol. 144v*] prior and convent and their successors against all people in perpetuity. Now for this gift, grant and, by this charter, confirmation, the said prior and convent have received us into their prayers. And so that this gift, grant and, by this charter, confirmation, may endure firmly and stably we have appended our seal to this present writing. With these witnesses: Sir Matthew de Melding [*Milden*], knight, John de Halingeberg', Richard Priur, Adam de Ylleye, clerk, Gilbert son of William, Anselm son of Salomon, Hugh son of Ralph, Symon de Stacwode, Matthew Marescall',[92] Salomon Marescallo, Walter son of Hugh, Richard Le Palmere, and many others.

---

[87] *Pryor* in B, fol. 144v; *Prior* in E, fol. 387r.

[88] *Marescall'* in B, fol. 144v; *Marescallo* in E, fol. 387r.

[89] No original charter extant; enrolled, as 'Charter of Anselm Abot concerning the homage of Hubert de Montecanisio with 6d. rent', in CCA-DCc/Register/B, fols 144r–v (thirteenth charter of twenty-seven enrolled) and CCA-DCc/Register/E, fol. 386v (thirteenth charter of nineteen enrolled, no. '1920').

[90] Dated as Charter 16 (?*c.* 1260s–1270s).

[91] Insertion in B, fol. 144r.

[92] *Marescall'* in B, fol. 144v; *Marescallo* in E, fol. 386v.

Charter 21.[93] Acknowledgement and quitclaim by Nicholas de Lelleseye of his right in 2½ acres of wood in Monks Eleigh (10 October 1276)

[*B, fol. 143r; E, fol. 385v*] Know, present and future, that I, Nicholas de Lelleseye [*Lindsey*], \son of Anselm de Lelleseye[94]/, have remitted, granted and penitently quitclaimed for me and my heirs in perpetuity to the religious men of the prior and convent of the church of Christ, Canterbury, and the successors of the aforesaid prior all the right and claim which I had [*B, fol. 143v*] or in any way in law could have in 2½ acres of wood with appurtenances in Monks Eleigh (*Ylleg' Monachorum*) which certain wood lies in breadth alongside the wood of the said prior and convent which is called Manhey on the east side and the way which leads from Milden (*Melding*) towards Kersey (*Kerseye*) on the west side and one head [*abuts*] on the land of Richard de Wathefeud [*Whatfield*], knight, which is called Wodecroft on the north side. To hold and to have all the aforesaid wood with all its appurtenances to the aforesaid prior and convent and the successors of the aforesaid prior in perpetuity so that neither I nor my heirs nor anyone for us or having on behalf of us any right or claim in the said wood with appurtenances in the future shall be able or ought to reclaim or sell the same. Now for having this remission, grant and quitclaim, the aforesaid prior and convent have given to me by the hand of Dom[95] William de Cerringe, then warden of the manor of Eleigh (*Illegh'*), 10s. sterling. In testimony of which thing, I have corroborated with my seal on this present writing on the Saturday next after the feast of Saint Faith the Virgin in the 4th year of the reign of King Edward [*I, Saturday, 10 October 1276*]. These being witnesses: Gilbert ate Tye, Walter de Finchesleg',[96] Anselm son of Salomon, Matthew Marscallo, Richard Baker (*Pistore*), Thomas ate Tye, Anselm Abot, Symon le Wylde, Symon de Grotene [*Groton*], John Polle, Salomon de Hygeleg',[97] Thomas le Forester,[98] and many others.

Charter 22.[99] Acknowledgement and quitclaim by Henry de Lelleseye of his right in 2½ acres of wood in Monks Eleigh (10 October 1276)

[*B, fol. 143v; E, fol. 385v*] Know, present and future, that I, Henry de Lelleseye [*Lindsey*], son of Anselm de Lelleseye, have remitted, conceded and penitently quitclaimed for me and my heirs in perpetuity to the religious men of the prior and convent [*E, fol. 386r*] of the church of Christ, Canterbury, and the successors of the aforesaid prior all the right and claim which I had or in any way in law could have in 2½ acres of wood with appurtenances in Monks Eleigh (*Ylleg' Monachorum*) which

93 CCA-DCc-ChAnt/I/223; enrolled, as 'Charter of Nicholas de Lelleseye concerning his right in 2½ acres of wood there', in CCA-DCc/Register/B, fol. 143r–v (sixth charter of twenty-seven enrolled) and CCA-DCc/Register/E, fol. 385v (sixth charter of nineteen enrolled, no. '1913'). See also Charters 22–23.

94 Inserted in B, fol. 143r.

95 The Latin word *dominus*, 'lord', can translate as 'Sir' in the case of knights or parish clergy (a courtesy title) but is here translated as 'Dom', the title given to monks such as those at Christ Church Priory, Canterbury.

96 *de Finchesleg'* in B, fol. 143v; *de Fincheglegh* in E, fol. 385v.

97 *de Hygeleg'* in B, fol. 143v; *de Yllege* in E, fol. 385v.

98 *le Forest'* in B, fol. 143v; *le Forester* in E, fol. 385v.

99 CCA-DCc-ChAnt/I/219; enrolled, as 'Charter of Henry de Lelleseye of his right in the same', in CCA-DCc/Register/B, fol. 143v (eighth charter of twenty-seven enrolled) and CCA-DCc/Register/E, fols 385v–386r (eighth charter of nineteen enrolled, no. '1915'). See also Charters 21 and 23.

certain wood lies in breadth alongside the wood of the said prior and convent which is called Manheye on the east side and the way which leads from Milden (*Melding*) towards Kersey (*Kerseye*) on the west side and one head [*abuts*] on the land of Richard de Wathefeld [*Whatfield*], knight, which is called Wodecroft on the north side. To hold and to have all the aforesaid wood with all its appurtenances to the aforesaid prior and convent and the successors of the aforesaid prior in perpetuity. So that neither I nor my heirs nor anyone for us or having on behalf of us any right or claim in the said wood with appurtenances in the future shall be able or ought to reclaim or sell the same. Now for having this remission, grant and quitclaim, the aforesaid prior and convent have given to me by the hand of Dom William de Cerring, then warden of the manor of Monks Eleigh,[100] 10s. sterling. In testimony of which thing, I have corroborated with my seal on this present writing on the Saturday next after the feast of St Faith the Virgin in the 4th year of the reign of King Edward [*I, Saturday, 10 October 1276*]. These being witnesses: Sir[101] Adam de Ylleg', Symon le Wilde,[102] Gilbert ate Tye, Walter de Finchesleg',[103] Anselm son of Salomon, Matthew Marscallo, Thomas ate Tye, Anselm Abot, Simon de Grotene [*Groton*], John Polle, Salomon de Hygeleg',[104] Thomas Forester and others.

Charter 23.[105] Acknowledgement and quitclaim by Thomas de Lelleseye of his right in 2½ acres of wood in Monks Eleigh (11 October 1276)

Know, present and future, that I, Thomas de Lelleseye [*Lindsey*], son of Anselm de Lelleseye, have remitted, granted and penitently quitclaimed for me and my heirs in perpetuity to the religious men of the prior and convent of the church of Christ, Canterbury, and the successors of the aforesaid prior all the right and claim which I had or in any way in law could have in 2½ acres of wood with appurtenances in Monks Eleigh (*Ylleg' Monachorum*) which certain wood lies in breadth alongside the wood of the said prior and convent which is called Manhey on the east part and the way which leads from Milden (*Melding*) towards Kersey (*Kerseye*) on the west part and one head [*abuts*] on the land of Richard de Wathefeld [*Whatfield*],[106] knight, which is called Wodecroft on the north part. To hold and to have all the aforesaid wood with all its appurtenances to the aforesaid prior and convent and the successors of the aforesaid prior in perpetuity, so that neither I nor my heirs nor anyone for us or having on behalf of us any right or claim in the said wood with appurtenances in the future shall be able or ought to reclaim or sell the same. Now for having this remission, grant and quitclaim, the aforesaid prior and convent have given to me by the hand of Dom William de Cerringe, then warden of the manor of Eleigh (*Illeghe*), 10s. sterling. In testimony of which thing, I have corroborated with my seal on this present writing on the Sunday [*sic*] next after the feast of St Faith the Virgin in the 4th year of the reign of King Edward [*I, Sunday, 11 October*

---

100 *Ylleg'* in B, fol. 143v; *Ylleghe* in E, fol. 386r.

101 In this instance, *dominus* has been translated as 'Sir', which was used as a courtesy title for parish clergy.

102 *Symon le Wilde* in B, fol. 143v; *Symone Le Wylde* in E, fol. 386r.

103 *de Finchesleg'* in B, fol. 143v; *de Fynchesleghe* in E, fol. 386r.

104 *de Hygeleg'* in B, fol. 143v; *de Ylleg'* in E, fol. 386r.

105 CCA-DCc-ChAnt/I/215; enrolled, as 'Charter of Thomas de Lelleseye about his right in the same wood', in CCA-DCc/Register/B, fol. 143v (seventh charter of twenty-seven enrolled) and CCA-DCc/Register/E, fol. 385v (seventh charter of nineteen enrolled, no. '1914'). See also Charters 21–22.

106 *Wathefeld* in B, fol. 143v; *Wathefeud* in E, fol. 385v.

1276]. These being witnesses: Sir Adam de Ylleg' [*Eleigh*], rector of the church of Bocking (*Bockyng*) [*Essex*];[107] Symon le Wilde,[108] Gilbert ate Tye, Walter de Finchesleg', Anselm son of Salomon, Thomas le Forester, Thomas ate Tye, Salomon de Hygeleg',[109] Anselm Abot, Simon de Grotene [*Groton*], John Polle, Matthew Marscallo, and many others.

Charter 24.[110] Grant by Richard son of Roger le Priur of rent of 1 mark for a pittance (20 November 1286–19 November 1287)

[*B, fol. 144r; E, fol. 386r*] Know, present and future, that I, Richard, son of Roger le Pryur[111] of Monks Eleigh (*Ylleya Monachorum*), have given, granted and by this my present charter confirmed to the prior and convent of the church of Christ, Canterbury, for my soul and the souls of my ancestors, 1 mark of silver annual rent in pure and perpetual alms for one pittance within the octave of the translation of Saint Thomas the Martyr [*E, fol. 386v*] annually to be taken wholly in their treasury at Canterbury in perpetuity from those who will hold the lands and tenements after my death which formerly were of William Fant and Hugh his brother in the vill aforesaid. And I, the aforesaid Richard, and my heirs and my assigns will warrant, acquit and defend the said rent to the said prior and convent as said above against all men and women in perpetuity. Also this rent and service to the said prior and convent from the aforesaid lands and tenements shall be accustomed to be paid first. And so that this my gift, grant, warrant and, by my present charter, confirmation, shall endure firmly and stably in perpetuity, I have appended my seal to this writing. With these witnesses: Sir Richard de Leleseya[112] [*Lindsey*], knight, Sir Adam de Ylleya, chaplain, John Pycot, Sir William de Cambes, chaplain, Matthew Marescallo, Gilbert de Tya,[113] Salomone Marescallo, Thomas Forester (*Forestar*), Walter de Fynchesleya, Anselm son of Salomon, and many others.

Charter 25.[114] Acknowledgement by John Pykot and Juliana his wife concerning the payment of a rent of 1 mark (20 November 1286–19 November 1287)

Know, present and future, that I, John Pycot, and Juliana my wife and our heirs and assigns are bound to pay to the prior and convent of the church of Christ, Canterbury, 1 mark of silver annual rent for one pittance within the octave of the translation of the blessed Thomas the martyr in their treasury at Canterbury in perpetuity from the

---

[107] *Bockyng* in B, fol. 143v; *Bockynge* in E, fol. 385v. He was still in office there in 1285 and may have remained so until his death in 1289 (Reaney, 'Early Essex Clergy' (1940), p. 79). See also Charter 11 (mid-thirteenth century).

[108] *Symon le Wilde* in B, fol. 143v; *Symone le Willde* in E, fol. 385v.

[109] *Salomon de Hygeleg'* in B, fol. 143v; *Salomon de Yllege* in E, fol. 385v.

[110] No original charter extant; enrolled, as 'Charter of Richard son of Roger le Priur concerning a 1 mark rent', in CCA-DCc/Register/B, fol. 144r (eleventh charter of twenty-seven enrolled) and CCA-DCc/Register/E, fols 386r–v (eleventh charter of nineteen enrolled, no. '1918'). See the next charter for an acknowledgement by the sitting tenants and Extent 7 for records relating to the rent being paid.

[111] *le Pryur* in B, fol. 144r; *le Priur* in E, fol. 386r.

[112] *Leleseya* in B, fol. 144r; *Lelleseya* in E, fol. 386v.

[113] *de Tya* in B, fol. 144r; *a Tya* in E, fol. 386v.

[114] No original charter extant; enrolled as 'Charter of John Pykot and Juliana his wife of the same mark rent' in CCA-DCc/Register/B, fol. 144r (twelfth charter of twenty-seven enrolled) and CCA-DCc/Register/E, fol. 386v (twelfth charter of nineteen enrolled, no. '1919'). See previous charter for their landlord's grant of their rent and Extent 7 for records relating to the rent being paid.

lands and tenements which formerly were of William Fant and Hugh his brother in the vill of Monks Eleigh (*Ylleya Monachorum*) which lands and tenements we hold out of the gift of Richard son of Roger le Priur in the vill aforesaid. And moreover all the rent and all other services from the said lands and tenements shall be accustomed to be paid first to the aforesaid prior and convent. In testimony of which thing we have appended our seal to this present writing. With these witnesses: Sir Richard de Leleseya[115] [*Lindsey*], knight, Sir Adam the chaplain of Eleigh (*Ylleya*), Gilbert his brother, Walter de Fynchesleya, Matthew Marescallo, Salomon Marescallo, Anselm son of Salomon, Thomas Forester (*Forestar'*), William Huneman, Salomon de Hyggeleya,[116] and many others.

Charter 26.[117] Grant by Thomas, son of Richard called Forster of Monks Eleigh of ½ acre of wood (20 November 1286–19 November 1287)

Know, present and future, that I, Thomas, son of Richard called Forster of Monks Eleigh (*Ylleg' Monachorum*), have given, granted and by this my present charter confirmed to the prior of the church of Christ, Canterbury and the convent of the same place and their successors in free, pure and perpetual alms, one half acre of my wood with appurtenances lying in Eleigh (*Ylleg'*) aforesaid, between the wood of the aforesaid prior and convent towards the east[118] and south and the land of William de Boytun towards the west and north. To have and to hold to the said prior and convent and their successors in free, pure and perpetual alms in perpetuity. And I, the aforesaid Thomas, and my heirs will warrant, defend and acquit the aforesaid half acre of wood with all its appurtenances to the said prior and convent and their successors against all people, Christian and Jewish, in perpetuity. And so that this my gift, grant, warrant, defence, acquittance and, by my present charter, confirmation, may be firmly upheld for ever, I have corroborated this my present charter with my seal in the 15th year of the reign of King Edward [*I, 20 November 1286–19 November 1287*]. With these witnesses: John de Belstede then bailiff of Eleigh (*Ylleg'*),[119] William de Boytune, Nicholas de Lelleseye [*Lindsey*], Matthew le Marscal, Thomas ate Tye, John at Tye, Adam ate Tye, John Polle, Salemann de Ylleg', Stephen Smith (*Stephano Fabro*), John ate Wode, clerk, and many others.

Charter 27.[120] Charter of the same concerning 1½ acres and 28 perches of meadow (20 November 1286–19 November 1287)

Know, present and future, that I, Thomas, son of Richard called Forestar' of Monks Eleigh (*Ylleg' Monachorum*), have given, conceded and by this my present charter

---

[115] *Leleseya* in B, fol. 144r; *Lelleseya* in E, fol. 386v.

[116] *de Hyggeleya* in B, fol. 144r; *de Ylleya* in E, fol. 386v.

[117] CCA-DCc-ChAnt/I/224; enrolled, as 'Charter of Thomas le Forstier concerning half an acre of wood', in CCA-DCc/Register/B, fol. 143v (ninth charter of twenty-seven enrolled) and as 'Charter of Thomas le Forester concerning half an acre of wood', in CCA-DCc/Register/E, fol. 386r (ninth charter of nineteen enrolled, no. '1916').

[118] Compass points in this charter are given in English.

[119] John de Belstede was a bailiff/steward rather than a reeve/bailiff/serjeant: see p. 45, footnote 12 respecting him under Accounts 1 (1285–86).

[120] No original charter extant; enrolled, as 'Charter of the same concerning 1½ acres and 28 perches of meadow', in CCA-DCc/Register/B, fol. 144r (tenth charter of twenty-seven enrolled) and CCA-DCc/Register/E, fol. 386r (tenth charter of nineteen enrolled, no. '1917').

24

have confirmed to the prior of the church of Christ, Canterbury, and the convent of the same place and their successors in free, pure and perpetual alms, 1½ acres and 28 perches of my meadow with appurtenances lying in Eleigh (*Ylleg'*) aforesaid, between the meadow of the heir of Salemann called Marscall' and the running water of Eleigh (*Yllegh'*) towards the north[121] and the messuage of William le Ver and the meadow of Heylewyse de la Tye towards the south. A head [*abuts*] on the meadow of the aforesaid Eylewyse[122] towards the west and on the bridge and street of Gedeford towards the east. To have and to hold to the aforesaid prior and convent and their successors in free, pure and perpetual alms in perpetuity. And I the aforesaid Thomas and my heirs will warrant, defend and acquit all the aforesaid meadow with all its appurtenances to the aforesaid prior and convent and their successors against all people, Christian and Jewish, in perpetuity. And so that this my gift, grant, warrant, defence, acquittance and, by my present charter, confirmation, may be firmly upheld for ever, I have corroborated this my present charter with the impression of my seal in the 15th year of the reign of King Edward [*I, 20 November 1286–19 November 1287*]. With these witnesses: William de Boytun'[123] [*Boyton, near Stoke-by-Clare*], Nicholas de Leleseye[124] [*Lindsey*], Master William de Basingeham, Symon Le Wylde, Thomas Berard, Matthew called Marscall', Thomas, John and Adam de la Tye, John Polle, Salemann de Hygel',[125] Stephen Smith (*Stephano Fabro*), John Clerk (*Johanne clerico*), and many others.

Charter 28.[126] Grant from Walter son of Hugh of Monks Eleigh to Robert Pig and Juliana[127] his wife of Monks Eleigh (*c.* 1270s–1280s)[128]

"[*Know, all, present*] and future that I Walter son of Hugh of Monks Eleigh (*Ylleia Monachorum*) have granted, given and by this my present charter confirmed [*to Robert*] Pig and Julian his wife of the same for their homage and service and for 14s. of silver which they have given me as a gersum fine [*1 rood of land*] in the same town lying in between my [*?land ?croft*] and the tract of open ground before my gate … towards the house of Robert Smith (*Faber*), whereof 1 head abutts on my land and the other head on the land of [*?Yner ?Christina*] del Broc with all … or may be in the said rod of land more or less. To have and to hold of me and the heirs of the said me and their heirs by Robert … Julian his wife or to whomsoever and whenever they may give, sell, bequeath or in any other way assign the said rood of

---

[121] Compass points in this charter are given in English.

[122] *Eylewyse* here in B, fol. 144r; *Heylewyse* in E, fol. 386r.

[123] *Boytun'* in B, fol. 144r; *Boytune* in E, fol. 386r.

[124] *Leleseye* in B, fol. 144r; *Lelleseye* in E, fol. 386r.

[125] *de Hygel'* in B, fol. 144r; *de Ylleghe* in E, fol. 386r.

[126] CCA-DCc-ChAnt/I/221 (original charter damaged); not enrolled in CCA-DCc/Register/B or CCA-DCc/Register/E. Text in double quotation marks is Michael Stansfield's transcription, which is reproduced here unedited.

[127] Charters 29 and 30 (both dated *c.* 1270s–1280s) name Robert Pig and his wife Hawise, rather than Juliana, as here, but Charter 25 (1286–1287) has a John Pykot and his wife Juliana. If Pykot is not a variant for Pig, or this is not a different wife, it might be a scribal error.

[128] Dated by a comparison of some of the people mentioned in the document with other witness lists in this volume. Subject matter, grantor and witnesses suggest a date close to Charters 29 and 30 (both dated *c.* 1270s–1280s). Thomas the forester is the grantor in Charters 26 and 27 (both dated 1286–87). Anselm son of Salomon witnessed Charters 16–20 (all *c.* 1260s–1270s), 21–23 (all dated 1276) and 24–25 (both dated 1286–87). John Poll(e) witnessed Charters 21–23 (all dated 1276) and 26–27 (both dated 1286–87).

land ... except to a house of religion ... to have in fee freely, quietly and in peace. Rendering thence jointly to me and my heirs 2[*d.*] at 2 terms annually that is at the feast of SS Peter and Paul 1d. and at the feast of St Michael 1d. for all [*services*], customs, suits to whatever court, aids and all scutages that may be demanded and I the said Walter and my heirs or ... assigns will warrant, defend and acquit the said rood of land with its appurtenances to the said Robert, Julian and their heirs [*against*] all people in perpetuity for the said service. With these witnesses: Thomas the forester, Gilbert brother of the same, Anselm son of [*?Solemann*], Adam the forester, Richard the marshall, John Poll', Robert Smith (*Faber*), Richard Ylger, Ralph de Nova Strata [*New Street*], Henry Babbe, [*?Walter*] de Mar, Peter son of the same, and many others."

Charter 29.[129] Grant from Reginald son of Walter of Monks Eleigh to Robert Pig and Hawise his wife (*c.* 1270s–1280s)[130]

"Know all, present and future, that I Reginald son of Walter of Monks Eleigh (*Illey Monachorum*) have given, granted and by this my present charter confirmed to Robert Pig and Hawise his wife and their heirs for their homage and service and for 10s. of silver which they have given me for a gersum fine 1 piece of arable land with its appurtenances just as were given to me lying in the town of Monks Eleigh that is in length lying between the land of the said Reginald on the one part and the land of Cristina de Broc on the other part and abutting at one head ... of Robert Smith (*Faber*) and at the other on the way leading towards the market place of Ker[*sey*] and to hold the said tenement with its appurtenances from me and my heirs by the said Robert ... and their heirs and to whom they might give, sell, bequeath ... freely, quietly, well, and in peace in fee and hereditarily rendering thence per year to me and my heirs 1 [*clove*[131]] for the customs and demands. And I the said Reginald and my heirs will warrant, acquit and defend the said ... Pig and Hawise his wife and their heirs or their assigns and their heirs for the said service against all men and women in perpetuity. In testimony of which thing I have appended my seal to this my writing. With these witnesses: Nicholas de Lelsey [*Lindsey*], Thomas his brother, Thomas le Foster, Robert Smith (*Faber*), John Ylger, Simon de Groton, John his son, Richard del Mere, Geoffrey Sparewe, and many others."

Charter 30.[132] Grant from Reginald son of Walter son of Hugh the Hayward of Monks Eleigh to Robert Pig and Hawis his wife of Monks Eleigh (*c.* 1270s–1280s)[133]

"May all present and future know that I Reginald son of Walter [*son of Hugh the hayward*] of Monks Eleigh (*Yllya Monachorum*) have given, granted and by this my present charter confirmed to Robert [*Pyg and Hawis*] his wife of the same town and their heirs for their homage and service and for 3s. [*as a gersum fine*] which they

---

[129] CCA-DCc-ChAnt/I/227A (original charter damaged); not enrolled in CCA-DCc/Register/B or CCA-DCc/Register/E. Like the previous charter, this is Michael Stansfield's transcript, unedited.

[130] Subject matter, grantor and witnesses suggest a date close to Charters 28 and 30 (both dated *c.* 1270s–1280s), as does the presence of witness Simon de Groton, who also witnesses Charters 16–18 (*c.* 1260s–1270s) and 21–23 (dated 1276).

[131] Probably one gillyflower clove: see Charter 11 (mid-thirteenth century) and Glossary.

[132] CCA-DCc-ChAnt/I/220 (original charter damaged); not enrolled in CCA-DCc/Register/B or CCA-DCc/Register/E. Like the previous two charters, this is Michael Stansfield's transcript, unedited.

[133] Dated as Charter 29 (*c.* 1270s–1280s).

have given to me ... 1 piece of land with its appurtenances containing in [*length*] 9 perches and in width ... on the street 1 perch and 4 feet at one head ... and in width 5 feet in one place and 2 feet at another place at another head ... in the [*vill*] of Monks Eleigh that is between my land and the land of the said Robert with one head abutting on the way which leads from the house of a certain [*?Alexander, ?Richard*] Ylger to the house of Robert Smith (*Faber*) and the other head [*abutts*] on the land of Robert Smith (*Faber*) ... certain piece of land with its appurtenances ... the heirs and assigns of the said Robert Pig and [*Hawis*] and their heirs ... freely, quietly, well and in peace ... Paying rent ... ½d at the feast of St Andrew the Apostle for all services, aids, customs ... asked for and I the said Reginald and my heirs or their assigns will warrant, acquit and defend the said piece of land with its appurtenances to the said Robert Pig ... or their assigns against all men ... In testimony of which I have appended my seal to this present charter. With these witnesses: Nicholas de ..., Thomas ..., John son of Simon, Robert Smith (*Faber*), [*?Nicholas ?Marescal*], Anselm ... Forestar, [*Stephen*] ... and John de Tya, Gilbert de Tya, Richard [*de*] ..., and many others."

Charter 31.[134] Agreement and grant by John atte Tye of 2s. free rent and a certain plot of land (1 November 1296)

May it be evident to all that on the feast of All Saints in the 24th year of the reign of King Edward [*I, 1 November 1296*] then it was agreed between the prior and convent of the church of Christ, Canterbury, on the one hand and John son of Thomas atte Tye of Monks Eleigh (*Illeghe Monachorum*) on the other, that is to say, that whereas the same prior and convent sought and demanded from the said John 13s. 4d. annual rent with appurtenances which the same prior and convent claimed, as the gift of Richard called Le Priur or someone else, the same prior and convent, for themselves and their successors, remitted and in all things quitclaimed to the aforesaid John and his heirs and his assigns all the aforesaid rent of 13s. 4d. with all the arrears and whatever else might accrue from the said rent in perpetuity. And now for this remission and quitclaim the aforesaid John has granted, given and confirmed to the aforesaid prior and convent a certain plot of his land which lies in length between the pasture of the said John towards the north on the one hand and the pasture of Stephen Smith (*Stephani fabri*) towards the south on the other. And one head [*abuts*] on the street which is called Fenstret and on the pasture of the aforesaid Stephen Smith. Which certain plot of land contains in length 40½ perches and in width 9 feet.[135] Saving to the said John and his heirs and his assigns free lopping of trees growing on both sides of the said plot without any limiting conditions or impediment from the said prior and convent and their successors in perpetuity. The aforesaid John grants and binds himself and his heirs to render to the said prior and convent and their successors, 2s. annual rent payable at 2 terms in the year, that is, at Easter, 1s., and at the feast of Saint Michael, 1s., issuing from a certain land called Fanteslond. And it is allowed that the aforesaid prior and convent and their

---

[134] CCA-DCc-ChAnt/M/418; enrolled, as 'Cyrograph of John atte Thye concerning 2s. free rent and a certain plot of land' in CCA-DCc/Register/B, fol. 145r (eighteenth charter of twenty-seven enrolled) and as 'Cyrograph of John atte Tye concerning 2s. free rent and a certain plot of land', in CCA-DCc/Register/E, fol. 387v (eighteenth charter of nineteen enrolled, no. '1925').

[135] The measurements, positioning and following clause about lopping trees on both sides sounds as if this plot of land was a lane.

successors may distrain the aforesaid land as often as the said rent of 2s. shall be in arrears, excepting any other rents and services normally owed and accustomed from the aforesaid land. In testimony of which thing the common seal of the convent of the aforesaid church and the seal of the said John have been appended in turn to this chirograph writing. Done on the day and year abovesaid.

Charter 32.[136] Agreement and exchange of lands by Stephen Smith and the prior and convent (7 September 1298)

Be it known by all, present and future, that on the 7th day of the month of September in the year of the Lord 1298, then it was agreed between brother John de Tanet [*Thanet*] then warden of the manor of Eleigh (*Illegh'*) on the one hand and Stephen Smith [*Stephanum Fabrum*] of Eleigh on the other, that is, that the aforesaid Stephen gave and granted to the prior and convent of the church of Christ, Canterbury, a certain plot of alder-holt containing in length between the mill and the bridge of the aforesaid prior and convent 10 perches of land and in breadth, 12 feet. To have and to hold to the aforesaid prior and convent and their successors under warranty of the said Stephen and his heirs in perpetuity. For which certain gift, grant and warrant the aforesaid brother John in the name of the aforesaid prior and convent gave and granted to the said Stephen a certain piece of their pasture at Holemed containing in length 7½ perches and in breadth 28 feet, lying next to the meadow of the aforesaid Stephen which is towards the east.[137] To have and to hold to the aforesaid Stephen and his heirs or his assigns freely, quietly, in perpetuity. In testimony of which thing the seal of the aforesaid brother John and the seal of the aforesaid Stephen have been appended in turn to this chirograph writing. Done the day and year abovesaid. With these witnesses: Simon le Wilde, Adam atte Hey, Adam son of Gilbert atte Tye, Simon son of Salomon le Marchal, Walter atte Lane, Thomas Berard, Walter called Merchant (*Waltero dicto mercatore*) of Eleigh (*Illegh'*), Thomas le Forester, Andrew his son, John Clerk (*Johanne clerico*) and others.

Charter 33.[138] Grant of excheated lands to John de Horwode, chaplain (13 February 1316/17)

To all the faithful in Christ to whom this present writing shall come, Henry, by divine permission prior of the church of Christ, Canterbury, and the chapter of the same place, greetings in the Lord for ever. Know us to have granted, demised and, by this present writing, confirmed to John de Horwode, chaplain, 1 messuage with the garden and curtilage adjacent and 6 acres of land with appurtenances in our vill of Eleigh (*Illegh'*) in the county of Suffolk (*Suthfolch*) which came into our hands through the felonies which John and William, sons of Stephen Smith (*Stephani Fabri*) of the same vill, committed, for which afterwards the aforesaid John abjured the kingdom of England and the aforesaid William was outlawed. To

---

[136] CCA-DCc-ChAnt/I/225; enrolled as 'Charter of Stephen Smith (*Stephani fabri*) concerning an exchange of certain lands' in CCA-DCc/Register/B, fol. 145r (nineteenth charter of twenty-seven enrolled) and CCA-DCc/Register/E, fol. 387v (nineteenth charter of nineteen enrolled, no. 1926).

[137] Compass points given in English in this charter.

[138] No original charter extant; enrolled, as 'Indenture between us and John de Horwode chaplain' in CCA-DCc/Register/B, fol. 145v (twenty-second charter of twenty-seven enrolled); not enrolled in CCA-DCc/Register/E.

have and to hold to the same John, his heirs and assigns from us and our successors by hereditary right in perpetuity rendering and making in respect of which, to us and our successors annually, all the services and customs owed and accustomed, in respect of which the said Stephen in the time when he held that tenement of us used to render and make for the same. And we the aforesaid prior and chapter and our successors will warrant all the said tenements with their appurtenances to the aforesaid John, his heirs and assigns, against all people in perpetuity. In testimony of which thing, we have appended our common seal to the part of this writing remaining in the possession of the said John, and the aforesaid John has appended his seal to the other part of this writing remaining to us. Given in our Chapter the 15th day of February in the year of the Lord 1316.

Charter 34.[139] Bond of Richard de Broghton (28 March 1326)

May it be evident to all by these presents that I, Richard de Broghton of Monks Eleigh (*Illeghe Monachorum*) have attorned myself to the prior of the church of Christ, Canterbury, and the convent of the same place for all services and customs owed to them for the lands and tenements which were formerly of John son of Stephen Smith (*Stephani Fabri*) in Monks Eleigh which came into the hands of the said prior and convent as their escheat for the felony of the aforesaid John son of Stephen and which were in my seisin on the day of the making of this writing. Concerning which lands and tenements I recognise for me and my heirs by these presents to be held of the aforesaid prior and convent and I am bound to them for doing all the services and customs owed and accustomed in respect thereof in future in perpetuity. Notwithstanding any letters or grants previously made or granted by the said prior and convent to anyone. In testimony of which thing I have appended my seal to this present writing. Given at Canterbury on the Friday next after the feast of the Annunciation of the blessed Mary in the 19th year of the reign of King E[*dward II*] son of *King Edward* [*Friday, 28 March 1326*]. With these witnesses: Sir John de Ifelde, knight, Thomas de Medmenham, William de Brannford [?*Bramford*], Bertram de Guytham, William le Hwyte, Roger de Cestr' [*Chester*], and others.

Charter 35.[140] Quitclaim by Richard de Broghton (28 March 1326)

May it be evident to all by these presents that I, Richard de Broghton, tenant of the prior of the church of Christ, Canterbury, concerning their manor of Monks Eleigh (*Illeghe Monachorum*) have remitted and released to the said prior and convent all kinds of actions, petitions, complaints and demands which I may have had against them for any reason before the day of the making of these presents. So that neither I, the said Richard, nor any in my name may bring any action, petition, complaint or demand against them as has been said in the future. In testimony of which thing I have made these my letters patent. Given at Canterbury on the Friday next after the feast of the Annunciation of the blessed Mary in the 19th year of the reign of King E[*dward II*] son of King E[*dward, 28 March 1326*]. With these witnesses: Sir

---

[139] CCA-DCc-ChAnt/Z/178; enrolled in CCA-DCc/Register/B, fol. 145v (twentieth charter of twenty-seven enrolled, no. 'xx'); not enrolled in CCA-DCc/Register/E.

[140] No original charter extant; enrolled in CCA-DCc/Register/B, fol. 145v (twenty-first charter of twenty-seven enrolled, no. 'xxj'); not enrolled in CCA-DCc/Register/E.

John de Ifeld, knight, Thomas de Medmenham, William de Brannford [*?Bramford*], Bertram de Guytham, John Quykman, and others.

Charter 36.[141] Grant from Matilda de Boyton to William ate Brok of Monks Eleigh and Cecilia his wife of land in Monks Eleigh (28 September 1360)

"May all present and future know that I Matilda de Boyton have conceded, given and by this my present charter confirmed to William ate Brok of Monks Eleigh (*Illeye Monachorum*) and Cecilia his wife one piece of arable land lying in the said Eleigh between the land of the lord prior and convent of Christ, Canterbury, on the one part and the land of Dyonisia de Boyton my mother on the other with one head abutting on the meadow of Michael de Burs [*Bures*]. To have and to hold the said piece of land with its appurtenances to the said William and Cecilia his wife, their heirs and assigns of the chief lord of the fee by the service thence customary and owed. And I the said Matilda and my heirs will warrant all the said piece of land with all its appurtenances to the said William and Cecilia his wife, their heirs and assigns in the said form against all people in perpetuity. In witness of which thing I have appended this my seal to this present charter. With these witnesses: Richard Forestar; Robert Gauge; Nicholas Hygeleye; Adam Cut; John Domlond [*?recte Donilond*]; and others. Given at the said Eleigh on Monday next after the feast of St Matthew the Apostle and Evangelist in the year of the reign of King Edward the third after the Conquest thirty-four [*28 September 1360*]."

---

[141] CCA-DCc-ChAnt/I/222 (original charter damaged); not enrolled in CCA-DCc/Register/B or CCA-DCc/Register/E. The text in double inverted commas is Michael Stansfield's translation, unedited.

II

EXTENTS

Early thirteenth century to early fourteenth century[1]

Extent 1. (1210–11)[2]

Eleigh (Illeghe). Salomon de Illeghe, Roger Prior, Robert son of Hugh, Robert son of Adam, jurors (*prepositi*) say that there is to be had in the same vill in respect of assize rents each year £8 11s. 8¼d. at five terms. And 2 hens at Christmas. And they say that Robert de Turnham[3] found nothing there in respect of stock neither in grain nor in utensils but the wardens of the manor recovered while he had custody 1 seam (*summam*) of wheat and 1½ seams of barley and 1 heap (*hoppam*) of the produce of the mill. And £2 11s. 6d. in respect of wood sold. And 15s. and 7d. in respect of hay sold. The same say that nothing else was found there on the aforesaid Tuesday.

Extent 2. Account of Deteriorations (*c.* 1213)[4]

Eleigh (Illege)

In respect of the deterioration of the buildings	£2.
In respect of the deterioration of the woodlands and bad sales (*de mala venditione*) [?of dead *wood*[5]]	£15.

The produce of stock

In respect of 4 cows for 6 years	£1 4s.
In respect of 90 (*iiiior xxti et x*) sheep	£18 and 15s.
In respect of 4 swine	£1 4s.

---

1   See Introduction, p. xxxv.
2   TNA, E 142/46 (formerly Exchequer K.R. Ancient Extents no. 46), catalogue reads 'Extent of the lands and the stock of Canterbury Priory in ... Monks Eleigh and Hadleigh, Suff; ... 12 John (Ascension Day 1210–the day before Ascension Day 1211).' It is one of a series relating to forfeited lands amongst the king's remembrancer's records in the Exchequer. Weller's translation (checked and edited here) is from Nichols' Latin transcript in *Custodia Essexae* (1930), Appendix B, p. 10. During King John's dispute with Pope Innocent, the property of the priory of Christ Church, Canterbury, was confiscated by the Crown for six years between 1207 and 1213. This extent reflects the poor administrative state of the manor at that time.
3   Robert de Turnham (Thurnham in other extents in the series) was the king's receiver who took office in September 1210, the surveys of the Canterbury manors being undertaken around Easter 1211 (see Nichols, '*Custodia Essexae*' (1930), p. 166; H. Summerson, 'Robert of Thornham (Turnham) (d.1211)', *ODNB* (2018).
4   CCA-DCc-Rental/38, being part of roll 2 of two parchment rolls (of five and three membranes), containing accounts of the priory's estates on their recovery from Crown seizure *c.* 1213. Latin. Translated by the current editor.
5   *Venditio* can mean 'the act of selling, a sale' and specifically a sale 'of dead wood from forest' (*DMLBS*). The addition of 'bad' here could imply fraudulent sales, or under-valued sales, as well as sales that should never have been made because the cutting of the wood damaged the woodland.

In respect of the deterioration of land not cultivated and badly cultivated for 5 years
£168 16s. 11d.
In respect of the sixth year \£34/ <£30> \£34/ 6s. and 4d.
<Total, £257 9s. and [?]8d.> Total, £241 6s. 3d.

Extent 3. (Mid- to late-thirteenth century, probably *c.* 1250)[6]

Extent of the manors of the lord prior and convent of the church of Christ, Canterbury, in the counties of Essex, Suffolk and Norfolk for a tenth of the lord King ...
Eleigh (*Ylleghe*). They say etc. that there is due here from assize rents in cash £8 9s. Also customs and works which are worth each year £4 10s. From heriots, reliefs and amercements of the court, 13s. From stock usually sold in the year with dairy, 12s. 4d. Also 1 water mill which is worth 15s. From the fruits of the garden and orchards (*gardini et [h]ortorum*),[7] 6s. 8d. Also 1 dovecote which is worth 1s. 8d. Also 9 acres of mowing meadow which is worth £1 2s. 6d, price of an acre, 2s. 6d. Also 6 acres of pasture which is worth 3s., price of an acre, 6d. Also 4 acres of alder-holt[8] which is worth 1s. Also 360 acres of arable land which is usually worth each year £9, price of an acre, 6d.
Total £25 14s. 2d.

Extent 4. Assize Rents (probably *c.* 1250–1260)[9]

Eleigh (*Yllege*)
For the term of St Thomas[10]	14s.
For the term of Palm Sunday	17s. 4d.
For the term of the Apostles Peter and Paul	£1 18s.
For the term of St Michael[11]	£3 13s. 11d. \[*illeg.*]/ 6¼d.
For the term of the blessed Peter in chains	£1 9s. 2¾d. (*iijqa*)

Total, £8 13s. ½¾d. [*sic*[12]].

---

6 CCA-DCc-RE/105, extent of all Canterbury's East Anglian manors, parchment roll, one membrane. Latin. Only Monks Eleigh's is translated here. It is difficult to date precisely. Although written in a late-thirteenth-century hand, it could have been re-copied from an earlier original. It is discussed in Nichols, '*Custodia Essexae*' (1930), pp. 169–74, which states that it must pre-date 1301, because Borley, acquired in that year, is not included. Nichols concluded that it was more likely to date from early in the priorate of Henry of Eastry (1284–1331). But the 1280s or 1290s seem too late for this extent on other evidence not used by Nichols. The valuations in this extent, as well as the acreages of land for arable, meadow and pasture, are all noticeably lower than those given for the manor of Monks Eleigh in Extent 5 (*c.* 1260–*c.* 1270). If we accept generally rising values of estates and commodities through the thirteenth century, this implies an earlier date than *c.* 1260–70 for this extent. A tentative date of *c.* 1250 is therefore suggested.
7 *Hortus* can mean 'garden', but also any enclosure of plants, such as an orchard, kitchen- or fruit-garden or even a vineyard (there *were* vines at Monks Eleigh: see Accounts 1 below).
8 Nichols, *Custodia Essexae* (1930), p. 172, translates *alneto* here as 'osier-bed'.
9 CCA-DCc-RE/87, fol. 6r of a parchment booklet of ten folios, formerly unfit for production but digitised images online via CCA's website. Comparing the assize rents with other extents and accounts, and assuming an increase in them over time, the date of this item is estimated to be *c.* 1250–1260.
10 In all later lists of assize rents, this term is the term of St Andrew.
11 This entry and the next are the wrong way round in this list.
12 The arithmetic is wrong here. Omitting the ambiguous and unclearly written 6¼d. addition for the Michaelmas term, the total comes to £8 12s. 5¾d., while including the 6¼d., it comes to £8 13s. 0d.

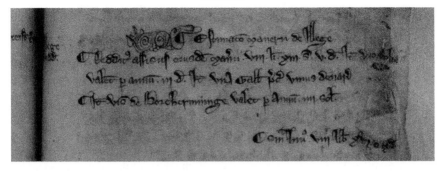

Plate 7. Extent 5 (c. 1260–c. 1270): beginning of the extent, with grotesque at start. This extent refers to the view of frankpledge on the manor of Monks Eleigh as the view of 'Borchtruminge', a word that might reflect the Canterbury scribe's Kentish vocabulary rather than local Suffolk usage. (CCA-DCc/Register P, fol. 119r) Photo: Dr Toby Huitson, CCA. Reproduced courtesy of the Chapter of Canterbury

Extent 5.[13] Valuation of the Manor of Eleigh (Illege) (*c.* 1260–*c.* 1270)[14]

[*H, fol. 160v; P, fol. 119r*]
　　　　　Valuation (*estimacio*) of the manor of Eleigh (*Illege*)
Eleigh (*Illege*) *Rents.* Assize rents of the same manor, £8 13s. 5d. Also two capons,[15] worth each year, 3d. Also one hen, price of 1d. Also a view of frankpledge (*Borchtruminge*),[16] worth each year, 4s. 　　　　　Total of these, £8 17s. 9d.

13　CCA/DCc/Register/P (probably compiled *c.* 1300–1330, possibly for or by Walter of Norwich, priory cellarer and monk-warden of the Essex custody *c.* 1304–1329), fols 119r–120r and CCA-DCc/Register/H (a composite volume containing items dating between 1150 and 1420), fol. 160v, comprising duplicate copies of a series of extents for the Essex custody manors, although only the Monks Eleigh extent has been translated here. Online digital images of CCA-DCc/Register/H can be accessed via CCA's website. The modern pencil foliation has been used here for both volumes (although in P there is also a contemporary Roman numeral foliation (*Cxxij recto–Cxxiij recto* (122r–123r), which has not been used here). Later fourteenth-century copies of the works and customs from this extent also exist in CCA-DCc/Register/B, fol. 148v and CCA-DCc/Register/J, pp. 112–13. The version in H is much more ornately produced, with marginal headings and initial letters in each paragraph picked out in red and blue ink. The version in P lacks the bright colours of H, but each of the Essex custody extents in it are headed with a pen-work grotesque (Plate 7).

14　Woods, *Medieval Hadleigh* (2018), pp. 93–95, 317 dates the corresponding Hadleigh extent in CCA-DCc-Register/H, fols 161r–v to *c.* 1260–*c.* 1270. As part of the same series, it seems logical to assume a similar date for this Monks Eleigh extent too, based on her evidence.

15　The text in H, fol. 160v clearly has *altilia*, from *altilis, ~e* '(fattened) fowl, capon' (*DMLBS*). In P, fol. 119r looks more like [*?*]*bolia*, although P's parchment pages have cockled and shrunk owing to fire damage in 1670 and there is a modern mesh repair just at this point, so the word is not clear there (see Plate 7). H, fol. 160v is preferred, as it agrees with later extents, which list two capons or hens in this position in the text.

16　Illustrated in Plate 7. See Glossary and Harvey, *Manorial Records* (1999), pp. 45–46; Nichols, 'Custodia Essexae' (1930), p. 80, citing Neilson, 'Customary Rents' (1910) (*recte* pp. 171–72). Neilson makes reference to the word *borgh* or *borgha* as a particularly Kentish term: 'the equivalent of tithing. A Kentish tithing is called a *borgha*, its capital pledge (head man of a tithing, or headborough) the *borghesealdor* and the chevage payment the *borghesealdorpeni*' (Neilson, 'Customary Rents' (1910), p. 171). This word might reflect Kentish, rather than Suffolk, usage by the scribe. See also the *OED* 'frank-pledge', 'borrow, n.(1a)', 'borrow, n.(3)' and 'trume/trome, v.'.

Works and customs [*B, fol. 148v; J, p. 112*]. Also there are in the said manor 21½ lands. And they owe the first ploughing for wheat and for oats on 107½ acres of land and they are worth £2 4s. 9½d., price for an acre, 7d.[17] Also they owe ploughing for three *benerthes*[18] for wheat and for oats and for fallow and by estimation they are worth £1 13s. 9d. Also they owe harrowing on 41 acres, and it is worth 3s. 5d., price for an acre, 1d.

Reaping.[19] Also they owe reaping at harvest-time (*in autumpno*) on 172 acres worth £2 3s., price for an acre, 3d. Also they owe carriage for all the corn of the same manor, that is to say, from the demesne, and it is worth each year, £1 6s. 10½d.[20]

Carriage service. Also they owe carriage for all the dung of the court (*curia*) and it is worth by common estimation, £1 1s. 6d, for doing which work the tenants of that manor will have [*P, fol. 119v*] 1½ seams of wheat, and that corn is worth 5s., price of a seam, 3s. 4d. Also they will have 112 herrings, price 7d., they will have also 8 cheeses, price 1s. 8d., price of each, 2½d., and thus with all counted and allowed, there remains clear to the lord, 13s. 4d.[21]

Bedrippes.[22] Also the said tenants ought to provide two *bedripes*[23] at harvest-time by 146 men and the said works are worth £1 7s. 8d., price for a man, 2d.,[24] for the doing of which works the said tenants will have 5 seams and 3b. of wheat and rye, and the said corn is worth, by common estimation, 17s. 11d. Also they will have for the first *bedrip* one beef carcass (*carcoys bovis*), price, 5s. They will have also for the second *bedrip*, 200 herrings, price, 1s. Also they will have for the first and for the second *bedrip*, 21½ cheeses and they are worth 2s. 9¼d. [*sic*], price of a cheese, 1½d.[25] They will have also for the first and for the second *bedrip* 2b. of peas and they are worth, by estimation, 5d. Also they will have salt and [?]garlic,[26] price, 1d., and thus there remains clear to the lord from the 2 *bedrip(p)es*, 5½¼d. Also the said tenants must gather a certain portion of straw and carry it into the lord's court and from it, thatch the lord's barns (*orrea*),[27] and this is worth, by estimation, 3s. 1¼d.

Mowing. Also they must mow, lift [*and*] carry the lord's hay, but that work produces nothing.

Transport service. Also they owe transport service to Ipswich (*Gipewycum*), but that work produces nothing.

---

17 £2 4s. 9½d. divided by 107.5 acres comes to 5d. for each acre, not 7d.
18 *Benerthes*: there is a Latinisation of this Middle English word, namely '*benertha* (ME *bene-erthe*), boon ploughing (cf. *bedertha, benripa*)' (*DMLBS*), which was a classic boon-work, but the ending in '-es' suggests the scribe is writing the English word here.
19 Marginal heading here is in H, fol. 160v but is not present in any of the other copies.
20 £1 3s. 10½d. (*xxiij s. xd. ob.*) in B, fol. 148v alone, probably due to a scribal error.
21 It should actually be 14s. 3d.
22 Marginal heading here is in H, fol. 160v but is not present in any of the other copies.
23 *Bedrippes* in H, fol. 160v, *Bedripes* in all other copies throughout. There is a Latinised version of this Middle English word in '*bederipa* (ME *bed-rip*), (day's service of) boon reaping (cf. *benripa, precaria*)' (*DMLBS*), but the scribe has put the plural in = '-es' ending, so he seems to have been writing the term in English.
24 Actually 2¼d. for each man.
25 Actually 2s. 8¼d. if the cheeses are worth exactly 1½d. each, but since 2s. 9¼d. divided by 21½ comes to 1.5465d. (decimal), 1½d. per cheese is close enough.
26 The scribes have written only *all'*, which might be garlic (*allium*) or perhaps more herrings (*allec*).
27 Or cover or thatch the lord's stacks of sheaves or ricks, as (*h)orrea* has that alternative meaning (*DMLBS*).

Also the said tenants owe, from the feast of St Michael until Easter, 312 works, and they are worth 13s. ¼d. [*sic*], price of a work, ½d.[28] And from Easter until the Friday in the week of Pentecost, they owe nothing in works. Also from the aforesaid Friday until the chains of St Peter, the said tenants owe 645 works and they are worth £1 6s. 10½d., price of a work, ½d.[29]

Also there are in the said manor 7 lands which are called mondaylands[30] and they owe [*P, fol. 120r*] each year 548 works and are worth £1 3s. 8d., price of a work, ½d.[31]

Total of these, £11 12s. 2¾d.

Valuation (extencio) of all the lands.[32] The valuation (*estimacio*) of all the arable land in the said manor, 463½ acres of land, from which they must take away 14 for the parson's tithes and thus there remain clear 449½ acres and they are worth, in common years, by estimation, £13 2s. 2½d., price for an acre, 7d.

Meadow. Also there are in the said manor 12½ acres of meadow and they are worth £2 3s. 6d., price for an acre, 3s. 6d. and the price of the half acre, 1s. 6d. [*sic*].

Pasture. Also there are in the said manor 10 acres of pasture and they are worth by estimation 15s., price for an acre, 1s. 6d. Also the profits of the garden with the curtilage, 13s. 4d.

Total of these [*the meadow and pasture*] with the curtilage, £3 11s. 10d.

Also for a certain mill   £1.

Sum total of the manor £38 5s. ¼d.

Extent 6. List of Works and Customs[33] (between 1285/86 and 1310/11)[34]

[*K, fol. 108r*]

---

28 The ¼d. is quite clearly written in the text, but a mystery, as the sum works if the 312 works are worth 13s.

29 If 21½ lands owed five works per week adding up to 645 works, there must have been six weeks counted in this extent (21.5 x 5 = 107.5. 645 ÷ 107.5 = 6) between the Friday in Pentecost (Whitsun week) and the feast of St Peter in chains (1 August). There can only be exactly six weeks between these two festivals in years with the latest possible date for Easter (25 April), which occurred in 1204 and 1451 but not in any years between.

30 *Mon*[n]*edeyeslond* in H, fol. 160v and P, fol. 119r; *monedeilond* in B, fol. 148v and J, p. 113.

31 The calculation is a fraction out: £1 3s. 8d. = 284d. ÷ 548 = 0.5182d., which is so close to being ½d. as to be negligible. However, ½d. x 548 = 274d. = £1 2s. 10d., which is 10d. less than the £1 3s. 8d. total.

32 Marginal headings in this section omitted from B, fol. 148v and J. p. 113.

33 This extent survives in several versions: two in CCA-DCc/Register B ('an old extent' on fol.148r; 'services and customs of the manor of Illegh' without the epithet 'old' on fol. 149r); one in CCA-DCc/Register J, pp. 111–12; one in CCA-DCc/Register/K, fol. 108r (modern pencil foliation, not the contemporary foliation '*lxxxviij*' (88r)) and two in CCA-DCc/Register/O, on fols 64r–v (modern pencil foliation at top right of recto, not the '44' and '232' at foot of recto) and fols 91r–v (modern pencil foliation at top of recto, not the contemporary foliation '*CC iiijxx xiij*' (293r) or '261' at the foot of the recto). Online digital images of Registers B, K and O are available via the CCA image gallery webpages (see Bibliography).

34 This list of works and customs can be dated to between 1285/86 and 1310/11 by reference to Adam de la Tye who appears in this extent with his un-named associates owing six works lifting hay. He also witnesses Charters 26–27 (1286–87) and appears in Accounts 1 (1285–86) in which Adam de la Tye and five named others owed six works as 'help in Skippesmedwe', the meadow where they made hay. By Accounts 2 (1310–11), Adam had gone, leaving his five other associates owing the same six works of 'help in the meadow called Skippesmed'. If he was [*?Adam*] atte Tye who defended a plea

35

Works and customs of the manors of the convent in the counties of Essex and Suffolk[35]
[*B, fol. 148r, fol. 149r; J, p. 111; O, fol. 64r; O, fol. 91r*] Eleigh *(Illeg')*[36]

At Eleigh *(Illeghe)*[37] there are 21½ lands and each land owes, from the feast of St Michael until Easter, 14½ works. Total, 312½ works.[38]

Also in respect of the same lands, from the Friday in the week of Pentecost until the feast of St Peter in chains, each week, from every land, 5 works. The total of the works being in accordance with the greatest and least [*time*] that separates the feasts (*secundum quod magis et minus distat inter festa*).[39]

Also in respect of the same lands, at Christmas, 41½ works.

Also in respect of 5 lands – mondaylands[40] – namely Turkyl,[41] Coupere,[42] Tollone,[43] Ayldred[44] and Keggel,[45] for each year 400 works, that is, for every land, 8 [*works*]. Also in respect of the land Colehog and of Agnes the widow, 96[46] works. Also in respect of the half land Wulmerd,[47] 48 works. Also in respect of the half-land of Thomas de Tya, 37 works. Also in respect of Adam de la Tye and his associates, 6 works, for lifting hay, 6 works.[48] The total of works from the mondaylands, 581 works.[49]

---

of trespass against Simon le Mareschal in Court Roll 1 (3 February 1305/6), his death must have been between 1305/6 and 1310/11. His presence dates this extent to between 1285/86 and 1310/11, with a possible narrowing to between 1285/86 and 1305/6.

[35] This general sectional heading occurs only in K, fol. 108r (in which this extent is written as one continuous paragraph). B, fol. 149r has the alternative singular heading of 'Services and customs of the manor of Illegh'. B, fol. 148r and J , p. 111 have the alternative heading 'Also an old extent'.

[36] B, fol. 148r, fol. 149r; J, p. 111 omit the marginal heading *Illeg'*.

[37] *Illeghe* in K, fol. 108r; *Ylleg'* in O (both versions), *Illegh* in all versions in B and J.

[38] This sum should be 311¾ works in total (21.5 x 14.5). J, p. 111 and B, fol. 148r omit the word 'works'.

[39] J, p. 111 and B, fol. 148r omit 'and least'. Extent 5 (*c*. 1260–*c*. 1270) gives 645 works worth £1 6s. 10½d. between these dates, in which the separation between the feasts is estimated as a nominal six weeks, without the 'more or less' proviso here (see p. 35, footnote 29 under Extent 5).

[40] *Monendayl'* in K, fol. 108r; *mondayl'* in O, fol. 64r, J, p. 111 and B (both versions); *Monedeyl'* in O, fol. 91r. They were probably named mondaylands because the services due from these lands were performed on Mondays (see Introduction, pp. xxxiv, xxxvi–xxxvii, on this and the longevity of the names of tenements).

[41] *Turkil* in B (both versions); *Turkyl* in all other versions. Turkilleslond is mentioned in Charter 7 (1222–1238) and the land of Thurkill (*Turekilli*) in Charter 5 (*c*. 1210/11–1234/35).

[42] Cowperesmundaylond in Rental 1 (1379–80), there comprising 13 acres, 1 rod of land, in several tenancies.

[43] Tollonesmundayland in Rental 1 (1379–80), there comprising 13 acres of land, in one tenancy. A William Tollune was granted 10 acres of land for 1s 6d. by Prior Geoffrey in Charter 3 (1191–1213).

[44] *Ayldred* in K, fol. 108r, O (both versions), and J, p. 111; *Ayldrede* in B, fol. 149r and *Aeldred* in B, fol. 148r. In Rental 1 (1379–80) it is in two parts: Ayredys mundaylond, comprising 19 acres of land and 1 acre of wood and second Ayredes mundaylond, containing 10 acres of land.

[45] *Keggel* in J, p. 111; K, fol. 108r; O (both versions) and B, fol. 149r; *Kegel* in B, fol. 148r.

[46] '16' in J, p. 111 and B, fol. 148r, both omitting the preceding 'four-score' (*iiijxx*).

[47] *Wulmerd* in K, fol. 108r; *Wlmed* in J, p. 111; B, fol. 149r and O (both versions); *Wlmer* in B, fol. 148r. Wlmar, a carpenter, was granted 3 acres of land for 2s. by Prior Geoffrey in Charter 3 (1191–1213).

[48] This repetition of '6 works' appears in K, fol. 108r, only: the scribe has probably simply repeated himself in error. K, fol. 108r quite clearly has 'for lifting hay' (*pro fenis levand'*), but all other versions equally clearly have 'dung' (*fimis*) not hay: probably a scribal error. It is almost certainly 'hay' as Adam de la Tye and five other men are named as performing six works as 'help in Skippesmedwe' (which presumably involved haymaking, as it was in a meadow) in Accounts 1 (1286–86).

[49] The total of 581 mondayland works does not include the six owed by Adam de la Tye and his associates.

Also in respect of the aforesaid 21½ lands, they owe ploughing, at the season of wheat, 53½ acres and 1 rood, that is to say, for each land, 2½ acres as gavelearth (*de gable*). Also in respect of the same lands, at the same season, 21½ acres as boon-ploughing,[50] that is,[51] for every land, 2 [*sic*] boons.[52] Also in respect of the same lands, at the fallowing of barley, 21½ acres as boon-ploughing.[53] Also in respect of the same lands at the season [*O, fol. 91v*] of oats, 53½ acres and 1 rood as gavelearth (*de Gavelerth*).[54] Also in respect of the same lands at the same season, 21½ acres, as boon-ploughing.[55] Also in respect of the same lands at the season of barley 10½ acres and 1 rood as boon-ploughing,[56] that is, for every land, 1 boon,[57] that is to say, half an acre. The total of acres ploughed as gavelearth[58] and boon-ploughing,[59] 182½ acres and 1 rood. Also the tenants owe [*O, fol. 64v*], in respect of the aforesaid lands, harrowing on 53½ acres and 1 rood as gavelearth[60] at the season for oats. Also the same [*owe*] at the same season, 21½ acres as boon-work.[61] Also the same [*owe*] at the season for barley, 10½ acres and 1 rood as boon-work.[62] Item, the same owe harrowing after the lord's plough by custom on 39½ acres. [*J, p. 112*] Also the aforesaid tenants are obliged to reap at harvest-time 86 acres of wheat[63] and 86 acres of barley and oats. The total of acres, 172[64] acres, that is, for every land, 8 acres. Let it be remembered that the work measurement of corn for wheat contains 2½b.; for rye and maslin, 4½b.; for barley, 5b.; for beans, 2½b.; [*B, fol. 148v*] for peas, 4½b.;[65] for oats, 7½b.[66]

Total of acres ploughed and sown by custom, 182½ acres and 1 rood.

Total of acres reaped by custom, 172 acres[67]

---

50 *De Benerthe* in K, fol. 108r; *de Beneerthe* in O (both versions); *de Beneherthe* in J, p. 111 and B, fol. 148r; *De Benerth* in B, fol. 149r (see Glossary).
51 *Hoc est* in O, fol. 64r, *videlicet* in all the other copies.
52 *Benes* in K, fol. 108r and B (both versions); *ben'* in O, fol. 64r; *bones* in J, p. 111 and O, fol. 91r, both meaning boons or boon-works.
53 *De Benerthe* in K, fol. 108r; *de Ben'* in O (both versions) and B, fol. 149r and *ben'* (omitting the *de*) in J, p. 111 and B, fol. 148r.
54 Only in this paragraph of this extent does the scribe write *gavelerth* (an English word, although sometimes Latinised) instead of the Latin equivalent of *gabulum* found otherwise in the rest of the documents in this volume where it appears in the form of *de gable, de gablo, de gabul', de gabulo* and *de gavel*.
55 *De bene* in K, fol. 108r; *de ben'* in O (both versions) and B, fol. 149r; *de beneherth* in J, p. 111 and *de benerth* in B, fol. 148r.
56 *De Benerth* in K, fol. 108r and B (both versions); *de beneerthe* in O (both versions); *de beneherth* in J, p. 111.
57 *Bene* in K, fol. 108r, O (both versions) and B, fol. 149r; *ben'* in J, p. 111 and B, fol. 148r.
58 *De Gable* in J, p. 111; K, fol. 108r; O (both versions); B, fol. 148r; *de Gabl'* in B, fol. 149r.
59 *Beneerth* in K, fol. 108r; *de bene* in O (both versions) and B, fol. 149r; *de ben'* in J, p. 111 and B, fol. 148r.
60 *De Gavelerthe* in K, fol. 108r; *de Gavel* in O (both versions) and B, fol. 149r; *de gavelerth* in J, p. 111 and B, fol. 148r.
61 *De Bene* in K, fol. 108r and O, fol. 91v; *de ben'* in J, p. 111; O, fol. 64v; B (both versions).
62 *De Bene* in K, fol. 108r; O (both versions) and B, fol. 149r; *de ben'* in J, p. 111 and B, fol. 148r.
63 '86 acres of wheat' omitted in J, p. 112 and B (both versions).
64 '172' in J, p. 112; K, fol. 108r; O, fol. 64v, B (both versions); '162' in O, fol. 91v, the latter presumably a simple scribal error since 8 acres x 21½ lands = 172 acres.
65 The entry for peas is omitted from B, fol. 149r.
66 8½ b. in B, fol. 148v.
67 These final two lines of this extent occur in B, fol. 149r only.

Extent 7. Various copies of extents and lists of services and customs[68] (late-fourteenth-century copies of earlier documents dating between *c.* 1260 and 1330)

[*B, fol. 147r; J, p. 108*]

Assize rents for Eleigh (*Illegh*)[69] [*c. 1310/11–c. 1329/30, probably towards the latter*[70]]

For the term of St Andrew the Apostle	14s. 7½d.
For the term of Palm Sunday	17s. 4d.
For the term of the Apostles Peter and Paul	£1 18s. 6d.
For the term of St Peter in chains	£1 9s. 2½¼d.
For the term of St Michael	£3 13s. 11½d.
From John ate Fen as a new [*rent*][71]	2s.
From Simon Tollon' as a new [*rent*]	2s.
For the site of[72] a certain smithy next to Gedeford	1d.
For 2 capons rendered 6d.	
From John ate Tye for a certain plot (*placia*) demised to him	8d.
From Adam ate Tye for a certain headland (*forera*) demised to him at Ravenescroft[73]	8d.
From Margery Forester for 1 rood of alder-holt demised to her which is an escheat of the lord after the death of Richard son of Stephen Smith (*Stephani fabri*)	6d.
From William de Higelegh for 1 headland demised to him	4d.

[*J, p. 109*] Total £9 4½¼d.

Allowances

Let it be remembered that the rector takes in the fields 7 acres of wheat[74] for a tithe. Also of oats, 7 acres, which 14 acres the lord is obliged to plough and sow and the rector is obliged to manure.

Also every ploughman takes 1 acre of wheat and 1 acre of oats for his pay each year. Also the reeve takes 1 acre of wheat and 1 acre of oats for his pay each year. It is allowed for the customary tenants to carry away dung by custom for the wheat, more or less according to the services they perform. Also for 2 boon-works at harvest-time, by custom, 3 quarters of wheat. Also for 2 boon-works by custom at harvest-time, 3 quarters of rye, that is to say, that from every bushel, for both

---

[68] This sequence of various different extents and lists of services and customs is copied, in two similar versions, CCA-DCc/Register/B, fols 147r–149r and CCA-DCc/Register/J, pp. 108–113. The versions in B and J also comprise copies of Extent 5 (*c.* 1260–*c.* 1270) as well as Extent 6 (between 1285/86 and 1310/11) entitled 'an old extent' (see Extents 5 and 6). Headings are centred in both B and J, and in red ink in B only.

[69] *Illeghe* in J, p. 108. This heading is omitted in B, fol. 147r.

[70] Dated by comparison to the lists of assize rents in the accounts included in this volume: those for Accounts 3 (1329–30) are much closer to the text of this extent than Accounts 2 (1310–11) in terms of the assize rents, which gradually increase over time, so this extent probably dates to just before 1329–30.

[71] 'As a gift' (*de dono*) in B, fol. 147r; 'as a new [*rent*]' (*de novo*) in J, p. 108, the latter agreeing with all other records of assize rents at this period in this volume.

[72] 'The site of' (*de situ*) omitted from B, fol. 147r.

[73] *Ravenesford* in B, fol. 147r; *Ravenescroft* in J, p. 108, and all other references to this rent in this volume.

[74] *Capit in campis vij acr' de frument'* in B, fol. 147r; *capit de fr[ument]o in campis vij acr'* in J., p. 109.

wheat and rye, 4 loaves of bread should be made and each man will have 1 loaf.[75] Also for beef (*carne bovina*) bought for the same customary tenants for the wheat boon-works by custom, 4s. 7d. Also for herrings bought for the oats boon-works by custom, 11d. Also for cheese bought for the same by custom, 1s. 11d.

Total of meat, fish and cheese, 7s. 5d.

Works

For 262 works in respect of the produce of 17½ lands from the feast of St Michael until Easter, that is, from each land for that time, 15 works, price of a work [*B, fol. 147v*] ½d. Also for 52 works in respect of the produce of 4 lands for that time, that is, from each land, 13 works, price of a work, ½d. Also in respect of the produce of the aforesaid 21½ lands at Christmas, 16½ works, price of a work, ½d. Also in respect of the produce of the said 21½ lands from the Thursday in the week of Pentecost until the first day of August, according to the time that takes, more or less,[76] that is to say, from each land, every week, 5 works, price of a work, ½d. Also for 400 works from the produce of 5 mondaylands[77] each year, that is, from every land, 80 works, price of a work, ½d. Also for 48 works from the half land Wlmer [*sic*] each year, price of a work, ½d. Also for 37 works from the half land of John ate Fen each year, price of a work, ½d. Also for 96 works from the land Colehog and of Agnes the widow each year, price of each work, ½d. Item for 6 works from the land of Robert Sacrist, William de Fynchislegh,[78] Robert Fuller, Philip Skarlet[79] and John Habbe[80] for help at Skyppsmed',[81] price of a work, ½d.[82] Total of works, price in money [blank]

Allowances

In allowance for the aforesaid 21½ lands for [*J, p. 110*] festival days and courts held, for days on which works are required between Pentecost and the first day of August, more or less, according to how [*long*] that happens to occur,[83] that is to say, for each land, each day, 1 work, price of a work, ½d.

---

75 B, fol. 147r has ...*videlicet quod de quolibet bussell' tam de frumento quam de siligie fiant iiijor* [*iiij in J., p. 109*] *panes et habebit qualibet* [*quilibet in J, p. 109*] *homo j pane'*. If each of the 48 bushels comprising the 6 quarters of grain was to make only four loaves of bread (at a rate of one loaf for every man), the loaves must have been intended to feed 192 men and have been improbably large. Perhaps this is rather an indication of the allocation of grain (rather than actual loaves) for each man to make the bread necessary to feed him during the harvest period.

76 Pentecost depends on the date of Easter, a moveable feast, so the number of weeks between it and 1 August varies each year.

77 *Mondeilandes* in B, fol. 147v; *mondeilondes* in J, p. 109.

78 *Fynchislegh* in B, fol. 147v; *Fincheslegh* in J, p. 109. William de Finchelegh appears in a similar list in Accounts 3 (1329–30), replacing the earlier Walter de Fynchelegh in the earlier Accounts 2 (1310–11), putting the date of this part of this extent between those two dates.

79 *Skarlet* in B, fol. 147v; *Scarlet* in J, p. 109. Philip Scarlet appears in the same list of men in Accounts 2 (1310–11), but by Accounts 3 (1329–30) the name is John Scarlet, possibly a son or other relative.

80 *Habbe* in both B, fol. 147v and J, p. 109, but Babbe in Accounts 1 (1305–6) and Accounts 3 (1329–30).

81 *Skyppsmed'* in B, fol. 147v; *Skippesmed'* in J, p. 109.

82 Adam de la Tye heads this list of haymakers in Accounts 1 (1285–86), is mentioned in Charters 26–27 (1286–87), but died between *c.* 1305/6 and 1310/11, so this part of the extent must date after 1310–11.

83 Another reference, differently expressed (*pervenir' contigerit*), to the variable period of time between the moveable feast of Pentecost and 1 August.

Threshing and winnowing

In the threshing of wheat, a greater or lesser service is to be done, depending on the amount of that grain, that is, for a work, 2½ bushels, price of a work, ½d. Also in the threshing of rye and peas, the service that is to be done concerning this crop [*is*] namely, for each work, 4½ bushels, price of a work, ½d. Also for barley and oats, the service that is to be done according to the quantity of this corn, more or less, [*is*] namely, for a work, 7 bushels, price of a work, ½d.

Expenses of works

Also[84] the making of watercourses. For holding the plough while the sower sowed after the plough of the lord and of the customary tenants at both seasons. For marling, mixing it with dung and spreading it, more or less accordingly as the work requires. For newly making ditches, more or less, that is, for every [?]perch (*virgat*[85]), 1 work, price of a work, ½d. For weeding grain, more or less, for a work, ½d. In spreading, gathering, making into heaps, and ricking hay, more or less, for a work, ½d. In reaping rye [*and*] barley before the first day of August, more or less, according to what each acre shall produce, that is, for each acre,[86] 1 work, price of a work, ½d. Also for binding [*sheaves*] on each acre, 1 work, price for a work, ½d. Moreover, after the first day of August no tenant to reap until the time for boon-work. For reaping peas before the first day of August, more or less, according to what each acre shall produce, that is, for an acre, 4 works, price for a work, ½d. For stacking wheat, barley, rye and other grains, more or less, according to what corn there shall be, for a work, ½d., the remaining works on other necessities are not to be put out for sale.

Ploughing

In respect of the issue of the aforesaid 21½ lands, 53 acres, 3 roods of ploughing as gavelearth (*de gablo*) at the winter season, price for an acre, 6d. Also concerning boon-works at the same season, 21½ acres, price for an acre, 6d.[87] With respect to ploughing upon the lord's land, more or less, if there be any residue, it is to be sold. Also with respect to the issue of the aforesaid 21½ lands, for ploughing at the fallowing of barley, 21½ acres, price for an acre, 6d. Also with respect to the issue of the aforesaid 21½ lands, at the season of oats and barley, 53 acres, 3 roods of ploughing as gavelearth (*de gablo*), price for an acre, 6d. Also at the same season, as boon-work, 21½ acres, price for an acre, 6d.

---

84 'Also' in B, fol. 147v; but 'in' in J, p. 110.

85 A virgate could be a variable measurement of length as here as well as of area. It could equate to the yard of 3 feet; but here it is more likely to approximate to 16½ feet, the measurement of length known as the rod, pole or perch. Witney states that this measurement derived from the ancient pre-Conquest 'yard' (Old English *gyrd*; Latin *virgata*, originally 'a yard-stick cut from coppice or straight saplings') the value of which changed according to place and over time. He cites an example from the Kent manor of Bishopsbourne, where cottars had to 'enclose four *virgates* around the lord's corn'. The use of *virgat'* here might reflect the Canterbury scribe's familiarity with the term in a Kent context (K.P. Witney, 'Kentish Land Measurements of the Thirteenth Century', *Archaeologia Cantiana* 109 (1991), p. 30).

86 Register B has 'work' for 'acre' here, presumably a scribal error.

87 Stansfield's translation ends here. The remainder of the text of this extent is translated by the current editor.

Harrowing

In respect of the issue of the aforesaid 21½ lands at the season of oats \and[88]/ barley, 75 acres, 1 rood to be harrowed as gavelearth (*de gablo*), price for an acre, ½d. Also at the same season, 39½ acres to be harrowed for the produce of the aforesaid 21½ lands after Christmas [*B, fol. 148r*] price for an acre, ½d. And they owe all this harrowing after [*J, p. 111*] the tenants' plough, for the doing of which service after the lord's plough they owe nothing.[89]

Reaping

In respect of the issue of the aforesaid 21½ lands in the winter season, 86 acres of reaping as gavelearth (*de gablo*), that is, for each land, 4 acres, price for an acre [*blank*]. Also concerning the same 21½ lands at the same season as boon-work, 43 acres of reaping, that is, for each land, 2 acres, price for an acre [*blank*]. Also at the season of oats and barley, 86 acres of reaping as gavelearth (*de gablo*), price for an acre [*blank*]. Also at the same season, as boon-work, 43 acres of reaping, price for an acre [*blank*].

Rents pertaining to the treasury [*after 1286–87*][90]

Robert de Monchensy at the feast of St Michael	6d.
Anselm Abbot for Hugh son of Ralph at the feast of St Michael	7d.
Adam son of Hugh, for the same Hugh at the feast of St Michael	4d.
Walter ate Mere, for the same Hugh, at the feast of St Michael	5d.
John Pykot, for Richard Prior, at the translation of St Thomas[91]	1 mark.

Also an old extent

For the 'old extent' copied at this point in Register B, fol. 148r–v and Register J, pp. 111–12 (omitted here), see the text edited at Extent 6 [*between 1285/86 and 1310/11*] above.

[*This paragraph must be after 1286–87.*[92]] From John Pykot within the octave of the translation of St Thomas the martyr, 13s. 4d.[93] In respect of the land of Richard Priur in Eleigh (*Illegh*), concerning the land which came from Hugh Fant and William his brother and is given for a pittance as it appears by charter.[94]

---

88 This 'and' is omitted altogether in B, fol. 147v; the 'and' is inserted above the text in J, p. 110.

89 *Et* [*debent* in B, fol. 148r; *debetur* in J, fol. 110] *tota ista herciatur' post caruc' tenent' qu' faciunt servic' post caruc' domini nichil debent.*

90 This paragraph is present in B, fol. 148r but is omitted from J, p. 111. It certainly dates from after Charter 19 (?*c.* 1260s–1270s) because Anselm Abbot, Adam son of Hugh and Walter de le/ate Mere, all paying rents to the treasury here, are all mentioned in that charter, by which Hugh son of Ralph grants their homage, service and rents to the prior. Robert de Monchensy who pays 6d. rent here may be the successor (or at least related) to Hubert de Montecanisyo whose 6d rent is granted in Charter 20 (?*c.* 1260s–1270s).

91 John Pykot's rent of 1 mark was due to be paid into the treasury at Canterbury on the feast of the translation of St Thomas Becket (7 July), as specified in Charters 24 and 25 (1286–87) above. See also the following 'old extent'.

92 Dated as after Charters 24 and 25 (1286–87) in the following footnotes.

93 The acknowledgement by John Pykot and Juliana his wife of the grant of this rent of 1 mark of silver (13s. 4d.) to the prior is in Charter 25 (1286–87).

94 The charter granting the pittance described here is Charter 24 (1286–87).

For the works and customs copied at this point in Register B, fol. 148v and Register J, pp. 112–13 (omitted here), see the text edited at Extent 5 (*c.* 1260–*c.* 1270) above.

[*B, fol. 149r*] Services and Customs of the Manor of Eleigh [*between 1285/86 and 1310/11*]

For the 'services and customs of the manor of Illegh' copied at this point in Register B, fol. 149r (omitted here), see the text edited at Extent 6 [*between 1285/86 and 1310/11*] above.

III

ACCOUNTS

1285 to 1482[1]

Accounts 1. Serjeant's account of J. (1285–86)[2]

[*Membrane 1, face*]
Account of J. serjeant of Eleigh from the feast of St Michael in the 13th year of the reign of King Edward [*I*] until the same feast in the year following [*29 September 1285–28 September 1286*].

Assize rents. The same [*serjeant*] answers for 14s. 7d. in rent for the term of St Andrew. And for 17s. 4d. in rent for the term of Palm Sunday [*7 April*]. And for £1 18s. 6¼d. in rent for the term of the Apostles Peter and Paul. And for £1 9s. 2½¼d. in rent in the term of St Peter in chains. And for £3 13s. 11½¼d. in rent for the term of St Michael.   Total £8 13s. 7½¼d.
The same answers for 7d. for 2 capons and 2 hens for rents sold.
                                                                                        Total by itself (*per se*).

Farm for a [*fixed*] *term.* The same accounts for 8s. for the mill put out to farm between the feast of the Apostles Peter and Paul and the feast of St Michael.
                                                                                        Total by itself.

Perquisites. The same answers for £1 12s. 6d. for perquisites of the court.
                                                                                        Total by itself.

Customary Works. The same answers for 7s. 4½d. for 14 acres 3 roods of ploughing released to the customary tenants. And for 6s. for 143 works sold. Total 13s. 4½d.
Herbage. The same answers for 15s. for herbage sold. And for 2s. for ditched pasture sold. And for £1 4s. for 3 casks of cider sold. And for £2 5s. for 4½ acres of wood sold. And for 2s. for 1 acre of underwood sold. And for 8s. for hay sold. And for 5s. for straw sold.   Total £5 1s.

Corn sold. The same answers for 7s. \6d./ for 1½ seams of wheat <of the chaff> sold, price of a seam, 3s. 4d.[3] And for £2 8s. for 9 seams of wheat sold, price of a

---

1   See Introduction, p. xxxviii.
2   CCA-DCc-BR/Illeigh/1. Parchment roll, two membranes, stitched together lengthwise, the customary works account being on the face of the second membrane. The serjeant 'J' might be John de Bosco who submitted accounts the following year (CCA/DCc/AS/26, not included herein) or John de Belstede, who appears within this account named as bailiff (and see p. 45, footnote 12).
3   The arithmetic is wrong here, whether or not the inserted 6d. after the 7s. is accounted for (the 6d. must be included to make the total for this sub-section add up correctly). If 1½ seams were valued at 7s. 6d., then the price of a seam should be 5s. (60d.) not 3s. 4d. (*40d.*) – has the scribe written *xld*

43

seam, 5s. 4d. And for £2 16s. 8d. for 10 seams of wheat sold, price of a seam, 5s. 8d. And for £10 1s. for 33½ seams of wheat sold, price of a seam, 6s. And for 16s. for 4 seams of barley sold. And for 10d. for 2b. of beans sold. And for 5s. 11½d. for 2 seams, 6b. of vetch sold, price of a seam 2s. 2d.   Total £16 15s. 11½d.

Stock sold. The same answers for 6s. 8d. for 1 ox sold. And for 6s. for 1 ox sold. And for 7s. for 1 ox sold. And for 19s. for 2 oxen sold. And for 10s. for 1 bull sold. And for 5s. for 5 calves of issue[4] sold. And for 12s. for 6 pigs sold. And for 6s. 5d. for 3 pigs sold. And for 2s. 3½d. for 11 geese sold, price of a goose, 2½d. And for 1s. for 8 capons sold. And for 6½d. for 6 ducks sold. And for 1s. for 300 eggs sold. And for 3s. for young doves sold. And for 2s. for 2 [?]pigs sold. And for 1s. 4d. for 2 [?]inferior [?]hams (*debilibus* [?]*pern'*) sold.   Total £4 3s. 2½d. [*sic*[5]]

Hides and skins. The same answers for 1s. 8d. for the hide of 1 bull [*dead*] of murrain, sold. And for 2d. for 2 skins of sheep [*dead*] of murrain, sold. And for 9d. for 3 wool fleeces, sold.   Total 2s. 7d.

Dairy. The same answers for £1 10s. from dairy sold.   Total by itself.

Total of all receipts, £39 10½d. [*sic*[6]]

Payments. Paid to Dom Randolph the treasurer at the feast of the nativity of the blessed John, £10 by tally. Paid into the treasury, £1 2s. by tally.   Total £11 2s.

For[7] the expenses of Dom S[*tephen*] de Ycham[8] and colleagues of the same at Eleigh (*Yllegh*) and [*Bury*] St Edmunds, £1 14s. <½¼> by tally. For the expenses of Dom R. Pucyn,[9] 3s. 8d. For the expenses of R, clerk of Dom S[*tephen*] de Ycham, 8d. For the expenses of Dom J. de Shamelesford[10] and J. de Lond'[11] on the Friday next after the feast of St Barnabas the apostle [*Friday, 14 June 1286*] in their passing through towards Norfolk, 4s. by tally. <del>For the expenses of Dom S[*tephen*] de Ycham and</del>

[40d.] instead of *lxd* [60d.]? And if it was worth 7s. (without the inserted 6d.), then the price of a seam would be 56d. (4s. 8d.). If the price of a seam really was 40d., then 1½ seams should be worth 5s. The alterations might have been made at audit in an attempt to make the figures add up correctly, but if so, they failed, and we can no longer interpret the story behind this entry. The crossing out of 'of the chaff' (*de Curall'*) and the reduced price of the wheat that replaces it in the text implies that it was wheat of inferior quality to the rest, if not actually chaff.

4 That is, produced, or born, in the current accounting year.

5 Actually £4 3s. 3d.

6 This total should actually be £39 0s. 10¼d. (if the original sub-totals above are added together) or £39 0s. 10¾d. (if the corrected sub-totals are added together).

7 *in* has been translated as 'for' following *DMLBS*, meanings 39, 'as, for, purpose' and 41 'expressing designation of something for use as'. 'For' sounds more natural in the context of these entries as well as agreeing with the initial construction of 'he answers (for)' *respondit* (*de*).

8 Probably Stephen of Ycham, mentioned as monk warden of the Essex custody in Hadleigh's manorial accounts in 1293–94 (Woods, *Medieval Hadleigh* (2018), p. 73). This is reinforced by the abbreviation of his first name as 'St.' towards the end of this current Monks Eleigh account. Ycham is probably Ickham, just east of Canterbury, by analogy with CCA online catalogue entry for CCA-DCc-ChAnt/I/23.

9 Probably Robert Poncyn or Poucyn, priory monk, who died in 1310 or 1312 (Searle, *Christ Church Canterbury* (1902), pp. 176, 178).

10 Probably Shalmsford in Chartham, another of the priory's manors, near Canterbury. John de Shamelysford, a priory monk, died in 1291 or 1292 (Searle, *Christ Church Canterbury* (1902), pp. 169, 175).

11 Probably one of two Johns de London, priory monks, the later of whom died in 1299 (Searle, *Christ Church Canterbury* (1902), pp. 173, 177).

~~Dom Randolph the treasurer upon the last view, 8s. 7d.~~> with the expenses of Dom S[*tephen*] de Ycham and Dom J. de Shamelesford and J. de Lond' since the feast of the apostles Peter and Paul on their return from Norfolk, <~~1s. 6d.~~> For the expenses of W. de Burne, clerk, for 1 visit, 10d. For the expenses of J. de Belsted, bailiff,[12] 2s. For the wages of the same, 13s. 4d. Total £ 3 1s. 1d.[13]

Corn bought. For 2½ seams of wheat bought, 11s. 3d., price of a seam, 4s. 6d. For 3 seams of rye bought, 12s., price of a seam, 4s. Also for 2 seams, 2b. of rye bought, 10s. 6d., price of a seam, 4s. 8d. Also for 3 seams, 3b. of rye bought for *metecorn*, 13s. 6d., price of a seam, 4s. Also for 4 seams, 1b. of rye bought for *metecorn* at harvest-time and for bread for the customary tenants, 13s. 9d., price of a seam, 3s. 4d. Also for 6 seams of oats bought, 14s., price of a seam, 2s. 4d. For 7 seams of oats bought, 17s. 6d., price of a seam, 2s. 6d. Also for 10 seams of oats bought, £1 5s. 10d., price of a seam, 2s. 7d. Also for 9 seams of oats bought, £1 7s., price of a seam, 3s. For 5b. of peas bought, 2s. 3½d, price of ab., 5½d.

Total £7 \7s./ 7½d.

Stock bought. For 1 ox bought, 15s.   Total evident.
For marling 4 acres of land, £1 1s. 7d.[14]   Total evident.
For half an acre of wood bought, £1 4d.   Total evident.

Plough costs. For 10 pieces of iron bought, 1s. 8d. Also for 2 pieces of iron bought, 5d. For half a sheaf of iron that is called *Osmund*[15] bought, 4½d. Also for 3 pieces of iron bought, 7½d. For 6½ sheaves of steel bought, 5s. 7½d. Also for 5½ sheaves of steel bought, 4s. 7d. For 4 new ploughshares made from iron in hand, 6d. For 9 strakes, 4 *restclutes* and 6 *stredelclutes* bought, 2s. 10½d. Also for 2 strakes and 2 *stredelclutes* bought, 8½¼d. For making new ploughs and repairing other ploughs together with making harrows and yokes, 1s, 6d. For shoeing oxen, 1s. For the shoeing of 1 ox, 4d. For 1 likewise, 2d. Also 2½ sheaves of steel bought, 2s. 1d. Also for shoeing \of stots, 7s./. Total £1 9s. 5½¼d.

Cart costs. For fitting 1 cart with axles,[16] 1d. For 2 pairs of traces [*made*] of hide, 2d. For 1 pair of hemp traces, 2½d. For 1 new rope for a cart, bought, 5d. For 8 *cartclut'*, bought and attached, 6d. <~~For the shoeing of stots, 7s.~~>[17] Total 1s. 4½d.

Costs of buildings. For the construction of 1 base for the axle of the mill and for the binding of the same axle with iron, 2d. Also for the wages of a carpenter for repairing the said mill, 3s. 6d. For boards cut for the same, 10d. For the repair of the spindle of the same mill, 3½d. For nails bought for the walls of the same mill,

---

12 The 'John de Belsted, bailiff', mentioned here and as a witness to Charter 26 (1286–87) (see p. 24) was a bailiff/steward (see pp. xxiv–xxvi. He appears in these accounts receiving expenses (including fodder for his horse) with the monk-warden and his party and is referred to as a former steward of the custody of Essex in John le Doo's 1309 extent of the manor of Milton Hall (Nichols, 'Milton Hall' (1929), p. 19). Belstead could be either the village of that name, originally Belstead Parva, 2½ miles south of Ipswich and 11 miles from Monks Eleigh, or Belstead Magna (now Washbrook) about 3½ miles south of Ipswich and almost 10 miles from Monks Eleigh.
13 The arithmetic is wrong here. Adding up all the figures, whether crossed through or not, comes to £3 8s. 7¾d. Adding only the figures not crossed out comes to £2 18s. 6d.
14 Something erased beneath the second 'x' of the 20s. and the 7d. added in a different hand and ink.
15 Written thus in English without abbreviation or Latin case ending.
16 Or an axle. The Latin here (*axanda*) uses the verb *axare*, 'to axle, i.e. to fit with axles or an axle' (*DMLBS*), so the number of axles fitted is not specified.
17 Crossed out here and inserted in previous entry.

3d. For the repair of the mill-bills, 3d. For improving the whole interior of the mill, 4d. For the roofing of the wardrobe and dovecote, 1s. 10d. Also for the roofing of other buildings on the estate, 1s. 2d. For repairing the lock of the grange, 3d. <For a lock bought at Halstead [?*Essex*] 1s.> Total 8s. 10½d.

Harvest-time expenses. For harvest-time expenses, £1 6s. 9½d. by tally against Thomas Forster. Total by itself

For meat bought for the wheat boon-work at harvest-time, 4s. 6d. For herrings bought for the oats boon-work at harvest-time, 1s. 4d. For cheese bought for both boon-works, 3s. 7d. Total 9s. 5d.

Serjeant's expenses and wages. For the expenses of the serjeant from the day \of St Andrew the apostle/ <the Thursday next after the feast of St Edmund the King [*Thursday, 21 November 1285*]> until the Monday next before the feast of St Peter in chains [*Monday, 29 July 1286*], both days included, £2 2d., taking for each week, 1s. 2d.[18]

Also for the expenses of the same from the Sunday next after the feast of the beheading of St John [*Sunday, 30 June 1286*] until St Michael's day, 4s. 8d. For the wages of the same, £1. For the wages of Thomas Forster at harvest-time, 4s. For the wages of Adam the reap-reeve, 2s. 6d. For the wages of the miller for the winter, 1s. For the wages of a cowherd and swineherd for the whole year, 3s. For the wages of a housemaid for the whole year, 2s.

For the expenses of the serjeant and the *famuli* on Christmas and Easter Days, 2s. <8d.>\10d./. Total £4 2d.

Small [expenses.] For 1 seam of great salt bought for the larder and kitchen, 1s. 8d. For iron for a manure fork and 1 fork for sheaves bought, 3d. For making shovels,[19] a spade and a manure fork, 2d. For iron bought for shovels and spades, 3d. For healing piglets and [?]bleeding[20] pigs, 5d. For cleansing oats for seed, 6d. For pruning vines and planting vine plants, 1s. For fencing the said vineyard, 2s. 8d. For mending a certain small metal pot,[21] 4d. For mending the oven, 2d. For making a certain trough for the pigs, 2d. For hooping 2 casks and 2 barrels, 4d. For mowing in the meadows, 4s. For cheese bought for the customary tenants removing manure, 11d. Also for herrings bought for the same, 6d. Paid to young men for carrying letters of Dom S[*tephen*] de Ycham and J. the bailiff to Deopham (*Depeham*) [*Norfolk*] and Bocking [*Essex*] on several occasions, 6d. For vegetable plants bought, 3d. For

---

[18] Near enough to 1s. 2d. per week. There are thirty-five full weeks between 30 November and 1 August.

[19] *Tribulum* can mean a threshing flail or a scoop or paddle of a waterwheel (*DMLBS*). Given the other implements here, a shovel is most likely. *Tribulis* here is clearly plural: the spade and manure fork (*vang' et furc' ad fimum*) are assumed to be singular given the price paid compared to the previous entry.

[20] The verb here is from *minuere*, meaning to make smaller, reduce in number, to let blood, to cut into smaller pieces, mince etc. (*DMLBS*). The work being paid for here, which also includes healing or curing (*sanand'*) piglets, sounds like the visit of the pig-man, working as both veterinarian and pig-sticker.

[21] *Pocynetta* here is probably a variant spelling of *pocene(t)tus* (ME *possenet*, OF *poçonet, pocenet*), a small (metal) pot, posnet (*DMLBS*).

platters, saucers and bowls[22] bought, 5d. For removing manure from the inner court and spreading it, 1s. For spreading marl, 4d.   Total 15s. 8¾d.[23]

Sum of all expenses £32 18s. 10½d.[24]
And thus he owes £6 2s.[25]

[Membrane 2 (stitched to the foot of membrane 1), face]

Works in detail. The issue of works from 17½ lands from the feast of St Michael until Easter, 262½ works, from each land, 15 works. Also from 4 lands for the same time, 52 works, from each land, 13 works. Also for the issue of works from the aforesaid 21½ \lands/ from the feast of Pentecost until the feast of St Peter in chains, 860 works, from each land for each week, 5 works.[26] Also for the issue of works from the aforesaid 21½ lands at Christmas, 41½ works. Also for the issue of works from 5 lands, that is to say, mondaylands, each year, 400 works, from each land, 80 works. Also from the half land of Wolmer, 48 works. Also from the half land of Thomas ate Tye, 37 works. Also from the land Colehog and of Agnes the widow, 96 works. Also from Adam de La Tye, Robert Sacrist, Walter de Finchelegh, Robert Fuller, Philip Skarlath and John Babbe for help in Skippesmedwe, 6 works.
Total 1,812½ works.[27]

Of which in allowance for 4 feast days and 2 courts held between the feast of Pentecost and the feast of St Peter in chains, 129 works.[28] Also for threshing 93 seams, 1b. of wheat, 298 works, that is, 2½b. for 1 work. Also for threshing 21 seams, 7½b. of rye, 39 works, that is, 4½b. for 1 work. For threshing 18 seams, 1b. of barley, 29 works, that is, 5b. for 1 work. Also for threshing 7½b. of beans, 3 works, that is, 2½b. for 1 work. Also for threshing 1 seam 5½b. of peas, 3 works, that is 4½b. for 1 work. Also for threshing 37½ seams of oats, 40 works that is 7½b. for 1 work. For making water courses, 36 works. For putting the mill in order, 28 works. For spreading manure, 8 works. For quarrying clay for the kitchen and for the oven, 12 works. For thatching before the feast of St Michael, 24 works. For 1 man going with the plough at the sowing of corn for 5 days, 5 works. For

---

22 Saucers might alternatively be salt-cellars. Bowls might possibly be cups as the Latin here (*ciph'*) is an alternative spelling for *scyphus*, vessel for food or drink, cup, goblet (*DMLBS*). Plurals have been assumed for all three commodities, although all are abbreviated so the number is unknown.

23 The arithmetic is wrong here. The total should be 15s. 10d. The ¾d. in the given total is not to be found anywhere in the text of this paragraph.

24 Actually £32 19s. 5½d. (a difference of 7d.) adding up the sub-totals as given above. However, the given sub-total respecting the expenses of the monk-warden and colleagues £3 1s. 1d. (*61s. 1d.*) is incorrect and should be either £3 8s. 7¾d. (adding up all the figures in that sub-section, whether crossed through or not) or £2 18s. 6d. (adding only the figures not crossed out). Taking these alternatives into account, the total should therefore be either £33 7s. ¼d (including crossed out figures in the monk-warden's expenses sub-section) or £32 16s. 10½d. (excluding the crossed out figures). Because the crossed out figures were presumably not allowed at the audit the total of £32 16s. 10½d. is probably to be preferred, which is 2s. less than the given total.

25 The sum is correct on its own given the figures: the sum given for receipts in this roll (£39 10½d.) minus the sum of payments (£32 18s. 10½d.) comes to £6 2s. However, if one uses the corrected editorial figures for both receipts and expenditure, then £39 0s. 10¾d. minus £32 16s. 10½d. comes to £6 4s. ¼d.

26 For this calculation to be correct, there have to be exactly eight weeks between Pentecost (Sunday, 2 June in 1286) and the feast of St Peter in chains. In 1286, the two dates were eight weeks and four days apart.

27 Actually 1,803.

28 Four feast days + two court days = six days without works x 21½ lands = 129 works respited.

breaking up the glebe for rye and barley, 24 works. For making an enclosure around Manhey, 22 works. For making 16 hurdles, 8 works. For pulling out and planting thorn-bushes, 16 works. For ditching 30 perches at Higeleye, 30 works. For making an enclosure around Bullockesfen and Skippesmede, 70 works. For digging and planting a new [*?*]enclosure (*impetim*) with beans, 40 works. For cutting under-wood for an enclosure and for the hearth, 34 works. For cutting down timber and wood for the paling of the vineyard, 8 works. For *rammyng'* for the same fencing, 8 works. For carrying and spreading manure within the aforesaid vineyard and for ditching around the vines, 12 works. For weeding corn, 432 works. For spreading and lifting hay, 112 works. For collecting branches for roofing buildings, 4 works. For the helpers in roofing, 6 works. For the sale of 144 works. For the reaping of 20 acres of rye, 40 works. For the binding of rye, 10 works. Also for the stacking of rye, 4 works and for the carting [*of it*], 2 works. For the stacking of barley, 6 works and for the carting of barley, 2 works. Also for the stacking of oats, 16 works and for the carting of oats, 6 works. Also for the stacking of wheat, 20 works and for the carting of wheat, 8 works. Also for the harvesting of 4 acres of peas, 16 works. Also for the harvesting of 1 acre of beans 10 works. Also for collecting apples, 31 works. For making cider, 8 works. For the sale of 144 works.　　Total [*blank*][29]

Ploughing. The same answers for ploughing on the aforesaid 21½ lands at the season (*ad seys*[*onam*]) of wheat, 53 acres 3 roods, of which 52 acres are ploughed, and sold, 1 acre 3 roods. Also concerning the same lands at the same season, 21½ acres as boon-work (*de bene*), of which 20½ acres are ploughed, and sold, 1 acre. Also concerning the same lands at the fallowing of barley, 21½ acres and all are ploughed. Also concerning the same lands at the season of oats, as gavelearth (*de Gable*), 53 acres 3 roods, of which are ploughed 44 acres 3 roods, sold, 9 acres. Also concerning the same lands at the same season, 21½ acres as boon-work (*de bene*), of which 19½ acres are ploughed, and sold, 2 acres. Also concerning the same lands at the <same> season of barley, 10 acres 3 roods, of which 9 acres 3 roods are ploughed and sold, 1 acre. Also concerning the same lands, for harrowing at the season of oats after the lord's plough, 41½ acres and all are harrowed.

Reaping. For reaping wheat from the aforesaid lands as gavelearth (*de Gable*), 86 acres and all were reaped. For reaping barley and oats from the aforesaid lands as gavelearth (*de Gable*), 96 acres and all were reaped.

[*Membrane 1, dorse*]
　"Eleigh (*Illeghe*). Account of the same J. for corn there for the year within written

Wheat. The same accounts for 93 seams" 1b. of wheat from the issue of the grange. And for 1 "seam 3½b." from the toll of the mill.
"And for 2½ seams bought."　　　　　　　　　Total 97 seams and ½b.
Of which. For "seed, 35"½ "seams" ½b.
In payment "to Saleman" the reeve[30] for 7 weeks, 7b.
In payment "to Thomas" Forster for the same time, 5b.
For bread for the customary tenants removing manure, 1½ seams.

---

[29] The final figure, for the sale of 144 works, is erroneously repeated, having been cited previously in this sub-section. Without the repetition, the works add up to 1,803, the same as the corrected sum in the previous sub-section.
[30] Presumably the reap-reeve, who was being paid for his harvest-time work.

For bread for the customary tenants at the wheat boon-work (*ad p[re]cem [sic] fr[ument]i*) at harvest-time, 3 seams.

For harvest-time expenses, 1½ seams.

Sold, 54 seams.   Total as above.

Rye. The same answers for 22 seams ½b. of rye from the issue of the grange.

And for 2 seams 3½b. from the toll of the mill.

And for 3½ seams received from the barley to pay the *famuli*.

And for 12 seams 6b. bought.   Total 40 seams 6b.

Of which. For seed, 5 seams 2b. In payment to 4 ploughmen and 1 cowherd from the feast of St Michael in the 13th year of the reign of King Edward until the same feast in the 14th year [*29 September 1285–28 September 1286*], 24 seams 3b., of which was taken by each of them, per 12 weeks, 9b.[31] In payment to the housemaid for the aforesaid time 3 seams 2b., which she took per 16 weeks, 1 seam.[32] In payment to the miller from the feast of St Michael in the year aforesaid until the Monday next after the feast of the apostles Peter and Paul [*Monday, 1 July 1286*], that is, for 39 weeks, 2 seams 3½b. taking for each week ½b. In payment to certain youths scattering [*seed in*] the furrows (*spargent' sulcos*) and to a harrower at the season of wheat and rye, 2b. Also in payment to a certain harrower at the season of oats and barley for 7 weeks, 3½b. Also in payment of 2 woodwards for the whole year, 1 seam 1b. For bread for the customary tenants for the oats boon-work (*precem*) at harvest-time, 3 seams. For harvest-time expenses, 5b.   Total [blank].[33]

Barley. The same answers for 18 seams 3b. of barley from the issue of the grange.
                                                                        Total evident.

Of which. For seed, 10½ seams. In payment for rye as appears above, 3½ seams. For feeding (*s[?us]tinend'*) piglets and capons, 3b. Sold, 4 seams.   Total as above.

Beans. The same answers for 7½b. of beans from the issue of the grange.
                                                                        Total evident

Of which. For seed, 4b. For planting,[34] 1½b. Sold 2b.   Total as above.

Peas. The same answers for 2 seams of peas from the issue of the grange.

And for 5b. bought.   Total 2 seams 5b.

Of which. For seed, 1 seam. For feeding[35] pigs, 1½ seams. For pottage, 1b.
                                                                        Total as above.

---

[31] Five people are paid 9b. for each twelve-week period (a nominal quarter of a year), but that adds up to only forty-eight weeks, rather than the full fifty-two weeks in the year. 9b. per twelve-week period (nine divided by twelve) comes to ¾b. per person per week. ¾ x 5 (for five people) = 3¾b. for all of them together per week, x fifty-two weeks in the year = 195b. per year, divided by eight (8b. per seam) = 24 seams, 3b.

[32] A complex calculation based once more on a forty-eight-week period, but this time expressed as three sixteen-week periods. Broken down to a weekly payment, the maid receives ½ a b. per week, which, over fifty-two weeks in the year, does indeed come to 3 seams 2b.

[33] These figures add up to 40 seams 8b., agreeing with the preceding sub-section.

[34] *DMLBS, plantatio,* 'act of putting into the ground, planting (cutting, seed or plant)'. This entry, differentiating between sowing and planting, might mean a difference between the broadcast sowing of seed and the deliberate planting of individual seeds (perhaps in a garden setting, rather than a field). Or perhaps the planting was of individually grown plants from seed.

[35] The verb used here (*depascend'*) is from *depascere,* 'to graze on, depasture' (*DMLBS*). The *OED* entry for 'depasture' implies that the pigs would have been feeding on the pea crop in the field, rather than on harvested peas. If so, the quantity of peas must have been estimated.

Vetch. The same answers for 3½ seams of vetch extracted from oats. Total evident.
Of which. For sustaining piglets, 6b. Sold, 2 seams 6b.   Total as above.

Oats. The same answers for 49 seams of oats from the issue of the grange.
And for 32 seams bought.
And for 1 seam 2½b. of the increment of oats bought.   Total [*blank*].
Of which. For seed, 54 seams. For meal for pottage, 2 seams. For feeding stots from
the Friday next before the feast of St Osyth the virgin [*Friday, 5 October 1285*] up
until the day of St Thomas the apostle, 9 seams 5b., each night 1b. Also for feeding
the same from the aforesaid day of St Thomas until the day of St Oswald the bishop,
4 seams 2½b., each night ½b. Also for feeding the same from the said day of St
Oswald until the day of St Ambrose, 4 seams 3b., each night 1b. Also for feeding
the same from the aforesaid day of St Ambrose until the day of the apostles Philip
and James, 1½ seams 1½b., that is each night ½b.
For feeding the horses of Dom S[*tephen*] de Ycham and the colleagues of the same
for their visit, together with a certain visit of Dom S[*tephen*] himself and Dom J.
de Shamelesford and J. de Lond' returning from Norfolk, 4 seams 3½b. For feeding
[*the horses of*] Dom R. Pucyn, 3b. Also for feeding the horses of Dom J. de Shamelesford and his colleagues going towards Norfolk, 3b. Also for feeding the horses of
the aforesaid Dom S[*tephen*] and Dom Randolph the treasurer upon their last view,
6b. For feeding the horse of J. de Belsted, bailiff, 5b.   Total [*blank*].

Concerning stock in the same year

Stots. The same answers for 9 stots of the remainders (*de rem'*).[36]
                                        And there remain[37] 9 stots.
And for 12 oxen of the remainders. And for 1 bought. And for 2 recruited (*adiunct'*).[38]
                                        Total 15.
Of which 5 sold.   And there remain 10 oxen.
2 bulls of the remainders. And 1 recruited.   Total 3.
Of which 1 sold. 1 [*died*] of murrain.   And there remains 1 bull.
9 cows of the remainders.   And there remain 9 cows
2 young oxen (*bovett'*) of the remainders. And recruited above.[39]
1 young bull of the remainders. And recruited above.[40]
3 heifers of the remainders.   And there remain 3 heifers.
4 calves, of issue from last year, of the remainders.
                  And there remain 4, of which, 3 bullocks and 1 heifer.
9 calves of issue from the present year. Of which 5 sold.
                        And there remain 4 calves of issue.
2 ewes of the remainders. Of which 1 [*died*] of murrain before shearing and lambing.
                        And there remains 1 ewe.
2 hoggets of the remainders.   And there remain 2 sheep.[41]
1 lamb, of issue from last year, of the remainders. Of which, 1 [*died*] of murrain
before shearing.   And none remain.

---

36 That is, brought forward from the previous year's account.
37 At the end of this accounting year.
38 That is, added, joined or transferred from the younger stock.
39 That is, two young oxen grew up and were recruited into the adult oxen, as shown a few lines above.
40 That is, one young bull was recruited into the bulls, as shown a few lines above.
41 The text here is 'sheep' (*multo*), which can mean sheep, mutton, ewe, ram or wether, not just 'hoggets'.

1 lamb of issue from the present year.   And there remains 1 female lamb.
        Total of the sheep, 4. And all have gone to Hadleigh (*Hadlegh*).
1 boar of the remainders.   And there remains 1 boar.
2 sows of the remainders.   And there remain 2 sows.
10 pigs and 28 piglets of the remainders.   Total 38.
Of which, 6 in the larder. 9 sold.   And there remain 23 pigs.
18 piglets of issue from this year. And 1 *kemeling*.[42]   Total 19.
Of which, 10 [*died*] of murrain.
    And there remain 9 piglets of issue, with the *kemeling*.
20 geese of the remainders. 28 of issue. Total 48.
Of which, 5 consumed by Dom S[*tephen*] de Ycham and his colleagues. 11 [*died*]
of murrain. 11 sold.   And there remain 21 geese.
21 capons of the remainders. Of which, 8 sold.   And there remain 13 capons.
23 hens and cockerels of the remainders. 25 of issue. 10 for perquisites.   Total 58.
Of which, 8 consumed by Dom St[*ephen*] and Dom R. Pucyn upon the account of
Saleman.
Also 11 consumed by the aforesaid Dom St[*ephen*] and his colleagues during their
visit afterwards. 9 [*died*] of murrain.   And there remain 30.
18 ducks of the remainders. 9 of issue.   Total 27.
Of which, 2 consumed by Dom St[*ephen*] and his colleagues during their visit. 6
[*died*] of murrain. 6 sold.   And there remain 13 ducks.
300 eggs of issue of the hens and ducks. And all were sold as below.
12 hams in the larder. Of which, 5 consumed by Dom S[*tephen*] and his colleagues
during their visit. Also 3 consumed at harvest-time. 4 sold.   And nothing remains.
[*Membrane 2, dorse, blank.*]

Accounts 2.[43] Serjeant's Account of Andrew le Forester (1310–11)[44]

[*Membrane 1, face*] Account of Andrew le Forester serjeant of Eleigh (*Illegh*) from
the feast of St Michael in the fourth year of the reign of King Edward [*II*] until the
same feast next following for one whole year [*29 September 1310–28 September
1311*].

Rents. He answers for 14s. 7d. rent for the term of St Andrew the apostle. And for
17s. 4d. for the term of Palm Sunday [*4 April*]. And for £1 18s. 6¼d. for the term
of the apostles Peter and Paul. And for £1 9s. 2½¼d. for the term of St Peter in

---

[42] ME *comeling*, 'a stray animal that joins another herd' (*MED*).

[43] CCA-DCc-BR/Illeigh/2. Parchment roll, three membranes, stitched together lengthways: stock
inventory on the third, small, membrane, which is roughly stitched to the foot of membrane 2.
On dorse is written in a [?]nineteenth-century hand, 'Illeigh, 4 Edw. I, 1276–7' and in pencil in a
twentieth-century hand below it, 'Illegh, Andrew Forester, 4–5 Edw. II'. Latin. Illustrated in Plate
8. For Weller's map of the demesne arable in the northern half of the manor upon which the tenants
would have worked, see Plate 9.

[44] The heading gives the king as 'E[*dward*]', which usually denotes the first king of a given name
and the labels indicate confusion over the king. From a comparison of the people mentioned in this
account who occur elsewhere, notably in Court Roll 1 (1305–1305/6), and from the length of the
list of assize rents (see Introduction, pp. xxviii–xxix), this account closely matches 1310–11 (4 Edw.
II), but not 1276–77 (which was, in any case, 5, not 4, Edw. I). However, the clinching evidence is
that this account refers to letters being carried to or for John Le Doo, steward of the Essex custody
1306–1326 at least, but certainly gone by 1334 (Nichols, 'An Early Fourteenth-Century Petition'
(1930), p. 301, n. 2) so the date is indeed 4–5 Edw. II, giving a 1310–11 date for the accounts.

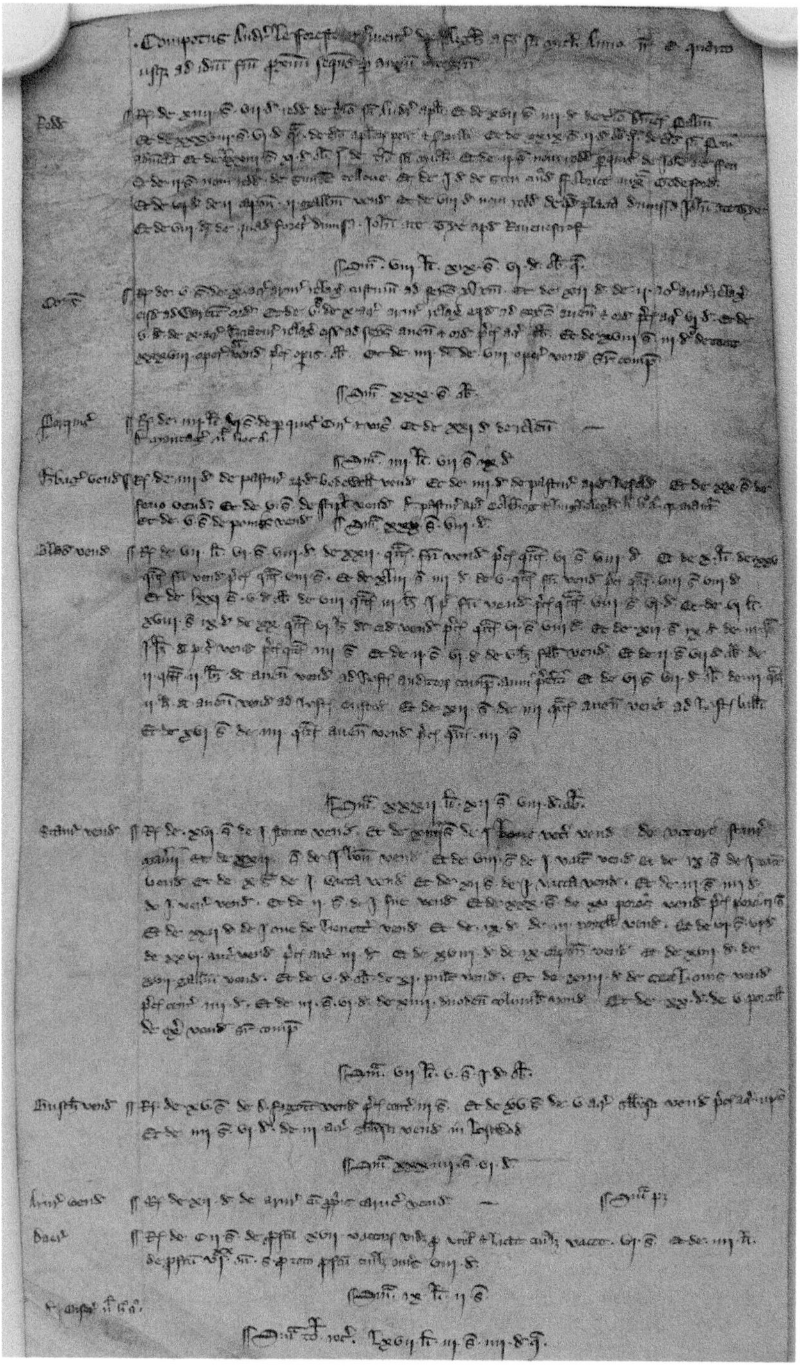

Plate 8. Accounts 2 (1310–11): beginning of the serjeant's account of Andrew le Forester. (CCA-DCc-BR/Illeigh/2) Photo: Dr Toby Huitson, CCA. Reproduced courtesy of the Chapter of Canterbury

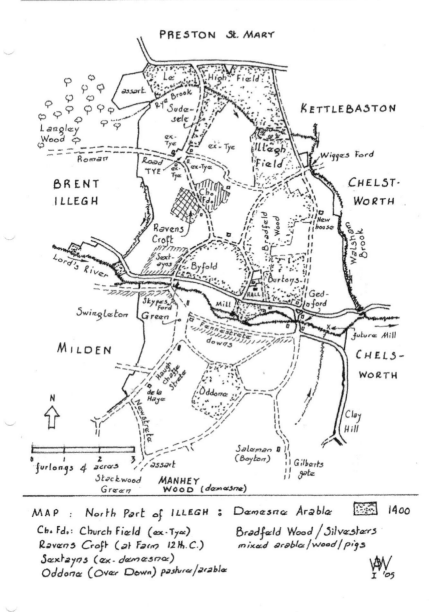

PRESTON St. MARY

Le
High Field
assart
R'a Brook
Sude-
sele
KETTLEBASTON

Langley
Wood
ex-
Tye
ex-Tye
Illegh
Field
Wigges Ford

Roman
Road
TYE
ex-Tye
ex-Tye
CHELST-
WORTH

BRENT
ILLEGH
Ch.
Fd.
New
house

Ravens
Croft
Bradfeld
Wood

Lord's River
Sext-
ayns
Byfold
Walsham Brook

Burtons

Swingleton
Skypes
Ford
Mill
HALL
Ged-
lo ford

Green
Fennestrete
downs
X
future Mill

MILDEN
CHELS-
WORTH

N
Haugh
de la
Haye
chasse
Strete
Oddona

Clay
Hill

0   1   2   3
furlongs 4 acres
assart
Saleman
(Boyton)
Gilberts
gate

Stackwood
Green
MANHEY
WOOD (demesne)

MAP : North Part of ILLEGH : Demesne Arable ▨ 1400

Ch. Fd.: Church Field (ex-Tye)   Bradfeld Wood / Silvesters
Ravens Croft (at Farm 12th.C.)   mixed arable/wood/pigs
Sextayns (ex-demesne)
Oddona (Over Down) pasture/arable

I '05

Plate 9. Weller's map of the northern half of the manor of Monks Eleigh, showing the location of demesne arable land, c. 1400. (Weller Archive, file 'Maps')

chains. And for £3 13s. 11½¼d. for the term of St Michael.[45] And for 2s. new rent acquired from John ate Fen. And for 2s. new rent from Simon Tollone. And for 1d. for the site of a certain forge next to Gedeford. And for 6d. for 2 capons and 2 hens sold. And for 8d. new rent from a certain plot demised to John ate Tye. And for 8d. for a certain headland demised to John ate Tye at Ravenescroft.

Total £8 19s. 6½¼d.

Customary [*works*]. He answers for 5s. for 10 acres of ploughing released from customary works at the winter season. And for 1s. for 2 acres of ploughing released from the same at the fallowing of barley. And for 5s. for 10 acres of ploughing released from the same at the season for oats and barley, price of an acre, 6d. And for 5d. for 10 acres of harrowing released from the same at the season for oats and barley, price of an acre, ½d. And for 18s. 3½d. for 438\½/ works sold, price of a work, ½d. And for 4d. for 8 works sold beyond the account.[46]   Total £1 10s. ½d.

Perquisites. He answers for £4 6s. for the perquisites of the court and view. And for 1s. 9d. for reliefs. For food allowances,[47] nothing for this year.   Total £4 7s. 9d.

Herbage sold. He answers for 4d. for pasturage at Bedewell', sold. And for 4d. for pasturage at Befold. And for £1. for hay sold. And for 5s. for straw sold. For pasturage at Colehog and Hughelegh [*sic*], nothing for this year because it is ploughed. And for 5s. for apples sold.   Total £1 10s. 8d.

Corn sold. He answers for £7 6s. 8d. for 22qr of wheat sold, price of a quarter, 6s. 8d. And for £10 for 25qr of wheat sold, price of a quarter, 8s. And for £2 3s. 4d. for 5qr of wheat sold, price of a quarter, 8s. 8d. And for £3 11s. 5½d. for 8qr 3b. 1 peck of wheat sold, price of a quarter, 8s. 6d. And for £6 18s. 9d. for 20qr 6½b. of barley sold, price of a quarter, 6s. 8d. And for 12s. 9d. for 3qr 1b. of peas sold, price of a quarter, 4s. And for 2s. 6d. for 5b. of beans sold. And for 2s. 7½d. for 2qr 2½b. of oats sold for entertaining the auditors of the accounts of the past year. And for 6s. 7½d. for 3qr 2½b. of oats sold for entertaining the warden. And for 12s. for 4qr of oats sold for entertaining the bailiff. And for 16s. for 4qr of oats sold, price of a quarter, 4s.   Total £32 12s. 8½d.

Stock sold. He answers for 16s. for 1 stot sold. And for 14s. for 1 old ox sold from the old stock of the manor. And for £1 2s. for 1 ox sold. And for 8s. for 1 cow sold. And for 9s. for 1 cow sold. And for 10s. for 1 cow sold. And for 12s. for 1 cow sold. And for 3s. 4d. for 1 boar sold. And for 2s. for 1 sow sold. And for £1 10s. for 15 pigs sold, price of a pig, 2s. And for 1s. 10d. for 1 sheep as a heriot, sold. And for 9d. for 3 piglets sold. And for 6s. 6d. for 26 geese sold, price of a goose, 3d. And for 1s. 6d. for 9 capons sold. And for 1s. 5d. for 17 hens sold. And for 5½d. for 11 pullets sold. And for 1s. 2d. for 350 eggs sold, price of a hundred, 4d. And for 3s.

---

45 This and preceding rents are the same as in Accounts 1 (1285–86). The ones following date from after that.

46 *super compotum*, literally 'upon/beyond the account', i.e. during the audit. Sometimes notional figures or accounting fictions could be added during the audit to make the accounts balance. This final sentence is in the same handwriting and ink as the rest of the account, so if it were added at the audit (and it *is* at the end of this sub-section, and there is space for it to have been added then) it must have been written by the same clerk fairly soon after he had compiled the rest of the account.

47 The text has *mancag'* here, an abbreviation for *mancagium*, which *DMLBS* suggests is the same word as *mensagium* [*mensa* + *agium*], 'table money, money for an allowance of food', citing as an example a phrase from 1284 that mentions the word together with perquisites.

6d. for 14 dozen doves sold. And for 1s 8d. for 5 piglets produced, sold beyond the account. Total £7 5s. 1½d.

Wood (busch') sold. He answers for 15s. for 500 faggots sold, price of a hundred, 3s. And for 15s. for 5 acres of underwood sold, price of an acre, 3s. And for 4s. 6d. for 3 acres of underwood sold in Losewod. Total £1 14s. 6d.

Ploughing sold. He answers for 1s. for ploughing-services with own ploughs (*arur' cum propris caruc'*),[48] sold. Total evident.

Dairy. He answers for £5 2s. for the profit of 17 cows, that is, for the calf and milk of each cow, 6s. And for £4 for the profit of 120 sheep, that is, for the whole profit of each sheep, 8d. Total £9 2s.
For cider nothing for this year.

Sum of all receipts £67 3s. 4¼d.

Payments. In respect of which, he paid the treasury of Canterbury £30 by 3 tallies. Total evident.

Lodging. For the expenses of the auditors of the account for the past year, 13s. 4d. Total evident.

External [expenses]. For letters of the lord prior and a writ of the lord king carried [*to or for*] John le Doo,[49] 1s. 4d., on 4 occasions.
For 1 man hired in place of the reeve at Henhow (*Henowe*) at the gaol delivery for 2 days, 4d.[50] Total 1s. 8d.

Expenses of the warden and bailiff. For the expenses of Dom S., warden, £4 6s. For the expenses of the bailiff, 18s. For the wages of the same, 10s. Total £5 14s.

Corn bought. For 7b. 1 peck of rye bought, 3s. 7½d. Total evident.

Stock bought. For 1 stot bought, £1 5s. 2d. For 1 ox bought, £1 4s. 1d. For 1 ox bought, £1 3s. 6d. For 1 cow bought, 13s. 4d. For 1 cow bought, 14s. 6d. For 1 cow bought, 12s. Total £5 12s. 7d.

Plough costs. For 2 ploughshares bought, 1s. 4d. For repairing 1 ploughshare, 6d. For 5 sheaves of steel, 3s. 11½d., price of a sheaf, 9½d. For 10 sheaves of steel bought, 8s. 4d., price of a sheaf, 10d. For 10 pieces of iron bought, 2s. 11d., price of a piece, 3½d. For 11 strakes, 2s. 3½d. For 11 *stradelclutes*, 1s. 10d. For 8 *restclutes*, 1s. For shoeing stots, 8s. For shoeing oxen, 1s. 3d. For making 6 new ploughs and repairing old ones, 2s. 6d. For making 1 new harrow, 1½d. Total £1 14s. ½d.

---

48 Unidentified tenants are paying cash rather than performing this labour service, but whether these are the demesne ploughs or the tenants' ploughs is ambiguous. My thanks to Prof. Mark Bailey for helping with this point.

49 John Le Doo steward of the Essex custody between 1306 and 1326 at least, although he was gone by 1334 (see Introduction, p. xxv).

50 Gaol delivery involved handing over for trial accused prisoners who were held in gaol pending their appearance in court, a duty that devolved upon the reeve, although a man was hired to deputise for him on this occasion. In 1305, the location of the king's courts (assizes and quarter sessions) for the eight and a half hundreds of the liberty St Edmund was moved from Cattishall in Great Barton to Henhow on Shire House Heath to the north-west of Bury St Edmunds (TNA, SC 8/140/6998 (petition); C 143/52/13 (inquisition); H.C. Maxwell Lyte (ed.), *Calendar of Patent Rolls, Edward I: Volume 4, 1301–1307* (London, 1898), pp. 360–99 (see membrane 20, 19 June 1305, Finden).

Cart costs. For 1 pair of wheels made from [?*the manor's*] own timber (*de meremio proprio*),[51] 1s. 2d. For fitting a cart with an axle, 3d. For 20 clouts for carts, with nails for the same, 1s. 8d. For grease for carts, 4d. For mending cart harness, 10d. For leather and hemp bought for the same, 6d.   Total 4s. 9d.

Costs of buildings. For roofing the oats grange in places, 1s. 8d. For covering with laths and roofing the bakehouse, 5s.   Total 6s. 8d.

Costs of the mill. For making a new inner wheel with a trendle for the same, 6s. 10d. For bindings bought for binding the same wheel, 1s. 4d.   Total 8s. 2d.

Fencing. For mending the paling between the hall porch and the kitchen and the paling of the pound, 2s. For 2 locks for the gates of Holemed, 5d.   Total 2s. 5d.

[Membrane 2, face] Mowing: For mowing 8 acres of meadow, 3s. 4d., for an acre, 5d.   Total evident.

Small [expenses]. For 4b. of salt, 1s. For 1 seed-sowing basket, 2d. For 2 sacks, 1s. 1d. For repairs in the vineyard, 6d. For making 1 new ladder, 6d. For castrating piglets, 6d.   Total 3s. 9d.

Harvest-time expenses. For the expenses of the serjeant, reap-reeve and *famuli* for 5 weeks at harvest-time, with the expenses of the lord warden, his colleagues and his *famuli* there for 4 days, £1 12s.   Total £1 12s.

Reaping. For herrings and cheese bought for the customary tenants clearing out the manure from the outer court, 1s. 5d., by custom. For meat bought for the wheat boon-work (*percar*[*iam*]) at harvest-time, 4s. 10d., by custom. For herrings bought for the oats boon-work at harvest-time, 1s. 3d., by custom. For cheese bought for both boon-works, 4s. 2d., by custom.   Total 11s. 8d.

Wages. For the wages of 1 reap-reeve at harvest-time, 3s. For the wages of one who is the cowherd and swineherd, for the year, 3s. For the wages of a maid,[52] 2s. For the wages of a shepherd, 5s. For the wages of a carter \for clearing out manure and marling/ for this year, 3s. For expenses and oblations (*oblationibus*) for the whole *famuli* for the days of Christmas and Easter, 4s.   Total £1.

Sum of all payments and expenses, £48 12s.

And he owes £18 11s. <4¼d.>[53]

Thus there is a profit of £48 11s.[54]

[Membrane 3, face: a small indented membrane attached at the foot of membrane 2.] Stock remaining in the manor of Eleigh (Illegh) at the feast of St Michael in the

---

[51] The timber could have been provided by either the unnamed carpenter or by the demesne, most likely the latter. My thanks to Prof. Mark Bailey for help with this point.

[52] In the 1285–86 accounts, the maid was specified as a housemaid (*ancille domus*); here she is simply a maid.

[53] The sum total of the charge (income, what the serjeant has received) of £67 3s. 4¼d. minus the sum total of the discharge (expenditure, what the serjeant has disbursed) of £48 12s. actually does come to £18 11s. 4¼d. (excess of charge over discharge, therefore liable to be paid by the serjeant to Canterbury), so it is unclear why the 4¼d. has been struck out here.

[54] This is the sum of the £30 paid into the treasury at Canterbury (see above in this account) plus the £18 11s. owed by the serjeant to the lord in the line immediately above. This type of calculation of profit at Canterbury is discussed in E. Stone, 'Profit-and-Loss Accountancy at Norwich Cathedral Priory', *Transactions of the Royal Historical Society*, 5th Series, 12 (1962), p. 29.

5th year of the reign of King Edward [*II*] [*29 September 1311*] at the beginning. Stots 8. Oxen 8. Bulls 1. Cows 17. Boars 1. Sows 2. Pigs 14. Piglets 17, Of which, 9 are half a year old, 8 are a quarter of a year old. Peacocks 5. Peahens 6. Young peacocks 3. Ganders 2. Geese 6. Capons 10. Cockerels 1. Hens 8. Chickens 20. Sacks 2. Ladders 1.

[*Membrane 1, dorse*]
    Account of Eleigh (*Illeg'*) for the fourth year of King Edward [*II, 1310–11*].

Wheat. He answers for 9qr of wheat of issue, measured by cantle in front of the stack (*cantell' coram tasso*). And for 42qr 1b. of issue from the eastern stack. And for 22qr of that measured by cantle, chosen for seed. And for 32qr of wheat of issue, from the western stack. And for 8qr of chaff of the same. And for 1qr 3b. from the issue of the mill.   Total 114½qr.
Of which, for sowing upon 132 acres, 33qr 2b., upon an acre, 2b. [*and*] 2b. more on the total. In payment to the serjeant for the year, except for 5 weeks at harvest-time, 5qr 7b. In payment to 1 reap-reeve for that time for a certain part of his wages, 1qr 3½b. 1 peck and taking as much rye as below. For mixing with rye as payment to the *famuli*, 8qr of inferior corn. Provided for the customary tenants clearing out the manure, 1½qr, by custom. Provided for the *famuli* at harvest-time, 1qr. Provided at the wheat boon-work at harvest-time, 3qr, by custom. For 60qr 3b. 1 peck sold.
                                                                                Total as above.
                                                                                And quit.

Rye. He answers for 27qr of rye of issue. \That is, from an acre, 1½qr.[55]/ And for 8qr of wheat chaff received as a payment. And for 5qr from the issue of the mill. And for 7b. 1 peck bought. Total 40qr 7b. 1 peck.
Of which, for sowing upon 20 acres, 5qr, upon an acre, 2b. In payment to the reap-reeve for the year, except for 5 weeks at harvest-time, for a certain part of his pay, 1qr 3½b. 1 peck, and he takes the residue at Hadleigh (*Hadlegh*). In payment to 4 ploughmen and 1 who is the cowherd and swineherd for the year, 21qr 5b., to each of them per 12 weeks, 1qr. In payment to the shepherd and the maid for the year, 6½qr, to both of them for a week, ½b. By custom to the shepherd at lambing time, 2b. In payment to one [*person*] scattering [*seed in*] the furrows (*spargent' sulcos*) in the winter season, 3b. In payment to one [*person for*] harrowing oats and barley for 6 weeks 3b. In payment to one carter for taking away manure from the inner court and out of the yard[56] and mixing the same with marl in the fields in various places for 16 weeks, 1qr 2½b. In payment to one [*person for*] driving away birds at the season of barley, 2b. By custom, to the woodward of Hitcham (*Hecham*), 4b. Provided for the oats boon-work at harvest-time, 3qr, by custom. Provided for the dogs of the court for the year, 2b. \Total delivered (*lib'*) 30qr 5½b.[57]/
                                                                                Total as above.
                                                                                And quit.

---

[55] This interpolation is added in the margin to the bottom left of the paragraph and perhaps fits best immediately after the first sentence of it, although it is not clear where within the paragraph it belongs.
[56] *Gardin'* here could mean 'garden', but *DMLBS* gives the alternative meaning of 'a yard (used for purpose other than cultivation)', so this is probably a farmyard.
[57] Inserted in the margin, at the bottom left of this paragraph.

Barley. He answers for 29qr 1b. of barley of issue.   Total evident.
Of which, for sowing upon 16½ acres, 8qr 2½b., upon an acre, 4b. [*and*] ½b. more
on the total. For 20qr 6½b. sold.   Total as above.
      And quit.

Peas. He answers for 6qr 2b. of peas of issue. Total evident.
Of which, for sowing upon 9½ acres, 2qr 3b. For sustaining pigs, 4b. For sustaining
doves, 1½b. For 3qr 1½b. sold.   Total as above.
      And quit.

Beans. He answers for 7b. of beans of issue. For planting in the garden, 2b. For
5b., sold.
      And quit.

Oats. He answers for 93qr of oats of issue. And for 7qr by estimation in sheaves.
      Total 100qr.
Of which, for sowing upon 129 acres, 56qr 3½b., upon an acre, 3½b. For meal for
pottage for the *famuli*, 2qr. For feeding 8 stots from the feast of St Faith the Virgin
until the feast of St Katherine for 50 nights, 6qr 2b. \for a night, 1b./ For the feeding
the same stots from the feast of St Katherine until the feast of the conversion of St
Paul for 61 nights, 3qr 6½b., for a night, ½b. For feeding the same from the feast
of St Paul until the feast of St Ambrose for 70 nights, 8qr 6b., for a night, 1b. For
feeding the same from the feast of St Ambrose until the feast of St John before the
Latin Gate for 31 nights, 1qr 7½b., for a night, ½b. \Total of fodder, 20qr 6b.[58]/
Sold for the entertainment of the auditors of the account for the past year, 2qr 2½b.,
sold. Sold for the entertainment of the warden, 3½qr, sold. Sold for the entertainment of the bailiff, 4qr, sold. For 4qr sold. For feeding oxen, by estimation, in
sheaves, 7qr.   Total as above.
      And quit.

Stock Account

Stots. He answers for 8 stots of the remainders. And for 1 bought.   Total 9.
Of which, 1 sold.   And there remain 8 stots.

Oxen. He answers for 8 oxen of the remainders. And for 2 bought.   Total 10.
Of which, 2 sold.   And there remain 8 oxen.

Bulls. He answers for 1 bull of the remainders.   And there remains 1 bull.

Cows. He answers for 17 cows of the remainders. And for 1 as a heriot. And for 3
bought.   Total 21.
Of which, 4 sold before calving.   And there remain 17 cows.
Let it be remembered about 120 sheep demised for profit.

Sheep. He answers for 1 sheep as a heriot and sold as earlier [*in this account*].

Boars. He answers for 1 boar of the remainders. And for 1 recruited from the pigs.
      Total 2.
Of which, 1 sold. And there remains 1 boar.

Sows. He answers for 2 sows of the remainders. And 1 recruited from the pigs.
      Total 3.
Of which, 1 sold.   And there remain 2 sows.

---

[58] Inserted in the margin, to the left of this line.

Pigs. He answers for 12 pigs of the remainders. And for 18 recruited from the piglets of the remainders.   Total 30.
Of which, 1 [*died*] of murrain. 15 sold.   And there remain 14 pigs.

Piglets of the remainders. He answers for 20 piglets of the remainders. Of which, 1 recruited into the boars. 1 recruited into the sows. 18 recruited into the pigs.
                                                                                And none remain.

[*Membrane 2, dorse*] *Piglets of issue*. And for <25> \30/ piglets of issue.
                                                                                Total evident.
Of which, 5 [*died*] of murrain. 3 sold for entertaining [*guests*] (*host'is*). 5 sold beyond the account. And there remain 17 piglets, of which, 9 are ½ year old, 8 are ¼ year old.

Peacocks. He answers for 4 peacocks, 6 peahens and 2 young peacocks of the remainders.   Total 12.
Of which, 1 [*died*] of murrain.   And there remain 5 peacocks and 6 peahens.

Young peacocks. He answers for 3 young peacocks of issue.
                                                          And there remain 3 young peacocks.

Geese. He answers for 2 ganders, 6 geese of the remainders. And for 31 of issue.
                                                                                Total 39.
Of which, 3 [*died*] of murrain. In expenses for [*?the household*[59]] at harvest-time, 2. 26 sold.   And there remain 2 ganders, 6 geese.

Capons. He answers for 12 capons of the remainders. And for 8 from the stock of pullets of issue.   Total 20.
Of which, 1 [*died*] of murrain. 9 sold.   And there remain 10 capons.

Hens. He answers for 1 cockerel, 8 hens of the remainders. And for 21 recruited from the pullets of the remainders.   Total 30.
Of which, 4 [*died*] of murrain. 17 sold.   And there remain 1 cockerel, 8 hens.

Chickens of the remainders. He answers for 24 chickens of the remainders. Of which, 3 [*died*] of murrain. 21 were recruited into the hens.   And none remain.

Chickens of issue. He answers for 35 chickens of issue. And for 6 from purchases (*perquis'*).   Total 41.
Of which, 2 [*died*] of murrain. 8 were made capons. 11 were sold for entertaining [*guests*].   And there remain 20 chickens.

Eggs. He answers for 350 eggs of issue. And sold as earlier [in this account].

Doves. He answers for 14 dozen doves of issue. And sold as earlier [in this account].

Works Account
He answers for 262½ works concerning the issue of 17½ lands from the feast of St Michael until Easter, that is, from each land, 15 works. And for 52 works concerning

---

[59] The text has *ad brigos*, which could translate as something like 'for/at brawls' ('*briga*, strife, dispute, brawl' (*DMLBS*)), which seems incongruous here. It might be a scribal error for the traditional Michaelmas geese being consumed by the household (*in menegos* in other accounts herein). Alternatively, it could be another term for a harvest goose, like the rip-goose or reap-goose that appears in the Cuxham manorial records (Harvey, *Manorial Records of Cuxham* (1976), p. 795).

the issue of 4 lands for the aforesaid time that is from each land 13 works. And for 903 works concerning the issue of 21½ lands from the Thursday in the week of Pentecost [*Thursday, 3 June 1311*] until the first day of August for 8 weeks 1 day in this year, that is, from each land, every week, 5 works. And for 41 works concerning the issue of the aforesaid lands at Christmas. And for 400 works from 5 monday-lands for the year, that is, from each land, 80 works. And for 48 works from the half-land of Wolmer for the year. And for 37 works from the half-land of Thomas ate Thie. And for 96 works from the land Colehog and of Agnes the widow for the year. And for 6 works from the land of Robert Sacrist, Walter de Fynchelegh, Robert Fuller, Philip Skarlet and John Babbe for help in the meadow called Skippesmed.

Total 1,845½ works.

Of which, in allowance from the aforesaid 21½ lands for 7 feast days, 1 court with view held on working days in this year between Pentecost [*30 May 1311*] and the first day of August, 186 [*sic*] works, that is, for each land, for each day, 1 work.[60] For threshing 113qr 1b. of wheat, 362 works, that is, 2½b. for a work. For threshing 27qr of rye, 48 works, that is, 4½b. for a work. For threshing 29qr 1b. of barley, 51 works, that is, 5b. for a work. For threshing 6qr 2b. of peas, 12½ works, that is, 4b. for a work. For threshing 7b. of beans, 2½ works, that is, 2½b. for a work. For threshing 93qr of oats, 99 works, that is, 7½b. for a work.   Total 761 works.[61] For making water courses, 51 works. For holding (*tenend*[62]) the plough while the sower sowed after the lord's plough at both seasons, 22 works. For spreading manure 40 works. For clearing turf on land for barley, 12 works. For repairing the breach in the mill-pond dam, 42 works. For ditching around Manhey, 12 works. For making 15 hurdles, 10 works. For weeding corn, 202 works. For spreading, gathering in and heaping into cocks hay from Prestowe, 25 works. For carriage of the same, 4 works. For spreading, gathering in and heaping into cocks hay from Gedeford and Skippesmed, 24 works. For collecting and stacking hay, 11 works. For reaping rye before the first day of August, that is, on 20 acres, 40 works. For binding the same, 20 works. For stacking rye, 3 works. For stacking wheat, 9 works. For stacking barley, 2 works. For stacking peas, 1 work. For stacking oats, 5 works. For reaping and binding \9 acres/ of peas, 36 works. For picking wheat and rye for seed, 67 works. Sold, 438½ works. Sold beyond the account 8 works.

Total 1,084½ works.

Sum of all works, allowances, expenses and sales, 1,845½ as above.[63]

Winter ploughing. He answers for 53 acres 3 roods of ploughing as gavelearth (*de gablo*) in the winter season concerning the issue of the aforesaid 21½ lands. And for 21½ acres of ploughing as boon-work on the same lands. Total 75 acres 1 rood.

---

60 Seven feast days + one court day = eight days without works x 21½ lands = 172 respited works by analogy with the same calculation in the 1285–86 accounts, not 186. For 186 to be the correct number of respited works, there would have to have been just over 8½ days without works, so this is probably just an error in the clerk's arithmetic. The ensuing totals in this section all use the erroneous figure of 186.

61 This sum total is correct if the number of works respited because of feast and court days is taken as the 186 given in error above. If the corrected figure of 172 respited works there is taken instead, this sum comes to 747 works rather than 761.

62 'Holding' here carries the additional sense 'to hold and control or guide, steer (plough, cart or similar)' (*DMLBS., tenere* (2), (3b)) and refers to the ploughman who ploughed in front of the seed sower.

63 1,831½ if the corrected figure of 172 from the respited works is taken, as above.

Of which, 65 acres 1 rood were ploughed. 10 acres sold.   And quit.

Fallowing. He answers for 21½ acres of ploughing at the fallowing of barley concerning the issue of the aforesaid 21½ lands.   Total evident.
Of which, 19½ acres were ploughed. 2 acres sold.   And quit.

Ploughing for oats. He answers for 53 acres 3 roods of ploughing as gavelearth (*de gablo*) at the season for oats and barley from the aforesaid 21½ lands. And for 21½ acres of ploughing as boon-work at the same season.   Total 75 acres 1 rood.
Of which, 65 acres 1 rood were ploughed. 10 acres sold.   And quit.

Harrowing. He answers for 75 acres 1 rood of harrowing as gavelearth and boon-work (*de gablo et precarie*) at the season of oats and barley. And for 39½ acres of harrowing after the lord's plough.   Total 114 acres 3 roods.
Of which, 104 acres 3 roods were harrowed. 10 acres sold.   And quit.

Reaping. He accounts for 86 acres of reaping wheat as gavelearth (*de Gabl'*). And for 86 acres reaping oats as gavelearth (*de Gablo*).   Total 172 acres.
And all was reaped.   And quit.

Accounts 3. Reeve's Account of William de Higgelegh (1329–30)[64]

[*Membrane 1, face*] Account of William de Higgelegh reeve of Eleigh (*Illegh'*) from the feast of Michaelmas in the third year of the reign of King Edward the third after the Conquest until the same feast next following [*29 September 1329–28 September 1330*].

Rents. The same answers for 14s. 7½d. in rents for the term of St Andrew the apostle. And for 17s. 4d. for the term of Palm Sunday [*1 April*]. And for £1 18s. 6d. for the term of the apostles Peter and Paul. And for £1 9s. 2¾d. for the term of St Peter in chains. And for £3 13s. 11d. for the term of St Michael. And for 2s. from John atte Fen for a new rent. And for 2s. new rent from Simon Tollon'. And for 1d. for the site of one forge at Gedeford. And for 6d. for 2 capons \2 hens/ sold. And for 8d. from John atte Tye for a certain plot demised to him. And for 8d. from Adam atte Tye for a certain headland demised to him at Ravenescroft.[65] And for 6d. from Margery le Forester for 1 rood of alder-carr demised to her as an escheat of the lord. And for 6d. new rent from William de Higgelegh for a certain headland demised to him. And for 16s. 8d. for 20 acres of land in Ravenescroft demised to Richard de Broktone.   Total £9 17s. ¾d.[66]

Customary [*works*]. He answers for 16s. for 32 acres of ploughing released from customary works at the winter season, price of an acre, 6d. And for 9s. for 18 acres of ploughing released from the same at the fallowing of barley, price of an acre, 6d. And for 13s. for 24 acres of ploughing released from the same at the season of oats and barley, price of an acre, 6½d. for harrowing. And for 10d. in respect of 20 acres of harrowing released from the same after Christmas for this year. And for

---

[64] CCA-DCc/BR/Illeigh/8. Parchment roll, two membranes, stitched together lengthways. Latin.
[65] Up to this point, these rents are the same as those in the account for 1310–11 (CCA-DCc-BR/Illeigh/2), although some of the assize rents here are ½d. or ¼d. different from the earlier ones for some reason.
[66] Actually £9 17s. 2¼d.

10s. 9d. for the carriage of manure released from the same. And for £1 9s. 3½d. for 703 small works sold, price of a work, ½d.   Total £3 18s. 10½d.

Perquisites. He answers for £3 1s. 6d. for levying perquisites of the court and view.
Total evident.

Corn sold. He answers for £4 8s. \8d./ for 14qr of wheat sold, price of a quarter, 6s. 4d. And for £7 12s. 3d. for 25qr \7b./ of wheat sold, price of a quarter, 6s. And for £6 6s. 5d. for 20qr 4b. of wheat sold, price of a quarter, 6s. 2d. And for 1s. 8d. for 2\½/ bushels of rye sold, price of a bushel, 8d. And for £4 15s. 2½\¼/d. for 17qr 2½b. of barley sold, price of a quarter, 5s. 6d. And for 2s. for 3b. of beans sold, price of a bushel, 8d. And for £1 6d. for 5qr 1b. of peas sold, price of a quarter, 4s. And for 13s. 7½d. for 6qr 6½b. of oats sold for entertaining [*guests*]. And for £5 9s. 10¼d. for 34qr 5½b. of oats sold, price of a quarter, 3s. 2d. And for 18s. 9d. for 3qr 6b. of wheat sold upon the account. And for 5s. 3d. for 1qr 1b. of barley sold.
Total £31 17s. 2½d.[67]

Stock sold. He answers for 8s. for 1 carthorse sold. And for 10s. for 2 old stots sold. And for 9s. for 1 cow sold. And for <[*?51*]> £2 6s.[68] \8d./ for 20 pigs sold, price of a head, 2s. [*?4*]d. And for 7s. for 28 geese sold, price of a goose, 3d. And for 2s. for 12 capons sold. And for 1s. 8d. for 20 hens sold. And for 9d. for 18 pullets sold, price of a head, ½d. And for 1s. 2d. for 350 eggs sold, price of a hundred, 4d. And for 3s. for 12 dozen young doves sold, price of a dozen, 3d. And for 4s. for 2 hides of cows [*dead*] of murrain, sold.   Total £4 13s. 3d.

Pasturage sold. He answers for 6d. for pasturage sold at Colehog'. And for 6d. for pasturage sold at Bedewelle. And for pasturage \at/ Bifold and of the street from Higgelegh nothing as it is fallow this year. And for 4s. for straw sold.   Total 5s.

Underwood (subbosc') sold. He answers for £1 10s. 4d. for 1,300 faggots sold, price of a hundred, 2s. 4d. And for 4s. for the branches and bark of 4 oaks felled in Manhey for laths for the new grange at Deopham (*Depham*) [*Norfolk*].
Total £1 14s. 4d.

Apples sold. He answers for 2s. for apples sold.   Total evident.

Dairy. He answers for £4 13s. 4d. for 14 cows demised for profit, that is, for the calf and milk of each cow, 6s. 8d. And for £5 for 120 sheep demised for profit, that is, for each sheep, 10d.   Total £9 13s. 4d.
Total of all receipts, £65 2s. 6¾d.[69]

Payments. In respect of which, he paid into the treasury of Canterbury, £42 by 3 tallies.   Total evident.

External [*expenses*]. Given to 1 young man going to Deopham (*Depham*) with letters of the lord warden \on 3 occasions/, 1s. Also given to the clerk of the hundred by order of the warden, 3s. 4d.   Total 4s. 4d.

<*Lodging.* ~~In expenses of Hugh the clerk sent by the convent into the custody~~> [*of Essex*] \because it is in the warden's tally/ <~~2s. for the term.~~   Total evident.>

---

[67] Actually £31 14s. 2½d.
[68] Written over the crossed through figure.
[69] Correct as a sum of the given sub-totals, but using corrected sub-totals it should be £64 19s. 8¾d.

Expenses of the warden and bailiff. In expenses of Dom J. de Valoynes,[70] warden, £3 18s. by tally. In expenses of the bailiff, £1 1s. 2d. by tally. In wages of the same, 10s.
Total £5 9s. 2d.

Corn bought. For 6qr \5½b./ of rye bought for paying the *famuli*, £1 11s. 1d., price of a quarter, 4s. 6d. Total evident.

Stock bought. For 1 carthorse bought, £1 6s. 8d. For 2 stots bought, £1 11s. For 3 cows bought, £1 13s., price of a head, 11s. Total £4 10s. 8d.

Plough costs. For making 6 new ploughs and for dressing timber and repairing old ploughs as task-work, 2s. 9d. For the wages of a smith for ironwork on the ploughs and for shoeing the stots and oxen for the year, £1 6s. 8d. Total £1 9s. 5d.

Cart costs. For 1 pair of wheels bought, 4s. For making 1 cart body, 8d. For 24 clouts with brad-nails, 2s. For 2 collars bought, 1s. For 2 pairs of traces bought, 8d. For 1 rope bought for a cart, 7d. For repairing old harness with [*?hemp or canvas*] (*can[n]evas'*), thread and flock bought for the same, 1s. 2d. For 1 horse hide bought, 1s. For cart grease bought, 1s. 6d., in consequence of the great carriage of timber for the new grange at Deopham (*Depham*). Total 12s. 7d.

Costs of buildings. For carpentry on 1 new door for the oats grange as task-work, 4s. For nails bought for the same, 6d. For 1 roofer roofing upon the oats grange and cresting [*it*] as task-work, 8s. 6d. Total 13s.

[*Membrane 2, face*] *Costs of the mill.* For lengthening the mill-spindle with purchased iron and repairing the cogs and spindle of the trundle wheel (*trendstavum*), 3s.
Total evident.

Mowing. For mowing 8 acres of meadow, 4s., for an acre, 6d. Total evident.

Small [*expenses*]. For 3b. of salt bought, 8d. For certain vines, 6d. For 2 sacks bought, 1s. For ironwork on 1 spade and a shovel, 3½d. For repairing 1 mattock, 2d. For repairing 1 copper pot, 17½d. Total 4s. 1d.

Making faggots. For making 1,300 faggots, 6s. 6d., for a hundred, 6d. Total evident.

Reaping. For beef meat bought for the customary tenants at the wheat boon-work at harvest-time, 4s. 7d., by custom. For herrings bought for the same at the oats boon-work by custom, 11d. For cheese bought for the same, 1s. 11d., by custom.
Total 7s. 5d.

Harvest-time expenses. In expenses of the reeve, reap-reeve and *famuli* for 6 weeks at harvest-time, with the expenses of the lord warden, his colleagues and *famuli* for 5 days, £2 4s. Total evident.
Allowed for this year on account of the long harvest and the long stay of the warden.

Wages. For the wages of one reap-reeve for the year, 6s. 8d. For the wages of one reap-reeve at harvest-time, 3s. For the wages of one carter for the year, 6s. 8d. For the wages of one who is a cowherd and swineherd for the year, 3s. For the wages of one maid for the year 2s. For the wages of one shepherd for the year, 5s. For the

---

[70] Possibly John Valeyns, priory monk, who died in 1337 (Searle, *Christ Church Canterbury* (1902), p. 179).

expenses and oblations for the whole *famuli* for the days of Christmas and Easter, 4s.   Total £1 10s. 4d.

Total of all expenses with payments, £61 8s. 7d.[71]

And thus he owes £3 13s. 11¾d.[72]

[*Membrane 1, dorse*]

Eleigh (*Illeigh*) in the third year of the reign of King Edward III [*1329–30*]. *Wheat.*[73] The same answers for [*an illegible number of quarters and bushels struck out*] \108qr 6b./ of clean wheat of issue \that is, for [*?an acre*], 1qr 1b./. And for 6qr of chaff of the same. And for 3qr from the produce of the mill. And for 2b. of damaged wheat in the corn.[74] And for 1b. [*of the remainder?*].

Total, 118qr 1b. And no more because the rector and *famuli* have 12 acres. Of which were sown upon 106 acres, 33qr, 4b., upon an acre, 2½b. [*and*] 3b. more on the total. For mixing with rye as payment to the *famuli*, from inferior wheat (*de corall' fr'i*), 6qr. In payment to the reeve for the year, except for 6 weeks during harvest-time, 5qr 6b., for a week, 1b. In payment to the reap-reeve for the year, except for 6 weeks during harvest-time, for half his pay, 1qr 3½b. And as much taken from the rye as below. Provided for the clearing out of the manure in the court, nothing for this year. Provided for the *famuli* at harvest-time, 1qr \2½b./, allowed on account of the long harvest/. Also provided for 2 boon-works at harvest-time, 3qr \by custom/. Sold, 60qr 3b. Given as the difference between razed and heaped measure, 3qr. Sold upon the account, 3qr 6b.   Total as above.

Rye. He answers for 21qr 2b. of wheat [*sic*] of issue \That is, to the fourth grain, more than 2qr 2b.[75]/. And for 6qr mixed with inferior wheat. And for 8qr from the produce of the mill. And for 6qr 5½b. bought. And for 2½b. in the difference between razed and heaped measure.   Total 42qr 2b.

Of which were sown upon 12 acres of land, 3qr 6b., upon an acre, 2½b. In payment to the reap-reeve for the year, for half his pay, 1qr 3½b. In payment to 4 ploughmen and one carter \and 1 who is the cowherd and swineherd/ for the year, 26qr, for each of them for every 12 weeks, 1qr. In payment to one shepherd and one maid for the year, 6qr 4b., to each of them for each week, ½b. By custom, to the shepherd at lambing time, 2b. In payment to one [*person*] scattering [*seed in*] the furrows (*spargent' sulcos*) for 6 weeks in the winter, 3b. In payment to one [*person*] for driving away birds at the same time and in the summer, 3b. Provided for 2 boon-works at

---

[71] Actually £61 9s. 7d.

[72] Correct for the given sub-totals but actually £3 10s. 1¾d. when corrected sub-totals are added together.

[73] This section forms part of the outermost area of the document when rolled and so some of the ink has rubbed and faded in places making some parts hard to decipher.

[74] The text here is *de dampn' fr*[*ument*]*is in blad'*, which could imply 'wheat damaged in the growing crop', in other words, damaged before harvest. This supports the idea of bad weather affecting the harvest in this year (and see footnotes for this account).

[75] This insertion is a reference to the yield of crop compared to the quantity of seed sown. In this case, 'to the fourth grain' indicates a four-fold yield, whilst the 'more than 2qr 2b.' indicates that the crop was 2qr 2b. more than four times greater than the amount of seed sown (J.S. Drew, 'Manorial Accounts of St Swithun's Priory, Winchester', *EcHR* 62 (1947), p. 31, citing Elizabeth Lamond (ed.), *Walter of Henley's Husbandry, Together with an Anonymous Husbandry, Seneschaucie and Robert Grosseteste's Rules* (1890), p. 71). According to Walter of Henley, 'rye should yield to the seventh grain', so the yield is less in these accounts than might have been expected, probably hence the annotation. Perhaps the extra-long harvest period mentioned in the harvest expenses above was due to bad weather, which led to a spoilt crop.

harvest-time, 3qr, by custom. Also provided for the dogs of the court, 2b. Sold 2½b. \Total paid, 34qr 7½b.[76]/ Total as above.

Barley. He answers for <25qr 5b.> \26qr 6b., that is, for an acre, 1qr 5b., because the rector has half an acre/ of barley of issue. Total evident.
Of which was sown upon 15 acres, 7qr 4b., upon an acre, 4b. Sold, 17qr 2½b. Given in the difference between razed and heaped measure, 6½b. Sold upon the account, 1qr 1b. Total as above.

Beans. He answers for 4b. of beans of issue. Of which was planted in the garden, 1b. 3b. sold. Total as above.

Peas. He answers for 7qr 5b. of peas of issue. \That is, to the third grain and a half, 5b. more.[77]/ Total evident.
Of which were sown upon 9 acres, 2qr 2b. upon an acre, 2b. 5qr 1b. sold. 2b. given in the difference between razed and heaped measure. Total as above.

Oats. He answers for 132qr 1b. of oats of issue \that is, for [*?an acre*], 1qr 1½b. more than 7½b./. And for 10qr given to the oxen in sheaves, by estimation.
    Total 142qr 1b. and no more because the rector and *famuli* have 12 acres.
Of which was sown upon 116 acres, 50qr, upon an acre, 3½b., less 6b. on the total. For meal for pottage 2qr. For feeding 8 stots from St Faith's day until St Edmund the king's day for 45 nights, 5qr 5b., for a night, 1b. And from the said day of St Edmund until the day of the conversion of St Paul, for 66 nights, 4qr 1b., for a night, ½b. And from the said day of St Paul until the day of St John before the Latin Gate, for 101 nights, 12qr 5b., for a night, 1b. For feeding 2 carthorses for the whole of the aforesaid time, that is, for 212 nights, 6qr 5b., for a night, 1 peck. For feeding oxen, by estimation, in sheaves, 10qr. Sold for entertaining the warden, 5qr 5½b. Sold by the bailiff, 1qr 1b. Given to the bailiff of the hundred, 1qr. Sold, 34qr 5½b. Given in the difference between razed and heaped measure, 8qr 5b., on account of which the bushels have accumulated. \Total fodder 29qr.[78]/ Total as above.

Stock Account

Carthorses. He answers for 2 carthorses of the remainders. And for 1 bought.
Total 3.
Of which 1 sold. And there remain 2 carthorses.

Stots. He answers for 8 stots of the remainders. And for 2 bought. Total 10.
Of which 2 were sold. And there remain 8 stots.

Oxen. He answers for 8 oxen of the remainders. And there remain 8 oxen.

Bulls. He answers for 1 bull of the remainders. And there remains 1 bull.

Cows. He answers for 14 cows of the remainders. And for 3 bought. Total 17.
Of which, 2 [*died*] of murrain. 1 sold. Total 3. And there remain 14 cows.

Sheep. He answers for 120 sheep of the remainders, demised for profit.
And there remain 120 sheep.

---

[76] Inserted in the margin, to the left of this paragraph.
[77] A reference to the yield again (see earlier footnote), which here is 5b. more than 3½ times the seed sown. According to Walter of Henley, peas should have yielded 'to the sixth grain' (i.e. a six-fold yield), so here again, the crop shows a reduction from the expected norm.
[78] Inserted in the margin, to the left of this paragraph.

Boars. He answers for 1 boar of the remainders. And for 1 recruited from the piglets of the remainders. Total 2
Of which 1 [*died*] of murrain. And there remains 1 boar.

[*Membrane 2, dorse*]
Sows. He answers for 2 sows of the remainders. And there remain 2 sows.

Pigs. He answers for 8 pigs of the remainders. And for 23 recruited from the piglets of the remainders. Total 31.
Of which 20 were sold. And there remain 11 pigs.

Piglets of the remainders. He answers for 24 piglets of the remainders. Of which, 1 was recruited into the boars and 23 into the pigs. And none remain.

Piglets of issue. He answers for 23 piglets of issue. Total evident.
And there remain 23 piglets, of which 13 were half a year old and 10 are suckling.

Peahens. He answers for 1 peahen of the remainders. And [*it died*] of murrain.
And none remain.

Geese. He answers for 2 ganders, 6 geese of the remainders. And for 30 of issue Total 38.
Of which, of issue, for the household, 2. Sold, 28.
And there remain 2 ganders, 6 geese.

Capons. He answers for 12 capons of the remainders. And for 12 made from the pullets of issue. Total 24.
Of which, 12 sold. And there remain 12 capons.

Hens. He answers for 1 cockerel, 8 hens of the remainders. And for 20 from the pullets. Total 29.
Of which, 20 were sold. And there remain 1 cockerel, 8 hens.

Pullets. He answers for 50 pullets of issue. Of which, 12 were made capons. 18 sold.
And there remain 20 pullets.

Eggs. He answers for 350 eggs of issue. And sold as earlier [in this account].

Doves. He answers for 12 dozen doves of issue. And sold as earlier [in this account].

Hides. He answers for the hides of 2 cows [*dead*] of murrain.
And sold as earlier [*in this account*].

Works Account

Works. He answers for 262 works from the issue of 17½ lands from the feast of St Michael until Pentecost, that is, from each land, for the same time, 15 works. And for 52 works from the issue of 4 lands for the same time, that is, from each land, 13 works. And for 946 works from the issue of the aforesaid 21½ lands from the Thursday in the week of Pentecost [*Thursday, 31 May 1330*] until the first day of August, for 8 weeks and 4 days for this year,[79] that is, from each land for each week, 5 works. And for 39 works at Christmas from the issue of the aforesaid lands. And for 400 works from the issue of 5 mondaylands for the year, that is, from each land 80 works. And for 48 works from the half-land of Wolmer for the year. And for 37

---

[79] The interval is actually eight weeks and six days, for which time period the calculation is correct.

works from the half-land of John atte Fen for the year. And for 96 works from the land Colehog and of Agnes the widow for the year. And for 6 works from the land of Robert Sacrist, William de Finchelegh, Robert Fuller, Philip Scarlet and John Babbe for help at Skippesmed. Total 1,886 works

Allowances. Of which, in allowances from the aforesaid 21½ lands for 3 feast days and for 1 court held on working days in this year between Pentecost and the first day of August, 86 works, that is, for each land, for each day, 1 work. Total evident.

Threshing. For threshing 111qr 3b. of wheat, \4b. of beans/, 358½ works, for a work, 2½b. For threshing 21qr 2b. of rye and 7qr 5b. of peas, 52 works, for a work, 4½b. For threshing 25qr 5b. of barley, 41 works, for a work, 5b. For threshing 126qr 6b. of oats, 135 works, for a work, 7½b. Total 586½ works.

Expenses of works. For making water courses, 16 works. For holding the plough while the sower sowed, 10 works. For mixing manure with earth, 36 works. For spreading manure, 8d. For making lute for ridging the oats grange, 4 works. For making gateways around Manhey, 8d. For making 40 perches of new ditch around woods at Hitcham (*Hecham*), 80 works. For scouring 40 perches of ditch at Le Fen, 40 works. For scouring 20 perches at Holemed, 20 works. For weeding corn 120 works. For spreading hay at Prestouwe and Skippesmed twice, collecting and cocking it, 52 works. For reaping 12 acres of rye after the first day of August, 48 works, for an acre, 4 works. For binding the same 12 works. For reaping \and binding/ 9 acres of peas, 36 works, for an acre, 4 works. For stacking wheat and rye, 9 works. For stacking barley and oats, 5 works. For stacking peas, 7 works. For 703 works sold. Total 1,200½ works.

Total of all allowances, expenses and sales, 1,886 works.
And quit.

Winter ploughing. He answers for 53 acres 3 roods of ploughing as gavelearth (*de gablo*) in the winter season concerning the issue of the aforesaid \21½/ lands. And for 21½ acres as boon-work at the same season. Total 75 acres 1 rood.
Of which, 43 acres 1 rood were ploughed upon the lord's land. 32 acres sold.
Total as above.

Fallowing. He answers for 21½ acres of ploughing for the fallowing of barley.
Total evident.
Of which, 3½ acres are ploughed upon the lord's land. 18 acres sold. And quit.

Ploughing for oats. He answers for 53 acres 3 rods ploughing as gavelearth (*de gablo*) at the season of oats and barley from the issue of the aforesaid 21½ lands. And for 21½ acres of ploughing as boon-work at the same season.
Total 75 acres 1 rood.
Of which, 51 acres 1 rood are ploughed. 24 acres sold. And quit.

Reaping. Let it be remembered concerning 87 acres of reaping wheat as gavelearth (*de gablo*) from the said 21½ lands, that is from each land, 4 acres. And concerning 43 acres of reaping wheat as boon-work at the same season from the aforesaid lands, that is, from each land, 2 acres. And for 86 acres reaping as gavelearth (*de gablo*) at the season of oats and barley. And for 43 acres of reaping as boon-work at the same season.

Total 258 acres. And all reaped upon the lord's land.
Eleigh (*Yllegh*)

Accounts 4. Serjeant's Account of Robert Framesden (1358–59)[80]

[*Membrane 1, face*] *Eleigh* (*Illegh*). Account of Robert Framesden, serjeant there from the feast of St Michael the archangel in the 32nd year of the reign of King Edward the third until the same feast next following for one whole year [*29 September 1358–28 September 1359*].

Rents. The same answers for 14s. 7½d. received for rents of the term of St Andrew the apostle. And for 17s. 4d. for rents of the term of Palm Sunday [*14 April*]. And for £1 18s. 6d. for rents of the term of the apostles Peter and Paul. And for £1 9s. 2¾d. for the term of St Peter in chains. And for £3 13s. 11½d. for the term of St Michael. And for 2s. for the rent of John ate Fen for the term of St Michael. And for 2s. for the rent of Simon Tollelone for the same term. And for 1d. for the site of a certain forge at Gedeford for the same \term/. And for 6d. for 2 capons and 2 hens for the same term. And for 8d. from John ate Tye for a certain plot demised to him. And for \8½d./ from Adam ate Tye for a certain plot at Ravenescroft. And for 1s. from Robert Gauge for 1 rood of alder-carr which is an escheat of the lord. And for 6d. from William Hygeleye for a certain headland demised to him.[81] And for 2s. from Henry Taylour for 1 rood of land demised to him in the field called Burton which Geoffrey le Smyth formerly had. And for 2s. from Alan Hod for 1 rood of land demised to him opposite \the court/ which was Thomas Clement's and the remainder in the lord's hand. And for 3s. from John Abot for a tenement formerly John Sadelar's, demised to him. And for 2s. from John Clement for a certain cottage at Swyngyldoun' demised to him from an escheat of the lord. And for 3s. 6d. from John Lyricok' for a certain cottage and 1 plot of land opposite the court demised to him which Robert Gauge held. And for 3d. from the same John for a certain small piece of land opposite the court demised to him. And for a building at Gedefford, nothing this [*year*] because it is in the lord's hand.   Total £9 13s. 9½¼d.[82]

Customary [*works*]. And for £1 10s. 6½¼d. received for 733½ small works sold, price of a work, ½d. And for 11s. for 22 acres of winter ploughing released from customary works, price of an acre, 6d. And for 3s. 9d. received for 7½ acres [*of ploughing at*] the fallowing of barley sold, price of an acre 6d. And for 10s. 3½d. for 19 acres of ploughing [*for*] oats and barley with harrowing, sold to the customary tenants, price of an acre, 6½d. And for 13s. 1d. received for 39 acres 1 rood of reaping sold to the customary tenants, price of an acre, 4d.   Total £3 8s. 8¼d.

Perquisites of the court. And for £2 19s. 3d. received for the perquisites of the court for this year.   Total £2 19s. 3d.

Corn sold. And for £2 13s. 4d. received for 8qr of wheat sold, price of a quarter, 6s. 8d. And for £2 6s. 10½d. received for 7qr 6½b. of wheat sold, price of a quarter, 6s.   Total £5 2½d.

Stock sold. And for 8s. 9d. received for 30 geese sold, price of a head, 3½d. And for 3s. received for 12 dozen doves sold, price of a dozen, 3d. And for 10d. received for 1 hide of 1 cow [*dead*] of murrain, sold. And for 1s. received for 1 hide of 1

---

[80] CCA-DCc/BR/Illeigh/21. Parchment roll, two membranes, stitched together lengthways. Latin.

[81] Up to this point, these rents are the same as those in Account 3 (1329–30), although some of the assize rents here are ½d. different from the earlier ones for some reason.

[82] Actually £9 13s. 10¼d.

stot [*dead*] of murrain, sold. And for 3d. received for the fleece of 1 sheep [*dead*] of murrain, sold. And for 3d. received for 2 skins of [*sheep dead*] of murrain, sold.
Total 14s. 1d.

Fleeces. And for £2 5s. received for 90 sheep fleeces sold, price of a fleece 6d.
Total £2 5s.

Pasturage and hay. And for 4d. received for pasturage at Byfold for this year. And for 8s. for hay sold. And for 5s. received for pasturage sold in the meadow at Gedeworth. Total 14s.[83]

Faggots. And for £5 5s. 9d. received for 2,350 faggots sold, with carriage, in Manhey, price of a hundred, 4s. 6d. Total £5 5s. 9d.

Dairy. And for £3 12s. received for 12 cows demised \at farm[84]/, price of a head, 6s., by agreement, with calves. Total £3 12s.

Garden. And for 14s. received for the fruit of the garden for this year. Total 14s.
Sum of all receipts, £34 5s. 9½d.[85]

Expenses

Payments. Of which he accounts for payment into the treasury by 1 tally against Dom Stephen de Monyngham, warden, £16 10s. Total £16 10s.

Warden and bailiff. In expenses of the warden, £2. In expenses of the bailiff, 10s. 3½d. by 2 tallies. In wages of the same, 10s. Total £3 3½d.

Corn bought. For 6qr of rye bought, £1 10s., price of a quarter, 5s. For 7qr of peas, £1 10s. 4d., price of a quarter, 4s. 4d. For 2qr 6b. of barley bought, 19s. 3d., price of a quarter, 7s. For 8qr 2b. of oats bought for provender, £1 7½d., price of a quarter, 2s. 6d. Total £5 2½d.

Stock bought. And for 1 stot bought, 13s. 6d. And for a cow bought, 10s. And for 2 calves bought for the dairy, 2s., price of each head, 1s. Total £1 5s. 6d.

Plough costs. For shoeing the plough horses, plough stots and oxen for the year £1 10s. Total £1 10s.

Cart costs. For 1 new pair of wheels bought for the dung cart, 6s. For 1 new cart made from the lord's timber, 1s. 6d. For fitting carts with axles on 5 occasions, 10d. For 3 axles bought for carts, 9d. For \16/ clouts with brad-nails bought, 2s. 8d. For 4 hurters bought, 8d. For repairing 2 pairs of *Lyns*,[86] 8d. For 1 cart-saddle bought, 1s. 1d. For repairing 1 cart-saddle, 2d. For 1 cart-rope bought, 1s. 4d. For 3 new collars bought, 2s. 4d. For 2 pairs of traces, 1s. 6d. For grease for carts, 1s. Total £1 6d.

Buildings and mill costs. For one man roofing upon the oats grange and *le stanhous* stable (*stabul'*) and the walls and in other places for 24 days, 6s., taking for a day, 3d. For one man hired for 29 days for covering the walls of houses and various other

---

83 Actually 13s. 4d.
84 That is, leased.
85 Actually £34 6s. 9½d. using uncorrected sub-totals above or £34 6s. 2d. using corrected sub-totals.
86 Written here in English, *lins*, *lyns*, a linchpin (*MED*), rather than Latin, which would have been from '*linca*, linchpin, axle' (*DMLBS*).

places by coping and plastering, 7s. 3d. For one old millstone bought, with carriage, and for bedding down the same, 9s. For repairing the mill-spindle, 2d.

Total £1 2s. 5d.

Mowing. For 10 acres of mowing at Prestowemed and Qwattysmed, 6s. 8d., price of an acre, 8d. Total 6s. 8d.

Small [expenses]. And for 3b. of salt bought, 1s. 6d. For 2 sacks bought, 2s. 2d. For 24 hurdles bought for the fold, 2s. For grease and pitch (*unct' et tarpis*) bought for the sheep, 2s. For ironwork for 1 shovel and 1 spade, 6d. For 1 rope bought for the well, 7½d. For making 1,850 faggots, 13s. 1¼d., for a hundred, 8½d. For planting poplar and blackthorn at Oddon and Costodilhech, 64 perches in length, 4s. 10d. For 1 barrow (*barwe*), 10d. Total £1 7s. 6½¼d.

Reaping. At the reaping and binding of 86 acres of various grains for this year by 2 boon-works, that is to say, for beef meat for the first boon-work for the wheat, 4s. 7d. And in allowance for the second boon-work, for the oats, 11d. In cheese bought for the same, 1s. 11d. Total 7s. 5d.

Harvest-time costs. In expenses for ale for the reapers and *famuli* for 6 weeks, £1 4s. 5d. Total £1 4s. 5d.

Wages (vadia). For the serjeant's wages nothing here, because he had extra payment in wheat for this year, because in future years he shall have 1s. 2d. a week, by agreement with the warden, and for stipend, £1 Total [*blank*].

[*Membrane 2, face*] *Wages (solid').* And for the wages of the reap-reeve for the year, 6s. 8d. And for the wages of one reap-reeve at harvest-time, 3s. For the wages for one carter for the year, 6s. 8d. For the wages for one cowherd for the year, 3s. For the wages for one shepherd for the year, 5s. For the wages for one maid for the year, 2s. For food and oblations for the *famuli* on the days of Christmas and Easter, 4s. Total £1 10s. 4d.

Sum of all payments and expenses, £34 5s. 3½¼d.
And he owes 5½¼d.[87]

[*Membrane 1, dorse*]
Eleigh (*Illegh*). Issue of corn there in the 32nd year [*of King Edward III.*[88]]

Wheat. The same answers for 72qr 3b. of wheat received from Richard Forster[89] by tally in razed measure. Total 72qr 3b.
Of which, was sown upon 31 acres 1 rood in the field called Illegh. Also upon 37½ acres in the field called Heyfeld. Also upon 32 acres in Oddon'. In total upon 100 acres 3 roods, 32qr 1½b., that is, upon an acre, 2½b., plus 5½b. on the total. In payment to the serjeant for the year, deducting therefrom 4 weeks in harvest-time, 6qr, taking for each week, 1b. Also provided for the expenses of harvest-time, 1qr. Also provided for 1 boon-work, 3qr. Also for maslin for the *famuli* as below, 13qr

---

[87] Actually 1s. 5¾d., if using uncorrected figures, or 10¼d. if using corrected ones.

[88] The regnal year 32 Edw. III covered 25 January 1357/58–24 January 1358/59 so a reminder (if one were needed) that the 'issue of corn' here derives from the harvest of 1358, at the beginning of the 1358–59 accounting year.

[89] Richard Forster or Forester appears throughout this account in terms that suggest he had been the lessee of the manor the previous accounting year (see Introduction, p. xxii).

4b. By custom, to the sower, 1b. Sold 15qr 6½b. And in the difference between razed and heaped measure (*avantag'*) of the same, 6b.   Total as above. And quit.

Rye. And for 6qr of rye received from R[*ichard*] Forester by tally in razed measure. And for 7qr 4b. from the profits of the mill. And for 6qr of rye bought. And 2½b. for the increment.[90]   Total 19qr 6½b.
Of which, was sown upon 10 acres, sown in various places, 3qr 6b., upon an acre, 3b. In payment to the *famuli* as below, 12qr 6½b. Also provided for 1 boon-work at harvest-time, 3qr. Also provided for the courtyard dogs 2b. Total as above. And quit.
Barley. And for 8qr of barley received by tally from R[*ichard*] Forester in razed measure. And for 2qr 6b. bought. And for 1b. for the increment.   Total 10qr 7b.
Of which, was sown upon 21½ acres, 10qr 7b., upon an acre, 4b., plus 1b. on the total.   Total as above. And quit.

Peas. And for 6qr of peas received by tally from R[*ichard*] Forester in measure as above. And for 7qr bought. And for 2½b. for the increment. Total 13qr 2½b.
Of which was sown upon 14 acres, 4qr 1b., upon an acre, 2½b., less 2b. on the total. Also for maslin for payment to the *famuli* as earlier [*in this account*], 9qr 1½b.
Total as above. And quit.

Oats. And for 54qr of oats received by tally from R[*ichard*] Forester. And for 6qr, by estimation, in sheaves by the same tally. And for 8qr 2b. bought as earlier [*in this account*].   Total 68qr 2b.
Of which, was sown upon 96 acres, 36qr 2b., upon each acre, 3b., plus 2b. on the total. For flour for the *famuli* for the year, 2qr. For the feeding of 2 cart horses from the feast of St Faith until the feast of the Invention of the Holy Cross, 6qr. For the feeding of 8 stots for the same time, 18qr. For the feeding of oxen, by estimation, in sheaves, 6qr.   Total as above. And quit.

Maslin for the famuli. And for 13qr 4b. of wheat. And for 12qr 6½b. of rye. And for 9qr, 1½b. of peas received above. Total 35qr 4b.
And from which in payment of the beadle (*beedelli*) for the year, deducting 4 weeks at harvest-time, 3qr, taking for each week, ½b. In payment to four ploughmen, one carter, one cowman, 26qr, each of whom taking per 12 weeks, 1qr. In payment to one shepherd, one maid for the year, 6qr 4b., each of whom taking per week, ½b.
Total as above. And quit.

Stock Account

Carthorses. And for 2 carthorses received from R[*ichard*] Forester.   Total 2.
And there remain 2 carthorses.

Stots. And for 9 stots received from R[*ichard*] Forester and for 1 bought. Total 10.
Of which 1 [*died*] in the murrain of the month of February, 1 in the murrain of the month of July.   And there remain 8 stots.

Oxen. And for 8 oxen received from R[*ichard*] Forester.   Total 8.
And there remain 8 oxen.

---

[90] *De incremento* here refers to the amount of grain covered by the difference between heaped and razed measure (M. Bailey, *The English Manor c. 1200–c. 1500* (Manchester, 2002), p. 118, n. 46, from an extract from F.M. Page (ed.), *Wellingborough Manorial Accounts, 1258–1323, from the Account Rolls of Crowland Abbey* (Northamptonshire Record Society 8, 1935), pp. 1–3).

Bulls and cows. And for 1 bull and 13 cows received from R[*ichard*] Forester and for 1 bought after calving just before the feast of Michaelmas.   Total 15. Of which 1 [*died*] of murrain before calving. And there remain 13 cows and 1 bull.

Calves. And for 2 calves bought from *le Deye* of which 1 [*was*] male.   Total 2. And there remain 2 calves.

Sheep. And for 91 sheep received from R[*ichard*] Forester.   Total 91. Of which 1 [*died*] of murrain before shearing and 2 after.   Total 3. And there remain 88 sheep.

Boars. And for 1 boar received from R[*ichard*] Forester.   Total 1. And there remains 1 boar.

Sows. And for 2 sows received from R[*ichard*] Forester. Total 2. And there remain 2 sows.

Piglets produced. And for 10 piglets from the issue of the sows, and no more because the serjeant \received/ the sows late from R[*ichard*] Forester.
                                    And there remain 10 piglets.

Ganders. And for 2 ganders received from R[*ichard*] Forester.   Total 2. And there remain 2 ganders.

Geese. And for 6 unmated female geese received from R[*ichard*] Forester. And for 35 of the issue.   Total 41. Of which 2 for the household[91] and 3 [*died*] of murrain and 30 sold.
                                    And there remain 6 unmated geese.

Hens and cockerels. And for 1 cockerel and 8 hens bought around the feast of Michaelmas.   Total 9.
                        And there remain 1 cockerell and 8 hens.

Doves. And for 12 dozen doves of the issue of the dovecote and no more because the serjeant had the key late.   And sold as earlier [*in this account*].

Fleeces. And for 90 sheep fleeces from the issue of the sheep.
                        And sold as earlier [*in this account*].

Hides. And for the hides of 2 stots and 1 cow [*dead*] of murrain as above. Total 3. Of which 1 was white-tawed to use for mending harness. 2 sold.
                                    And none remain.

Fleeces. And for one fleece [*from a sheep that died*] of murrain.
                        Total 1. And sold as earlier [*in this account*].
                                    And none remain.

Small skins.[92] And for 2 small skins [*from animals that died*] of murrain.
                        Total 2. And sold as earlier [*in this account*].
                                    And none remain.

Garden. And from the garden nothing here, because earlier [*in this account*] in cash.

---

[91] The text has '*in menegos*', probably from '*managium*' meaning 'household' (*DMLBS*). It is possible that in this context these two geese were provided for the customary Michaelmas or harvest-time feast.

[92] Almost certainly lambskins, agreeing with the two sheepskins sold above in this account.

Faggots. And for 2,350 faggots made in Manhey, of which 500 were made by the *famuli* and the rest as task-work and sold as earlier [*in this account*] and none remain.

Works Account

[*Membrane 2, dorse.*] Works. The same answers for 262½ works concerning the issue of 17½ lands from the feast of St Michael until the feast of Pentecost, that is, for each land, 15 works, and for 52 works concerning the issue of 4 lands for the same time, from each land, 13 works. And for 752½ works concerning the issue of the said 21½ lands from the Thursday in the week of Pentecost until the day of St Peter in chains, for 7 weeks this year, that is, from each land for each week 5 works. And for 35 works concerning the issue of the aforesaid 17½ lands at Christmas, from each land, 2 works. And for 400 works from 5 mondaylands for the year, from each land 80 works. And for 48 works from the half-land Wolmeres for the year and for 37 works from the half-land of John ate Fen for the year. And for 96 works from the land Colehog and of Agnes the widow of each year. And for 6 works from the land of Robert Sacrist and others for having helped at Skyppesmede.

Total 1,689 works.

Allowances of works. Of which in allowance on 21½ lands for 3 feast days falling this year on work days between the feast of Pentecost and St Peter in chains. And for one court in the same [*period of*] time. 86 works for each land, for each day, 1 work. Total 86.

Expenses of works. And for 72qr 3b. of wheat threshed and winnowed as works, 230½ works, for every 2½b., 1 work. For 6qr of rye, 6qr of peas, threshed and winnowed as works, 21 works, for every 4½b., 1 work. And for 8qr of barley threshed and winnowed as works, \13 works, for every 5b., 1 work. And for 54qr of oats threshed and winnowed as works[93]/, 58 \works/, for every 7½b., 1 work. For one man scattering [*seed in*] the furrows (*spargent' sulcos*) at the time of the sowing of wheat, 36 works. For one scaring off the birds at the time of the sowing of wheat and barley, 42 works. For one ditch newly excavated as works at Costo-dilhach and Oddon', 64 perches in length, 128 works, price of a perch, 2 works. For holding the plough while the sower sowed, 12 works. For spreading manure, 16 works. For spreading and lifting hay at Prestouwemed and Qwattismed, 46 works. For reaping and binding 14 acres of peas, for which reaping, with the mondaylands, 56 works, for every acre, 4 works. For various *brekkys*[94] around Manhey, 4 works. For collecting rods for roofing buildings, 4 works. For digging clay for repairing buildings, 6 works. For collecting straw, 21 works. For the restoration of the vines, 6 works. For one man serving the roofer for 24 days, 48 works. For hedges around the garden, 6 works. For uprooting brambles, 7 works. For stacking wheat and rye, 10 works. For stacking barley, peas and oats, 8 works. For weeding corn, 91 works. Sold 733½ works. And quit.

Winter ploughing. And for 53 acres 3 roods as gavelearth (*de Gabul'*) in the winter season concerning the issue of the aforesaid 21½ lands, that is, for every land, 2½

---

[93] Insertion at this point is written in left margin.
[94] Probably a reference to work on breaches to the boundary around Manhey Wood, although it could imply unspecified work in 'brakes' (*OED*, 'brake, n.2 ... A clump of bushes, brushwood, or briers; a thicket').

acres. And for 21½ acres ploughing as boon-work at the same season concerning the same. Total 75 acres 1 rood.
Of which, 53 acres 1 rood was ploughed upon the lord's land in this year. Sold 22 acres. And quit.

Fallowing. And for 21½ acres of ploughing barley on the same land according to custom. Total apparent.
Of which, 14 acres was ploughed upon the lord's land in this year. Sold 7½ acres.

Ploughing for oats. And for 53 acres 3 roods as gavelearth (*de Gabul'*) at the season for oats and barley concerning the issue of the aforesaid land. And for 21½ acres as boon-work at the same season. Total 75 acres 1 rood.
Of which, 56 acres 1 rood was ploughed upon the lord's land in this year. Sold 19 acres. And quit.

Harrowing. And for 75 acres 1 rood as gavelearth (*de Gabul'*) and boon-work at the season for oats and barley. For harrowing between Christmas and the Purification, nothing for this year because nothing was ploughed. Total 75 acres 1 rood.
Of which, 56 acres 1 rood of harrowing was harrowed upon the lord's land. Sold 19 acres. And quit.

Reaping. And for reaping 86 acres of wheat as gavelearth (*de Gabul'*) on the aforesaid 21½ lands, that is, for every land, 4 acres. And for 43 acres as boon-work at the same season, that is, for every land, 2 acres. And for reaping 86 acres as gavelearth (*de gabul'*) at the season for oats and barley, that is, from every land, 4 acres. And for 43 acres as boon-work at the same season. Total 258 acres.
Concerning what was reaped and bound upon the lord's land, that is, for wheat, rye, barley and oats, 218 acres 3 roods. Sold 39 acres 1 rood as before. And quit.

Accounts 5. Serjeant's account of William atte Hel (1379–80)[95]

[Membrane 1, face] Eleigh (Illegh'). Account of William atte Hel, serjeant there from the feast of St Michael in the 3rd year of the reign of King Richard the second after the conquest of England until the said feast next following for one whole year (*29 September 1379–28 September 1380*).

Assize Rents. The same answers for £29 7s. 4½d. and ½ of \¼d./ for assize rents, works and customary works sold to the tenants for this year for the first time.
Total £29 7s. 4½ and ½ of ¼d.

Cottagers' rents.[96] And for 2s. from Simon Tollelone for the term of St Michael. And for 8d. from John atte Tye for a certain plot of land demised to him. And for 8[d.] from Adam ate Tye for a certain plot at Ravenescroft. And for 1s. from Robert Gawge for 1 rood of alder-carr coming from an escheat. And for 4d. from William Hygelegh' for a certain headland demised to him. And for 3s. from John Abot as a new rent for the messuage of John Sadeler coming from an escheat at the terms of Easter and St Michael. And for 2s. from John Clement for a cottage coming from an escheat demised to him at the same terms. And for 2s. from Alan Hood for 1 rood of land demised to him opposite the court. And for 2s. from Henry Teilour for

---

[95] CCA-DCc/BR/Illeigh/32. Parchment roll, two membranes, stitched together lengthways. Latin.
[96] There are several inked strokes through this whole paragraph, as if to cancel it.

1 rood of land demised to him in the field called Burtons at the same terms. And for 3s. 6d. from John Lyrekoc for a certain plot of land demised to him opposite the court. And for 3d. from the same John for a certain plot of land demised to him there at the same terms. And for 8s. from the same John for a certain garden called Northapultone demised to him. And for 6d. from John Wendecole for Kynggesfen. And for £1 1s. 2½d. for cottagers' rents. Total £1 1s. 2½d.

Leases. And for 16s. at the Easter term from Thomas Marchant for a certain wood called Losewode demised to him at farm. And for 9s. from John Clerk atte Tye for the year for 18 acres of land handed over to him at farm in Sudesele for 40 years, this year being the second, for an acre, 6d. And for 10s. for the year from Nicholas Seg for 20 acres of land in Ravenescroft handed over to him at farm for the term of his life, for an acre, 6d. And for [*9s. 4d.*] from James atte Tye for 16 acres of land handed over to him at farm in Oddone for 40 years, this year being the first, for an acre, 7d. Total £2 4s. 4d.

Perquisites of the court. And for £1 15s. from perquisites of the court for this year. Total £1 15s.

Corn sold. And for £1 15s. for 5qr 2b. of wheat sold, for a quarter, 6s. 8d. And for 16s. for 4qr of rye sold, for a quarter, 4s. And for £6 2s. for 30qr 4b. of barley sold, for a quarter, 4s. And for 13s. 4d. for 4qr of dredge sold, for a quarter, 3s. 4d. And for 12s. for 4qr of peas sold, for a quarter, 3s. And for 2s. 2d. for 1qr 5b. of oats sold for entertaining [*guests*], for a quarter, 1s. 4d. Total £10 6d.

Stock sold. And for 8s. for 1 bull sold. And for £2 6s. 4d. for 25 sheep sold after shearing, for a head, 22½d. And for 6d. 8d. for 4 piglets of the remainders, sold, for a head, 1s. 8d. And for 3s. 4d. for 10 piglets of issue sold, for a head, 4d. And for 2s. 1d. for 5 piglets of issue sold, for a head, 5d. Total £3 6s. 5d.

Hay and pasturage. Nothing for this year.

Dairy. And for £4 13s. for the farm of 15 cows and 1 heifer, for a cow, 6s. And for the profit from 1 cow, nothing, because [*she is*] sterile. And for 6s. for the farm of 6 unmated geese. And for 4s. for the farm of <six> \8/ hens. Total £5 3s.

Wool sold. And for £2 12s. 8d. for 79 fleeces of sheep sold, for a fleece, 8d. And for 9s. 3d. for 111 fleeces of lambs sold, for each fleece, 1d. Total £3 1s. 11d.

Hides and skins. And for 8d. for the hide of 1 stot [*dead*] of murrain, sold. And for 17s. 1d. for 41 sheep skins sold, for a skin, 5d. And for 4d. for the skins of 3 lambs produced, sold. And for 2d. for 4 skins, sold. Total 18s. 3d.

Wood and faggots. And for 16s. 8d. for 20 *lind*[97] sold, 10d. apiece. And for 13s. 4d. for 10 ash trees sold, 1s. 4d. apiece. And for £2 5s. for 1,000 faggots sold, for a hundred, 4s. 6d. with carriage. Total £3 15s.

External [*receipts*]. And for £2 for the cart place. And for £1 13s. 4d. for one old building sold. Total £3 13s. 4d.

Sold beyond the account. And for £2 16s. \8d./ for various things sold beyond the account. Total £2 16s. 8d.

---

[97] Linden or lime trees (*Tilia europaea*), or the wood of the lime.

Total of all receipts £67 3s.[98]

Payments. In respect of which, he accounts for payments into the treasury of the church of Christ, Canterbury by tally, £20. Total £20.

Warden and bailiff. In expenses of Dom William Woghope, warden for the time being, £3. In expenses of Clement Spice, steward, 7s. In fees of the same for the year, 10s.   Total £3 17s.

Corn and stock bought. For 2 stots bought, £1 4s. For 3 calves of issue, bought with cows,[99] 3s. For 21 sheep bought before shearing, £1 10s., for a head, 1s.6d., less 1s. 6d. on the total. For 4 ewes bought after shearing, 6s., for a head, 1s. 6d. For 40 lambs of the remainders, bought after shearing, £2 17s., for each head, 1s. 5d., less 4d. on the total. For 100 lambs of issue, bought at Lawling (*Lallyngg'*) before shearing, £3 15s., for a head, 9d.   Total £9 15s.

Plough [*costs*]. For ironwork on the ploughs and shoeing the stots, with the wages of the smith, £2 for this year because the serjeant is owed 10s. in rent for the smith's lands. For carpentry work on the ploughs, 2s. 8d.   Total £2 2s. 8d.

Cart [*costs*]. For shoeing cart-horses for the year, 10s. For 1 new pair of wheels bought for the cart, 7s. 6d. For new ironwork on the same, £1 4s. For 12 *cartcluts* bought, 2s. 6d. For 2 pairs of traces bought, 1s. 2d. For a white-tawed hide bought for harness, 1s. For 4 ells of beaver fur bought for a collar, 1s. For a cart axle, 2s. For grease bought, 1s. 4d. For 1 rope bought for the carts, 8d.   Total £2 11s. 2d.

Buildings and mill [*costs*]. For 2 men hired for 20 days for repairing, roofing and ridging and daubing the *sepecot*,[100] 13s. 4d., taking for a day, 8d. For hiring a roofer with his boy for 12 days for repairing various buildings within the manor, 8s., taking for a day, 8d. For hiring a carpenter for repairing the walls of the cart stable, 5d. For ramming the same, 8d. For taking up 6 acres of straw, 4s., for an acre, 8d. For hiring a carpenter for making 1 new dovecote, £1 13s. 4d. For 100 nails bought for the buildings, 4d.   Total £3 1d.

Small [*expenses*]. For food and oblations for the *famuli* on the days of Christmas and Easter, 4s. For 2b. of salt bought, 1s. 8d. For 1 wheel bought for the hand cart, 6d. For 1 fan bought, 1s. 4d. For grease and pitch bought for ointment for the sheep with lambs, <2s. 6d.> \1s. 6d./ For milking and shearing 190 sheep and lambs with treatment given to the sheep, 2s. For 36 hurdles bought, 3s. For 1 seed-sowing basket bought, 6d.   Total 14s. 6d.

Threshing and winnowing. For 37qr 7b. of wheat and rye threshed, 12s. 7d., for a quarter, 4d. For 90qr of barley, dredge, peas and oats threshed, £1 2s. 6d., for a quarter, 3d. For winnowing 127qr 7b. of various grains, 10s. 7½¼d., for a quarter, 1d.   Total £2 5s. 8½¼d.

---

[98] This total is right for the uncorrected sub-totals above, but should be £68 5s. 11d. if the sub-total of the 'cottage(r)s' *rents*' is really £2 7s. 1½d. Both sums ignore the 'and ½ of ¼d.' of the assize rents sub-total.

[99] That is, bought with their mothers.

[100] The scribe writes the English word for a sheep-cote or sheep-shed here, rather than the Latin *bercaria*. For medieval sheep-cotes, see C. Dyer, 'Sheepcotes: Evidence for Medieval Sheepfarming', *Medieval Archaeology* 39, issue 1 (1995), pp. 136–64.

Ditching and enclosing. For making 6 perches of new ditches in Mellecroft, 2s. 6d., for a perch, 5d. For making an enclosure around the garden and various other places, 2s. 8d. For making an enclosure around Manhey, 2s. 8d. For 1 wall newly made between the gate and the cowshed, 10s. 8d., by contract. For covering and coping the same, 5s. Total £1 3s. 6d.

Weeding and mowing. For weeding corn for this year, 6s. 8d. For mowing 7 acres of meadow at Prestowe, 4s. 8d., for an acre, 8d. For spreading, gathering and lifting the same, 2s. For mowing 5 acres at [*?Ronweyn*], 3s. 4d., for an acre, 8d. For spreading, gathering and lifting the same, 2s. Total 18s. 8d.

Expenses of boon-works. For expenses of boon-works, nothing for this year because the customary works are in cash as above.

[*Membrane 2, stitched below the first, face*]
Reaping. For 23 acres of wheat, 18 acres of mixed corn, 30 acres of peas and 27 acres of oats, in total 98 acres, reaped and bound, £3 5s. 4d., for an acre, 8d. For 20 acres of barley, reaped and bound, £1, for an acre, 1s. Total £4 5s. 4d.

Harvest-time [*expenses*]. For the expenses of the serjeant, hayward, one reap-reeve and of others of the *famuli* for 4 weeks during harvest-time, £1 10s. For the wages of one reap-reeve, <5s.> \4s./. For 8 pairs of gloves bought, 1s. 4d.
Total £1 15s. 4d.

Wages (*vadia*). For the wages of the serjeant for the year, except the 4 weeks at harvest-time since he was then given food allowance, £2 16s., taking for a week, 1s. 2d. For the stipend of the same for the year, £1. Total £3 16s.

Wages (*solid'*). For the wages of the reap-reeve for the year, 10s. For the wages of the carter for the year, 10s. For the wages of the cowherd for the year, 5s. 4d. For the wages of the shepherd, nothing for this year as the serjeant paid because he had the sheep for the lord. For the wages of the three *famuli* ploughing for this year, £1 11s., because they did not harrow the corn in the field, each of them taking for the term, 2s. and at harvest-time, 5s. Total £ 2 16s. 4d.

External [*expenses*]. For external expenses for 94 days by several men for making 1 new rental, £3 8d. For 10 acres of fallow land 10s. Also for giving to one man making the new rental, 10s. Total £4 8d.

Allowances. In allowance for Sadeler's land and tenement, nothing, as it pays a new rent. Total [*blank*].
Total of all expenses and payments, £63 23¾d.
And he owes £4 12¼d. Of which is respited for the rent of Ralph Walssham, 13s. 4d.
And thus he owes net[101] £ 3 7s. 8¼d.

Also he owes £1 1s. for arrears for the first year of King Richard [*II, 1377-78*].
And thus he owes net £4 8s. 8¼d.

[*Membrane 1, dorse*] Eleigh (*Illegh'*).
Issues of the corn there in the 3rd year of the reign of King Richard the second after the Conquest [*1379–80*]

---

[101] *Et sic debet de claro.* This translation follows Harvey, *Manorial Records of Cuxham* (1976), p. 55.

[*Wheat*][102] The serjeant answers for 36qr 7b. of wheat from the issue of 52 acres sown in the year, valued by razed measure, threshed as task-work for this year ... [*illeg.*] ... in cash as appears below, deducting from which 7 acres for tithes and 3 acres for the stipends of the *famuli*, that is from an acre, 7b. and no more ... [*illeg.*] ... mildew (*meldew*).[103]   Total 36qr 7b.

Of which, was sown upon 30 acres, 9qr 4b., upon an acre, 2½b., plus 1b. on the total. By custom, to the sower, 1b. Also for mixing with rye for making maslin, 4qr. For boon-work expenses nothing for this year because the custumary works are put out to cash, as earlier [*within this account*], this year. For harvest expenses, 1qr. For paying the beadle for the year, 3qr 2b., taking for a week, ½b. For paying the *famuli* as below, 14qr. Sold, 5qr.   And quit.

Maslin. And for 4qr of wheat received as above. And for 2qr of rye received as below.

Total 6qr. And the total sown upon 18 acres, upon an acre, 2½b., plus 3b. on the total.
                                                      And quit.

Rye. And for 6qr of rye from the issue of 6 acres sown in the year worth by measure as above,[104] that is, from each acre, a quarter.   Total 6qr.

Of which, mixed with wheat for making maslin, 2qr. Sold, 4qr.   And quit.

Barley /£1 4s.\ And for <42>\48/qr of barley from the issue of 24 acres sown in the year worth by measure as above, that is, from an acre, 1qr 6b.   Total 48qr.

Of which, was sown upon 20 acres, 10qr, upon an acre, 4b. Sold, 30qr 4b. In the difference between razed and heaped measure of the same, 1qr 4b. /and beyond the account, 6qr <4b.> for [*blank*]\.   And quit.

Dredge /6s. 8d.\. And for <four> \6/qr of dredge from the issue of 4 acres sown in the year worth by measure as above, that is, from an acre, <1qr> \1qr 4b./.
/Sold beyond the account, 2qr for [*blank*]\.

Total 4qr sold as earlier [*within this account*].
                                                      And quit.

Peas /18s.\. And for <fourteen> \20/qr of peas from the issue of 20 acres sown in the year worth by measure as above, that is, from an acre, <6b. less 1qr on the total 1 qr> \1qr/ and no more because of a deficiency in the field.   Total 20qr.

Of which, was sown upon 30 acres, 10qr, upon an acre, 2½b., plus 5b. on the total. Sold, 4qr and beyond the account 6qr for [*blank*].   And quit.

Oats /8s.\. And for <36> \40/qr of oats from 50 acres sown in the year worth by measure as above, deducting from which 7 acres for tithes and 3 for the stipends of the *famuli* of which by estimation in sheaves, 6qr, that is, from an acre, 1qr <less 4qr on the total>.   Total 40qr.

Of which, was sown upon 34 acres, 10qr 5b., upon an acre, 2½b. For the fodder of 4 cart horses for the year, 5qr. For the fodder of 4 stots for the year, 10qr. For fodder for oxen (*bov'*), by estimation in sheaves, 6qr. For meal made for pottage for the

---

[102] This section forms part of the outermost area of the document when rolled so some of the ink has rubbed and faded in places, making some parts hard to decipher.

[103] Written in English, from *mildeu, meldeu*, 'fungus growth on plants, mildew; also, blight of any kind' (*MED*).

[104] Presumably by razed measure.

famuli, 2qr. For the steward's expenses, 6b. Sold for entertaining [*guests*], 1qr 5b., and beyond the account, 4qr for [*blank*].   And quit.

Mill multure. And for 12qr of multure from the farm of the mill for the year. And all paid to the *famuli*.   And quit.

Paid to the famuli. And for 14qr of wheat received as above as payment to the *famuli*. And for 12qr of mill multure received for the same.   Total 26qr.
Of which, in payment to a carter, three ploughmen, one cowherd, [*one*] who is the maid of the manor and one shepherd for the year, 26qr, each taking for each 12 weeks, 1qr.   And quit.

Stock Account

Cart horses. And for 4 cart horses of the remainders.   Total 4.
                                    And there remain 4 cart horses.

Stots. And for 4 stots of the remainders. And for 2 bought.   Total 6.
Of which, 1 [*died*] of murrain. Also 1 was stolen by night.   Total 2.
                                         And there remain 4 stots.

Oxen. And for 6 oxen of the remainders.   Total 6.
                                          And there remain 6 oxen.

Bulls. And for 2 bulls of the remainders.   Total 2.
Of which, 1 was sold.   And there remains 1 bull.

Cows. And for 16 cows of the remainders. And 1 recruited [*from the heifers*].
                                                      Total 17.
                                            And there remain 17 cows.

Heifers. And for 1 heifer of the remainders recruited into the cows as above.
                                            And none remain.

Calves of the remainders. And for 3 calves of the remainders.   Total 3.
                                          And there remain 3 calves.

Calves of issue. And for 3 calves of issue, bought with cows.   Total 3.
                                          And there remain 3 calves.

Wethers. And for 21 wethers bought before shearing. And for 36 recruited [*from the hoggets*]. T   otal 57.
Of which <25> \29/ were sold after shearing.   Total <25> \29/.
                                   And there remain <32> \28/ wethers.

Rams. And for 2 rams received from the recruits [*from the young rams*]. Total 2.
                                           And there remain 2 rams.

Ewes. And for 2 ewes of the remainders. And for 15 recruited [*from the gimmers*]. And for 4 bought after shearing.   Total 21.
                                           And there remain 21 ewes.

Young rams. And for 3 young rams of the remainders.   Total 3.
Of which, 1 [*died*] of murrain before shearing. Also 2 recruited [*to the rams*] as above.   Total 3.
                                            And none remain.

Hoggets. And for 57 hoggets of the remainders. Of which 20 [*died*] of murrain before shearing. Also 1 devoured by dogs after shearing. Also 36 recruited into the wethers. Total 57.

And none remain.

Gimmers. And for 35 gimmers. Of which 20 [*died*] of murrain before lambing. Also 15 recruited into the ewes as above. And none remain.

Lambs of the remainders. And for 2 lambs of the remainders. And for 40 bought after shearing. Total 42.

And there remain \1 young ram, 40 hoggets/ and 1 gimmer.

Lambs of issue. And for 13 lambs of the issue of the ewes and no more because 4 ewes were sterile in so far as they were sick. And for 100 bought at Lawling (*Lallyng'*) before shearing. And for 5 added to the same. Total 118. Of which 7 [*died*] of murrain before shearing 7. Also 4 [*died*] of murrain after shearing. Total 11.

And there remain 107 lambs.

Total of all sheep with lambs 200 <four>.

Boars. And for 1 boar recruited [*from the piglets*].   And there remains 1 boar.

Sows. And for 1 sow of the remainders.   And there remains 1 sow.

Piglets of the remainders. And for 5 piglets of the remainders.   Total 5.
Of which, 1 recruited into the boars. Sold, 4.   Total 5.

And none remain.

Piglets of issue. And for 15 piglets of the issue of the sows.   Total 15.
Of which 1 [*died*] of murrain. Sold, 10.   Total 11.

There remain 4 piglets.

Ganders and geese. And for 2 ganders and 6 unmated geese of the remainders. And of issue from them, nothing here because earlier [*within this account*] in cash. And there remain \2 ganders and 6/ unmated geese.

Cockerels and hens. And for 1 cockerel and 8 hens of the remainders. And of issue from them, nothing here because earlier [*within this account*] in cash. And there remain 1 cockerel and 8 hens.

Doves. And of the issue of the doves, nothing, because the dovecote [*is*] in ruins.

[*Membrane 2, dorse*] *Wool.* And for 79 fleeces sold, from the issue of the sheep. And for 111 fleeces of lambs of the issue of the same. And all sold as earlier [*within this account*]. And none remain.

Hides and skins. And for the hide of 1 stot [*dead*] of murrain. And for the skins of 1 young ram, 20 hoggets, 20 gimmers and 7 lambs of issue. And for the pelts of 4 lambs of issue. And all sold as earlier [*within this account*].   And none remain.

Faggots. And for 1,000 faggots made in this year and sold as earlier [*within this account*]. And none remain.

Garden. Of the profits of the garden, nothing for this year.
In respect of works and customary works, nothing here, because earlier [within *this account*] in cash for this year for the first [*time*].
[*Account ends here*]

Accounts 6. Account of Adam Turnour, farmer of the manor of Monks Eleigh (1478–80)[105]

[*Fol. 47v*] *Monks Eleigh* (*Illeigh Monachorum*). View of the account of Adam Turnour, farmer there, from the feast of St Michael the archangel in the 18th year of the reign of King Edward IV to the same feast in in the 20th year of the reign of the same lord king, that is, for two whole years (*29 September 1478–28 September 1480*).

Arrears. Nothing, because he received the account quit, as shown at the foot of his account.

Farm. But the same burdens himself of his own free will with £82 for the said farm for 2 years, that is, for the year ending at the feast of St Michael the archangel [*in the*] 19th [*year of the reign of King Edward IV, 1479*], £40. And for the year ending at the feast of St Michael the Archangel [*in the*] 20th [*year of the reign of King Edward IV, 1480*], £42, as shown by indenture. Total £82.

Cash paid. In respect of which the same accounts for paying to Thomas Humfrey, warden of the manors [*of the Essex custody*] in his progress in the Easter term in the 19th year of Edward IV [*1479*]. £16.
[*fol. 48r*] And to the same warden at Canterbury by the hand of Robert Thorp on the last day of June in in the said 19th year [*30 June 1479*]. £1 16s. 8d.
And to the same warden in his progress in the term of St Michael in the abovesaid 19th year [*1479*]. £13.
And to the same warden on 15 November in the said 19th year [*1479*]. £3 16s. 8d.
And to the same warden in his progress in the Easter term in the 20th year [*of the reign of King Edward IV, 1480*]. £8 13s. 4d.
And to the same warden on 27 June in the said 20th year [*1480*]. £9 10s.
Total £52 16s. 8d.

Repairs. And paid to Thomas Slaughter for making the gate of the aforesaid manor, 10s. And paid to the same for repairs to the stable and cow shed (*neethows*[106]) and for annexes of the aforesaid buildings by an engrossed agreement, 6s. 8d. And paid to John atte Wode, smith, for 6 *Doggis* of iron, for the same work, 4s. 4d. And paid to Richard Baron of Milden (*Mildyng*) for 3,000 flat tiles bought, price of 1,000, 3s. 8d., 11s. And paid for the carriage of 5 cartloads of flat tiles, 2s. And paid to John Goldyng of Semer for 3 quarters of burnt lime, price of a quarter, 1s. 2d., 3s. 6d. And paid to John Rede for 500 *Tielpynnes*, 10d. And paid to the same John for 1,000 *prigge*, 10d. And paid to the same John Rede, tiler, and to Andrew Pilberowe his servant, for 8 days, taking between themselves for each day 10d., 6s. 8d. And paid to John Sonday for splitting 100 laths, 2d. And to the same for splitting [*stakes for*] le Pale and for making 4 [*sic*] gates for 7 days, taking for a day 6d., 3s. 6d. And paid to John atte Wode for 200 *ffyvepenynail*, 10d. And to the same for 5 *Hamys* and 5 *Eyes* for the aforesaid gateways, 5d.[107] And paid for *Bryk* bought for *le Stok*[108]

---

[105] CCA-DCc-MA 6, fols 47v–48v (pencil foliation at foot of each recto page). One of a number of farmers' accounts covering 1478–83 in a parchment volume (201ff.) in the series of miscellaneous accounts. Latin.
[106] The scribe uses the East Anglian dialect word for a cow-shed (*OED*).
[107] Five hooks and five eyes, but above, only four gates.
[108] Possibly a dialect word for the place at the back of the fireplace, or immediately above it (E. Moor, *Suffolk Words and Phrases* (Woodbridge, 1823), p. 400). This entry implies that there might have

81

and the *herth* in the hall, 4d. And paid to Simon Elyot, plasterer, for working about various repairs there for 2 days, 8d. And paid to Peter Ballard for repairs to the wall opposite the churchyard (*cimiterii*), 2d.   Total £2 1s. 11d.[109]

Costs of the water mill. And paid to Thomas Slaughter for repairs to the old mill wheel, 1s. 6d. And paid to John atte Wode for 100 *iiij penynail*, 4d. And paid for sharpening the spindle of the aforesaid mill, 2s. And paid to Simon Kempe for *shredynge*[110] the mill wheel and for repairing *le Waterlane*[111] and *le Coggewhele*, 18s. And paid for *spekynges* bought for the same mill, 1s. 9d. And paid to John Chirche for ramming *le flodegates* for 2 days, taking for a day, 4d., 8d. And for making *le ffate* of the aforesaid mill, 2s. 4d. And paid for sharpening the spindle of the aforesaid mill for a second time, 2s.   Total £1 8s. 7d.

[*fol. 48v*] Total of allowances and payments, £56 17s. 2d. And he owes £25 2s. 10d. Of which he paid upon the termination of this view, made on the 10th day of October in the said 20th year [*of the reign of King Edward IV, 1480*], £9 6s. 8d. besides (*ultra*) 6s. 8d.[112] received for the expenses of the warden and his *famuli* and horses being at Borley (*Borlee*) for one day and one night, that is, the 15th day of October in the said 20th year [*1480*] with the promise of the said Adam for £8 6s. 8d. to be recovered from the same Adam, which promise was not observed. And he owes £15 16s. 2d.

Accounts 7. View of the account of Andrew Vyncent, farmer of the manor of Monks Eleigh (1481–82)[113]

[*Fol. 138v*] Monks Eleigh ([*Illei*]gh [*Monac*]horum). View of the account of Andrew Vyncent, farmer there, from the feast of St Michael the archangel in the 21st year of the reign of King Edward IV until the same feast in the 22nd year of the same lord king for one whole year [*29 September 1481–28 September 1482*].

[*Arrears.*] Nothing, because the first year.[114]   Total nothing.

[*Farm.*] But the same burdens himself of his own free will with £42 for the farm of the said manor for the year, thus demised to him for a term of years by indenture.
                    Total £42.
                    Total of all £42.

---

been two hearths requiring brick, one in the centre of the hall (as was still common at this period) and another against a wall, requiring a fireproof back (*le Stok*), therefore possibly with a chimney, although no chimney is mentioned here.

[109] These figures add up to £2 11s. 11d. not £2 1s. 11d. But the clerk has actually taken £2 11s. 11d. in adding up his total below, so the sub-total of xljˢ xjᵈ must be a scribal error.

[110] That is, shaving off parts of the mill-wheel to prevent it catching when in motion or to make it fit into a space.

[111] The water channel driving the mill-wheel.

[112] This 6s. 8d. has not been used to make the total of what Turnour owes below.

[113] CCA-DCc-MA 6, fols 138v–139r (modern pencil foliation at foot of each recto, earlier foliation at top right of recto is fols 191v–192r). One of a number of farmers' accounts covering 1478–83 in a parchment volume (201ff.) in the CCA series of miscellaneous accounts. Latin. Foredges of this volume have been trimmed, probably during the binding or re-binding process, cutting off the beginnings of the left-hand marginal annotations on verso pages and those in the right-hand margins of the recto pages.

[114] This was Andrew Vyncent's first year as lessee of the manor so there are no arrears to carry over.

[*Cash*] paid. Concerning which the same accounts for paying to Thomas Humfrey, warden of the manors [*of the Essex custody*], in his progress in the Easter term in the 22nd year of Edward IV [*1482*] as it appears in the sealed bill sealed by the said warden.   £17.

Total £17.

[*Lodging.*] And for lodging for the said warden for one day and one night, for his household and his horses.   4s.

Total 4s.

[*Repairs.*] And the same accounts for paying William Maryott for hewing *bord-loggys* for planks, 1s. 7d. And paid for sawing 700 feet of boards, 7s. And paid for hewing *bordstokkys* for a wall, 1s. And for sawing the same containing 400 feet of board, 4s. And for sawing 300 feet of *evysbord*, 1s. 6d. And to John Rannson for *groundsellyng* for *le Cotys* for 3 days, 1s. And for meals[115] for the same, 7½d. And to Geoffrey Hobard for making the doors of the cottage there, 1s. And paid to Thomas Slawter for fixing one beam above *le Mille Dam*, 1s. And paid to the said Thomas and another 2 men for *bordyng* a wall there for one day, 1s. 6d. And to the same for *Groundsellyng, nedelyng*[116] and making *le undirframe*[117] for the long stable for 14 days, 14s. And for meals for the same for the aforesaid time and for those who were present at the time of the raising of the said work, 10s. And paid for *splyntyng*[118] and daubing the said stable and elsewhere where necessary, 3s. 4d. And for roofing *le Carthows*, 2s. And for straw, *Brochis*[119] and *byndynges* for the said work, 1s. And paid for 3,000 flat tiles, 12s. And for 1 quarter of burnt lime, 1s. 2d. And for sand, 2d. And for 1,000 *lathnayll'*, 10d. And for *evisbord nayll* and *spekyngez*, 4d. And for tiling on the small house facing the street, 4s. And for 5,000 *Tielpynnez*, 9d. And for daubing the said house and *le Cotys* abovesaid, 1s. 6d. And for keys for the doors of *le* [*fol. 139r*] *Cotes* and for the wall, 1s. And for hooks, hinges and staples (*hamyis, henges & stapill'*) for the same, 1s. And for nails, (*clav'*), hasps and staples (*haspys & stapill'*) for *le Byfold gate, le Poundgate & le East Cartegate*, 8d. And for [*blank, ?two words omitted*] the well there, 1s. 4d. And for 5 *stoklokes* for the doors, 2s. And for carriage of timber for the aforesaid long stable and for the labour of me and my men at various times in the autumn, labouring about the said stable, 5s. And for 1 millstone bought for the mill there, £2 10s. And for carriage of the same, 3s. 4d. And for construction and ramming concerning the *le milledam*, 10d. And for my expenses carrying the court rolls from Eleigh (*Illeigh*) to Canterbury, 4s. And paid to Thomas Groundshewe for his expenses towards London and for one hired horse, 3s. 4d.   Total £7 3s. 9½d.

Total paid and allowed, £24 7s. 9½d.

---

[115] *Mensam*, literally 'table' or food and drink, in the sense of 'bed and board'.

[116] *Nedelyng*, which looks like a specialist English word inserted in the Latin text. The *MED* and *OED* suggest 'something done of necessity' or 'with force', but the *DMLBS*'s 'nedelum, a post used as a temporary support for a wall' makes more sense, in which case a Latin word has been anglicised and should be read here as 'supporting'.

[117] *Le undirframe*, presumably an under-frame or foundation frame. Since a number of people were present at the raising of the building, this could refer to the basic box-framing of the whole building, which would require communal effort to raise and join it together.

[118] *OED*, 'to cover, furnish or construct with splints or thin strips of wood etc.'

[119] *DMLBS*, 'broca, -us, ... pointed stick, skewer, ... thatching-pin'. Thatching-pin seems the most likely.

And he owes £17 12s. 2½d of which he paid upon the termination of this view, made on the 10th day of October in the said 22nd year [*of the reign of King Edward IV, 1482*], £17.   Total £7 3s. 9½d.

IV

BUILDING ACCOUNTS

1343 to 1466[1]

Building Accounts 1.[2] Extract from the account of William de Higelegh serjeant of Monks Eleigh from Michaelmas 1343 to the same feast 1344 for one whole year

Buildings (Dom'). And for roofing the hall (*aule*) and oats grange (*grang' aven'*) and cresting (*crestand'*) the same 16s. And for 1 new gateway (*porta*) made at Coufen 3s.   Total 19s.

Building Accounts 2.[3] Extract from the account of William de Hygele serjeant there from Michaelmas 1345 to the same feast following for one whole year

Building costs. For 1 man employed to repair the roof of the dovecote in total, 5s. For nails (*clav'*) bought for the same, 8d. For 1 roofer with his assistant (*auxil'*) roofing the said dovecote for 4 days, 1s. 6d., per day for him and his assistant, 4½d.
                                                                          Total 7s. 2d.

Mill. And for 1 stone (*petr'*) bought for the mill, £1 6s. For carrying the same from Ipswich to Eleigh (*Illegh*), 8d.   Total 7s. 2d.

Building Accounts 3.[4] Extract from the account of Robert Framesdenne, serjeant there from Michaelmas 1359 to Michaelmas 1360 for one whole year

Buildings. For repairing the pantry (*panetria*), 6s. 2d. For repairing 1 gateway, 6d. For 1 man roofing the hall, grange, walls, and other places where it was necessary for 40 days, 10s. taking per day, 3d. For daubing (*dabur'*) the stable, 3s. 9½d. For hinges (*heng'*) and hooks (*hok'*) bought for the door of the hall, 1s. For 1 carpenter employed repairing the mill, 4s. 9d. For daubing the same, 3s. 6d. For repairing the [?] (*remo*) of the mill, 1s. For 1 iron wheel (*circulo ferr'*) for the mill beam (*trave*), 1s. 6d, For 1 [*man*] roofing the mill for 10 days, 3s. 4½d taking per day, 4d. For 1 chest (*arca*) bought for receiving the tolls (*toloneo*), 2s. 6d. For wheels (*rot'*) and cogs (*coggys*) bought, 7s. 1d.   Total £2 5s. 2d.

---

[1] See Introduction, pp. xlii–xliii and Plate 2. The extracts comprising this section are the original translations made in the 1990s by Michael Stansfield. The current editor has edited them for formatting purposes, but they have not been checked against the original documents. Other building accounts can be found within the comprehensive accounts in the previous Section III.

[2] CCA-DCc-BR/ Illeigh/19.

[3] CCA-DCc-BR/Illeigh/20.

[4] CCA-DCc-BR/Illeigh/22.

Ditching (foss') and fencing (clausar'). For 3 men digging and planting (*ponent'*) thorns (*spinas*) in 1 ditch at Sextaynesfeld containing 56 perches for 10 days, 7s. 6d. <del><taking per day, 3½d.></del>   Total 7s. 6d.

Expenses of the chamber (cam'). For 18,000 tiles (*tegul'*) bought for the chamber, £3 16s. 8d., per 1,000, 4s. 3d. with carriage. For 12 quarters of lime bought, 12s. For 6,000 lath nails (*lathenayl'*) bought, 10s. 4d. For door nails (*dorenayl*) bought, 1s. 6d. For 1,500 laths made, 2s. 4d. For 150 nails for corner tiles (*cornertegil*) bought, 6d. For 1 tiler (*tegulator*) employed roofing the chamber, 18s. For 1 carpenter employed to repair the chamber for 6 days, 1s. 9d., taking per day, 4½d.

Total £6 3s. 1d.

Building Accounts 4.[5] Extract from the account of Robert Framesdenne serjeant of Monks Eleigh from Michaelmas 1365 to Michaelmas 1366 for one whole year

Buildings. For a roofer employed on the grange, 1s. 3d. For roofing and cresting the [*grange*] (*gang'*), 5s. For roofing the dovecote building, 1s. 8d. For repairing 1 door (*hostio*), 4d.   Total 8s. 3d.

Building Accounts 5.[6] Extract from the account of Robert Framesdenne serjeant of Monks Eleigh from Michaelmas 1366 to Michaelmas 1367 for one whole year

Buildings. For repairing the mill 5s. 2d. For 3,000 tiles bought, 13s. 6d., per 1,000, 4s. 6d. For 1 quarter and 4 bushels of lime bought, 1s. 6d. For a tiler employed to repair the kitchen (*coquina*) and granary (*granari*), 5s. 8d. For 1 roofer employed for roofing the grange and oxhouse (*boveria*), 3s. 4d. For daubing (*doband'*) the walls, 1s. For boards (*bordis*) sawn for the mill, 4s. 6d.   Total £ 1 21s. 8d.

External (forinc'). For 1 ditch made at Burtone besides the customary works as extra 8s. ...

Building Accounts 6.[7] Extract from the account of Robert Framesdenne serjeant there from Michaelmas 1367 to Michaelmas 1368 for one whole year

Buildings. For 1 roofer employed repairing the hall and grange, 5s. 4d. For repairing the walls of the grange, 1s. For a carpenter employed repairing the grange 1s. 4d.

Total 7s. 8d.

External. For 1 ditch scoured (*scurlond'*) and for trees planted at Sodeselemedwe and at Oddone, 6s. 10d. For 2 gateways made 4s. 2d.

Building Accounts 7.[8] Extract from the account of Robert Framesdenne serjeant of Eleigh from Michaelmas 1368 to Michaelmas 1369 for one whole year

Buildings. For sawing boards bought for the floodgate (*flodgat'*), 6s. For a roofer employed for 2 days, 9d.   Total 6s. 9d.

---

5   CCA-DCc-BR/Illeigh/23.
6   CCA-DCc-BR/Illeigh/24.
7   CCA-DCc-BR/Illeigh/25.
8   CCA-DCc-BR/Illeigh/26.

Ditching and fencing. For repairing the pound (*pondf'*), 12s. For fences[9] (*sepibus*) made 3s. 10d. For repairing 1 bridge 1s. 4d.   Total 17s. 2d.

Building Accounts 8.[10] Extract from the account of Robert Framesdenne serjeant there from Michaelmas 1370 to Michaelmas 1371 for one whole year

Buildings. For a roofer employed for 16 days roofing buildings, 5s. 4d. taking per day, 4d.   Total 5s. 4d.

Ditching and fencing. For trees planted at Oddone, 7s. 6d.   Total 7s. 6d.

Building Accounts 9.[11] Extract from the account of Robert Framesdenne serjeant there from Michaelmas 1371 to Michaelmas 1372 for one whole year

Buildings. For 1 roofer employed for 12 days repairing the grange, 4s. taking per day, 4d. For a carpenter employed repairing the stable, 8d. For a roofer employed roofing the walls, 2s. 8d. For a roofer employed repairing the hall, 1s. 6d.
                    Total 8s. 10d.

Mill. For timber felled (*prosternend'*) for wheels for the mill and the floodgate, 8d. For trimming (*scapul'*) the same, 8d. For sawing the same, 8s. 6d. For a carpenter employed making the wheels and floodgate, 5s. 6d. For making the mill shaft with nails bought, 3s. 4d.   Total 18s. 8d.

Ditching and fencing. For making a gateway from the pound, 6d.   Total 6d.

Building Accounts 10.[12] Extract from the account of Robert Framsdenne serjeant there from Michaelmas 1372 to Michaelmas 1373 for one whole year

Buildings. For a carpenter employed repairing 1 stable, 1s. 4d. For making a manger and rack in the same, 1s. 4d. For a roofer employed repairing the hall and grange with [?] [*satiem*] 5s. 4d.   Total 8s.

Mill. For 1 millstone bought, £3. For expenses incurred in transporting the same 2s.
                    Total £3 2s.

Ditching and fencing. For fences made, 1s. 4d. For repairing the great gateway, 1s. For repairing the windows (*fenistra*) of the kitchen, 6d.   Total 2s. 10d.

Building Accounts 11.[13] Extract from the account of William atte Hel serjeant there from Michaelmas 1375 to Michaelmas 1376 for one whole year

Buildings. For 1,000 tiles bought, 4s. 4d. For a tiler employed with his boy (*garcione*) for 4 days repairing the chamber, 2s. 8d. taking per day, 8d. For 1 quarter of lime

---

9   More probably fences than the more usual translation of hedges, since they are cited here as being made rather than planted.
10 CCA-DCc-BR/Illeigh 27.
11 CCA-DCc-BR/Illeigh/28.
12 CCA-DCc-BR/Illeigh/29.
13 CCA-DCc-BR/Illeigh/30.

bought, 1s. 6d. For a roofer employed for 14 days repairing the grange and walls 4s. 8d. taking per day, 4d.   Total 13s. 2d.

Ditching and fencing. For 1 bridge made next to the mill called Mellebregge, 13s. 4d. For 1 ditch scoured there, 2s. For 2 walls crested, 3s. 4d. For 3 new gateways made for various fields (*campis*), 10s. For iron wheels for the same, 1s. 3d.

Total £1 9s. 11d.

Building Accounts 12.[14] Extract from the account of William atte Hel serjeant there from Michaelmas 1377 to Michaelmas 1378 for one whole year

Buildings. For a carpenter employed enlarging (*ampliand'*) 1 *sepecot*[15] with 1 old building, 10s. For roofing the same, 8s. For 400 laths made for the same, 8d. For 1600 lath nails (*latteneil*) bought for the same, 2s. per 100, 1½d. For 100 other nails bought, 4d. For [?]straw (*straumen*) bought for the same, 10s. For a carpenter employed making 1 new wheel for the mill, £1. For various ironwork bought for the same, 7s. For 2 new doors made for the dairy (*deyr'*) building, 1s. For hinges and hooks with nails bought for the same 1s, 4d.   Total £3 4d.

Ditching and fencing. For repairing the gateway of the manor next to the road (*strat'*) 1s.   Total 1s.

Building Accounts 13.[16] Extract from the view of the state of John North farmer there from the morrow of Michaelmas 1400 to the morrow of Michaelmas 1401 for one whole year

Building costs. For 6,500 flat tiles (*tegul' plan'*) bought, £1 15s. 9d., per 1,000, 5s. 6d. For 10 quarters of burnt (*usti*) lime bought,14s., per quarter, 1s. 5d. For 1 tiler with his boy employed for 21 days tiling in places where necessary, 15s. 9d. taking between them per day, 9d. For 100 laths bought for the same, 1s. For 1 man employed for 7 days cleaning the ditch around the grange and ramming (*rammand'*) the underpinning (*suppositura*) of the same grange with lute (*luto*), 2s. 4d. taking per day, 4d. For 1 carter (*carecta*) employed for 2 days carrying lute and sand (*zabulo*) for the same, 2s. For digging lute, 4d. For 1 carter employed for 1 day carrying timber for the repair of the well (*putei aquatici*), 1s. For nails bought for the same 6d. For 1 carpenter employed for 21 days for 21 days [*sic*] for felling and cutting the said timber and repairing the said well, 10s. 6d. taking per day, 6d. For 6 cartloads of straw bought with carriage, 9s. For 1 roofer with his boy for 8 days roofing the grange and oxhouse, 8s. 8d. taking between them per day, 1s. 1d. For 2 carpenters employed for 6 days for making and repairing [?] (*proseperibus*) and bins (*bynnys*), 4s. each taking per day, 4d. For 1 carpenter employed for 1½ days propping up (*stonchonand'*) and silling (*sellando*) the wall of the said grange on the south side, 10d. taking per day, 6d. For 1 man employed for 4 days daubing (*dauband'*) the said wall, 1s. 4d. taking per day, 4d. For 5 bolts (*seruris*)[17] bought for the doors of the 2 granges, granary (*granar'*) and for the little gateway next to the door of the

---

[14] CCA-DCc-BR/Illeigh/31.
[15] The English word for a sheep-cote or sheep-shed (*MED*; and see Dyer, 'Sheepcotes: Evidence for Medieval Sheepfarming' (1995), pp. 136–64.
[16] CCA-DCc-BR/Illeigh/33.
[17] Or locks, padlocks.

kitchen and for the door of the chamber next to the buttery (*boteller'*) with hasps (*haspis*), staples (*stapul'*) and keys (*clavis*) for the same, 1s. 6d. For 1 rope (*corda*) bought for the well, 1s. For 1 man employed for 4 days repairing the underpinning of the oxhouse, 1s. 4d. taking per day, 4d.   Total £5 10s. 9d.

Mill costs. For 1 man employed for 2 days digging lute for ramming the mill, 8d. taking per day, 4d. For 1 man employed for 16 days for digging, ramming and repairing *le Bay* of the said mill, 5s. 4d. taking per day, 4d. For 13 boards bought for the same, 4s. 8d. For 1 carter (*curtena*) employed for 2 days carrying lute for the same, 2s. For repairing 1 shaft, 1s. 8d.   Total 14s. 4d.

Ditching. For cleaning 16 perches of ditch at Mellane, 3s. 4d., per perch, 2½d. For cleaning 35 perches around Horsfeld, 5s. 10d., per perch, 2d. For 1 man employed for 11 days for cleaning ditches at Mellecroft, 3s. 8d., taking per day, 4d.
                     Total 12s. 10d.

Building Accounts 14.[18] Extract from the view of the state of William Bacoun farmer there from the morrow of Michaelmas 1406 to the morrow of Michaelmas 1407 for one whole year

Building costs. For 2 new gateways made as per contract in total for the outer (*exteriori*) and inner (*interiori*) court (*cur'*), 7s. 8d. For 300 nails bought for the same, 1s. 6d. per 100, 6d. For hooks and doorbands (*gumphis & vertinellis*) bought for the same in addition to the old iron, 1s. 4d. For timber felled for the same, 5d. For the carriage of the timber for the same 1s. 4d. For 1 labourer employed for 1 day for digging the foundation (*fundo*) there for setting (*imponend'*) the [?]gate-posts (*gatstoggis*) and [?]wallings (*sporis*), 4d. For 1 labourer employed for 1 day ramming the said foundation and for carrying [?]lime/lute (*lom*) for the same, 4d. For 1 carpenter employed for 3 days for silling (*celland'*) the small stable and for repairing [?] (*lez mamores*), 1s. 1½d., taking per day, 4½d. For daubing the walls of the same, 8d. For carrying clay (*argillo*) for the same, 4d. For hooks and door-bands for 1 hatch (*hacche*) for the door of the hall, 8d. For 1 carpenter employed for making 1 hatch there for 1 day, 4½d. For 1 hook and 1 doorband bought for the gateway of the garden, 4d. For hasps and staples bought for the old grange and Mellecrofgate and Byfolgate, 6d.   Total 16s. 11d.
Mill costs. For 1 carpenter employed for 2 days repairing the mill, 9d. taking per day, 4½d. For 100 nails bought for repairing the mill wheel, 6d. For carrying clay and lute for ramming the same mill, 6d. For 2 labourers employed for 2 days for ramming *Le Bay* of the same mill 1s. 4d. each taking per day, 4d. For digging lute and clay for the same, 4d. For lengthening (*elongand'*) the shaft of the mill, 8d.
                     Total 4s. 2d.

Building Accounts 15.[19] Extract from the view of the state of Thomas Malcher farmer there from Michaelmas 1427 to Michaelmas 1428

Mill costs. For mending (*emend'*) the cog wheel (*la coghwel*), 2s. 4d. And for mending the bridge next to the mill, 1s. And for repairing the walls next to the

18 CCA-DCc-BR/Illeigh/34.
19 CCA-DCc-MA/132, r.3.

churchyard (*cimiter'*) there, 2s. For nails (*clav'*) bought for the mill, 8d. For mending the spindle of the mill, 1s.   Total 7s.

Building Accounts 16.[20] Extract from the view of the state of Thomas Malchyer farmer there from the morrow of Michaelmas 1429 to the morrow of Michaelmas 1430

Repairs. And for 1 carpenter employed for making (*fac'*)[21] 1 new building for the dairy (*le deiorye*), £1 6d.[22] And for 3,000 tiles (*tegul'*) bought for the same building, 13s. 4d.[23] And for the underpinning (*supposicione*) and daubing of the said building, 6s. 4d. And to sawyers (*sarratoribus*) for sawing boards (*asser'*) for the same building, 2s. And for 1 carpenter employed repairing the doors of the grange (*grang'*) there, 6d.   Total £2 2s. 8d.[24]

Mill costs. And for 1 carpenter employed for mending the mill wheels (*rota*) there, 9s. 6d. with nails bought for the same. And paid (*solut'*) for scouring (*scuracione*) the mill pond (*stagnium*) there, 13s. 6d.   Total £1 3s.

Building Accounts 17.[25] Extract from the view of the state of Thomas Maalcher farmer as above (Michaelmas 1430 to Michaelmas 1431)

And for 1 carpenter employed repairing the stable, 1s. 8d. And for 1 plasterer (*daubatori*) employed for the same, 1s. And for 1 tiler (*tegul'*) employed repairing the grange 1s. And for burnt lime (*calce uste*) bought for the same, 6d. And for 1 roofer (*coopertori*) employed roofing the same, 1s. 8d. And for 1 fence (*pale*) newly made in the court (*cur'*) there, 4s.   Total 19s. 10d.

Building Accounts 18.[26] Extract from the view of the state of Thomas Malechere farmer as above (Michaelmas 1432 to Michaelmas 1433). The right half of most of this account is missing

Building expenses. And for 8 ridge tiles (*festewes*) bought for repairing the grange there ... bought for the same, 4s. Item for 1,000[27] tile pins (*tyelpynnys*) bought ... for the same, 13s. 6d. And for 1 tiler (*tegulator'*) ... Item for laths split (*findend'*) for the same ...   Total ...

Mill costs. For a labourer employed ramming (*raumyng*) ... mending the mill wheels there, 8d. ... of the same, 1s. 8d. And for mending the mill dam ... 4d.

Total 5s. 8d.

---

[20] CCA-DCc-MA/133, r.4, formerly CCA document reference BR LAW 21 (r.2).
[21] Cancelled.
[22] Interlineated.
[23] 4d. interlineated above 6d. cancelled.
[24] 10d. cancelled.
[25] CCA-DCc-MA/134, r.2, formerly CCA document reference BR CLI 55 (r.2).
[26] CCA-DCc-MA/136, r.5.
[27] Interlineated.

Building Accounts 19.[28] Extract from the view of the state of Thomas Malechere farmer there as above (Michaelmas 1434 to Michaelmas 1435)

Mill costs. And for a labourer employed mending the mill dam there by contract (*ex convenc'*) in total, 15s. 3d.   Total 15s. 3d.

Building Accounts 20.[29] Extract from the view of the account of Thomas Malchere farmer there from Michaelmas 1437 to Michaelmas 1438

Mill costs. The same accounts for payments to a certain roofer (*tect'*) and his servant[30] (*servient'*) working on the roof of the said mill <each of them> for 2 days taking per day, 5d. and [*blank*]. And for his servant carrying (*tractant'*) straw for the same for the same time taking per day, 4d. – 8d. And paid for the collaring (*colering*) of the shaft (*spindel*) of the same mill, 1s. 2d. And paid to 1 carpenter for making 1 pair of trundle-wheels (*trendell*), 6d. And for timber bought for the same, 8d. And paid for timber bought for thence making cogs (*scarioball'*), 12d. And paid for making and repairing the mill pond (*stagnum*), 1s.   Total 5s. 10d.

Repairs of the manor. And paid for 1,500 tiles bought for repairs of the grange of the manor, 6s. 6d. And paid for 1 bolt (*sera*) bought for the door of the hall of the manor, 6d.   Total 7s.

Building Accounts 21.[31] Extract from the view of the account of Andrew Shopp farmer there from Michaelmas 1449 to Michaelmas 1450

Repairs. And paid to Andrew Sparwe and John Sorell carpenters employed each of them for 4 days working around the erection of a chamber (*camere*) and for the [*?*] boarding (*le Bierding*) of the same, each of them taking per day, 6d., 4s. And paid for 100 nails bought for the same, 6d. And paid for 1 cartload of sand bought for the tiling (*tegulatura*) of the buildings, 4d. And for 2 bushels of burnt lime bought at Cosford for the said cause (*caus'*), 6d. And paid to Thomas Wright tiler (*tegulatori*) employed for 1 day tiling the granary, 5d.[32] And to the same for tiling the hall and chamber for 2 days, 10d. And paid to John Caldewell and John Rolfe for ditching (*fossatur'*) and [*?*] making (*posicione*) 335 perches of ditch (*fosse*) and [*?*] (*virectum*[33]) around le heighfeld by contract made with the same by order (*precept'*) of the [*monk*] warden (*custod'*) taking per perch, 3d., £4 3s. 9d. And paid to John Dervy and John Rolfe for gathering 2,400 stakes (*stakis*) for fencing (*clausur'*) the same [*?*] (*virectum*), for each 100, 1½d., 3s. And paid for 1 carter (*carect'*) employed for 3 days carrying the said stakes taking per day 2s., 6s. And paid to 1 carter employed for 3 days for the carriage of the said [*?*] (*virectum*) from Fynbarwe [*?Finborough*] to the said work taking per day, 2s., 6s. And paid for 950 [*?*] (*tenet*) bought for fencing the said [*?*] (*virectum*), price per 100 with carriage, 3s. 6d., £1 13s. 3d. And paid to John Caldewell and John Rolfe for making the hedges (*sep'*) of the said [*?*] (*virectum*) by contract made with the same, 14s.   Total £7 12s. 7d.

---

28 CCA-DCc-MA/138, r.2.
29 CCA-DCc-BR/Illeigh/35.
30 'his servant' cancelled.
31 CCA-DCc-MA/144, r.1.
32 6d. cancelled.
33 Probably herbage or hay, given the name of the field.

Memorandum that there remains at Eleigh (*Illeigh*) 9 [*?*]ash (*rowell*) boards, 34 oak boards. Item 2 new braces (*brases*) for [*?*]eaves (*de eves*) weigh [*blank*] pounds.[34]

Building Accounts 22.[35] Extract from the view of the account of Thomas Tornour farmer there from Michaelmas 1454 to Michaelmas 1455 for one whole year

Repairs. And for making new walling from earth (*nov' pariet' de terra*) towards the common way and containing 11 perches, price per perch, 4s., £2 4s. And paid for [*?*] (*lez watelyng*) of the same, 3s. 4d. And paid for [*?*]splitting rods (*sprendel'*) and [*?*] bending them (*bend'*), 2s. And paid for straw bought, 4s. And paid to Richard Grene the thatcher (*tector*) for the positioning (*posicione*) of the same with his servants (*servientibus*) by contract in total, 14s. And paid for making of a new door (*hostii*) and for repairs in the kitchen, 4s. And paid to John Mors carpenter for repairs to the stable for 15 days, per day, 7d., 8s. 9d. And paid to John Norys carpenter employed for 16 days per day 7d., 9s. 4d. And paid for 4,000 tiles with carriage, price per 1,000, 4s. 8d., 18s. 8d. And paid to John Cabow tiler (*tegulator'*) for the positioning of the same, 12s. And paid to John Prikke for 4,000 prig nails (*prigg'*), 4s. And paid to John Norys for making [*?hurdles*] (*clat'*) 4,000, per 1,000, 2s., 8s. And paid for 5 quarters of burnt lime price per quarter, 1s. 4d., 6s. 8d. And for carriage of the same 2s. And paid to John Warner plasterer (*daubator'*), 4s. And paid for sand, 2s. And paid for digging clay with carriage, 2s. And paid for making [*?*] the mill vat (*lez mellefat*), 2s., 6s.   Total £7 2s. 11d.

Building Accounts 23.[36] Extract from the view of the account of Thomas Tornour farmer there from Michaelmas 1455 to Michaelmas 1456 for one whole year

Repairs. And paid to John Norays for 10,000 tile pins (*teylpynnys*), price per 1,000, 2½d. – 2s. 1d. And paid to William Bocher for making a new [*?*]axle (*yaxtr'*), 13s. 10d. And paid to John Aunsell for ironwork bought for the mill, 7s. 1½d. And paid to John Smyth for braces (*brasis*) and ironwork, 4s. And paid for cogs and trundle-wheels (*trendelys*), 2s. And paid for 1 bolt (*cera*), 3d. And paid for carriage of the [*?*]axle (*le yax*), 9d. And paid to Andrew Sparow carpenter employed for 4½ days, taking per day, 6d., 2s. 9d. And paid to John Aunsell for hasps (*haspis*), hinges (*hengis*) and nails (*clav'*), 1s. 6d. And paid to John Martyn and his colleague (*socio*) sawyers (*sarrat'*) for sawing 800 boards, price per 100, 1s. 2d., 8s. 6d. And paid to John Broun carpenter for making a new gateway (*porte'*) at Eleigh wood (*silvam de Illegh*) with with [*sic*] all other expenses by contract in total, 13s. 4d. And paid for 1 quarter of burnt lime, 1s. 4d. And paid for pargetting (*pargetyng*), 1s. 8d. And paid for 2 cartloads of sand, 8d. And paid to John Der for repairs to the kiln (*le kelne*), 1s. And paid to John Aunsel for 1 bolt, 3d. And paid to John Smyth for making a new brace (*brasse*), 1s. 3d. And paid to Richard Meller for making the cog-wheel (*coggewhell*) and the cog timber (*cogtymbir*), 6d. And paid to John Cherche for ramming (*rammyg'*), 1s.   Total £3 3s.[37]

---

[34] This section is all marginalia.
[35] CCA-DCc-MA/148.
[36] CCA-DCc-MA/149.
[37] 4d. cancelled.

Allowances. And the same seeks allowance for 14s. 4½d for rent from William Donton for headacre (*hedacr'*) and others which of old (*ab antiquo*) used to pay per year, £2 1s. ½d. now by agreement (*per composit'*), £1 6s. 8d.　　　Total 14s. 4½d

Building Accounts 24.[38] Extract from the view of the account of Adam Turnour farmer there from Michaelmas 1460 to Michaelmas 1461

Repairs of the mill. And he accounts for (*computat*) payment to William Jacob of Ipswich for 1 mill stone (*lapide molar'*), £2 14s. 4d. And paid to Robert Clerk of Kersey, 3s. And paid to Richard Belcham for [?] (*spilys*) for the [?] (*le goyon*) of the [?]axle (*le extre*), 2d. And paid for the casting (*le castyng*) of clay and [?][39] for the mill, 2d. And paid to 1 carter for carriage of the same, 7d. And paid to John Cherch employed for 2 days for ramming at the floodgate (*le floodgate*), taking per day, 5d., 10d. And paid to John Fowle for mending the ground gate (*le groundgatez*) of the mill, 4d. And for nails bought for the same work 2d.

Repairs of the manor. And he accounts for payment to Richard Couper of Bildeston for [?] (*le moryng*) of the [?]vat (*la fatys*) and for nails bought for the same, 3d. And paid to John Mos and John Deer for hedging (*le heggyng*) around the Manney (*le manney*) by contract in total, 3s. And paid to the same John Mos for 2 [?] (*killen*) hurdles (*herdels*), 1s. 4d. And paid to John Cherche for mending the oven (*clibam*) in the bakery, 5d. And paid to Andrew Grene and John Pilberewe employed for 5 days plastering (*daubatura*) the stable and the walling towards the churchyard there taking per day for food and wages, 8d., 3s. 4d. And paid to Richard Grene thatcher employed for 10 days thatching (*tegend'*)[40] the old grange there taking per day for wages and food, 5d., 4s. 2d. And paid to Thomas Lod labourer employed for 10 days assisting the said thatcher taking per day for wages and food, 4d., 3s. 4d. And paid for 5 cartloads of straw for the said grange per cartload, 10d., 4s. 2d. And paid to William Breton carpenter employed for 4 days making 1 [?]stile (*stile*) in Mill Croft (*le millecroft*), taking per day, 6d., 2s. And paid to Walter Cabawe of [*Brent*] Eleigh ([ ]*nt Illegh*) for 4,000 tiles with carriage remaining (*remanentibus*) in a future year, 16s. And paid to John Sawyer of Ash (*Asshe*) for 3 quarters of burnt lime remaining in a future year[41] per quarter, 1s. 4d., 4s. And paid to 1 carter employed for ½ day carrying sand (*aren*'[42]) 7d. And paid for the casting of the same 2d.

Total £5 2s. 4d.

Building Accounts 25.[43] Extract from the view of the account of Adam Turnour farmer there from Michaelmas 1463 to Michaelmas 1464 for one whole year

Repairs. And paid to Thomas Slaughter carpenter employed repairing the old grange for 2 days, taking per day, 6d., 1s. And paid to John Abell mending the manger (*manger*) together with nails bought for the same, 2d. And paid to John Martyn for sawing 200 feet of boards (*asser*), per 100, 1s. 4d., 2s. 8d. And to John Shus for

---

[38]　CCA-DCc-MA/150, r.1.
[39]　There is a hole here, probably only one word missing.
[40]　*deserviend'* cancelled.
[41]　This phrase interlineated.
[42]　Probably '*harena*, sand, building sand' (*DMLBS*).
[43]　CCA-DCc-MA/152.

making 1,000 laths, 1s. 4d. And paid to John Rowte for 2,000 tiles bought, price per 1,000, 4s. 4d., 8s. 8d. which tiles together with 500 tiles bought in another year will remain in a future year.

Repairs of the mill. And paid to William Breton millwright (*millewright*) employed for 3 days mending the old mill wheel there, 2s. And for nails bought for the same work, 8d. And for mending the flood gate (*la floodgatez*), 1s. 4d. And paid to John Bocher millwright for 23 days employed making a new wheel for the said mill, taking per day, 10d., 19s. 2d. And paid to the son of the said John Bocher employed for 21 days, taking per day, 6d., 10s. 6d. And paid to John Martyn for sawing 150 feet of board, 1s. 8d. And for 200 nails bought, 10d. And paid to Thomas Dunnyng for the [?] (*le shotyng*) of 1 brace, 2s. And paid to Thomas Breton for mending the dam (*la damme*), 1s. And for nails bought for the floodgate, 4d. And paid to John Aschele for ramming, 8d. And paid to John Deer and John Cherche for plastering the walling of the said mill, 1s. 8d. And allowance to the same for the said mill standing vacant and not being occupied for 11 days at the time of the repairs, 1s. 8d.

External (forinsec) repairs. And paid to Thomas Chapeleyn for enclosing (*clausur'*) 240 perches of hedge (*sep'*) at Manney, per perch, ½d. – 10s.   Total £3 7s. 4d.

Building Accounts 26.[44] Extract from the view of the account of Adam Turnour farmer there from Michaelmas 1465 to Michaelmas 1466 for one whole year

Repairs. And he accounts for payment to Thomas Slaughter for making a door (*ostii*) for the sheep-cote (*le shepcote*), 3d. And for nails bought for the same door, 1½d. And paid to John Sumpter and John Chapeleyn for making an oven, 7d. And paid to Thomas Slaughter for making a gateway (*porte*) for the pound, 6d. And paid to John Abell for nails bought for the same gateway, 2d. And for 1 iron hasp, 1½d. And paid to Richard Grene thatcher employed for 7 days taking per day, 5d., 2s. 11d. And paid to William Balard his servant (*servienti*) employed for the same 7 days, taking per day, 4d., 2s. 4d. And paid to John Havell for 1,000 lath nails bought, 10d. And paid to Nicholas Wade employed for 7 days plastering the old grange, taking per day, 4d., 2s. 4d. And paid to John Shelyng for 2,000 tiles bought, 8s. 8d. And paid for the erection of a wall next to the churchyard, 6d. And paid to Thomas Wryght plasterer employed for 3 days plastering the same wall, taking per day, 4½d., 1s. 1½d. And paid to Nicholas Wade employed for the same work for 3 days, 1s. 1½d. And paid to John Bette for sawing 200 of eaves-boards (*evysbord*), 1s. And paid to Thomas Wright tiler (*tegulator'*) employed with his servant for a day tiling the granary there, 10d. And paid [*sic*] And paid for mending the door of the <grange> there, 2d.

Repairs to the mill. And paid to William Bretoun millwright employed for 9 days making the floodgate, the shute (*le shotez*) and keying (*keying*), taking per day, 8d., 6s. And paid to his servant employed for 12 days, taking per day, 6d., 6s. And paid to the same William Breton and his servant[45] employed for 12 days for the same work, taking per day between them, 1s. 2d., 14s. And paid for sawing 700 boards for the said work, price per 100, 1s. 1d., 7s. 7d. And paid for the carriage of 7 cartloads of timber from Manney to the said mill, price per cartload, 6d., 3s. 6d. And paid for a

[44] CCA-DCc-MA/153.
[45] Interlineated.

carter from Manney to the same mill, that is Thomas Friday, 2s. 4d. And paid for 1 carter employed for 6 days for the carriage of the timber to the said mill, taking per day, 1s. 8d., 10s. And paid for the felling of the timber, 8d. And paid for food/fodder (*cibar'*) used (*expendit'*) by the carter, 1s. And paid to John Osteler for sawing 800 boards, 8s. And paid to John Benet employed with his 2 colleagues for 6 days ramming at the [?]shute (*le shete*) taking per day between them, 1s., 6s. And paid for nails bought, 11d. And paid to William Breton and his colleague for mending the top (*capit'*) of the mill, 6d. And paid to William Breton for cog timber (*coggetymber*), 6d. And paid to John Godard with his 13 colleagues employed for 5 days cleaning the pond of the said mill, taking per day between them, 5s. 10d., £ 1 9s. 2d. And paid to John Slaughter millwright employed for repairing the mill for 31 days, taking per day, 8d., £1 8d. And paid to his servant employed for 29 days for the same work, taking per day, 6d., 14s. 6d. And paid to his other servant employed for the same work for 18 days, taking per day, 6d., 9s. And paid to Thomas Slaughter employed for 15 days cutting (*cissur'*) and splitting (*dolatur'*) the board logs (*bordloggez*) and preparing them for sawing, taking per day, 7d., 8s. 9d. And paid to William Lambard for 400 nails bought, 1s. 8d. And to John Prikke of Stowe for 200 nails bought, price per 100, 7d., 1s. 2d. And to the same John for 100 nails bought, 5d. And paid for the carriage of lute (*luti*) with 1 tumbrel for 4 days, 4s. 8d. And paid to John Pilbergh and William Endyrby employed for 4 days for stubbing (*le stub-byng*) the said lute, taking per day, 8d., 2s. 8d. And paid to John Bette for sawing 1,400 boards and splitting (*splittyng*) the timber, 14s. And paid to Thomas Wright and his colleague employed ramming and keying (*caying*) for 2 days taking per day between them, 10d., 1s. 8d. And paid to Nicholas Wade and his colleague employed for 1 day [?]hedging (*sepiacione*) the dam, 4d. And paid to Slaughter employed with his [?] (*trice*) for 3 days helping the carter, taking per day, 10d., 2s. 6d. And paid to Thomas Chapeleyn for enclosing 16 perches of hedge in the Manney, 8d.

Total £11 3s. 11d.

Allowances. And allowed to the same as the said mill stood unoccupied at the time of the repairs for 5 weeks that is according to the annual value of 13s. 4d. – 1s. 4d.

Total 1s. 4d.

V

COURT ROLLS

1305/6 to 1422 and 1545[1]

Court Roll 1.[2] (4 October and/or 25 October 1305, 3 February 1305/6 and 21 March 1305/6)

Eleigh. A court there, held on the Monday \next after the feast of St Michael [*probably Monday, 4 October 1305*]/ next before the feast of the apostles Simon and Jude in the [*partly illeg., probably 33rd*] year of the reign of King Edward [*probably Monday, 25 October 1305*].[3]

Essoins
[*Damaged*] [*essoins him/herself*] of the common [*suit*]   by Geoffrey Pecche.
[*Damaged*] atte Fen of the same   by William Segersteyn.
[*Damaged*] of the same   by William le [?]Haiwarde.
[*Damaged*], chaplain, of the same   by Ro[*?bert*] [*illeg.*].
[*Illeg.*] le [*illeg.*] of the same   by Adam Abot.
[*Illeg.*] le [*illeg.*] of the same   by Simon Chapman.
[*Illeg.*] atte Tye of the same   by Richard Mont'.
[*Damaged.*] William Chapman [*rest of line illeg.*].
[*Damaged.*] Stephen [*rest of line illeg.*].
[*six lines illeg.*].
[*Damaged.*] Margaret le Forester has a day against the next [*court*] to show how she has entered into one acre of land of the lord's fee [*illeg.*] she did fealty. And she has handed over a charter. Therefore in respect of which [*illeg.*].
[*About fourteen lines illeg.*]
[*Damaged.*] [*illeg.*] pledge, William Broun.

---

1   See Introduction, p. xliii.
2   CCA-U15/14/18 (former CCA document number '48826' and incorrect date '1361' written on dorse in a nineteenth-century hand). Parchment roll, one membrane. Latin. Very badly damaged by damp, with several holes and much of the top right section missing. Three, possibly four, courts, probably incomplete.
3   These dates are ambiguous and are estimated on a number of features of the manuscript. The court(s) beginning here should be earlier than the one (or possibly two) on the dorse (identified as the dorse by the annotated nineteenth-century document reference, which implies long-standing rolling, probably from the bottom upwards, based on the greater wear and tear at the top of the membrane). The final court on the dorse is clearly 3 February 1305/6 (34 Edw. I), so this first court must date from the preceding autumn (1305) given the saints' days cited, and be in the regnal year 33 Edw. I (20 November 1304–19 November 1305). The difference between the dates here suggests that either both courts are being recorded together, or that the earlier court was cancelled (although the date is not crossed through) and replaced by one on the inserted later date. There might therefore be either one or two courts recorded under this heading.

[*Damaged.*] It was presented by the inquest that Thomas Ayleward held of the lord [*illeg.*] John son of the same Thomas is his heir in respect of the same [*illeg.*] [*?heriot*] one horse, price 1s. 6d. according to the custom of the manor [*illeg.*] fealty to the lord for entry [*illeg.*].

[*Damaged.*] William Broun [*illeg.*] did fealty to the lord for himself and for Alice his wife for one piece of land [*illeg.*] in a garden which he acquired from Geoffrey, son of [*illeg.*] of the lord's fee. And he showed a charter by which the same [*illeg.*]. And he did fealty for the same.

[*Damaged.*] Sely le Fullere gives to the lord for [*illeg.*] for a trespass in the lord's wheat and forestalling Andrew le Forester [*illeg.*] suit of court [*?*]saving the pledges Simon Donyland and Andrew le Forester.

[*Illeg.*] The jurors present that William Broun \brewed/ and sold against the assize and did not [*illeg.*], pledge, Richard Abot.

[*Amercement*] *8d.* Also they say that Amanda Calle did likewise. Therefore in mercy.

[*Damaged.*] Thomas atte Brok pays a fine to the lord because he did not come to roof upon the lord's grange and thus his fine, pledge, Richard Abot.

[*Damaged.*] Richard Grehound brewed and sold against [*the assize*]. Therefore in mercy.

[*Damaged.*] Roger de Meldyngges did likewise. Therefore in mercy.

[*Damaged.*] Thomas le Koc did not come to roof upon the lord's grange, thus his fine, and he is subject to the lord for service and by custom for \6 years, pledge, John at Church. And it is ordered to distrain [*him*].

[*Damaged.*] Cristiana le Slaythtere brewed and sold against the assize, pledge Stephen Smith.

[*Damaged.*] William Chapman did likewise.

[*Damaged.*] Alice Monckes did likewise. Therefore in mercy and more than once.

[*Damaged.*] William Segesteyn did likewise and more than once.

[*Damaged.*] Thomas le Coliere did likewise. And he did not serve as [*ale*] taster, therefore in mercy.

[*Damaged.*] Sely le Fullere did likewise and more than once.

[*Amercement*] [*?*]*3d.* Ralph Abot did likewise and more than once.

[*Illeg.*] Andrew le Forester did likewise.

[*Illeg.*] John at Church did not come to work, that is, to roof upon the lord's grange and he is subject to the lord's service, pledges, Thomas Cokes and Nicholas Huneman.

[*Illeg.*] A day. By the election of the whole court, Adam atte Hey, Stephen Smith and John de Geywode, clerk, were elected to office as [*?*]chief pledges (*prepositi*). And they have made pledges to come before the Lord Warden at his next coming to receive their office, by pledge of each to the others.

Amercement 6d. Richard Abot, ale-taster, because he has not done his duty.

Amercement 6d. John atte Lane for the same.

[*Illeg.*] Osbert Hothard for default.

[*Illeg.*] William de Boyton for the same.

[*Illeg.*] Mareschal for the same.

[*Illeg.*] Adam Mareschal for the same.

[*Illeg.*] The tenants of the lands of Robert de Brenne for the same.

[*Illeg.*] The tenants that Robert le Sekefayn [*illeg.*].

Affeerors: Adam atte Hey, Stephen Smith.

Total: 15s. 7d.

[*Dorse.*] Court of Eleigh (*Yllegh*) in the 33rd year.[4]
[*Damaged*] in a plea of debt. And the pledges are the aforesaid Andrew le Forester and Adam atte Hey.
[*Three lines illeg.*]

Eleigh (*Yllegh*). A court there, held on Thursday, the morrow of the purification of the blessed Mary in the 34th year of the reign of King Edward [*I, 3 February 1305/6*]

Essoins
John de Geywode [*essoins himself*] of the common [*suit*]   by John son of Simon.
Richard Coleman \[*illeg.*]/ [*illeg.*] and Simon Le Mareschal   by [*illeg.*]
William Broun [*essoins himself*] of the common [*suit*]   by Richard Abot
[*About six lines damaged and illeg.*]
Adam atte Hey, plaintiff, presents himself against Robert Calle in a plea of debt and [*rest of line and next line illeg.*].
Again [*illeg.*] Simon le [*illeg.*].
Again [*?it is ordered*] to distrain Sewall Babbe [*illeg.*] to show how he has entered into the lord's fee, pledge William le Schopland.
Again it is ordered to destrain Adam atte Hey the elder to respond to Adam atte Hey the younger in a plea of debt [*illeg.*] Adam atte Hey the younger [*illeg.*]. And he has a day, etc. And the pledges are John le Koc and Thomas [*illeg.*].
A day. A day is given [*illeg.*] between Thomas atte Brok, plaintiff and Nicholas Honeman, defendant in a plea of debt [*illeg.*] to come to court without essoin.
[*A day.*] A day is given between Simon le Mareschal plaintiff and Nicholas Honeman defendant in a plea of debt until the next court, to come without essoin.
Complaint. Ordered. Simon le Mareschal complains of John le [*?*]Forester of Brent Eleigh (*Yllegh Combusta*) in a plea of debt. And the pledges to prosecute are Andrew Le Forester and Thomas Le Messor. And it is ordered to distrain the said John for all things until he presents himself through a surety to answer the aforesaid Simon in the plea aforesaid.
Complaint. The same Simon complains against Adam atte Tye in a plea of trespass. And the pledges to prosecute are John le Doo[5] and Andrew le Forester. And it is ordered to distrain the said Adam to answer the said Simon in the aforesaid plea.
The same Simon complains against John Skot in a plea of debt. And the pledges to prosecute are Andrew Le Forester and Thomas Le Messor. And it is ordered to distrain the said John for all things until he presents himself for judgement through a surety to answer the said Simon in the aforesaid plea.
Complaint. Thomas [*?*]le Br[*?oces*] complains against Anselm le Bakestere in a plea of debt. And the pledges to prosecute are Walter atte Lane and [*?Thomas le Kok*]. And it is ordered to distrain the said Anselm until he attaches himself to respond to the same Thomas in the aforesaid plea.
Amercement 6d. Simon le Mareschal gives to the lord as a fine for a trespass made in the lord's wood at Manhey with his pigs, pledge Simon Donyland.
Amercement 3d. Adam Le Coliere gives to the lord as fine for making too many defaults of suit of court, saving half an acre of land which the same Adam [*?acquired*

---

4   Edw. I, 20 November 1304–19 November 1305. The heading indicates a continuation of the first court from the recto side of the membrane rather than any new court.
5   Steward of the Essex custody in 1306–26. See Introduction, p. xxv.

99

from Adam] le Fullere of Stratford [*St Mary*] and Katherine his wife, of the lord's fee, pledge, Simon Donylond. And he has done fealty to the lord in respect of the same.

Amercement 6d. The tenants of the lands of Simon Le Wilde for default of suit of court, in mercy.

Amercement [?]3d. William de Boytone for the same.

Amercement 3d. Hugh [?]Buckes for the same.

        Affeerers: Simon le Mareschal, [*one other name, illegible*].

               Total [*illeg.*].

Eleigh (*Illegh*). A court there held on the Monday next before the feast of the Annunciation of the blessed Mary in the year of [King] Edward abovesaid [*34 Edward I, Monday, 21 March 1305/6*]

Essoins

John de Geywode [*essoins himself*] of common [*suit*]   by William Broun. 2nd.[6]

Simon son of Matthew le Mareschal for the same   by John atte Lane. 1st.[7]

Richard Coleman defendant against Simon le Mareschal in a plea of debt

                              by Benedict Aubery.

John le Skot defendant against Simon Mareschal plaintiff in a plea of debt

                              by John atte Fen.

Adam son of Geoffrey [?]defendant against Simon Mareschal in a plea of trespass

                              by Saloman atte Tye.

Adam le Colhirde [*illeg.*] John Alhoc against Robert Calle in a plea of debt

                              by Geoffrey Pecche.

Again it was ordered to distrain Simon Cock until he has done fealty to the lord. Therefore [*illeg.*].

Court Roll 2.[8] (*?c.* 1349–50)[9] *Head of membrane missing, no title, first ten lines of what survives are badly damaged and largely illegible*

[*Damaged*] [*Sa*]leman Donylonde one croft of land containing [*damaged*] William de Hygeleye formerly held for the term of his life [*damaged*] paying rent in respect of which to the lord each year of 1s. a year [*damaged*] and he did fealty. And the aforesaid Saleman [*illeg.*].

---

6   That is, essoined for the second time.

7   Essoined for the first time.

8   CCA-U15/12/19 (former CCA document number '53988' stamped and '37/45' written on dorse in a nineteenth-century style and hand). Parchment roll, one membrane. Latin. Very badly damaged by damp; head and right edge missing. Probably two courts with dates missing.

9   This court must pre-date Court Roll 5 (23 February 1351/52), but not by more than about eighteen months. At this court, Thomas Clement claims his late father Robert's lands and immediately surrenders them back to the lord to have them re-granted to hold jointly with his wife, Cecilia. Thomas and Cecilia sold them on 23 February 1351/52 (which must therefore be after the current court). Also at this court William de Boyton's death was reported and his heriot respited pending further enquiry, which was ordered on 23 February 1351/52 when William's inquest jury was appointed. The number of deaths and enquiries into tenants needing to show their rights in holding tenements in the current court roll are consistent with it dating to around the short-term aftermath of the Black Death, which swept through Suffolk in the late spring and summer of 1349. A date of around the latter half of 1349 or sometime in 1350 seems the most likely, therefore.

[*Damaged*] [*Sal*]eman de Donylond came and did fealty to the lord for land [*damaged*] as his charter more fully testifies etc.

[*Damaged*] Babbe who holds of the lord one cottage and one croft of land [*damaged*] Margery Babbe is respited until the next [*court*] etc. because it is unknown [*damaged*].

Ordered. It is ordered to distrain Thomas le Webbe to show how he has entered into [*the lord's fee*] [*damaged*].

Fealty. William de Walsham did fealty to the lord for the tenements which he holds of the lord in the vill of [*damaged*].

[*Illeg.*] Thomas Clement came and gave security to the lord for a relief as above for the tenements of Robert his father. And he did [*fealty*] [*damaged*].

[*Illeg.*] John atte Cherche came and gave security to the lord for a relief as above. And he did fealty.

[*Illeg.*] John Aylward, Robert Munchensy, John Broun and John Petyt acquired from Adam Skot 6 acres of land in [*Monks Eleigh, damaged*] did fealty. And it is ordered to distrain the other feoffees etc. to do fealty to the lord etc. And afterwards [*damaged*].[10]

Heriot, 1 ox, price, [illeg.]s. 7d. Nicholas Buk, who held of the lord a half-land of land (*demylond terre*), lately died, after whose death [*damaged*] [*widow of*] the said Nicholas asked to hold the said land as her free bench[11] according to the custom of the manor which was granted [*damaged*].

Heriot 1 cow, price, 4s. Ordered. Avice Cartere who held of the lord 5 acres of warland (*v acras Ware terre*), formerly of Thomas atte Tye [*?on the day she died*] [*damaged*] [*heriot*] 1 cow, price as [*written*] before.[12] And for a relief, 6d. And it is ordered to distrain the tenants of the said land to do fealty to the lord [*damaged*] his wife, son and heir of the said Avice.

Heriot, 1 horse, price [illeg.]. Thomas Berard, chaplain, who held of the lord 10 acres of warland (*Ware terre*), lately died, after whose death 1 horse [*?was taken as heriot*] [*damaged*] [*as written*] before. And John, brother of the said Thomas, who acquired the said land, did fealty to the lord etc.

Heriot 1 ox, price 6s. 8d. Thomas de Hygeleye died seised of one house with appurtenances. And he gives to the lord for heriot by his [*?*]free will 1 ox [*damaged*]. And Joan, wife of the same Thomas, who holds the said house as her free bench according [*to the custom of the manor*] etc. did fealty to the lord etc.

[*Ordered*]. It is ordered to distrain Adam Serviant and Basilia his wife and Joan sister of the same Adam to show how they have entered [*damaged*].

Fine 2s. 6d. Thomas Sparwe gives to the lord as a fine for licence to marry Agnes his daughter outside the vill as [*written*] before.

Fine 2s. John Gauge gives to the lord as a fine for the same for Roisia his \daughter/ within the vill as [*written*] before.

Ordered. It is ordered to distrain John \afterwards he did fealty[13]/ Hoberd of Kettlebaston to show how he has entered into the lord's fee and to make his homage to the lord [*damaged*].

Again (*adhuc*), it is ordered to distrain Alan atte Hel to show how he has entered into the lord's fee and to make fealty to the lord etc.

---

10 This sentence is in a different hand in different ink, so probably added later.
11 A widow's right of her deceased husband's property during her lifetime, analogous to dower.
12 That is, in the margin.
13 Added in another hand later.

Heriot. Again, the heriot which is subject to demand after the death of William de Boyton, as is evident in the court aforesaid [*damaged*] [*?respited*].

Again, the heriot exacted after the death of Margery le Parker, as is evident in the same court aforesaid, respited, etc.

Ordered. Again, it is ordered to distrain <Thomas> \John[14]/ Berard and \his/ associates with him \and he did fealty[15]/ [*damaged*] to show etc. And he did fealty etc. And [*damaged*].

Again, it is ordered to take back into the lord's hand 2 cottages with their appurtenances which Cecilia Babbe held of the lord [*damaged*].

[*Illeg.*] And to distrain Robert Munchensy John Broun and John Petit to do fealty to the lord etc. [*damaged*]

Amercements 2s. 9d. Ralph Swyft \3d./, John Huberd \3d./, John Berard \3d./, Margaret Boyton \3d./, Alice Chapman \3d./ [*damaged*], Simon Chapman \3d./, Roberty Munchensy \3d./, Ralph Swyft, Thomas le Rede \3d./, Robert Wulfare \3d./, William [*damaged*] \3d./, for default of suit of court, in mercy.

Amercements 5s. John Donylonde \6d./ puts himself [*in mercy*] for trespassing in the lord's [*illeg.*] with various of his animals. John Sparwe \3d./ for the same there. [?] Adam \[?]1d./ [*damaged*] there. Katherine atte Fen \2d./ for the same there. Simon de Lelesey \4d./ for the same with his animals in the lord's wheat. [*Illeg.*] [*?*]2d [*damaged*] there. Lucy de Beche \2d./ for the same there. Adam Cut \2d./ for the same there with 1 cow. The executors \3d./ of William de Hygel[*eye*] [*damaged*] [*for the same*] in the lord's rye and Michael de Bures \2d./ for the same in the lord's wheat with 2 oxen.

Amercements 6d. Robert Gaugge \3d./ and[16] John Sparwe \3d./ ale tasters because they did not do their duty, in mercy.

Amercements 4s. 5d. John Broun \3d./, Hugh le Skynnere \3d./, Adam Cobold \3d./, Thomas le Melnere \4d./, Thomas [*?atte Tye*] \3d./, [*?Robert Gauge*] \3d./ [*damaged*] Personn \3d./, Richard de Halle \3d./, Adam Pikke \3d./, Matilda Heyward \3d./, John Clement \3d./, William Fant \3d./, John [*damaged*] \3d./, Nicholas Joseph \4d./ brewed and sold against the assize. Therefore the same in mercy. Also John [*?Lacy \3d./*] likewise. William [*damaged*] \3d./ [*?likewise*] … Puddyng.

Amercements 9d. Robert Gauge \3d./, William Personn \3d./, Richard de Halle \3d./ for baking against the assize.

Amercement 1d. John [*sic*] Lacy because [*he is a*] regrator (*regratatrix*)[17] of ale against the assize.

Memorandum that Sir Edmund de Cranele granted to Robert Gauge and John le Clerk 2½ acres of land [*damaged*] to the use of the prior of the church of Christ, Canterbury and the convent of the same place, which certain [*damaged*].

[*Illeg. total*]

[*Dorse*] [*Damaged. At least two lines illeg.*]

[*Damaged*] [*?To this court*] came John Huberd and showed a charter by which he acquired from Henry Bererad [*damaged*] land of the lord's fee. And he did fealty.

---

14 Added in a different hand and ink later.
15 Added in a different hand and ink later.
16 Repeated.
17 The name is clearly written as the masculine *Johannes*, and he appears elsewhere in the Monks Eleigh records, but the Latin for regrator is equally clearly written in the feminine, *regratatrix*.

[*Damaged*] [*?To this court came Sayer ate Wayour*] and showed his charter by which he acquired from Alice le [*damaged*]. And he did fealty.

[*Four lines too damaged to make sense of.*]

[*Damaged*] Robert Clement died seised of 2½ acres of land [*damaged*] Thomas his son and heir did fealty.

[*Damaged*] [*?ate Cherch*] died seised of 1 messuage and 7 acres of land [*damaged*] [*?his heir and*] did fealty.

[*Damaged*] did fealty for a tenement acquired from James le Melnere.

[*Damaged*] Margaret his wife did fealty for a tenement acquired from Adam Cut and Thomas [*damaged*].

[*Damaged*] Thomas Clement and [*no blank space, no name*] surrendered into the lord's hand one cottage [*damaged*] of the said Thomas and Cecilia his wife and took the said cottage [*illeg. damaged*] [*?for his life*] to him and his heirs according to the custom of the manor and they gave as a fine as [*written*] before. And they did fealty.

[*Damaged*] [*?to distrain Nicholas le*] Foster to do fealty for a tenement acquired from Edmund de Cranele.

[*Damaged*] It is ordered to distrain William son of Leticia de Gaywod for a tenement acquired from Nicholas le Taylour and John [*?*]Berchalk, John [*?*]Fost, William Bentleye and John Whyteplays for the tenement formerly of William de Berton [*damaged*] le Webbe \afterwards did fealty/ to show how, etc. Robert Munchasy', John Petyt [*damaged*] [*?for a tenement formerly of Adam*] Skot. And Alan atte Helle \and he did fealty/ to show, etc.

[*Damaged*] [*?The lord granted*] out of his hand 1 rood of land with 1 house built on it which was formerly of Peter Bray [*?to Robert*] Offrey to have and to hold of the lord, by the rod, to the aforesaid Robert, his heirs and assigns for service [*damaged*] owed etc. And he gave to the lord as a fine as [*written*] before. And he did fealty.

[*Damaged*] Margaret Babbe respited to respond until the next [*court*] because she has entered into tenements which [*illeg.*] etc.

[*Damaged*] Ralph Swyt \3d./, John Broseyhard \3d./, Edmund Beneyt \3d./, Adam Maschal, chaplain \3d./, John Buk \3d./, [*?*]Robert Padebrok \3d./, Robert Munchasy \3d./ and Ralph Swyt \3d./, Robert Munchasy, John Chapman \3d./ for default of suit of court, in mercy.

[*Damaged*] Thomas le Webbe is distrained to show how he entered into the lord's fee [*illeg.*] to show how he and the widow of Thomas Gauge and Walter [*illeg.*] etc.

[*Illeg.*] At this court it is declared that the land which was given to Robert Gauge and John Clerk by Sir Edmund de Cranele to the use of the lord prior of Christ [*Church*], Canterbury, was sold by the said Robert and John to John Broke for £1 2s. 6d. And it is ordered to distrain the aforesaid John atte Broke to do fealty.

Total of this court £1 13s. 3¼d.

Court Roll 3.[18] (*c.* 1350–51–1350/51: probably some weeks before 24 January 1350/51 and 19 March 1350/51)[19] Much of the head including title missing with severe damage from damp to the top quarter of the roll. First twenty or so lines completely illegible

[*Illeg.*] Nicholas Higeleygh for trespassing in the lord's wheat [*illeg.*].

[*Illeg.*] John Donilond for trespassing in the lord's wheat [*illeg.*].

[*Illeg.*] John Sparwe for trespassing there [*illeg.*].

[*Illeg.*] John Mundham for trespassing in the lord's corn at Oddon [*illeg.*].

[*Illeg.*] Nicholas [*illeg.*] for trespassing [*illeg.*] It is ordered [*illeg.*].

[*Illeg.*] Nicholas Higleygh for trespassing with his pigs in the lord's peas. It is ordered [*illeg.*].

[*Illeg.*] The same Nicholas in the lord's peas at [*?*]Bradefield [*illeg.*].

[*Illeg.*] Simon de Leleseye for the same there. It is ordered [*illeg.*].

[*Illeg.*] [*?*]Master John for the same there. It is ordered [*illeg.*].

[*Illeg.*] John Sparwe \3d./, Robert Gauge \3d./, tasters of ale because they do not do their duty [*illeg.*].

[*Illeg.*] John Dul \6d./, Adam Spencer \6d./, William Vant \3d./, John Brisete \3d./, John Liricok \3d./, Robert Gauge \3d./, [*damaged*] Nicholas Josep \puts himself [*in mercy*]/, Thomas Clement \6d./, John Greigrom \3d./, William Person \[*illeg.*]d./, Adam Pikk \3d./, brewers and have broken the assize.

[*Illeg.*] Robert Gauge \3d./, John Greigrom \3d./, bakers and have broken the assize [*illeg.*]

Total of this court 10s. besides the value of 3qr 4b. of wheat and [*illeg.*]

Eleigh (*Illeigh*). A court there held on the Saturday next after the feast of St Gregory in the 25th year of the reign of King Edward the Third [*Saturday, 19 March 1350/51*]

[*Essoins*]

[*Illeg.*] [*essoins him/herself*] of common [*suit*]	[*illeg.*]
[Illeg.] de Leleseye, of the same	by Adam Chapman.
[*Two lines illeg.*]	
[*Illeg.*] John [*?*]Berard [*essoins himself*] of common [*suit*]	by William ate Brok.
[*Illeg.*] Adam [*illeg.*], chaplain, of the same	by Thomas le Webbe.
[*Illeg.*] of the same	by Thomas ate Tye.
[*Illeg.*] of the same	by Stephen le Deye.
[*Illeg.*]	by John Mundham.
[*Illeg.*]	by Gilbert le Heldere.

---

[18] CCA-U15/14/20 (former CCA document number '53,988' stamped and '3/46' written on dorse in a nineteenth-century style and hand. Also on foot of dorse as a label upside down, 'Concerning the years 24 and 25 [*Edw. III*]' (*De anno xxiiij et xxv*) in a fourteenth-century hand). Parchment roll, one membrane. Latin. Very badly damaged by damp, parts of head and margins missing, anything written on dorse (apart from labels) completely illegible. Two courts with views of frankpledge.

[19] The date of the second court depends on which feast of St Gregory is intended: 12 March, his death, is more likely than 3 September, his ordination as pope, because no specification is given for the feast. The date of this court is probably Saturday, 19 March 1350/51, rather than 10 September 1351. The contemporary label on the dorse is for 24 and 25 Edw. III: the second court is definitely dated 25 Edw. III (25 January 1350/51–24 January 1351/52), so the first court (without heading or date) is presumed to be from 24 Edw. III (25 January 1349/50–24 January 1350/51). Having the second court on 19 March 1350/51 and the undated first court several weeks earlier but in the preceding regnal year would nicely fit all the parameters.

John Haberd of the same	by William Personn.[20]
[*Illeg.*] le [*?*]Tailour of the same	by John le Taliour.
[*Illeg.*]	by John le Taliour.
William [*?*]Ancy of the same	by John Donylond.
John le Sadilere for the same	by John Brenn.

[*One line illeg.*]

[*Illeg.*] *Amercement* [*?*]*d.* Ordered. John ate Brokes complains of John le Sadilere in a plea of trespass, pledge to prosecute, William ate Broke. And the aforesaid John le Sadilere was attached by pledge of John Gauge and he has not come, therefore the same in mercy, and it is ordered to cause the aforesaid John le Sadilere to appear by a better pledge before the next [*court*].

Fine [*?*]*2s. Fealty.* Robert Gauge surrendered into the lord's hand 32 perches of land with buildings built thereon, to him and his heirs, and the lord put into possession thereof Thomas Clement and Cecilia his wife, to have and to hold, at the lord's will, to the same Thomas and Cecilia, their heirs and assigns, according to the custom of the manor, saving the right, etc. And they gave to the lord for entry as [*written*] before and they did fealty.

Fine [*?*]*. 6d. Annual rent 1s. Fealty.* The lord granted out of his hands one rood of alder-holt, which Margaret la Forester held of the lord for the term of her life which is parcel of Smetheslond, to Robert Gauge and Joan his wife, to have and to hold at the lord's will to the same Robert and Joan, their heirs and assigns, rendering for the same annually at the feasts of Easter and St Michael in equal portions, 1s. And they gave to the lord as a fine for entry as [*written*] before, and they did fealty.

Amercements 1s. 3d. From Robert Ilger \3d./, Roesia Ilger \3d./, Richard Cnappok \3d./, John Petyt \3d./ for default of suit [*of court*], in mercy, Margery de Boyton \3d./ for the same, in mercy.

Amercements 1s 4d. The same Robert \4d/, Roys[*ia*] \4d/, Richard \4d/ and John \4d/ because they did not warrant [*their*] essoins from the last court, in mercy.

Total of this court 9s. 4d. besides 1s. from rent of land each year.

[*Dorse: nothing now legible except labels.*]

Court Roll 4.[21] (between 19 March 1350/51 and 23 February 1351/52)[22] Head very badly damaged, part missing. Title of court and first ten lines or so damaged or illegible

Heriot 1 horse, worth 6s. 8d. Relief, 1s. 10¾d. Heriot 1 cow, worth 6s. 8d. It was found by the inquest that Salomon Donylond who [*four words illeg.*] of the lord on

---

20 Or possibly Parsonn: the initial abbreviation usually stands for *per* but can also indicate *par*.

21 CCA-U15/15/12 (former CCA document number '58,988' stamped and '18/46' written on dorse in a nineteenth-century style and hand). Parchment roll, one membrane. Latin. Badly damaged by damp. Two courts, headings missing.

22 Precise dating of this court roll is impossible, but is probably *c.* 1350–51. Most of the people named in it also appear (some of them often) in several different court rolls dated between 1350/51 to 1373/74. Thomas Donylond, who appears for the first time in this court roll as a new tenant, and otherwise only relatively rarely between 1351/2 and 1361 (Court Rolls 5 and 7, see pp. 109 and 114), was reported dead at the court dated 24 September 1361 in Court Roll 8 (see p.120). If the William de [*?*]Bocton mentioned as recently dead in the current court roll is really William de Boyton (although it shows no sign of a medial 'y'), then the current court roll could be of similar date to Court Roll 5 (23 February 1351/52), in which an inquest jury was appointed to enquire into the recently dead William de Boyton's holdings in the manor. The pot and pan mentioned in connection with William

the day on which he died [*damaged*] in Sweyneslond, in respect of which for a relief of 9d. and as a heriot 1 horse worth 6s. 8d. as [*written*] before. The same Salomon [*damaged*] land of the tenement of Thomas ate Tye in respect of which, for a relief 1d. and 1 acre of Smetheslond in respect of which [*illeg.*] [*damaged*] that is, 10 acres of warland (*x acr' war'*) in respect of which, for a relief according to custom, 1s. and 1 cow [*illeg.*] as a heriot, worth half a mark [*damaged*] acres of bond (*native*) land lying at Losemede. Therefore it is ordered \the same/ to be retained in the lord's hand until etc. And it is ordered that [*?*]John Donylond [*damaged*] to do fealty to the lord because it was found by the inquest that the same John is the nearest heir of the same Solomon [*damaged*].

Ordered. It is ordered to distrain Alice Legiard and Thomas son of [*illeg.*] to show how they entered into the lord's fee, etc. Also Alice atte [*?*]Peek [*damaged*].

Also Thomas Donylond for the same, Andrew Dexter for the same, Thomas Schail for the same, William Gawgde [*?for the same*] [*damaged*] Forster, Henry Forster for the same.

View [*of frankpledge*] there held on the day and year abovesaid

Capital pledges. Adam Cut, Peter [*illeg.*], John [*?Ayl*]ward [*illeg.*], John [*?*]Donylond [*damaged, illeg.*], Thomas le [*?*]Wylde, William [*illeg., damaged*].

Common fine, 4s. To the lord as a fine as before.[23]

Also they present that they gave to for the view [*of frankpledge*] as a fine as before.

Amercement 6d. Also they present that John Broun made a trespass upon Alice Sparwe for which the said Alice raised hue [*damaged*].

Amercement 6d. Also that Peter A[*illeg.*] made an illegal recovery (*fec' rescuss'*) [*rest of line illeg.*].

Amercement [?]6d. Also that William atte Tye beat [*?*]John Dul against the peace [*damaged*].

Amercement [?]6d. Also that John Dul committed hamsoken on William atte Tye whereby [*illeg.*].

Amercement 4d. Also that the said John Dul drew blood from the aforesaid William, therefore the same in mercy.

Amercement 6d. Also that William Wynk drew blood from John Aylward, in respect of which the hue was unjustly raised upon the said William, pledge, Richard Forster.

Amercement 4d. Also that John Aylward raised hue upon [*Edmund or Edward*] (*Ed'm*)[24] the chaplain unjustly.

Amercement [illeg.]. Also that Nicholas le Smeth took away [*illeg.*] sheaves of the lord's wheat worth 1d., the lord's reaper raised hue upon the said Nicholas unjustly, pledge William le [*illeg.*].

Amercement [?]6d. Also that Thomas Clement drew blood from [*illeg.*] Sweyn for which hue was raised upon [*damaged*].

Wynk in the second of the courts in this current court roll is probably the same case as in Court Roll 5 (23 February 1351/52), where the matter is mentioned 'again' (*ad huc*), so this current roll probably pre-dates Court Roll 5 and comes immediately after Court Roll 3 (the last court of which is dated 19 March 1350/51).

23   That is, as written immediately before, in the marginal heading, with the added understanding that it was paid 'as before' at previous courts. The common fine was probably the same as the 'cert money' found elsewhere. See Bailey, *The English Manor* (2002), pp. 181, 226 and his glossary pp. 242, 244 and Neilson, 'Customary Rents' (1910), pp. 168–69.

24   Probably [*Edmund or Edward*] Co(o)k, chaplain (see p. 109, footnote 30).

Amercement 3d. Also that John son of Robert Pykele committed hamsoken upon John atte [*?*]Pirie therefore [*illeg.*] pledge [*blank space*].

Amercement [*?*]*1d.* Also that the same John Pikele drew blood from Alice Greyberd.

Amercement [*?*]*1d.* Also that the same John Pikele made an illegal recovery from the said Alice Greyberd.

Amercement [*?*]*2d.* Also that the same Robert [*sic*] Pikele made an unlawful way over the land of John ate Pirie, therefore the aforesaid Robert in mercy.

Amercement [*?*]*2d.* Also that John le Coupere drew blood from Simon Puddyng, therefore the said John in mercy, pledge, Thomas Clement.

Amercement 6d. Also that William the chaplain of the parish drew blood from Henry le Taliour, in respect of which the hue was unjustly raised upon the said William, pledge, John [*illeg.*].

Amercement [*?*]*6d.* Also that Thomas le Parker struck John Holle against the peace in respect of which the hue was unjustly raised against the said Thomas, pledge, John Donylond.

Amercement [*?*]*1d.* Also that William de Peyton dwells within the precincts of the place [*but*] is outside a tithing, therefore etc.

Amercements 1s. Nicholas Dughty \3d./ for the same, Sayer atte Wayour \3d./, John le Clerk \3d./, John le Schepherd \3d./ for the same, therefore in mercy.

Amercement [*illeg.*]. Also that William [*?*]Fam', butcher [*illeg.*].

Amercement [*illeg.*]. Also that John le Slaghtere does likewise.

Bakers [*illeg.*]. John Greygrom \3d./, William Personn \3d./, Robert Gauge \3d./ baked and sold against the assize.

Brewers. Amercements 5s. 9d. John Greygrom \6d./, Robert Gauge \¼d./, William Personn \6d./, Richard Dul \3d./, William le Skynnere \3d./, Adam le Spenser \6d./, John Dul \6d./ [*illeg.*], John le Slaghtere \3d./, Nicholas [*?*]Doughty \3d./ Alan [*illeg.*] \6d./, John [*illeg.*] \3d./, Letitia la Hore[25] \3d./, William [*?*]Schepherd \¼d./, [*probably two or three names illeg.*] Smert, Thomas Clement \6d./, John Sparwe \6d./ and Adam Pikke \3d./ brewed and sold against the assize. Nicholas Joseph \6d./ for the same.

Amercements 3s. 4d. Also they present that William Vant[26] made an unlawful way over the lord's land with his cart [*illeg.*] fields called Heifeld Illeye and Hodingfeld. Therefore etc.

Amercement [*?*]*6d.* Also John Sparwe \6d./ and Robert Gauge [*are*] [*ale*] tasters and have not done their duty etc.

Amercements [*illeg.*]. Thomas Heym, \Simon/ Kyng, Richard Cnappok because [*they are*] tithingmen and made default.

[*Dorse.*] [*Head very badly damaged, part missing. Apparently a new court, but damage has removed title.*]

[*Damaged.*] [*Essoins illeg.*] [*Final column of pledges for essoins only, which comprises*] Simon Fynches[*?leigh*], William Personn, John atte Wode, Henry de Swelnetham, [*illeg.*].

[*Damaged*] that is, one pot (*ollam*) and 1 pan (*patenam*), [*?*]upon (*super*) William Wynk to respond to [*illeg.*] [*Margaret Calewdon*[27]] [*illeg.*].

---

25 Probably 'Letitia with the grey (hoary) hair' rather than 'Letitia the whore'. My thanks to Dr Keith Briggs for the clarification.

26 Probably Fant.

27 Name supplied from Court Roll 5 (1351/52), where an order is made 'again' respecting this case.

[*Damaged*] in a plea of debt and levy more etc.

[*Damaged*] le Sadeler' puts himself in mercy for licence to settle with John att Brok in a plea of trespass, etc.

[*Damaged*] Wink made default, therefore etc.

[*Damaged*] for the same, therefore etc.

[*Damaged*] A day is given for [*illeg.*] Simon Querdelyng plaintiff and William Wynk defendant to come [*illeg.*] without essoin.

The inquest says that John Sadeler acquired [*land*] of the lord's fee of Keneseggeslond. And it is ordered to distrain the said John to show the form of his entry etc.

Amercements 2s. 6d. Also they say (*dicunt*) that William Skynner \6d./ [*illeg.*], Robert [*?*]Anfrey/Ausrey \6d./, Margery Joseph \6d./, Rosia le Vox \6d./, Alice Hod \3d./, Amy le Vox \3d./ gathered the lord's pannage. And [*?the jurors to take a day to certify*] [*illeg.*].

Amercements 4s. 6d. Also that John Donylond \6d./, Nicholas Hygeleye \3d./, John Sparwe \6d/, Simon Kyng \6d./, William Ancy \3d./, the parson \6d/ of the church of Eleigh (*Illeye*), Katherine ate Fen \6d./ did damage in the pannage and in the corn of the lord, therefore etc.

Fine 10s. To this court came Robert Wlleward and surrendered into the lord's hand one messuage with the buildings built upon it, with appurtenances, to the use of Roysia Sparwe to have and to hold to the same Rois' for the term of her life. And after the death of the said Rois' the said tenement with its appurtenances are to remain to Joan and Katherine daughters of the said Rois' to hold to the same, their heirs and assigns, at the will of the lord, according to the custom of the manor, saving the right, etc. And she gave to the lord as a fine as [*written*] before. And she did fealty etc.

[*Amercement ?1s. 3d.*] John Parker \3d/ made default of suit of court, therefore, etc. John Borard \3d./ for the same, [*?*]Richard [*illeg.*] \3d./ for the same, Margery de Boyton \3d./ for the same, Adam Mascal \3d./ chaplain for the same. Therefore in mercy etc.

[*Illeg.*] William de [*?*]Bocton held on the day that he died.

Brewers

[*Amercements*] [*damaged*] 6d. Adam Pycke \6d./, John Greygrom \6d./, Cecilia Raven \6d./, Joan le Gerl \3d./, Margaret Dul \3d./, Margery Joseph \3d./, Sayer ate Wayour \3d./ brewed and sold against the assize, therefore etc.

Bakers

[*Damaged*] Cecilia Raven \3d./, John Greygrom \3d./ bakers, sold bread against the assize, therefore, etc.

Ale Tasters

[*Damaged*] Robert Gauge \3d./, John Sparwe \3d./, tasters of ale, do not do their duty, therefore etc.

Affeerers: John Gauge, Robert Gauge. Total of this court £1 2s. 10d.

Court Roll 5.[28] (23 February 1351/52)[29]

Court held there on the Thursday next after the feast of St Peter's chair in the 26th year of the reign of King Edward the Third [*Thursday, 23 February 1351/52*]

Essoins

Katherine atte Fen [*essoins herself*] of common [*suit*]	by John Gauge 1st
John Godale of the same	by Simon Prynche 1st
Adam Cut of the same	by Richard atte Pyrie 1st
John Choney of the same	by John de Holemere 2nd
John Huberd of the same	by William Personn 1st
Thomas Donylond of the same	by John Donylond 1st

[*Bracketed to the right of all six entries above*] Affeered

Fealty. John Chapman of Eleigh (*Illeye*) and Agnes his wife did fealty to the lord for one piece of land with appurtenances which they acquired from Robert Gauger and Joan his wife.

Fealty. John Reyner and Margaret his wife did fealty to the lord at this court for one piece of land which they acquired from [*Edmund or Edward*] (*Ed'*)[30] Cook, chaplain.

[?]*Fine 1s. 6d.* Thomas Clement surrendered into the lord's hand one cottage with one rood of land adjacent next to the King's highway leading from Gedeworthe towards Brent Eleigh (*Brende Illeye*) from him and his heirs in perpetuity. And in respect of which, the lord put into possession Alan Hood and Alice his wife. To hold to the same Alan and Alice, the heirs and assigns of the same Alan, of the lord according to custom etc. by service etc. saving the right. And they give to the lord as a fine for entry as [*written*] before. And they did fealty.

Amercement 4d. Nicholas Hygeleye puts himself [*in mercy*] for trespassing in the lord's rye with his 3 horses and 3 bullocks on 4 occasions.

Amercement 3d. John Donylond puts himself [*in mercy*] for trespassing in the lord's rye with his sheep.

Amercement 3d. Thomas Sparwe puts himself [*in mercy*] because one of his household trespassed in the lord's wood of Manhey, lopping and carrying away etc.

Ordered. It was found that Simon de Leleseye [*Lindsey*] trespassed in the aforesaid wood of Manhey with his 24 animals. Therefore it is ordered to distrain the said Simon to be at the next court to answer concerning the aforesaid trespass etc. And for pannage of his 12 pigs.

Amercement 3d. John Clerk puts himself [*in mercy*] for licence to settle with Thomas Reyner in a plea of debt.

Amercement 3d. Thomas Sparwe gives to the lord for pannage of his 2 pigs.

---

28 CCA-U15/15/1 (former CCA document number '48824' written on dorse in a nineteenth-century hand). Parchment roll, one membrane. Latin. Torn in places and damaged near head and right foot, written on one side only. One court.

29 Almost certainly Thursday, 23 February 1351/52 (based on the feast of the chair of St Peter at Antioch, 22 February), but just possibly Thursday, 24 January 1352/53 (based on the lesser-known alternative feast of St Peter's chair at Rome). Edward III's twenty-sixth regnal year ran from 25 January 1351/52 to 24 January 1352/53.

30 The Latin abbreviation here (*Ed'*) could be either. In Suffolk, Edmund was a much more common name than Edward owing to the influence of St Edmund and his shrine at Bury St Edmunds.

Increase 1 piglet. It was found by the inquest that 1 piglet came, as increase (*exit '*),[31] on to the lord's land on the morrow of St Michael last past and it is worth 1s. 8d. Therefore it is ordered etc.

Ordered. It was found that Geoffrey Gylessone trespassed in the lord's pannage at Manhey with his 12 pigs. Therefore it is ordered to distrain etc.

Fine 4s. Robert Aumfrey surrendered into the lord's hand one rood of land with one building built upon it which were formerly of Peter Bray, from him and his heirs in perpetuity. And in respect of which, the lord put into possession Thomas Reyner. To hold to him and his heirs, of the lord, according to the custom etc. for service etc. saving the right etc. And he gives to the lord as a fine for entry as [*written*] before. And he did fealty.

Amercement 3d. Thomas Reyner puts himself [*in mercy*] for trespassing in the lord's wheat with 1 horse.

Fealty. John Donylond and Margery his wife and Matilda their daughter came to this court and did fealty to the lord for one piece of land which they acquired from [*Edmund or Edward*] (*Ed'o*) Cok, chaplain.

Amercement 3d. Ordered. John Greygrom because he fell into a plea of debt against John Cabau, in mercy. And it is ordered to levy 3s. 4d. of the principal debt and damages from the said John Greygrom to the benefit of the said John Cabau, which was recovered against him in the aforesaid plea.

Amercement 3d. Ordered. The same John Greygrom because he fell into a plea of trespass against the said John Cabau, in mercy. And it is ordered to levy 1s. in damages from the said John Greygrom to the benefit of the aforesaid John Cabau which was recovered against him in the aforesaid plea.

Amercement 6d. Nicholas Cranelee \3d./, chaplain and Adam Marscal \3d./, chaplain, because they did not warrant their essoins at the last court, in mercy.

Ordered. And it is ordered to distrain the same Nicholas and Adam, to save the default, etc.

Respited. On behalf of the parties, the plea between Simon Querdelyng plaintiff and William Wynk defendant in a plea of contract is put in respite to the next [*court*] etc.

Ordered. Again, it is ordered to retain one [*illeg.*] pot and one iron pan (*patell'*) taken, that is to say, from William Wynk and more taken from Margaret Calewedon in a plea of debt.[32]

[*Illeg.*] John Gauge, Robert Gauge, John Reyner, William le Smyth, John Taillour, Peter atte Brok, John Donylond, William Auty, Peter Anselote, Thomas Webbe, John Cabau and William Personn, sworn as an inquest [*jury*] [*damaged*] [*to report*] at the next court to certify to the lord how many acres of free land and how many acres of customary land [*William de*] Boyton held on the day on which he died.

Amercement 1s. 3d. Richard le Parker \3d./, John Berard \3d./, Margaret de Boyton \3d./, William le Sweyn \3d./, Adam le Heldere \3d./ [*damaged*] [*for default of*] suit of court, in mercy. And it is ordered to distrain the said tenants to save the default.

Total, 9s. 4d

---

31 The stray piglet is being counted as an additional animal or increase (*exitus*) to the livestock of the manor.

32 This case also mentioned in Court Roll 4 (*?c.* 1350–51).

Court Roll 6.[33] (29 July 1359)

Eleigh (Illeyghe). Court with view [*of frankpledge*] held there on the Monday next before the feast of St Peter, that is to say, in chains in the 33rd year of the reign of King Edward the third [*Monday, 29 July 1359*]

Essoin
Robert [*?*]Gauge [*essoins himself*] of common [*suit*]   by John Gauge, 1st
Showed charter. Fealty. John Donilond showed by his charter how he acquired one piece of land from Simon le Kyngh. And he did fealty.
Showed charter. Fealty. John Cabau and Alice his wife showed by a charter how they acquired three pieces of land in Kettlebaston to them and <~~their~~> the heirs of the said John. And they did fealty.
Showed fealty. Alice [*damaged*] showed how she acquired one piece of land from Simon Kyng. And she did fealty etc.
Amercement 3d. [*Damaged*] puts himself [*in mercy*] for licence to settle with Adam atte Medewe in a plea of trespass.
Amercement [illeg.]d. The same Adam puts himself [*in mercy*] for the same with the aforesaid Thomas in the aforesaid plea.
Amercement 3d. The same Thomas puts himself [*in mercy*] for the same with the same <~~Thomas~~> Adam in a plea of trespass.
Amercement 6d. Robert Pekele puts himself [*in mercy*] for trespassing in the lord's wheat with 1 horse.
Amercement 6d. The parson (*le par'*) of the church of Eleigh (*Illeygh*) for trespassing in the lord's corn with his ox and his horse, by pledge of the bailiff.
Amercement 11d. Nicholas de Hygeleyghe puts himself [*in mercy*] for trespassing in the lord's wheat, oats, peas and pasture with his various animals, by pledge of John Domolond [*?recte Donilond*].
Amercement [illeg.]d. William Fant for trespassing in the lord's corn with 1 cow, by the pledge of John Petit, reap-reeve.
Amercement [?]2d. John Liricok puts himself [*in mercy*] for the same with 1 cow, by the pledge of Nicholas Hygeleyghe.
Amercement 6d. John Donilond puts himself [*in mercy*] for trespassing in the lord's corn and pasture with his animals by the pledge of the aforesaid.
Amercement 1s. 3d. Felicia Deye puts herself [*in mercy*] for the same with cows and geese in the lord's wheat and oats by the pledge of the bailiff.
Ordered. Again it is ordered to distrain Richard [*?*]Bataille to come to the next [*court*] to show etc. And to do [*fealty*] etc. And [*?to be informed as to his tenure*] for the lands he acquired, (*facere tenetur' pro terr' cten' perquis'*) etc.
Amercement 3d. John Reyner puts himself [*in mercy*] for licence to settle with Thomas Stonhard in a plea of debt, by the pledge of John Petit, reap-reeve.
Amercement 6d. Robert [*?*]Pekele puts himself [*in mercy*] for licence to trespass [*sic*] in the lord's oats and meadows with his animals, by the pledge of the bailiff.
Amercement 4d. John Reyner puts himself [*in mercy*] for licence to settle with John atte Tye in a plea of trespass, by the pledge of the aforesaid.
Amercement 3d. The same John puts himself [*in mercy*] for licence to settle with John Ber' [*?Berard*] in a plea of trespass by the pledge of the aforesaid.

---

33 CCA-U15/15/2 (former CCA document number '48825', 'Illegh' and (erroneously) '1360' written on dorse in two different nineteenth-century hands). Parchment roll, one membrane. Latin. One court.

Amercement 4d. Matilda Boyton \1d./, Alice Meller' \1d./, [?]Christina [?]Sweyn \1d./, Agnes [?]Ancey \1d./ put themselves [*in mercy*] for trespassing in the lord's meadows by the pledges of each other.

Respited. A day is given to Simon le Kyng, Nicholas Foster, John Bolemere, William Denford and Alice Saleman formerly the wife of Simon de Leleseye, that they should appear at the next [*court*] to show etc. how etc.

Amercement 10d. John de Stowe puts himself [*in mercy*] for licence to settle with Sayho' atte Wayour in three pleas of trespass, by the pledge of the bailiff.

Amercement 10d. William Skynnere puts himself [*in mercy*] for trespassing in the lord's oats with his cows by the pledges of John Clement and the bailiff.

Chief pledges

Adam Cut	John atte Tye	\<Thomas Well\>\John de Bresete/	John Sparwe
William Smyth	John Doniland	William Fant	Thomas Sparwe
John Aylward	Thomas Heym	\<Peter atte Brook\> \John Abot/	Richard Dul

Common fine 4s. [*Illeg.*] [*the chief*] pledges present that they give to the lord as the fixed (*certe*) common fine as of ancient custom etc as before.

Amercement 3d. Also they say that Peter Amphelote has 1 ditch not cleaned out. Therefore etc.

Amercement 3d. Also they present that Robert [?]Doreman assaulted Matilda Knappok. Therefore.

Amercement 3d. Also they present that the aforesaid Matilda [?]justly[34] raised hue upon the said Robert. Therefore etc.

Amercement 1s. Also they present that William atte Brook assaulted John le Buk and drew blood from him. Therefore etc.

Amercement 1d. Also they present that Elena atte Fen struck Roger Grotene. Therefore etc.

Amercement, 1d. Also they present that the said Roger justly raised hue upon the said Elena. Therefore etc.

Amercement 3d. Also they present that Matilda [?]Wyntour unjustly raised hue upon Richard Dul. Therefore etc.

Amercement 3d. Also they present that John Wage unjustly struck John Driver. Therefore etc.

Ordered. Also they present that John Ferthyng broke the liberties of the lord. Therefore etc.

Amercement 3d. Also they present that John atte Fen has 2 ditches not cleaned out. Therefore etc.

Amercement 3d. Also they present that John atte Tye assaulted Robert Fant. Therefore etc.

Amercement 3d. Also they present that the said Robert justly raised hue upon the said John. Therefore etc.

Amercement 3d. Also they present that John Slautere justly raised hue upon John atte Tye. Therefore etc.

---

34 The ink has worn away or lifted off the surface in this area. It does not look as if there is room for this word to be 'unjustly' (*iniuste*).

Amercement 2d. Also they present that Geoffrey Hoptone committed hamsoken on John atte Fen. Therefore etc.

Amercement 6d. Also they present de Boyton's tenants have two ditches not cleaned out. Therefore etc.

Amercement [illeg.]d. Also they present that John de Berneye has 2 ditches not cleaned out. Therefore etc.

[Illeg.]. Also they present that the tenants of Becheslond have 1 ditch not cleaned out. Therefore etc.

Turn over

[Dorse] Amercement 3d. Also they present that Nicholas Hygeleyghe struck Agnes *[?]*Heese. Therefore etc.

Amercement 3d. Also they present that the said Agnes justly raised hue upon the said Nicholas. Therefore etc.

Amercement 3d. Also they present that the said Nicholas struck William Morice. Therefore etc.

Amercement 3d. Also they present that the said William justly raised hue on the said Nicholas.

Amercement 6d. Also they present that the rector of the church of Eleigh (*Illeyghe*) committed hamsoken on Nicholas Hygeleyghe. Therefore etc.

Amercement 3d. Also they present that Dennis atte Tye has 1 ditch not cleaned out. Therefore etc.

Amercement 6d. Also they present that John Huberd has 1 building built upon John Cabaau's road. Therefore etc.

Amercement 3d. Also they present that Pernel (*Petronilla*) Skynnere justly raised hue upon Roger Cobold and Agnes Capup *[damaged]*.

Amercement 3d. Also they present that John atte Cheche committed hamsoken on John Cabaau. Therefore etc.

Amercement 6d. Also they present that Alan Hood assaulted Simon Puddyng. Therefore etc.

Amercement 3d. Also they present that the said Simon justly raised hue upon the aforesaid Alan etc. Therefore etc.

Amercement 1s. Also they present that William le Heldere \3d./, John son of Robert Gauge \3d./, John Cosgrave \3d./, and John Smerr \3d./ are of age etc. and dwell within etc. and are not in a tithing. Therefore etc.

Amercement 3d. Thomas Heym for his false claim against Adam atte Medewe.

Amercement 3d. Also they present that the same Thomas made an encroachment upon the king's highway. Therefore etc.

Amercement 6d. William Hard, because he struck the servant of Robert Framelysdene and drew blood from him, in mercy because *[?it is ordered]* (*quia sit precer'*) by the chief *[pledge]*.

Amercement 3d. Also they present that the said servant justly raised hue on the said William. Therefore etc.

Amercement 3d. Also they present that Thomas Reyner put back into possession (*fecit reseissum*) Stephen le Fox. Therefore etc.

Amercement 2d. Also they present that Agnes Cut made a *[?]*seizure[35] *[illeg.]* Therefore etc.

---

[35] The text has *str'*, possibly *strictura*, 'seizure, distraint' (*DMLBS*).

Amercement 3d. Also they present that a member of William atte Brook's household struck Stephen Sparwe. Therefore etc.

Amercement 3d. Also they present that the said Stephen justly raised hue upon the said household member. Therefore etc.

Amercement 1s. 6d. Also they present that Robert Hut \3d./, William Personn \3d./, Thomas son of Adam atte Tye \3d./, John Wreyghte \3d./, John [?]Knyth \3d./, Simon le Kyng \3d./ are tithingmen and have defaulted. Therefore etc.

Amercement [blank]. Also they present that Geoffrey atte Halle \6d./, Thomas Heym \3d./, John Greigrom \9d./, Matilda atte Ty \3d./, John Lyricok \1s./, John Dul \1s./, Robert Gauge \3d./, John Raach \3d./, John Stowe \6d./, Leticia Hert \3d./, Nicholas Josep \3d./, Sayher atte Wayour \3d./ and William Smyth \3d./ are brewers and sell against the assize. Therefore, etc.

Amercement 9d. Also they present that John Greigrom \3d./, Geoffrey atte Halle \3d./, John Lyricok \3d./ are bakers and sell against the assize.

Amercement 2s. Also they present that William Fant \1s./, John Slautere \1s./ are butchers and sell short meat. Therefore etc.

A day [illeg.]. A day is given to all the chief pledges to certify the presentment made on the rector at this [court], that is to say at the next [court] under penalty, as [written] before [in the margin], [illeg.] of them to come without essoin etc.

Amercements 1s. Also they present that John Sparwe \6d./ and John Dul \6d./ are ale-tasters and did not do their duty. Therefore etc.

Amercement [illeg.]d. William de Walsham gives to the lord as a fine for suit of court, respited until the next [court]. Given as [written] before.

Total of this court and view [of frankpledge] £1 14s.

Affeerers: William Smyth, John Sparwe. Sworn.

Court Roll 7.[36] (12 April and 8 [recte 9] August 1361)

[Damaged] A court there, held on the Monday next after Hokeday[37] in the 35th year of the reign of King Edward III [Monday, 12 April 1361]

Essoins

William Mone [essoins himself] of common [suit]	by William Lerycok 1st
John Buk of the same	by Thomas atte Brook 1st
John Godhale of the same	by Adam Cut, 2nd
John Greygrom of the same	by Adam Poleyn, 1st

Amercement 3d. Thomas Donylond because he did not warrant his essoin, in mercy.

Ordered. It is ordered at this [court] to distrain Richard Bataill against the next [court] to show how he entered into the lord's fee etc.

Fealty. Simon Kyng comes to this court and showed a charter by which he entered into the lord's fee etc.

A day. Nicholas Forester again has a day until the next [court] to show how he entered into the lord's fee etc.

---

36 CCA-U15/15/3 (former CCA document number '53988' stamped and '40/46' written on dorse in a nineteenth-century style and hand). Parchment roll, one membrane. Latin. Very badly damaged by damp at head, foot and right side of recto. Two courts. Palimpsest, with evidence of earlier court roll entries on dorse underneath current entries, especially top half.

37 Hoke Day was the second Tuesday after Easter, which in 1361 was on 6 April.

114

Amercement 6d. Ordered. John Bulmere \quit/, William Denford \3d./ and Alice Saleman \3d./, formerly the wife of Simon Leleseye, had a day [*given*] at the last court until this [*court*] to show how they entered into the lord's fee and they have not come. Therefore the same in mercy. And it is ordered to distrain against the next [*court*] the aforesaid John, William and Alice to show how they entered into the lord's fee etc.

A day, penalty £1. Again, a day is given to all the chief pledges until the next leet to certify the encroachment made by the rector of this church of Illeigh under penalty of £1 etc.

Amercement 6d. Simon Kyng puts himself [*in mercy*] for trespassing in the lord's wheat with his cows, by the pledge of the bailiff.

Amercement 3d. Walter Heyward puts himself [*in mercy*] for trespassing in the lord's pasture with his horses, by the pledge of John Sleigter.

Amercement 3d. Thomas Reyner puts himself [*in mercy*] for trespassing in the lord's wheat and rye, that is to say, in the shocks (*schokkes*) etc.

Amercement 10d. Nicholas Hegeleigh puts himself [*in mercy*] for trespassing in the lord's wheat and rye with his sheep and pigs, by the pledge of the bailiff.

Amercement 3d. John Petit puts himself [*in mercy*] for trespassing there with his animals, by the pledge of the same.

Amercement 3d. William Fant puts himself [*in mercy*] for the same there with 1 cow, by the pledge of the same.

Amercement 3d. John Donylond puts himself [*in mercy*] for trespassing in the lord's wheat with 16 sheep by the pledge of the same.

Amercement 3d. John Stowe puts himself [*in mercy*] for licence to settle with John Wyndecole in a plea of trespass, by the pledge of the bailiff.

Amercement 3d. John atte Fen puts himself [*in mercy*] for licence to settle with Simon Qwerdlyng in a plea of trespass, by the pledge of John Petit.

Amercement 3d. Geoffrey Hopton and his pledge to prosecute, because they did not prosecute against John Petit in a plea of trespass, in mercy [*damaged*].

Amercement 3d. Thomas Heym, chief pledge, for default, in mercy etc.

[*Damaged*] The jurors present that Peter atte Brook acquired one quarter of the land[38] called Godhynesquarter and [*damaged*] Gaywodesquarter etc.[39] Therefore it is ordered to distrain the said Peter against the next [*court*] to show how he entered into the lord's fee [*damaged*].

[*?*]*Heriot worth 13s. 4d.* Also they present that William atte Brook who held of the lord \one messuage and/ 1 warland acre of customary land (*acr' War' de terr' Custum'*) \jointly [*damaged*]/ [*damaged*] worth 13s. 4d. And because there are no heirs to follow it is ordered to seize [*the property*] into the hand of the lord etc. And to answer [*damaged*] [*?for the issues*].

Heriot. Ordered. Also they present that the same William who held of the lord 20 acres of free land jointly with Cecilia his wife [*damaged*] as a heriot etc. And

---

38 This could either mean 'one quarter of the [*quarter-*]land called Godhynesquarter' (which was itself a quarterland, and in multiple occupation in Rental 1, 1379–80) or 'the [*whole of the*] quarterland called Godhynesquarter'. The Latin *unum q[u]arter' de terre voc[at] Godhynesquarter* is ambiguous.

39 Godhynesquarter and Gaywodesquarter are entered together as two quarter-lands (Goodynggesquarter and Gaywodequarter), making up a half-land in Rental 1 (1379–80). Their names might reflect those of earlier tenants (such as Robert Godhyne (see Charter 18, *?c.* 1260s–1270s), John de Geywode, clerk (see Court Roll 1 (1305–6)) or Leticia de Gaywod (see Court Roll 2, *c.* 1350) or one of their relations. See also p. 119, footnote 44 to Godȝineslond in Court Roll 8 (1361–62).

because the said Cecilia [*?has*] no other heir to follow etc. it is ordered to seize the said land [*damaged*] for the issues etc. Until etc.

[*Damaged*] *1s. 6d. Heriot.* Also it is presented that Dennis atte Tye who held of the lord 36 acres of free [*?land*] [*damaged*] has animals etc. And to this court comes Thomas atte Tye son and heir of the said Dennis and [*damaged*] [*?asked to be accepted as tenant*]. And he gave to the lord as a relief 1s. 6d. [*damaged*].

Fine 1s. Fealty. At this court the lord granted to John Donylond 2 acres and 1 rood of land from the demesne [*damaged*] on the one hand and the land of the said John on the other. To hold to the same John and his heirs [*damaged*] annually to the lord 1s, 10½d. at the two \usual/ terms of the year in equal portions and making common [*damaged*] to have as is shown, by the pledge of the bailiff. And he did fealty.

[*Total of this*] court 6s. 9d., price of the heriots [*damaged*]

Eleigh (*Illeigh*) [*damaged*]. [*A court and view held there*] on Monday the 8th day of the month of August and in the [*illeg.*] year of the reign [*of King Edward III*] [*Monday, 8* [*recte 9*] *August 1361*].[40]

It is ordered again to distrain Richard Bataill against the next [*court*] to show how he entered into the lord's fee etc.

Showed a charter. Fealty. To this court came Simon Kyng and showed a charter by which he had entered into the lord's fee in [*damaged*] acquired from Thomas atte Tye in the vill of Eleigh (*Illeigh*) etc.

[*Illeg.*] Again, Nicholas Forester has a day until the next [*court*] to show how he entered into the lord's fee etc.

Ordered. It is ordered again to distrain John Bulmere \[*?*]dead/, William Denford and Alice Saleman formerly the wife of Simon Leleseye [*damaged*] to show how they entered into the lord's fee etc.

It is ordered again to distrain Peter atte Brook against the next [*court*] to show how he entered into the lord's fee [*damaged*].

Issues. It is ordered again for the issues to be answered for, concerning 50 acres of customary land [*damaged*].

[*Damaged.*] John Donylond puts himself [*in mercy*] for trespassing in the lord's wheat with [*illeg.*].

[*Damaged.*] Thomas atte Tye puts himself [*in mercy*] for trespassing in the lord's oats with 3 calves, by the pledge of John Donylond.

[*Damaged.*] John Farthing puts himself [*in mercy*] for trespassing in the lord's oats with his horse and ox, by the pledge of Robert Frammesden.

---

[40] The part of the title to this court that would include the regnal year is missing due to ancient damp damage. One might assume that being quite clearly (and unusually) dated by day and month (Monday, 8 August) immediately after the clearly dated court of Monday, 12 April 1361, this court too would be from 1361, but 8 August in 1361 was on a Sunday, not a Monday. 8 August *was* on a Monday in 1362, however. If 1362 is the correct date, then the two courts on this roll were held sixteen months apart and the two courts comprising Court Roll 8 (1361–1361/62) fall between the two courts of this roll, which seems unlikely. If Monday, 8 August is a scribal error for Monday, 9 August, then that puts this court back into 1361, four months after the first court on this roll and just over six weeks before the first court of Court Roll 8 (24 September 1361). This seems more logical, although it has to be said that the dorse of this court roll shows evidence of being a palimpsest (see below), so there might have been some muddle concerning which parchments to use to record courts at that time. On balance, it seems more sensible to assume a scribal error and to correct the date of this court to Monday, 9 August 1361.

[*Damaged.*] for trespassing in the lord's wheat with his beasts, sheep and pigs, by the pledge of William S[*illeg.*].
[*Foot of membrane damaged and missing*]

[*Dorse*][41]

Again, as earlier

Amercement 3d. Simon Kyng puts himself [*in mercy*] for licence to settle with William Peyton in a plea of debt, by the pledge of William Peyton.

Amercement 3d. Simon Kyng puts himself [*in mercy*] for licence to settle with John Smert in a plea of debt by the pledge of the bailiff.

[*Illeg.*] Nicholas Hegeleigh puts himself [*in mercy*] for trespassing in the lord's oats with his horses, beasts and 60 sheep by the pledge of Thomas atte Tye.

[*Amercement*]. [*illeg.*] The same Nicholas puts himself [*in mercy*] for trespassing in the lord's wheat with 9 pigs, by the pledge of the aforesaid.

Amercement [*damaged*]. The same Nicholas puts himself [*in mercy*] for the same there with his oxen by the pledge of the aforesaid.

[*Damaged*]. The same Nicholas puts himself [*in mercy*] for trespassing in the lord's wheat and peas with his household, by the pledge of the aforesaid.

[*Damaged*]. [*The jurors*] say that Stephen Bacon, Richard Skreyk, Walter Beneyt and John Kakebred acquired from [*Edmund or Edward*] (*Ed'o*) son of Benett 5 acres [*? of customary land*] with appurtenances in the vills of Kettlebaston (*Ketelbeston'*) and Hitcham (*Heecham*) and Eleigh (*Illeigh*) etc. Therefore it is ordered to distrain the said Stephen, Richard, Walter and John before [*?the next court to show*] how they entered into the lord's fee etc.

[*Damaged*]. Also they present that John son of John Huberd, who held of the lord 1 messuage and 2½ acres of customary land, of the land called Ravenesland, and who [*damaged*] next heir, it is ordered to seize the said tenement into the lord's hand etc. and to answer for the issues etc. until etc.

[*Damaged*]. Nicholas Hegeleigh, Thomas atte Tye \[?]dead[42]/ and John Donylond \[?]dead/ acquired one parcel of one messuage and one quarter and 1 acre of warland (*acr' War'*) with appurtenances in Eleigh (*Illeigh*) etc. \of the lord's fee from William Sweyn/. Therefore it is ordered to distrain the said Nicholas, Thomas and John against the next court to show how they entered into the [*lord's*] fee [*damaged*] by right \voluntarily/ one cow for a relief worth 2s.

[*Damaged*]. Gauge and Thomas Sparwe acquired one quarter of the land called Sweyneslond from John Sparwe with appurtances [*illeg.*] the lord's fee etc. Therefore it is ordered to distrain the said Robert and Thomas against the next court to show how they have entered into the lord's fee etc.

[*Damaged*] acquired one piece of land with appurtenances in Eleigh (*Illeigh*) from John atte Fen etc. Therefore it is ordered to distrain the said John [*damaged*] to show how how he entered into the lord's fee etc.

---

[41] This side of the parchment membrane shows signs of it being a palimpsest, at least from the top down to about the middle. Very faint lines of writing are visible, going underneath the heading and current lines of writing. They are not writing 'grinning through' from the other side, because odd words can still be read and they are the right way round. Some words that can be identified, such as 'pledge' and 'distrain', suggest that this side of the membrane once served as a court roll, and that it has been re-used for this court.

[42] This and the next insertion added later in a different ink.

117

[*Damaged*] acquired half a rood of land with appurtenances in Eleigh (*Illeigh*) \from John Donilond/ from the land of [?]Antyes/Ancyes of the lord's fee etc. Therefore it is ordered [*damaged*] to show how he entered into the lord's fee etc.

[*Damaged*]. It is ordered [*to distrain*] Thomas Heym \defendant/ and Geoffrey de Halle, plaintiff in a plea of debt until the next [*court*] to come without essoin.

[*Damaged*] by the inquest against Walter Heyward in a plea of trespass, in mercy, etc. And it is ordered to raise [*damaged*] to the use of the said Walter etc.

[*Chief pledges*]

John Donylond	John de Bresete	Robert Gauge	}
[*Damaged*] Thomas Heym	<del>William Fant</del>\dead/	<del>Thomas Sparwe</del>\dead/	} Sworn
[*Damaged*]	John Abot	Richard Dul	}

[*Damaged*] [*they*] give to the lord for the fixed (*cert'*) common fine as of ancient custom etc, as is evident etc.

[*Damaged*] [*?raised hue*] upon Nicholas Hegeleigh unjustly etc. Therefore the same in mercy.

[*Damaged*] upon [?]Simon [?]Bryan unjustly etc. Therefore etc.

[*Three lines damaged and illeg.*]

[*Damaged*] raised the hue upon John Petit justly etc. Therefore etc.

[*One line, damaged and illeg.*]

[*Damaged*] Gauge and Thomas Sparwe jointly [*have*] 1 ditch at Lelesmed etc. Therefore etc.

[*Damaged*] and William Walsham have a certain ditch not cleaned out at Le Piek Lane to the nuisance etc. Therefore etc.

Also [*they present*] Thomas atte \Tye/ has a certain ditch not cleaned out at Sextaynesfeld to the nuisance, etc. Therefore etc. And he is ordered to put it right [*?before the next court*] [*damaged*].

[*Damaged*]. Also they present that John atte Fen has not cleaned out his ditch at Mellelane to the nuisance of those passing by etc. Therefore etc. And he is ordered to put it right before the next [*court*].

[*Damaged*] they present that John atte Fen and Michael de Bures obstruct the water-course opposite Thomas Webbe's. Therefore etc.

[*Damaged and illeg.*] 1 ditch [*illeg.*] at Sextenes not cleaned out etc. Therefore etc.

[*Damaged*]. Adam [?]Wynter has 1 ditch not cleaned out at [*illeg.*] to the nuisance etc. Therefore etc.

[*About ten lines mutilated and illegible, and the foot damaged and part torn off. This roll ends here.*]

Court Roll 8.[43] (24 September 1361 and 17 January 1361/62)

Eleigh (Illeigh). A court there, held on the Friday next after the feast [of St Matthew the apostle in the 35th year of the reign of King Edward the Third] [Friday, 24 September 1361]

---

43 CCA-U15/15/4 (former CCA document number '48827', 'Illeigh' and '1362' written on dorse in a nineteenth-century hand). Parchment roll, one membrane. Latin. Some holes in places, especially near foot and some damp damage. Two courts.

Essoins

John atte Fen [*essoins himself*] of common [*suit*]	by John Gauge.
John Godale of the same	by Adam Cut.
John Buk of the same	by William Mone.
John Abot of the same	by Simon Bryan.
John Aylward of the same	by John Sextayn.

Showed charter, fealty. Peter atte Brook came and showed a charter by which he entered into the lord's fee in 1 messuage and 1 quarter land called *Godʒineslond*[44] with appurtenances in Eleigh (*Illeigh*) at Stakwod. And he did fealty etc.

Amercement 1d. Thomas Heym puts himself [*in mercy*] for licence [*to settle*] with Geoffrey de Hall in a plea of debt by the pledge of John Cabaw.

Showed charter. Fealty. To this court came Thomas Chonay and showed a charter by which he acquired land and a tenement with appurtenances from John Chonay in the vill of Hitcham (*Heecham*) etc. And he did fealty etc.

Ordered. It is ordered again to distrain Richard Bataill against the next [*court*] to show how he has entered into the lord's fee etc.

A day. Again Nicholas Forester has a day until the next [*court*] to show how he has entered into the lord's fee etc.

Ordered. It is ordered again to distrain William Denford and Alice Saleman, lately wife of Simon Leleseye, against the next [*court*] to show how they have entered into the lord's fee etc.

Showed a charter. Fealty. John Bolle came to this court and showed a charter by which he had entered into the fee etc.

Ordered, issues. It is ordered again to answer for the issues from 50 acres of customary land and for the issues of 20 acres of free land of which William atte Brook died [*seised*] etc. and to answer for the issue etc. until etc.

Ordered. It is ordered again to distrain John Goodhale against the next [*court*] to answer to the lord for a trespass in the lord's wheat with 1 sow and 2 pigs etc. to the damage of 3s. 4d. etc.

Fealty. To this court came Thomas Huberd, brother of John Huberd, and asked for \1 messuage and/ 1 acre and 3 roods of customary land [*?as promised*]. And because it was found by the inquest that he is truly the heir and of the nearest of the said John and of full age, he was accepted for the tenement. And he did fealty etc.

Amercement 6d. Ordered. Simon Kyng, because he withdrew from court proceedings against Richard Dul in a plea of debt, in mercy. And it is ordered to levy from the goods and chattels of the said Simon, 6d, to the use of the said Richard etc. which was recovered etc.

Ordered. It is ordered again to distrain Stephen [*?*]Bacon, Richard Skreyk, Walter Beneyt and John Cakebred against the next [*court*] to show how they have entered into the lord's fee and acquired from [*Edmund or Edward*] (*Ed'o*) fitz Benett etc. in

---

44 The scribe has written Godʒineslond, using the Old and Middle English letter yogh 'ʒ', probably in error for the letter wynn (p), which would give the modern version of the name 'Godwineslond', although other references to this land do not confirm this overtly. The quarterland probably takes its name from a former tenant who might have been Robert Godhyne (a witness to Charter 18, *?c.* 1260s–1270s) or a relative. In Court Roll 7 (1361), Peter atte Brook acquired Gadhynesquarter and part of Gaywodesquarter, which appear together in Rental 1 (1379–80) as two quarter lands called 'Goodynggesquarter and Gaywodequarter'. Clearly, by 1379–80 Godʒineslond/Gadhynesquarter has mutated into Goodynggesquarter. Perhaps the local pronounciation of the name at the heart of this land was something between 'Godwin' and 'Goodyng'.

the vills of Kettlebaston (*Kedelberston*), Hitcham (*Heechham*) and Eleigh (*Illeigh*) etc.

\A day, penalty, half a mark/ It is ordered again to distrain Nicholas Hegeleigh against the next [*court*] to show how he entered into the lord's fee etc.

It is ordered again to distrain Robert Gauge against the next [*court*] to show how he entered into the lord's fee etc.

It is ordered again to distrain John Reyner against the next [*court*] to show how he entered into the lord's fee etc.

Amercement 3d. John de Stowe puts himself [*in mercy*] for a trespass in the lord's oats with pigs, by the pledge of William Smyth.

Ordered. It is ordered \again/ to distrain Thomas Reyner against the next [*court*] to answer to the lord for a trespass in the lord's oats and bullimong (*bulmong'*) with his pigs etc.

Amercement 3d. John atte Tye puts himself [*in mercy*] for a trespass in the lord's corn with 2 pigs, by the pledge of the bailiff.

Amercement 1d. Saher atte Wayour puts himself [*in mercy*] for the same with 1 pig, by the pledge of the aforesaid.

Amercement 2d. Walter Heyward puts himself [*in mercy*] for the same with pigs, by the pledge of Adam Cut.

Amercement 3d. Nicholas Josep puts himself [*in mercy*] for the same by the pledge of the aforesaid.

Heriot 1 ox, 8s. \A day, penalty, [*?half a*] mark/ The jurors say that Ralph atte Gate chief [*pledge*] and [*Edmund or Edward*] (*Ed's*) Parker acquired one messuage and 40 acres of customary land from John Donylond and indeed after the decease of the said John, as a heriot, 1 ox worth 8s [*was given*] according to the law by free will etc. Therefore it is ordered to distrain the same Ralph and [*Edmund or Edward*] against the next [*court*] to show how they entered into the lord's fee etc.

Heriot 1 pig, 1s. 6d. Also they say that Thomas Donylond, who held of the lord one messuage and 3 acres of customary land, recently died, after whose death, as a heriot, 1 pig worth 1s. 6d. for which the bailiff is charged. And now comes Alice, lately wife of the said Thomas, and claims the said tenement with appurtenances as her free bench etc. And because they say that it is the custom (*usus*) of this manor, it is granted to the same, etc. And she did fealty.

Heriot 1 horse, 10s. \[*Illegible insertion, worn or rubbed out*]/ Also they say that John Abot, John Brysete and William atte Tye acquired one messuage and 30 acres of customary land from Thomas atte Tye etc. and after the decease of the said Thomas as a heriot 1 horse worth 10s. according to the law, voluntarily etc. Therefore it is ordered to distrain the said John, John and William against the next [*court*] to show how they entered into the lord's fee etc.

[*Illeg.*] Also they say that Thomas Sparwe, who held from the lord one messuage and 12 acres of land, recently died, after whose death, as a heriot, 1 pig, worth 1s. etc. And whereupon, for the said 12 acres, comes Alice lately wife of Thomas and claims them as her free bench etc. And because the inquest say that it is the custom of this manor, it is granted to her etc. And she did fealty etc. And so the messuage is ordered to be seized into the hands of the lord etc. And to answer for the issues etc. Until etc.[45]

---

[45] The scribe has written a number of abbreviated stock legal phrases here that do not agree with each other. If Thomas's widow Alice was indeed entitled to the property as her free bench by the custom

[*Illeg.*] The same say that John Slautere, Nicholas Josep' and William atte Tye acquired 6 acres of customary land with appurtenances from William Fant etc. Therefore it is ordered to distrain the said John, Nicholas and William against [*the next court to show*] how they have entered into the lord's fee etc.

Turn over

[*Dorse*]

Again as before

Ordered. Also they say that Robert Gauge, Thomas Fuller and Ralph atte Gate, chief [*pledge*], acquired one messuage and 3 acres of land from John Lacy, of the lord's fee. Therefore it is ordered to distrain the said Robert, Thomas and Ralph against the next [*court*] to show how they entered into the lord's fee etc.

Total of this [*court*] 1s. 7d., 1 ox as a heriot worth 8s., 1 pig worth 1s. 6d., 1 horse worth 10s. and 1 pig worth 1s.

Eleigh (*Illegh*). General court there held on the Monday next after the feast of St Hilary in the 35th year of the reign of King Edward the third [*Monday, 17 January 1361/62*].

Showed a charter. Fealty. To this court [*came*] Saxena, lately wife of John Parker of Bures and showed a charter by which she entered into the lord's fee etc. \for the term of her life/. And she did fealty etc.

Fine, 6d. Saxena, lately wife of John Parker, gives to the lord as a fine for having rendered suit of court \for the year/ as is evident, by the pledge of Adam Cut.

Fealty. Cecilia atte Brook came and showed a charter by which she entered into the lord's fee etc. And she did fealty etc.

Showed a charter. Fealty. Adam Cut and Alice his wife came to this court and showed a charter by which they entered into the lord's fee etc. And they did fealty to the lord etc.

Showed a charter. Fealty. To this court came Robert Gauge and showed a charter by which he entered into the lord's fee etc. And he did fealty to the lord etc.

Amercement 9d. Thomas Reyner puts himself [*in mercy*] for trespassing in the lord's oats and corn with his pigs, by the pledge of William Smyth.

Showed a charter. Fealty. John Abot and John Bresete came to this court and showed a charter by which they entered into the lord's fee etc. And they did fealty etc.

Showed a charter. Fealty. To this court came Alice, lately wife of Thomas Sparwe, and showed a charter by which she entered into the lord's fee for life etc. And she did fealty to the lord etc.

Ordered. It is ordered to distrain Robert Gauge and William Smyth to show how they entered into the lord's fee, in the tenement formerly of John Lacy etc.

Ordered. It is ordered again to distrain Richard Bataill against the next [*court*] to show how he entered into the lord's fee etc.

Ordered. It is ordered again to distrain John Godale against the next [*court*] to answer to the lord for trespassing in the lord's wheat with 1 sow and 2 pigs to the lord's damage of 3s. 4d.

---

of the manor, as stated by the inquest jury, and she did fealty, then the property should not have been seized into the lord's hand and no-one else needed to answer for its issues. Perhaps the final 'until etc.' implies that the property *would* be seized if she did not pay the heriot.

121

<*Amercement 9d.* Thomas Reyner puts himself [*in mercy*] for trespassing in the lord's corn with his pigs, by the pledge etc.>

Ordered. It is ordered again to distrain Stephen [*?*]Bacon, Richard Skreyk, Walter Benett and John Cakebred to show how they entered into the lord's fee etc.

A day, penalty half a mark. A day is given until the next [*court*] for Nicholas Hegeleigh to show how he entered into the lord's fee etc. Under [*the penalty*] that appears etc.

Ordered. It is ordered again to distrain John Reyner against the next [*court*] to show how he entered into the lord's fee etc.

A day, penalty 13s. 4d. A day is given to Ralph atte Gate, chaplain and [*Edmund or Edward*] (*Ed'm*) Parker until the next [*court*] to show how they entered into the lord's fee etc. Under the penalty that appears etc.

Ordered. It is ordered again to distrain against the next [*court*] John Slauter, Nicholas Josep and William atte Tye to show how they entered into the lord's fee etc. [*then, in a different ink and hand*] for a tenement formerly of William Fant etc.

Amercement 6d. Margaret Donylond puts herself [*in mercy*] for a trespass in the lord's pasture with 12 pigs, by the pledge of William Smyth.

Amercement 3d. Alice atte Piek puts herself [*in mercy*] for the same with 6 pigs by the pledge of Adam Cut etc.

Amercement 4d. John Clark puts himself [*in mercy*] for the same with 8 pigs by the pledge of John Clement.

Amercement 1s. John Lericok puts himself [*in mercy*] for the same and for a trespass in the lord's curtilage with 3 sows, by the pledge of William Smyth.

Amercement 6d. The same John puts himself [*in mercy*] for cutting the lord's trees without licence etc. by the pledge of the aforesaid.

Amercement 4d. John Clerk puts himself [*in mercy*] for a trespass in the lord's wheat with 2 cows and 2 bullocks by the pledge of John Clement.

Amercement 3d. Nicholas Hegeleigh puts himself [*in mercy*] for a trespass in le Launde, in the wood and in le Fen of the lord with his sheep, by the pledge of the bailiff etc.

Amercement 3d. John Clerk puts himself [*in mercy*] for licence to settle with Cecilia atte Brook in a plea of debt by the pledge of John Clement.

Amercement 6d. Alice Donylond for her unjust complaint against John Clerk in a plea of trespass, in mercy.

[*Amercements*] *3s. 9d.* Cecilia atte Brook \2s./ for 15 pigs, Nicholas Hegeleigh \6d./ for 6 pigs, William Chapman \1s./ for 8 pigs and John atte Cherche \3d./ for 1 sow going into the lord's wood at pannage time etc.

Heriot worth 1s. 6d., fealty. The jurors present that Thomas Heym, who held of the lord 1 messuage and 10 acres of land, recently died, after whose death the lord's heriot [*is*] 1 calf worth 1s. 6d. And now comes Thomas Heym, related by blood to the said Thomas [*illeg.*] the said tenement as of right and his inheritance. And because [*illeg.*] is accepted for the tenement. And [*illeg.*] as is evident. And he did fealty.

Also they present that Sir Andrew de Sakevill, knight, John Olyver of S[*illeg.*] and Robert [*illeg.*] acquired 1 messuage and thirteen acres of land from Sir Ralph atte Gate[46] and [*Edmund or Edward*] Parker etc. which tenement was lately held by

---

46 He appears as a chaplain (above in this court roll) and of Bricett in 1367 and 1368 (Court Rolls 14 and 15) with the courtesy title 'Sir' then used for parish clergy.

John Donylond. Therefore it is ordered to distrain the said Sir Andrew, John and Robert to show how they entered into the lord's fee. And that [*illeg.*] at the next [*damaged, illeg.*].

Ordered. Also they present that [*?John ?Brodeye*], John Clod and Adam Cut acquired 1 acre and 1 rood from Andrew Dexter etc. Therefore it is ordered to distrain the said John, John and Adam against the next [*court*] to show how they entered the lord's fee etc.

[*End of roll, probably incomplete.*]

Court Roll 9.[47] (31 July 1363)

Eleigh (*Illeygh*). A court with view [*of frankpledge*] there, held on the Monday next after the feast of St James the apostle in the 37th year of the reign of King Edward the third [*Monday, 31 July 1363*]

Essoins

John Godhale \[*illeg.*] next[48]/ defendant against John called Jolyfiakke in a plea of debt   by John Man.

Amercement 1s. Adam Cut puts himself [*in mercy*] for John Godhale for trespassing in the lord's wheat with beasts etc.

Ordered. Again it is ordered to distrain Stephen Bacon, Richard Skreyk, William Benett and John Cakebred against the next [*court*] to show how they have entered into the lord's fee etc.

Ordered. Again \again/, John Reyner, against the next [*court*], to show how he has entered into the lord's fee etc.

Amercement 2s. Robert Frammesden puts himself [*in mercy*] for Nicholas Hegeleigh for trespassing in the lord's oats with his pigs and geese etc.

Amercement 1s. John Clerk puts himself [*in mercy*] for trespassing in the lord's wheat with 6 beasts by the pledge of John Brysete.

Amercement 3d. John Reyner puts himself [*in mercy*] for licence to settle with John Barker in a plea of debt, in mercy, by the pledge of John Clement.

A day. A day is given to Adam Cut \puts himself[49] [*in mercy*]/, defendant, and Robert Pykele, plaintiff, in a plea of trespass until the next [*court*] to come without essoin.

Amercement 3d. John Buk puts himself [*in mercy*] for trespassing in the lord's wood with his beasts, by the pledge of John Abot etc.

Fealty. To this court came John atte Tye and showed a charter by which he has entered into the lord's fee etc. And he made oath etc.

Fealty. To this court came Richard atte Tye and showed a charter by which he has entered into the lord's fee etc. And he made oath etc.

Fealty. To this court came Alice, lately the wife of John Broun, and showed a charter by which she has entered into the lord's fee etc. And she made oath etc.

Fealty. To this court came Alice, lately the wife of John Broun, and showed a charter by which she has entered into the lord's fee acquired from William de Akenham of

---

47 CCA-U15/15/5 (former CCA document number '48828', '1364' and 'Illeigh Manor, Court Rolls, Temp. Edw. III' written on dorse in a nineteenth-century hand). Parchment roll, two membranes, one fragmentary, both very badly damaged by damp. Latin. One court.
48 Written in a different ink, added later.
49 Added later.

Hadleigh, Peter atte Tye, Thomas atte Tye and John Hunte of Lindsey (*Lelseye*) etc. And she made oath etc.

Fealty. To this court came Christina, lately \the wife/ of William Sweyn, and showed a charter by which she has entered into the lord's fee etc. And she made oath etc.

Fealty. To this court came Peter atte Tye of Lindsey (*Lelseye*) and John his son and showed [*a charter*] by which they have entered into the lord's fee etc. And they made oath etc.

Fealty. To this court came Matilda who was formerly the wife of Andrew Dexter and showed a charter by which she entered into the lord's fee etc. And she made oath.

Amercement 3d. Ralph Swyft puts himself [*in mercy*] for trespassing in the lord's corn with 8 calves by the pledge of Robert Frammesden etc. [*Damaged*]

Heriot 1 ox worth 13s. 4d. Showed a charter. Fealty. The jurors present that Nicholas Hegeleigh who held of the lord one messuage, 1 quarter of the land called [*damaged*], 1 quarter-land from Lyggardesland containing 13 acres,[50] 5 acres of Hutteslond, 21 acres 1 rood [*damaged*] and 25 perches of land, 3 acres, 3 roods of Hunmanneslond, 2 acres 1 rood and 16 [*damaged*] [*perches*] in Monemedwe, 6 acres of land with 1 grove of the mundayland of Wolmeresland [*damaged*] with 1 grove containing 1 acre of Aylredesland and [*blank space*] acres of land of [*damaged*] formerly abbuting, after his death, as a heriot, 1 ox worth 13s. 4d. And to this [*?court came*] [*damaged*] of the deceased and showed a charter by which s/he[51] is joined in the said tenements with the said Nicholas etc. And [*damaged*].

Fealty. To this court came John Abot and Roisa his wife and showed how they have entered [*damaged*] fealty etc.

Chief pledges

<Adam Cut> \John Bresete/	John atte Tye	Robert Gauge	John [*damaged*]
William Smyth	<John de Bresete>	Richard Dul	John [*damaged*]
John Aylward	John Abot	Robert Taylour	<John> \Adam/ Poleyn

Common fine 4s. All the chief pledges present that they give as the common fine as is evident as of ancient times [*damaged*].

Amercement 6d. Also they present that John Petit committed hamsoken [*?against John atte Fen upon which*] [*damaged*] etc. Therefore etc.

Amercement 9d. Also they present that Matilda wife of John Teyler assulted Alice atte Peek [*damaged*] etc. Therefore etc. by the pledge of John Teyler etc.

Amercement 1d. Also they present that William Lerycok assulted Joan Anall, [*?*] Christina [*damaged*] [*raised*] hue justly by the pledge of John Teyler etc.

Amercement 1d. Also they present that William Wynter obstructed the watercourse at Peek to the great [*?*]nuisance [*damaged*].

---

[50] *1 q*[*ua*]*rt' terr' de Lyggardeslond cont' xiij acr'* is ambiguous. It could imply that the land comprised one quarter of the land called Lyggardeslond. However this does not fit with the fact that in Rental 1 (1379–80) Leggardeslond is described as half a customary land comprising a total of 26 acres, ½ rood, 10 perches, of which Margaret Higeliegh then held 13 acres, 16 perches, which is approximately half of the half-land. It has therefore been translated in the sense that the 13 acres effectively comprise a quarter-land (half of a half-land) belonging to Ly/eggardeslond.

[51] The joint tenant may well have been the Margaret Higeliegh (perhaps his wife) who held at least some of these properties in 1379–80 (see previous footnote).

Turn over

Again, as earlier

Amercement 3d. Also they present that Simon Kyng made 1 pit at Le Cangel, etc. to the great nuisance of the neighbourhood etc. Therefore etc.

Amercement 3d. Also they present that Adam Simon still has 1 ditch not cleaned out at Sodeselelane to the nuisance etc. Therefore etc.

Amercement 2d. Also they present that Alice atte Peek has 1 ditch not cleaned out there to the nuisance of passers-by (*ad noc' transeunt'*) etc. Therefore etc.

Amercement 3d. Also they present that Richard atte Tye has 1 ditch not cleaned out at Ravenescroft to the nuisance etc. Therefore etc.

Amercement 1d. Also they present that Michael de Bures has 1 ditch not cleaned out opposite Thomas Webbe's to the nuisance etc. Therefore etc.

Amercement 6d. Also they present that William Chapman and Robert Pekele have 1 ditch not cleaned out opposite Schepkotecroft etc, to the nuisance etc. Therefore the same in mercy etc.

Amercement 3d. Also they present that John Petit has 1 ditch not cleaned out in the king's highway at Petitessloo etc. Therefore etc.

Amercement 1d. Also they present that William Wynter has 1 ditch not cleaned out at Doyescroft etc, to the nuisance etc. Therefore etc.

Amercement 2d. Also they present that Adam Cut and John Godhale have one ditch not cleaned out in Mellelane etc. to the nuisance of the passers-by etc. Therefore etc.

Bakers

Amercements 6d. Also they present that John Hervy \3d./ and Geoffrey de Halle \3d./ are bakers and bake and sell against the assize etc. Therefore the same in mercy.

Brewers

Amercement 4s. 4d.[52] Also they present that John Hervy \1s./ common [*?brewer*] \clerk/, John de Stowe \1s./ common [*?brewer*], John Lerycok \6d./ common [*?brewer*] \bailiff/, John Dul \1s./, John Clement[53] \6d./, William atte Tye \3d./, Adam Spencer \6d./, Cristina Sweyn \3d./, John atte Medwe \3d./, William Morice \1d./, Thomas Reyner \3d./, Nicholas Josep \3d./, <del>Leticia Hert</del> \acquitted by the bailiff because poor/, John Whepsted \3d./ and Robert Gauge \3d./ are brewers and sell against the assize etc. Therefore etc.

Ale tasters

Amercements 6d. Also they present that Thomas Reyner \3d./ and John Clement \3d./ are ale tasters and do not do their duty etc. Therefore etc.

Butchers

[*Damaged*] Also they present that John Bresete is a butcher and sells unclean meat etc. Therefore etc.

[*Damaged*] Also they present that John son of Thomas Reyner \1d./, Henry Fox \ because he came/ are dwellers within the precincts of the leet and are outwith a tithing etc. Therefore etc.

---

[52] The amercements in this section actually add up to 6s. 4d.
[53] His name is surrounded by a curly bracket.

[*Damaged*] [*John*] Clerk and Richard Dul are elected to the office of ale taster etc. And they took their oath etc.

[*Damaged*] Also they present that Thomas Huberd obstructed a certain common way to the nuisance. Therefore etc. And he is ordered to put it right etc.

[*Damaged*] \A day/ is given again to Nicholas Forster until the next [*court*] to show how he entered into the lord's fee.

[*Damaged*] Ralph atte Gate, John de Bresete, John Abot and John Lacy acquired one parcel of land [*damaged*] [*?*]esland containing 5 acres and 2 acres in Moorwall of the said land and 1 acre called Schezingacre of the said land [*damaged*] [*?*]nktel, 3 roods from Smytheslond and in Cuttescroft, 1 acre, 1 rood of pasture of Nether-houslond [*damaged*] and pasture containing half an acre etc. Therefore it is ordered to distrain the said Ralph, John, John and John Lacy against [*damaged*] [*the next court, to show*] how they entered into the lord's fee etc.

[*Damaged*] Clerk puts himself [*in mercy*] for unjustly making ways across the lord's land by the pledge of John Bresete etc.

[*Damaged*] A day is given to Robert Gauge and his associates until the next [*court*] to show how they entered into [*the lord's*] fee [*damaged*].

[*Damaged*] Thomas Huberd to repair a certain way etc. as is evident in the preceding court etc. And it is ordered to distrain the said Thomas [*damaged*] to come to the next [*court*] showing how that way has been repaired etc.

[*Damaged*] at the next [*court*] how John Bren died etc. and how much he held of the lord etc.

Total of this court with view, 19s. 6d. and 1 ox as a heriot worth 13s. 4d., / re[*?tained*] for the stock of the lord[54]\. Affeerers: Adam Cut, John Cabaw. Sworn. [*Membrane 2 too fragmentary to be made sense of. This court roll ends here.*]

Court Roll 10. (between 31 July 1363 and 18 April 1364)[55] *Head of membrane and top right of face missing and damaged, no heading.*

Chief pledges
[*Damaged*] William Smyth [*illeg., damaged*]   John Aylward [*illeg., damaged*]

Common fine 4s. All the chief pledges present that they give as the common fine as [*of ancient custom*] [*damaged*].

Amercement 3d. Also they present that John Abot of Bildeston (*Byldeston*) obstructed [*damaged*] [*illeg.*] etc. Therefore etc.

Amercement 3d. Also they present that John Abot has one ditch not cleaned out [*damaged*] etc. Therefore etc.

---

54 Inserted afterwards in a different ink.

55 CCA-U15/15/13 (former CCA document number '53,988' stamped and altered to '53,989' and '3/6' written on dorse in a nineteenth-century style and hand). Parchment roll, one membrane. Latin. Badly damaged by damp, head missing. One court. This court roll is damaged, and there is no heading to give the date of the single court recorded on it. CCA's catalogue gives an over-arching dating period of *c.* 1350–*c.* 1375. However, it is very similar in content and personnel to Court Roll 9 (31 July 1363), to the extent that it is almost certainly the court immediately following that one, and before that of Court Roll 11 (18 April 1364). John Clerk and Richard Dul who are in this court presented for not doing their duty as ale tasters were elected to office at the court of 31 July 1363 but were still not doing their duty by 18 April 1364. Many of the presentments for having ditches not scoured out in this court are for the same people and presented in the same order as those in the court of 31 July 1363.

Amercement 3d. Also they present that John Sparwe has one ditch not cleaned out [*damaged*].

Amercement 3d. Also they present that <Richard> \Peter/ atte Brook has one ditch not cleaned out [*damaged*] to the damage of the passers-by etc. Therefore etc.

Amercement 4d. Also they present that Roger Maskal obstructs a water course *apud* [*damaged*].

Amercement 3d. Also they present that the same Roger has one ditch not cleaned out [*damaged*].

Amercement 1d. Also they present that Thomas Webbe has one ditch not cleaned out [*damaged*].

Amercement 3d. Also they present that the tenants of the tenement formerly of John Donylond have one ditch not cleaned out [*damaged*] to the nuisance etc. Therefore etc.

Amercement 3d. Also they present that the tenants of the tenement of John Donylond obstruct a water course [*damaged*] to the nuisance etc. Therefore etc.

Amercement 3d. Also they present that the tenants of the tenement formerly of Nicholas Hegeleigh obstructed [*damaged*].

Amercement 2d. Also they present that Simon le Kyng has one ditch not cleaned out [*damaged*].

Amercement 2d. Also they present that Simon Kyng made one pit at le Cangel to the great damage etc. Therefore etc.[56]

[*Amercement* [?]*d.*] Also they present that Alice atte Peek has 1 ditch not cleaned out at Sodesellane to the nuisance of the passers-by etc. Therefore etc.

[*Amercement* [?]*d.*] Also that Richard atte Tye has one ditch not cleaned out at Raveneslane etc. Therefore etc.

[*Amercement* [?]*d.*] Also they present that Michael de Bures has one ditch not cleaned out opposite Thomas Webbe's [*damaged*].

[*Amercement* [?]*d.*] Also they present that John atte Fen has 1 ditch and 1 [*illeg., damaged*].

[*Amercement* [?]*d.*] Also they present that William Chapman and Robert Pekele have one ditch not cleaned out [*?opposite Schepkotecroft*[57]].

[*Amercement* [?]*d.*] [*?Also they present that John Petit has one*[58]] ditch not cleaned out at Petiteslond etc. Therefore etc.

[*Amercement* [?]*d.*] [*?Also they present that William Wynter*] has one ditch not cleaned out at [?]Doyescroft.

[*Amercement* [?]*d.*] [*?Also they present that Adam Cut and*] John Godhale have one ditch not cleaned out [*?in Mellelane*].

[*Damaged*]. dung in the King's highway to the nuisance of the passers-by etc. Therefore etc.

[*Amercement* [?]*d.*] [*illeg.*] in the common way to the nuisance etc. Therefore etc.

[About *6 lines illegible at foot of membrane.*]

Turn over

[*Dorse*]

Again, as before

[*About six lines illegible at head of membrane*]

---

[56] This and following presentments for uncleansed ditches also appear in Court Roll 9 (31 July 1363).

[57] Location as given in Court Roll 9 (31 July 1363).

[58] Editorial insertions in this and the following two entries supplied from commensurate entries in Court Roll 9.

Bakers

Amercements [illeg.]. Also they present that John Hervy \6d./, Geoffrey de Halle \6d./ are bakers and baked and sold against the assize. Therefore etc.

Brewers

Amercement 5s. 3d.[59] Also they present that John Hervy \1s./, John Stowe \1s./, John Dul \1s. otherwise bailiff/, John Clement \1s./, common [*?brewer*] [*illeg.*], Geoffrey atte Halle \3d./ twice, John Clerk \3d./ likewise, John Lerycok \6d./ twice, Alice Taylour \3d./ likewise, Nicholas Joseph \[*illeg.*]d./, [*?*]Letitia Hart likewise, Anna Mundham \3d./ likewise, Simon Chapman \3d./ twice, Robert Gauge \3d./ likewise, William Skynnere \3d./ likewise, John Chapman \3d./ likewise, Adam Spencer \3d./ twice and [*damaged*] sold ale against the assize. Therefore etc.

Ale Tasters

Amercements 6d. Also they present that John Clerk \3d./ and Richard Dul \3d./ are ale tasters and [*damaged*] [*?do not do their duty*].

Butchers

Amercement 7d. Also they present that John Bresete \6d./, Robert [*?*]Fant \1d./ Henry [*damaged*]. Therefore the same in mercy etc.

Affeerers [*damaged*]

Total of this court [*damaged*]

Court Roll 11.[60] (18 April 1364)

[*Damaged*] [*Court held*] on the Thursday next before the feast of St George in the 38th year of the reign of King Edward the Third [*Thursday, 18 April 1364*]

[*Damaged*] John Godenhale puts himself [*in mercy*] for licence to settle with John called Jolfjakke in a plea of debt by the pledge of Adam Cut etc.

[*Damaged*] Adam Cut puts himself [*in mercy*] for licence to settle with Robert Pykele in a plea of trespass by the pledge of Robert Framesden etc.

Amercement 3d. Again it is ordered to distrain Stephen Bacon, Richard Skreyk, William Benett and John Kakebred against the next [*court*] to show how they entered into the lord's fee etc.

[*Damaged*]. Again it is ordered to distrain John Reyner against the next [*court*] to show how he entered into the lord's fee etc.

A day. Again a day is given to Nicholas Fester [*sic*] until the next [*court*] to show how he entered into the lord's fee etc.

Showed a charter. Fealty. To this court came Sir Ralph, chaplain of the parish of Monks Eleigh (*Illeigh Monachorum*), and the rest named in a certain charter and they showed a certain charter by which they entered into the lord's fee, into the land and tenement acquired from Adam Cut etc. And they did fealty to the lord etc.

Showed a charter. Fealty. To this court came Thomas le Fullere and Margaret his wife and showed a certain charter by which they entered into the lord's fee, into the

---

[59] The amercements in this section add up to more than 5s. 3d, but as some are illegible, the exact sum cannot be ascertained.

[60] CCA-U15/15/7 (former CCA document number '48830' written on dorse in a nineteenth-century hand). Parchment roll, one membrane. Latin. Badly damaged by damp. One court.

land and tenement acquired from John Lacy and Alice his wife etc. And they did fealty to the lord etc.

Showed a charter. Fealty. To this court came Nicholas Seg and showed a certain charter, by which he entered into the lord's fee, into a cottage built in Illeigh acquired from John Bolle etc. And he did fealty to the lord etc.

A day. Again a day is given to Robert Gauge and his associates until the next [*court*] to show how they entered into the lord's fee etc.

Ordered. Again it is ordered \to distrain/ Thomas Huberd, or the tenants of the tenement of the said Thomas, that they be at the next [*court*] to show why they and John Cabaw and himself are not obliged to repair a certain way etc.

Amercement 3d. John Clerk puts himself [*in mercy*] for trespassing in the lord's wheat with cows and bullocks etc, by the pledge of John Bresete etc.

Amercement 3d. William Page puts himself [*in mercy*] for the same there with his [?]cow by the pledge of the same.

Amercement 1d. 1 bushel of rye. Richard Dul puts himself [*in mercy*] for a trespass in the lord's rye with 8 beasts by the pledge of the aforesaid [*illeg.*] 1 bushel of rye etc.

Amercement 1d., 1 bushel of rye. John Lerycok puts himself [*in mercy*] for the same there with 4 cows, by the pledge of Robert Gauge etc. [*Illeg.*] 1 bushel of rye etc.

Fealty. To this court came John Abot of Bildeston (*Byldeston*) and Alice his wife. And they did fealty to the lord etc.

Showed a charter. To this court came John Aylward and Juliana his wife and showed a certain charter by which they entered into the lord's fee. And they did fealty to the lord etc.

Ordered. "At the last court a day was given for an inquest [*damaged*] what lands John Bron held on the day that he died. They say on oath that the said John held [*damaged*] jointly with his wife Alice all his lands and tenements by service unknown [*damaged*] Alice is to be distrained to do fealty at the next court etc."

[*Ordered.*] The jurors present that William Loofham acquired one acre of land with appurtenances from Dionisia formerly the wife of John Wrighte. Therefore it is ordered to distrain the said William against the next [*court*] to show how he entered into the lord's fee etc.

Ordered. Also they present that John Knoost acquired a certain land called Palmereslond from Alice Waryn. "It is ordered to distrain the said John to show at the next court how he had thus entered into the lord's fee etc."

Ordered. Also they present that Richard Sparwe held from the lord, by the rod, one messuage [*damaged*] the aforesaid Richard. Therefore it is ordered to seize the said land into the lord's hand and distrain [*damaged*] concerning the aforesaid waste.

A day \inquest/. A day is given to the inquest until the next [*court*] to prove and certify whether John Whepsted [*damaged*].

Also the abovesaid jurors present that John Rycher, sub-bailiff of the half hundred[61] of Cosford on 14th [*day of March*[62]] [*in the*] 38th [*year*] of the reign of the present King [*1363/64*] entered the liberty of the church of Christ of Canterbury at Monks Eleigh (*Illeigh Monachorum*) and without the bailiff of the lord archbishop or the bailiff of the prior, the lord of this manor or the constable of the aforesaid vill, took John atte Tye [*damaged*] and imprisoned him under a certain custody until he

---

[61] Half-hundred written twice, once before and once after Cosford.

[62] Month taken from Stansfield's translation.

made a fine to the steward of St Edmund of 3s. 4d. and to his clerk \and Laurence Porterose/ of 1s. Therefore to take counsel etc.

Also they present that Laurence Porterose, bailiff of the hundred of Babergh (*Babberugh*) and Cosford came to Monks Eleigh on the 20th day of the month of November in the 35th year of the reign of the King then [*1361*] and by colour of his office entered the house of John Chapman of the same place, to make an attachment, that is, to take John Scharp without the bailiff of the archbishop or of the prior or the constable of the aforesaid vill against the liberty of the church of Christ, Canterbury, and to the injury of the same etc. Therefore to take counsel etc.

Counselled. Also they present that William Cokerel, sub-bailiff of the hundred of Bebergh came to the aforesaid Monks Eleigh within the liberty of the church of Christ, Canterbury, and levied from the aforesaid vill, 1s. 8d. In which sum the said vill was liable to amercement at the tourn of the steward of St Edmund at Babergh for defaulting on the same, which certain amercement pertains to the said prior etc. Therefore to take counsel etc.

Amercement 3s. 4d. Also they present that John Lerycok is a brewer and brews, and he does not wish to become ale taster [*?or*] to do his duty separately as bailiff, taster and constable, against the will of the lord etc. And the said John is present in court and puts himself in the lord's grace by the pledges of John Bresete and John Clement etc. And it is ordered to seize into the lord's hands all the lands and tenements of the said John etc. [*Damaged*] etc. until etc.

[*Damaged*] John Lerycok \2s./ and John Dul \6d./ are brewers and [*illeg. and damaged*].

[*Three lines damaged and illegible at foot of membrane*]

[*Dorse*]

Again of the court before

Amercement 1s.[63] Also the aforesaid jurors within written present that John Lerycok \clerk, 1s./, John Dul \[*illeg.*], 1s./, John Stowe \6d./ and [*damaged*] \6d./ are [*?common*] brewers and sell against the assize. Therefore the same in mercy etc.

Amercement 3s. Also it is presented that Alice Bron \3d./, Alice Sparwe \3d./, John Clement \6d./, Adam Spencer \6d./, William Skynnere \3d./, John Scharp \3d./, Robert Gauge \3d./, John Lacy \3d./, Simon Chapman \3d./ and Richard Dul \3d./ are brewers and sell against the assize etc. Therefore etc.

Amercement 6d. Also they present that Richard Dul \3d./ and John Clerk \3d./ are ale tasters and did not do their duty etc. Therefore etc.

Amercement 6d. Also they present that John Harvy \3d./ and Geoffrey de Halle \3d./ are bakers and bake and sell against the assize etc. Therefore etc.

Amercement 6d. Also they present that Thomas Hubard \3d./ and the tenants \3d./ of the tenement of Boyton are suitors of court and have defaulted etc. Therefore etc.

Total of this court 12s. 6d., the price of 2 bushels of rye aforesaid

Affeerers: Adam Cut, Richard Dul

---

[63] The amercements in this section actually add up to 3s.

Court Roll 12.[64] (29 July 1364)

Eleigh (Illeigh). Court with view [*of frankpledge*] there, held on the Monday next after the feast of St James the apostle in the 38th year of the reign of King Edward the third [*Monday, 29 July 1364*]

Showed a charter. Fealty. To this [*court*[65]] came Nicholas Forster, clerk, and showed a certain charter by which he entered into the lord's fee, into the land and tenement \with appurtenances/ acquired from Alice formerly \wife/ of Simon de Lelseye [*Lindsey*], that is to say, 1 quarter of the land called Auncelislond etc. And he did fealty to the lord etc.

Showed a charter. Fealty. To this court came John Bresete, John Abot, Robert Gauge and William Smyth of Monks Eleigh (*Illeigh Monachorum*) and showed a certain charter of enfeoffment by which they entered into the lord's fee, into one piece of meadow called Breggend (*?an enclosed projection, proict' includit[ur]*) etc. And they did fealty to the lord etc.

Ordered. It is ordered at this [*court*] to distrain Stephen Bacon, Richard Skreyk, William Benett and John Cakebred against the next [*court*] to show how they entered into the lord's fee etc.

[*Ordered.*] At this [*court*] it is ordered to distrain Thomas Huberd, or the tenants of the tenement of the said Thomas, that they be at the next [*court*] to show why they and John Cabaw and himself are not obliged to repair a certain way etc.

Showed a charter. Fealty. To this court came William Lofham and Agnes his wife and showed a certain charter of enfeoffment by which they entered into the lord's fee, into one messuage and 1 parcel with its appurtenances acquired from Denis son of a certain William atte Fen. And they did fealty to the lord, etc.

Ordered. It is ordered at this [*court*] to distrain John Knoost[66] against the next [*court*] to show how he entered into the lord's fee etc.

Ordered. It is ordered at this [*court*] to distrain Richard Sparwe against the next [*court*] to answer to the lord in respect of making waste [*?in his tenement*] etc.

Amercement 3d. William Page puts himself [*in mercy*] for a trespass in the lord's oats with his sheep by the pledge of the bailiff.

Amercement 3d. Robert Pekel puts himself [*in mercy*] for a trespass in the lord's wheat in Bradefeld with 3 horses by the pledge of the bailiff.

Amercement 1d. William Page puts himself [*in mercy*] for a trespass in the lord's corn with 6 beasts by the pledge of the bailiff.

Amercement 1d. Alice atte Peek puts herself [*in mercy*] for a trespass in the lord's oats with 15 sheep, by the pledge of [*illeg.*].

Amercement 3d. John Clerk puts himself [*in mercy*] for a trespass in the lord's oats with [*illeg.*].

Amercement 3d. John Lerycok puts himself [*in mercy*] for a trespass in [*illeg.*].

Ordered. The jurors present [*about eight to nine lines illegible because of damp damage and the rest of the membrane torn off. Nothing written on the dorse except labels, so this court ends abruptly here*].

---

64 CCA-U15/15/6 (former CCA document number '48829' and incorrect dates '1365' and '37 Edw. III' written on dorse in a nineteenth-century hand). Parchment roll, one membrane. Latin. Badly damaged by damp, written on face of membrane only. One court.

65 The scribe has mistakenly written 'charter' (*cartam*) here instead of 'court' (*curiam*).

66 Probably the same man as the John Gnost reported as having fled in Court Roll 13 (1365 or 1366).

Court Roll 13.[67] (31 July 1365 or 30 July 1366)[68]

Eleigh (Illegh). [Court and view of frankpledge held there on the] [?]Thursday next \after/ the feast of St James the apostle in the [*damaged*] year of the reign of King Edward [*III, either 31 July 1365 or 30 July 1366*]

[*Damaged*] showed a certain charter by which John Sparewe son of Thomas Sparewe enfeoffed the same with one piece of land [*damaged*] in the vill of Monks Eleigh (*Iillegh [sic] Monachorum*) between the land of Richard Forester on the one hand and the land of Robert Taylour and the said John [*damaged*] according to the form of the statute. Therefore he is admitted a tenant of the lord and did fealty etc. [*Damaged*] [*To this court came*] [*illeg.*] and Basilia[69] his wife and showed a certain charter according to the form of the statute by which they acquired from Thomas Haym of Kettlebaston (*Ketilb'*) [*damaged*] acres of land in the vill of Kettlebaston (*Ketilb'ston'*) of the lord's fee etc. and \the aforesaid Adam/ did fealty etc.
[*Damaged*] To this court came John Chapman and showed a certain charter according to the form of the statute by which he acquired from John Slauhttere of Monks Eleigh (*Illegh Monachorum*) and Thomas Morse of Nayland (*Neylond*) all the lands and tenements which were of the aforesaid John Slauhtter and Thomas, of the lord's fee and he did fealty etc.
[*Damaged*] To this court came John Chapman of Monks Eleigh (*Iillegh Monachorum*) \and John Bolle of the same/ and showed a certain charter according to the form of the statute by which he acquired from Alice Salman of Preston one cottage with a certain curtilage adjoining in the vill of Eleigh (*Illegh*) of the lord's fee and they did fealty etc.
Ordered. [It is ordered], as many times [*before*], to distrain John Reyner against the next [*court*] to show how he entered into the lord's fee etc.
Ordered. Issues (exit') 6d. a year. [It is ordered] to distrain John [?]Gnost[70] to show how he entered into the lord's fee etc. And now it is declared by the court \that/ the said John has fled and nobody occupies the said [*land*] in his name. Therefore

---

67   CCA-U15/14/19 (former CCA document number '53988' stamped and '42/46' written on dorse in a nineteenth-century style and hand). Parchment roll, one membrane. Latin. Badly damaged by damp. One court, after 25 July in whichever year it is, incomplete.

68   This court must date between 31 July 1363 (the first court in Court Roll 10) and 14 January 1366/67 (the first in Court Roll 14) so almost certainly either 31 July 1365 or 30 July 1366. It must post-date the court of 31 July 1363, at which Christina, widow of William Sweyn, took a tenancy: she appears here as Christina Sweyn, who had recently married John Colkyrke, both of them being admitted to the tenancy of the same property. The Thursday after St James' day would be within a week after his feast day of 25 July, so it cannot be 1364 as there is already a court dated to the Monday after St James' day (Court 12, 29 July) in that year. At the current court, one 'John Whepsted called Smart' is reported to have acquired a cottage from William Wynter and was ordered to show how he had acquired it. 'John Smert of Whepstede' showed his charter of acquisition of a messuage from William Wynter of Saxthorpe, Norfolk in Court Roll 14 (14 January 1366/67), so this current court must predate that one. William Chapman and Robert Pykele were amerced at the current court for having a ditch at Boyton not scoured and were ordered to put it right before the next court under a penalty of 1s. 6d. At the court of 14 January 1366/67, the two paid a fine of 3d. each for respite of suit of court, the implication being that they were doing so to avoid the penalty, so this current court pre-dates that of 14 January 1366/67.

69   Basilia is an uncommon name: this couple might be the Adam Serviant and Basilia his wife who are mentioned in Court Roll 2 (*?c.* 1349–50).

70   Probably the same man as the John Knoost who was ordered to be distrained to show how he entered his holding at the court of 29 July 1364 (Court Roll 12).

it is ordered to seize the said land into the lord's hand and concerning its issues to answer to us etc. And the bailiff says that he has demised the said land for 6d a year.
Fealty. To this court came John Hervy, John atte Chirch of Kettlebaston (*Ketelb'ston*) and Thomas Reyner of Eleigh (*Illegh*) and showed a certain writing which testifies that Thomas Hoberd of Preston released all his right which he had in all the lands and tenements which Ralph Sweft the younger formerly acquired by charter from the same Thomas and they asked to be admitted and they were admitted and did fealty to the lord etc.
Ordered, issues. It is ordered, as elsewhere, to answer for the issues of 1 messuage and 1 rood of bond (*native*) land which John Bally and Rosia his wife alienated without the lord's licence to a certain Simon Deney.
Fealty. To this court came John Colkyrke who took to wife Christina Sweyn and did fealty to the lord etc. for a tenement which he holds of the lord by the right of the same Christina.
Amercement 3d. William Page puts himself [*in mercy*] for trespassing in the lord's meadow with his horses by the pledge of John son of Adam atte Tye etc.
Amercement 2d. John Colkerke puts himself [*in mercy*] for making a trespass on the lord by making an unlawful way over the lord's wheat in Illeghfeld by the pledge of John Petyt etc.
Amercement 1d. Simon Kyng puts himself [*in mercy*] for trespassing with his bullocks in Sodesele by the pledge of the bailiff etc.
To answer, heriot. It was found by inquest, taken by virtue of his office by the steward, on the oath of the whole homage jury [*who*] say on their oath that Saher atte Wayour, who held of the lord jointly with Alice his wife one messuage with appurtenances, to hold to the same Saier and Alice and the heirs of the same Saier for service etc. lately on the day [*he died*] etc. after whose death the lord seized one cow worth 10s. calling it a heriot. And because Alice was joined (*coniun[c]ta est*)[71] with the said Saier therefore the said cow was delivered to the said Alice until etc. by the pledges of John Whepsted and Adam Cut for the return of the said cow or its price with the agreement of the lord, which was done. And because the said Alice has not done fealty to the lord, therefore she is distrained against the next [*court*] etc.
Ordered. Also they say that John Abbot of Bildeston (*Bildeston'*) acquired from John Sparwe 2½ acres of land called Littelecroft, parcel of Palmerslond. And John Aylward acquired from Margaret Kalwedon the younger 1 cottage with appurtenances, parcel of Merislond and also from William Mone 2 pieces of land and 1 piece of garden with 1 piece of land with a piece of garden likewise, parcel of Bolleslond and another piece of land is parcel of Reinoldesquarter. And that John Whepsted called Smart[72] acquired 1 cottage with appurtenances from William Wynter. And that John Reyner acquired from Richard Forster half a rood of pasture with appurtenances. And that John Stannard acquired from John atte Chirche 13 feet of land, because all the said lands are of the lord's fee and they have not shown [*how they have entered into them*] etc. Therefore etc.
Amercement 1s. Also they present that the tenants of the tenement of Nicholas Hegelegh \3d./ and of the tenement of John Ive \3d./ and the tenants of the tenement

---

71 Joined as joint tenants as well as joined in marriage.
72 He appears also as John Smert of Whepstead in Court Roll 14 (1367).

Boyton \3d./, the tenants of the tenement of John Clement \3d./ are suitors [*of the court*] and made default.[73] Therefore etc.

Now concerning the view [*of frankpledge*], the day and year above written

Capital pledges

John Brisete	<del>John Whepsted</del> \the aforesaid in place of John atte Tye[74]/	Richard Dul	Thomas Fuller	}
				}
				}
				} Sworn
William Smyth	John Abbot	Robert Taylour	John Clerk	}
John Aylward	Robert Gauge	John Chapman	Adam Poleyn	}
	John son of Adam atte Tye			}

Common fine 4s. All the chief pledges present that they give for the common fine for a single year as is shown etc.

Amercement 1s. John atte Tye, chief pledge, summoned, because he has not come. Therefore in mercy, etc. However he remains a chief [*pledge*].

Amercement 10d. Ordered. Also they present that William Morice \3d./, William Page \2d./, William son of William atte Tye \1d./, Walter Whepsted \1d./, Simon Bron \1d./, William son of Saiher atte Wayour \1d./, and John Chaunceler \1d./ are resident and outside a tithing. Therefore etc.

Amercement 1s. Ordered. Also they present that John Abbot of Bildeston continues [*to have*] 2 ditches next to Sadelersbrigg not cleaned out, to the nuisance etc. Therefore etc. And he is ordered [*to put them right*] under penalty of 2s. etc.

Amercement [?]6d. Ordered. Also they present that John [*damaged*] obstructed 1 ditch next to le Laye to the nuisance etc. Therefore etc. And he is ordered to put it right before the next [*court*] under penalty of 1s.

Amercement [?]1s. Ordered. Also they present that Roger Mason obstructed the common water course at Brokesgate to the nuisance etc. Therefore etc. And he is ordered to put it right before the next [*court*] under penalty of 2s.

Amercement 6d. Ordered. Also they present [*that*] the same Roger has 1 ditch lying near Ilgerslegh not cleaned out etc. to the nuisance [*etc.*]. Therefore etc. And he is ordered to put it right before the next [*court*] under penalty of [?]2s.

Amercement [?]2d. Ordered. Also they present that William Chapman and Robert Pykele have 1 ditch at Boyton not cleaned out to the nuisance etc. And he is ordered [*to put it right*] before the next [*court*] under penalty of 1s. 6d.

Amercement 3d. Also they present that John Petyt has 1 ditch at [?]Pettessle not cleaned out to the nuisance [*etc*]. Therefore etc. And he is ordered [*to put it right*] under penalty of [*illeg.*].

---

73 That is, they all owe suit of court, but have not attended as required.

74 This insertion *predicta loco Johannis atte Tye* does not make sense, although its placing in the text here is clear: if John Whepstead was made a chief pledge in the place of (*loco*) John atte Tye, why is John Whepstead's name crossed through? The addition of John, son of Adam atte Tye to the foot of the column of names indicates that what the clerk really means is that John (son of Adam) atte Tye has replaced John Whepstead as a chief pledge.

Amercement 3d. Also they present that John Stowe has 1 ditch at Doysescroft not cleaned out to the nuisance [*etc*]. Therefore etc. And he is ordered [*to put it right*] under penalty of [*?*]1d.

Amercement 6d. Also they present that William Wynter has 1 ditch at le Peeke not cleaned out to the nuisance [*etc*]. Therefore etc.

Amercement 3d. Also they present that Michael de Bures has 1 ditch opposite Thomas le Webbe's not cleaned out. Therefore etc.

Amercement 6d. Also they present that John atte Fen has 1 ditch at Melle[*?lane*] not cleaned out. [*Illeg.*]

Amercement 3d. Also they present that John atte Tye has 1 ditch at Seggesslow not cleaned out. [*Illeg.*]

[*Amercement*] *1d. Ordered.* Also they present that Alice atte Peek has 1 ditch at Sodeselelane not cleaned out to the nuisance. Therefore etc.

Amercement 5d. To put right. Also they present that Margaret Higelegh has 1 ditch at Sodeselelane and 1 ditch at [*?*]Hunnemannescroft not cleaned out [*illeg.*].

Amercement 2d. To put right. Also they present that Simon Kyng has 1 ditch at le Kangle not cleaned out [*illeg.*].

Amercement 3d. Also they present that Richard ate Tye has 1 ditch at Sexteyesfeld not cleaned out to the nuisance. Therefore etc.

Amercement 3d. To put right. Also they present that Margery Donylond has 1 ditch opposite D[*illeg.*]yscroft not cleaned out, to the nuisance. Therefore etc.

Amercement 3d. To put right. Also they present that Margaret Higgelegh has 1 ditch at [*?Lang*]croft not cleaned out, to the nuisance. Therefore etc.

Ordered. Also they present that the lord prior has 1 ditch at Ravenescroft and 1 ditch at [*illeg.*]. 1 ditch at le Launde not cleaned out to the nuisance. Therefore he is ordered to put them right before the next [*court*] etc.

Ordered. Also they present that the aforesaid lord prior is obliged to repair one [*?bridge*] at le Melle lane [*illeg.*] [*?to be able*] to carry 5 men and he has not repaired it, to the nuisance. Therefore he is ordered to put it right before the next [*court*].

[*Amercement*] [*?*]*1d.* Also they present that William Morice assaulted Alice wife of Simon Deneys drawing her blood against the peace, for which the said Alice raised hue upon the aforesaid William. Therefore etc. by the pledge of Richard Dul.

Also they present that William Liricok beat John ate Mede and drew his blood against the peace Therefore etc. by the pledge of Richard Dul.

Also they present that William Morise made an assault with a knife and drew blood from Robert le Fant against the peace. Therefore etc. by the pledge of Richard Dul.

[*Also*] they present that the same William Morise drew blood from [*illeg.*] Mede against the peace. Therefore etc. by the pledge of the aforesaid.

[*Also they present that*] William Liricok \2d./, Robert le Fant \2d./ [*illeg.*].

[*Bottom of the membrane torn off, so this roll ends here.*]

Court Roll 14.[75] (14 January 1366/67; 29 July, 30 September 1367)

[*Membrane 1, face*] *Eleigh* (*Illegh*). A general court of the prior and convent of the church of Christ, Canterbury, there held on the Thursday next after the feast

---

75 CCA-U15/15/8 (former CCA document number '48823', 'Illeigh' and '1367' written on face of membrane 2 in a nineteenth-century hand). Parchment roll, two membranes stitched together at head

of St Hilary in the 40th year of the reign of King Edward the Third [*Thursday, 14 January 1366/7*]

Essoin

John Godale [*essoins himself*] of common [*suit*]   by Robert Pyrye.
Fine [*illeg.*].

Fine 3d. Thomas Marchaunt give to the lord as a fine for the same as is apparent etc.

Fine 3d. John atte Cherche give to the lord as a fine for the same as is apparent etc.

Fines 6d. William Chapman \3d./ and Robert Pykele \3d./ give to the lord as a fine in respect of the tenement Boyton for respite of suit of court [*illeg.*] as is apparent etc.[76]

Showed a charter. Fealty. John Aylward the elder came to this court and showed a charter by which he acquired two pieces of arable land lying in the vill of Eleigh (*Illegh*) in the field called Honemanesfeld, of which one piece contains 1 acre and half a rood of land and is of Boleslond and the other piece contains 1½ acres and is of Reynoldeslond, from William Mone of Lindsey (*Lelleseye*) to have to the aforesaid John and his heirs of the chief [*lords of the fee*] etc. to hold etc. in perpetuity. And he was admitted to the tenement and did fealty etc. which is of the lord's fee etc.

Showed a charter. Fealty. Alice Peek of Monks Eleigh (*Illegh Monachorum*) came to this court and showed a charter by which she acquired from Ralph atte Gate of Bricett, chaplain, [*?*]8 acres of land and 1½ acres of wood of Sweyneslond and 1 acre and 1 rood of land from Salmaneslond, to have and to hold to her and her heirs of the chief [*lords of the fee*] etc. in perpetuity etc. And she was admitted. And she did fealty etc. because of the lord's fee etc.

Showed a charter. Fealty. John Smert of Whepstead (*Whepstede*) came to this court and showed a charter by which he acquired from William Wynter of Saxthorpe (*Saxthorp*) [*Norfolk*] a messuage which was formerly William Chapman's containing 1 rood of Scarlateslond to have and to hold to the aforesaid John, his heirs and assigns, of the chief [*lords of the fee*] etc. in perpetuity etc. And he was admitted. And he did fealty etc. which is of the lord's fee etc.

Showed a charter. [*Fealty*]. John Clerk and Matilda his wife came to this court and showed a charter by which the same [*Matilda*] when she was single, by the name of Matilda Sparwe, acquired from Robert Gauge 4 acres of land with a way called le Smaleweye, 1½ acres of meadow and 7 roods of wood which are of Sweyeneslond. To hold and to have to the aforesaid Matilda for her whole life and after her death to Thomas her son, his heirs and assigns, in perpetuity. And she was admitted. And she did fealty. And also she showed another charter by which the same Matilda acquired from the same Robert three pieces of land from Sweyneslond lying in a croft called Sweynescroft which was formerly John Sparwe's and two pieces of pasture called [*?*]Ferthingespightel and Gibbesmedwe of Sweyneslond. To have and to hold to the aforesaid Matilda for the term of her life and after her death to John her son, his heirs and assigns in perpetuity. And also she showed another charter by which the same Matilda when she was single acquired from the same Robert one piece of meadow, that is to say, 3 roods of Hutteslond and half an acre of Sweyneslond.

(membrane 1 written on face only, membrane 2, both face and dorse written on). Latin. Three courts.

[76] The tenants of the tenement of Boyton were presented for defaulting on their attendance at court on 18 April 1364 (see Court Roll 11). William Chapman and Robert Pykele were amerced for having a ditch unscoured at Boyton in Court Roll 13 (1365 or 1366).

To have and to hold to the aforesaid Matilda, her heirs and assigns in perpetuity, of the chief [*lords of the fee*] etc. of the lord's fee. And they were admitted as tenants. And did fealty etc.

Showed a charter. [*?*]*Fealty.* Simon [*sic*] Chapman and Margaret his wife came to this court and showed a charter by which they acquired from John Lay 1 acre and 3 roods of Smetheslond of the lord's fee. To have and to hold to the aforesaid John [*sic*] and Margaret, their heirs and assigns, in perpetuity, of the chief [*lords of the fee*] etc. And they were admitted etc. And did fealty.

Showed a charter. Fealty. John Aumfrey and Agnes his wife came to this court and showed a charter by which they acquired from John Stowe and Isabella his wife one messuage with the buildings erected upon it in Eleigh (*Illegh*), parcel of Agneysmondaylond the Wedwe, of the lord's fee. To have and to hold to them and their heirs in perpetuity, of the chief [*lords of the fee*] etc. And they also showed another charter by which the same had acquired from William Wynter of Saxthorpe [*Norfolk*] one piece of land called Doysecroft containing 3½ acres of land, of which 3 acres [*are*] of Tynteslond and half an acre is from [*?*]Smytheslond. To have and to hold to them, their heirs and assigns in perpetuity, of the chief [*lords of the fee*] etc. which is of the lord's fee etc. And they were admitted as tenants. And did fealty etc.

Ordered. John de Benton complains against John Reyner in a plea of trespass. And in respect of which, the plaintiff [*says*] that on the Wednesday next after the feast of Epiphany in the said 40th year of the reign of King Edward the Third [*Wednesday, 13 January 1366/67*] the said John Reyner incited his dog to bite the sheep of the aforesaid John de Benton in such a way that by that attack 1 sheep of the aforesaid John was killed, to his damage of 2s. And in respect of which he brings forward his suit etc. And the aforesaid John Reyner said that he was in no way guilty thereof. And for this he puts himself on the country. And another [*illeg.*]. Therefore an inquest was taken etc. who say on their oath that the aforesaid John Reyner is guilty thereof to the damage of 1s. 4d. Therefore it is found that the aforesaid John de Benton should recoup his aforesaid damages etc. And the aforesaid John Reyner in mercy, etc. And it is ordered to raise the aforesaid damages from the aforesaid to his use etc.

Amercement 3d. Simon Kyng because he attacked (*incidit versus*) Agnes Donylond in a plea of trespass and that her corn and grass to the value of 1s. was eaten by one of his horses etc, for which it is ordered to raise to the use of the aforesaid Alice etc. in mercy.

Amercement 2d. The same Alice for falsifying her claim against the same Simon in a plea of trespass, in mercy.

Amercement 1d. William Lofham because he attacked Simon Kyng in a plea of trespass to his damage of 3d. in mercy. And it is ordered to raise the aforesaid damages to the use of the aforesaid Simon etc.

Amercement 3d. Ordered. The same Simon because he attacked the same William and Agnes his wife in a plea of trespass, in such a way that he beat and wounded the same Alice on the Monday next after the feast of Pentecost in the 40th year [*of the reign of King Edward III, Monday, 25 May 1366*], the aforesaid Agnes [*repeated*] etc. to her damage of 3s. 4d. in mercy. And it is ordered to raise the aforesaid damages to the use of the aforesaid [*Alice*] etc.

Penalty. Simon Kyng, because he threatened the same William Lofham to come in person and find pledges for himself for good behaviour towards him and others under penalty of 3s. 4d. etc.

A fine called merchet 2s. 6d. The jurors present by virtue of their office that John Chapman tenant of the lord gives to the lord as a fine for his daughter Alice marrying outside the vill, as of ancient custom as usual etc.

Ordered. The same present that John Abot, John Whepsted, John Reyner, Thomas Abot, Roger son of Stephen and Richard de Lofham acquired [*land*] in various places of the lord's fee and have not shown the lord how they entered etc. Therefore it is ordered to distrain the same to show [*this*] before the next [*court*] and to do fealty for it to the lord etc.

Fine 1s. John Lerecok makes a fine to the lord for trespassing in his corn and grass very often as is apparent etc.

Fine 3d. John Whepsted gives as a fine for respite of suit of court until the next [*court*] as is apparent etc.

Amercements [illeg.]. Also the aforesaid jurors present that Geoffrey atte Halle \4d./ common [*brewer*], John Hervy \4d./ common [*brewer*], Margaret Hod \[*illeg.*] 6d./, John Dul \[*?*]hen, 4d./ common [*brewer*], Robert Gauge\3d./, [*?*]Roger [*?*] Hart \[*?*]2d./, Thomas Reyner \3d./, John Lyricok \3d./, John Benton \[*illeg.*]/, John Clement \3d./, Adam Spencer \3d./, William Skynnere \3d./, Christina [*?*]Fant \3d./, Henry Slauhtere \3d./ are brewers and sold ale against the assize. Therefore in mercy.

Amercements 4d. The same present that Geoffrey atte Halle \2d./ and John Hervy \2d./ are bakers and sold bread against the assize. Therefore the same in mercy.

Amercement 6d. The same present that Thomas Fullere \3d./ and John Wendecole \3d./ are tasters of bread and ale and have not done their duty. Therefore in mercy.

[Ale-]Taster. Also they present that John Clement is the most suitable for the office of [*ale*] taster in place of Thomas Fullere who was [*?*]sworn to the said office.

Amercement 5d. John Petyt \1d./, John Mellere \2d./ and John Dul \2d./ put themselves [*in mercy*] for trespassing in the lord's wheat with their pigs etc.

[Illeg.] Again it is ordered to distrain John atte Cros and Egidia his wife, John Abot \showed⁷⁷/ of Bildeston (*Bildiston*) and Richard le Clerk [*damaged*] to show how they entered into the lord's fee in various places as appears in the preceding court and to do fealty to the lord etc.

Affeerers: John Clerk, John Wendecole

Total of this court, besides the fee of the clerk and bailiff, 10s. 2d.

[*End of membrane 1 face. Nothing is written on dorse of membrane 1.*]

[*Membrane 2, face.*] Eleigh (*Illegh*). Court with view [*of frankpledge*] of the lord prior and convent of the church of Christ, Canterbury, there "on the Thursday next after the feast of St" James the apostle [*25 July*] in the 41st year of the reign of King Edward the third [*29 July 1367*].

Essoins

Margaret Hyggelegh [*essoins herself*] of common [*suit*]   by William [*?*]Peytenyn.

John atte Fen of the same   by Thomas Webbe.

John le Buk of the same   by John Abot.

John atte Tye senior of the same   by Robert Gauge.

Richard Dul of the same   by "John de Bresete".

Geoffrey de Halle of the same   by John atte Cherche.

[*Bracketed to the right of all six entries above*] Affeered for the 1st time (1° Aff')

---

⁷⁷ Annotation added later.

Showed a charter. Fealty. John Broun and Margaret his wife came to this court and showed a charter by which they had acquired from "John Abot" of Eleigh (*Illeigh*) one messuage with a certain piece of arable land adjacent, a projection enclosed from the land of Godhynesquarter lying between the land of the said John Broun on both sides, one head abutting upon the land of Peter atte Tye and the other upon the street (*stratum*) called Stakwodestrete to hold to them and their heirs, of the chief [*lords of the fee*], etc. And they did fealty etc.

Showed a charter. Fealty. William atte Ware of Lindsey (*Lelleseye*) and Joanna his wife came to this court and showed a charter by which [*they acquired from*] "Peter atte Tye and John" Lyvene of Lindsey all the lands and tenements which they formerly held of the gift and feoffment of the said Joan in the vill of Monks Eleigh (*Illeigh Monachorum*) of the land of Godhyneslond, to hold to them and the heirs of the aforesaid Joan, of the chief [*lords of the fee*], etc. which are of the lord's fee. And they did fealty, etc.

Showed a charter. Fealty. Ralph atte Gate of Bricett (*Bresete*), chaplain, came to this court and showed a charter by which the same acquired from Ralph Leggard of Eleigh (*Illegh*) two pieces of land lying in Eleigh (*Illeigh*), of which one piece lies between the land of William Wynter on the east side and the land of a certain John Donylond, and the other piece of land is called le Leeye and lies between the wood called O3framynesgrove on the one hand and the land of Simon Kyng on the other. To hold to him and his heirs, of the chief [*lords of the fee*] etc, of the lord's fee of Maskaleslond. And he did fealty etc. And also he showed another charter by which he acquired from John Stowe of Monks Eleigh (*Illegh Monachorum*) one built messuage lying in Eleigh (*Illegh*) aforesaid between the meadow of Simon Chapman on the south side and the king's highway leading towards Ipswich (*Gipwycum*) on the other, of a mondaylond, of the lord's fee. To hold of the chief [*lords of the fee*], to him and his heirs. And he did fealty etc.

Showed a charter. Fealty. John Abot senior of Bildeston (*Bildyston*) and Alice his wife and Margaret, daughter of the aforesaid John Abot, came to this court and showed a charter by which they had acquired from John Sparwe, son of Thomas Sparwe of Eleigh (*Illegh*), one croft of arable land, just as it is enclosed with hedges and ditches between the land of John Abot cordwainer (*cordewaner*) on the one hand and land formerly of John Broun on the other, from the land of Palmereslond, of the lord's fee, etc. To hold to them and their heirs of the chief [*lords of the fee*] etc. And they did fealty etc.

Showed a charter. Fealty. John Slauhtere, William Smyth, William atte Tye, John Chapman and Ralph atte Gate, chaplain, came to this court and showed a charter by which they had acquired from Margaret Cut her reversion of the lands and tenements after the death of Adam Cut her father in the vill of Eleigh (*Illeigh*) which are of the land formerly of Amiel de Becche, of the lord's fee. To hold to them and their heirs of the chief lords of the fee etc. Upon which the said Adam, being present in court, was examined, well knowing that he was appointed attorney for the aforesaid John, William, William, John and Ralph etc. And the same were admitted to the tenements as above. And they did fealty etc.

Showed a charter. Fealty. Simon de Salle, rector of the church of Monks Eleigh (*Illeigh Monachorum*), came to this court and showed a charter by which he had acquired from William Wynter of [?]Barningham (*Bermyngham*)[78] three pieces of

---

[78] Probably Barningham (Suffolk) or possibly one of the Norfolk Barninghams.

land lying in Eleigh (*Illegh*) aforesaid in the field called Burton, of which one piece lies between the land of the church of Eleigh (*Illegh*) aforesaid on both sides and another piece lies between the land of the said church on the one hand and the land of the lord prior and convent on the other and the third piece lies between the land formerly of John atte Tye on the one hand and the pasture of Richard Forster on the other, which are of the land of Palmereslond, of the lord's fee. To hold to him and his heirs of the chief lords of the fee etc. And he is admitted to the tenements. And he did fealty etc.

Acquired. Ordered. It was found by the inquest, taken by virtue of their office, that John Abot of Eleigh (*Illegh*) \showed [*a charter*]/ acquired from John Buk one messuage and "one" acre of land and [*damaged*] and from Richard Forster one piece of land of the lord's fee. Also that John Davy acquired from John Buk one piece of pasture. And that Thomas Webbe acquired from John Reyner one garden etc. Also that John Dul acquired from John Chapman 11 acres of land of Ilgereslond. And that John Clerk acquired from Simon Kyng 2 acres of land. Also that Alice Saleman acquired from John Chapman and John Bolle a cottage with a garden. Also that Ralph Prest acquired from Ralph Leggard two pieces of land etc. concerning which the above to show charters, therefore, etc. Also that John Whepstede acquired from William Wynter one messuage situated on three acres of land. Also that Rose Hard and others acquired from Thomas Fullere and Nicholas Josep' one cottage. Also that William de Ware of Lindsey (*Lelleseye*) \showed [*a charter*]/acquired from Peter atte Brook all his lands and tenements, etc. concerning which the above to show [*their charters*] etc. Also that John Broun \showed [*a charter*]/ acquired from John Abot of Eleigh (*Illeigh*) one messuage with a certain piece of land adjacent for which the above showed a charter and did fealty etc. all of which lands and tenements aforesaid are of the lord's fee. Therefore it is ordered to distrain those who have not shown charters against the next court, to do fealty to the lord etc.

Amercement 7d. William Page puts himself [*in mercy*] for trespassing in the lord's wheat, by estimation half a bushel of wheat,[79] with his oxen.

Amercement 5d. John Clerk puts himself [*in mercy*] for trespassing in the wheat and rye with 5 beasts, by the pledge of John Clement.

Amercement 3d. Robert Deye puts himself [*in mercy*] for trespassing in the wheat with his cows.

Stray 1s. Ordered. The jurors present that a certain piglet, worth 1s., has come into the possession of the lord as a stray (*stray*).

Ordered. It is ordered that the bailiff distrain all who have acquired [*land*] from the lord's fee and not shown the lord a charter as is apparent in the aforesaid court, to do fealty to the lord. And to execute all orders contained in the last court and view and not executed etc. And to raise all debts and damages recovered as is apparent in the previous court etc.

Ordered. It is ordered to distrain John Abot, John de Whepstede, John Reyner, Thomas Abot \[*illeg.*]/, Roger son of Stephen and Richard de Lofham and John atte Cros and Egidia his wife and Richard le Clerk of Kersey (*Kerseye*) to show how they entered into the lord's fee in various places and to do fealty, etc.

---

79 Presumably the estimated amount of damage done to the crop by the animals.

Now the view [*of frankpledge*]

Common fine 4s. All chief pledges, that is to say, John Bresete, John Aylward, Robert Gauge, Richard Dul, John Chapman, John [*?*]Clerk, William Smyth, John Abot, John son of Adam Tye, Robert Taillour, Thomas Fullere, Adam [*?*]Poleyn, [*say*] that they give for the common fine for themselves and their tithings on the day of the view [*of frankpledge*] as is apparent etc.

Amercements 8s. 3d. [*illeg.*]. Also they present that Geoffrey de Halle \clerk, 1s. 6d./ and John Hervy \[*?*]hen, 1s./, John Dul \1s./, John Clement\1s./, Alice, wife of Saier atte Wayour \3d./, Simon Chapman \3d./ [*illeg.*] Mundham \3d./, Leticia Hert \3d./, John de Stowe \3d./, Thomas Veyse \3d./, William Serviens \3d./, John Whepstede, Henry le Fox \3d./, Nicholas Joseep' \3d./, [*?*]Richard Hard \3d./, Thomas Reyner \3d./, William Smyth \3d./, Alice, wife of Henry Taillour \3d./, John Lyricok \3d./, Margaret Hod \7d./, Simon Deneys \2d./, Adam Spencer \3d./, [*?*]John Melnere \ [*?*]3d./, William Skynnere \3d./, Rose Gauge \3d./, Nicholas Seg \3d./, Richard Dul \3d./ and Richard de Lofham \3d./ are brewers and brewed ale against the assize and are in mercy.

Amercement 6d. Also they present that John Wendecole \3d./ and John Clement \3d./ are tasters of ale and have done their duty negligently. Therefore in mercy.

Amercement 6d. Also they present that John Hervy is a common baker and baked bread and sold it against the assize. Therefore in mercy.

Amercement 3d. Also they present that John de Bresete is a butcher and sold meat outside the burgh (*extra burgam*).[80] Therefore in mercy.

Amercement 6d. Also they present that Simon Deneys \[*illeg.*]/, William Page \2d./, Henry Gardyner \2d./ and William son of [*damaged*] atte Tye are resident within the lord's liberty for one year and one day and are outwith a tithing. Therefore the same in mercy. And it is ordered to distrain them [*damaged*] etc.

Amercement 6d. Also they present that Stephen of the household (*manupastus*)[81] and William Page made an unlawful recovery from the bailiff. [*Damaged, therefore in*] mercy.

Amercement 3d. John Clerk chief pledge made default. Therefore in mercy.

Ordered. It is ordered to distrain William son of Sayer atte Wayour and Walter Whepstede [*damaged, until*] the next [*court*].

Election of [*Ale-*]*Tasters.* Also they present that John Lyrycok and John Wendecole are the most suitable for the office of ale taster than any others.

Amercement 3d. Also they present that Alice Sparwe raised hue upon John Sparwe unjustly. Therefore in mercy.

Amercement 4d. Also that Richard [*?*]Pasper drew blood from John Peryndon of Milden against the peace and he is attached by the pledge of [*damaged*].

Amercement 6d. Also they present that Nicholas Ketyl beat William Wyng against the peace for which the same William raised hue upon him [*damaged*].

---

[80] The text has *burgam*, although Monks Eleigh was not a town or borough, fortified or otherwise. The term may derive from '*borga* [AS *borg*] , frankpledge, tithing, group of households with collective legal responsibility (in Kent and Sussex a territorial unit)' (*DMLBS*). If so, it implies the area within the jurisdiction of the manorial view of frankpledge (and see also p. 33, footnote 16). Alternatively, it could reflect the local terminology of Suffolk villages, however small, calling themselves 'towns' until well into the eighteenth century.

[81] Literally 'Stephen fed by hand'. Although not stated, the household to which he belonged might have been the bailiff's, making Stephen one of the manorial *famuli*.

Amercement 3d. Also that John Gauge struck John Reyner for which he justly raised hue upon him. Therefore in mercy.

Amercement 3d. Also they present that John Broun dragged a furrow through the middle of the meadow of Couperesmondaylond by which [*?the water, damaged*].

Amercement 4d. Also they present that Roger Maskal has one ditch next to his horse-pond (*waieram*) not cleaned out and further they present [*damaged*].

Amercement 7d. Also that the same Roger has one ditch at La Leye not cleaned out to the nuisance etc. And further they present that he has not mended [*illeg.*].

Amercement 4d. Also they present that John atte Fen has one ditch at La Hoolstrete not cleaned out, to the nuisance etc. Therefore in mercy.

Amercement [*illeg.*]. Also they present that John Dul \6d./ made an encroachment with a cottage upon the common way. And that the same John \6d./ diverted the water there by which the way is flooded to the nuisance etc. Therefore in mercy. It is ordered by all the chief pledges themselves that the aforesaid encroachment be removed.

Amercement [*illeg.*] Also they present that Christina Vant deposited dung in the common way to the nuisance etc. Therefore in mercy. And they further present that she has not put it right. Therefore it is ordered that she rectify it before the next court under penalty of [*?*]3s. 4d.

Amercement [*illeg.*]. Also they present that John Reyner has one ditch not cleaned out at Le Fenstrete, to the nuisance etc. Therefore in mercy.

Amercement [*?*]4d. Also they maintain that William Wynter has one ditch not cleaned out at Le Peek. Therefore in mercy and further they present [*?he has not put it right, damaged*].

Turn over

"Memorandum of a certain cow delivered" to the warden as a heriot after the death of Thomas atte Brook "worth 8s. 4d."

[*Membrane 2, dorse.*]

Again, as before

[*About eight to ten lines illeg.*]

Eleigh (*Illeigh*). General Court held there "on the Thursday next after the feast of St Michael in the 41st year of the reign of King Edward the third" [*Thursday, 30 September 1367*]

Essoins

John atte Fen [*essoins himself*] of common [*suit, damaged*].

John Goodhale of the same [*damaged*].

Robert Gauge of the same [*damaged*].

John Buk of the same [*damaged*].

[*Illeg.*] Richard Dul has not warrantied [*his essoin, illeg.*].

[*Illeg.*] "The tenants of the lands and tenements of" Parkeres give to the lord as a fine for suit of court for the year.

Amercement 3d. [*?Geoffrey Gilssone gives to the lord as a fine for the same*].

Amercement 3d. William atte Ware gives to the lord as a fine for the same.

Amercement 3d. William Chapman gives to the lord as a fine for the same for Boyton's tenement.

Showed a charter. Thomas Syward of Monks Eleigh (*Illegh Monachorum*) came and showed a charter by which he acquired from John Reygner of Eleigh (*Illegh*) one

142

messuage lying in the vill aforesaid from the land [*?he worked*] (*opar'*) land lying between the meadow of the lord prior and the pasture of Michael de Bures together with 1 pasture adjacent [*?to the demesne*]. And since the said charter was made according to the form of the statute, he is admitted. And he did fealty.

Showed a charter. John Abot showed a charter by which the same and Roesa his wife acquired from John Buk of Eleigh (*Illeigh*) one built messuage with a croft adjacent and a wood called Bukkesgrove of Baxtereslond, one piece of land called Cokyscroft and 2 pieces of land in Bukkysschrubbis from the land of Rolf, one piece of land called Bukkeslegh from Knappokeslond and [*illeg.*] the wood called Bukkesgrove aforesaid containing 16 feet in width. To hold to the said John Abot and Roesa and their heirs in perpetuity. And since the charter was made according to the form of the statute they were admitted. And they did fealty.

[*Illeg.*] John Sparwe of Stakwode gives to the lord as a fine for respite of suit of court for 1 year as is apparent.

[*Illeg.*] Roger Maskal \3d./, Thomas Reyner \3d./, John Hervy \3d./, Richard Lofham \3d./, John atte Cherche \3d./, Simon Kyng \3d./ are suitors [*of this court*] and defaulted. Therefore in mercy.

Brewers

Amercements [*illeg.*]. Ordered. The jurors present that John Dul \3d./ common [*?brewer*], Robert Deye \6d./ and John Hervy \[*illeg.*]d./, Geoffrey de Halle \3d./, Richard de Lofham \3d./, Simon Deneys \3d./, Nicholas [*?*]Joseep \3d./, John Clement \3d./, Adam Spencer \3d./, John Petyt \3d./, Laurence Cartere \1d./ are brewers and sold ale against the assize. Therefore in mercy.

[*Illeg.*] Also they present that Geoffrey de Halle is a baker and breaks the assize. Therefore in mercy. And John Hervy "is a butcher and breaks the assize".

It is ordered the bailiff must execute all the orders contained in the last court etc.

[*Illeg.*] *Fine.* "The jurors" seek "a remit to present" at the next [*court*] many tenants of Smytheslond who hold by making iron for the lord for the whole apparatus pertaining to 2 ploughs "for the coulter" and the ploughshare each year, of which land John Bresete holds a parcel, who asks that it be apportioned etc. And he gives as a fine [*blank*].

[*Manicule*]. *Ordered. Issues.* It is ordered to seize into the lord's hand 1 piece of pasture at Ravenescroft, 1 piece of pasture at Sextenesfeld which Richard atte Tye holds by the rod. And 2 acres of land which Simon Tollelone holds by the rod. And 1 headland atte Mersh which William Wynter holds by the rod and to answer for the issues until etc. for that they have not taken them in court, from the lord's hand, nor have they [*illeg.*] by licence of the lord etc.

Affeerers: John [*?*]Abot, John [*?*]Wendecole
Total, "5s. 10d."

Court Roll 15.[82] (24 July, 2 October 1368; 17 September 1369)

Eleigh (*Illeigh*). A court with view [*of frankpledge*] there held on the Monday in the vigil of St James the apostle in the 42nd year of the reign of King Edward the third [*Monday, 24 July 1368*]

---

82 CCA-U15/15/9 (former CCA document number '48831', 'Illeigh' and '1369' written on dorse in nineteenth-century hand). Parchment roll, one membrane. Latin. Damaged by damp. Three courts with views of frankpledge.

Amercement 3d. Robert Gauge \came/ and John Buk because they have not warranted their essoins, in mercy.

Showed a charter, fealty. William Lofham, taylor, came to this court and showed a charter by which he acquired a certain curtilage lying in Eleigh (*Illegh*) [*damaged*] land formerly of John atte Fen and a tye called Illegh Tye, of the lord's fee, of Fenneslond. To hold to himself and his heirs of the chief lords of the fee. And he was admitted. And he did fealty etc.

Showed a charter, fealty. Richard, son of a certain Matthew de Lofham, came and showed a charter by which he acquired from Thomas Choney of Hitcham (*Hecham*) all his free lands and tenements in the vill of Hitcham of the fee of the lord of Eleigh (*Illeigh*). To hold to him and his heirs of the chief lords etc. And he was admitted for the holding. And he did fealty etc. And this is of Loseslond.[83]

Amercement 3d. Robert Chok puts himself [*in mercy*] for licence to settle with Nicholas Mowyere in a plea of contract. Therefore in mercy, by the pledge of Nicholas Ketyl.

Amercement 2d. John Reyner puts himself [*in mercy*] for licence to settle with Thomas Reyner in a plea of debt. Therefore in mercy, by the pledge of John Clement.

Amercement 2d. The same John puts himself [*in mercy*] for licence to settle with John Lacy in a plea of debt. Therefore in mercy.

Amercement 3d. William Page puts himself [*in mercy*] for trespassing in the lord's wheat with 2 oxen.

Amercement 3d. Ralph de Hitcham (*Hecham*) puts himself [*in mercy*] for trespassing in the oats with his bullocks. Therefore in mercy.

Showed a charter, fealty. Nicholas Ketyl of Thorpe Morieux (*Thorp Moryaux*) and Anne his wife came to this court and showed a charter by which they acquired from John Abot of Monks Eleigh (*Illeigh Monachorum*) and Roesia his wife one messuage with the buildings erected upon it and with a certain piece of arable land adjacent in the aforesaid vill of Eleigh (*Illeigh*), of the lord's fee, of the land called Rolfeslond. To hold to them and their heirs of the chief lords of the fee etc. And they were admitted for the holding. And did fealty etc.

Fealty, showed a charter. John Davy came here into court and showed a charter by which he acquired from John Buk of Monks Eleigh (*Illeigh Monachorum*) one cottage and one piece of land called Humbilbankyscroft, of the lord's fee, from a mondayland. To hold to him and his heirs of the chief lords of the fee. And he was admitted. And he did fealty etc.

Amercement 3d. John Smert puts himself [*in mercy*] for trespassing in the lord's pasture with his sheep. Therefore in mercy.

Amercement 3d. John Clerk puts himself [*in mercy*] for trespassing in the lord's wheat with 3 horses. Therefore in mercy.

Amercement 3d. The same John puts himself [*in mercy*] for trespassing with his beasts in a pasture. Therefore in mercy.

Fine 2s, fealty. The lord granted out of his hands to Richard atte Tye two pieces of pasture with the hedges and ditches set out thereupon, in respect of which, 1 piece [*is*] of Sexteynesfeld and the other piece, of Ravenescroft. To hold to him and his offspring (*sequel'*)[84] of the lord, by the rod, according to the custom of the manor,

---

83 Loseland was property belonging to the manor of Monks Eleigh lying in Hitcham.

84 *Sequela* means literally 'followers', although it can be used for the offspring or brood of both livestock and unfree villeins on a manor, this language being a sure mark of derogatory attitudes to

at the will of the lord. And for ancient service, that is, rendering 1s. 4d. a year. And he did fealty etc.

Showed a charter, fealty. John Clerk of Chelsworth came to this court and showed a charter by which he acquired two pieces of land of Dextereslond from Ralph atte Gate, chaplain. And he also showed another charter by which he acquired from Simon le Kyng of Eleigh (*Illeigh*) one piece of land with a way called le Cangel for carrying and driving, of the land of Sweyneslond. To hold to him and his heirs, of the chief lords etc. And he was admitted. And he did fealty etc.

Ordered. The jurors present that Robert Taillour, William de Peytoo [*sic*] and John Mellere acquired from John Sparwe one messuage and four acres of land, of a mondayland. Therefore it is ordered to distrain them for fealty.

Ordered. Also that John Bolle acquired from John atte Fen one acre of arable land of Vanteslond. Therefore, it is ordered to distrain [*him*] for fealty.

Ordered. Also that John Reyner acquired from Thomas Webbe one orchard with appurtenances. Therefore, it is ordered to distrain [*him*] etc.

Relief 2½d. Also that Ralph Swyft the elder who held of the lord four acres of land of Tenteslond for service and custom, etc. closed his last day.[85] And that Ralph his son and heir is of full age. And gave to the lord as a relief as is shown.

Showed a charter, fealty. John Dul came to this court and showed a charter by which he and Margaret his wife acquired a grove called Ilgeresgrove and a croft and meadow called Ilgeris adjacent with appurtenances, of Ilgereslond, from John Chapman of Monks Eleigh (*Illeigh Monachorum*). To hold to him and his heirs, of the chief lords etc. And he was admitted. And he did fealty.

Ordered. It is ordered to distrain Richard Forster to answer to the lord for trespassing in the wheat and in the rye with his pigs and beasts continuously.

Total, 4s. 3½d.

Common fine, 4s. John Bresete, John Aylward, Robert Gauge, John Wendcole, John Dul, John Clerk, William Smyth, John Abot, John son of Adam Tye, Robert Taillour /Richard Dul\, Thomas Fullere, Adam Poleyn /[*illeg.*]\ capital pledges, sworn, present that they give as the common fine for themselves and their tithings as of the custom, as is shown.

Amercement 3d. Also they present that Margaret wife of John Reyner beat John Chapman on the head and drew blood. And Agnes his wife justly raised hue upon her and finds a pledge, namely John Bresete.

Amercement 2d. Also that the same Margaret brought in [*a crop from*] the close of Isabel Gerl against the peace and took away peas for which the same Isabel justly raised hue, by the pledge aforesaid.

Amercement 2d. Also that Margaret Coyfe raised hue upon Andrew Lyrycok unjustly.

Amercement 2d. Also that the same Margaret raised hue upon Richard atte Chambre unjustly.

Amercement 2d. Also that John Clerk assaulted Simon Kyng against the peace for which the same Simon justly raised hue.

Amercement 2d. Also that Simon le Kyng raised hue upon John Mellere unjustly.

---

unfree tenants (Peter Coss, 'Neifs and Villeins in Later Medieval England', *Reading Medieval Studies* 40 (2014), pp. 196, 198). The usual legal formula here would be 'to hold to him and his heirs'.

85 'Closed his last day', that is, he died. The Latin phrase used here, *diem clausit extremum*, is the name of the writ to the Crown's escheators, which commenced the formal proceedings of an inquisition *post mortem*.

Amercement 3d. Also that Thomas, servant of Thomas Fullere, took doves by snares (*ingenia*), namely 27.

About a waif 2s. 6d. Also that [*damaged*] in the manner of a thief [*?stole*] two pieces of linen (*linthianua*)[86] and 1 *Chalon*[87] and 1 [*?*]blanket (*whytyl*)[88] worth 1s. 8d. and 10d. \in d[*illeg.*]/ fled [*damaged*] dismissed after [*?*] himself (*dimisit post se*) [*damaged*].

Amercement 3d. Also that Adam Spencer is accustomed to fish with his net in the lord's river and he took from the lord's pond a young pike (*pykerel*) [*damaged*].

Amercement 3d. Also that a member of the household, Walter Whepstede, fished similarly in the lord's river. Therefore, in mercy.

Amercement 4d. Also that John Bresete \3d./ and Henry Slaughtere \1d./ are butchers and sell meat outside the town. Therefore in mercy.

[Turn over]

[*Dorse*]

Amercement 3d. Also that John atte Fen has a ditch in le Mellelane not cleaned out, to the nuisance [*etc*]. Therefore in mercy. And he is ordered to put it right [*damaged*].

Amercement 3d. Also that [*blank space*] Roger [*no surname stated*] has one ditch at la Legh not cleaned out. Therefore [*illeg.*].

Amercement 2d. Also that John atte Fen has a ditch at Holstrete not cleaned out, to the nuisance. Therefore in mercy. And he is ordered to put it right.

Respited. John Dul has not put right an encroachment made with one house situated upon the common way to the nuisance etc. [*Illeg.*] respited [*damaged*].

Amercement 1s. 1d. Also that William atte Tye \3d./, John Buk \3d./, William de Peyton \3d./, John atte Cherche \3d./ and John Schapp \1d./ are tithingmen [*and*] make default. Therefore [*in mercy*].

Amercement 5s. 2d. [*illeg.*]. Also that [*at least two full names damaged and illeg.*] Dul, Katherine Clement \8d./, Elena le Deye \8d./, wife of Geoffrey de Halle \8d./, John Hervy \[?]hen (*Gall'*) 9d./, [*damaged*] Lofham, Peter Joye \[?]3d./, Alice Wayour \3d./, Amya Mundham \3d./, Simon Chapman \3d./, Roesia Hard \3d./, Nicholas Joseep' \3d./, [*damaged*] Cristina de Boyton \1d./, Adam Spencer \4d./, William Skynnere \1d./, Stephen [?]Pages \1d./, William Page \4d./, James atte Tye \3d./ are brewers and brew and sell ale against the assize. Therefore in mercy.

Amercement 6d. Also that John Wendecole \3d./ and John Lyricok \3d./ are ale tasters and have not done their duty. Therefore in mercy.

Amercement 6d. Also that John Hervy \3d./ and Walter de Halle \3d./ are bakers and sell bread against the assize. Therefore in mercy.

Amercement 1d. Also that Richard de Lofham is a regrater and sells against the assize. Therefore in mercy.

Total £1 11½d., price of a [illeg.]

Eleigh (Illeigh). General court there held on the Monday next after the feast of St Michael the archangel in the 42nd year of the reign of King Edward the third [*Monday, 2 October 1368*]

---

[86] Probably a variant of *linteamen*, a linen cloth, or *linteanus*, 'of or pertaining to linen' (*DMLBS*).

[87] Probably *chalo*, 'cloth of Chalons-sur-Marne, 'chalon', 'shalloon', blanket (*DMLBS*).

[88] Probably *whitel*, 'a blanket or covering' (*MED*).

Essoins

John Swift [*essoins himself*] of common [*suit*]   by James Stace.
Roger Maskal, Matilda Dextere of the same
                                   by Robert Frammesden and Thomas Mess'.
John atte Fenn, Thomas Reyner of the same by John Wendecole and Robert Reyner.
John Slaughtere of the same   by John Boydyn.
[*Bracketed on the right against all the above essoins*]   Affeered [for the] 1st [time].
Fines 2s. 8d.[89] The tenant of the tenement of Parkeres \vacant/. The tenant of the tenement of Boytones \6d./. John Abot \4d. of Bildeston (*Bild'*)/, Geoffrey Gilesson \3d./, John Buk \6d./, William atte Ware \4d./, Thomas Heym \6d./. The tenant of the tenement of Peter Aumflot \2d./, for fines for suit of court respited until the feast of Michaelmas.

Amercement 6d. John le Clerk puts himself [*in mercy*] for trespassing in the wheat with 2 cows. Therefore in mercy.

Amercement 1 quarter of wheat and 6s. 8d. Richard Forester puts himself [*in mercy*] for trespassing in the wheat and in the rye with his pigs and beasts continuously and [*the damage is*] estimated at 1 quarter of wheat.

Ordered. The jurors present that Roger Webbe acquired from Nicholas Seg 1 ruinous cottage containing 1 rood, of the lord's fee.

Amercement 3d. Also that John Smert trespassed in the straw of the oats with his sheep by the pledge of John Slaughtere.

Amercements 1s. 7d. Also that John Dul \clerk, 6d./, John Clement \4d./. Adam Spenser \3d./, Robert Deyne \3d./, Anne Mundham \3d./, John le Clerk \3d./, John Greygrom \[?]hen (*Gall'*), 6d./, Geoffrey Halle \3d./ are brewers and sell ale against the assize. Therefore in mercy.

Amercements 6d. Also that Geoffrey de Halle \3d./ and John Greygrom \3d./ are bakers and sell bread against the assize. Therefore the same in mercy.

Election of reeves. Also the aforesaid jurors elected William de Peytoo and John atte Tye to office as [?]chief pledges (*prepositi*).

Amercements 2s. 9d. The tenant of the tenement formerly of Edmund Beneyt \3d./, Roger son of Steven \3d./, Richard Mayheu \3d./, the tenant of the tenement of Parkeres \3d./, John Godale \3d./, Richard atte Tye and [*blank space*] John son of Adam atte Tye \3d./, Simon Deneys \3d./, the tenant of the tenement Sparwes \3d./, John Colkyrke \3d./, John Whepstede \3d./ for default of suit of court, in mercy.

Amercement 6d. Also that John Wendecole \3d./ and John Lyrycok \3d./ are tasters of ale and have done their duty badly (*male*). Therefore in mercy.

Complaint. Stephen le Coo complains about Seman Hogoun \puts [*himself in mercy*]/ in a plea of debt, pledge to prosecute, John Clement. And the defendant [*is*] attached for the King by the pledge of [*blank*].

Complaint [?]cancelled. John le Kyng complains about the same Seman in a plea of debt, pledge to prosecute as above. And attached as above on which day he asked for a day until the next court [*illeg.*]. And it was granted. \The bailiff [*illeg.*] by the pledge of Robert Gauge./

Total for the court 14s. 11d.[90]

---

[89] Actually 2s. 7d.
[90] Michael Stansfield's translation ends here, so this court roll has been completed by the current editor.

Eleigh (Illegh). A court there held on the Monday next before the feast of St Matthew the apostle in the 43rd year of the reign of King Edward the third [*Monday, 17 September 1369*].

Essoin

John atte Fen [*essoins himself*] of common [*suit*]   by John Peg 2nd

Heriot 1 horse ordered. Relief ½d. The jurors present that Richard Forster, who held of the lord one messuage and certain lands and tenements etc. died after the last court, after whose death came into the possession of the lord as a heriot 1 horse worth 2 marks. And they say that Simon is the son and nearest heir and of the age of 14 years [*illeg.*] and of full age by custom etc. to receive his land. Therefore, to distrain for relief and fealty etc. And he gives as a relief ½d. for hall and chamber etc.

Ordered. Issues [*with manicule pointing to 'issues'*]. Also they say that the same Richard died seised of 1 rood of pasture opposite Whepstedes, held by the rod. Therefore it is ordered to seize [*it*] into the hand of the lord until the heriot is paid etc. And to answer for the issues.

Ordered. Also they say that the same Richard enfeoffed Walter Kersoner and others of certain lands and tenements as is shown in a schedule (*cedula*).[91] Therefore it is ordered the same be distrained for fealty.

Fealty, showed a charter. Letitia le Hert came here to court and showed a charter by which she acquired from John Reyner one cottage with appurtenances in Eleigh (*Illegh*), of Smytheslond. To hold to her, her heirs and assigns in perpetuity of the chief lords etc. And she was admitted. And did fealty.

Ordered. Also that Ralph atte Gate, chaplain, and others acquired from John Slaughtere one messuage \with appurtenances/ of Smytthyelond. And that John Abot \ [*illeg.*]/ and another acquired from John Petyt one messuage and 10 acres of land with appurtenances of the lord's fee. Therefore to distrain for fealty.

Amercement 6d. Roger Maskal has not warranted his essoin. Therefore in mercy.

Amercement 3d. Seman Hogoun puts himself [*in mercy*] for licence to settle with Stephen le Seg in a plea of debt. Therefore in mercy by the pledge of Robert Gauge.

Respited. The jury seek a respite until the next [*court*] concerning [*damaged*] Simon King plaintiff and John Clerk in a plea of trespass [*damaged*] (s)he destroyed the corn of the same Simon with his/her beasts to the damage of half a mark or not, just as etc. And [*damaged*].

Ordered. It is ordered to distrain Ralph Swyft for fealty etc. after the death of his father etc. [Blank] distrained. Therefore in mercy for fealty etc.

Total of the court [illeg.]

[*Upside-down, at foot of membrane, possibly as a label*] Bailiff of Eleigh (*Illegh*) [*illeg.*]

---

[91] Presumably a rental of some kind.

Court Roll 16.[92] (between 25 January 1371/72 and 2 August 1372; 2 August 1372)

Eleigh (Illiegh). Court of the lord [*damaged*] held on the Monday next after the feast [*damaged*] [*in the*] 46th [*year of the reign of king Edward third* [*between 25 January 1371/72 and 2 August 1372*[93]]

Essoins

[*Damaged*] [*essoins him/herself*] of common [*suit*]	by Robert his/her son
John Colkirke [*essoins himself*] of common [*suit*]	by Robert Dexstere

Ordered to retain 3s. 4d. [*damaged*] Roger Glasewryghte \puts himself [*in mercy*] by the pledge of the bailiff/ to answer John Clerk in a plea of contract and more to take until etc. [*Damaged.*]

Fine 1s. 7d. William de Boyton \4d./, John Abot \3d./, the tenant of Parkeres in Hitcham (*Heecham*) \6d./, Geoffrey atte Cherche \3d./ and John Chapman \3d./ give to the lord as a fine for suit of court respited for a year as is apparent, by the pledge of the bailiff.

New rent 6d. [*sic*]. To this court came John Wendecole and took from the lord the whole vesture[94] \called [?]Ascherker/ of a certain alder-holt called Kynggesfen belonging to the lord, to have and to hold to the same John Wendecole and to his heirs, of the lord, by the rod, at the lord's will, according to the custom of the manor, rendering for which to the lord and his successors annually at the terms of Easter and St Michael the archangel 6d. in equal portions. And let it be remembered that the herbage and pasturage of the said alder-holt belongs to the aforesaid John and ought always to belong by ancient right.

Ordered. Amercement 1s. 2d. Richard \Dul/ for 10 animals in the lord's oats \1s./ and for 100 of his sheep all together (*conjunctibus*) in the lord's pasture at Oddon. \ Ordered to distrain [*illeg.*] \\puts himself [*in mercy*] by the pledge of Robert Gauge// [*illeg.*] next court to show etc./.John Clerk \2d./ for his animals and sheep in the lord's rye, by the pledge of Nicholas Seg'.

Inquest. Ordered. Inquest taken by the steward by virtue of his office on the oaths of John Brysete, William Smyth, John Aylward, John Abot, Robert Gawge, John Wendecole, Robert Taylor, Adam Poleyn, John Clerk, John Dul, Nicholas Josep and John Broun, sworn, who say on their oath that Laurence Porteroose, Symon Holdayn, Walter Maryoun and John Copee acquired from Ralph Swyft all his tenements both of the fee of the lord and of the fee of others etc. and of which there are of the lord's fee 5 acres and more of the land called Tentislond and 1 acre and 1 rood of the land called Berardislond and in respect of which his service [*is*] in arrears (*aretro*) by many years. And no-one has shown a charter nor done fealty to the lord. Therefore it is ordered they be distrained against the next court to show etc. and do fealty etc.

Showed a charter. Also they say that Geoffrey de Hall' acquired from Thomas Heym all his lands and tenements in Kettlebaston (*Ketilberiston*) of the lord's fee, that is

---

[92] CCA-U15/15/10 (former CCA document number '48832', 'Illeigh' and '1373' written on the dorse in a nineteenth-century hand). Parchment roll, two membranes, stitched end-to-end. Latin. Damaged by damp. Two courts with views.

[93] The regnal year of 46 Edw. III was 25 January 1371/72–24 January 1372/73, so this court must be between the beginning of that regnal year, 25 January 1371/72, and the following court, dated 2 August 1372.

[94] *Vestura*, 'what grows upon or covers the land' (*DMLBS*).

to say, of the land called Raven of Wigge[95] and of the land called Mantonefrelond, who came and showed a charter in which, according to the form of the statute, it is laid down. Therefore he was admitted tenant of the lord. And he did fealty.

[*Illeg.*] *Ordered.* Also they say that John Brysete, Robert Gawge, William Smyth, and John Kyng acquired from Thomas le Fuller all his tenement of the lord's fee and no-one has shown [*a charter*] to the lord nor done fealty. Therefore it is ordered that they be distrained against the next court to show etc. and to do fealty etc.

Ordered. Also that John Clerk acquired from Simon Kyng and Alice Cut acquired from Richard Calle, Richard Clerk and Richard Smyth the half-land called Fichattislond and a half-land of customary land (*customarlond*) from various lands and no-one has shown [*a charter*]. Therefore [*it is ordered*] to distrain against the next court etc.

Amercement 1s. Also they say that John son of Adam atte Tye \3d./, Richard atte Tye \3d./, the tenants of Richard Forster's tenement \3d./ and Roger Webbe \3d./ are suitors and made default. Therefore etc.

Amercements 4s. 9d. Also they say that Geoffrey de Halle \6d./, Robert Deye \3d./, Thomas Reyner \3d./, William Skynner \3d./, John Clerk \3d./, Seman Hogoun \ clerk, 6d./, John Dul, \bailiff, 6d./, Adam Spencer \6d./, John Gawge \3d./, Richard Dexstere \3d./, Avicia Brodeye \3d./, Nicholas Seg \3d./, John Taylor \3d./, "John Bolle \3d./, John Sturmyn", miller (*mellere*) \3d./, William Payn \3d./, Robert de Wecyngg \3d./, "James atte Tye \3d./, Alice atte Wayour \3d./" brew and sell ale against the assize. Therefore etc.

Amercement 6d. [*illeg.*]. Also that Geoffrey de Halle \2d./, Seman Hogoun \2d./, and John Harvy \2d./ are bakers and bake and sell bread against the assize.

Amercement 6d. Also that Richard Dul \3d./ and Nicholas Josep \3d./ are [*ale-*]tasters and do not do their duty. Therefore etc.

Election of [*ale-*]*taster.* Also all the abovesaid jurors elect John Clerk to the office of [*ale*]taster in the place of Richard Dul and he is sworn into the aforesaid office.

Showed a charter. To this court comes Agnes daughter of Robert Gawege and John Slawghtere of Monks Eleigh (*Illieghe Monachorum*) and showed their charter by which they acquired from Simon, rector of the church of Eleigh (*Illiegh*) aforesaid, all the lands, meadows and pastures with their hedges and ditches and all their appurtenances variously lying in the vill aforesaid which the aforesaid Simon formerly had as the gift and enfeoffment of William Wynter and Matilda his wife of Barningham (*Berningham*), John Slawghtere abovesaid, John Abot, John Colkirke of Eleigh (*Illiegh*) aforesaid and Ralph atte Gate of Bricett (*Brysete*), to have to them and their heirs in perpetuity. And which said charter was made according to the form of the statute and they were admitted to the said tenement. And did fealty.

Total of this court 9s. 6d.

Affeerers – Robert Gawge, Richard Dul

[*An additional piece of parchment stitched below this, but nothing written on it on this side.*]

[*Dorse*] *Eleigh* (*Illiegh*). Court with view of the lord [*damaged*] held on the Monday next after the feast of St Peter [*damaged*] [*Monday, 2 August 1372*[96]]

---

[95] Rental 1 (1379–80) on p. 194 describes this as a full customary land called Raveneslond and Wyggeslond.

[96] Dated on the assumption that it is after the undated first court, but within the forty-sixth regnal year of Edward III (25 January 1371/72–24 January 1372/73), therefore in 1372, if the feast is St Peter in

Essoin

John atte Cherche [*essoins himself*] of common [*suit*] [*damaged*]

Showed a charter, fealty. John Clerk showed a charter according [*?to the form of the statute by which he acquired*] from Simon Kyng one piece of land and one wood (*buscam*) adjacent [*damaged*] from the land of Hunmanneslond and he asked to be admitted and was admitted [*damaged*].

Showed a charter, fealty. Robert Gawge showed a charter according to the form of the statute [*by which*] he acquired from John Gawge his father [*damaged*] arable with pasture adjoining and hedges and 1 piece of meadow called Litlemedwe containing in total [*damaged*] land called Baxstaresquarter and he did fealty.

Showed a charter, fealty. Robert Gawge showed a charter made according to the form of the statute by which Robert himself, his wife Joan [*?*]jointly [*damaged*] acquired from John Bresete and his associates one messuage and two crofts of land, of which 3½ acres [*are*] of [*?Smythesland*] and the residue from Scarlattislond, to hold to them and their heirs in perpetuity. And they did fealty.

Fines 5d. Matilda Dexstere \2d./, John Swyft \3d./ give to the lord as a fine for suit of court respited for a year as is shown, by the pledge of the bailiff.

Showed a charter, fealty. Edmund Baker of Framlingham Castle (*Framlyngham Castell*) and John Beverlee of the same showed a charter made according to the form of the statute by which they acquired from Alice formerly wife of Adam Cut all her lands and tenements both of the lord's fee and of other lords in Monks Eleigh (*Illiegh Monachorum*) and Lindsey (*Lelleseye*). And they did fealty to the lord.

Showed a charter, fealty. John son of Robert Gawge showed a charter made according to the form of the statute by which he acquired from Alice Cut half an acre of land of the lord's fee. And he did fealty to the lord and it is called Doughtyescroft and is of the land called Smethislond. And he is to do fealty to the lord [*sic*].

Amercement 3d. Roger Glaswryghte puts himself [*in mercy*] for licence to settle with John Clerk in a plea of contract by the pledge of the bailiff.

Amercement 6d. Richard Dull puts himself [*in mercy*] for trespassing against the lord with 100 sheep all together (*coniunctibus*) in Oddon without licence by the pledge of Robert Gawge.

Amercements 1s. Thomas Reyner \3d./ puts himself [*in mercy*] for 3 cows in the wheat and rye by the pledge of Adam Spencer. Richard Dull \3d./ for 16 animals in the lord's wheat at Ravenescroft by the pledge of Adam Spencer. The same Richard \4d./ for 60 sheep in the wheat and pasture by the pledge of the aforesaid. John Reyner \2d./ for 1 cow and 2 bullocks in the corn and pasture.

View [*of frankpledge*] there the day and year as above

Chief pledges, common fine 4s. John Brysete, John Aylward, Robert Gawge, John Wendecole, Adam Poleyn, John Clerk, William Smyth, John Abot, John son of Adam atte Tye, John Broun, John Whepsted, John Dull, chief pledges, sworn, present that they give as the common fine for the year for themselves and for their tithings, as is evident. [*Illeg.*]

Amercements 3s 2d. Penalties. Also they present that William atte Ware \3d./ has a ditch at Lelleseyecros and Stephen le Fox \1d./ has 1 ditch there not cleaned out to the nuisance. And that William Chapman \2d./ has 1 ditch next to Piggiscote at the corner of [*?*]Magiscroft not cleaned out. And that John Whepsted \2d./ has 1 ditch at

---

chains (1 August) is meant.

Doysiscroft. And that Edmund Cut \2d./ has 1 ditch at Bradefeldelane. And that John Reyner \1d./ has 1 ditch in le Fenstrete opposite his alder-holt. And that Richard atte Tye \4d./ has 1 ditch at Ravenescroft \he is ordered to put it right under penalty of 3s. 4d./. And that John Davy \3d./ obstructs the common water course opposite his gateway to the nuisance. And Roger Mascall \1d./ has 1 ditch opposite [?Read] isappulton. And that Margaret Higgeliegh \3d./ has 1 ditch at Honymannes. And that Margaret Donylond \9d./ has 1 ditch at Clerkis and 2 ditches at Honymannes. Richard atte Tye \because above/ for 1 ditch at Ravenescroft. And that John atte Fen \6d./ has 2 ditches at le Mellelane. And that Alice Peek \1d./ has 1 ditch at Sudesle-lane not cleaned out, and many more to the nuisance. Therefore etc.

Ordered. Also that the lord prior has 1 ditch at Byfooldegatte not cleaned out to the nuisance. Therefore it is ordered to be put right.

Ordered. Also that the lord prior obstructs the common way of the tenement [?]Duls at le Launde, to the nuisance [*illeg.*]. Therefore etc.

Amercement [?]6*d. because bloodshed (quia ex').* Also that John, friend of Alice Sparwe, beat the said Alice and John her son and drew blood against the peace. And that the aforesaid John immediately fled and never returned. Therefore etc.

Amercements 6d. Also that Robert Taylour \3d./ beat John Sparwe [*?against the peace, and he*] raised hue upon the said Robert [*illeg.*], by the pledge of William de Peyton. And that Alice Sparwe \3d./ unjustly raised hue upon Robert Taylour. Therefore etc.

Amercement 6d. Also that Robert Berte drew blood from Richard Dull against the peace [*and*] that he justly raised hue upon him etc.

Amercement 1d. Also that James Skynnere drew blood from Rosia wife of John Gawge against the peace.

Amercement 1d. Also that Margery Sturmyn drew blood from William Clement against the peace. Therefore in mercy etc.

Amercement 6d. Also that John le Kou drew blood from Rosia Querdelyng against the peace because [*illeg.*].

Amercement 1d. Also that William Morisce drew blood from John Sturmyn, miller (*mellere*), against the peace. Therefore etc.

Amercement 4d. Also that John Reyner \1d./ made a recovery unjustly on John Dull against the peace. And that the said John Reyner \2d./ unjustly raised hue upon the said John Dull. And that John Dull justly raised hue upon John Reyner \1d./ by the pledge of John \Wendecole/.

Also that Robert Frammesden the lord's bailiff entered the close formerly of Richard Forster without licence and there intended to take various animals namely as distraint for arrears of rent and services owed from the tenement lately of the said Richard to him, that the same Robert had the power to take as sufficient distraint out of the said close \up to/ the value. And that the same Robert unjustly raised hue against William Skynner making an illegal recovery upon the said Robert on the occasion aforesaid [*illeg.*].

Amercement 6d. Also that John le Vant, chaplain, assaulted Robert Frammesden the lord's bailiff against the peace, for which Robert Gawge [*illeg.*] justly raised hue upon the said John. Therefore etc. by the pledge of William \Skynner/ and [*illeg.*].

Amercement 3d. Also that Andrew Liricok committed one hamsoken (*hamsokne*) upon Henry Rach against the peace for which he raised hue upon the said Andrew. Therefore etc. by the pledge of William Skynnere and John Taylour.

Amercement 3d. Also that John Colkirke assulted Simon Kyng against the peace for which the said Simon justly raised hue \the said John [*illeg.*] and by the pledge of John [*illeg.*]/.

Amercement [*blank*]. Also that Nicholas Smyth drew blood from Edmund Brasyer against the peace. Therefore etc.

Amercement 3d. Also that John Brysete is a butcher and sells meat to be consumed against the statute. Therefore etc.

Amercements 6d. Also that Nicholas Josep \3d./ and John Clerk \3d./ are [*ale-*]tasters and do not do their duty. Therefore etc.

Amercements 7d. Also that Geoffrey de Halle \3d./, Robert Danyel \3d./, and John Harvy \1d./ are bakers and bake etc. [*illeg.*].

[*Second membrane stitched to the foot of the first at this point.*]

Amercement 10d. Also they present that Geoffrey de Hall \6d./, Alice Taylour \3d./, Adam [*?*]Spencer, \bailiff, 6d./, Robert Danyel \4d./, John Huyn \4d./, Simon Chapman \3d./, Leticia Hert \2d./, Nicholas Josep' \3d./, Margery Fullere \3d./, Robert "Wetyngg" \3d./, Robert Berte \2d./, John Dull \3d./, John Clement \3d./, John "Michel, Simon [*?*]Hodman \2d./, William Skynner" \2d brewed and sold ale against the assize. Therefore etc.

[*Amercements 4d.*] Also that Richard atte Chambre \1d./, Henry Fox \1d./ and William atte Ware \2d./ are [*?*]tithingmen [*?and made default of suit of court*]. Therefore the same and their chief [*pledges*] in mercy.

[*Illeg.*] Also that John Clerk \1d./, John le Koo \1d./, Roger Stannard \1d./, John Taylour \1d./, [*illeg.*], Henry Gardyner \1d./, Walter Whepsted \1d./, John Michel \1d./ are resident and outside a tithing [*Illeg.*].

Amercement [*?*]2d. Also that John Whepsted [*illeg.*].

Also that John Dul [*?has*] a [*?*]common [*?*]building at Swynggildon 10 perches long and 8 perches wide [*illeg.*].

Election of [*ale-*]taster. Also John Clement is elected to the office of ale-taster in place of John Clerk [*damaged*].

Showed a charter. John Grey showed a charter made according to the form of the statute by which he acquired from Alice Waryn 1 messuage with a garden of the land called Palmereslond in Eleigh (*Illiegh*). And he did fealty to the lord.

Total of this court and view, "£1 1d."

Affeerers: Nicholas Josep [*illeg.*]

Court Roll 17.[97] (23 January 1373/74)

Eleigh (*Illeigh*). General court [*damaged*] there held on the Monday next before the feast of the conversion of St Paul [*damaged*] in the 47th year [*of the reign of King Edward III, Monday, 23 January 1373/74*]

Essoin

William [*damaged*] [*essoins himself of common suit*]   by Simon Querdelyng.
The showing of a charter [*illeg.*]. *Fealty.* John Aylward [*damaged*] by which he acquired from Peter Amyel one piece of land with its appurtenances in Eleigh

---

97   CCA-U15/15/11 (former CCA document number '53,988' stamped and '17/46', 'Illeigh Manor Court Roll 47 H 3rd' [*date erroneous*] written in a nineteenth-century style and hand). Parchment roll, one membrane. Latin. Very badly damaged by damp, partly fragmentary. One court. This court roll, not translated by Stansfield for Weller, has been translated by the current editor.

(*Illeigh*) [*damaged*] from Andrew son of Simon Kyng of Monks Eleigh (*Illiegh Monachorum*) and Joan his wife, showed a charter according [*to the form of the statute*] by which he acquired from John <Ch> Wepstead and John Brysete all their messuages and tenements with their appurtenances which were formerly of Simon Kyng in Monks Eleigh (*Illegh monachorum*) which are parcel of the land called Leggeardislond [*illeg.*]. To hold to them and the heirs of their bodies. And in default of issue of their bodies then [*illeg.*] of Simon Kyng and his heirs in perpetuity. Henry atte Marssh of Monks Eleigh (*Illiegh monachorum*) showed a charter made according to the form of the statute by which he acquired from Nicholas Forster one and a half acres of land of the lord's fee. And John son of Robert Gawge and Juliana his wife showed a charter made according to the form of the statute by which they acquired from Ralph atte Gate, chaplain, and John Slawghtere of Bricett (*Brysete*) one messuage with its appurtenances in Eleigh (*Illiegh*) of fee, to hold to them and the heirs of their bodies etc. And they asked to be admitted. And Stephen atte Marssh showed a charter made according to the form of the statute and by which he acquired from Nicholas Forster one croft of land called Boleynescroft of the lord's fee. And he asked to be admitted. And all were admitted. And they did fealty.

[*Damaged.*] William atte Tye and John Clement ale-tasters \with the chief jurors/ present that Richard atte Tye \2d./, Nicholas Seg \3d./, Laurence [*?*]Hart \[*illeg.*] [*?*]exonerated./, Simon Chapman \3d./, Henry Slawghtere \3d./, Alice daughter of Henry Taylour \3d./, Alice Cut \2d./, Matilda Deye \[*illeg.*] [*?*]exonerated / and Richard Mayhiewe \3d./, [*damaged*] Halle \6d./, John Greygrom \1d./, John Gawge \6d./, Margaret Dull \[*?*]by the clerk, 6d./, Rosia Hard \by the bailiff, 6d./ are brewers and brew and sell [*against*] the assize.

[*Damaged.*] all [*damaged*] present that Geoffrey of Halle[98] \6d./ and John Gawge are bakers and bake and sell bread [*against the assize*].

[*Damaged.*] William atte Tye \3d./ and John Clement \3d./ are ale tasters and do not do their duty. Therefore etc.

[*Damaged.*] [*Inquest*] taken as of their office [*illeg.*] by the oaths of John Brysete, William Smyth, John Aylward, John Abott, Robert [*?*]Gawge, [*damaged*] Seg, John Wendecole, John Broun, Adam Poleyn, John Whepsted, John Clerk and John [*?*] Dul, /chief pledges sworn who say\ [*damaged*] that Robert Po[*damaged*] [*damaged*] Poleyn one piece of land of the lord's fee. And that Thomas [*?*]Abot [*damaged*] John Abot his father one messuage and one piece of land adjacent of the lord's fee. And they have not shown [*damaged*] [*how they entered*] [*damaged*] and have not done fealty. Therefore etc.

[*Damaged.*] John Davy, who held of the lord 1 messuage and 1 [*?*]piece of land called Bolesquarter and 1 acre [*damaged*] [?]mondaylond [*damaged*] lately closed his last day [*died*] (*nuper diem suum clausit extremum*). And they say that the afore-said tenements are heriotable but [*damaged*] the aforesaid John Davy had no animals at the time of his death, but 7 days before his death he had [*damaged*] should be paid. Therefore it is ordered to distrain the tenement for sufficient heriot to the lord or for sufficient [damaged]. And that Christina, who was wife of the aforesaid John Davy [*?*]had [*damaged*] in the aforesaid messuage and acres of land [*c. 1½ lines damaged*] mundaylond [*damaged*] hold all the land whole as her free bench [*several lines damaged or illeg.*].

---

[98] 'of Halle' written in English throughout this court roll.

[*Damaged*] of Kettlebaston (*Ketilberston*), Richard Mayhiew \2d./, John Parker \4d./, John Abot of Bildeston \2d./, Geoffrey son [*damaged*] \2d./, [*damaged*] de Boyton \2d./, [*damaged*] as fines [*damaged*] until the next court after the feast of St Michael [*damaged*].

[*Remaining part of membrane, probably about 6 lines, too damaged and illeg. to make sense of.*]

[*Dorse*]

Eleigh (*Illyegh*) Court Roll [*damaged*][99]
Again, concerning this court [*damaged*]

Chief pledges. Common fine 4s. John Brysete, William Smyth, <~~John Aylward~~> \ William Peyton/, [*damaged*] Robert Gawge, <~~Nicholas Seg~~> \John Whepistead/, John Wendecole, John Broun, <~~Adam Poleyn~~> \William atte Tye/, Geoffrey of H[*alle*], [*illeg.*] clerk, and John Dull, chief pledges aforesaid present that they give to the lord as the common fine for this single year [*illeg.*].

Amercement 2d. Also they present that William Sexteyn \[*?*]because he has [*?*] nothing, [*?*]2d./ [*and*] [*?*]Dennis Wynk beat Richard Dull and drew his blood against the peace. Therefore etc.

Amercement 3d. Also they present that John Rawnyld beat William atte Tye the younger and drew his blood against the peace. Therefore etc. by the pledge of William [*illeg.*].

Amercement 6d. Also they present that John Reyner the younger beat Alice atte Wayour and drew her blood against the peace. Therefore etc.

Amercements 5s 1d. Also they present that John Broun \3d./, Nicholas Ketill \3d./, Thomas Ponder \2d./, Robert Beerte \2d./, John Clement \2d./, Andrew Hard, John le Koo \2d./, Maria Skynnere \2d./, Robert the chaplain \[*?*]/, Alice Taylour \1d./, William Skynnere \1d./, Joan la Skynnere \1d./, Robert Gawge \3d./, Letitia Hert \1d./, Richard atte Chambre \1d./, Alice Sayher \1d./, Nicholas Josep' \3d./, Henry Rach \1d./, John Cuttyng \3d./, Laurence Cartere \1d./, Nicholas Seg \3d./, Richard atte Tye \1d./, Andrew Kyng \3d./, Robert atte Medewe \3d./, Richard de Lavenham \6d./, Geoffrey of Halle \[*?by the clerk*], 6d./, John Gawge \ [*?wife sworn*], 6d. by the bailiff/, John Dull \[*?wife sworn*], 6d., by the clerk/, Adam Spencer, \[*?wife sworn*], 6d./, Henry Rach \[*illeg.*], 3d./ are brewers and brewed and sold ale against the assize. Therefore etc.

Amercement 3d. Also that Geoffrey of Hall is a baker and baked and sold bread against the assize. Therefore etc.

Amercement 3d. Also that John [*illeg.*].

Amercement 3d. Also that John Clement and William atte Tye are [*ale-*]tasters and do not do their duty. [*Damaged*].

Amercement 1d. Also that Christina Davy has 1 ditch at Humbilbank not cleaned out to the nuisance [*damaged*].

Amercement 3d. Also that Nicholas Ketill has 2 ditches in Manheylane not cleaned out to the nuisance [*damaged*].

Amercement 3d. Also they present that Nicholas le [*damaged*] unjustly obstructed the common way of the lord [*damaged*] and the church at [*damaged*].

Amercement 1d. Also that John P[*damaged*] has one ditch at [*damaged*].

Amercement 2d. Also that John Brodeye \puts [*himself in mercy*]/, Nicholas Ketill \puts [*himself in mercy*]/, Robert Ketill \puts [*himself in mercy*]/, Robert Reyner

---

[99] Apparently a contemporary label.

155

[*damaged*] Dilwyk, John Clerk \puts [*himself in mercy*]/ are resident and outwith a tithing. Therefore etc.

Amercement 3d. Also that John Whepsted [*damaged*].

Amercement 1d. Also that Margery Fullere [*damaged*] called Fynchelieghestret [*damaged*].

Amercement 1s. Also they present that Nicholas Ketill unjustly [*Remaining* [*?*]*six lines of the membrane too damaged to make sense of*].

Court Roll 18.[100] (1 August 1413)

[*Damaged*] [*Court and*] view of frankpledge held there on Tuesday, the feast of St Peter in chains in the first year of the reign of King Henry [*V, Tuesday, 1 August 1413*[101]]

Essoins

[*Damaged*] of Burye [*Bury St Edmunds*] [*essoins him/herself*] of common [*suit*]
by Thomas Davy.

[*Damaged*] Porter the younger of the same	by Andrew Kyng.
Thomas atte Stone of the same	by John North.
John Ward of the same	by Thomas Kyng.
John atte Medwe of the same	by William Ayleward.
John Prymchet of the same	by John Wendecole the younger.
John Bakere of the same	by John Davy.

[*Damaged*] puts himself [*in mercy*] by the pledge of John Beneyt for licence [*to settle*] with John Chapeleyn in a plea of debt. Therefore the same Richard in mercy.

[*Damaged*] [*?*]Seg [*and*] Simon Brodeye in mercy because the same have not responded to Roger Mellere \not [*?*]prosecuted (*non pros'*)/ in a plea of debt. And they are ordered to come to the same etc.

[*Damaged*] pledge of John Chapman because the same has not responded to John Bonmays in a plea of debt. And it is ordered etc.

[*Damaged*] for licence [*to settle*] with John Chapman in a plea of debt.

[*Damaged*] Webbe in mercy for licence [*to settle*] with John Sare in a plea of debt.

[*Damaged*] by the pledge of John Chapman in mercy because the same has not responded to Richard Smyth, shoemaker, \not [*?*]prosecuted./ in a plea of debt. And it is ordered [*damaged*] by the inquest that Roger FitzStevene \3d./, John [*?*]Wayn, cordwainer \3d./, Thomas Peytone, chaplain \3d./, Simon Bakere \3d./, [*damaged*] William atte Tye, chaplain \6d./, Robert Reyner \[*illeg.*]/, John Bonde \3d./ and John Whepestead \3d./ are in \default/ of suit of court.

---

[100] CCA-U15/15/14 (part 1). This reference covers two separate parchment court rolls, each of one membrane (former CCA document number '48833', 'Monks Illeigh' and 'Roll 1416, 1420' written on dorse of both membranes in a nineteenth-century hand). Here Court Roll 18 comprises the first membrane (court dated 1 August 1413), Court Roll 21 the second (court dated 1 August 1419). The two have been separated in this volume because there are other courts between these dates. Latin. Badly damaged by damp.

[101] If the king is Henry V, then the date is 1 August 1413, but if it is Henry IV, it is 1 August 1400. It cannot be Henry VI as there is already a court close in date to 1 August 1422 (the third court in Court Roll 22 is dated 2 August 1422). 1413 has been chosen as it agrees with the nineteenth-century endorsement, which was probably written when the court roll was in better physical condition and more legible than it is now.

[*Damaged*] Clement languishing at the point of death (*in extremis*) outwith this court surrenders into the hands of John Coo, clerk, a tenement [*damaged*] chaplain, John Hoberd and other tenants of the lord, according to the custom of the manor, one cottage with appurtenances formerly [*damaged*] Mellecroft and formerly of John Clement. And it renders each year 2s. at the usual terms to the use of John Wendecole the younger and Simon [*damaged*] to whom seisin of which has been handed over, by the rod, to hold to the same John and Simon and to their heirs, by the rod, at the will of the lord, [*damaged*] custom. And they did fealty to the lord. And they give to the lord as a fine as is evident in the heading.[102]

[*Damaged*] Also they present that John Webbe \4d./ with 2 pigs in the summertime, Alice Blok \3d./ with 1 horse, John Coo, clerk, \8d./ with 2 cows Roger [*damaged*] \3d./ with 1 cow and 2 bullocks, trespassed in the lord's pasture in Mellecroft. Therefore the same in mercy.

[*Damaged*] present that Thomas Wryghte of Lindsey (*Lelesey*) broke the hedge[103] at Brookhalle and has not repaired it again for which [*damaged*]. Fostar trespassed in the lord's underwood in Manhey. Therefore the said Thomas in mercy.

[*Damaged*] [*Geoffrey*] Hoberd puts himself [*in mercy*] for trespassing with his oxen in the lord's wood of Manhey several times. Therefore the same Geoffrey in mercy by the pledge of Thomas Calle.

[*Damaged*] [*Richard*] Byllyng puts himself [*in mercy*] for the same with 1 horse in the lord's pasture several times. Therefore the same Richard in mercy.

[*Damaged*] Cobold puts himself [*in mercy*] for the same with his sheep in the lord's pasture in Heyfeld several times. Therefore the same in mercy.

[*Damaged*] puts himself in mercy for the same with 3 cows in the lord's wood and le Launde. Therefore the same John in mercy.

[*Damaged*] [*?Bakere*] puts himself [*in mercy*] for the same with 1 horse in the lord's [*illeg.*] Byfeld [*illeg.*] in wintertime. Therefore the same in mercy.

[*Damaged*] [*?Reyner*] puts himself [*in mercy*] for the same with 1 horse in the lord's peas in Illyefeld. Therefore the same in mercy.

[*Damaged*] [*?Thomas H*[*illeg.*]] puts himself [*in mercy*] for the same with 11 pigs and piglets in the lord's peas there. Therefore the same in mercy.

[*Damaged*] puts himself [*in mercy*] for the same with 1 sow and 6 pigs in the lord's peas there. Therefore etc.

[*Damaged*] [*puts himself in mercy*] for the same with 15 cows in the lord's peas there and in le Heyefeld. Therefore the same in mercy.

[*Damaged*] for the same with 4 horses and others of his animals in the lord's pasture at Custodilhach. Therefore the same in mercy.

[*Damaged*] for the same with his pigs in the lord's peas and [*?*]hay[104] in le Heyefeld. Therefore the same in mercy.

[*Damaged*] for the same with his animals in the winter pasture in Heyefeld. Therefore the same in mercy.

---

[102] The marginal heading is missing for this entry.

[103] The Latin word (*?*)*hayve* is indistinct but could be related to, or a variant of, *haia*, 'a hedge'; *hayo*, 'to enclose with a hedge' implying some kind of hedged enclosure. A boundary hedge is most likely meant here.

[104] The writing is indistinct, but could be *haras* (*hara*, 'a coop, animal enclosure, such as a pig-stye') or possibly *hayas* (*haia*, 'an enclosure in forest', 'hay', (with reference to Hereford Hayes) although there was no forest law in Monks Eleigh). Given the location of le Heyefeld, it is probably a Latinisation of the ME *hei*, 'hay' (*DMLBS, MED*).

[*Damaged*] "Walter Cobold" puts himself [*in mercy*] for the same with his sheep in the lord's peas and [*?*]hay in le Heyefeld.

[*Damaged*] puts himself [*in mercy*] for the same with 1 horse in the lord's pasture in Suddesele. Therefore the same in mercy.

[*Damaged*] puts himself in mercy for the same with 1 horse in the lord's oats several times. Therefore the same in mercy.

[*Damaged*] that Andrew Kyng and his associates acquired 1 piece of meadow from John Brysete of the lord's fee who [*damaged*].

[*Damaged*] court came John Wendecole the younger and showed a certain charter by which the same Robert atte Medwe and John North acquired from John [*?*]Brysete all his lands and tenements in the vills of Eleigh (*Illye*) and Milden (*Meldyng*) which certain charter is made under the form of the statute. And they did fealty to the lord.

[*Damaged*] To this court came Geoffrey atte Cherche and showed a certain charter by which he acquired from John atte Cherche his father all his lands and tene-ments, meadows, pasturage and pastures which he had and held on the day of the making of the aforesaid, in the vill of Kettlebaston which certain charter was made under the form of the statute. And he did fealty. And he showed another charter by which he acquired from Geoffrey Cabow of Preston, Ralph Cabow of Brettenham (*Brethinham*) and John Cabow of Kettlebaston (*Ketilberstonn*) two pieces of arable land lying in the croft which John atte Cherche enclosed which formerly was [*?*]held by John Cabow of the lord's fee, which certain charter was made under the form of the statute. And he did fealty to the lord.

[*Chief pledges*]

John North	John Shoppe	John Davy	Robert Heyward
John Wendecole the younger	John Nytyngale	Richard Reyner	John Webbe
Robert Fullere	John Ayleward	William Shoppe	[*damaged*] [*?chaplain*].

[*To the right of the chief pledges' names, bracketed against them*] Sworn.

[*Damaged*], *7d.* The abovesaid chief pledges present that Andrew Page \3d./, John Wendecole the elder \5d./, John Bonde the elder \3d./, John Bonde the younger \3d./, John Valli \3d./, Richard Smyth, shoemaker (*sowtere*) \3d./, Nicholas Smyth \[*illeg.*], John Deye \3d./, Alice Blok, Andrew Vally \3d./, Robert Moteslo \2d./, John Sawyer \[*?*]3d./, Geoffrey Boch \3d./, John Bette, fuller (*fullar'*) \[*?*]3d./, William Puddyng \ [*illeg.*]/, John Merssh \3d./, John Warde \3d./, John son of John Blak \3d./, [*?*]Robert [*?*]Aylewarde \[*illeg.*]/, [*?*]Robert son of [*illeg.*] Cook \3d./, John Webbe the younger \3d./, John Elyngham \3d./, John Stouk \3d./, Roger Webbe \3d./, John son of John Hoberd \3d./, and Roger FitzStevene \4d./, [*?for making default of suit of court*]. Therefore the same in mercy.

Amercement 1s. And that John \3d./ son of William Shoppe, Thomas Stanton \3d./, John Bows \2d./ and Thomas Wryghte \3d./ have stayed within the precincts of the leet for 1 year and one day and are of the age of 12 years and more and are not in a tithing. Therefore the same in mercy.

Amercement 6d. And that John Wendecole the elder made an assault upon Thomas Stantone against the peace. Therefore the said John in mercy.

[*Illeg.*] And that John Davy the younger beat Agnes Stantone against the peace. Therefore the said John in mercy.

[*Illeg.*] And that John Chapman made an assault upon John Stowk and drew blood from him against the peace. Therefore the same in mercy.

Amercement 2s. And that William Browstere of Lavenham committed hamsoken upon John Curtays, taylor, carrying off a pot of his against the peace.

Amercement 2d. And that John Pretown, taylor, drew blood from John Chapman against the peace. Therefore the same in mercy.

Amercements [?]6d. And that Thomas Hoberd \3d./ and John Lytyl Coo \3d./ are ale-tasters and carry out their duty badly. Therefore the same in mercy.

Amercements 6s. 2d. And that William Astele \8d./, Thomas Kyng \1s./, Richard Smyth \6d./, Isabell Mutslo \1s./, Andrew Hard \1s./, Thomas Gant \1s./, John Hoberd \8d./ and John Coo, clerk, \4d./ brew ale and break the assize. Therefore the same in mercy.

Amercements 2s. 7d. And that John Noche \3d./, John Cabow \3d./, John Davy \[*illeg.*]d./, William Vally \3d./, Adam Bretown \3d./, Thomas Calle \4d./, Roger Reyner \3d./, Henry Bakere \3d./, John Davy \3d./ and Thomas Levyng \3d./ are brewers and sold ale against the assize. Therefore the same in mercy.

Amercement 1s 6d. And that Thomas Kyng \3d./, Richard Smyth \3d./, Isabell Mutslo \3d./, Andrew Hard \3d./, Thomas Gant \3d./ and William Osteler \3d./ are regraters of bread \against the assize/.

Amercement 2s. And that Thomas Brown \1s./ and Thomas Mows \1s./ have [?] regrated (*attularunt*) bread against the assize. Therefore the same in mercy.

Amercement 8d. And that John Waryn has 1 ditch not cleaned out at Warestrete to ·the nuisance. Therefore the same in mercy.

Amercement 1s. And that Simon Foster has 1 ditch not cleaned out at Hoddone to the nuisance. Therefore the same in mercy.

Amercement 1s. And that the tenants of the tenements of John Brysete have 1 ditch not cleaned out at Holstrete. Therefore the same in mercy.

Amercement 6d. And that John Webbe has obstructed his watercourse opposite the land of John Brysete. Therefore the same in mercy.

Amercement 6d. And that John North has 1 ditch not cleaned out at Manefeld to the nuisance. Therefore the same in mercy.

Amercement 6d. And that John Wendecole the younger has 1 ditch not cleaned out at Magotiscroft to the nuisance. Therefore the aforesaid in mercy.

Amercement 6d. And that Robert Fullere has 1 ditch not cleaned out at Petytes. Therefore the same in mercy.

Amercement 6d. And that John Porter has 1 ditch not cleaned out at opposite [?] Morewall. Therefore the same in mercy.

Amercement 6d. And that the tenants of Gedeford have one ditch not cleaned at [?] Mabbecroft to the nuisance etc.

Turn over and see the back.

[*Dorse*] *Amercement 3d.* And that Thomas Peytone, chaplain, [*damaged*].

Amercement 3d. And that John Porter has 1 ditch [*damaged*].

Amercement 2d. And that Geoffrey Hoberd has 1 ditch not cleaned out opposite [*damaged*].

Amercement 3d. And that John Coo, clerk, has one ditch not cleaned out in Moileland, to the nuisance etc. Therefore the same [*in mercy*].

Amercement 3d. And that Margery Stanhard obstructed her watercourse in the marsh opposite Langeleywode to the nuisance [*damaged*].

Amercement 3d. And that the tenants of Walshams have one ditch not cleaned out opposite Cuttiscroft to the nuisance [*damaged*].

Elected to office. Simon Fullere and John Webbe were elected [*?ale-tasters*] [*damaged*].

Total of this court with leet, £2 7s. 11d.

Court Roll 19.[105] (1 August 1414)

Monks Eleigh (Illeigh Monachorum). Court with view of frankpledge there, held on Wednesday, the feast of St Peter in chains in the second year of the reign of King Henry the fifth [*Wednesday, 1 August 1414*]

[*Essoin*]
Robert Barkere of Chelsworth (*Chelsworthe*) [*essoins himself*] of common [*suit*] by John Warde

[*Blank space left for up to two or three lines.*[106]]
[*Damaged*] Burye \3d./, John Porter the younger \3d./, "Thomas atte Ston \3d,/ Robert atte" Medwe \3d./, John Prymchet \3d./ and [*?*]Robert Bakere \3d./, because they did not warrant their essoins.[107] Therefore etc.

[*Damaged*] because he does not proceed with his complaint against Simon Brodeye in a plea of debt. Therefore etc.

[*Damaged*] Richard Smyth, shoemaker, because he does not proceed with his complaint against John Chapman in a plea of debt, therefore etc.

[*Damaged*] It is ordered, as elsewhere, to distrain John Chapman by a better pledge, to respond to John Bonmays \did not [*?*]proceed/ in a plea of debt.

[*Damaged*] It is ordered to distrain Andrew King and his associates to show [*how*] they have entered into 1 piece of meadow acquired from John Brycete and \for fealty/.

[*Damaged*] And also to attach John Taylour to respond to William Grey \did not [*?*] proceed/ in a plea of debt. And John Arcott to respond to Nicholas [*damaged*] \did not [*?*]proceed/ in a plea of contract against [*illeg.*].

Amercement [*illeg.*]. John Smyth puts himself [*in mercy*] for licence [*to settle*] with Thomas Kyng in a plea of debt by the pledge of Thomas Calle therefore etc.

Amercement 3d. Thomas Hard puts himself [*in mercy*] for licence [*to settle*] with Warin Cordewaner in a plea of debt, by the pledge of Andrew Hard, therefore etc.

Amercement 3d. Thomas Calle puts himself [*in mercy*], [*damaged*] because he does not proceed [*with his complaint*] against John Wolleman in a plea of debt, therefore etc.

Amercement 3d. The same Thomas, because he did not proceed [*with his complaint*] against Simon Hard in a plea of debt, therefore etc.

---

[105] CCA-DCc-ChAnt/I/259, stamp of 'Chapter Library, Canterbury' on face; incorrectly endorsed '1415'. Parchment roll, one membrane. Latin. Badly damaged by damp. One court with view of frankpledge.

[106] The blank space left here suggests that perhaps some of the court roll was pre-written, with space left for those essoined who would not be known until the court actually commenced.

[107] In other words, they did not come to the court, nor did they provide sureties for not coming. This must relate to earlier essoins because Robert Bakere did produce a surety at this court.

Amercement [*illeg.*]*d.* Also Geoffrey Hoberd \6d./ with oxen and cows, John Ayleward \[?]4d./ with 2 calves, William Tylwyt \4d./ with 1 calf, put themselves [*in mercy*] for trespassing in the underwood in Manhey [*Wood*], therefore etc.

[*Amercement*] [*illeg.*]*d.* Simon Bakere \3d./ with his sheep, John Coo, clerk \3d./ with 1 cow, Roger Reyner \4d./ with 2 cows put themselves [*in mercy*] for trespassing in the underwood of the lord, in the alder-holt called Hoogfen, therefore etc.

Amercement 4d. [*Illeg.*] Clerk puts himself [*in mercy*] for trespassing with his pigs in the lord's pasture in Mellecroft, therefore etc.

Amercement 6d. Thomas Sparwe puts himself [*in mercy*] for trespassing with 1 sow and 6 piglets in the lord's meadow called Prestowemedwe, therefore etc

Amercement 9d. John Porter \3d./ with 1 pig, Roger Reyner \3d./ with 2 pigs, John Holm \3d./ with his hens, put themselves [*in mercy*] for trespassing in the lord's wheat \in Burtons/.

Amercement 9d. [*Illeg.*] \6d./ with 2 pigs, Nicholas Gylle \3d./ with 1 pig, put themselves [*in mercy*] for trespassing in the lord's barley at Custodilhach,[108] therefore etc.

Amercement [?]*3d.* John [?]Schoppe puts himself [*in mercy*] for trespassing in the lord's oats in Byfold, therefore etc.

Amercement 1s. Katherine Deye \3d./ with 3 pigs, Thomas Hard \6d./ with 1 sow and her piglets, John Webbe \3d./ with 2 cows, put themselves [*in mercy*] for trespassing in the lord's wheat in Tolhouswente,[109] therefore etc.

Amercement [*illeg.*]. Katherine Deye puts herself [*in mercy*] for trespassing with 1 horse in the lord's wheat in Tolhouswente, therefore etc.

Amercement [*illeg.*]. Alice Blok puts herself [*in mercy*] for trespassing [*illeg.*] \with 1 cow/ in the lord's pasture in Hallegardyn, therefore etc.

Amercement [*illeg.*]. [*Illeg.*] puts him/herself [*in mercy*] for trespassing with 1 horse [*illeg.*] in the lord's pasture, therefore, etc., by the pledge of Andrew Hard, etc.

[*Illeg.*] To this court came [*Richard Cobb*] and Margery his wife, she being examined on her own privately, and they surrendered into the lord's hand one and a half roods of land "of the lord's demesne" in Mellecroft lying between the land formerly of Richard Blok on the one hand and the lord's land on the other. And the rent in respect of which, each year, 2s, to the behoof[110] of William Shoppe the younger, Andrew Shoppe and Thomas Hoberd. To whom the lord delivered seisin thereof. To hold to the same William, Andrew and Thomas and their heirs, of the lord, by the rod, at will etc. And they give as a fine as above. And they did fealty.

[*Illeg.*] *fealty.* To this court came Richard Cole and John Hoberd and they surrendered into the lord's hand one rood of land lying in Mellecroft lengthways between the land formerly of John Clement on the one hand and the land of Alice Blok on the other hand, to the use of [*William*] Shoppe, Andrew Shoppe and Thomas Hoberd. To whom the lord delivered seisin thereof, to hold to the same William, Andrew and Thomas and their heirs, from the lord, by the rod, at will etc. And they give for a fine as above. And they did fealty.

Amercement 5s. 6d. The inquest presents that the tenants of the lands called [*illeg.*], John Burye \3d./, Thomas atte Ston \3d./, John Waryn \3d./, Thomas Peytone \3d./, clerk, the tenants of Brownys tenement, Thomas Webbe \3d./, John Wendecole the

---

108 Literally something like the warden's wicket, or gate-keeper's hatch.

109 A went is a field with a path or road running through it. The tollhouse might have belonged to a bridge.

110 In later Latin legal documents, the formulaic phrase *ad usum et opus* becomes in English documents 'to the use and behoof (of)'. Here, the scribe has omitted *usum*.

younger \3d./, the tenants of the tenement Dullys \3d./, Robert atte Medwe \3d./, John Hoberd \3d./ for the tenement Tyye, the tenants of the tenement Whepstedes \3d./, Robert Barkere \3d./ John Hoberd \3d./ for the tenement formerly of Stephen Fox, the same John \3d./ for the tenement formerly of Walter Cakebred, Roger Mellere \[?]3d./, John [?]Gedeford, clerk \3d./, Robert Heyward \3d./ Richard atte Tye \3d./, Margery Stanhard \3d./, "Hugh Ive" \3d./ the tenants of the tenement formerly of John Halle owe suit of court and have defaulted. Therefore etc.

Amercement [*illeg.*]. Thomas Hard puts himself [*in mercy*] for making waste upon [*damaged*] of the same hedges at Lytilhegelye [*damaged*] of the same hedges, therefore etc.

[*Damaged*] puts himself [*in mercy*] for trespassing [*illeg.*] in the lord's [*illeg.*] therefore etc.

[*Damaged*] Richard [*illeg.*] puts himself [*in mercy*] for trespassing [*illeg.*] [*?in the lord's*] grass (*herbagium*) in Prestowemede, therefore etc.

Capital pledges

John North	John Davy	Thomas Sowe	}	
John Schoppe [*illeg.*]	Roger Reyner	Geoffrey Hoberd	}	Sworn
John [*illeg.*]	William Shopp	John Wendecole the elder	}	
John Aylward	John Webbe	John Warde	}	

Common fine 4s. All of the aforesaid chief pledges present that they give for the common fine as of ancient custom, as is evident in the [*marginal*] heading.

[*Illeg.*] And that John Wendecole the younger \6d./ Robert [*damaged*], John Shoppe \6d./, Robert Heyward \[*illeg.*]d./ are chief pledges and made default [*of suit of court*].

Amercement 6d. And that the tenants of the tenement Brownys [*damaged*] Sadilerisbregge to the nuisance etc. Therefore etc.

Amercement [*illeg.*]. And that Thomas Peytone, clerk, [*trespassed*] by digging clay (*fodend' argillum*) from the common way next to Brownisgate to the nuisance etc. therefore etc. And he is ordered to fill it in before the next [*court*].

[*Illeg.*] And that Thomas [?]Calle \3d./ dug [*illeg.*] 1 pit in the common way opposite Burtone therefore etc.

[*Illeg.*] And that Thomas Gant \3d./ did likewise there. And it is ordered etc. under penalty for each one of them 6s. 8d.

Amercement [*illeg.*] And that John Wendecole the younger has 1 ditch not cleaned out at Pykkiscroft in length etc, therefore etc.

Amercement [*illeg.*] And that Simon Foster has 1 ditch not cleaned out at Hoddone to the nuisance etc. therefore etc.

Amercement [*illeg.*] And that the same Simon obstructed a water course at Brodefeldebrook therefore etc.

Amercement [*illeg.*] And that the tenants of the tenement [?]Walshams have 1 ditch not cleaned out opposite Hellycroft in length etc, therefore etc.

Amercement [*illeg.*] And that Simon Fullere and John Webbe are ale tasters and carry out their duty badly therefore etc.

Amercements [*illeg.*] And that John Rowe \3d./ and Thomas Wryghte \6d./ have dwelt within the precincts of the leet for 1 year etc. and are outwith a tithing therefore etc.

Amercements [*illeg.*] And that Robert Hayward \3d./ John Vally \3d./, Richard Smyth, shoemaker \6d./, John Deye \3d./ formerly servant of Alice Blok, Thomas \3d./ servant of Robert Fullere, Roger Sayer \[*illeg.*]d./, John Bette \3d./ fuller, William Cole \3d./, John Coo the elder \3d./, Roger Webbe \3d./ are in a tithing and make default therefore etc.

[*Illeg.*] And that Thomas Kyng \[*illeg.*]d./, Robert Mutslo \[*illeg.*]d./, "Thomas Gant, John Ho"berd \[*illeg.*]d./, Andrew Hard \1s./, John Derby \1s./ and Thomas Wryghte \[*illeg.*]d./ [*are*] common brewers and sold ale against the assize.

[*Illeg.*] And that John Noche \3d./, William Astele \3d./, Adam Bretown \3d./, John Bette, fuller (*fullere*) \3d./, "Thomas Hoberd, William" [*illeg.*], Thomas Calle \3d./, Roger Reyner \3d./, John Grene \3d./, John Coo, clerk \[*illeg.*]d./, Anne Sosteyn \10d./, Roger [*damaged*] are brewers and broke the assize.

[*Damaged*] [*John*] Coo, clerk, Thomas Brown \1s./, Thomas Mowe \1s./ are bakers and [*?*]produced (*attulerunt*) bread within [*damaged*] against the assize, therefore etc.

[*Damaged*] And that Thomas Kyng \3d./, Robert Motslo \3d./, Thomas Gant \3d./, John Hoberd, Andrew Hard \7d./, John Derby and [*damaged*] Wryghte are regrators (*regraciatric'*) of bread and sold against the assize.

[*Damaged*] To this court came John Pylcrek son of William Pylcrek and did fealty to the lord for various lands and tenements which fell to him as his inheritance after the death of the aforesaid William. And [*damaged*] associates and by the custom of the manor.

Turn over

[*Dorse*] [*?*]Presentments. Also the inquest presents that Andrew [*?*]Stanhard acquired [*?1 acre of free land from John Boule*].

And that William Shoppe [*?acquired 1 piece of free land*] from the same John.

And that John Webbe acquired from John Wendecole the younger a piece of land called Litil Hoddone.

And that John Derby acquired one cottage with a curtilage adjacent from Thomas [*?*]Mundekyn.

It is ordered to distrain [*them*] against the next [*court*] to show how they entered into their lands. And for doing fealty to the lord.

[*Damaged*] Affeerers: Thomas Hoberd, John Webbe. Sworn.

Court Roll 20.[111] (1 August 1415)

[*Damaged.*] Court with view of frankpledge there held on Thursday the feast of St Peter in chains in the third year of the reign of King Henry the fifth [*Thursday, 1 August 1415*]

[*Essoins*]

[*Damaged*] [*essoins him/herself*] of common [*suit*]	by John Cabaw.
[*Damaged*] Castelyn of the same	by Adam Turnour.

---

111 CCA-U15/15/15 (former CCA document number '53,988' stamped and '13/46' and 'Illey Court Roll 3 H. 5' written on dorse in a nineteenth-century style and hand). Parchment roll, one membrane. Latin. Poor condition, some areas missing or illegible. One court.

[*Damaged*] Ketyl of the same   by Thomas Kyng.

[*Damaged*] [*?*]*ordered*, Thomas Haughey, plaintiff and Thomas Gant, defendant, in a plea of detention of his chattels. Ordered.

[*Damaged*] Gemneys because he does not proceed in his complaint against John Chapman in a plea of debt. Therefore etc.

[*Damaged*] Grey because he does not proceed in his complaint against John Taillour in a plea of debt. Therefore etc.

[*Damaged*] puts himself [*in mercy*] for licence to settle with John Sare of Lavenham in a plea of debt. Therefore etc.

[*Damaged*] Meller puts himself [*in mercy*] for licence to settle with Thomas Haughey in a plea of debt. Therefore etc.

[*Amercement*] [*damaged*]. John Hamond puts himself [*in mercy*] for licence to settle with John Broun of Bildeston (*Byldeston*) in a plea of debt. Therefore etc. By the pledge of John Slaughtere.

Amercement 9d. John Coo the elder puts himself [*in mercy*] for licence to settle with John Beneyt in 3 pleas of debt, contract and trespass. Therefore etc.

Amercement 9d. Ordered. Thomas Calle because [*illeg.*] for his recognizance against Thomas Haughey in a plea of debt, that is to say, for 3 bushels of wheat, 60 door nails (*dornayl'*) and 60 window nails (*wyndownayl'*) which it is ordered [*?to be seized*]. And the same Thomas Calle in mercy.

Amercement 3d. John [*?*]Benete [*damaged*] against John Chapeleyn in a plea of debt. Therefore etc.

Amercement 3d. John Cole because he did not proceed as plaintiff against John [*?*] Hony in a plea of contract. Therefore etc.

Amercement 3d. Ordered. John Coo, clerk, because [*damaged*] against Thomas Kyng in a plea of debt, that is to say, the detention of chattels, that is to say, 1 cow, which it is ordered to be raised \[*illeg.*] 3d. [*illeg.*]/. And the same John in mercy.

Amercement 3d. Nicholas Smyth because he did not proceed in a complaint against John Harcourt in a plea of contract. Therefore etc.

Amercement 4d. William Ayleward puts himself [*in mercy*] for trespassing with 4 cows at various times in the lord's peas in Hygeleighwente. Therefore etc.

[*Amercement*] *3d.* The same William for the same with his sheep in the lord's oats in Mapylcroft etc.

[*Amercement*] *3d.* The same William for the same with his pigs in the lord's peas there. Therefore etc.

Amercement 3d. The farmer[112] of the cows of Walshams for the same with his horse in the lord's wheat. Therefore etc. by the pledge of Thomas Kyng.

Amercement 3d. Roger Reigner puts himself [*in mercy*] because he trespassed with cows in the lord's pasture at various times. Therefore etc.

Amercement [*?*]*2d.* Nicholas Smyth for the same with one \horse/ in the lord's pasture in Mellecroft. Therefore etc.

Amercement \[*illeg.*]/ *3d.* Simon Smyth for the same with 1 cow and 1 calf in the lord's pasture. Therefore etc.

Amercement 3d. John Bomsted for the same with 1 cow and 1 calf in the lord's pasture. Therefore etc.

Amercement 3d. Simon Bakere for the same with 4 cows in the lord's pasture. Therefore etc.

---

[112] That is, lessee.

Amercement [?]*3d.* John Heyward for the same with [*damaged*] cows in the lord's pasture. Therefore etc.

Amercement 3d. John Coo, clerk, for the same with cows in the lord's pasture in Mellecroft. Therefore etc.

Amercement 6d. Geoffrey Hoberd for the same with his beasts in the wood called Manhey. Therefore etc.

Amercement 6d. John Ayleward \the elder/ for the same with his beasts in the lord's wood there. Therefore etc.

Amercement 1s. Simon Forster for the same with sheep and calves in the lord's wood there. Therefore etc.

Amercement 3d. Simon Bakere for the same with one horse there for one month. Therefore etc.

Amercement 4d. Nicholas Gylle for a trespass by carrying away peas at harvest-time out of the lord's field without licence. Therefore etc.

Amercement 3d. The same Nicholas for trespassing with his pigs at various times in the lord's peas in Byfold. Therefore etc.

Amercement 4d. John Davy for the same with one horse in the lord's pasture in Manhey. Therefore etc.

Amercement 4d. Thomas Wryghte for the same with one horse in the lord's pasture there. Therefore etc.

Amercement 2d. William Tylwhit for the same with one bullock in the lord's pasture there. Therefore etc.

Amercement 3d. John Davy the elder for a trespass because he carried away 1 cart load of rods out of Manhey for 1 building [*at*] Vanteland without licence etc.

Amercements [*blank space*]. Thomas Calle \2d./, Thomas Gant \2d./, William Clement \2d./, John Haw \2d./ because they cut underwood there without licence and carried it away without licence. Therefore the same in mercy.

Amercement 3d. Roger Meller puts himself [*in mercy*] for trespassing with one horse in the lord's pasture in various places. Therefore etc.

Amercement 3d. John Petycoo for the same with one horse in the lord's pasture in Manhey. Therefore etc.

Amercement 6d. William Calle of Lindsey (*Lelsey*) for trespassing by lopping and carrying away underwood out of Manhey without licence. Therefore etc.

Amercement 2d. Richard Benorthern for trespassing with two pigs in the lord's pasture. Therefore etc.

Amercements 3s. 3d. It was found by the inquest that [*illeg.*] John Burys \3d./, Thomas Ston \3d./, John Waryn \3d./ \[*illeg.*]/, Margaret Broun \3d./, John Vendecole the younger \3d./ for the tenement [?]Wryghtys [*illeg.*] and John Vendecole the elder \3d./ [*illeg.*], John Whepstead \[*illeg.*]/, Robert Fuller \3d./, Roger Meller \3d./, [*illeg.*], Richard Tye \3d./, Robert Reigner \3d./, Hugh Ive \3d./, John Halle \3d./, John Ronde the younger \3d./ [*illeg.*], William [*illeg.*], Alexander Kylle \[?]4d./ and Simon Cuttyng \4d./ owe suit of court and made default. Therefore etc.

Chief pledges

John [?]North	Roger Reigner	Geoffrey Hoberd	}
John [*illeg.*]	William Schoppe	John Warde	}
John Nytingale	John Webbe	John Hoberd	} Sworn
John Davy	Thomas Sparwe	John Shopp	}

Common fine 4s. All the abovesaid chief pledges present that they give as the common fine as is apparent in the [*marginal*] heading.[113]

Amercements [*?*]*s. 1d.* Also they say that Thomas Kyng \1s./, John Davy \1s./, Robert Mutslo \1s./, Thomas Calle \1s./, Thomas Gant \1s./, John Hoberd \8d./, Andrew Hard \1s./, John Derby \1s./, Thomas Wryghte \1s./ [*are*] common brewers and broke the assize of ale. Therefore etc. And that John Dogat \3d./, Thomas Levyng \3d./, John Damysell \3d./, James [*?*]Slork, Thomas Alfrych \3d./, Alice Fuller \3d./, Roger [*?*]Canteren \[*illeg.*]d./, John Prynchat \3d./, William Ayleward \3d./, John Cabaw \3d./. They brewed there and broke the assize of ale. Therefore etc.

Amercement 6d. And that Simon Fuller \3d./ and John Webbe \3d./, ale-tasters, do not do their duty. Therefore etc.

Amercement [*illeg.*]. And that John Derby \3d./, John Mutslo \3d./, "Thomas Broun" \1s./, Thomas [*?*]Moris \1s./ and William Slaughtere \1s./ regrate bread within the vill and sell against the statute. Therefore etc.

Amercement 1s. 6d. And that Thomas [*illeg.*] \6d./, Richard Mutslo \6d./, "Andrew Hard" \3d./, John Davy \3d./, Robert Mutslo, Thomas Calle \2d./, Thomas Gant \3d./, Andrew Hard sell bread against the statute. Therefore etc.

Amercement [*illeg.*]*d.* And that John Vyndec[*?ole*] [*damaged*] made default. Therefore etc.

[*Two lines illeg.*]

Amercement 6d. And that Robert Reigner has one ditch not cleaned out at Hunmanescroft. Therefore etc.

[*One line illeg.*]

Amercement [*illeg.*]. And that the tenants of Richard atte Tye hold one ditch there next to [*damaged*].

[*Remainder of this side of the membrane, about twenty lines, damaged and/or illeg.*]

[*Dorse*] *Amercements 1s. 6d.* Also the said chief pledges say that John Bette \6d./, Thomas Gant \3d./, Thomas Hoberd \3d./ and John Curteys \6d./ [*illeg.*] against the peace. Therefore etc.

Amercement 3d. And that John Curteys assaulted John Davy against the peace. Therefore etc.

Amercement 3d. And the same John Davy assaulted the said John Curteys against the peace etc.

Amercement 3d. And that John Stouke against the peace assaulted Margaret Grey and [*?*]drew blood. Therefore etc.

Amercement 3d. And that Margaret Grey against the peace assaulted the said John Stouke. Therefore etc.

Amercements 3s. And that John Bonde the younger \3d./, Richard Benorthen \3d./, John Vally \3d./, William Lyncolne \3d./, Roger Sayer \3d./, [*damaged*] John Coo the elder \3d./, John Boble \3d./, Richard Byllinges \3d./, John Wyndecole \3d./ the younger, John Taillour \3d./ and John [*damaged*] made default. Therefore etc.

Amercements 1s. 6d. And that John Rous \3d./, Thomas Wryghte \3d./, Walter Ancey \3d./, William Myle \3d./, William [*Archer*] \3d./ and that Richard Cabaw [*damaged*] [*dwell within*] the precincts of the leet and are outwith a tithing. Therefore etc.

Amercement 6d. And that John Curteys against the peace assaulted John Broun and drew blood. Therefore etc.

---

[113] That is, the marginal heading, so 4s.

Elected. John Warde and Roger Reigner are elected to the office of constable and are sworn.

Again concerning the court as before

Fealty. To this court comes Andrew Page son of John Page and asks to be admitted to one tenement and certain free land which Richard atte Tye held for the term of his life. And to one free tenement formerly of John atte Tye, of which he is the nearest heir, as it is said. And thus it is found by the homage. And he is admitted to hold to him and his heirs. And he did fealty to the lord. And nothing as a relief, as it is said, according to the custom of the manor.

Fine 10s. To this court came Alice Blok, Robert Fuller and Thomas Calle and surrendered into the lord's hand one "messuage" with buildings erected upon it, as of ancient times called Lyrycokkysgardyn lying in Monks Eleigh (*Illeigh Monachorum*) and "one piece of meadow" called Squattysmedewe with appurtenances lying opposite Mellecroft, quit from them and their heirs as the lord "might do thereof" by will, excepting however from it one cottage with one piece of curtilage, parcel of the said messuage of Lyrycokksgardyn, just as it is bounded and the same is certified, that the aforesaid Alice, Thomas and Robert Calle have reserved to them and their heirs. And upon this, at the instance of the court, the lord granted to Nicholas Blok the aforesaid messuage and meadow with appurtenances, the cottage with its curtilage previously excepted, from the day given by this court until the feast of St Michael the archangel now next in the future and from the following feast of St Michael the archangel until the same feast then next following, rendering for the same to the aforesaid Alice within the aforesaid terms £2 at the terms of Easter and St Michael in equal portions, on account of which the said Alice according to the agreement will acquit the said Nicholas of all services and customs for the same for the whole of the aforesaid term [*damaged*]. And after the aforesaid feast of St Michael the archangel at the end of the aforesaid term the aforesaid messuage and meadow with their appurtenances excepting the cottage with its curtilage aforesaid will remain to Robert Mutslo and Isabelle his wife to hold to the same Robert and Isabelle and their heirs, of the lord, by the rod, at the lord's will, by the services and according to the custom of the manor. And rendering each year to the aforesaid Alice, during the life of the same Alice, £1 at the feasts of Easter and St Michael the archangel equally. And finally paying to the aforesaid Alice or her certain attorney, £20 of legal money within the term of 10 years next following after the aforesaid feast of St Michael at the end of one year next after the feast of St Michael the archangel then next following, that is to say, for each year £2 at the feasts of Easter and St Michael the archangel in equal portions during the term of the said 10 years. And if it happens that the aforesaid Robert Mutslo and Isabelle or their heirs default in the payment of the aforesaid £20 or in the payment of the said £1 at any of the aforesaid terms for 6 weeks next following against the provisions aforesaid in part or in total, that then the aforesaid Alice or her attorney are allowed, by licence of the lord, to re-enter into the aforesaid messuage and meadow with their appurtenances and to hold the same as before without any contradiction whatsoever, with the proviso however that if the aforesaid Alice within the term of St Michael the archangel next after the feast of St Michael the archangel now next in the future should die, that then by the agreement the aforesaid £2 reserved to the said Alice will be paid by the said Nicholas as has been said earlier after the death of the said Alice in part or in total to be paid faithfully to the said Robert Mutslo and Isabelle and their heirs or their attorneys by the said Nicholas in the form aforesaid, acquitting the aforesaid Nicholas of the services and customs thereby accruing as the said Alice would have been acquitted him. And reserving furthermore that it is fully allowed for the aforesaid Robert Mutslo and Isabelle and their heirs [*?to detain certain moneys from the issues*] of the aforesaid messuage and meadow for repairs to the buildings there and for making repairs to the enclosures without any cost and by right to him the aforesaid Nicholas and by any pretext introduced. And it was granted to the aforesaid Robert Mutslo and Isabelle seisin of the same, to hold the aforesaid after the said term of St Michael at the end, etc. [*illeg.*]. And the said Robert Mutslo and Isabelle give to the lord as a fine as is evident in the heading. And they did fealty.

[*?It is ordered*] to distrain Andrew Stannard to show how he entered in to the lord's fee, that is to say, one free messuage which he acquired from John [*illeg.*]. And for doing fealty etc. And Andrew Kyng and his associates to show how they entered into a free tenement formerly of John Whepsted and for fealty, etc. And to execute the orders of the last [*illeg.*].

Amercement 3d. John Holm because [*illeg.*] against John Chapman in a plea of trespass, that is to say, [*damaged*] it is ordered to raise [*damaged*].

Amercement 3d. Thomas Kyng puts himself [*in mercy*] for licence to settle with John Coo, clerk, in a plea of [*?*]debt [*illeg.*].

[*This court ends here*].

Court Roll 21.[114] (1 August 1419)

[*Damaged*] with leet there held on the Tuesday the feast of St Peter in chains in the seventh year of the reign of King Henry the fifth [*Tuesday, 1 August 1419*]

[*Damaged*] "Margery" Stanhard puts herself [*in mercy*] for trespassing with her cows in the lord's pasture in Illeigfeld on two occasions. Therefore the same in mercy.

[*Damaged*] "Thomas" Sparwe for the same with his cows on one occasion in the lord's wheat in Suddyssele. Therefore etc.

"*Amercement*" 6d. John Bonde for the same with his cows on one occasion in the lord's wheat in Byfold. Therefore in mercy.

[*Damaged*] [*Amercement*] 1d. John Roice for the same with his cows on several occasions in the lord's oats in Heighfeld. Therefore etc.

[*Damaged*]. Robert Talbot for the same with his pigs in the lord's pasture in Mellecroft. Therefore etc.

[*Amercement*] 1d. The same Robert for the same with his cows in the lord's pasture there and [*illeg.*] Therefore etc.

[*Damaged*]. [*Illeg.*] for the same with 2 pigs in the lord's pasture there. Therefore in mercy.

[*Damaged*]. Thomas Kyng for the same with pigs [*illeg.*] in the lord's pasture in Mellecroft in the wintertime. Therefore etc.

---

[114] CCA-U15/15/14 [*part 2*]: this reference covers two separate parchment court rolls, each of one membrane (former CCA document '48833', 'Monks Illeigh, Roll 1416, 1420' written on dorse of both membranes in a nineteenth-century hand). Court Roll 18 comprises the first membrane (court dated 1 August 1413), Court Roll 21, here, the second (court dated 1 August 1419): the two have been separated in this volume as there are other courts between these two dates. Latin. Badly damaged by damp.

Amercement [*illeg.*]. Robert Smyth for the same with his pigs in the lord's wheat in le Burton on several occasions. Therefore etc.

Amercement 3d. Thomas Lylye for the same with his pigs in the lord's wheat there. Therefore in mercy.

Amercement 1s. Geoffrey Hoberd for the same with his beasts on several occasions in the lord's wood in Manhey. Therefore etc.

[*Illeg.*]. John Ayloof for the same with his beasts on several occasions. Therefore etc.

[*Illeg.*]. John [*?*]Bene[*t*] for the same with one cow in the lord's oats in Heighfeld. Therefore etc.

[*Illeg.*]. [*Illeg.*] for the same with his cows in the lord's oats there. Therefore etc.

[*Damaged*] [*Illeg.*] Cobold for the same with his sheep in the lord's wheat in Seddysele. Therefore etc.

[*Damaged*] [*Illeg.*] for the same with his [*illeg.*] on several occasions in the lord's pasture. Therefore etc.

[*Damaged*] [*Illeg.*] de Preston trespassed [*illeg.*] with his cart. Therefore etc.

[*Damaged*] [*Illeg.*] for trespassing with one horse in the lord's pasture on several occasions [*illeg.*].

[*Damaged*] [*Illeg.*] Webbe puts himself [*in mercy*] for licence to settle with Robert Talbot in a plea of debt. Therefore in mercy.

John Prynchat because he did not proceed in a complaint [*illeg.*].

[*Amercement*] [*?*]d. [*Illeg.*] puts himself [*in mercy*] for licence to settle with John Ward in a plea of debt. Therefore etc.

[*Illeg.*] John Bonde, plaintiff and John Shoppe \the elder/, defendant, in a plea of trespass, by the pledge of the next.

[*Remainder of this side of this membrane illegible due to damage caused by damp.*]

[*Dorse*]

Again concerning the leet

Brewers 11s. 2d. Also they present that Thomas Gant \1s./, [*illeg.*] Stanhard \3d./, John Stanhard, Robert Mutslo \1s./ [*damaged*] Kyng \1s./, Robert Gaweg [*sic*] \1s./, John Derby \6d./, [*illeg.*]Thomas Hoberd \3d./, Thomas Calle [*illeg.*] Brown \3d./, Robert Fuller \3d./, William Shopp \3d./, Thomas Alfrych \3d./, John Damysell \3d./, William Freman \3d./, Robert [*damaged*], John Webbe \3d./, John B[*?*] \3d./, Simon Smyth \3d./, John Coo, clerk \3d./, John Cabaw \3d./, Geoffrey Cabaw \3d./, [*damaged*] Halle \3d./, are brewers and break the assize of ale. Therefore etc.

Amercement [*illeg.*]*d.* And that John Derby \4d./ [*illeg.*] break the assize of bread. Therefore etc.

Amercement 1s. 7d. And that Thomas Brown \8d./, Thomas [*illeg.*] \8d./ and [*illeg.*] Holdeyn are bakers and [*illeg.*].

Election. William Shopp the younger is elected with Thomas Alfrych into the office of ale-taster and were sworn.

Amercement 1s. Also they say that John Davy \6d./ and William Tyrwhit \6d./ [*illeg.*] against Manhey [*illeg.*]. Therefore in mercy. And he is ordered to put it right before the next [*court*] under penalty [*illeg.*] 6s 8d.

Amercement 1s. And that John Roice obstructed a certain way in Kettlebaston (*Ketilberston*) belonging to the lord \and/ the rector of Eleigh (*Illeigh*) [*illeg.*] ditch. And he is ordered to appear against the next [*court*] under penalty of 10s.

Fealty. John Chapelayn, Simon Fuller and John Wyndecole the younger showed a certain charter by which they acquired from John Bonde and William Shoppe one piece of land in Monks Eleigh (*Illeigh Monachorum*) to hold to them and their heirs. And they did fealty to the lord.

Fealty. John Coo, Robert Fullere and Thomas Hoberd show a charter by which they acquired from John Hoberd and Geoffrey Hoberd certain lands in Oddoune and elsewhere, to hold to them, their heirs and assigns, for which they did fealty to the lord.

Amercement 1s. 9d (*xxjd.* [*sic*]) Also they say that Thomas *Bryghtʒene*[115] \3d./, Roger Sayer \3d./, John Betts, fuller (*fullere*) \6d./, William Puddyng \6d./, William [?]Slawghtere \3d./, [*damaged*] Fanit \3d./, Geoffrey Hoberd, John Noche \3d./ are in default of a tithing. Therefore the same in mercy.

Total of the court and leet [damaged]

Court Roll 22.[116] (2 September, 21 October 1420; 2 August 1422)

[*Paper roll*] [*Monks Eleigh. Court*] with leet held on the "Monday" on the morrow of St Giles in the 8th year of Henry V [*Monday, 2 September 1420*]

[*Essoins*]

[*Damaged*] Pylcrek [*essoins himself*] of common [*suit*]	by John Prynchat
[*Damaged*] Simon Fuller of the same	by John Shopp
[*Damaged*] Davy of the same	by Richard Davy

[*Damaged*] [*John*] Chapman and Margaret his wife complain against John [?]Holm in a plea of debt [*damaged*] that is to say, of 1s. 8d. of the [*illeg.*] of the said Margaret to the damage of 1s. And [*illeg.*]

[*Damaged*] \[*Illeg.*]/ The same John Chapman against John [?]Holm in plea of debt of 1s. 8d. for [*illeg.*] to the damage of 1s. And [*illeg.*] by the pledge of [*illeg.*].

[*Damaged*] Richard Cole \does not proceed/ against John Coo the elder of Fenstrete in plea of debt.

[*Damaged*] Zakysle complains against John Erl in a plea of trespass. And the same Zakysle puts himself [*in mercy*] by the pledge of Thomas Gant.

[*Damaged*] rector of Eleigh (*Illeigh*) against Thomas Gant in a plea of debt. And the same Thomas puts [*himself in mercy*] [*damaged*].

[*Damaged*] puts himself [*in mercy*] for trespassing with sheep or beasts in the wheat on various [*illeg.*].

[*Damaged*] for the same with [?]animals on several occasions in the peas in Byfold.

[*Damaged*] for the same with 1 pig in the peas there.

[*Damaged*] 2 pigs in the lord's peas there.

[*Damaged*] Coo, clerk, for 2 pigs in the pasture in Mellecroft.

[*Damaged*] for 4 pigs [*illeg.*] in the peas and oats in Byfold.

[*Damaged*] pigs in the peas there.

[*Damaged*] beasts in the wood of Manhey.

[*Damaged*] with his beasts there.

[*Damaged*] with his beasts in the woods there.

[*Damaged*] John Cole [*illeg.*] against John Prynchat in a plea of debt of 6s. [*illeg.*] which it is ordered to be raised etc.

---

[115] No name is obvious whether the yogh (ʒ) is transliterated as 'g' or 'y'.

[116] CCA-U15/15/16 (former CCA document number '53963' and '8/10' written on dorse of paper roll in a nineteenth-century hand). Two rolls: one paper (1420, draft), one parchment (1422, fair copy). Latin. Paper roll damaged badly in places, with much of left side missing. Parchment roll badly damaged by damp in places, some holes, some ink flaking off. Three courts, with leet.

[*Damaged*]. John Baker, chaplain, and John Wyndecole the younger, executors of the testament of John Wyndcole of Monks Eleigh (*Illeigh Monachorum*) against John [*?*]Salter \puts himself [*in mercy*]/ of Buxhall (*Buxhale*) in a plea of debt [*illeg.*] to answer John Kyng.

[*Damaged*]. John [*?*]Coverour against William Taverney [*?*]taylor ([*?*]*taillour*) in a plea of debt. And [*damaged*].

\[*Damaged*]. \+ concerning common fine [*?*]chief pledges heard in the last leet firstly placed in the leet./

[*Damaged*]. William Shopp the younger against John Wyndcol the younger, John Stanhard, Geoffrey Hoberd [*damaged*] John Shopp.

[*Damaged.*] Sir Thomas Meer \6d./, Aug' Duncan \3d./, <Robert Marchant>, William Peyton \3d./, Simon Casteleyn \3d./, John North \3d./ and Robert Ketyl \3d./ and John Ayleward \3d./ and John Wyn[*?decole*] \3d./, John Coo the elder \3d./, <John Ayleward> and <John> <Robert> <Barker>, Roger Meller \3d./, [*illeg.*] Hugh Yve \3d./, Roger Fizstevyn \3d./ and John Halle \3d./ for default of suit [*of court*] (*sect' pro def'*).

[*Damaged.*] John Cole because [*illeg.*] against John Skut in a plea of debt.

[*Damaged.*] John Grene [*illeg.*] against John Taillour in a plea of debt, that is, in 6d [*damaged*] ordered to raise etc.

[*Damaged.*] John Marchant for [*illeg.*].

[*Damaged.*] [*William Shopp*] the younger and Thomas Alfrych \3d./ ale-tasters do not do their duty.

[*Damaged.*] John Damysell \3d./ and [*?*]Halbert Hard \3d./ and John <Ty> Pye \3d./ [*damaged*] William Taverner \3d./ and Thomas Sharp \3d./ and Joanna Browistere \3d./ and John [*damaged*] \3d./ [*damaged*] Skylmay and Henry Baker \3d./ and Thomas Gant \1s./ and Robert Motslo [*damaged*] \1s./, q. \1s./, Thomas Lylye \1s./ and Thomas Kyng \1s./ and Robert Calliot \1s./ and John Derby \1s./ and John Stanhard \3d./ and John Mole \3d./ and the same brew and break the assize.

[*Damaged.*] that Thomas Broun \8d./, Thomas More \8d./ and Thomas Bogays \<6d, 6d,> 8d./ bake [*damaged*] break the \assize of bread./, John Derby \8d./ for the same.

[*Damaged.*] Robert Motslo was examined in court \<surrendered into the hand of the lord> by the hand of Thomas Malch[*er*] the lord's [*illeg.*]/ in the presence of John Hoberd, John Shopp, William Shopp and other tenants and Isabell wife of the said Robert Motslo at the instance of the court was examined alone and secretly, surrendered into the lord's hand one messuage with buildings erected upon it of ancient time called Lyricokkysgardyn lying in Illeigh aforesaid and one piece of meadow called Squattysmed with appurtenances lying opposite Mellecroft quit to her and her heirs to them whole just as Robert and the same Isabell formerly had it out of the surrender of Alice Blok, Robert Fullere and Thomas Calle to the use of Andrew Stannard, John Neve, John Stannard and William Stannard to whom seisin thereof was delivered. To hold to them and their heirs \of the lord, by the rod, at the will of the lord, according to the custom of the manor/ reserving however to the aforesaid Alice Blok by a certain agreement \under penalty as agreed/ in the said court aforesaid \with leet here held/ on Thursday, the feast of St Peter in chains in the 3rd year of the reign of abovesaid King Henry [*1415*].[117]

Ordered. [*Damaged.*] It is ordered to seize into the lord's hand certain land and pasture which was held by the rod that Roger Reigner alienated to John Bumsted.

---

[117] See Court Roll 20 (1 August 1415).

Fealty. The inquest present that Roger Reyner acquired 1 free croft from John Wyndecole son of the late John Wyndcole who showed a charter to him and Thomas Hoberd and their heirs. And he did fealty.

[*Damaged.*] And that Aug' Duncan acquired a free tenement called Boyton from Thomas Greyve and others. And And he is ordered [*to do*] fealty.

Ordered. [*Damaged*] that <Robert> William Prior acquired from Robert Heyward 1 cottage tenement and free land. And he is ordered to be distrained.

Order for fealty. And that Andrew Sparwe acquired 1 piece of land from Thomas Sparwe.

Order for fealty. And that Thomas Whersted alienated to John Hoberd and other free land etc.

Fealty. And that John Wyndecole the younger lately died holding from the said lord 1 messuage and free land from this manor, for service [*?jointly with*] [*illeg.*] who did fealty.

[*Dorse*] *Amercement 3d.* Ordered. And that [*illeg.*] 1 ditch not cleaned out at Gaugyslane in length etc. And it is ordered that [*he puts it right*].

Amercement 3d. Ordered. Also the same for another ditch at Paiekatistrete in length \[*?*]8 perches/. And it is ordered 3s. 4d.

Amercement 6d. Also the same assaulted Alice Byllynges and drew blood. And [*illeg.*].

Amercement 3d. William Taverner drew blood from [*illeg.*] Chapman.

Amercement <3d.> 3s. 4d. <Adam Turnour> John [*?*]Forster [*?*]beat Adam Turnour and drew blood.

Amercement 3s. 4d. John Crokyshale drew blood from Roger [*illeg.*].

[*Damaged.*] Talbot appropriated a parcel of the king's highway and of the church opposite the tenement Puddynges placing [*illeg.*] another way. And a penalty of 10s. is ordered.

[*Damaged.*] And that the same Robert spreads [*illeg.*].

Elections. John Bomsted, John Hervy ale tasters. Andrew Stanhard, William Shopp, constables.

[*Damaged.*] William Taverner \3d./, William Cabaw \3d./, Clement Walays \3d./, John [*?*]Bence \3d./, fuller, John North \3d./, John [*?*]Taverner the elder \3d./, John [*illeg.*] \3d./, Roger Fizstevyn \3d./, John [*?*]Noch \3d./, John Rakedeux \3d./, Robert Reigner tithingmen, for default [*of suit of court*].

[*Damaged.*] common fine, 4s.

Affeerers: William Shopp, John Chapeleyn

[*Damaged.*] [*Monks Eleigh.*] Court held on the Monday next after the feast of St Luke the evangelist in the 8th year of Henry [*V, Monday, 21 October 1420*]

Essoins

[*?*]Thomas [*?*]Edneys [*essoins himself*] of common [*suit*]   by T. Malcher.
Simon Forster of the same   by John Ward.

[*Damaged.*] *3s. 4d.* Roger Reigner came into court and surrendered into the lord's hand 4½ acres and ½ rood of land of the demesne in Le Burton, quit from him and his heirs, so that the lord might do his will therewith, which is held of the lord for service, 4s. 3d. And the lord re-granted the said land to the aforesaid Roger, John Bumsted, Thomas Hoberd, to hold to them and their heirs, of the lord, by the rod, at the will of the lord, according to the custom of the manor. And seisin thereof was delivered to them. And they give as a fine for entry.

[*Damaged.*] The tenants of the tenement Walshams \3d./ <Aug' Duncon>, the tenants of Thomas [*?*]Boxtan' \3d./, <John [*?*]Waryn> the tenants of the land of John Waryn \3d./ and William Peyton \3d./, Adam Turnour \3d./ and Robert Ketyl \3d./, William Tylwyth \3d./, John Davy \3d./, Simon Baker \3d./, John Wyndcol \3d./ the elder, [*damaged*] and John Whepstead, John Prynchat \3d./, William Tye \3d./, chaplain, Roger Meller \[*?*]2d./, <Ro> Walter [*?*]Richard [*illeg.*] \3d./ and John Waltham \3d./ and Robert Reigner \3d./, Hugh Ive \3d./, Roger Fiz Stevyn \3d./, <John Bonde> and Andrew Page \3d./ and William Shopp suitors [*of this court*] for default [*of suit of court*], John Wyndcol the elder \3d./ for the same.

Amercement 6d. John Pilcrek and John Davy for not warranting essoins.

Amercement 3d. John Chapman for unjustly complaining against John Holm in a plea of debt.

[*Damaged.*] It is ordered that the said John [*?ought*] to show [*how*] he entered into land formerly of John Halle.

[*Damaged.*] John Chapman and Margaret his wife do not proceed against John Holm in a plea of debt.

Amercement 6d. Robert Motslo \[*illeg.*] T. Malcher/ against John Sawyer in 2 pleas of debt. And the first by the pledge of the said John [*damaged*], it is ordered.

[*Damaged.*] John Hoberd, John Wyndcol, Andrew Stanhard, Geoffrey Hoberd, Robert Fuller, William Shopp the younger, Thomas Sparwe, Simon Fuller, John Webbe, Thomas Hoberd, Roger Reigner, John North, John Noche who are not in a tithing.

[*End of this court and roll.*]

[*Parchment roll, damaged.*] [*Monks Eleigh.*] Court with leet there, held on the Monday next after the feast of St Peter in chains in the tenth year of the reign of King Henry the fifth [*Monday 2 August 1422*]

[*?*]*Essoin.* William Clandysle, defendant, against John Chapman in a plea of debt, by Robert Talbot.

Amercement [*damaged*]. Richard Talbot puts himself [*in mercy*] for trespassing with his pigs in the pasture of Mellecroft. Therefore etc

Amercement [*damaged*] Kyng for the same with his pigs in the pasture there. Therefore etc.

Amercement [*damaged*]. John Coo, clerk, for [*the same with*] 2 pigs in the lord's wheat in Byfold. Therefore etc.

Amercement [*damaged*]. Roger Reyner for [*the same with*] his beasts at various times in the lord's wood in Manhey. Therefore etc.

Amercement 6d. [*?*]Simon Forster for the same with various of his beasts in the lord's wood there. Therefore etc.

Amercement [*damaged*]. [*Illeg.*] atte Cherche for the same with 2 beasts in the lord's wood there. Therefore etc.

Amercement [*damaged*]. [*Illeg.*] Coo for the same with 2 oxen in the lord's wood there. Therefore etc.

Amercement [*damaged*]. Thomas Sparwe for the same with beasts in the lord's peas in Illeigefeld. Therefore etc.

[*Damaged.*] John [*illeg.*] for the same with beasts in the meadow of Prestow, by pledge. Therefore etc. By the pledge of William Prior, clerk.

173

[*Damaged.*] John Hoo, plaintiff, against John Coo the elder in a plea of debt. And the same John Coo puts himself [*in mercy*]. Therefore etc.

[*Damaged.*] [*?*]Thomas Bogays, plaintiff, against John Coo the elder in a plea of debt. And the same John puts himself [*in mercy*]. Therefore etc.

[*Damaged.*] puts himself [*in mercy*] for licence to settle with Thomas Bogays in a plea of debt. Therefore etc.

[*Damaged*] Reyner, plaintiff, against John Pypere \1 pledge/ in a plea of debt, pledge to proceed, the bailiff etc. And [*?on behalf of the parties*] they have a day until the next court. And [*illeg.*] it is ordered John [*damaged*].

[*Damaged*] and John Sawyer \puts [*himself in mercy*]/ defendants in a plea of debt until the next [*court*] etc.

Amercement [*damaged*]. John Hoberd, plaintiff, against John Grenefeld in a plea of trespass. And the same John Hoberd did not proceed. Therefore etc.

Amercement 3d. [*Damaged*] puts himself [*in mercy*] for licence to settle with Roger [*?*]Josefe in a plea of debt. Therefore etc.

Amercement 3d. [*Damaged*] puts himself [*in mercy*] for licence to settle with the said Roger in a plea of debt. Therefore etc.

Amercement [*damaged*]. [*Illeg.*] puts himself [*in mercy*] for licence to settle with Thomas [*?*]Greyve in a plea of debt. Therefore etc.

Amercement [*damaged*]. [*Illeg.*] puts himself [*in mercy*] for licence to settle with Simon Baker in a plea of trespass. Therefore etc.

Amercement [*damaged*] puts himself [*in mercy*] for licence to settle with the said Simon in a plea of trespass. Therefore etc.

Amercement [*damaged*] puts himself [*in mercy*] for trespassing for licence to settle with the said Simon in a plea of trespass. Therefore etc.

Amercement [*damaged*]. John [*?*]Prior puts himself [*in mercy*] for licence to settle with Robert Talbot in a plea of trespass. Therefore, etc, by the pledge of John Wyndecole.

Amercement 3d. John Kyng puts himself [*in mercy*] for licence to settle with William Archer in a plea of debt. Therefore etc.

Amercement 3d. William Archer puts himself [*in mercy*] for licence to settle with John Kyng in a plea of debt. Therefore etc.

A day. A day is given to John Ward, plaintiff and Thomas Hoberd, defendant, in a plea of trespass until the next [*court*].

Amercement 3d. John Grenefeld does not proceed in a complaint against John \ Hoberd/ in a plea of debt. Therefore etc.

Amercement 3d. John Warde does not proceed in a complaint against Thomas Hoberd in a plea of trespass. Therefore etc.

Amercement 6d. Adam Turnour for unjustly complaining against Simon Smyth in 2 complaints of trespass. Therefore etc.

Amercement 3d. Thomas Hoberd did not proceed in a complaint against John Ward in a plea of trespass [*damaged*].

Fealty. John Noche of Kettlebaston (*Ketylberston*) and Alice his wife show a charter according to the form [*of the statute*] by which they acquired from Geoffrey Cabaw one messuage and half an acre of land in Kettlebaston, to have and [*to hold*] [*damaged*]. And they did fealty to the lord.

Inquest. Taken by virtue of their office by the oaths of John North, John Shopp, Robert Fuller [*damaged*] Stanhard, Simon Fuller, Thomas Gant, John Coo, clerk, Thomas Alfrych, Henry Baker, Thomas Calle and John [*damaged*], tenants of the land of the lady Phillipa \6d./ for the land formerly of Thomas Moor, clerk, Augustine Dunton \3d./, Hugh Ive \3d./, Roger Fitzstevyn \3d./, tenants holding the land formerly of William [*damaged*] Casteleyn \3d./, Roger Reygner \3d./, for the tenement Swyftys, the same Roger for the tenement of Isabel Reigner and the rector of the church of Eleigh (*Illeigh*) \3d./ are suitors of court and make default [*of suit of court*]. Therefore it is ordered [*damaged*].

Ordered. And that John Warde acquired 1 croft of free land [*damaged*] of Andrew Kyng whom it is ordered to distrain to do fealty against the next [*court*].

[*Ordered.*] And that John Porter \1 pledge/ acquired from Robert atte Medwe the tenement Fennys freely. And it is ordered to distrain the said John to do fealty to the lord etc.

Ordered. And it is ordered to distrain John Sawyer \1 pledge/, John Hoberd and Thomas Calle to show how they have entered into one cottage formerly of John Prynchat and for fealty.

A day. A day is given for the inquest upon \under penalty of 6s. 8d./ their oaths etc. [*damaged*], William Puddyng \does not proceed./ [*illeg.*] sold to the same William by William Tye, chaplain, at the last feast of Christmas [*damaged*] without licence of the same William Puddyng by force and arms [?]removed (*elongavit*) to the damage of William himself of 1s. [*illeg.*] the same William by John Hoberd his attorney here in the court [*damaged*] etc.

Death. Fine 8s. Fealty. Also it is found by the chief pledges whose names are contained within that Andrew Page, who lately died, held of the lord one croft of land called [?]Runenystye containing about 16 acres of land with a parcel of pasture adjacent, for service and [?]8s. and of which he died seised. And after his death, John atte Tye of Lavenham, kinsman of the said Andrew, is his nearest heir and is of full age, who, being present in court, sought admittance. And he was accepted as tenant, to hold, to him and his heirs, of the lord, by the rod, at the will of the lord, according to the custom of the manor. And seisin thereof is delivered to him. And he gives as a fine as above. And he did fealty.

Fine 8s. Fealty. And at the instance of the lord, John surrendered into the lord's hand the stock and the said parcel of pasture so that the lord might do his will therewith. And concerning these at the same court the lord granted out of his hand the croft and parcel of pasture aforesaid to the use of Robert Wellyng, the said John atte Tye, Thomas Hoberd the younger \and Thomas [?]Malcher/ to whom the lord handed over seisin thereof. To hold to the same Robert, John, Thomas Hoberd \and Thomas/ and their heirs, of the lord, by the rod, at the will of the lord, according to the custom of the manor. And they give to the lord as a fine for entry as above. And they did fealty.

[?]*Ordered* [*illeg.*] *and relief. Relief* [*illeg.*]. And that the same Andrew Page held from the lord one messuage and around 40 acres of free land by service etc. when he closed his last day. And after his death the aforesaid John atte Tye entered into the said messuage and land by right of inheritance to that which the same Andrew died seised. And that the same \John/ immediately after his entry \into the said messuage and land/ made an enfeoffment thereof to Robert Wellyng and others whom it is ordered to distrain to show how they entered into the same and to do fealty to the lord at the next [*court*]. And the said John atte Tye gives to the lord as a relief as is apparent in the heading etc.

Chief pledges

John Wyndecole the elder	John Wyndecole	Thomas Hoberd	}
John Webbe	John Hoberd	John Davy	}
Thomas Sparwe	William Shoppe	John Chapeleyn	}
John Cabaw	Geoffrey Hoberd	William Ayleward	}

Sworn

Common fine 4s. They present that they give to the lord as the common fine as of ancient custom as is evident in the heading.

Amercement 6d. And that John Chapman \3d./ and Andrew his brother \3d./ against the lord king's peace made an assault on John [*illeg.*] and drew blood. Therefore the same in mercy.

Amercement 6s. 8d. And that Thomas Wryghte \6s. 8d./ of Lelsey and John Sket \ [*?*]3d./ of Kersey against the lord king's peace entered the demesne and unjustly distrained 2 horses \from John [*illeg.*]/ and took them by force and arms and abducted them out of this liberty [*?to the contempt of the lord*] etc. Therefore in mercy.

[*Dorse*]

Still relating to the court and leet as before

Amercement 6d. Ordered. Also they present that Adam Turnour made an encroachment, appropriating to himself parcel of the lord's common and of his tenements at Swyngyldene [*damaged*] hedge erected [*illeg.*] King's highway there. Therefore the same in mercy. And he is ordered to remove it before the next leet under penalty 6s. 8d.

Amercement 2s. 1d. And that Thomas Broun \8d./, Thomas Mone \8d./, John Cocat \6d./ and Robert Talbot \3d./ baked and sold bread within the precincts of this leet [*damaged*].

Brewers, 8s. 11d. And that Thomas Gant \1s./, Simon Smyth \6d./, Robert Motslo \6d./, Thomas Lylye \8d./, Thomas Kyng \1s./, Robert Talbot \1s./, John Cocat \6d./, John Derby \6d./ [*damaged*], John Beneyt \3d./, Matilda Skut \3d./, William Shopp the younger \3d./, John Coo, clerk, \3d./, John [*illeg.*] \3d./, John [*illeg.*]\3d./, John [*illeg.*] \3d./, John [*illeg.*] \3d./, [*damaged*], John Cabaw \3d./, Herman Taillour \3d./ and John Grenefeld \3d./ are brewers and broke the assize of ale. Therefore the same in mercy etc.

Amercement 6d. And that John Bomsted \3d./ and Thomas Alfrych \3d./ are aletasters [*?and have not done their duty*] [*damaged*].

Amercement [?]2s. 9d. And that John Bonde the younger \3d./, Thomas [*illeg.*] \3d./, Robert Fullere, Robert Talbot \3d./, Robert Mutslo \[*illeg.*]d./, Roger Reigner \3d./, [*?*]Robert Cabaw \3d./, Adam Brete \3d./, [*?*]Thomas [*?*]Hoberd the younger \[*illeg.*] d./, Roger Fiz Stevyn \3d./, Robert son of Roger Reigner \3d./ and John [*illeg.*] \3d./ made default [*of suit of court*]. Therefore the same in mercy.

Amercement 1s. And that Robert Treweman \3d./, Robert Hervy \3d./, Thomas Grym \3d./, and Thomas Bocher \3d./ [*?*]dwell within the precints of the leet and [*are not in*] a tithing. Therefore etc.

Elections. [*Illeg.*] Hoberd is elected to the office of constable with William Shopp and they are sworn.

[*Illeg.*] and William Archer are elected ale-tasters and are sworn. [*Leet ends here.*]

Court Roll 23.[118] (19 October 1545)

"[*Fol. 23r*] *Monks Eleigh* (*Illeygh Monachorum*). Court with leet held there on Monday next after the feast of St Luke the Evangelist in the year of the reign of Henry the Eighth by the grace of God King of England, France and Ireland, defender of the faith and supreme head of the Church in England and Ireland 37 [*Monday, 19 October 1545*]

"Essoins nil

"Jurors.

"James Hubberde gent. Richard Hubberde William Hubberde Nicholas Hubberde

"John Folkes   Richard Goodale   Stephen Chapleyn Richard Strutte

"John Gentylman   Simon Stansby   Robert Goymer   John Barrett

"*Fealty.* To this court came Robert Ryce son and heir of Robert Rice gent and showed a certain copy [*of a court roll*] for one piece of meadow lying at Skyp-pyscrofte containing by estimation 4 acres and for 5 acres of land called Woodfeld now parcel of Woodfelde with appurtencances in Illyghe which the said Robert Rice father and Robert Ryce son took together at the court held here on the Monday of the feast of St Peter Advincula in the year of the reign of Henry the Eighth now King 22 [*Monday, 1 August 1530*] as in the roll of the court is more fully shown. And the said Robert Rice son does fealty to the lord.

"*Fine of 1s.* It is presented to this court by the homage that Robert Gale surrendered out of court to the lord's hand by the hand of Richard Goodale a villein tenement (*nat' ten'*) by testimony of Richard Strutt that is held of the lord and others by homage according to the custom of the manor 1 cottage with its appurtenances containing 1 rod parcel of Burton lying next to the King's highway in Eleigh (*Illyghe*) which the said Robert Gale took in year 29 of the lord Henry the Eighth now King [*1537–38*] as in the roll of the court is more fully shown to the work and use of John Jentylman and his heirs to whom seisin has thence been given to hold to him, his heirs and assigns by rod at the will of the lord according to the custom of the manor etc saving the right etc. And he gives the lord the fine etc. And he does homage to the lord etc.

"*Fine of 9d.* To this court came Richard Strutte and in full court surrendered into the lord's hand 1 cottage parcel of le Cherche Strete Rowe with its appurtenances with a certain way to the spring (*fontem*) there for carrying water as much and as often as was necessary without any impediment. Which certain cottage and other premises appertaining to it the said Richard took here in court on Monday in the vigil of St Matthew the Apostle in the year of the reign of the lord Henry the Eighth now King 32 [*Monday, 20 September 1540*] [*fol. 23v*] as in the roll of the court is more fully shown to the work and use of Hugh Wilson and his heirs to whom seisin has now been given. To hold to his heirs and assigns by service of 9d. each year and suit of court by rod at the will of the lord according to the custom of the manor etc saving the right etc. And he gives the lord the fine etc. And he does homage to the lord etc.

"*Fine of 2s. 10d.* It was presented to this court by homage that William Colman out of court surrendered to the lord's hand by the hand of Simon Stansbye a villein tenement by testimony of Richard Strutte that is held of the lord and others by homage according to the custom of the manor a villein tenement called le Swanne formerly

---

[118] CCA-U15/15/17, fols 23r–24r. Latin. This court roll could not be checked by the editor so remains as translated by Michael Stansfield.

of Peter Salkge with its appurtenances in Le Churche Strete in Eleigh (*Illyghe*) next to the tenement formerly of Thomas Malther and the land of this manor on the one part and the land lying beneath (*subtus*) the great grange there on the other part and containing in length 2 perches and 4 feet and in width at one end 2 perches and 8 feet and at the other end 2 perches and 12 feet as the survey and bounds there show. Which certain tenement and other premises with their appurtenances the said William took here in court on Thursday in the feast of St Peter ad vincula in the year of the reign of the lord Henry the Eighth now King 25[119] as in the roll of the court is more fully shown to the work and use of Stephen Umfrey and his heirs to whom seisin has now been given. To hold to him, his heirs and assigns by service of 2s. 10d. each year and suit of court by rod at the will of the lord according to the custom of the manor etc saving the right etc. And he gives the fine to the lord etc. And he does homage etc.

"*Fine of 2s. 10d.* To this court came Stephen Umfrye and in full court surrendered in to the hand of the lord 1 villein tenement called le Swane formerly of Peter Sawye and formerly of William Colman with its appurtenances in Le Cherche Strete in Eleigh (*Illyghe*) next to the tenement formerly of Thomas Malcher and the land of this manor on the one part and the land lying under the great grange on the other part and containing in length 2 perches and 4 feet and in width at one end 2 perches and 8 feet as the survey and bounds there show to the work and use of William Lawman and his heirs to whom seisin has been given. To hold to him, his heirs and assigns by service of 2s. 10d. each year by rod at the will of the lord according to the custom of the manor etc however under this following condition that is that if the said William Lawman, his heirs, executors or assigns pay to the said Stephen Humfrey, his executors or assigns or their assigns £9 sterling now and in the form following that is at Christmas next following after this court £2, at Christmas then next following £2, and annually at Christmases following £2 until £8 of the £9 have been fully [*fol. 24r*] paid and the Christmas then next following £1 in full payment of the said £9 then this surrender stands fully effective and corroborated. And if there is any deficiency in the payment either in part or in whole at any of the Christmases then it will be quite permissible for the said Stephen his heirs or assigns by licence of the lord to reenter the said tenement called Le Swane and its parcels and enjoy them in their own right this surrender notwithstanding. And the said William gives the lord the fine etc. And he does homage etc.

"*Verdict of the court in mercy for 6s. 3d.* They say on oath that Thomas Jerman,[120] knight, 6d., John Spryng, esquire, 6d., Elizabeth Bendysshe widow 3d., William Rysbye 3d., [*blank*] Alyngton, esquire, 6d., William Grome 3d., John Rydar gent. 3d., Walter Clearke, gentleman, 3d., Thomas Cournour 3d., John Barfete 3d., Nicholas Vynsent 3d., Richard Dockett 3d., [*blank*] Danyell gentleman 3d., William Sterthope 3d., John Clopton gentleman 3d., Thomas Halybrede 3d., Robert Alyngton 3d., Hugh Rushe 3d., Robert Allexander 3d., John Grene 3d., John Johnson 3d., and Christopher Rausham 3d. owe suit of court and have made default. Each of them is in mercy as is shown in the head.

"*Death of a tenant.* And they say that [*blank*] Corbolde has died since the last court and he held certain villein land and that William Corbolde is thence his next heir.

---

[119] The feast of St Peter in chains, 25 Henry VIII was on Friday, 1 August 1533, so the Thursday must have been the vigil of the feast, or the year, wrong.

[120] Sir Thomas Jermyn of Rushbrook, died 1552.

"*Verdict of the leet for the common fine of 4s.* The jurors say that they give to the lord for the common fine the usual amount as of old as is shown in the head etc.

"*In mercy for 2s. 9d.* And they say that Thomas Elles 3d., Nicholas Hubberd junior 3d., Thomas Hubberd 3d., John Grene 3d., John Wells 3d., Robert Pelticane 3d., William Sherewoode 3d., John Growse 3d., Thomas Bronde 3d., John Andrewe 3d. and John Halsyll senior 3d. owe suit of leet and have made default. Each of them is in mercy etc.

"*Election.* And they have chosen John Clopton and Richard Hubberde to carry out the office of subconstable of the vill of Monks Eleigh (*Monks Illyghe*) for this next year."

Court Roll 24. Monks Eleigh, rough court minutes and estreats (1586, 1588, 1589, 1590)[121]

[*Fol. 46r*] [*Latin*] *Monks Eleigh* (*Illigh Monacorum*). Court with leet held 16 May 1586

a fine of Ellyce Pettycan for Olivers 2s. 6d.

a fine of Thomas Lummys for Boores \and Barrardyes, 3s. 8d./ 13s. 4d.

[*Manicule*] for the common fyne 4s.

of Frances Clopton for a fyne of Hiefeildes 5s.

[*English*] The estreat in the 28th year of the reign [*of Queen Elizabeth I*], 16 of Maye 1586

Common Fyne 4s.

[*Illeg.*] Robert Cutler, Lucke Melton, John Herte, Nycolas Heywarde, Edward Coocke, Wylliam Teylor, Lenerde Kembolde, Robert Monynges, James Hobart, Robert Symson, Lenerde Rusche, John Grene, John Lorde and Robert Alden, eyther[122] of them, 3d.   3s. 6d.

Edward Hyll, Rychard Goymer and Thomas Ward are commanded to scoore [*scour*] a water corse from Byfeild Gate on this syde St John Baptyst,[123] upon payne of eyther of them, 3s.

Mr Scynner commanded to macke hys dytche agaynste Walnutte Croft, [*by the feast of*] All Saints, payne of 5s.

Wylliam Heyward commanded to macke hys dytche agaynste Inderbyes [*by the feast of*] All Saints, payne 5s.

John Herte commanded to score a sluse agaynste Wasche Medo [*by the feast of*] St John Baptyste 5s.

Corte Baron

of Francis Clopton for fyne of Hyghe Fyld 5s.

of Elys Petycan for fyne of [?]Olyvers 2s. 6d.

of Thomas Lummas and An[n] hys wyffe for fyne of Bores and Baraways 3s. 4d.

the ballye commanded to dystreyne the eyers of Ny[cholas] Sprynge, gentleman for a relyfe

Sum of the corte, 18s. 4d.

---

121 CCA-U15/15/17, fols 46r–48r. In a paper booklet containing rentals, rough court minutes, estreats and memoranda, by the steward George Chettynge and some re-copied, catalogued as 1544–90, in poor condition. A mixture of Latin and English.

122 At this period, 'either' could mean any number of people, not merely a choice between two.

123 That is, before the feast of St John the Baptist.

George Chyyttyng [*steward*]

[*fol. 46v*] [*Latin*] *Monks Eleigh* (*Illie Monacorum*). 1587. At the court with leet there held on Tuesday, that is, 28th day of April in the 29th year of Queen Elizabeth

[*English*] *Fyne, 15s.* of Thomas Hubberde of Milden (*Myldynge*) for a fine for hys tenement with the appurtenances called Brykotts, Domynickes Medow and Domynyckes Garden   15s.

Fyne 4s. of Mistress Alyce Huberde wydowe for a tenemente called Brondes with hyr appurtenances   4s.

Fyne 4s. For common fine   4s.

Sute fine. Sute fine Mistress Danyell, 4d.; Mr Teylor, 4d. and of John Nunne, 4d.

Sum 1s.

Let it be remembered there remayneth unreceyved 3d. for amercyamente of Leonarde Kembolde and 3d. for Robert Sympson dewe at the coorte laste before thys.

1 of Maye in the 30th year of the Queen, 1588

of Jeffrye Colman for fyne of Stanbyes   14s.
of Mr Northefyld for fine of the Bull   5s.
of <Thomas Rise> \Jeffrye Colman/ for lysens to let Stanbys to Ralfe   1s. 4d.
of Raffe Golberde for fine of Cutlers   1s.

Monks Eleigh (*Ely Monacorum*). 13th May in the 31st year of the reign of Queen Elizabeth, 1589

Received of John Bright for his fine of Stansbyes   14s.
Received of Wylliam Hie, clarke, for his fine of Struttes, late Andrewe Chaplyns 3s.
Received of Robert Yonge for his fyne of hys tenemente called Sheellynges   2s. 6d.
Received for the common fyne   4s.

Monks Eleigh (*Mounkesellye*). The extreete of the leete and coorte there holden the 13 daye of Maye in the year of the reigne of our sovereign Ladye Elizabeth by the grace of god of Englande, France and Irelonde, Quene, Defendor of the faythe etc. 31st [*year 1589*].

Common Fyne 4s. Firstly for the common fine as appereth on the heade.

Amercements 2s. Also that Edwarde Whittipoll, gentleman \3d./, George Waldegrave, gentleman \3d./, Edwarde Doylye, gentleman \3d./, Nicholas Huberd, gentleman \3d./, Robert Cutler of Ipswiche \3d./, Thomas Coe of Boxford (*Boxeforde*) \3d./, John Dey \3d./ and John Lorde \3d./ doe owe sewte to this coorte and have made defawlte this daye. Therefore every one of them are ordered as severally appereth upon there heades.

[*Fol. 47r*] *Respecte of suite 8d.* Also of Elizabeth Rytche, wydowe \4d./ and of Luke Melton \4d./ for respett of suite as appereth severally upon there heades.

Ordered. Also that Leonard Kembolde hathe not sufficiently mended hys dyche nexte Oxepasture by twoe dayes woorke of one man. Therefore he is commanded to fynishe the same with all convenient speede.

Amercement 3s. 4d. Penalty £1. Also that Richarde Aggas dothe keepe a common alehowse and dothe receyve into the same gestes of ill behaviour, and keeping ill rule in the tyme of devine service to the prophanynge of the lordes daye and to the ill ensample and offence of all his neighbours. Therefore he is amerced 3s. 4d. And he is commanded that he do not offende hereafter in the lyke upon payne of   £1

Penalty set 10s. Also Leonard Rushe is commanded to remove one cartehowse that standeth upon the common called Stackwoode Greene over agaynste his howse to

the greate anoyance of his neighbours before the feaste of the natyvite of our lorde
God upon peyne of   10s.

Penalty set, £2. Also that John Lorde hathe letten his tenement at the Tye to one
John Chynerye, a man of ill fame and conversation to the greate anoyance of all his
neighbours. Therefore the sayd John Lorde is commanded to remove owte of his
sayd tenement the sayd John Chinerye before the feaste of St Michell the archayn-
gell nexte comynge upon peine of   £2

Fine 14s. Also of John Brighte for the fyne of one messuage late Dixons with a
peece of meadow called Swatts Meadow and one peece of lande parcell of the hall
garden which he latelye had of the surrendor of Jeffery Colman   14s.

Fyne, 3s. Also of Wylliam Hie, mynister, for the fine of [*a*] cotage as it lyeth in
Eleigh (*Elighe*) afforesayd in a certayne streete called the Churche Streete which he
lately had of the surrender of Andrew Chaplen   3s.

Fine 2s. 6d. Also of Robert Yonges for the fine of one tenement custemarye called
Schellinges in Eleigh (*Ellighe*) afforesayd which he lately had of the surrendor of
John Nunne   2s. 6d.

Ordered. The baylyfe is commanded to destrayne John Grymwoode to be heere
at the nexte coorte to doe his fealtye and other services for fower score [*80*] acres
of lande which the sayd John latelye purchased of Nicholas Springe gentleman
deceased, as parcell of his mannor of Loose Hall and holden of this mannor.

Ordered just as the other. The baylyff is lykewyse commanded as heretofore to
destrayne John Prycke, parson of Kettlebaston (*Ketlebarston*), to be heere at the
nexte coorte to doe his fealtye and other services for a certayne parcell of lande
holden free of this mannor lyeinge in Kettlebaston which he lately had of the
purchase of James Chaplen.
                        Extracted by George Chitting, steward [*signature*]

[*Fol. 47v*] Monks Eleigh (*Mounkes Elleighe*). 1590. An abstracte of the leete and
generall courte there holden the 19 daye of Maye in the 32nd yere if the reigne
of our soveraigne ladie Elizabeth, by the grace of God of Englande, France and
Irelande, Quene, defender of the faythe etc.

Common fine 4s. Firstly for the comon fyne   4s.

Amercement 8d. Peine sett £2. Also that Wylliam Jefferey at dyverse and sondrye
tymes hathe secretlye receaved and taken into his howse one Johan Coocke an idle
and vagrant person and a woman of ill conversation. Therefore he is amersed 8d.
and he is commanded that hereafter he shall not so doe upon peyne of   £2

Peine sett 5s. Also that the landholders of Oxepasture is [*sic*] commanded sufficiently to scooure and make cleane a dytche nexte unto Davies Fenne, that the water
may passe owte of Davies Slowghe before the feaste of the natyvite of our lord god
nexte comynge upon payne of   5s.

Peine sett 5s. Also John Harte is commanded to skowre his dytche nexte unto Whit-
lande and also to shrewde[124] and loppe his trees which to doer dreepe the highe waye
there before the sayd laste recited feaste upon payne of   5s.

Peine sett 10s. Also Leonarde Rushe is commanded to skowre hisdiche over bothe
sydes of the waye leaddinge from Springes Greene towardes Laylaund Gate before
the laste recyted feaste upon payne of   10s.

---

124 To shred, prune or cut back (*MED*).

Amercements 2s. Peine sett £4 [*sic*]. Also that Richarde Aggas \1s./ and Stephen Cchaplyn [*sic*] \1s./have received and taken into their howses at dyverse and sondrye tymes, certeine vagrante and ydle persons beyinge of ill fame and conversation and them have retained as guestes contrarye to the lawe in that case provided etc. And therefore thay are amercied as severally appereth upon there heades. And thay are commanded that from henceforthe they shall no mare so doe upon peine to either of them   £2 [*sic*].

[*Fol. 48r*] *Peine sett 10s.* Also Jhon Goodale is commanded to skoowre the dytche in his yarde as heretofore hathe byn used that the water maye passe owte of the highewaye there before the feaste of all Sayntes nexte comynge upon payne of   10s.

Amercement 3s. 4d. Also that Isaacke Mylles dyd make an affray and dyd drawe bloodde upon Rafe Golderd agaynste the peace of our sovereigne ladye the Queene and therefore the sayd Isaacke is amercied   3s. 4d.

Peine forfett 3s. 4d. Also that Thomas Cole hathe stollen wood and the same hathe sowlde in bundells, that is, syxe bundells on a daye contrarye to an order and a by lawe in this Cowrte made and sett downe whereupon he hathe forfett a payne of 3s. 4d. which the balyff is commanded to levie of the goodes and cattells of the sayd Thomas.

The Courte

For respite of suit one shilling. Also of the Lady Ritche for respitt of suite of courte for this yeere   4d.

Also of Wylliam Taylor, minister, for the lyke for this yeere   4d.

Also of Luke Melton for the lyke 4d.

Fyne £1. Also of Robert Ryece, gentleman, for a fine of one peece of meadowe lyeinge at Skyppes Crosse conteynynge 4 acres. And also for one fyne parcell of lande called Wooddefielde containing 5 acres holden by copy of coorte rolle of this mannor which discended unto hym after the decease of Robert Ryce, gentleman, hys late father.[125]   £1

Fyne 5s. Also of John Cutter, gentleman, for a fine of one cottage and a garden customarye which he had of the surrendor of Richard Chaplen   5s.

Fyne 1s. Also of Robert Snape and Dorathie hys wyefe for a fine of one peece of lande nowe buylded, late parcell of a cottage and a gardeine customarie which thay had of the surrendour of John Chapleyne   1s.

Fyne 6s. 8d. Also of Thomas Ranson for a fyne of one tenement customary called Barretts which he had of the surrendor of John Harper and Maryon hys wyefe, mother unto the sayd Thomas   6s. 8d.

Extracted by George Chettynge, steward [*signature*]

---

[125] For further information about Robert Ryece, see **p. 000, footnote 99** and **p. 000, footnote 103**.

VI

RENTALS

1379–80 to 1683[1]

Rental 1. (1379–80)[2]

This rental is clearly dated 3 Richard II (22 June 1379–21 June 1380) and the expenses for making it are in Accounts 5 (29 September 1379–28 September 1380). The overlap gives a period for first making it of 29 September 1379–21 June 1380. Further narrowing of the date would be speculative and is probably pointless: the accounts tell us that expenses were paid for '94 days by several men' to make it, so it was clearly an extended exercise as weather and the jurymen's usual work allowed. The finely written register copy (see Plate 10) was annotated on one occasion later in in a single ink and tiny, spidery handwriting, inserting the names of later tenants above the names of most of the original 1379–80 tenants. About twenty-five of the original tenants are unannotated, so they must still have been tenants at the annotation date, which is difficult to ascertain exactly. A few of the inserted names are mentioned in the few court rolls that survive for the early fifteenth century: William Prior, clerk (Court Roll 22: courts of 2 September 1420 and 2 August 1422), Thomas Malcher, lessee of the manor 1419–38 (2 September 1420) Andrew Schopp lessee of the manor 1449–50 (Court Roll 19, 1 August 1414) and William Archer (Court Roll 22, 2 August 1422) for example. But most of the annotated names do not appear in any court rolls, so either they did not happen to appear before the courts in the surviving court rolls after 1380 or they first became tenants after 1422 (the date of the last court roll surviving before 1545). Perhaps the best estimate for the date of the annotations would be the 1410s–1420s, about a generation after its first creation. See also Introduction, p. l on annotated surveys generally.

[*Fol. 149v, in red ink*] Rental of the manor of Monks Eleigh (*Illegh Monachorum*) drawn up by the tenants of the same in the time of brother William Woghope[3] warden there in the third year of the reign of King Richard the second [*22 June 1379–21 June 1380*]. Clerk Thomas Rydle. [*In black ink hereafter*]

---

[1]   See Introduction, p. xlvii.

[2]   CCA-DCc/Register/B, fols 149v–157r. Modern pencil foliation used here – contemporary foliation (black ink) is one folio behind the pencilled one.

[3]   Probably the William Woghope, priory monk and a monk-warden, who died 1397 (Searle, *Christ Church Canterbury* (1902), p. 182).

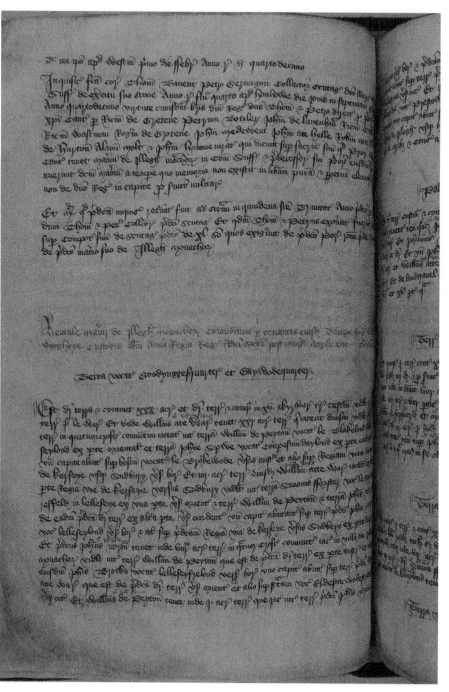

Plate 10. Page showing the beginning of the registered enrolment of Rental 1 (1379/80) with heading in red ink (CCA-DCc/Register/B, fol.149v). Photo: Dr Toby Huitson, CCA. Reproduced courtesy of the Chapter of Canterbury

Land called Goodynggesquarter and Gaywodequarter

It is half a land and contains 30½ acres of land and accounts for 15 *akyrwar* of custumary land, that is, 2 acres of land equals *le War*.[4] And in respect of which William ate War \now John Reve[5]/ holds 21 acres of land which lie separately, that is, [*?17 acres*] of land in 4 crofts joined together lying between the land of William de Peyton called le Blakelond de Leleseylond on the east side and the land of John Sparwe called Couperesmundaylond on the west side, with one head abutting upon the wood called Le Bro\o/kewode towards the south and the other upon the king's highway leading from Kersey (*Kerseye*) towards Sudbury towards the north. And 4 acres of land of the same William atte War \John Reve/ lie on the other side of the king's highway from Kersey towards Sudbury, that is, between the land of Simon Forster called le Speteleresfeld in Lindsey (*Lelleseye*) on the one hand towards the east and the land of William de Peyton and the land of John Brown of the same aforesaid half-land on the other hand towards the west, with one head abutting upon the land of the aforesaid John Brown called Lelleseylond towards the north and the other upon the aforesaid king's highway from Kersey towards Sudbury (*Sudbery*) on the south side. And the aforesaid John Broun \now John Reve/ holds thereof 8 acres of land in 4 crofts joined together lying in the vill of Monks Eleigh (*Illegh Monachorum*), that is, between the land of William de Peyton which is of the aforesaid half-land on the south side and the land of the same John Brown called Lelleseyfrelond towards the north, with one head abutting upon the land of the aforesaid William atte War which is of the aforesaid half-land towards the east and the other upon the street called Eldestacwodestrete towards the west. And William de Peyton \now John Reve/ holds thereof 1 acre of land which lies between the land of the aforesaid John Broun on [*fol. 150r*] the one hand towards the north and the aforesaid king's highway leading from Kersey towards Sudbury (*Sudbery*) on the other hand towards the south, with one head abutting upon the land of the aforesaid William atte War towards the east and the other upon the common way called Eldestacwodestrete towards the west. And John de Bures \now William Rokewode/ holds thereof half an acre of pasture lying at Prestowe, that is, between the lord's meadow called Prestowemedewe on the one hand towards the west and the meadow of Robert Gawge on the other hand towards the east, with one head abutting upon the King's highway leading from Sudbury (*Sudbery*) towards Bildeston towards the north and the other upon the river running from Eleigh (*Illegh*) to Hadleigh (*Hadliegh*) towards the south. And in respect of which is owed for the rent called landgavel, 1s. 6d. And for works and customs valued in cash, 10s., that is, for every acre thereof, 4½d. each year. Total 11s. 6d.

Palmereslond at Stacwode

It is half a customary land and contains 15 *akyrwar* of land and in number of acres, 30 acres of customary land. And in respect of what is held thereof, the tenants of a certain John Abot \now William Prior, priest/ hold 10½ *akyrwar* and containing in number of acres, 21 acres of land. And John Broun \now John Reve/, Robert Taillour and William atte War hold thereof 4½ *akyrwar*. And one John Broun holds 5 acres of land and Robert Taillour \now John Reve/ holds thereof 3½ acres of land and William atte War \John Reve/ holds thereof half an acre of custumary land. And

---

4   For *akyrwar* and *Le War*, see Glossary and Introduction, pp. xlix–l.
5   Or possibly John Rene.

in respect of which, as free rent each year, 5d. And for landgavel, 1s. 6d. And for works and customs valued in cash, 10s., that is, for every acre 4½¼d. and a 15th part of a farthing. Total 11s. 11d.

Land called Kenseghlond

It is a quarter of 1 land containing 17 acres, 1 rood of land. And it renders for landgavel each year, 9d. And as free rent, 4d., and for services and customs valued in cash, 5s. each year. And in respect of what is held thereof, the tenants of John Abot \now William Prior, priest/ hold thereof in demesne, 8½ acres and ½ rood and 8 perches of land. And John atte Broke \now William Hobert/ holds thereof 4 acres and 8 perches of land. And John \now William/ Aylward holds thereof 3 roods of land which were formerly of Robert Schephierd. And Margaret Hyggelyegh \now Thomas Malcher/ holds thereof half an acre of meadow in Langeliegh. And in the lord's hand [are] 3 acres, 1 rood and 9 perches of land by escheat by the death of Isabell Knappok and they stand in the hand of the tenant of the tenement formerly of John Abot \now of William Prior, priest/ at farm by court roll as appears elsewhere, that is, for every acre, 5¼d., less in itself, ½d. And in respect of what relates to the lord (*super dominum*), as touched upon. Total 6s. 1d. except for the lord.

Land called Bakstereslond

It is a quarter of 1 land and contains 19 acres 3½ roods of land. And it renders for landgavel each year, 9d. and for other free rent nothing, in respect of works and customs valued in cash each year, 5s. And in respect of which Edmund Ravenyld \now William Prior, priest/ holds thereof 7 acres and John Abot \now William the priest/ holds thereof 8 acres and half a rood of land. The tenants of Brokes \now William Hobert/ [hold] 2½ acres. Simon \now Richard/ Forster holds thereof 1½ acres as mesne tenant between the lord and Robert Gawge. And the tenants of Dony-lond \now John Laghard/ hold thereof 3 roods of meadow at Sodisele, price of each acre, 3½d. Total 5s. 9d.

Land called Howeslond Rolf[6]

[*fol. 150v*] It is a full custumary land and contains 30 *akyrwar* and in number of acres, 80 acres 3 roods of land, in respect of which for *le War*, 2 [*acres*], 3 roods. And it renders for landgavel each year, 3s. And as free rents each year 3s. And for works and customs valued in cash each year, £1. And in respect of which Simon \ now Richard/ Forster holds 13½ acres. The tenants of a tenement formerly of John Abot \now of William Prior, priest/ hold thereof 17½ acres. And John \now William/ Aylward holds thereof 10½ acres. Peter Aunselote \now William Prior/ holds thereof 10 acres. Thomas Pachet \now William Prior/ holds thereof 10 acres. The tenants of a tenement formerly Brokes \now William Hobert/ hold thereof 9 acres. Thomas \ now John/ Ketyll holds thereof 2 acres and 1 rood. And John Bron \now John Reve/ holds thereof 8 acres, price of each acre, 3¾d. and ½ of ¼d. Total £1 6s.

Land called Mereslond

It is a quarter of 1 land and contains, in number of acres, 14 acres and 6 perches of land. And it renders for landgavel, 9d. And as free rent 1½d. And for works and

---

6 Probably named after Hugh Rolf/Radulphus otherwise Hugh son of Ralph who grants or witnesses several charters in the mid-thirteenth century. See Charters 11–12, 14, 16–20.

customs valued in cash 5s. And in respect of which John North, who holds the tenement formerly of John Abot \now of William Prior/, holds 14 acres of land with a messuage built on the same. And John \now William/Aylward holds thereof 6 perches of land, price of each acre, 5d., plus ½d. on the total.   Total 5s. 10½d.

Land called Gokyeslond

It is half a customary land and contains 15 acres and accounts for 15 *akyrwar* of land and it lies opposite the gate of Brokes. And it renders for landgavel, 1s. 6d. And for works and customs valued in cash, 10s. And whereof the heirs of Brokes \ now William Hobert/ hold 14 acres of land. And Simon Forster \now Richard Foster [*sic*]/ holds thereof 1½ [*sic*] acres of land, price of each acre, 9d.   Total 11s. 6d.

Land called Brokesquarter

It is a quarter of 1 custumary land and contains 7½ acres of land, which land the heirs of Brokes \now William Hobert/ hold with a messuage built upon it. And in respect of which, it renders for landgavel each year, 9d. And for customary works valued in cash, 5s., price of each acre, 9¼d., less ¼d. and ½ of ¼d. on the total.
                                                    Total 5s. 9d.

Land called Rolveslond atte Newestrete[7]

It is a quarter of one custumary land and half a *War* and contains 8 *akyrwar* of land and in number of acres, 13 acres and 3 roods of land, of which for *le Ware*, 1½ acres and ½ rood. And in respect of which for landgavel and for customary works valued in cash, 6s. 2d., that is, for landgavel for the quarter land, 9d. And for works and customs valued in cash for the same quarter land, 5s. And in respect of which the heirs of Brokes \now William Hobert/ hold 8½ acres and ½ rood. And John North \now William Prior, priest/, who holds a tenement formerly of John Abot, holds thereof 5 acres and ½ rood of customary land, price of each acre, 5¾ and ½ a ¼d.
                                                    Total 6s. 2d.[8]

Land called Bolysquarter

It is a quarter of 1 custumary land and contains 11 acres, 1 rood and 2 perches of land. And of which for landgavel, 9d. [*fol. 151r*] each year. And for works and customs valued in cash, 5s. each year. And in respect of which Thomas atte Broke \now William Hobert/ holds 1 acre, 1 rood and 12 perches. The tenants of Brokys hold 1 acre of land formerly of Margaret Hamond. Christina Davy \now T[*?homas*] Gant/ holds thereof 1 acre and 1 rood of land formerly of Nicholas Sparwe. And John \now William/ Aylward holds thereof 7½ acres and 30 perches of land, price of each acre, 5¾d. and ½ a ¼d.   Total 5s. 9d.

Land called Reynoldeslond

It is a quarter of 1 custumary land and contains 7½ *akyrwar* and in number of acres, 15 acres and 5 perches of land. And in respect of which the heirs of Brookes \now William Hobert/ hold thereof 14½ acres and ½ rood and 5 perches of land. And in the lord's hand, 1½ roods which John Smert \now William Tilhwyt/ holds by the

---

7   Probably the same new street from which Ralph de Nova Strata, witness to Charter 28 (*c.* 1270s–1280s), took his appellation, therefore not so new in 1379–80.

8   The arithmetic is wrong here: 9d. for landgavel plus 5s. for works and customs in cash comes to 5s. 9d. (as in the following quarterlands), not 6s. 2d.

rod, etc. And landgavel is 9d. each year. And for works and customs valued in cash, 5s., price of each acre, 4½d. and ½ of ¼d. Total 5s. 9d.

Land called Ilgereslond

It is a full custumary land and contains 30 *akyrwar* of land and in number of acres, 41 acres of land, that is, for *le War*, 1 acre, 1½ roods and 4 perches of land. And it renders for landgavel each year, 3s. And for services and customs valued in cash each year, £1 And in respect of which the heirs of Brokes \now William Hobert/ hold 8 acres and 3 roods of land. John Dul holds thereof 12 acres of land. Thomas Ponder \now William Tilhwyt/ holds thereof 11 acres of land. John de Bures \now William Rokewode/ holds thereof 6 acres and 3 roods of land. And the tenants of the tenement \now William Prior, priest/ formerly of John Abot hold thereof half an acre of wood next to the wood of Kenseghes. And in the lord's hand by escheat, half an acre of wood at Manhey and 1½ acres of meadow at Gedefordebregg, price of each acre, 6½¼d., in respect of what relates to the lord (*super dominum*), 1s 1½d. for the 2 acres etc.

Total £1 1s. 10½d. And no more here because 1s. 1½d. relates to (*super*) the lord as above.

Land called Ildereslond

It is a quarter of 1 land and contains 15½ acres of land. And it owes for landgavel each year, 9d. And for services and customs valued in cash, 5s. And in respect of which John de Bures \now William Rokewode/ holds thereof 10 acres of land which are called Heyescroft. Thomas Ponder \now William Tilhwyt/ holds thereof 4 acres of land with a toft. And Richard Dul \now William Hobert/ holds thereof 1½ acres of land, price of each acre, 4½d. Total 5s. 9d.

Land called Smyththelond

It is a certain custumary land and is accustomed to work the iron of the 2 ploughs of the lord each year and now is rented out by custom by the lord for 10s. a year for all services except suit [*of court*]. And John Brysete \now William [?]*Deele*/ holds the aforesaid tenement for the services aforesaid, etc. Total 10s.

Land called Tentyslond

It is a full custumary land and contains 30 *akyrwar* of land and in number of acres, 46 acres of land, of which for *le Ware*, 1½ acres, 4 perches and 3 parts of 1 perch. And it renders for landgavel each year, 3s. [*fol. 151v*] And for works and customs valued in cash, £1 And in respect of which Thomas Munchesy \now Malcher/ holds 6 acres. Nicholas Hyggeleygh holds thereof 1 acre and 1 rood of meadow. John Whepstede \now Grigge/ holds thereof 3 acres of land, 1 acre and 1 rood of meadow. John ate Tye \now Simon Fuller/ holds thereof 1½ acres of land. Nicholas Seg \now Andrew Schoppe/ holds thereof 1 rood of wood formerly of Alexander Auty. John ate Fen \now Porter/ holds thereof four acres of alder-holt, meadow and pasture. Simon Forster \now Richard Foster/ [*holds thereof*] 1½ acres of meadow at Prestowe. And John de Bures \now William Rokewode/ holds thereof 27½ acres of land, meadow and pasture, price of each acre, 6d. Total £1 4s. [*sic*][9]

---

[9]   The rent here should total £1 3s. (*iijs.* and *xxs.*) not £1 4s.

Land called Fanteslond

It is half a custumary land and contains 15 *akyrwar* of land and in number of acres, 24½ acres of land. And it renders as free rent each year, 2s. And for landgavel each year, 1s. 6d. And for works and customs valued in cash, 10s. And in respect of which John de Bures \now William Rokwode/ holds 3 roods of land built with 3 cottages. John Baker \now T[*?homas*] Lylye/ holds thereof [*?½*] acre of land with a messuage built [*on it*]. John Reyner \now Webbe/ holds thereof ½ acre, ½ rood and 14 perches of pasture called le Founteynes Appylton. Isabell Gerl \now William Archer/ holds thereof 1 rood with a cottage built on the same. Margaret Sexteyn holds thereof 6 perches of land. John Wendcole \now Tavernour/ holds thereof ½ rood of land. John Bolle \now Wyndecole/ holds thereof 1 acre and 3 roods of land. Christina Fant \now John Wyndecole/ holds thereof 2 acres of land. John Petyt \ now T[*?homas*] Hobert/ holds thereof [*?2*] acres and ½ rood of land. John atte Fen \now John Porteyr/ holds thereof 8 acres of land. And in the lord's hand by escheat, 2 roods of land, of which 1 rood is built for the use of the lord with 1 cottage and the other rood is demised to John Wendcole the younger \now [*?*]Bemays/ and his heirs by the rod for 2s. a year, price of each acre, 6½d. and ½ of ¼d., in respect of what relates to the lord (*super dominum*), 3¼d. and a 4th part of ¼d.

Total 13s. 2¾ and a 4th part of ¼d.

Land called Fennesquarter with Sygaryscroft

It is a quarter of one custumary land and contains 7½ *akyrwar* and in number of acres, 12½ acres of which for *le War*, 1 acre and 3 roods of land. And it renders for landgavel each year, 9d. And for works and customs valued in cash, 5s. a year, which whole aforesaid tenement John ate Fen \now Porteyr/ holds, price of each acre, 5½¼d. And the same John [*holds*] 1 messuage at le Fennes. And in respect of which he renders to the lord as free rent each year, 4d.   Total 6s. 1d.

Land called Colyereslond

It is half a custumary land and contains 15 *akyrwar* of custumary land and in number of acres, 24 acres of custumary land, in respect of which for *le Ware*, 4 acres and 1 rood, 2 perches and 3 parts of 1 perch. And it renders for landgavel each year, 1s. 6d. And for services and customs valued in cash each year, 10s. And in respect of which James ate Tye \now John Coo holds it/ holds 10 acres and 6 perches of land in separate parcels, that is, in Colyerysdoune, 8 acres; in Oddon', 2 acres; in le Gardisyerd (*Gardiȝerd)*, 6 perches of land. And John Wendcole holds 2 acres and 3 roods. And Thomas Ponder \now John Wencole/ holds thereof 2 acres and a rood. And John Brisete holds thereof 2 acres, 2½ roods and 5 perches of which in Oddone, 2 acres; in le Pykedecroft \now T[*?homas*] Hobert/, 3½ roods and 5 perches. And John Lanerok \now Thomas Hobert/ holds thereof 3 acres and 3 roods in Oddone. And Simon \now Richard/ Forster holds thereof ½ acre of meadow in Oddon' Medewe by the [*?*]headlands[10] of Oddon'. And Richard Dul \now William Hobert/ holds thereof 1½ acres and 6 perches [*fol. 152r*] in Oddon'. And John de Bures \now William Rokwode/ holds thereof 1 acre of land and 1 rood in le Mellepond next to le Swannesnest. And Robert Frammesden \now Talbot/ holds thereof

---

[10] This word is ambiguous. It is written as *che(u/n)(c/t)a* with an abbreviation above that looks like a + sign. It could be *chevica*, from chevicium, 'headland'. An alternative might be 'by the sheds or cotes' (*cheta*).

3½ roods of land formerly of Matilda atte Tye. And William atte Tye \now Robert Talbot/ holds thereof 3 acres and 1 rood of land and pasture with ½ acre and ½ rood of Cecil' Cut. And John Swyft \now T[?homas] Malcher/ holds thereof 1 acre and 3 roods. And John atte Tye \now T[?homas] Davy/ holds thereof 16 perches of land at Fenstret. And John Cakebred \now T. Gant/ holds thereof 1½ acres. And the lord of Chelsworth (*Chelesworth*) holds thereof 1½ roods of meadow, price of each acre, 4d. and a 4th part of ¼d.   Total 11s. 6d.

Land called Salmanneslond le Ryche
It used to be a full custumary land and contains 30 *akyrwar* of customary land. And now it is in the hand of William de Boyton \now Augustine Dunton holds it/ freely by charter of the lord for 9s. 4d. a year and suit [*of court*] for which, with all other services, is to be paid at the 4 terms of the year.   Total 9s. 4d.

Land called Gambyslond
It is half a custumary land and contains 15 *akyrwar* of custumary land and lies next to Manhey. And it renders for landgavel each year, 1s. 6d. And for works and customs valued in cash, 10s. And which whole aforesaid tenement William de Boyton \now Augustine Dunton/ holds. And he renders services as appraised, etc. And common suit of court.   Total 11s. 6d.

Land called Manefeldlond
It is half a custumary land and contains 15 *akyrwar* of land and in number of acres, 28 acres of land, of which for *le War*, 1 acre, 3½ roods. And it renders for landgavel, 1s. 6d. And for works and customs valued in cash each year, 10s. And in respect of which William ate Tye \now Augustine Dunton holds it/ holds 21 acres of land. And Cecil' Cut \now Augustine Dunton/ holds thereof 3½ acres of land. And John Godale \now Augustine Dunton/ holds thereof 3½ acres of land, price of an acre, 4½¼d. and 3 parts of ¼d.   Total 11s. 6d.

Land called Auncelislond
It is a full custumary land and contains 30 *akyrwar* of land and in number of acres, 120 acres of land, of which for *le War*, 4 acres. And it renders for landgavel each year, 3s. And for works and customs valued in cash each year, £1 And in respect of which Simon \now Richard/ Forster holds 51½ acres of land, meadow and pasture in separate parcels. And William atte Tye \now Adam Breton/ holds thereof 24 acres, 1 rood. Robert Gawge holds thereof 8 acres. Richard Dul \now William Hobert/ holds thereof 8 acres of land. And the tenants of Cherchemedewe hold thereof 1 acre and 1 rood of meadow at Tollelones. And Simon Chapman \now John Hobert/ holds thereof 1½ acres of meadow at Gedeforderee. And John Godale \now Augustine Dunton holds it/ holds thereof 7 acres and 3 roods of land and wood, of which 1 acre and 1 rood [*are*] wood. And Cecil' Cut \now Augustine Dunton holds it/ holds thereof 3 acres and 3 roods. And the tenants \now T[?homas] Malcher/ of Hygelieghes hold thereof 9 acres. And the tenants of Boytones \now Augustine Dunton/ hold thereof 8 acres of land and meadow, price of each acre, 2¼d. and a 4th part of ¼d.   Total £1 3s.

[*Fol. 152v*] Land called Smetheslond
It is half a custumary land and contains 15 *akyrwar* of land and in number of acres, 31 acres and ½ rood, in respect of which for *le War*, 2 acres 12½ perches. And it renders for landgavel, 1s. 6d. And for works and customs valued in cash, 10s. And

in respect of which, Robert Gawge \now T[*?homas*] Gant/ holds 3 acres. And in the lord's hand by escheat [*?1*] rood besides is in the hand of the aforesaid Robert Gawge, to him and his heirs by the rod for 1s. a year. And Simon Forster \now Richard Foster/ holds thereof 5 acres. And John Whepstede \now Grigge/ holds thereof 4 acres and ½ rood. John Donylond \now Laghard/ holds thereof 2 acres and 1 rood lying at Tollelones. And William ate Tye \now Adam Breton/ holds thereof 8 acres and 3 roods which were formerly of Alice Cut in dower and after her decease remained to Simon Forster. And the aforesaid William atte Tye holds thereof of land formerly Cut's, 2½ acres of land. And John Goodale \now Augustine Dunton/ holds thereof 1 acre of land. And Cecil' Cut holds thereof ½ acre of land. And Simon Chapman \now John Hobert/ holds thereof 2 acres of land. And Henry Bekyswell \ now T[*?homas*] Malcher/ holds thereof 3 roods of land. And Ralph de Walsham \ now the Earl of Suffolk (*Southfolche*)/ holds thereof 1 acre of land in Henlyeghcroft, price of each acre, 4½d.   Total 11s. 6d.

Land called Smeremongeresland

It is half a custumary land and contains 15 *akyrwar* of land and in number of acres, 10½ acres of land, meadow and pasture. And in respect of which, for *le War*, 1½ acres, less 3 roods on the total. And it renders for landgavel each year 9d. And for works and customs valued in cash, 5s. And in respect of which Simon \now Richard/ Forster holds [*?9*] acres of land, garden, pasture and alder-carr. And William Smyth \now John Porteyr/ holds thereof 1½ acres of meadow, price of each acre, 6½d. and 3 parts of ¼d.   Total 5s. 9d.

Land called Palmereslond at Gedeford

It is half a custumary land and contains 15 *akyrwar* of land and in number of acres, 31 acres and 1 rood of land, whereof for *le War*, 2 acres and 12 perches, plus 2 perches on the total. And it renders for landgavel, 1s. 6d. And for works and customs valued in cash 10s. And in respect of which the tenants of Hygelyegh \now Thomas Malcher/ hold 15 acres of land. And Simon Forster \now Richard Foster/ holds thereof 5 acres. And John atte Tye \now T[*?homas*] Hobert/ holds thereof 5 acres, 1 rood of land. Alice atte Wayour \now John Sayer/ holds thereof 3 roods of land. And Thomas \now Roger/ Reyner holds thereof 2 acres. And John Reyner the younger holds thereof 1½ acres of land. And Simon Chapman \now John Hobert/ holds thereof 1 acre 3 roods, price of each acre, 4¼½d. [*sic*] and a 4th part of ¼d.
                                                      Total 11s. 6d.

Land called Lanelond

It is a full land and contains 30 *akyrwar* of land and in number of acres, 56 acres, of which for *le War*, 1 acre 3 roods and 13 perches of land. And in respect of which the tenants \now T[*?homas*] Malcher/ of Hygelyeghes hold 34 acres of land, meadow and pasture and wood. John Whepstede \now Grigge/ holds thereof 14 acres of land. John Donylond \now Laghard/ [*fol. 153r*] holds thereof 4 acres and 1 rood of land and wood. Ralph de Walsham \now the Earl of *Suffolk* (*Suff'*)/ holds thereof 1 acre and 1 rood of land. Thomas \now Roger/ Reyner holds thereof 1 acre of land and ½ acre of meadow. And Simon Chapman \now John Hobert/ holds thereof [*?1*] acre of land. And it renders for landgavel, 3s. And for services and customs valued in cash, £1, price of each acre, 4½¼d. and 3 parts of ¼d.   Total £1 3s.

Land called Mascalislond

It is a full custumary land and contains 30 *akyrwar* of land and in number of acres, 46 acres, 3 roods, of which for *le War*,1½ acres and 7 perches of land and 3 parts of 1 perch. And it renders for landgavel, [*?3*]s. And for services, works and customs valued in cash each year, £1 And in respect of which the tenants \now T[*?homas*] Malcher/ of Hygelighes hold 11 acres of land, meadow, pasture and wood. John Colkirke \now Andrew Schoppe/ holds thereof 8½ acres of land and pasture. John Clerk \now Kynge/ holds thereof 5 acres of land. Nicholas Seg holds thereof 2½ acres of land. Margery Donylond \now John Laghard/ holds thereof 19 acres and [*sic*] land and pasture. And Ralph de Walsham \now the Earl of Suffolk (*Sutfolch*)/ holds thereof 3 roods of wood called Mascaliswode, price of each acre, 6¼d.

Total £1 3s.

Land called Priouresquarter

It is a quarter of one land and contains 7½ *akyrwar* and in number of acres, 15 acres of land, whereof for *le War*, 2 acres. And it renders as free rent each year, 8d. And for landgavel, 9d. And for works and customs valued in cash, 5s. Which certain land the tenants of the tenement formerly of Nicholas Hygeliegh \now Andrew Schoppe/ hold all the aforesaid tenement called Priouresquarter, price of each acre, 5¾ plus ¼d. on the total.

Total 6s. 5d.

Land called Tyelond at Ravenescroft

It is a quarter of one custumary land and contains 7½ acres of land, whereof for *le War*, 1 acre. And it renders for landgavel each year, 9d. And for works and customs valued in cash, 5s. And in respect of which Margery Donylond \now John Laghard/ holds 6 acres 1½ roods of land with a cottage built on the same. William Lofham \ now Margaret Stanhard/ holds thereof ½ rood. Richard ate Tye \now Simon Fuller/ holds thereof 1 acre of land, price of each acre, 9¼d.

Total 5s. 9d.

Land called Honymanneslond atte Tye

It is 10 *akyrwar* of custumary land and contains, in number of acres, 13½ acres and 10 perches of which for *le Ware* 1 acre, 1 rood and 17 perches. And it renders for landgavel each year, 1s. And for works and customs valued in cash, 6s. 8d. And in respect of which Richard atte Tye \now Simon Fuller/ holds 5 acres, 3 roods and 10 perches of land. Margery Donylond \now John Laghard/ holds thereof 1 acre of land. And Margaret Hyggelyegh \now T[*?homas*] Malcher/ holds thereof 3 acres 3 roods and 8 perches of land. And John Clerk \now Kynge/ holds thereof 2 acres, 12 perches of land and 1 rood of wood formerly of Simon Kyng. And Ralph de Walsham \now the Earl of Suffolk (*Southfolch*)/ holds thereof ½ acre and ½ rood of pasture [*fol. 153v*] at Suttis which was formerly of Richard Forster, price of each acre, 7d.

Total 7s. 8d.

Land called Swyneslond

It is a full custumary land and contains 30 *akyrwar* of land and in number of acres, 46 acres of land and 5 perches, of which, for *le War*, 1½ acres and 5 perches. And it renders for landgavel, 3s. And for works and customs valued in cash, £1 And in respect of which John Clerk \now Kyng/ holds 8½ acres and 1 perch. And 2 acres and 3 roods of meadow, pasture and wood which were formerly of John Sparwe. And John Colkirke \now T[*?homas*] Malcher/ holds thereof 15½ acres and 4 perches of land and 1½ acres of meadow, pasture and wood. And Alice Peek \John Kyng/

holds thereof 8 acres of land and 1½ acres of meadow and wood. And Simon Kyngg holds thereof 6 acres of land. And the aforesaid John Clerk holds thereof, as his own demesne (*de suis propriis dominicis*), 2 acres and 1 rood of land, price of each acre, 6d. Total £1 3s.

Land called Salmanneslond atte and Thomas atte Tye

It is 20 *akyrwar* of custumary land and contains, in number of acres, 35 acres, 1 rood and 13 perches of land, whereof, for *le War*, 1 acre, 3 roods 2½ perches, plus 3 perches on the total. And it renders for landgavel each year, 2s. And for works and customs valued in cash, 13s. 4d. And in respect of which Margery Donylond \John Laghard/ holds 2 acres and 5 perches of land. And John Clerk \now Kyng/ holds thereof 9 acres, 1 rood and 25 perches with the carter's cottage, which cottage renders as free rent, 3d. each year, the price of other services proportionate to the aforesaid rent. And William Lofham \Stannard/ holds thereof 1 acre with his messuage. And Nicholas Hygelyegh \T[*?homas*] Malcher/ holds thereof 21 acres, 1 rood and 17 perches of land, price of each acre, 5¼d. less 1½d. on the total.

Total 15s. 7d.

Land called Leggardyslond

It is half a custumary land and contains 15 *akyrwar* and in number, 26 acres, ½ rood, 10 perches, of which, for *le War*, 2½ acres and 1 rood, less 10 perches on the total. And it renders for landgavel each year, 1s. 6d. And for works and customs valued in cash, 10s. And in respect of which Margaret Higeliegh \T[*?homas*] Malcher/ holds 13 acres of land and pasture and 16 perches which were formerly of John the son of John atte Fen, and lie in a field called le Marsshlond and Ketelesliegh. And Simon \John/ King holds thereof 10 acres of land and pasture with a messuage and wood. And the same Simon \now John/ Kyng holds thereof in le Kangyl 1 acre, 3 roods, 14 perches of land. And William Page \now Robert Talbot/ holds thereof 2 acres lying in le Wynsislond which were formerly of Adam atte Tye, price of each acre, 5¼d. and ½ of ¼d. Total 11s. 6d.

Land called Hutteslond

It is 10 *akyrwar* of custumary land and contains, in number of acres, 42 acres and 3 roods of land, of which, for *le War*, [*fol. 154r*] 4 acres, 1 rood and 4 perches. And it renders for landgavel each year, 2s. And for works and customs valued in cash, 13s. 4d. And in respect of which Margery Donylond \now John Laghard/ holds 22½ acres of land with a messuage and and [*sic*] 5 acres of land formerly of William ate Fen and 2 acres of land and ½ rood of land formerly of Adam Cut. And William Page \now Robert Talbot/ and Richard atte Tye hold thereof 10 acres of land with a messuage which were formerly of John ate Tye. And Ralph de Walsham \now the Earl of Suffolk (*Sutfolch'*)/ holds thereof 2 acres of land formerly of Richard de Walsham lying next to the highway leading from Walshambregg towards le Reebregg. And John Clerk \now Kyng/ holds thereof 3 roods of pasture formerly of Richard Forster at Sodesele, price of each acre, 4¼d. and a 4th part of ¼d.

Total 15s. 4d.

Land called Berardislond

It is 10 *akyrwar* of custumary land and contains, in number of acres, 17½ acres and 5 perches of land, of which, for *le War*, 1 acre, 3 roods and ½ perch of land. And it renders for landgavel, 1s. And for works and customs valued in cash 6s. 8d.

And in respect of which Roger fitz Steven holds 12 acres of land and meadow. And Thomas Munchensy \now Malcher/ holds thereof 1 acre and 1 rood of land which were formerly of Ralph Swyft. And John \now Th[*omas*]/ Crowe holds thereof 1 acre and 1 rood of land. And Geoffrey *of Halle*[11] \now John Derby/ holds thereof 1 acre and 1 rood of meadow. And Robert ate Medewe \now John Cabaw/ holds thereof 1 acre, 3 roods and 5 perches of land, price of each acre, 5d. and a 4th part of ¼d. Total 7s. 8d.

Land called Raveneslond and Wyggeslond[12]
It is a full custumary land and 5 *akyrwar* more and thus is reckoned 35 *akyrwar* of custumary land and contains, in number of acres, 43 acres of land, of which, for *le Ware*, 1 acre and 1 rood. And it renders for landgavel each year, 3s. 6d. And for works and customs valued in cash £1 3s. 4d., that is, for landgavel for the full land, 3s. And for the 5 *akyrwar*, 6d. And for works and customs valued in cash for the aforesaid full land each year, £1 And for the aforesaid 5 *akyrwar*, for works etc, 3s. 4d. And in respect of which Ralph de Walsham \now the Earl of Suffolk (*Sutfolch*)/ holds 17 acres, 1½ roods whereof of meadow, 1 acre and 1 rood. And John ate Chirche \Derby/ holds thereof 6 acres of land, 1 acre of meadow. And Geoffrey de Halle \now Ralph Cabaw/ holds thereof 4½ acres and 13 perches of land and 2 acres of meadow. And John Cabaw holds thereof 10 acres and ½ rood of land. And the tenants of the tenement formerly of William Hyggeslyegh \T[*?homas*] Malcher/ hold thereof 1½ acres of land lying next to the cross called le Spylmannescrouch which Bekeswell lately held, price of each acre, 7½d. and ½ of ¼d. Total £1 6s. 10d.

Land called Parkeryslond with Looselond and Chonyeslond in Hitcham (*Heecham*)
It is a certain full land and formerly [*?held by works*[13]] (*quondam operaria*) and a long time before this time the lord by his judgement granted the whole of the aforesaid land called Parkerislond to the ancestors of Thomas Marchaunt of Bildeston (*Byldeston*), which aforesaid Thomas holds the aforesaid tenement. And he renders thereof to the lord annually at the usual terms £1 2s. for all services except suit [*of court*]. And Geoffrey Taylour \now T[*?homas*] Marchant/ holds [*erasure covered by a horizontal line*] a certain land called Peperispyghtyl lying at the gate of Parkerysweye in Hitcham (*Heccham*). And he renders in respect of it each year, 6d. And Richard Mayhew \now John Chapman/ holds [*erasure covered by a horizontal line*] 6 acres of land formerly of Adam Chonehey in Hitcham (*Heecham*). And he renders in respect of it each year at the usual terms, 3s. Total £1 5s. 6d.

[*Fol. 154v*] Land called Mantoneslond
It is free land and contains, in number of acres, 12 acres. And in respect of which there falls to the lord as free rent at the usual terms, 3s., that is, for each acre, 3d. And in respect of which Ralph de Walsham \now the Earl of Suffolk (*Soutfolchie*)/ holds 4 acres and 3 roods of land and 1 acre of meadow. And John Ive \now

---

[11] Given in English here, but as *de Halle* elsewhere.
[12] Called 'Raven of Wigge' in Court Roll 16 (1371/72–1372), above, p. 150.
[13] The contrast in tenure is probably the point here, and the entry is meant to imply that this holding is now subject to a cash rent to cover all services, but was formerly held 'by works'.

Hugh Coyk/ holds thereof 4 acres which were formerly of John Beneyt. And John [*?Cabaw*] holds thereof 3 acres, 1 rood of land, each acre valued as above.

Total 3s.

Land called Nethyrhouslond

It is free land and contains 7 acres of land. And it renders to the lord annually at the usual terms as free rent 3s. [*6d.*]. And in respect of which John Clerk \now Kyng/ holds 1 acre and 3 roods of land. And the tenants of [*the tenement of*] Bekeswell \now T[*?homas*] Malcher/ which was formerly of William de Hyggelyegh, hold thereof 5 acres and 1 rood of land, price of each acre, 6d.   Total 3s. 6d.

Land called Antyeslond

It is free land and contains 7 acres, 1½ roods and 8 perches of land. And it renders to the lord annually at the usual terms as free rent, 6s. 9½¼d. And in respect of which Margery Donylond \now T[*?homas*] Humme/ holds 4 acres and [*?14*] perches of land. And Richard ate Tye holds thereof in Wencesfeld 2 acres. And Nicholas Seg holds thereof 1 acre and 14 perches of land. And Roger Webbe holds thereof 1 rood of land, price of each acre, 11d.   Total 3s. 9½¼d.

Land called Fynchelieglond

It is free land[14] and contains 2 acres of land lying next to le Cowfen. And it renders to the lord annually at the usual terms as free rent, 2s. and 1 man at hay time to turn and work the hay for 1 day at hay time in the meadow of Prestowe, which certain land John Cuttyng \now Teyler/ holds. And pays [*rent*] and performs [*services*] as is aforesaid.   Total 2s. and 1 man for 1 day in the meadow.

Land called Soutereslond

It is free land and contains less than 2 acres of land which William Smyth \now John Porteyr/ holds wholly in his measure of land. And he renders in respect of it to the lord annually at the usual terms as free rent, 2s. 6d. and 1 man for 1 day in the meadow called Skyppesmedewe to turn and work the hay. Total 2s. 6d. and 1 man for 1 day in the meadow.

Land called Fychattyslond

It is free land \and/ contains 16 acres of land. And in respect of which, it renders to the lord annually at the usual terms as free rent, 16s. And in respect of which, William atte Tye \Adam Breton/ holds 12 acres and 35 perches of land. And Cecil' Cut \now Augustine Dunton/ holds thereof 2 acres of land. And John Goodale \now Augustine Dunton/ holds thereof 1 acre, 3 roods and 5 perches of land, price of each acre, 1s.   Total 16s.

[*Fol. 155r*] Land called Skarlatteslond

It is free land and contains 3 acres of land and in respect of which it renders to the lord each year at the usual terms as free rent, 2s. And in respect of which Robert Gawge \now John Porteyr/ holds 2 acres with a messuage. And Simon \now Richard/ Forster holds now 1 acre of land, price of each acre, 8d.   Total 2s.

---

14 For Weller's map of free land in the valley of the River Brett at the centre of Monks Eleigh (including most of those on this page), see Plate 11.

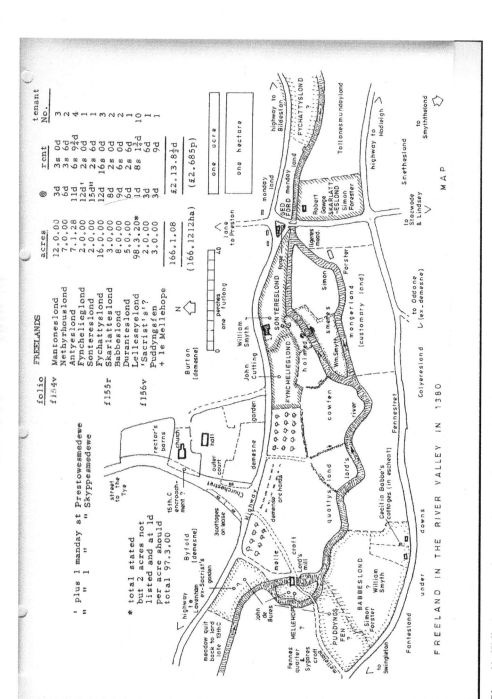

Plate 11. Weller's annotated map and notes of manorial free land in the valley of the River Brett at the centre of Monks Eleigh in 1380 (Weller Archive, file 'Maps')

Land called Babbeslond

It is free land and contains 8 acres of land. And it renders to the lord each year at the usual terms as free rent, 6s. And in respect of which William Smyth \now John Portyr/ holds 6 acres of land. And Simon \now Richard/ Forster holds thereof 2 acres, price of each acre, 9d. Total 6s.

Land called Duranteslond

It is free land and contains 5 acres of land and abutts upon Buckeswode towards the south and upon le Droveweystrete towards the north. And it renders to the lord each year at the usual terms as free rent, 2s. 6d. And the tenants of the tenement formerly of John Abot \now William Prior, priest/ hold the whole of the aforesaid land. And they render as is aforesaid, price of an acre, 6d. Total 2s. 6d.

Land called Lelleseyelond

It is free land and contains, in number of acres, 98 acres and 3½ roods of land. And it renders to the lord each year at the usual terms as free rent, 8s. 2½¼d. And in respect of which Simon \now Richard/ Forster holds 60 acres, of which, in Asshwell, 17 acres; in Lelleseye croft and Patbrook, 23 acres; in le Lyegh, 6 acres; in the field called Aylmeslond lying between the land land [*sic*] called Bromescroft on the south side and the street called Leyeghstrete leading from Stacwode towards the church of Lindsey (*Lelleseye*) on the other side, 8 acres of land and 4 acres of wood next to Manhey in Pyscescroft and 1 acre of wood in a grove next to le Overkangyl of which one head abutts upon le Leyegh towards the south. And John \now William/ Aylward holds thereof 18 acres of land. And John Bron \now John Reve/ holds thereof 9 acres of land. And William de Peyton \John Reve/ holds thereof 5 acres of land. And Stephen Fox holds thereof 2 acres lying next to Hyppynggescrouch at Hyppyngges Appylton. And the tenants of the tenement formerly of John Abot \William Prior, priest/ hold thereof 2 acres of land next to Hobkyneslond. And Geoffrey Gyleslond holds thereof ½ acre and ½ rood. And Richard Clerk of Kersey (*Kerseye*) holds thereof 1½ roods. And the heirs of Brokes \now William Hobert/ hold thereof 1½ roods of wood. And the lord prior of the church of Christ, Canterbury holds thereof 1½ acres of wood, price of each acre, 1d.

Total 8s. 1¼½d., and no more because 1½d. relates to (*super*) the lord.

Land called Sparwesmundaylond

It is 1 *mundaylond* and contains 13 acres of land. And it renders to the lord each year at the usual terms, 7s. 6d., from which, 10d. for *Brewyngselver*. And 6s. 8d. for 80 works. And Robert \now John/ Ketyll holds all the aforesaid [*land*]. And he renders as is aforesaid, price of each acre, 6½¼d. and 3 parts of ¼d. Total 7s. 6d.

[*Fol. 155v*] Land called Cowperesmundaylond

It is 1 *mundaylond* and contains 13 acres 1 rood. And it renders to the lord each year at the usual terms, 7s. 6d. And from which for *Brewyngsilver*, 10d. And for 80 works, 6s. 8d. And in respect of which William Peyton \now John Reve/ holds 5 acres of land. And John Broun \now J[*ohn*] Reve/ holds thereof 2 acres of meadow. And Robert Taylour \now William Prior, priest/ holds thereof ½ acre of meadow. And John Buk \now William Prior, priest/ holds thereof 1½ acres of land and pasture. And Alota Sparwe \William Prior holds/ holds thereof 4 acres and 1 rood of land, price of an acre, 6¾d. and a 4th part of ¼d. Total 7s. 6d.

Land called Fennesmondaylond

It contains 6 acres and a rood of land. And it renders each year as in 45 works, 3s. 9d., price of a work, 1d. And in respect of which Joan Brembyl \now William Prior, priest/, Roisia and Alice \Walter [*?recte William*] Prior/ her sisters hold in Broodokcroft 3 acres, [*?1*] rood. And the heirs of Brokes \William Hobert/ hold 2 acres. And Christina Davy \T[*?homas*] Gant/ holds 1½ acres, price of each acre, 6¾d. Total 3s. 9d.

Land called Tollonesmundaylond

It is 1 *mundaylond* and contains 13 acres of land. And it renders to the lord each year at the usual terms for *Brewyngselver*, 1s. 6d. And for 80 works, 6s. 8d. And the price of a work, 1d. Which certain *mundaylond* Margery Donylond \now William Archer/ holds wholly and she renders as is aforesaid. Total 8s. 2d.

Land called Ratonerysmundaylond

It contains 1 acre of land. And it renders to the lord each year at the usual terms as in 76 works, 6s. 4d., price of a work, 1d. And in respect of which Margaret Josep \now Simon Smyth/ holds 1 rood, built upon. And Thomas Reyner \now Roger Reyner/ and Richard Galyot hold thereof ½ acre of land with 2 cottages built on the same. And in respect of which the aforesaid Richard holds 10 perches of land. And Richard ate Ponde \now John Sawyer/ holds thereof 15 perches of land. And Thomas Porter \now John Sawyer/ holds thereof [*?25*] perches of land. And they render between them as is aforesaid. Total 6s. 4d.

Land called Anneysmundaylond le Wydewe

It contains 2 acres, 4 perches. And it renders to the lord each year at the usual terms as in 68 works, 4s., price of a work, 1d.[15] And in respect of which Simon \now Richard/ Forster holds 1 acre, 1 rood and 32 perches. And Simon Chapman \now John Hobert/ holds thereof 1½ roods. And John Gawge \now Hobert/ holds thereof ½ rood and 8 perches. And William atte Tye \Adam Breton/ holds thereof 4 perches of land. Total 4s.

Land called Wolmerys mundaylond

It is a certain land called a *mundaylond*. And the heirs of Brokes \now William Hobert/ hold it wholly and on which land their barn is built. And it renders as free rent, 2s. And for 48 works, 4s., price of a work, 1d. Total 6s.

Land called Ayredys mundaylond

[*Fol. 156r*] It is a certain [*land*] called a *mundaylond* which land the tenants of a tenement formerly of Nicholas Hyglyegh \now William Archer/ hold. And it contains 19 acres of land and 1 acre of wood. And it renders to the lord as a rent called *Brewyngsylver*, 10d. And for 80 works, price of a work, 1d.[16] In respect of which William Page \now Robert Talbot/ holds a certain parcel [*of land*] for which he renders 10d. for 10 works, price of each acre, 4½d. Total 7s. 6d.

---

[15] Sixty-eight works at 1d. each comes to 5s. 8d., not 4s. If the scribe mis-copied *lx viij* (68) instead of *xl viij* (48) in error, that would explain the mistake.

[16] No total is given for these eighty works.

Land called the second Ayredys mundaylond

It is a certain land called a *mundaylond* and it contains 10 acres of land. And it renders to the lord \as/ a rent called *Brewyngselver*, 10d. and 6s. 8d. for 80 works, price of a work, 1d. And in respect of which Nicholas Seg \T[*?homas*] Humme/ holds 3 acres with his messuage in le Reedeles. And the tenants of a tenement formerly of Nicholas Hygliegh \T[*?homas*] Humme/ holds thereof 7 acres, price of each acre, 9¼d. and 3 parts of ¼d., less ¼d. and 3 parts of ¼d. on the total.

Total 7s. 6d.

Land called Quattyslond

It is a quarter of one custumary land and contains 7½ *akyrwar* and in number of acres, 9 acres of land, of which, for *le Ware*, 1 acre, 1 rood. And it used to [*have*] works and render for landgavel as much as the rest of the lands. And now it is in the lord's hand and it lies between the lord's demesnes, that is, in Mellecroft between the way from Cowfen on the one hand and le Mellelane on the other hand. And it is now worked by the lord's servants.   Total nothing, because in the lord's hand.

Rent from the Rectory of Illegh

The rector of Monks Eleigh [*Illegh Monachorum*], whoever he shall be, holds of the lord a certain wall and a certain part of his curtilage in the rectory of Illiegh aforesaid. And in respect of which, he renders to the lord each year at the usual terms, 1s.   Total 1s.

Tenements held by the rod at the lord's will according to the custom of the manor
Geoffrey Huberd holds 1 cottage at Burton next to Gedeford by the rod. And he renders each year at the usual terms, 2s. Alice Hood holds 1 cottage next to the cross near the gates of the manor of Illiegh by the rod. And she renders each year 2s. Beatrice Lyricoc holds 1 cottage next to Byfold by the rod and renders each year, 2s. Stephen Parker holds 1 cottage next to Byfold by the rod and he renders each year, 1s. 6d. John Ravenyld holds 1 cottage at Overstacwode by escheat of the lord as part of Bolysquarter by the rod and he renders each year, 2d. The tenants of the tenement formerly of John Abot hold 3 acres, 1 rood and 9 perches of land of the tenement formerly of Kensegh, which Isabel Cnappok lately held, and it fell into the lord's hand by escheat and John Abot took it by the rod from the lord holding at will according to the custom of the manor etc. And it renders each year at the usual [*terms*] 3s. And Robert Gawge holds ½ rood of land by the rod from Smythyslond which fell into the lord's hand by escheat and he renders to the lord each year, [*fol. 156v*] 1s. Simon Forster holds 1½ acres of meadow by the rod at Gedeford of the land Ilger which fell into the lord's hand by escheat and he renders each year at the usual terms 3s. Margery Donylond holds 2 acres of pasture at Tollelones by the rod. And she renders in respect of it to the lord each year at the usual terms, 2s. And the same Margery holds 1 acre and 3½ roods of pasture at le Heyghefeld from the lord by the rod and she renders for the same each year at the usual terms, 1s. 10½d. And Richard atte Tye holds 2 parcels of the lord's demesne, holding by ancient grants from 2 different [*manor*] wardens by the rod at will and he renders to the lord each year at the usual terms, 8d. And John Wendecole the younger holds 1 rood of land from Fanteslond by the rod which fell into the lord's hand by escheat. And in respect of which, he renders to the lord each year at the usual terms, 2s.   Total £1 1s. 2½d.

Farms [*leases*] of land

John Clerk owes for 18 acres of land of the lord's demesne in Sodesele each year, farmed for the term of 40 years, at the usual terms, 9s., price of an acre, 6d. Nicholas Seg owes for 20 acres of land of the lord's demesne at Ravenescroft each year for the term of 40 years at the usual terms, 10s., price of an acre, 6d. James atte Tye owes for 16 acres of land of the lord's demesne in Oddon' each year farmed for the term of 40 years, at the usual terms, 9s. 4d., for an acre, 7d. And Thomas Marchaunt of Bildeston (*Byldyston*) holds from the lord at farm a certain plot of land called Illieghwode in Hitcham (*Heecham*) for a term of years and he renders each year at the usual terms, 16s. Total £2 4s. 4d.

Chychelotescroft

It is 3½ *akyrwar* of land and contains, in number of acres, 7 acres of land, of which, for *le War*, 2 acres of land and it renders for landgavel each year, 4¼d. And for services and customs valued in cash, 2s. 6½¼d. and which aforesaid tenement John Bryset \Wyndecole/ holds and does service as is aforesaid. Total 2s. 11d.

Blentesfeld

It is 3 *akyrwar* of custumary land and contains, in number of acres, 6 acres of land, of which, for *le War*, 2 acres of land, which were formerly of Richard Forster. And it renders for landgavel each year 3½d. And for services and customs valued in cash, 2s. 2½d. And which aforesaid tenement John de Bures \now William Rokewode/ holds. And he pays [*rent*] and does services as is aforesaid. Total 2s. 6d.

Free land formerly of William Basyngham and Puddyngesfen with le Mellehope John de Bures \William Rokewode/ holds 2 acres of free land which was formerly of William Basyngham, in respect of which he renders each year at the usual terms as free rent, 6d. Also the same John de Bures holds certain land called Puddyng-gesfen and le Mellehope which contain less than 3 acres of land and which afore-said land called Puddynggesfen and le Mellehope Michael de Bures and Richard Forster lately jointly held. And he renders as free rent each year, 9d., as the aforesaid Michael and Richard used to pay. Total 1s. 3d.

[*Fol. 157r*] Pyggescroft

It is 4½ *akyrwar* of custumary land and contains, in number of acres, 9 acres of land, of which, for *le War*, 2 acres of land. And it renders as free rent each year, 6d. And for landgavel each year, 5½d. And for services and customs valued in cash, 3s. 3½d. And which aforesaid tenement Nicholas Ketyll \now Roger Reyner/ holds and pays [*rent*] and does services as aforesaid, that is, for each acre 5½d. and ½ of a ¼d. Total 4s. 3d.

Rental 2. (*c.* 1503–*c.* 1513)[17]

Weller assumed this rental dated from c. 1510 on the basis of the CCA catalogue, which dated the volume into which it was re-copied as having been written between 1462 and 1515. Other Essex custody rentals in it are specifically dated between 1488 and 1514, but the Monks Eleigh rental is not dated. Its dating is more complex than it seems, not least because it is a fair copy enrolment of a rental that was annotated in its original form, but these annotations were recopied without differ-

---

17 CCA-DCc/MA 33 fols 43v–50v.

entiation, making them difficult to spot and date too. The original rental must have been made before 1504 and annotated after that date since there is an entry relating to 'William Foorthe now Robert Foorth of Hadleigh (Hadley) the elder ...' (see p. 208): William was the original tenant and the 'now Robert Foorth ...' indicates an insertion after William died in 1504,[18] although the fair copy does not differentiate what was clearly an insertion in the original rental. The inclusion in the rental of title of knight to the tenant James Hobart, attorney-general to Henry VII, indicates that it was made (or an undifferentiated insertion made) between his knighting on 18 February 1503 and death on 24 February 1517.[19] Thomas Hoberd or Hobart of Layham (possibly the Thomas Hobard who was the surveyor making the rental), another tenant in this rental and a nephew of Sir James, died between making his will on 14 March 1513/14 and its probate on 3 November 1515, so the rental must pre-date his death between those two dates.[20] Henry Wyatt (noted at the end of the rental as 'Master Wyott', paying the rent for Loose Hall in Hitcham) was granted the lease of the 'manor' of Loose Hall in 1492 and was knighted in 1509, indicating the rental was made between those two dates.[21]

Another clue to the dating of Rental 2 comes towards its end, in what sounds like additional material to the original manuscript (although it is not differentiated in the re-copied text) where this heading appears above a short indented list of some holdings:

> *These parcels of rents Thomas Hobard has not inserted in this book in the same way, however, [because] the present farmer [lessee] collects and is in possession [of them] according to the confession of Andrew Vyncent formerly farmer there.*

Andrew Vyncent 'formerly farmer' was the lessee from 1482/83 to 1496–97, or perhaps even as late as 1503–4 (see Table 5 on p. xlii) in comparison with 'the present farmer', who is unnamed in the rental but must be John Warde. Warde's dates as lessee are hard to pin-point: he could have taken office as early as 1496–97 or as late as 1503–4 and lasted until either 1513–14 or 1519–20, or some point in between. These lease periods and the changeovers of farmers suggest that Rental 2 might well have been first made for the commencement of the lease of John Warde, c. 1503 and annotated after 1504 for an unknown period but probably until c. 1513. It was then re-copied into the volume in which it now survives at some time before 1515.

[*Fol. 43v*] Rental compiled by Thomas Hobard.[22]

Monks Eleigh (*Illegh Monochorum*). The rector of Monks Eleigh holds by copy [*of a court roll*] 2 parcels of land now enclosed within the rectory there. 1 parcel of the

---

[18] TNA, PROB 11/14/325, PCC will of William Foorth of Hadleigh, made 2 August 1504, proved 25 October 1504.

[19] E.W. Ives, 'Hobart, Sir James (d.1517)', *ODNB* (2004). See also p. 210, footnote 36; pp. 213–14.

[20] TNA, PROB 11/18/224, PCC will of Thomas Hobbart of Leyham, Suffolk, made 14 March 1513/14, proved 3 November 1515. See also p. 203, footnote 27 and p. 214 below.

[21] H.C. Maxwell Lyte, J.G. Black, and R.H. Brodie (eds), *Calendar of Patent Rolls, 1485–91* (London, 1914), p. 433. 1492, September 13 (my thanks to Edward Martin for this information and reference); C. Burrow, 'Sir Thomas Wyatt (*c.* 1503–1542), Poet and Ambassador' (sub-section on Sir Henry Wyatt (*c.* 1460–1536)), *ODNB* (2004). See also p. 215 below.

[22] Either Thomas Hobard of Fen Street, Monks Eleigh, or Thomas Hobard of Layham (d. 1515), both of whom appear as tenants in this rental. For further information on the latter, see p. 203; see also footnote 20, above.

same is called Berneyerd and pays each year, 1s. at the usual [*terms*[23]] of the manor. And the other parcel just as it extends from the cottage of John Burch, formerly of Roger Bunche, chaplain, enclosed by one wall as far as the end of the same wall on the north side and it renders each year at the terms, 2d. 1s. 2d.

John Burche holds by copy [*of the court roll*] one built cottage containing by estimation about half a rood and 3 perches of land formerly of Roger Bunche, chaplain with one footpath containing in width five feet and in length five perches extending from the said cottage as far as the king's highway leading from Lavenham to Ipswich (*Gippm'*). And the aforesaid cottage with its appurtenances lies between the graveyard of Illegh aforesaid and the lord's land called Burtonfeld and was formerly parcel of Burton. And it renders each year at the terms. 4d.

John Shilling holds one cottage by native [*tenure*] (*native*),[24] with various workshops (*shopis*) belonging to the same and gardens attached to it, of which 2 \ small/ parcels were newly taken from the lord's hand and are now called Le Boole, formerly in the tenure of Andrew North and before that of Thomas Breton and lying between the site of the lord's manor on the one hand and the cottage of the said John Shilling called Le Swanne formerly of Henry Galiott and before that of William Hobart of Stakwod on the other hand. And it renders each year at the usual terms etc. with the aforesaid 2 parcels lately newly taken at 4d. a year. 2s. 1d.

And the same holds by native [*tenure*] one cottage now called Le Swann with gardens and one [?]barn (*lathm'*[25]) belonging to the same from ancient times, and also with another small parcel lying on the south side of the great barn of the lord's manor, formerly taken out of the lord's hand for a rent each year of 2d. And the aforesaid cottage lies between the cottage called Le Boole on the one hand and the king's highway on the other hand. And it renders each year from ancient times, 2s. 8d., sum in total. 2s. 10d.

John Rutlond holds one cottage by native [*tenure*] formerly Foulys, with a garden belonging to the same formerly of Richard Hobart and before that of John Foule and it lies between the cottage called Le Swann on the one hand and the cottage of Walter Coteler on the other hand. And it renders each year at the usual terms of the manor 6d.

Walter Coteler holds by native [*tenure*] one cottage with a garden attached formerly of Richard Hobart and before that of John Sumpter and it lies between the cottage now of John Rutlond on the one hand \and/ the lord's land lately taken by copy [*of the court roll*] into the hand of Thomas Stannesby called Le Teyntouryerd on the other hand. And it renders each year at the usual terms 10¼d.

Joan Pyghtell holds by native [*tenure*] one small cottage called Le Almeshous formerly of Richard Hobert, just as it lies between the cottage of Walter Coteler on the one hand and Le Teyntouryerd on the other hand formerly of Thomas Stannesby. And it renders each year at the terms 1d.

[*Fol. 44r*] Simon Stannesby holds one parcel of land by native [*tenure*], called Le Teyntouryerd formerly taken out of the lord's hand by Thomas Stannesby father of

---

23 The text has *terr'*, 'land', here, which is probably a scribal error, given the context.

24 Literally 'by birth' (*native*), a reference to unfree tenants being bondsmen or villeins 'by blood' or by birth, and applying also to land held by unfree, or villein, tenure.

25 Or possibly *lathiu'* (*lath* plus three minims in a script that does not always dot its 'i's). Most probably ME *lathe*, a barn, granary or storehouse (*OED, MED*); or alternatively, *latha*, a variant of *lata* or *lada*, 'a leat, watercourse, channel' (*DMLBS*). See also p. 207. Later rentals note that this tenement has an orchard, so perhaps it means 'orchard'. If so, its origin is not known.

the said Simon and it lies between the lord's land on the one hand and the messuage and garden of Walter Coteler on the other hand. And it renders each year at the terms

6d.

Christina Shoppe, formerly the wife of Robert Shoppe, widow, holds one parcel of land by native [*tenure*], called Le Saffronpane containing by estimation around 3 roods formerly of the demesnes of the manor called Burton, just as it lies between the cottage of John Bayly on the one side and the lord's land on the other hand. And it renders each year at the terms 1s.

John Bayly holds by native [*tenure*] one cottage with a garden attached formerly of Thomas Breton and before that of Robert Wyncoll, just as it lies between the messuage of Andrew Vincent formerly Robert Shoppe on the one hand and a parcel of land now of Christina Shoppe called Le Saffronpane on the other hand. And it renders each year at the usual terms 13½¼d.

Andrew Vyncent holds by native [*tenure*] one messuage with various houses, buildings, gardens and 1 croft of land belonging to the same formerly of the demesnes of the manor, of Burton[26] formerly of Robert Shoppe and before that of William Shoppe father of the said Robert just as it lies between the messuage of John Bayly on the one hand and the messuage and garden of William Clerke on the other hand. And it renders each year at the terms 3s.

William Clerke holds by native [*tenure*] one messuage in which he now dwells with a garden and curtilage belonging to the same formerly of Robert Wyncoll just as it lies between the cottage of Thomas Aleyn on the one hand and the messuage of Andrew Vyncent on the other hand. And it renders each year at the terms

1s. 8d.

Thomas Aleyn holds by native [*tenure*] one cottage with a garden attached formerly of John Burch' and before that of Richard Hobart of Stakwod and it lies between the cottage of William Clerke on the one hand and the cottage of Thomas Gentylman on the other hand. And it renders each year at the terms 1s.

Thomas Gentylman holds by native [*tenure*] one cottage with a garden formerly of John Burch and before that William Hobart just as it lies between the cottage of Thomas Aleyn on the one hand and the messuage of Hugh Thurgor formerly of John Tyler the younger on the other hand. And it renders each year at the terms 1s.

Thomas Hobart[27] holds by copy [*of the court roll*] 5 cottages with 2 small houses called Almeshouses once of Andrew Kyng called from ancient times Chirchestret Rowe just as they lie between the cottage and curtilage of John Boor, parcel of Chirchestrett, on the one hand and the land of the lord called Byfold on the other hand and abutting to the east upon Le Chirchestrett. And it renders each year at the terms [*blank*].

[*Fol. 44v*] John Boore holds by native [*tenure*] one messuage with a curtilage containing around half an acre called parcel of Chirchestrett Rowe formerly of William Hobart of Gedeford and before that of Andrew Grigge and before that

---

26 That is, part of the piece of land called Burton, which was part of the demesne of the manor. See also Christina Shoppe's entry just above.

27 Thomas Hoberd (d. 1515) of Layham, nephew of Sir James Hobart (d. 1517). He bequeathed to his widow Elizabeth 'londis called Pages with 2 litill [?]cotes [*cottages*], lying in Munkesilly on[e] of them that Jamys Richardson dwellith in and the other that Pilberghe['s] wife dwellith in Chirche Strete Rowe, the other 2 tenementis lying at the upper ende of the said Rowe to go for the dwellyng of almes folkis after the will of my ffather' (TNA, PROB 11/18/224, PCC will of Thomas Hobbart of Leyham, Suffolk, made 14 March 1513/14, proved 3 November 1515). See also p. 201. His father is a key character in section VII. See pp. 295–302.

of Andrew Kyng just as it lies between the cottage of Thomas Hobart, parcel of Chyrchestrett Rowe, on the one hand and the king's highway leading from Lavenham towards Bildeston (*Bilston*) on the other hand and the east head of the same abuts upon Chirchestrett. And it renders each year at the terms   [*blank*].

Alan Briget holds by native [*tenure*] one cottage with a garden adjacent and a parcel of land called Le Orchyerd and also another parcel lately newly taken out of the lord's hand formerly parcel of Mellecroft containing by estimation around 1 rood just as it lies between Le Mellelane on the one hand and a footpath leading from Mellecroft gate towards the church on the other hand. And it renders each year for the messuage and Le Orcheyerd with appurtenances 4s. And for the aforesaid parcel newly taken 1s. 8d. Sum total in chief   5s. 8d.

John Bregge holds one small cottage called Le Almeshous lying between the gate called Melcroftegate, that is, between the footpath leading from Mellecroftgate towards the church on the one hand and the cottage now of Andrew Vynsent on the other hand. And it renders each year at the terms   2d.

Andrew Vynsent holds by native [*tenure*] one messuage with a garden attached and a parcel of land lately newly taken from the lord's hand containing by estimation around 1 acre formerly parcel of Mellecroft just as it lies between the cottage of John Bregge called Le Almeshous on the one hand and the cottage of William Breton lately acquired from the said Andrew on the other hand. And it renders each year, that is to say, for the messuage and garden, 3s. 4d. And for the other parcel lately newly taken, 1s. 8d. Sum total as in chief   5s.

William Breton holds by native [*tenure*] one cottage with a garden attached \ formerly[28]/ of Andrew Vyncent and before that of Thomas Turnour, just as it lies between the messuage of the said Andrew, a short while ago of Thomas Turnour, on the one hand and the cottage formerly of William Shoppe now of John Downyng in right of his wife, formerly the wife of the said William Shoppe, on the other hand. And it renders each year   8d.

John Downyng holds by native [*tenure*] as in the right of Agnes his wife, formerly the wife of William Shoppe, 1 messuage with a garden attached, formerly of the said William Shoppe just as it lies between the cottage of William Breton on the one hand and the cottage of Alice Shoppe widow formerly belonging to the said cottage now Downyng's on the other hand. And it renders each year.   1s.

Alice Shoppe widow holds by native [*tenure*] one cottage with a garden attached formerly of Andrew Shoppe her husband, just as it lies between the cottage formerly of William Shoppe her son now of John Downyng on the one hand and the cottage of John Webbe on the other hand. And it renders each year at the terms   1s.

[*Fol. 45r*] John Webbe holds by native [*tenure*] 1 cottage with a garden attached formerly of Richard Alysaunder and before that of William Shoppe just as it lies between the cottage of Alice Shoppe widow on the one hand and the messuage of the said Richard Alysaunder on the other hand. And it renders each year at the terms
1s.

Richard Alysaunder holds by native [*tenure*] 1 messuage with a garden attached with another parcel formerly newly taken out of the lord's hand containing around [*no measurement given*], just as it lies between the cottage of John Webbe and Le Mellecroft now of Andrew Vynsent on the one hand and the messuage of Simon Stannesby formerly of Thomas Stannesby and before that of Thomas Tyler the elder

---

[28] Interlineated in a different hand.

on the other hand, one head abutting the same abutting [*sic*] upon the deep stream, the other head [*abutting*] upon the way leading from Lavenham towards Bildeston (*Bylston*) on the other hand. And it renders each year for the messuage, 5s. And for the new parcel, 5d. Sum in total   5s. 5d.

Simon Stannesby holds by native [*tenure*] 1 messuage with various buildings, gardens, ponds, dyehouse (*dyhous*) and meadows belonging to the same formerly of Thomas Stannesby father of the said Simon and before that of Thomas Tyler the elder, called from ancient times Lyrcokkes gardyn and the aforesaid meadow called Squatys medowe and [*which*] were formerly parcel of Mellecroft. And the said messuage with appurtenances lies between the messuage and garden of Richard Alysaunder formerly of William Shoppe the elder on the one hand and the messuage and garden of Thomas Stannard on the other hand. And the aforesaid meadow contains by estimation around one and a half acres just as it lies between the meadow of Richard Alysaunder formerly parcel of Mellecroft on the one hand and the meadow of Robert Rosshebroke on the other hand. And it renders each year at the usual terms for all the aforesaid parcels   7s. 6d.

Thomas Stannard holds by native [*tenure*] 1 cottage with a garden and orchards (*orchyerdes*) belonging to the same containing by estimation around half an acre just as it lies between the garden and Le Pondyerd of Simon Stannesby on the one hand and the cottage of Robert Rosshebroke which he holds \from/ the lord by native [*tenure*], formerly of John North, on the other hand. And it renders each year at the terms   1s. 2d.

Robert Rosshbroke holds by native [*tenure*] one cottage with a garden attached, formerly of John North, just as it lies between the cottage of Thomas Stannard on the one hand and the messuage and curtilage in which the said Robert dwells on the other hand. And it renders each year at the usual terms   4d.

The same Robert holds freely one messuage in which he now dwells with a garden attached formerly of John Stannard and before that Root's, with an annual value of   3d.

[*Fol. 45v*] The same Robert holds by native [*tenure*] one meadow called Cowfen and another parcel of fen together in closes near his messuage. And the same now extends just as it lies between the meadow formerly of Thomas Stannesby on the one hand and the meadow or free pasture between William Hobart's and before that of John Tyler on the other hand and abutting at the southern head upon the deep stream and the other head upon Le Dyhous and it renders each year   5s.

John Hobart son of William Hobart holds freely one messuage with gardens, orchards (*orcheyerdes*), pastures together in closes, also one meadow from ancient times called Smethis which is enclosed by the common water flowing all around it formerly of William Hobart father of the said John and before that of John Tyler the elder and previously of Robert Fuller. And the said messuage, with appurtenances, lies between the messuage and pasture of Robert Rosshebrook on the one hand and the messuage and pasture of Thomas Abbott formerly Smythis on the other hand and abuts at the northern head on the common way leading towards Bildeston (*Bylston*). And it renders each year for the said messuage with appurtenances, 2s. 4d. And for the said meadow since it lies enclosed by flowing water, 10d. Total   3s. 2d.

Hugh Thurgour holds freely one messuage with one rood of land belonging to the same formerly of Thomas Cobold and before that of John Tyler the younger just as it lies between the messuage of Thomas Gentilman towards the west \on/ the one hand and the messuage of Robert Barett formerly of William Asshelee on the other hand, one head of the same abutting upon the king's highway leading towards

Bildeston (*Bilston*) on the south side and the land of William Ayleward formerly of John Burch which he holds from the lord by native [*tenure*], on the north side. And it renders each year for the said messuage and free land   1s. 3d.

The same holds one parcel of land by native [*tenure*], containing by estimation around half a rood, belonging to the same messuage adjacent, just as it lies between the free land of the said Hugh belonging to the said messuage on the one hand and the land of William Ayleward formerly of John Burche which he holds by native [*tenure*] on the other hand and both heads of the same abut upon the land of the said Ayleward formerly of John Burch which he holds by copy [*of the court roll*]. And it renders each year   4d.

Robert Baret holds freely 1 messuage with a garden adjacent containing by estimation 1 rood formerly of Andrew North and before that of William Asshelee just as it lies between the messuage of Hugh Thurgour on the one hand and the messuage of William Ayleward once of William Asshelee on the other hand, one head of the same abutting upon the king's highway leading towards Bildeston (*Bilston*) on the south side and the other head abbuting upon the land of William Ayleward on the other hand. And it renders each year   8d.

[*Fol. 46r*] William Aylewarde holds freely one messuage with one rood of land belonging to the same formerly of John Burch and before that of John Calle [*and*] of Agnes his wife and once of William Asshelee the elder just as it lies between the messuage of Robert Baret on the west side and the messuage of Hugh Thurgour on the other side, one head of the same abutting on the king's highway leading towards Bildeston (*Bilston*) on the south side and the land of the same Hugh on the north side. And it renders each year   8d.

The same holds by native [*tenure*] one close of arable land with one piece of pasture at the south end of the same close containing by estimation around 4 acres formerly parcel of Burton just as it lies between the land of Andrew Vynsent which he holds from the lord by native [*tenure*], formerly of Robert Shoppe on the west side and a small grove (*virgult'*) called Tyes grove now of Nicholas Hobart on the east side. And it renders each year.   4s.

Hugh Thurgour holds freely 1 messuage with a garden and curtilage adjacent called from ancient times Smythis and Chapmans containing by estimation around half an acre formerly of William Hobard and before that of John Hobard just as it lies between the messuage of William Ayleward formerly of John Burche on the west side and the king's highway leading towards Hegelyes on the east side, one head of the same abutting on the king's highway leading towards Bildeston (*Bilston*) on the south side on the one hand and a close once called Bolours now of the said Hugh on the north side. And it renders   1s. 2d.

Nicholas Hobart holds freely 1 messuage in which the said Nicholas now dwells, with 1 parcel of land belonging to the same containing by estimation around half an acre formerly of William Hobart father of the said Nicholas and before that of Thomas Hobart father of the said William <~~William~~> just as it lies between the king's highway leading towards Hegelyes on the west side [*and*] the land of the said Nicholas formerly of Richard Cobold \and/ before that of John Hobart the elder on the east side, one head of the same abutting upon the king's highway leading towards Bildeston (*Bilston*) on the south side and the land of the same once called Hoggesgardyn on the north side. And it renders   10d.

The same holds freely one parcel of land adjacent to the aforesaid messuage containing by estimation around 1 acre with one croft \of land/ adjacent to the same

206

containing around 2 acres with one [*?*]barn (*lathe*)[29] and a messuage adjacent once called Mundoms formerly of John Hobart the elder just as it lies between the said messuage of the said Nicholas on the one hand and land belonging to the tenement Hogelyes called Regners Croft on the east side, one head of the same abutting on the king's highway leading towards Bildeston (*Bilston*) on the south side and land belonging to Hogelyes on the north side. And it renders each year   1s. 6d.

[*Fol. 46v*] The same holds freely 1 meadow lying next to Chelsworth Bridge (*Chellesworth Bregge*) containing by estimation around 1 acre formerly of William Hobart father of the said Nicholas just as it lies between the king's highway leading towards Bildeston (*Bilston*) on the one hand and the common stream flowing from the mill called Coboldes mille towards the mill of Chelsworth (*Chellesworth*) on the other hand, one head of the same abutting on the meadow of William Foorth formerly of Thomas Cobold on the west side and the other head upon the said stream on the east side. And it renders each year   [*Blank*].

The same holds 1 croft of land called Webbiscroft containing by estimation around 7 acres formerly of William Hobart father of the said Nicholas just as it lies between the meadow of William Hobart of Fosteres called Dulles on the south side and the land of Roger Alysaunder formerly of Thomas Hobart of Fenstrett which he holds from the lord by native [*tenure*], on the north side, one head of the same abutting on the land of the College of Denston called Longepastur' on the east side and the other head abutting on the land of the said William Hobart called Dullys on the west side. And it renders each year   2s. 11d.

The same holds freely one parcel of land upon which one smith's forge (*Smythishous*) is built with one cottage adjacent containing by estimation around 12 perches formerly of the aforesaid William Hobart father of the said Nicholas just as it lies between the king's highway leading towards Bildeston (*Bilston*) on the north side and the king's highway leading towards Hadleigh (*Hadley*) on the south side. And it renders each year   4d.

John Wood holds freely one messuage in which he now dwells with a garden and curtilage adjacent containing by estimation around 1 rood once called Gantes formerly of William Hobart and Thomas Hobart father of the said William just as it lies between the king's highway leading towards Bildeston (*Bilston*) on the north side and the stream flowing towards Chelsworth (*Chellsworth*) on the south side, one head of the same abutting upon the messuage of the said John formerly of John Hobart and afterwards of Richard Cobold on the east side and the king's highway towards Le Smyth on the west side. And it renders each year   4½d.

The same holds 1 garden by native [*tenure*], with 1 parcel of free land now enclosed called Padokhall containing by estimation around half \a rood/ in which are contained 2 fish ponds (*Stues*), formerly of Thomas Breton just as they lie between the king's highway leading towards Hadleigh (*Hadley*) on the one hand and the lord's meadow belonging to Fosteres on the other hand. And it renders each year   2d.

The same holds one messuage with one dovecote attached and a parcel of pasture adjacent formerly of Richard Cobold and before that of John Hobard containing by estimation around one acre just as it lies between the king's highway leading towards Bildeston (*Bilston*) on the north side and the common stream flowing towards Chelsworth (*Chellesworth*) on the south side, one head of the same abut-

---

29   Probably a barn. See p. 202, footnote 25 above.

ting upon the messuage of the said John Wood in which he now dwells on the west side and the messuage of Ralph Forth formerly Coboldes on the east side. And it renders each year   18½d.

[*Fol. 47r*] William Foorthe[30] now Robert Foorth of Hadleigh (*Hadley*) the elder holds freely one mill with various buildings adjacent to the same with various parcels of land and meadow belonging to the same containing around 18 acres formerly of Thomas Cobold and before that of William Alysaunder called from ancient times Northes and the aforesaid mill, pasture and meadow lie together between the king's highway leading towards Bildeston (*Bilston*) on the north side and the way leading towards Hadleigh (*Hadley*) on the south side, one head of the same abutting upon the pasture of John Wood on the west side and the meadow of Nicholas Hobart and the messuage of Henry Munnynge formerly of John Burch and before that of Henry Cobold on the east side. And one croft of land of the same called Coboldes Croft lying between the king's highway leading towards Bildeston (*Bilston*) on the south side and land belonging to Hegelyes on the north side. And it renders each year £1

The same holds one piece of meadow by native [*tenure*], containing around 1 acre and 1 rood formerly of Richard Alysaunder just as it lies between the free meadow formerly of Thomas Cobold now of the said William on the north side and the common stream leading towards Chelsworth (*Chellesworth*) on the south side. And it renders each year   2s.

Henry Munnyng holds freely 1 messuage with a garden attached and one acre of arable land called Barkers Acr' just as the said messuage and garden lie together between the pasture of William Foorth on both sides, one head of the same abutting upon the king's highway leading towards Bildeston (*Bilston*) on the north side and the aforesaid [*Barkers*] Acre lies in the field called Colboldesfeld between the pasture of John Hobart on the south side and the land of William Foorth on the north side, one head of the same abutting upon the pasture of Agnes Tymperley widow on the east side and upon le meer called Amyelesmeer on the west side. And it renders each year   2s. 2d.

The tenants of the late Agnes Tymperley, hold freely 1 parcel of meadow lying next to Chelsworth Bridge (*Chellesworthbregge*) next to the stream there on the east side, formerly Porter's, father of the said Agnes and contains by estimation around 3 roods and it renders   2d.

The heirs of the late Thomas Slawter hold freely one tenement next to the bridge of Gedford containing by estimation around 1 rood formerly of John Hobard just as it lies between the stream next to the aforesaid bridge and the tenement called Porters now belonging to Cistille, lately daughter of John Fastolff. And it renders each year   ½¼d, inquire.[31]

Cistilla Fastolf[32] holds one tenement called Porters and before that Cooes lying next to the aforesaid tenement called Slawters with various parcels of land with one

---

[30] D. 1504. His will made bequests to his wife Margaret, son Robert, daughter Elizabeth and her husband Thomas Baldry of London. Sir James Hobard was supervisor (TNA, PROB 11/14/325, PCC will of William Foorth of Hadleigh, made 2 August 1504, proved 25 October 1504). The beginning of this entry is all written in a fair hand, but it reads as if it were simply re-copied from a draft in which William Forth was the tenant and still alive (the draft being before 1504, therefore), with an annotation written later updating the tenancy to his son (and see dating note for Rental 2 on **p. 000**).

[31] The annotation here by the compiler of the rental states his intention to enquire further into this rent or entry.

[32] She appears elsewhere in this rental as a more plausible Cecillia (see **pp. 000, 000**). A Dame Cecilia Falstolf was the last prioress of Bungay Priory, 1532–36 (*VCH Suffolk* 2, p. 82). As a nun, she would

dovecote lying together with the same, just as it extends between the way [*fol. 47v*] leading from Gedfordbregge towards Hadleigh (*Ladley* [*sic*]) on the one hand and the stream leading towards the mill formerly called Coboldes Mille on the other hand. And one close called Smythis Crofte and another croft in the upper part of the same close just as it lies between the king's highway leading towards Boytons manor on the east side and land belonging to the tenement called Fosteres now belonging to the College of Denston on the west side and also 1 parcel of pasture lying between the land of Boytons on the one on the one [*sic*] hand and a close called Petytes formerly of William Hobard on the other hand. And it renders each year   7s. 8d.

The College of Denston hold (*tenent*) freely one messuage called Fosteres next to the bridge of Gedford with all the lands belonging to the same and the pasture lying in Monks Eleigh (*Illegh Monochorum*) and also various lands, meadows, feedings, pastures called Lellesey [*Lindsey*] Croftes and 1 parcel of meadow which is held of the lord by native [*tenure*], lying next to the aforesaid bridge, that is to say, between the stream on the north side and the aforesaid messuage on the south side and it renders each year   £2 16s.

And also he holds (*tenet*) around one acre of meadow lying on the west side of Prestowmedowe now demised to John Ward bailiff at farm.[33] And it renders each year   2s. 8d.

Thomas Baldry of London holds 1 tenement now called Boyton manor with all the lands, meadows, pastures, feedings, woods with its appurtenances lying in Monks Eleigh (*Illegh Monochorum*) formerly of Robert Foorthe of Hadleigh (*Hadley*) and before that of William Dunton. And it renders each year   £1 6s. 8d.

And he also holds 1 croft called Piggyscote Croft, inquire where it lies.[34] And it renders each year   4s. 3d.

And also he holds at farm one piece of land formerly of the demesne of the manor containing by estimation around 10 acres called Parkfeld Pece and it lies between 1 grove called Bettisgrove on the south side and the land of the lord which William Hobard holds in farm from the lord. And it renders each year   10s.

And William Hoberd the younger holds at farm 1 piece of land lying on the north side of the aforesaid piece called Parkfeld containing by estimation around 4 acres just as it lies between the way leading from Eleigh (*Illegh*) towards Hadleigh (*Hadley*) on the west side. And another parcel of land belonging to the tenement Fosteres on the other side and he used to pay rent to the lord each year for 1 meadow belonging to the same land on the north side of the aforesaid road. And between the meadow of Thomas Hobard on the west side and the meadow called Parkmedowe on the east side. And he used to pay rent each year of   10s.

[*Fol. 48r*] And Thomas Hobard of Layham (*Leyham*) holds 1 piece of meadow containing by estimation around 2 acres just as it lies between the land of Robert Foorthe the elder of Hadeley on the one hand and the said meadow called Parkmedowe on the other, one head of the same abutting upon the stream on the north side and the other head on the way leading towards Hadleigh (*Hadeley*) on the south side.   [*Blank*].

---

not have been able to hold property in person, so if she were the same woman, she presumably held it before she took the veil.

[33] 'Demised … at farm', i.e. leased.

[34] The text here is *quer' ubi*. Presumably the original compiler's 'note to self', here copied into the register without differentiation from the main text.

Simon Kempe holds freely one messuage with various parcels of land belonging to the same formerly of Richard Grene lying at Stakwood containing by estimation around five acres. And it renders each year   4s. 6½d.

Andrew Vynsent holds by copy [*of the court roll*] one cottage lying at Stakwood with one garden attached formerly of John Croxale. And it renders each year   4d.

William Brooke holds freely one garden lying at Stakwood opposite the tenement of Thomas Sprynke containing by estimation around 1 rood. And it renders each year   1½d.

Thomas Hobard of Layham (*Leyham*) holds freely one tenement lying in Stakwod formerly of Walter Hobard and before that \of William/ Hobard father of the said Walter and before that Brokes with various pieces of land, meadow, feedings, pasture, wood and a grove (*virgult'*), containing by estimation around, with Dullys, 100 acres. And it renders each year   £2 5s. 3d.

The same holds one parcel of land lately acquired from Simon Kempe containing around 1 acre called Humbelbancke lying next to the Cross of Stakwood.   2d.

The same holds 1 messuage lying in Stakwood formerly of Thomas Ayleward with various closes, lands, woods and pastures[35] belonging to the same, containing by estimation around [*blank*] acres. And it renders each year   [*Blank*].

Be it remembered [*in English*] that ther' is a parcell of lond in Stakwood late Thomas Aylewardes which John Hobard occupied lying by Knapolislane. Thomas Hobard of Layham (*Leyham*) payethe therfor' in Aylewardes parcell   [*Blank*]

[*In Latin*] Andrew Vyncent holds freely one parcel of land called Newlondhall with various parcels of land belonging to the same, containing by estimation around 8 acres, formerly of John Deer' lying in Stakwood. And it renders each year   8s.

[*Fol. 48v*] Thomas Sprynge holds freely two closes of land lying next to Stakwood formerly of John Croxale of which one close lies between the land of Thomas Hobard of Layham (*Leyham*) called Dulles on the one hand and the king's highway leading from Stakwood towards Swyngildon on the other hand and the [*other*] close lies, etc.   6s.

The same holds one tenement lying at Stakwod formerly of John Tyler and before that of William Prior, chaplain, with various lands, meadows, feedings, pastures, a grove (*virgult'*) belonging to the same tenement. And it renders each year
£1 14s. 2d.

The heirs of John Martyn late of Hadleigh (*Hadeley*) hold freely one tenement called Brommys lying next to Stakwod with various pieces of land, meadow, pasture, wood and a grove (*virgult'*) lying altogether containing by estimation around [*no measurement given*] etc. And it renders each year   £1 5s. 1d.

The wardens of the Guild of the Blessed Mary of Monks Eleigh (*Illegh Monochorum*) hold freely one close called Chirchcroft containing around 1½ acres lying next to the footpath leading towards Stakwod on the one hand and the land of James Hobard,[36] knight, on the other hand. And it renders each year   1s.

Robert Lee esquire holds one tenement lying upon Swyngildon hill towards Stakwod called Wyncols with all the lands, meadows and pastures with their appurtenances lying together just as they lie between the way leading towards Stakwod

---

35 Plurals have been assumed here, although all the types of property are abbreviated (*claus' terr' boss' et pastur'*), and so could be translated as any variant of various close(s) (of) land(s), wood(s) and pasture(s).

36 Sir James Hobart, lawyer, judge and attorney-general to Henry VII, knighted 18 February 1503, died 24 February 1517 (Ives, 'Hobart, Sir James (d.1517)', *ODNB* (2004)).

on the one hand and the land of Thomas Hobard called Dullys on the other hand with one close of land called Le Down and also one piece of meadow lying next to le cawsy leading towards Swyngildon. And it renders each year   14s.

The same holds freely various parcels of land lying next to Bureswood and another parcel called Blenfeld with various meadows and pastures which extend from Skyppisbregge towards Brent Eleigh (*Brendylly*) on both sides of the water there as far as Skyppismedow and also one close of land called Pyrlishill containing by estimation around five acres just as it lies between the king's highway leading towards Brent Eleigh (*Brendilly*) on the one hand and the land of Thomas Hobard called Pagys on the other hand. And it renders each year   £1 8s. 7d.

William Hobard of Swyngildon holds freely one tenement with one garden and pasture and land adjacent to the same and also various parcels \of land/, meadow, pasture and a grove (*virgult'*) called from ancient times Le Parva Dullys formerly of Richard Hobard and before that of Lelyes. And it renders each year   7s. 6d.

[*Fol. 49r*] Cecillia Fastolf[37] holds freely one tenement lying in Swyngildon called Fennys formerly of Agnes Tymperley and before that of John Porter with all the lands, meadows and pasture belonging to the same just as they lie between the stream flowing from the mill called Monks Eleigh mill (*Munckislygh mill*) towards Skyppisbregge on the one hand and Swyngildon grene on the other hand. And 1 close of land containing by estimation around 5 acres lying on the south side of the way heading towards Little Waldingfield (*Waldingfeld parva*) and in the middle of her tenement. And it renders each year   8s. 8d.

John Hobard holds by copy [*of the court roll*], with, as it is said, 2 closes of land next to Le Down with other land and pasture which he holds freely containing around 12 acres inquire how many,[38] just as it lies between Webbes croft belonging to Nicholas Hobard on the one hand and the land called Fosteres on the other hand [*see next entry for joint rent*]

And Roger Alexaunder holds one messuage lying in Fenstret formerly of Thomas Hobard of Fenstret with Le parcel of Le Down lying next to the said tenement with one cottage and a piece of pasture called Le Fenn containing around 3 acres. And all these aforesaid parcels pay

[*bracketed together with the paragraph immediately above*] 7s.

The same Roger holds one piece of land parcel of Le Down with 1 croft lately acquired from Richard Grene by Richard Alexaunder father of the said Roger containing by estimation around 3 acres. And it renders each year   1s. 8d.

John Bronde holds by native [*tenure*] one messuage with a garden attached lying in Fenstret formerly Bemays, that is to say, between the king's highway there on the one hand and the meadow of Nicholas Hobard formerly of William Hobart on the other hand. And it renders   2s.

Thomas Hobard of Layham (*Leyham*) holds all the lands, meadows, and pastures called Pagis[39] at Le Tye containing around [*blank*] acres with one parcel of land now in the hand of William Inderby formerly parcel of Ravens croft, by copyhold tenure (*copi hold*), 20 acres held from the lord by native tenure. And it renders each year   £1 3s.

---

[37] See p. 208, footnote 32.

[38] The text has *quer' quantum'* ('enquire how many') here, another example of the original compiler's annotation to the text that the copyist has not differentiated.

[39] See p. 203, footnote 27.

William Sharpe holds freely one messuage with a garden and a close of land attached to the same just as it lies at Le Tye between the land of Pagis on the one hand and the tenement formerly of Thomas Kyng on the other hand and 2 closes of land with one way belonging to the same extending from Le Tye aforesaid towards Eleigh (*Ily*) [*blank*] that is to say as far as Boyscroft and it renders each year 2s. 8d.

Thomas Kyng holds freely one messuage with a garden attached and one croft of land adjacent to the same at Le Tye aforesaid, that is to say, between the messuage of William Sharpe on the one hand and the messuage and land formerly of John Chapleyn now Emeline Rande daughter of the said John on the other hand and it renders each year 1s. 7d.

[*Fol. 49v*] John Kynge holds freely 2 crofts of land with one parcel of meadow at Le Tye containing around 5 acres just as it lies between the land of James Hobart, knight, on the one hand and the land formerly of Bendyste now of Andrew Vyncent on the other hand and it renders 4s.

Emelina Rande daughter of the late John Chapleyn holds freely one messuage with a garden attached with one piece of land adjacent to the same containing in total around 3 acres just as it lies between the messuage of Thomas King on the one hand and the land called Ravenscroft on the other hand, one head abutting upon Le Tye leading towards Antystret and it renders each year 2s. 4d.

William Clopton, knight, holds freely one messuage lying at Le Tye formerly of William Jacob and before that of Robert Thorpe and before that of John Stannard with various closes of land and pasture belonging to the same containing around [*blank*] acres. And it renders each year £1

The same holds one piece of land by copy [*of the court roll*] lying in (*en*) Le Highfeld containing 20 acres and lying on the west side of the same field. And it renders each year 5s.

The same holds by copy [*of the court roll*] one close of land containing around 4 acres formerly in the tenure of Gunse just as it lies between the aforesaid piece of Highfeld on the one hand and land belonging to the said William Clopton on the other hand, one head of the same abutting upon the close called Tylepetclose belonging to the manor of Swyftes on the north side and it renders each year 4s.

The same holds another piece of pasture containing around one acre and 1 rood just as it lies between the land of the said William on the one hand and Le 20 Acre parcel of Highfeld held by copy [*of the court roll*] now of the said William on the other hand and it renders each year 8d.

The same holds one tenement recently built upon, formerly of Thomas Benstye and before that of Thomas Davy with various gardens and crofts belonging to the same. And it renders each year 3s. 6d.

Andrew Vyncent holds freely two pieces of land with one piece of meadow containing around 4 acres just as it lies and abutting upon Le Highfeld towards the north and the land of John Kyng towards the south. And it renders each year 1s. 6d.

William Sharpe holds freely one messuage lying at Le Tye with one garden adjacent formerly of Richard Bereve just as it lies towards Le Tye. And it renders each year 3d.

[*Fol. 50r*] Robert Lee holds freely one parcel of garden lying next to the aforesaid messuage on the one hand and the lane heading towards Highfeld on the other hand. And it renders each year 3d.

James Hobard, knight, holds one tenement lying at Le Tye formerly of Andrew Grigge and before that of Andrew Kinge with various lands, meadows, feedings, pastures belonging to the same. And it renders each year   18s. 3d.

The same holds various parcels of land formerly Gunsis just as it lies etc.
     7s. 3d., inquire.

Thomas Chapleyn holds freely one messuage formerly of William Chapleyn lying at Le Tye with various \lands/ belonging to the same. And it renders each year   8s. 4d.

The same Thomas holds freely one messuage in which he now dwells with one croft of land belonging to the same containing around 4 acres formerly of Robert Chapleyn father of the said Robert [sic]. And it renders each year   2s. 4d.

The same holds freely one messuage once built upon called Mascalles formerly of Robert Fenys, knight, and afterwards of Thomas Hobard, esquire, and afterwards of Robert Rosshebrooke with all the lands and pastures belonging to the said tenement. And it renders each year   £1 10s.

The same holds one parcel of land formerly parcel of Woodfeld formerly taken by Robert Rosshebrook by copy [of the court roll] containing by estimation 6 acres. And it renders each year   [blank].

Robert Parker holds one cottage formerly of John Byrche lying in Antistrett containing around 1 rood and it lies between the way on the one hand and the land of John Parker on the other hand. And it renders each year   4d.

And the aforesaid Thomas Chapleyn holds 1 cottage lying in Antystrett containing around 1 rood formerly of Robert Lyon and before that of John Manwood. And it renders each year   2d.

John Parker holds freely one messuage with various pieces of land and pasture containing in total around 7 acres by estimation formerly of Thomas Duncen and before that Hunnes lying in Antistrett. And it renders each year   8s.

[Fol. 50v] William Inderby holds freely one messuage lying in Antistrete formerly of Rose Bursted with a certain piece of land belonging to the same containing around 8 acres. And it renders each year   5s. 4d.

The same holds by native [tenure] one parcel of Ravenscroft containing around half an acre.   6d.

Richard Ree the younger holds one messuage lying at Antystret formerly of Adam Turnour and before that of Thomas Tyler and before that of William Schoppe with certain lands, meadows [and] pastures belonging to the same. And it renders each year 14s.   8d.

The same holds a certain parcel of land called Le Pertalle[40] containing around [blank] acres   2s. 3d.

The same holds by copy [of the court roll] 1 meadow containing around 2 acres next to Skippisbrege formerly of William Shopp. And it renders each year   5s.

The same holds by copy [of the court roll] 1 croft called Kyngiscroft containing around five acres. And it renders each year   4s. 2d.

Laurence Martyn holds one tenement called Higelyes formerly Gunsis with all the lands belonging to the same and one croft called Litilhegelies held from the lord by native [tenure]. And it renders each year   £1 5d.

---

[40] Or possibly Le Partell: the abbreviation at the beginning of this name could be par or per for pightle.

These parcels of rents Thomas Hobard has not inserted in this book in the same way, however, [*because*] the present farmer [*lessee*] collects and is in possession [*of them*] according to the confession of Andrew Vyncent formerly farmer there.

Kettlebaston (*Ketylberston*) hall	16s.
Master Wyott	£1 2s.
[*In English*] Divers of Thomas Hobard's native [*tenure*] parcels, [*then, in Latin*] how much profit to be inquired into. And for Aylewardes	[*blank*].
John Ston	3s.
Mr Robert Lee	4s.
John Cabowe and William Cabowe	3s. 5d.
Robert Rorchebrok	2s. 6d.
Nicholas Hobard, native [*tenure*] profits	[*blank*].
John Bore, native [*tenure*] profits	[*blank*].
Also [*in English*] for Galyottes medowe late Rochebrok	4s. 6d.

Rental 3. (*c.* 1525)[41]

The dating of this rental is problematic so these notes go into some detail to try to determine a likely date. It is an amalgamation of two rentals that are so similar in their details that they must be very close in date. The main text (CCA-U63/70455/1) is a full year's rental explicitly dated as Michaelmas, 17 Henry VIII, 29 September 1525. It looks like an original document of that date, with annotations made later in a different hand and ink. The secondary text (CCA-U15/15/17, fols 48v–50r, the differences in which are foot-noted in the text), is a partial later sixteenth-century copy of a half-year's rental made from a faded and worn original: the copy ends suddenly before the end with the copyist's comment that 'There is more in the rentall but the letters beinge worne owte no more canne be redde.' This secondary copy is dated in the Latin heading by the copyist as being 'for the half year ending at Michaelmas renewed 27th day of the month of September in the 31st year of the reign of King Henry the eighth', which should be 27 September 1539. However, the copyist, or an annotator, has inserted in English next to this date 'which was 1544 [sic]'. The annotation of it being 1544 seems to be an error: the copyist mis-reading the regnal year might be another, although the regnal year is written out in full in words rather than numerals. But a close comparison of the tenants and rents in this rental with that dated 29 September 1525 shows that in fact this '1539/1544' rental must actually be a little earlier than the 1525 rental, though not by much: '1539/1544' has as a tenant 'Harry Munnynge nowe Thomas Torner', whilst 1525 has 'Thomas Turnour for Munnynges'. Henry Munnynge(s) may well be the man of that name of Nedging, who died in 1521, implying that the two documents making up Rental 3 date from before and after that date.[42] In similar fashion, '1539/1544's'

---

[41] Comprising two documents (and see the dating notes): the main text is CCA-U63/70455/1 (former CCA document number '70,455' stamped and '1/53' written on the dorse in a nineteenth-century style and hand, together with 'Monks Illeigh Rental 1526 [*sic*]'), part of a deposit, made in 1966, by the Church Commissioners (CCA-U63). Paper booklet, 7pp. Latin. Secondly, incorporated as footnote annotations to the main text as it is almost identical, is a mis-dated half-year's rental (CCA-U15/15/17, fols 48v–50r). Marginal annotations in a different hand and ink, added later, are shown as insertions thus \.../ at the beginnings of lines. Running totals at the foot of each page are added in the same hand and ink as the annotations.

[42] TNA, PROB 11/20/287, PCC will of Henry Munyng of Nedging, made 16 October 1521, proved 29 November 1521. His will does not specify land in Monks Eleigh, but he did leave money bequests

*Secylye Fastolpe nowe Mr Sprynges' becomes 1525's 'Master Spryng for Fastolles':
both individuals are hard to identify and date, but respecting Secylye Fastolpe, see
p. 208, footnote 32. Overall, if the date of the main text really is 1525, then both
dates given for the rental of '1539/1544' must be wrong.*

*But is the 1525 date for the main text correct? In both the rentals making up
Rental 3, Sir James Hobart is listed as a tenant, with his knightly title, indicating
a date between 1503 when he was knighted and 1517 when he died. Likewise,
Thomas Hoberd (d. 1515) is also in both, indicating a date before 1515. These two
men also help to date Rental 2 (c. 1503–c. 1513) (see the dating note to that on pp.
200–1), yet most of the tenants in the two rentals making up Rental 3 (which are
very similar) are sufficiently different from those in Rental 2 to suggest a number of
years (easily a decade or more) between them in time. Another dating hint comes
from the presence of Thomas Baldry of London as the tenant of Boyton Hall in
both of the Rental 3 rentals. He was the son-in-law of William Foorth of Hadleigh
(d. 1504) (see the dating notes for Rental 2 on pp. 201, 208, footnote 30 above) as
well as the city of London alderman of that name who was lord mayor of London
1523–24, knighted c. 1524, died around August 1534 and whose grand-daughter
married the 2nd Baron Rich.[43] Neither of the Rental 3 rentals notes Baldry's knight-
hood, however, thus suggesting a date for both of them as prior to 1524.[44]*

*But to muddy the waters, there are two different and incongruous tenants of
Loose Hall, Hitcham, in the two rentals comprising Rental 3: Robert Bramfielde
in the earlier, mis-dated, '1539/44' rental and Sir Robert Chamberleyne in the
supposed 1525 version. Robert Bramfield is otherwise unknown (as a tenant of
Loose Hall or elsewhere), but Sir Robert Chamberleyn was a well-known Yorkist
who was executed in 1491 for his part in the Perkin Warbeck rebellion.[45] This seems
like a very unlikely mistake for a scribe to make in a 1525 rental (thirty-four years
after Chamberleyn's execution), especially as Chamberleyn's successor, Henry
Wyatt, keeper of the king's jewels, who was granted Loose Hall in 1492, is listed in
Rental 2 (see p. 201), but there he is, and his presence is inexplicable if the 1525
date is correct, or even close. Sir Robert certainly held Loose Hall at his death, as
it was listed amongst his properties in his inquisition post mortem in 1492, which
also states that Henry Wyott, esq. [sic] had taken the issues and profits of the manor*

---

to Robert Rice (who certainly did hold property in Monks Eleigh) and his family.

[43] A.B. Beaven, 'Chronological List of Aldermen: 1501–1600', in *The Aldermen of the City of London
Temp. Henry III – 1912* (London, 2 vols, 1908, 1912), pp. 20–47.

[44] Boyton or Buyden Hall Manor is noted by Copinger as a separate manor in Monks Eleigh, and he
cites Davy, mis-stating 'that Sir *William* Baldrey, knight, of London was lord and was succeeded by
his son and heir George Baldrey who died in 1540, when the manor passed to his daughter and heir
Elizabeth who was married to Robert Rich, 2nd Baron … son of Richard Rich, Baron Rich and Lord
Chancellor of England' under Henry VIII [Copinger, *Manors of Suffolk* 1, p. 163]. Although Copinger
gives the wrong first name of Baldrey, the descent of the manor through Thomas's descendants
confirms that the former lord mayor of London is the right Thomas, and not one of his contemporary
name-sakes (his younger brother, also called Thomas Baldry, died *c.* 1524–25, but was 'of Ipswich'
and its MP). The lord mayor's younger son and a nephew were both also Thomas Baldries (they
died *c.* 1539 and *c.* 1535 respectively). His grand-daughter, Elizabeth (née Baldry), Lady Rich, held
Boyton Hall in the 1583 rental and all of her properties were in the hands of Joshua Warde in the
1599 rental, agreeing nicely with Lady Rich's death in 1591.

[45] Copinger (*Manors of Suffolk* 3, p. 177) does not mention Sir Robert Chamberleyn in respect of Loose
Hall. However, Copinger does refer to him (*Manors of Suffolk* 1, p. 182) as lord of the manor of
Casteles in Polstead at the end of the fifteenth century (although he does not mention his execution),
where he was succeeded by his widow Elizabeth until her death on 23 May 1517, followed by Sir
Robert's son Sir Ralph Chamberleyne (d. 4 March 1523), then his son Edward Chamberleyne.

since Sir Robert's death.[46] *After Wyatt's death in 1536, his son, Sir Thomas, disposed of it to Sir Ralph Warren in 1538.*[47] *Perhaps both of the Rental 3 documents are actually re-copyings (perhaps more than once removed from the original) of a rental that was made a little earlier than 1525 (maybe c.1515 at the latest, based on the presence of Sir James Hobart and Thomas Hoberd), and mis-dated, or re-made in 1525. If the scribe also had earlier rentals to hand that have not survived, perhaps he simply re-copied Sir Robert Chamberleyn (whose name, and infamy, had been largely forgotten by then) as the tenant for Loose Hall from one of them in error.*

Another incongruity is the inclusion in both versions of Rental 3 of Lawrence Martyn who appears as tenant of Hegelynges in Rental 3. He must be the man of that name of Long Melford who died between 1516 and 1518 and left 'Higgelles and Reyners ... in Monkysylly' to his son Roger in his will.[48] *This again pushes the 1525 dating back a few years, although it is possible that out of date material was being re-copied here too. Whatever the facts of the matter, the dating of Rental 3 is still problematic, although it is believed to be in its proper place within the chrono-logical pecking order within this volume. A date of c. 1525 has been adhered to for editorial purposes, although it should be borne in mind that this is a date open to amendment in the light of further research.*

[*p. 1*] [*Latin*] Rental there at the feast of St Michael the archangel in the 17th year of the reign of Henry VIII [*29 September 1525, but see dating notes above*] for a whole year

[*English*[49]] Firstly, the parson for lond leying ageynst Manney Wode	1s.2d.
Adam Goodale for the Bull late Goddardes	2s. 1d.
Robert Alisaunder for the Swanne	2s. 10d.
Robert Heyward for his mansyon	1s. 4d.
Same for Fennys with Swyngeldon Grene now Master Spryng for the year	8s. 8d.
Thomas Hobert for 3 tenementes in the Church Rowe	5s.
John Ceywey[50] for his tenement late Boores	1s.
Richard Goodale for his tenement late Boores[51]	1s.
John Rudland now Cutlers	6d.
\now 1s. 4d./ John Stritt[52] for his cotage	1s.
Robert Goymer for his cotage late Shoppys	1s.
Rowland Lay sumtyme Bretons	8d.
Same for a medow late Vyncentes[53]	5s.
For Our Lady Gyld Land	1s. 1d.

---

[46] For Sir Robert's inquisition *post mortem*, see C. Flower, M.C.B. Dawes and A.C. Wood (eds), *Calendar of Inquisitions Post Mortem, Hen. VII*, 3 (London, 1955), p. 378, entry 672; p. 382, entry 683: my thanks to Edward Martin for this information and reference, and for his help in trying to disentangle this conundrum.

[47] Copinger, *Manors of Suffolk* 3, p. 177.

[48] TNA, PROB 11/19/183, PCC will of Laurance Martyn of Long Melford, made 14 November 1516, proved 16 December 1518.

[49] The rental is written in English sprinkled with a few Latin words and annotations that for the most part have been silently translated, except where problematic.

[50] John Berywey in CCA-U15/15/17, fol. 48v.

[51] Recorded as 'hys cottage late Boores' in a different position in CCA-U15/15/17, fol. 49r.

[52] John Strutt in CCA-U15/15/17, fol. 48v.

[53] 'The same Rowlande for Andrewe Vyncentes' in CCA-U15/15/17, fol. 48v.

Roger Alysaunder 5s.	4d.

£1 17s. 4d.

[*p. 2*] Symon Stanesby	7s. 2d.
Same for his Teyntour Yard	6d.
\now is in the new rental/ Old Hunte late Alice Caxtons[54]	4d.
\now is [?]renewed/ John Warde for Asselottes[55]	8d.
Lawrence Couper for Russhebrookes	3d.
Same for old Russhebrookes	5s.
Same for Alice Shoppys	1s.
William Colman for a cotage late Russhbrokes	1s. 2d.
Alice Cage	4d.
Same for Galyottes Medow	4s. 6d.
Master Bendissh[56] for Old Hoberdes	8s.
\<deceased (*defunct*) in the new rental>/ John Fullar for Clerkes	1s. 8d.
Roger Shyllyng	1s. 1½d
Nycholas Vincent for his father[57]	3s.
\deceased/ Thomas Aleyn	1s.
Thomas Gentilman in Ferrors	1s.
\deceased/ Alyngton for Cobaldes[58]	1s. 7d.
\deceased/ Geffrey Hobert for Abbottes	5s.
William Statout[59] for Wardes	6d.
Yonge Baret for Scottes Croft	2s. 6½d
William Hobart for Burches	8d.
Same for Calliscroft	4s.

£4 8s. 4d.

[*p. 3*] \deceased/ Thomas Tyler for the Churchmedow[60]	6d.
[*deceased/*] Same for his Mansyon[61]	4d.
Nicholas Hobart for his Mansion	10d.
Same for Mundys[62]	1s. 6d.
Same for Webbyscroft	2s. 11d.

---

54 Alyce Caston in CCA-U15/15/17, fol. 48v and in later rentals.

55 Astleyes in CCA-U15/15/17, fol. 48v.

56 Mr Wylliam Bendyshe in CCA-U15/15/17, fol. 48v. Possibly the brother of Thomas Bendyshe of Topsfield Hall, Hadleigh, whose son Rauffe married Dorothy, the daughter and heiress of Thomas Hobert of Leyham (see p. 203, footnote 27) (W.C. Metcalfe, *Visitations of Essex Made by Hawley, 1552; Hervey, 1558; Cooke, 1570; Raven, 1612 and Owen and Lilly, 1634* (London, 1878), p. 316). If so, this is another illustration of different members of family networks investing in properties in Monks Eleigh. If he was the same as the William Bendisshe or Bendish of Leyham, whose nuncupative will was made on 4 July 1528 and proved in PCC on 9 July 1528, he must have died between those two dates (TNA, PROB 11/22/549).

57 'Andrew Vyncente now Nicholas Vyncente' in CCA-U15/15/17, fol. 48v.

58 'Arlingeton for Cobboldes' in CCA-U15/15/17, fol. 48v.

59 Ottertowt in CCA-U15/15/17, fol. 48v, which is probably a copyist's error for the surname Startup. The 1524 subsidy has a William Stertowt, which itself might be a mis-reading or variant of the surname Startup, which occurs in relation to this property in Rental 4 (*c.* 1544–45), CCA-U15/15/17, fol. 51r.

60 'for the Church Meadowes sometymes called Burches' in CCA-U15/15/17, fol. 49r.

61 'for his dwellinge' in CCA-U15/15/17, fol. 49r.

62 Mundyll in CCA-U15/15/17, fol. 49r.

Same for Wyntye Burton[63]	3s. 2d.
\deceased in the new rental £1 2s./ Master Foorthe for the mill	£1.
\deceased/ Thomas Turnour for Munnynges[64]	2s.
William Corbold for Cages	4½d.
Same for Paddok Hall	2d.
Same for the Parkfeld and the Medow	£1.
Same for Coboldes	1s. 6½d
\<del>deceased</del>>/ Master Spryng for Fastolles[65]	7s. 8d.
Lawrence Martyn[66] for Hegelynges	1s. 6½d.
Same for Davyes Grove	1s.
Same for Hogfen[67]	1d.
The Colage of Denston for Fosters[68]	£2 13s. 8d.
\<del>finished (defunct')</del>>/ Same for Prestow Medow	2s. 8d.
Thomas Elyot for Kempys in Milden (*Meldyng*)[69]	4s. 4d.
John Davy for Newlond Hall	4s.
Thomas Plome for Holmes[70]	3d.
\deceased/ William Brook	1½d.
[*p. 4*] Thomas Hobert for Wat' Hobardes[71]	£2 5s. 3d.
Same for Humbilbanck[72]	4d.
Same for Aylwardes	7s. 9d.
Master Spryng for Croksales[73]	6s. 4d.
Same for Priours	£1 14s. 2d.
Same for Wyncolles	14s.
Same for Bowres Grove	£1 8s. 6d.
Same for Cabowys	1s. 6d.
Master Martyn for Brownes	£1 5s. 1d.
Sir William Clopton for Thorpys	£1 8d.
Same for a parcel in Hyefeld	5s.
Same for Gausys Land[74]	2s.
Same for Bestneys	5s.
Same for another parcell	8d.
\deceased/ Thomas Kyng for his tenement[75]	1s. 6d.
\deceased/ The Wife of Thomas Chapleyn for Parkers	4d.
Same for Lyons	2d.
Same for John Parkers	8d.

---

63 Wynterburton in CCA-U15/15/17, fol. 49r.

64 'Harry Munnynge nowe Thomas Torner' in CCA-U15/15/17, fol. 49r.

65 'Secylye Fastolpe nowe Mr Sprynges' in CCA-U15/15/17, fol. 49r.

66 This was Lawrence Martyn of Long Melford, who left 'Higgelles and Reyners ... in Monkysylly' to his son Roger in his will (TNA, PROB 11/19/183, PCC will of Laurance Martyn of Long Melford, made 14 November 1516, proved 16 December 1518).

67 'Hogfen lyenge betweene Illighe and Chelsewoorthe [*Chelsworth*]' in CCA-U15/15/17, fol. 49r.

68 Forsters in CCA-U15/15/17, fol. 49r.

69 'now Mr Clarkes' added in CCA-U15/15/17, fol. 49r.

70 'John Holmes nowe Plommes' in CCA-U15/15/17, fol. 49r.

71 'Water [*Walter*] Hubertes' is the name of a tenement in CCA-U15/15/17, fol. 49r.

72 Humblebankes in CCA-U15/15/17, fol. 49r.

73 'Thomas Sprynge for Cocksalls' in CCA-U15/15/17, fol. 49r.

74 Gouselond in CCA-U15/15/17, fol. 49r.

75 'lyenge by Mr Hubbarte' added in CCA-U15/15/17, fol. 49r.

The Wedow Parker for Cutlers[76]	10½d
Sir Jamys Hobart	18s. 3d.
Same for Gousislond	6s. 7d.

£8 7s. 7d.

[*p. 5*] Stephen Chapleyn for his father	2s. 2d.
Same for William Chapleyns	8s. 4d.
Same for Pages	£1 2s.
Same for Shoppys \or Sharpes/[77]	5s.
Same for Mascalles	£1 10s.
Same for a parcel in Wodefeld	2s. 6s.
\for new rental it is 4s./ Same for Skyppismedow[78]	3s.
Same for a parcel in Hyefeld[79]	1s. 6d.
William Seman for Emme Randes[80]	2s. 4d.
John Kyng	4s.
\now enrolled in new rental/ Same for Thurgoes[81]	1s. 2d.
\now enrolled in new rental/ William Sharp for his dwellyng	3d.
Same for Stannardes	2s. 8d.
John Goddard for Endyrbyes[82]	5s. 4d.
Richard Ree for his mansion[83]	14s. 8d.
Same for Kingiscroft	4s. 2d.
Thomas Clerk for Bregettes[84]	4s. 10d.
Same for a medow late William Hoberdes	3s.
Same for [?]Dominic's (*dns'*) Gardyn[85]	1s.

Swyngyldon grene

William Hobert for Letyes[86]	7s. 6d.
\for new rental it is 4s./ John Brond[87]	2s.
[*p. 6*] John Hobert for a parcel called Alowden[88]	7s.
Geffrey Hobert for Godales in Fenstret	10d.
The Almes Hows at the Milcroft Gate	2d.
The Almes Hows late Stevynsons	2d.

---

[76] 'The same Chaplens wyfe for Cutlers nowe Wydowe Parkers' in CCA-U15/15/17, fol. 49v.

[77] 'Shopps sometime Reys' in CCA-U15/15/17, fol. 49v.

[78] 'late Andrewe Vyncentes' added and the rent for the half-year, 1s. 6d. in CCA-U15/15/17, fol. 49v.

[79] 'The same Steven for Andrew Vyncentes in Highe Fielde' in CCA-U15/15/17, fol. 49v.

[80] 'The same Steven [*Chaplen*] for Emme Randes now Seman' in CCA-U15/15/17, fol. 49v, where the tenement Emme Randes is listed amongst Stephen Chaplen's holdings immediately above here.

[81] Thurgoys in CCA-U15/15/17, fol. 49v.

[82] 'John Goddarde for [*blank*] now Rysbyes' in CCA-U15/15/17, fol. 49v.

[83] 'Richarde Reve for his message [*messuage*] now Rysbye' in CCA-U15/15/17, fol. 49v.

[84] Brockettes in CCA-U15/15/17, fol. 49v.

[85] 'Domynyngs Garden' in CCA-U15/15/17, fol. 49v. The Latin abbreviation here *dns'* has been translated as 'Dominick's' by analogy with this tenement's name in later rentals: the name may be an anglicisation of the written Latin term for 'the lord's garden' or 'the demesne garden' (*dominus* or *dominicus*).

[86] 'Wylliam Hobbart for landes now Mr Ryce' in CCA-U15/15/17, fol. 49v.

[87] Probably the name of the tenement.

[88] 'John Hubbert for a pastor called Alowden by Webbis Crofte' in CCA-U15/15/17, fol. 49v.

Plome[89] of Milden (*Meldyng*) for Webbiscroft[90]	3s.
Thomas Baldry of London (*Lundon*) for Boyton Hall	£1 6s. 8d.
Same for Piggescote Croft	4s. 3d.

Kettlebaston (*Ketilberston*) and Hitcham (*Hecham*)

John Folkys for my lady of Lincoln[91]	16s.
The Church Medow[92]	7d.
Sir Robert Chambyrleyn[93] for Loos Hall	£1 2s.
Thomas Wellam	3s.
Thomas Crowe[94] for Berardes[95]	4s. 8d.
Same for Illy Close[96]	6d.
Same for Martyns	1d.
Richard Hacche for Ransons[97]	1s. 4d.
John Whyte for Adams	5s.
Same for Leys	6d.
John Cabow theelder	2d.
Same for Howys	6d.
[*p. 7*] Master Vynes for Sharfeld	1s.
Same for Darbyes	3s. 7d.
Gregory Cook for Illy Clos	5s. 8d.
Monks Eleigh (*Monkecely*) Myll	£2 13s. 4d.

£11 3s. 1d.

£34 9s.[98]

---

89 Possibly the William Plom listed as being assessed to pay 5s. on £10 in the 1524 subsidy return, or a relation (S.H.A. Hervey (ed.), *Suffolk in 1524, Being the Return for a Subsidy Granted in 1523, with Map of Suffolk in Hundreds* (Suffolk Green Books 10, 1910), p. 19).

90 'for Ely Crofte otherwyse called Webbys' in CCA-U15/15/17, fol. 49v.

91 'John Folkes for my lady of Lyncolnes for Walsomyes now Honnynges' in CCA-U15/15/17, fol. 50r. Margaret, Countess of Lincoln, widow of John de la Pole (*c*. 1460–87), Earl of Lincoln, daughter of Thomas FitzAlan, 17th Earl of Arundel and his wife Margaret (née Woodville), sister to Elizabeth Woodville, Edward IV's queen. Lady Lincoln was still alive in 1524, when she was bequeathed her father's great turquoise ring in his will (R. Horrox, 'Pole, John de la, earl of Lincoln (*c*. 1460–1487)', *ODNB*, (2004); TNA, PROB 11/21/478 PCC will of Thomas Arundell Erle of Arundell, proved 29 November 1524).

92 'The parson for the Towne Meadowe' in CCA-U15/15/17, fol. 50r.

93 Robert Bramfield was the tenant in CCA-U15/15/17, fol. 50r. The only candidate for Sir Robert Chambyrleyn seems to be the knight of that name executed for his part in the Perkin Warbeck rebellion in 1491 (see dating notes on pp. 215–16).

94 Possibly Thomas Crowe of Kettlebaston, d. 1527 (V.B. Redstone, 'Calendar of Pre-Reformation Wills, Testaments, Probates, Administrations, Registered at the Probate Office at Bury St Edmunds' *PSIAH* 12, no. 3 (1906), p. 202).

95 Barrardes in CCA-U15/15/17, fol. 50r.

96 The names of the tenements in this and the following entry are left blank in CCA-U15/15/17, fol. 50r.

97 This entry, and those following, are omitted from CCA-U15/15/17. The late sixteenth-century copyist notes at this point, 'There is more in the rentall but the letters beinge worne owte no more canne be redde' before 'The somme of this Rentall £37 18s. 2d.'

98 £37 18s. 2d. in CCA-U15/15/17, fol. 50r.

Rental 4.[99] (c. 1544–45)

This follows on almost seamlessly (save for the insertion of the annotation 'This is with owte date') and in the same copyist's hand from the undated Monks Eleigh rental (mis-dated as '1539/1544') that forms part of Rental 3 (CCA-U15/15/17, fols 48v–50r, and see above pp. 214–16). Its original must date between 1544 and 1548, the former perhaps being more likely in that 1544 was added as an erroneous annotation to the heading of the '1539/1544' component of Rental 3, which immediately precedes it. There are a few suggestions in the text that help to clarify the date. Denston College, mentioned as a tenant, was dissolved in 1548. Richard Strutt held his cottage (in this rental and Court Roll 23) between 20 September 1540 and 19 October 1545 (see p. 177 above). Margery Ryce (née Waldegrave) appears in it holding several properties as the widow of Robert Ryce I (d. 10 August 1544) before Robert Ryce II took over the tenancy on 19 October 1545 (Court Roll 23, 1545).[100] These indicate a date for the rental between 10 August 1544 and 19 October 1545.

[*Fol. 50r*] *Monks Eleigh* (*Illeygh monachorum*)

	This is with owte date
From Robert Goymer for Le Bull	1s. ½d.
From the same for a cottage formerly Layes	2s. 10d.
Also for Prestow Meadowe	1s. 4d.
From the parson for land lying against Manneywoode	7d.
From Robert Heywarde for a mansion	8d.
From the Widow Corbolde for Fennyslyer	4s. 4d.
From the same for Cobboldes	9¼d.
Also for Paddockes Hall	1½d.
From the aforesaid	2¼d.
From Stephen Chapleyn for the cottage Rosshebrokes	7d.
Also for Parkers	2d.
Here the rental is torn for one sum (*hic dilaceratur Rentale pro una summa*)	
Also for Vyncentes in Highefilde	9d.
Also for Boyton Hall	13s. 4d.
Also for Pyggessgate Croffe [*sic*]	2s. 1½d.
From John Springe esquire for Porters	3s. 10d.
Also for Pryors	17s. 1d.
Also for Wyncolles	7s.
Also for Bowers Grove	14s. 3½d.
Also for Barrardes	2s. 4d.
\Note/ Also for Cockesalls	3s. 2d.
\Note/ Also for Cabbowes	9d.
[*Fol. 50v*] From Benedict Hasyll for Parkefielde and Le Medowe	10s.
From Robert Newlande for 3 tenements in Le Churche Rowe	2s. 6d.

---

[99] CCA-U15/15/17, fols 50r–51v. Latin. This rental is part of a late-sixteenth-century book in rather poor condition, containing various draft court minutes, estreats and copy rentals and follows on from part of Rental 3 (see dating notes for Rental 4).

[100] See also C.G. Harlow, 'Robert Ryece of Preston, 1555–1638', *PSIAH* 32, no. 1 (1970), pp. 43–69, especially the family tree between pp. 46 and 47. Robert Ryece II was the father of Robert Ryece III (1555–1638), the antiquarian and author of the *Breviary of Suffolk, 1618*, edited and published by Hervey in 1902 (see Bibliography and p. 222, footnote 104).

From Hugh[101] in Brent Eleigh (*Brendely*) for the tenement <Barrardi>	4d.
From Nicholas Hubbert for Cuttlers	3d.
Also for Higgelens	9s. 2½d.
Also for Davys Grove	6d.
Also for Hogge Fenne	1d.
Also for a pasture called Alloden	3s. 6d.
From the Widow Parker for <Chapl> Cuttelers	5d.
From John Strutte for a cottage	6¼d.
From Richard Strutte[102] for a cottage called Shopps	6d.
From John Bronde for Le Gylde Lande[103]	6½d.
From Ro [*sic*] Roger Alysander	3s. 8d.
From Symon Stannysbye	3s. 7d.
here in a damaged section (*in dilaceratione*) another sum is missing	
From Hunte for Alice Castons	2d.
From Thomas Halybrede for Rosshebrookes	1d.
Also for Olde Rosshebrookes	2s. 6d.
Also for Alice Shoppes	6d.
From Alice Cage \of Bury [*St Edmunds*]/	2d.
Also for Gallettes Medow	2s. 3d.
From John Warde for Asselees	4d.
From John Barrett formerly Wardes	10d.
From Roger Sheelinge	6½¼d.
From Nicholas Vyncente	1s 6d.
From Thomas Allyn	6d.
From John Jentylman	6d.
From John Andrewe for Arlington	9½d.
From Margery Ryce for Olde Hobbertes	4s.
Also for Chaplyns	1s. 1d.
Also for William Chaplens	4s. 2d.
Also for Mascalls	15s.
Also for Shoppes formerly Reyes	2s. 6d.
Also for a parcel at Woodfielde	1s. 3d.
Also for Skyppysmeadowe[104] formerly Andrew Vyncentes	1s. 6d.

---

[101] Surname omitted in the copying.

[102] Richard Strutt was admitted as tenant to a cottage, probably this property, on 20 September 1540 and surrendered it at the manorial court on 19 October 1545 (see Court Roll 23).

[103] Le Gylde Lande was formerly held by the parish's Guild of Our Lady, which, like all other parish guilds in England, must have been abolished by 1547, following attempts since 1545. If the dating of this rental as *c.* 1544–45 is correct, there are two implications concerning this tenement. Either the guild was suppressed early and John Bronde acquired it after its confiscation by the crown commissioners, the name Le Gylde Lande having become a mere tenement name rather than reflecting its tenant or usage. But if the guild was not abolished until 1547, then Brond might have been either a sub-tenant or trustee appointed by the parish to hold it, which raises the intriguing possibility that this was done with a view to concealing it from the crown commissioners. A tenement of the same rent as Le Gylde Lande appears in Rental 5 (1580/81) (see p. 225) and afterwards as Marie or Marye Crofte, preserving the memory and name of the Guild of Our Lady in a less overt manner for a Protestant age.

[104] Robert Ryce I, d. 10 August 1544, and his son Robert Ryce II, d. 1590, father of the antiquarian Robert Ryce III, jointly took tenancy of a piece of meadow at Skyppyscrofte, with other properties on 1 August 1530. Robert Ryce I died in 1544. At a manorial court on 19 October 1545, Robert Ryce II came to do fealty as sole tenant. Margery Ryce (née Waldegrave), the tenant listed here, was the

222

Also for William Hubberde for Bondes[105]	3s. 6d.
[*Fol. 51r*] From Robert Alysander for Abbottes lately of Geoffrey Hubbard	2s. 6d.
From William Startuppe for Wardes	3d.
Here, a missing sum	
From Barrett the younger for Scottes Crofte	1s. 3d.
From William Hobarde for Burches	4d.
From the same for Callis Crofte	2s.
From Thomas Tyler for Le Churche Medowe	3d.
From Richard Hubbert for a mansion	2d.
Also for Bryckettes	2s. 6d.
Also for Le Medowe	1s.
Also for [?]Dominic's (*dns '*)[106] garden	6d.
From James Hoberde for a mansion	5d.
Also for Mundyll	10d.
Also for Webbes Crofte	1s. 5½d.
Also for John Bronde[107]	1s.
Also for Wynterburton	1s. 7d.
Also for Walter Hobardes	£1 2s. 7½d.
Also for Humblebankes	2d.
Also for Aylewardes	3s. 10½d.
From Richard Gooddale for a cottage	6d.
From Froste for le Myll	10s.
From Henry Munninge now Turner[108]	1s.
From the College of Denston[109] for Fosters	£1 6s. 8d.
From Ellyat for Kempys in Milden (*Meldynge*)	2s. 2d.
From John Darby[110] for Newlande Halle	2s.
From John Holmes now Plommes[111]	1½d.
From John Bronde for William Brooke	½¼d.
Here another missing sum	
From William Clopton for Thorpes	10s. 4d.
Also for a parcel in Heighe Fielde	2s. 6d.
Also for Gosselonde	1s.

---

second wife of Robert Ryce I (she later married John Gray and had five children with him, so she was presumably younger than her first husband) who is clearly paying the rent as *de facto* tenant here, so perhaps her stepson Robert Ryce II (born before 1536) had still not fully taken over the running of his inheritance. See Harlow, 'Robert Ryece of Preston, 1555–1638' (1970) and above, p. 221.

[105] It is not clear whether this property was held by William Hubberde, or Margery Ryce. 'Also' at the beginning of the entry suggests the latter, but the format of the entry suggests the former. William Hubberde might therefore be either the name of the tenement, named after a former tenant, or the present tenant of the land called Bondes.

[106] See p. 219, footnote 85.

[107] That is, the tenement known as John Bronde named after a present or previous tenant.

[108] The late-sixteenth-century copyist is copying later annotations to the original here.

[109] Established 1475, suppressed 1548. See above, p. 221.

[110] Earlier rentals call the tenant of Newland Hall John Davy and this late-sixteenth-century copyist might well have written the name 'John Darby' here in error because there was a tenant of this name in 1599.

[111] This seems to push back the date of this rental, since the 1525 rental has 'Thomas Plome for Holmes', and this one implies that Plomme is a recent annotation to the original. It is more probably an error by the late-sixteenth-century copyist.

Also for Bensons	2s. 6d.
Also for another parcel	4d.
From Thomas Kynge for his tenement	9d.
Also Pagis	11s.
From John Greene	4s.
[*Fol. 51v*] From the Widow Seman for Randes	1s 2d.
From Master Rysbye	£1 7s. 5d.
From John Kynge the elder	1½d.
From John Hasyll for Thourgost	4½d.
From Robert Allysander for Le Swanne	1s. 5d.
From Alice Bronde for Le Almeshowse	1d.
From Master Allington	5d.
From the Widow Hale	1s 6d.

Kettlebaston (*Ketlebarston*) and Hitcham

From Christopher Ranson for [*sic*] <Ranso> parson for Le Towne Medowe	3½d.
From Robert Springe for Loose Hall	11s.
From Thomas Welham	1s. 6d.
From Alyngton for Ely Close	3d.
Also for Martens	½d.
From Robert Hatche for Ransheams	8d.
From John Whyte formerly Adams	2s. 6d.
From the same for Lees	3d.
From John Cabowe	1d.
From the same for Le Howse	3d.
From Master Vynes for Sharefielde	6d.
Also for Darbyes	2s. 9½d.
From Gregory Cooke for Eelys Cloose	2s. 10d.
Total of the aforesaid – £34 5s.	

Rental 5. (25 January 1580/81)[112]

[*Fol. 56v reversed*] [*English, with scattered Latin phrases*] This half year gatherer [*sic*] of Monks Eleigh (*Monkes Illighe*) rentes is renewed this 25 of Januarye in the 23rd yere of the Quenes Majeste Elizabeth by the grace of God etc. 1580.

***** *Mr Cutler*. Firstly, of Robert Cutler, gentleman, for Wyncolls late Master Springes   7s.

---

[112] CCA-U15/15/17, fols 56v–55v, in back of volume, reversed. One of a number of rentals, court minutes and memoranda some re-copied, some in draft, in a paper book of various court records 1544–90, in poor condition. This rental is properly a rent collection record, arranged by tenants' names, which are in the left margin. The number of half-years' rents paid are indicated in the margin, bracketed against all of each tenant's holdings: for each tenant's entry, a horizontal line is drawn in the margin, with short vertical lines above and below it, each vertical half-line indicating a half-year's rent paid as well as making it clear how many full years' rent has been paid (a vertical line both above and below the horizontal one). A dot instead of a vertical line presumably indicates a half-year's rent not paid. This is represented in the text by asterisks before the tenants' names, which represent the number of half-years' rents paid, for example: ***** = five half-years' rents paid. The number of half-years' rents covers the period between this rental (arranged by tenant for ease of rent collection) and Rental 6 (1583), which is arranged by tenement.

The same for Bowers Grove	14s. 3½d.
The same for Fennes	4s. 4d.
The same for the lytle yarde by the Tye	2d.
[*Total*]	£1 5s. 9½d.
***** *S. Blomfyld*. Symonde Blomefeilde for Priors	17s. 1d.
for Croxsalls	3s. 2d.
for Abbotts	2s. 6d.
for Geytes	2¼d.
for Woodes late Corboldes	9¼d.
for Padocke Hall	1½d.
for the Bull	1s. ½d.
for Stertops	3d.
for parte of Brownes	3s. 1½d.
for Porters	3s. 10d.
<for Topshops> \Clementes/[113]	2d.
The same for Boores	4d.
The same for Goodales \Barawayes/	6d.
The same for parcell of the Mylle late [*damaged*] Chaplens	3s.
[*Total*]	£1 16s. 1d.
***** S. Hobart. Stephen Hobart for Fosters	£1 6s. 8d.
for Allen Downe Feilde	3s. 6d.
for parcel of Parke Feilde	2s. 6d.
* for Mr E. Doyle his 2 tenementes[114]	2s. 6½d.
The same for Vinsentes	1s. 6d.
The same for Byrches	4d.
For Caves Crofte	2s.
[*Total*] £1 19s. ½d \	£1 16s. 6d./
***** J. Man. <Jhon> \James/ Manne for Marie Crofte[115] late Hobartes	6½d.
***** J. Heyward. Jhon Heywarde for Asleses	4d.
tenement late Jentlemans	6d.
tenement late Allingtons	9½d.
tenement in the chyrche yearde * Parson Whytwell/[116]	2d.
[*Total*]	1s. 9½d.
***** Jhon Nunne for Shellinges	6 ½¼d.
***** J. Clopton. Jhon Clopton gentleman for Thorpes	10s. 4d.
for Highe Feilde	2s. 6d.
for Gawes Londe	1s.

---

[113] With a horizontal line linking back to a separate marginal note of five half-years' rents paid for this tenement. Presumably Richard Clementes (who appears in Rental 6 (1583) as the tenant of Topshops) acquired it soon after this collection record was made, because he paid five half-years' rents.

[114] With a horizontal line linking back to a separate marginal note of four half-years' rents unpaid, fifth half-year's rent paid. Edward Doyle presumably only acquired this property in the fifth half-year after the beginning of the rental, so probably early in 1583: he appears in Rental 6 (1583) as the copyhold tenant of The Almes Tenement, comprising four [*sic*] tenements in Church Street Row.

[115] In previous rentals, a tenement known as Le Gylde Land or the land of the parish Guild of Our Lady (see p. 222, footnote 103).

[116] With a horizontal line linking back to a separate marginal note of four half-years' rents unpaid, fifth rent paid. Like Edward Doyle, above, Parson Whytwell presumably acquired this property early in 1583. As John Whytell, clerk, he appears in Rental 6 (1583) holding several properties including this one, here named as Chyrcheyard Tenement.

an other parcell	4d.
for Benstedes	2s. 6d.
[*Total*] 16s. 8d.	
[*Fol. 56r reversed*] ***** N. Hobart. Nicholas Hobbart gentleman for Pages	11s.
for Huntes	9d.
***** James Hobart. James Hobbart gentleman for his mancon \called Mondams/	
	5d.
an other parcell \Parsonage Croft otherwise \Wynter/ Burtons/	11d.
Webbes Crofte	1s. 5½d.
for Brondes	2s.
for Burtons	1s. 7d.
Walter Hobbarts	£1 2s. 7½d.
Humble Blanckes	2d.
for Aylewardes	3s. 10½d.
[*Total*]	£1 13s. ½d.
***** H Scynner. Henry Skynner gentleman for 2 tenementes called Rushebroockes	
	2s. 7½d.
for Schops	6d.
for Scottes Crofte[117]	1s. 3¼d.
Alce Cages	2d.
Gallettes Medows	2s. 3d.
[*in right margin, before the sum total against the previous four entries, scribbled in a different hand and ink*] 6s. 10d. [*and below it*] £1 8s. 3d. [*sic*]	
The same for Lyons late Mr Honynges	1d.
for Vinsentes	9d.
for divers other parcells	£1 7s. 5d.
[*Total*]	£1 15s. ½¼d.
***** \Robert/ Goodale for Parkers of Chaplens	2d.
***** Robert Ryce. Robert Ryce \now Sterne/ for Olde Hobartes	4s.
for Chaplens	1s. 1d.
William Chaplens	4s. 2d.
Mascalles	15s.
Schopps sometyme Rees	2s. 6d.
for 5 acres in Woode Feilde	1s. 3d.
Scips Medowe late Vynsentes	1s. 6d.
[*Total*]	£1 9s. 6d.
Marten.[118] Master \Umfrye/ Marten esquier for Higlens	10s. 2½d.
Davies Grove <6d.>	6d.
Hogge Fenne	½d.
[*Total*]	10s. 9d.
**** L[*ord*] Rytche. Robert Lorde Ryche for Boyton Hall	13s. 4d.
for Pigges Crofte	2s. 1½d.

---

[117] In the left margin is a horizontal line linking either this or the following property (the line is ambiguously placed) to a marginal note of five half-years' rents paid for one of them. This might indicate a sale of one of them shortly after this collection record was made. All of Henry Skynner's properties listed here are annotated as having passed to Luke Melton and then John Darby in Rental 6 (1583), so perhaps Melton purchased one of the properties in 1580 and the others in 1583, after Rental 6 had been first written.

[118] Number of rents paid is indistinct.

Jhon Chaplen for Kemps	2s. 2d.
William Hobbertes at Swyngleton	3s. 7d.
the pease [*piece*] under Mannie Woode \call'd the Tufte/	7d.
[*Total*] \[?]Another place/	£1 1s. 9½d.

***** W. Teylor. <del>\<John></del> \Wylliam/ Teylor, clerke, for a cotage called Rushe-broockes late Jhon Chaplens   7d.

***** Robert Chaplen. Robert Chaplen for his parte of the Mylle	8s.
for Turners	1s. 1d.
[*Total*]	9s. 1d.
***** <del><Nicholas></del> \John/ Chaplen for Parkers	5½¼d.
***** Wydow Chaplen for the Downe	5d.

[*In right margin, in a different hand and ink, bracketed with the previous entry*] 11½d. [*and*] 6d. [*illegible*]

***** Andrewe Chaplen for the tenement Struttes	6d.
for the yearde	2d.
[*Total*]	8d.
***** Richard Chaplen for the tenement late Richard Struttes with the waye	10d.
[*Fol. 55v reversed*] ***** <del><Thomas></del> \Wydow/ Ranson for Barretts	10d.
***** N. Heyward. Nicholas Heywarde or his mother for Brycottes	2s. 5d.
for the Medowe	1s. 6d.
Dominickes Garden	6d.
[*Total*]	4s. 5d.
***** J Dyxson. <del><Jhon></del> Dyxon for Stanesebies	3s. 7d.
for the Teynter Yearde	3d.
[*Total*]	3s. 10d.
***** Ralphe Wrighte for his parte of Brownes	9s. 5d.
***** Jhon Greene for his parte of Parke Feilde	7s. 6d.
***** Jhon Greene for Parkers \for his parte/ <del>4s.</del>	1s. 5d.
\Thomas Waynflet his parte of Parckers	2s. 6d./
***** <del><William></del> \Thomas/ Laman for the Swanne	1s. 5d.
***** William Heywarde for Leyes	2s. 6d.
***** Robert Nightingall for Heywardes	8d.
**** <del><Powlinge></del> \[?]Werde/ for the Clocke Medowe	3d.
***** Plummer for Newlande Hall	2s.
**** <del><Thomas></del> \John/ Havell for a tenement late Olyvers	1½d.
**** Wylliam \Old [?]Wyncolles/ Sherman <del><late></del> \now/ Wydow \Mans/ <del><Cunstables></del>	1½¼d.
***** Thomas Lawdam	6d.
***** Thomas Wayneflett	4d.
***** <del><Wydowe Kynge></del> \Francis Clopton/ for Stansbyes	1½d.
***** Jhon Lorde for Eme Randes	1s. 2d.
***** <del><Stephen></del> \Joone/ Golberde \wydo/ for Cutlers	3d.
Sir Robert Jerny [?*Jermy*] knighte for a parcell of Prestowe Medowe	1s. 4d.
*** Adken for the tenement at the Mylle Gate	1d.
***** Thomas Clarke for Ellighe Crofte in Milden (*Myldynge*)	1s. 6d.
***** William Smythe for Tylers	2d.
***** Jhon Whitwell, clerke, for Byxbies late Robert Byxebies	3s. 8d.

Kettlebaston (*Ketlebarston*)

***** <~~Corder~~> \Gybson/ for Darbies	2s. 9d.
***** Sympson for Hatches	8d.
***** The Towne Medowe	3d.
***** James Chaplen for Whites	2s. 6d.
the same for Leyes	3d.
[*Total*]	2s. 9d.
***** Roger Cabbowe for Rusches	4d.
***** Robert Branson for Cabboes	10d.
of T. Wynnyf for Barretts	2s. 4d.
of Mihell Flegge for Crowes	3d.

[*in right margin, bracketed against the preceding two entries*] deteyned

Hitcham (*Hytcham*)

**** Mr George Waldegrave gentleman for Blockes	½d.
the same for Sheire Feilde	6d.
***** Nicholas Springe gentleman for Loose Hall ~~11s.~~ \	9s. 8d./
***** Thomas Rusche for his parcell	1s. 6d.
***** Thomas Bantofte for Illig\h/e Close	5s. 4d.
\Furthermore, Barrard. John Heyward for parcell of Loosehall	1s. 4d./

Rental 6. (24 June 1583)[119]

[*Fol. 2r*] *Monks Eleigh* (*Illyghe monacorum*). this halfe yeres rentall made and renewed the 24 daye of June and in the 25 yere of the reygne of our sovereyne ladye Quene Elisabethe etc. [*1583*].

Thalmes [*The Alms*] Tenement. Firstly, Wylliam Adkyn holdethe by copye one tenement called the Almes Howse with a garden ther to adjoyninge lyenge by Melcrofte Gate, abutting upon the demaynes of this manor called Melcrofte towerdes the sowthe and upon the Towne Streate towerdes the northe and rent for the half year,

1d. 1d.

Priors. Symon Blomfylde holdethe frelye one mesuage called Priors with serten londe, medow, \wood/ and pastor therto apperteynynge containing by estimation in oll 90 acres abutting <~~abutt²~~> upon Stackewoode Streate towardes the este, in parte etc. and upon the londe late Sir Wylliam Sprynges now in the tenure of John Mendham, gentleman in parte, of the londe of Margarett Danyell wydow in parte, of the londe of Thomas Hobart in parte, and of the londe parsell of Brownes now in the tenure of the sayd Symon in parte towerdes the weste and upon the londe of Ralfe Wryght late Roger Martens gentleman called Brownes towardes the sowthe, and upon the queen's hyghewaye ledynge from Stackewoode towardes Swyngledon in

---

[119] U15/15/17, fols 2r–21r. One of a number of rentals, court minutes and memoranda, re-copied or draft, in a paper book of various court records 1544–90 (in poor condition). It was made by Robert Ryce, bailiff of the manor (see p. 221, footnote 100; p. 222, footnote 104). Throughout, there are annotations that were clearly added later to prepare the new rental of 1599 (Rental 7): the ink is different from the main body of the current rental and despite some of the marginal annotations being in a fine italic hand (chiefly annotations to tenement names) the same annotator writes in a mixture of italic and secretary hands elsewhere. Throughout the rental, there are circles, crosses and dashes that indicate some kind of checking off of entries, the purpose of which is now obscure but may relate to rents paid. These have not been transcribed here.

parte, upon Newlondehall in parte, and upon the londe of Robert Cutler gentleman in parte, towardes the northe and rent, 15s. 6d. 15s. 7d.

Parsell Priors. The same lyckewyse holdethe frelye one other erable close as parsell of Priors with a grove containing [*fol. 2v*] conteynynge [*repeated*] 8 acres by estimation, abutting upon the waye called the Lye Lane towardes the sowthe, and upon Priors Grene towardes the weste and rent, 1s. 6d. 1s. 6d.

Croxsalles. The same lyckewyse holdethe frelye one other pease [*piece*] of londe called Croxsalles, parsell of Sprynges containing by estimation 5 acres abutting upon the Quenes hyghewaye ledynge from Stackewoode towardes Monks Eleigh (*Monckesillye*) towardes the northe, and upon the lordes wood called Manneye Woode towardes ye sowthe, 1s. 7d. 1s. 7d.

Parsell croxsalles. The same Symonde lyckewyse holdethe frelye one other parsell of londe and parsell of the sayd Croxsalles containing by estimation 5 acres, abutting upon the queen's hyghewaye ledynge from Milden (*Myldinge*) to Swyngledon Grene towardes the weste and upon the londe of James Hobart gentleman towardes the este, 1s. 7d. 1s. 7d.

Parsell off Brownes. The same lyckewyse holdethe frelye serten londe, medow and pastor containing by estimation 20 acres late Roger Marten gentleman, and beyinge parsell of Brownes, abutting upon the fyrste sayd londes called Priors now beynge the londe of the sayd Symon towardes the este, and upon the grove of Thomas Hobart in parte and upon ye londe of Thomas Appleton gentleman in parte towerdes the weste and rent, 1s. 7d. 1s. 7d.

Parsell off Brownes. The same Symonde lyckewyse holdethe frelye serten londe, <medow> and pastor beynge lyckewyse latelye parsell of Brownes containing by estimation 20 acres, abutting upon the fyrste sayd parsell of Priors londe now the londe of the sayd Symond, towardes the weste, and upon the londe of John Stephens towardes the este and rent for the half year, 1s. 6½d. 1s. 6½d.

Corboldes. The same lyckewyse holdethe frelye his mancion howse, with the appertynances by estimation, 1 acre and a half, called [*fol. 3r*] by the names of Gaytes Woodes and Paddockehall, late Corboldes adjoynynge to the river by Gedford Brydge towardes the sowthe, and upon the queen's hyghewaye ledynge from Bildeston (*Byldeston*) towardes Lavenham towardes the northe, which sayd sundrye parselles ben owghte of memorye to devyde. Be it remembered, ther is also one ortecharde or pondyarde containing by estimation 1 roode and is parsell of thes premysses, and abutts upon the lordes ryver towardes the northe, and adjoynethe unto the sayd Gedforde Brydge and rent, 1s. 1d. 1s. 1d.

Chaplens Medow /the other peece lyeth nexte the myll dam conteyneth 3 acres\ The same Symon holdeth frelye 5 acres by estimation of medow late Robert Chaplens, by Coboldes Myll, abutting upon the ryver towardes the sowthe est, and upon the Quenes hyghewaye ledynge from \Chelsworth (*Chelsworthe*) Brydge/ Bildeston (*Byldeston*) to Lavenham towardes the northe, 3s. 3s.

Porters. The same Symon holdethe frelye one mesuage called Porters otherwise Sprynges with 18 acres by estimation of londe in 2 partes, wherof the howse and one of the sayd partes abutt upon the ryver of the lorde towardes the northe, and upon ye queen's hyghewaye ledynge from Gedforde Brydge to Hadleigh (*Hadleye*) towardes the sowthe, and the other fylde abutt[*s*] upon the queen's hyghewaye ledynge from Gedforde Brydge to Boyton Hall towerdes the este, and upon the londe now Thomas Sterne in parte, and of Stephen Hobart in parte towardes the weste, and rent togider, 3s. 10d. 3s. 10d.

Stertops. The same Symon holdethe frelye one mesuage called Stertops, with a yarde containing by estimation 3 roodes, abutting upon the Ryver of the lordes towardes the sowthe, and upon the Towne streate towardes the northe,   3d. 3d.

Abbotes /Cawdam:\ The same holdethe frelye one mesuage \called/ the Clyckett \now decayed/ otherwise Abbottes late Alexanders abuttynge upon the Ryver of the lord towardes the sowthe, and upon the Towne streate towardes the northe and rent,
2s. 6d. 2s. 6d.

/it contains by estimation 1 acre bysydes almoste a roode or 20 pole solde by S: which S for 3 pepper carnells in a year and 4d. rente to be paid to the r[?].\

[Fol. 3v] The Bull /Northefielde:\ The same Symon holdeth by copye of corte roll one tenement called the Bull with the appertynances abut[ing] upon the Chyrches-treate towardes the weste, and upon the howse and garden of Thomas Laman towardes the sowthe este, and upon ye londe of ye lordes of this manor towardes the northe and rent,   1s. ½d. 1s. ½d.

Boores /Thomas Rafe, inquire. Cornys\ The same Symon holdethe by copye of corte roll 2 tenementes with thappurtynances called Boores, and Barawayes beynge now occupyed togider, and abutting upon the Cherchestreate towardes the este, and upon the londe of the lordes called Byfolde towardes the northeweste, and upon the queen's hyghewaye ledynge from Bildeston (*Byldeston*) to Lavenham towardes the sowthe and rent,   10d. 10d.

Kemps. /John Chaplen the mynister had this and solde it to <Mr Soe> S. Blom-filde\ John Chaplen holdeth frelye one mesuage called Kemps at Stackewoode with 3 sundrye parselles of grownde containing by estimation 7 acres abutting upon Stackewoode streate towards the weste, and upon the londe of James Hobart called Cattes Crofte towardes the este and rent,   2s. 2d. 2s. 2d. \inquire/

V. [*sic*] Hobartes.[120] /Katheren Chap' [*Chaplen*] wydowe\ The same holdethe frelye one mesuage called Wylliam Hobartes at Swyngledon with serten londes, medow and paster lyenge in 2 partes containing by estimation 16 acres which mesuage with 4 acres of the forsayd grondes [*grounds*] abutt upon Swyngledon Grene towardes the weste, and upon the londe of Thomas Nutt in parte, and upon the londe of Robert Cutler \gentleman/ in parte towardes the este, the reste of the forsayd londe by estimation 12 acres medow and pastor called Dulles lyethe in \4/ severall parselles adjoynenge with a severall waye therto belongynge, 3s. 7d. 3s. 7d.

Parckers. \Stephen Chaplen the younger (*Junior*)/ The same John Chaplen holdethe by copye one tenement called Parckers, with a yarde containing 1 roode and a half abutting upon the towne streat towardes the sowthe, and upon the demaynes of the manor beynge the hall yarde towardes the northe,   5½¼d. 5½¼d.
/Snape hathe now parcel herof.\

/Robert Snape holdeth by coppy one peece of grownde containing by estimation 3 poole in lengthe and 2 pole in breadthe with a poore howse newly thereon erected parcell sometyme of the tenemente called Parkers, abuttinge upon the towne streete towardes the sowthe and the demeanes of the mannor beinge the hall yarde towardes the northe and renteth   1d.[121]\

---

[120] Probably intended to be the tenement known as William Hobarts, which Katheryn Chaplyn held in 1599 (Rental 7). There was another tenement called Walter Hobart's, which appears to have been sub-divided, discussed in more detail in Rental 7.

[121] This inserted paragraph relating to Parckers is virtually identical to the entry for this tenement in the 1599 rental, the handwriting and spelling also being very similar, evidence that the annotations to this 1583 rental were made in preparation for that of 1599.

[*Fol. 4r*] Boyton Hall /Josuah Warde, Symon Blomfilde 60 acres, Mr Saltner\ Dame Elysabeth Rytche holdeth frely her manor called Boyton Hall with dyvers londes, medows and pastors containing by estimation 7 score [*140*] acres abutting upon the lordes woode called Manneye Woode in parte towards the sowthe and upon the londe called Fosters towardes the northe, and upon a close called Kemps in parte, and upon the Quenes hyghewaye ledyinge from Gedforde Brydge to Stackewood in parte towardes the weste and upon the waye ledynge from Monks Eleigh (*Monckesillyghe*) to Hadleigh (*Hadleye*) towardes the easte,   13s. 4d. 13s. 4d.

Pyggescrofte. The same Ladye Rytche holdethe frelye one close called Pygges crofte \now Reyners/ containing by estimation 10 acres abutting upon the hyghewaye ledynge from Gedforde Brydge to Stackewoode, towerdes the easte and upon the londe called Fosters towardes the weste,   2s. 1½d. 2s. 1½d.

The Tufte. The same ladye holdethe frelye one pease of londe under Manneye Woode called the Tufte containing by estimation 4 acres and abutting upon the sayd Mannie Woode towardes the sowthe, and upon the londes of Boyton Hall towardes the northe   7d. 7d.

Coboldes Myll. Robert Chaplen holdeth frelye the water myll called Coboldes Myll with 3 acres of pastor by estimation abutting upon the river towardes the sowthe, and upon the Quenes hyghewaye ledynge from Lavenham to Bildeston (*Byldeston*) towardes the northe, and 3 acres by estimation of londe and medo abutting upon the sayd river and mell dam towardes the northe, and upon the queen's hyghe waye ledynge from Gedforde Brydge to Hadleigh (*Hadleye*) towardes the sowthe, and upon the londe late Sir Wylliam Sprynges knyghte called Porters towardes the weste and rent   2s. 2s.

[*Fol. 4v*] Mell Medow /Blomfielde hathe this. Inquire\ The same Robert holdeth frelye 3 acres of medow by estimation abuttynge upon the ryver towardes the sowthe and upon Turners garden in parte, and the medow of Symon Blomfylde late parsell of the same medow in parte towardes the northe and rent   2s. 2s.

Melfylde. The same Robert holdethe frelye Melfylde containing by estimation 16 acres abutting upon the queen's hyghewaye ledynge from Lavenham to Bildeston (*Byldeston*) towerdes the sowthe, and upon the londe parsell of Hyglens towardes the northe, and upon a lytell medow late Sir Wylliam Sprynges knyght towardes the este, and upon the londe parsell of the sayd Hyglens towardes the weste,   3s. 3s.

Walsehams Medow. The same holdethe frelye one longe medow containing by estimation 3 roodes, abutting upon the river called Walsehams towerdes the este and upon the forsesayd Melfyld <medow> towardes the weste,   1s. 1s.

Turnors. The same Robert holdethe frelye one ortechard or garden called Turnors containing by estimation 1 acre abutting upon the sayd hygewaye ledynge from Lavenham to Bildeston (*Byldeston*) towardes the northe, and upon the abovesayd 3 acres of medow called Mell Medow towardes the sowthe and rent,   1s. 1d. 1s. 1d.

Harpe Downe /Robert Offoode\ Kateren Chaplen wydow holdethe frelye one crofte of erable londe in manner of a harpe containing by estimation 2 acres and a half called the Downe and abutting upon the bonde londe of this manor in the tenure of Steven Hobart called Alendownefylde towards the sowthe and upon the queen's hyghewaye called Fen streat towardes the northe, and rent, 5d.   5d.

Struttes /Barthelmew Marchante. Sr. <~~Hye~~>¹²²\ Andrew Chaplen holdeth by copye one tenement late Struttes with a garden therto apperteynynge, abutting upon the bonde londe of this manor in the tenure of John Whyttell clerke, towardes the sowth, and upon the towne streate towardes the northe, and the sayd tenement rent for the half year, 6d., and the sayd garden, 2d., total 8d. 8d.

[*Fol. 5r*] Rychard Strutes /<~~J. Cutler.~~> John Offwoode\ Rychard Chaplen holdethe by copye one tenement late Rychard Struttes with a serten waye and with a gardayne to the same adjoynynge abutting upon the bonde londe of this manor in the tenure of John Whyttell, clerke, towardes the sowth, and upon the Towne streat towardes the northe, and rent, 10d. 10d.

Thorps. John Clopton gentleman holdethe frelye his mancyon howse called Thorps, with dyvers londes, medos and pastors therto adjoynynge, that is, 1 pytell and one erable close called Gatcrofte, containing 8 acres, 3 pytelles therto adjoynynge called Dedmans Layes, with a lytell grov\e/ on the este syde on the same fylde, and another lytell grove on the weste syde of the same fylde next Langeleye Woode containing 9 acres, one medow called Lytell Valeye containing 3 roodes, and 2 fyldes called Langeleye Fyldes, adjoynynge to Langeleye Woode containing 10 acres in total, 28 [*sic*] acres and rent \10s. 4d./ <~~2s. 6d.~~> 10s. 4d.

Benstedes. The same John also holdethe frelye Benstedes Yardes containing 1 acre, 3 pytelles called Benstedes Croftes containing 8 acres, one other erable close called Waterforow, adjoynynge to the forsayd pytelles containing 8 acres, and one headelonde medow called the Bygg Valeye containing 3 acres, in total, 20 acres, 2s. 6d. 2s. 6d.

Lytle Tyle Pettes. The same John holdeth frelye one lytell erable pytell called Lytell Tylepettes adjoynynge to the forsayd Langeleye Fyldes towards the sowthe, and upon the londe of Sir Robert Jermen, knyght, called Gret Tylepettes towards the northe containing 1 acre by estimation, 4d. 4d.

Hyghfylde. \F.C.¹²³/ The same John Clopton holdethe by copye one erable fylde called Lytell Hyghefylde containing by estimation 15 acres, and abutting upon the queen's hyghewaye ledynge from <~~ledynge~~> Lavenham to Kettlebaston (*Ketle-baston*) towardes the northe, and upon the londe¹²⁴ medo of the sayd John called the Valeye Medow towardes the sowthe, 2s. 6d. 2s. 6d.

[*Fol. 5v*] Gaweslond otherwise Stubbey /John Parker. F.C.\ The same John Clopton holdethe by copye and as he saythe dowtethe whether the same be fre or copye, one erable fylde called Gaweslond otherwise Stubbeyefylde containing by estimation 5 acres, and abutting upon the sayd Hyghefylde towards the este and upon the lond of the sayd John called Langeleyes towards the weste and rent, 1s. 1s.

Stansebyes /John Parker\ Francis Clopton gentleman holdeth frelye one tenement called Stansebyes, with a garden of londe therto apperteynynge containing by estimation 1 roode, and abutting upon the grene called Monks Eleigh Tye (*Monckeselye Tye*) towardes the sowthe, and upon the londe of John Clopton gentleman called Benstedes yards towardes the weste, and upon the hyghewaye called Tye lane towardes the este and rent, 1½d. 1½d.

---

¹²² The crossed-out name may be William Hye, clerk, referred to in Rental 7 (1599) as a tenant of other properties, but not this one. The 'Sr.' could refer to the custom of giving clergy the honorific title of 'Sir'.

¹²³ Possibly Francis Clopton.

¹²⁴ Should this be 'longe'?

Topschops. Rychard Clementes holdethe frelye one tenement latelye decayed, and now newlye re-edyfyed \beeinge a smythes forge/ called Topschops near Gedforde Brydge, abuttynge upon the queen's hyghewaye rownde abowght and rent, 2d.   2d.

Clocke Medow. The towne of Monks Eleigh (*Monckeselye*) holdethe frelye one close of pastor called the Clockemedow containing by estimation 1 acre and a half abutting upon the Wagarde Brydge towardes the sowthe, and upon Oxpastour towardes the north, and upon the queen's hyghe waye \on/ bothe the other sydes, 3d.   3d.

Wyncolles. Robert Cutler, merchant, and one of the portemen of the towne of Ipswich, do [ac]knowledge to holde frelye, all that his mesuage or tenement called Wyncolles lyenge upon Swyngledon Hyll with all the londes medows and pastors to the same belongynge containing by estimation 50 acres, wherof [*fol. 6r*] the mooste parte abutts upon the common waye leadynge from Swyngledon to Stackewoode towardes the weste, and upon the londe of James Hobart gentleman called Dulles towerdes the easte, one erable fylde therof called the Downefylde containing by estimation <10 acres> 11 acres abutting upon the rent of Thomas Nutt in parte, and upon the Downe Pytell in parte in the tenure of the sayd Thomas Nutt towardes the north, and upon a serten severall waye ledynge to Lytell Dulles and Webbescrofte towardes the sowthe, and one medow containing 2 acres and a half by estimation, lyenge by the foote cawseye [*causeway*] ledynge from Swyngledon towardes the lordes myll, and also 3 severall parselles of medow called the Hopps containing by estimation 1 acre 1 roode, abuttynge all upon the river of the lord towardes the northe, all which sumtyme wer Rychard Le[e] esquire, and latelye Sir Wylliam Sprynges knight and rent, 7s.   7s.

Bowers. The same Robert Cutler lyckewyse holdethe frelye dyvers parsells of londe, medow and pastor called Bowers, or Bowersgrove, containing by estima-tion 7 score [*140*] acres, wherof one fylde is called Blenfylde, abutting upon the sayd comon waye ledynge from Swyngledon to Stackewood towardes the easte and dyvers medows and pastors of bothe sydes of the river of the lorde runnynge from Brent Eleigh (*Brentillye*) \to/ Scyppscrosse Brydge, and also one close erable called Pyrlynge Hyll containing by estimation 5 acres, abutting upon the queen's hyge waye, ledynge from Monks Eleigh (*Monckesillyghe*) to Brent Eleigh (*Brentil-lyghe*) towardes the sowthe, and upon the londe of Nycolas Hobart gentleman called Balonde towardes the northe, all which were sumtyme [*of*] the sayd Robert Le[e] and latelye Sir Wylliam Sprynge, knyghte, 14s. 3½d.   14s. 3½d.

[*Fol. 6v*] Fens. More the sayd Robert holdethe frelye one tenement called Fens in Swyngledon with all the medows, londes and pastors to the same appertey-nynge containing by estimation 22 acres, wherof the greteste parte abuts upon the ryver of the lorde towardes the northe, and upon Swyngledon Grene, in parte, and serten tenements ther in parte, towerdes the sowthe, and one pease of erable londe containing by estimation 5 acres now called Fordes Clioose abutting upon the londe of the said Robert Cutler towardes the sowthe, and upon the queen's hyghewaye ledynge from Swyngledon to Little Waldingfield (*Lytell Waldyngefylde*) towardes the northe, latelye Sir Wylliam Sprynges, knight, before that Ceselye Fastalfe, before that Agnes Tymperle[y], and fyrste John Porter, 4s. 4d.   4s. 4d.

Ty Gate Yarde. The same Robert Cutler lyckewyse holdethe frelye one parsell of one garden late of the sayd Robert Le[e], and lastelye the sayd Sir Wylliam Springes knight, lyenge at Monks Eleigh (*Monckesillye*) Tye Gate, abutting upon the tenement of Francis Clopton gentleman, called Stansebyes towardes the weste, and upon the queen's hyghewaye ledynge from Monks Eleigh (*Monckesillyghe*) Tye to Preston towards the este, and rent, 2d.　　　　　　　　　　　　　　　　　2d.

Thalmes [*The Almes*] Tenement. Edward Doyle gentleman holdethe by copye 4 tenements in Cherche Streat Row adjoynynge, abutting upon the same Cherche Streate towardes the easte, and upon the demaynes of this maner called Byfolde towardes the northeweste, 2s. 6½d. Let it be remembered that the 2 uppermooste of thes tenements ben the almes almes [*sic*] ho[*u*]ses by the gyfte of Thomas Hobart, gentleman, deseased [*deceased*].　　　　　　　　　　　　　　　　　　　2s. 6½d.

Stansebyes /Brighte\ John Dyxson holdethe by copye one mesuage called Stansebyes wythe serten pondeyardes therto adjoynynge and apperteynynge, with a me-[*fol. 7r*] medow [*sic*] adjoynynge to the sayd yarde containing by estimation to geder 3 acres, the sayd medow abutting upon the ryver of the lord towardes the sowthe, and the sayd mesuage <up> upon the towne streat towardes the northe, 3s. 7d.

　　　　　　　　　　　　　　　　　　　　　　　　　　　　　　　　　3s. 7d.

Teynter Yard /Brighte\ The same John Dyxson lyckewyse holdethe bye copye one pease of pastor called the Teynter Yarde abutting upon the sayd towne streate towardes the sowthe and upon the demaynes of this manor towardes the northe containing by estimation 1 roode and a half, 3d.　　　　　　　　　3d.

Illyghe Crofte /John Daniel.\ Margaret Danyell wydow holdethe frelye one parsell of pastor beynge now a buschye pastor called Illyghe Crofte containing by estimation 4 acres and abutting upon the londe of the sayd Mistress Danyell towardes the weste, and upon the londe of Symon Blomfylde towardes the east, and northe, and sowthe syde upon the londe of the sayd Symon, 1s. 6d.　　　1s. 6d.

Cutlers /Rafe, gentleman\ Joone Golbert wydow holdethe by copye for terme of her lyffe one tenement called Cutlers, with a garden, abutting upon the towne streate towardes the sowthe and upon the bonde garden of Thomas Laman the younger, parsell of the Swan towardes the northe and rent, 3d.　　　　　　　　3d.

Parckers. Robert Goodale holdethe frelye one tenement or cotage called Parckers Tenement with a garden and ortecharde therto apperteynynge containing by estimation 3 roodes, and abutting upon the queen's hyghewaye ledynge from the Tye towardes the chyrche towardes the northe and upon the londe now Thomas Waynflett, late parsell of Parkers, towardes the sowthe and rent, 2d.　　　　　2d.

[*Fol. 7v*] Parkers /William Hobberd, College[125]\ John Grene holdethe frelye as yet in the ryght of his mother one mesuage bylded called Parckers, with the gardens, and one pytell therto adjoynynge containing by estimation 1 acre and a half abutting upon the queen's hyghewaye ledynge from Monks Eleigh (*Monckesillye*) Tye towardes the chyrche ther towardes the northe, and the fylde of now Thomas Waynflett and of late perteynynge to the sayd mesuage called Kyngescrofte towardes the sowthe and rent, 1s. 6d.　　　　　　　　　　　　　　　1s. 6d.

Parckefylde. John Grene of *Chelseforde*[126] holdethe bye copye one fylde called Parckefylde, now devyded ynto 2 partes containing by estimation 12 acres abutting up upon the bonde londe of the manor of Beaumonds (*Bemondes*) in Lindsey (*Lenseye*) in the tenure of Stephen Hobart in parte, and upon the londe of Boyton Hall in parte called Dedacar towardes the weste, and upon the Quenes hyghewaye ledynge from Monks Eleigh (*Monckes Illye*) to Hadleigh (*Hadleye*) towardes the easte, with one medow called Parckefylde Medow containing 1 acre and 3 roodes

---

125 Listed in Rental 7 (1599) as 'Parkers Colledge': see there for the reason for the name change.
126 Probably an error for nearby Chelsworth, although it could alternatively be Chillesford near Orford.

by estimation, and abutting upon the ryver towardes the northe and upon the laste sayd hyghewaye towerdes the sowthe and rent, 7s. 6d.   7s. 6d.

Fosters. Stephen Hobart holdethe frelye all that his mancion howse called Fosters with all the londes therto apperteynynge, and containing by estimation 5 fvye score [*100*] acres, lyenge and for the mooste parte adjoynynge unto his sayd mancion howse and rent, £1 5s. 8d.   £1 5s. 8d.

Byrches. The same Stephen holdethe frelye one mesuage called Byrches with the appertynances, containing by estimation half an acre abutting upon Monks Eleigh (*Monckesillyge*) streat towardes the sowthe, and upon the bonde londe of this maner called Caves Crofte towardes the northe, 4d.   4d.

[*Fol. 8r*] Pond Medo. The same Stephen Hobart holdethe bye copye one medow called Ponde Medow containing by estimation 3 acres abutting upon the ryver of the lordes towerdes the northe and upon the londe of Fosters towardes the sowthe, 1s.   1s.

Alendowne. The same Stephen holdethe by copye a fyld called Alen Downe containing by estimation 18 acres abutting upon the hyghewaye ledynge from Gedforde Brydge to Swyngledon towardes the northe and upon the londe parcelles of Fosters towardes the sowthe and rent, 3s. 6d.   3s. 6d.

Parckefylde. The same Stephen holdethe by copye a parsell of Parckefylde containing by estimation 5 acres, abutting upon great Parckefylde towardes the sowthe, and upon the bonde londe of the manour of Beaumonds (*Bemondes*) in Lindsey in the tenure of the same Stephen called the Grendle or Slade towardes the weste, 2s. 6d.   2s. 6d.

Vynsentes. The same Stephen holdethe by copye one mesuage called Vynsentes with a pytell of londe containing by estimation 2 acres abutting upon the towne streate towardes the sowthe, and upon the demaynes of the manor called Burton towardes the northe, 1s. 6d.   1s. 6d.

Cavescrofte. The same Stephen holdethe by copye Caves Crofte containing by estimation 4 acres abutting upon Byrches aforsayd towardes the sowthe and upon \the londe/ of <James Hobart gentleman> \John Coppyn in right of his wife, wydd[*ow*] Alce/ called Parsonage Crofte towerdes the northe and rent, 2s.   2s.

Mondams /Alyce Hoberde. John Coppin in right of his wife\ James Hobart holdethe frelye his mancions howse called Mondams with the yarde and a lytell crofte containing by estimation 5 acres abutting upon the towne streate towerdes the sowthe, and upon the londe called Hyglens now Robert Monyng gentleman towardes the northe, 5d.   5d.

[*Fol. 8v*] W. Burtons /Alyce Hoberd, Coppin in right of his wife\ The same James holdethe frelye 2 peces of londe <with> \some tymes/ a grove called Parsonage Crofte otherwise Wynter Burtons containing by estimation 15 acres abutting upon the queen's hyghewaye ledynge from Monks Eleigh (*Monckesillye*) to Preston towardes the este and upon the demaynes of this maner called the Ballyffes Grove towards the weste and rent, 11d.   11d.

Webbes /S. Hobberd\ The same James holdethe frelye one pease of londe called Webbes Crofte containing by estimation 8 acres abutting upon the lond \late/ of John Chaplen called Dulles Medow towardes the sowthe and upon the bonde londe of this maner called Alendowne in the tenure of Stephen Hobart towardes the northe, 1s. 5½d.   1s. 5½d.

Walter Hobartes. \Coe/ /this is devyded, John Chaplen John Whittell[127]\ The same James holdeth frelye his mesuage called Walter Hobartes at Stackewoode with dyvers parsells of londe, medow and pastor containing by estimation 50 acres adjoynynge to geder [*together*] and abutting upon the queen's hyghe waye rownde abowght on everye syde and rent for the half year. £1 2s. 7½d.   £1 2s. 7½d.

Humblebanckes /Coe [*repeated*]\ The same holdethe frelye one pease of londe called Humblebanckes lynge at Stackewoode, containing by estimation 3 roodes, abutting upon the queen's hyghewaye ledynge to Leye Lane, towardes the sowthe and upon the londe of the sayd James called Walter Hobartes towardes the northe, 2d.   2d.

Aylewardes /Coe\ The same holdethe frelye one mesuage called Aylewerdes with serten londe, medow and pastor containing by estimation 25 acres, abutting upon the Hoames, by Mannye Wood towardes the este, and upon the grene ledynge to <abutt² hereon> Leye Lane towardes the weste, 3s. 10½d.   3s. 10½d.

Burtons /Coe\ The same holdethe frelye one mesuage called Burtons with his appertynances, unserten wher it lyethe but supposed by the owner to lye at Stackewood and rent for the half year, 1s. 7d.   1s. 7d.[128]

[*Fol. 9r*] Brondes /Alyce Hoberd, Coppin in right of wife\ The same James Hobart holdethe by copye of corte roll one tenement called Brondes with his appertynances containing by estimation 1 rood and abutting upon the queen's hyghewaye called Fens Streate Lane towardes the sowthe, and upon the medow of the same James called Gauge Brydge Medow towardes the northe, 2s.   2s.

Let it be remembered that the tenant supposethe that here he paye to motche rente.

Huntes /Wm Hobert\ Nycolas Hobart gentleman holdethe frelye one mesuage \ called/ Huntes, with a crofte of londe, and one pytell of pastor containing by estimation in all 3 acres, abutting upon the grene commonly called Monks Eleigh (*Monckes Illye*) Tye towardes the northe, and upon the londe of the same Nycolas Hobart called Ravens Crofte towardes the sowthe, 9d.   9d.

Pages /Wm. Hobert\ The same Nycolas holdethe frelye serten londe, medow and pastor called Pages, wherof one fylde is called Pages Fylde, containing 18 acres, one yarde called Pages Yarde, containing 1 acre, one pytell of pastor adjoynynge called Pages Pytell containing half an acre, one pastor called to Longepastour containing 4 acres, one erable fylde called Balonde containing 12 acres, one erable close called Ravens Crofte with a parsell of medow which to geder [*together*] contain 18 acres, one medow called Scypps Crosse Medow containing 1 acre and a half, one medow called Gryges Medow containing 2 acres and one other lytell medow called Lytell Prestow Medow containing 1 acre and a half, in total, 58 acres to geder [*together*], all which rent for the half year, 11s.   11s.

Let it be remembered that the lordes macke clayme to Ravens Crofte at this daye, to be holden of them by copye, wherupon the same is now seased.

[*Fol. 9v*] Jentlemans /Hughe Woode\ John Heywarde holdethe by copye one cottage with a garden containing 1 roode late Jentlemans, and abutting upon the bonde londe of this manour in the tenure of Thomas Lawdam towardes the northe, and upon the towne streate towardes the sowthe, more he lyckewyse holdethe by

---

[127] See the note at the end of the entry for Catts Crofte and Reades in this rental, below.

[128] Inserted above this total is *frustra*, 'in vain, to no effect'. Presumably a bad debt that could not be collected, perhaps because no-one knew where it lay.

copye one pease of an ortecharde containing half a roode, abutting upon Burches in the tenure of Stephen Hobart, towardes the northe and upon the fre tenement of the sayd <John Heywarde> \Andrew Hoberte/ sumtyme John Tylors towardes the sowthe, 6d.   6d.

Alyngtons Asleses /Andrewe Hubberd\ More the sayd John Heywarde holdethe frelye 2 tenements wherof one is called Alyngtons, the other Asleses, adjoynynge to geder, and abutting upon the londe called Byrches in the tenure of Stephen Hobart in parte, and upon the sayd bond londe parsell of the ortecharde in the tenure of <the sayde John> \Hughe Woode/ in parte towardes the northe, and upon the towne streat towardes the sowthe, and rent for the half year, that is, for Alyngtons, 9½d. and for Asleses 4d., in total, 1s. 1½d.   1s. 1½d.

Leyes /Andrewe Hubberde\ Wylliam Heywarde holdethe by copye one tenement with his appertynances, and one medow and hopyarde therto belongynge containing by estimation 2 acres called Leyes abutting upon the towne streate ryght agaynste the chyrche streate or grene towardes the northe, and upon the ryver of the lorde towardes the sowthe, 2s. 6d.   2s. 6d.

Bryckottes /<Thomas> /George\ Hubberd.\ Nycolas Heyward holdethe by copye of cort roll, one tenement, garden and ortshard [*orchard*] called Bryckottes containing by estimation half an acre, and abutting upon the Quenes hyghewaye ledynge from Lavenham to Bildeston (*Byldeston*) towardes the northe and upon the demaynes of this manour called Melcrofte \sometyme Hall Crofte/ Pastor towardes the sowthe, 2s. 5d.   2s. 5d.

[*Fol. 10r*] Dominickes Medo /George Hubberd\ The same Nycolas holdethe by copye one medow called Domynyckes Medo containing by estimation 2 acres and abutting upon the laste sayd hyghewaye towardes the northe, and upon the common ryver of the lorde nere the mell dam towardes the sowthe, 1s. 6d.   1s. 6d.

Dominickes Garden /George Hubberd\ The same Nycolas holdethe by copye one garden or medow, beynge an ortecharde, containing by estimation half an acre, called Dominickes Garden, and abutting upon the sayd hyghewaye towardes the northe, and upon the common ryver of the lordes towardes the sowthe and rent, 6d.   6d.

Olyvers /Pettican\ John Havell \Ellice Pettican/ holdethe by copye one tenement in Stackewoode Streate called Olyvers with an ortecharde therto adjoynynge containing half an acre by estimation, abutting upon the londe \sometyme/ of James Hobart gentleman \and now of Thomas Coe/ called Reyners towards the weste and upon Stackewood Streate towardes the easte, 1½d.   1½d.
Let it be remembered that a lytell pease of this ortecharde is supposed by Havell to be freholde.

Lytell Prestow. Sir Roberd Jermyn knyght holdethe bye copye one pease of medow containing by estimation half an acre lyenge in the corner of the medow of the sayd Sir Robert called Lordes Medow apperteynynge to his manor of Brent Eleigh Hall (*Brentillye Hall*), the sayd half an acre of medow abutting upon the ryver ther towardes the sowthe, and upon the sayd medow called Lordes Medow in parte, and upon the medow of the sayd Sir Robert called the Checker Medow in parte towardes the northe, 1s. 4d.   1s. 4d.

Swan /<William Heywarde> John Heyward \5d./ John Sheder 1s.\ Thomas Laman the yonger holdethe by copye one tenement called the Swan, with a garden and ortecharde ther to apperteynynge containing by estimation half an acre, the sayd tenement abutting upon the Chyrchestreat towards the weste, upon the towne streat

237

towards the sowthe, and the sayd ortchard and yardes upon the Bull in parte, and
upon the hall berne [*barn*] in parte towards the northe, 1s. 5d.   1s. 5d.

[*Fol. 10v*] Em' Randes /M \Robert/ Lenton\ John Lorde holdethe frelye (yn the
ryght of his wyffe) one mesuage called Em' Randes, with a croft of londe and
pastour therto adjoinynge, containing by estimation 3 acres and abutting upon the
queen's hyghewaye ledynge from Monks Eleigh (*Monckes Illye*) Tye, to Monks
Eleigh (*Monckes Illye*) Chyrche, towards the northe, and upon the londe of Nycolas
Hobart called Huntes towards the sowtheweste, 1s. 2d.   1s. 2d.

 Gerdyns /Nicholas Yonge\ Thomas Lawdam holdethe by copye one tenement
late Gardyns with half an acre of londe, abutting upon the Townestreate towards the
sowthe, and upon the bonde londe of this maner called Barrettes Ortchard in parte,
and upon Caves Crofte in parte towardes the northe, 6d.   6d.

 Hyglens. Robert Monnynge gentleman holdethe frelye one mesuage called
Hyglens, sumtyme Lawrence Martens with an ortcharde and garden therto
adjoynynge containing by estimation 2 acres with one erable fylde called Lytell
Hyglens containing by estimation 8 acres, adjoynynge nere unto the sayd mesuage,
one other erable cloose now called Dufhowse Cloose containing by estimation 7
acres, and adjoynynge on the sowthe syde of the sayd mesuage, 2 severall medows
containing eche of them 2 acres, abutting upon ~~was~~ Walshams Ryver, 2 parselles of
corse medow or pastour adjoynynge called The Slades, adjoynynge upon the sayd
~~was~~ Walsehams Ryver containing to geder 3 acres by estimation, one other erable
cloose called Bull Cloose containing by estimation 9 acres, one other erable cloose
now lately devyded ynto 2 partes called the Melfylds containing to geder 24 acres,
one other erable cloose called Longecrofte containing by estimation 10 acres, with
a medo to the ende of the sayd crofte adjoynynge containing by estimation 2 acres,
in total in all to gether by estimation ~~60 acres~~ 70 acres, 10s. 2½d. 10s. 2½d.
yt is supposed by the owner that this rent scholde not be so motche by 1s., everye
half year.

 [*Fol. 11r*] Davys. The same Robert lyckewyse holdethe frelye one pastor or
grove, with an erable close therto adjoynynge containing in the hoole [*whole*] 10
acres by estimation called Davys Pastor abutting upon the demaynes of this manor
called the Hyghe Fyldes towardes the northe, and upon the sayd demaynes called
Illyghe Fylde towardes the sowthe and rent for the half year, 6d.   6d.

 Hogfen. The same Robert lyckewyse holdethe frelye one medow called Hogfen
containing 2 acres abutting upon parsell of the sayd Hyglens called Dufhowse Close
towardes the weste, and upon one of the forsayd 2 medows, apperteynynge to the
sayd Hyglens towardes the easte, and rent, ½d.   ½d.

 Marye Crofte. James Man holdethe frelye one pese of erable londe called Marye
Crofte containing by estimation 1 acre and a half, abutting upon the hyghewaye
leadynge from Monks Eleigh (*Monckesillye*) to Boxford (*Boxforde*), towardes the
easte, and upon the londe of Robert Cutler gentleman towardes the weste and rent,
6½d.   6½d.

 Davys Yard /Blomefilde\ Robert Man of Kersey (*Kerseye*) holdethe frelye
one pytell of pastor called Davyes Yarde containing 1 roode and a half, abutting
upon Stackewoodestreat towardes the weste, and upon the londe of James Hobart
gentleman in 3 partes, that is, sowthe, este, and northe and rent, 1½¼d. 1½¼d.

 Schelynges /<~~Robert~~> Yonge\ John Nut holdethe by copye one tenement called
Schelynges with his appertynances abutting upon the bonde londe of this maner
called Vynsentes towardes the northe, and upon the towne streate towerdes the
sowthe, and rent for the half year, 6½¼d.   6½¼d.

[*Fol. 11v*] Heywardes /Edward Coocke the alehowse sometimes\ Robert Nytyngall holdethe by copye one tenement called Heywardes with a garden and ortcharde containing by estimation 1 roode, abutting upon the lordes demeanes called Byfolde towardes the weste and upon the Chyrche Streate towardes the easte, 8d.   8d.

Barrettes /Cuthbert Atkynson\ Maryan \Thomas/ Ranson wydow holdethe by copye, for terme of her lyffe one tenement called Barrettes with an orthechard and garden therto apperteynynge containing by estimation 1 acre abutting upon the towne streate towardes the sowthe, and upon the bonde londe ~~lond~~ of this maner called Vynsentes towards the northe, 10d.   10d.

Mascalles. Robert Ryce now ballye [*bailiff*] of this maner and macker [*maker*] herof, holdethe frelye, one mesuage sumtyme bylded called Mascalles, with thes parselles of londe medow and pastor and woode, here folowynge and therto belongynge, that is one fylde called Mascalles Fylde containing by estimation 9 acres, Mascalles Grove 4 acres, Mascalles Yardes 1 acre and a half, Mascalles Pytell 2 acres, Northefylde 7 acres, Thysleye Fylde <~~5 acres~~> 12 acres, Wagarde Fylde 5 acres, Stubbeyefylde 5 acres, Sondpett Fylde 2 acres and a half, and 2 peces, at one place adjoynynge, in Lytell Woodefylde 2 acres, in total to geder by estimation 50 acres and rent for the half year, 15s.   15s.

Chaplens. The same Robert lyckewyse holdethe frelye one capytall mesuage called Chaplens with the yarde and one pastor therto adjoynynge containing by estimation 6 acres, and one erable fylde called Homayne Crofte containing by estimation 7 acres, and abutting upon the Tye Grene, towardes the weste, and upon the londe of the sayd Robert called Reyners in parte, and upon Mascalles in parte towardes the easte and rent, 4s. 2d.   4s. 2d.

[*Fol. 12r*] Reyners. The same Robert lyckewyse holdethe one tenement called Reyners now used for a backehowse [*bakehouse*], adjoynynge to the forsayd tenement called Chaplens, with one pease of pastor called The Backehowse Yarde containing 1 acre and a half and one fylde and close of pastor called Reyners Pytelles containing by estimation 6 acres and abutting upon the forsayd grene called Monks Eleigh (*Monckes Illye*) Tye, towardes the weste, and upon the londe latelye Rysbyes, now Henrye Scynners gentleman towardes the este, 1s. 1d.   1s. 1d.

Scypps Medow. The same Robert Ryce holdethe by copye one medow called Scypps Crosse Medo containing by estimation 4 acres, sumtyme devyded in 2 partes, lyenge upon the queen's hyghe waye ledynge from Brent Eleigh (*Brentillye*) to Monks Eleigh (*Monckillyghe*) towardes the northe, and upon the common ryver towardes the sowthe, and rent for the half year, 4s.   4s.

Woodfylde. The same Robert lyckewyse holdethe by copye one pease of erable londe in Lytlewoodfylde containing by estimation 5 acres, and abutting upon the fre londe of the sayd Robert called Mascalles Harpe in parte, and upon the hye waye in parte towardes the weste, and upon the demayns of the lorde called Hyglens Fylde towardes the este, and upon the demaynes of the lordes called Great Woode Fylde towardes the sowthe, and upon the fre londe of the sayd Robert called Mascalles Ponde Pece in the same fylde towardes the northe, 1s. 3d.   1s. 3d.

Bendysches /John Daye\ Thomas Sterne holdethe frelye one capyetall mesuage called Bendysches with one pese of pastor adjoynynge containing by estimation 3 acres abutting upon the towne streate towardes the northe and upon the severall runynge water of the sayd Thomas in parte, and upon the lordes ryver in parte towardes the sowthe, 1s. 3d.   1s. 3d.

[*Fol. 12v*] B. Medow[129] /<del>Bendyshes</del>> John Daye\ The same Thomas lykewyse holdeth frelye one medow containing by estimation 2 acres belongynge to the sayd mesuage, and abutting upon the sayd severall runnynge water of the sayd Thomas, towardes the northe, and upon the lordes ryver, now almoste londed[130] and decayed, towerdes the sowthe este, 1s.   1s.

Petytes /Blomfild\ The same Thomas lyckwyse holdethe frelye one close of pastor called Petytes containing by estimation 6 acres, abutting upon the waye ledynge from Gedforde Brydge to Boyton Hall towardes the weste, and upon the bonde londe of Anthonye Cage, gentleman, perteyninge to his maner of Beaumonds (*Bemondes*) in Lindsey (*Lenseye*), and now in the tenure of Symon Blomfylde, towardes the este, 7d.   7d.

Dowtys /John Daye\ The same Thomas also holdeth frelye one cloose of erable londe called Dowghtyes containing by estimation 6 acres, and abutting upon the hyghe waye ledynge from Gedforde Brydge to Boyton Hall, towardes the weste, and upon the londe of Symon Blomfylde in parte, and upon the londe of Boyton Hall called Dedacre in parte towardes ye este, 8d.   8d.

Goddon /John Daye\ The same Thomas also holdethe frelye one other severall close of erable londe called Goddon Lond containing by estimation 5 acres, abutting upon the londe of Symon Blomfylde late Sir Wylliam Sprynges, parsell of Porters, towardes the easte, and upon the londe of Stephen Hobart, apperteynynge to Fosters, towerdes the weste, and rent, 6d.   6d.

Ruschebroockes /L[*uke*] Melton, John Darby\ Henrye Scynner gentleman holdethe frelye one mesuage sumtyme Ruschebroockes, with an ortechard and a garden therto adjoynynge containing by estimation half an acre, abutting upon the bonde londe of this maner in the tenure of the sayd Henrye called Cowfen towardes the sowthe, and upon the townestreat towardes the northe, 1½d.   1½d.

[*Fol. 13r*] Cowfen /L[*uke*] Melton\ The same Henrye holdethe by copye one medow called Cowfen containing by estimation 4 acres abutting upon the ryver of the lorde towardes the sowthe, and upon the sayd mesuage of the said Henry called Ruschebroockes towerdes the northe, and rent for the half year, 2s. 6d.   2s. 6d.

Teynter Yard /L[*uke*] Melton\ The same Henrye holdethe by copye one pese of <del>past</del> pastor late parsell of Burtons sumtyme Schopps now called the Teynter Yarde containing 1 acre by estimation, abutting upon the bonde londe of this maner in the tenure of Stephen Hobart called Vynsentes towardes the northe, and upon the towne streate towardes the sowthe, 6d.   6d.

Scottes Crofte /L[*uke*] M[*elton*]\ The same Henrye holdethe frelye one pease of erable londe containing by estimation 5 acres called Scottes Crofte, abutting upon the londe of Boyton Hall called Dedacre towardes the este, and upon the queen's hyghewaye ledynge from Monks Eleigh (*Monckesillyghe*) to Boyton Hall towerdes the weste and rent, 1s. 3¼d.   1s. 3¼d.

Cages /<del>H. Skynner</del>> L[*uke*] M[*elton*]\ The same \H[*enry*]/ holdethe by copye 1 mesuage with a curtylage late parsell of Lurcockes sumtyme Cages, abutting upon the bonde londe of this maner in the tenure of the sayd Henrye called Cowfen towardes the sowthe, and upon the townestreat towardes the northe, 2d.   2d.

---

[129] Bendishes Meadowe in Rental 7 (1599).

[130] 'Londed and decayed' presumably refers to the river rather than the meadow, and possibly implies that the river had become silted up, or made into land at this location (see *OED*, 'land' v.). The River Brett as it flows through Monks Eleigh has had various and braided channels over the centuries, as a comparison between maps of various periods shows.

240

Galettes Medows /L[*uke*] M[*elton*]\ The same Henrye Scynner holdethe lyck-ewyse by copye serten ruscheye medows called Galettes Medows containing by estimation 5 acres, abutting upon the ryver of the lordes towardes the sowthe, and upon the queen's hyghewaye ledynge from Monks Eleigh (*Monckesillye*) to Lavenham towardes the northe, and rent for the half year, as my boockes do schew, 2s. 3d.   2s. 3d.
Let it be remembered that Mr Scynner dothe saye that he owght not to paye so motche rent.

[*Fol. 13v left blank*] [*Fol. 14r*] Kyngescroft /George Gardiner\ The same Henrye holdethe bye copye one pease of erable londe late Rysbyes called Kyngescrofte containing by estimation 8 acres abutting upon the demaynes of this maner called Sextens Fylde towardes the sowthe, and upon the londe of Nycolas Hobart gentleman called Ravenscrofte or Ravens Crofte Medow towardes the northe and rent, 2s. 1d.
                                                                                        2s. 1d.

Manor. The same Henrye holdethe frelye one capytall mesuage wheryn he now dwellethe called the manor, with 30 acres by estimation of londe and pastor there-unto adjoynynge, and abutting upon the londe of Robert Ryce called Thysleye-fylde in parte, and Mascalles in parte towardes the northe, and upon the quenes hyghewaye ledynge from Monks Eleigh (*Monckesilly*) Tye to the churche towardes the sowth, 7s. 10d.   7s. 10d.

Kynges or Hobardes. The same Henrye holdethe frelye one decayed mesuage of olde called Kynges and after Hobardes, lyenge at Monks Eleigh (*Monckesil-lyghe*) Tye Gate with 50 acres by estimation of londe, medow and pastor therto adjoynynge, abutting upon the bonde londe of this maner in the tenure of John Clopton gentleman in parte called Lytell Hyghefylde, and upon the demaynes of this maner called Hyghefylde in parte, and upon the bonde londe of this maner called Susselles in parte, towardes the northe, and upon the grene called Monks Eleigh (*Monckesillye*) Tye in parte, and upon the londe of Robert Ryce in parte towardes the sowthe, 12s. 10d.   12s. 10d.

Scherps /Queere [*enquire*] heere for Goodwyn who hathe bowghte the howse\ The same Henrye holdethe frelye one mesuage called of olde Scherps lyenge at Monks Eleigh (*Monckesillye Tye*), wheryn one Nycolas Hasell dothe now dwell, with 9 acres by estimation of londe and pastor therto [*fol. 14v*] belongynge lyenge in 2 partes, abutting upon the londe of Nycolas Hobart gentleman called Huntes, in parte, and upon his londe called Pages in parte, towardes the sowthe weste, and upon the queen's hyghewaye ledynge from Brent Eleigh (*Brentillye*), to Monks Eleigh (*Monckesillye*) Tye towardes the northe, 2s. 6d.   2s. 6d.

Indrebyes. More the sayd Henrye holdethe frelye one tenement called Indrebyes with 11 acres <of> by estimation of londe, medow and pastor therto belongynge, abutting upon the londe of Nycolas Hobart gentleman called Ravens Crofte towardes the weste, and upon the Quenes hyghewaye ledynge from the Manour Hyll at the Three Waye Lete to Scypscrosse Brydge, and to Swyngledon towardes the easte and rent, 3s.   3s.

Susselles. The same Henrye Scynner holdethe by copye one cloose of pastor with a medow therto apperteynynge called Susselles containing by estimation 20 acres and abutting upon the queen's hyghewaye ledynge from Monks Eleigh (*Monckes Illye*) Tye towardes Preston towardes the weste and upon the londe of the sayd Henrye towardes the este and rent for the half year, 10s. Let it be remembered that this is no parte of the ballyes collectyon or charge.

Tylors /Wylliam Hye\ Wylliam Smythe holdethe frelye one tenement called Tylors lyenge in the towne streat with a garden and ortecharde containing by estimation 1 roode and a half, abutting upon the lordes ryver towardes the sowthe, and upon the sayd towne streat towardes the northe, 2d.   2d.

Ruschebroockes. Wylliam Teylor, clerke, holdethe bye copye one tenement with a garden called Ruschebroockes late Chaplens, and abutting upon the towne streate towardes the northe, and upon the \bonde/ medo of this maner in the tenure of Henrye Skynner gentleman towardes the sowthe and rent, 7d.   7d.

[*Fol. 15r*] Newlond Hall. John Tornor the yonger holdethe frelye one mesuage called Newlonde Hall with 3 acres of londe by estimation and abutting upon the queen's hyghewaye ledynge from Stackewoode towardes Milden Grene, towardes the northe este and upon the londe of Robert Cutler gentleman towardes the weste and upon the londe of Symon Blomfylde towardes the sowthe, 2s.   2s.

Byxbyes. John Whyttell, clerke, holdethe by copye one tenement late Byxbyes with a garden and a medow therto adjoynynge containing by estimation 2 acres and a half and abutting upon Monks Eleigh (*Monckesillye*) Streate towardes the northe and upon the ryver of the lordes towardes the sowthe, 3s. 8d.   3s. 8d.

Chyrcheyard Tenement. The sayde Mr Whyttell holdethe by copye one tenement with a garden and a serten footewaye therto adjoynynge abutting upon the chercheyarde towardes the weste, and upon Burton Crofte, beynge the demaynes of this maner, towardes the este, 2d.   2d.

Parckers, otherwise Sedges /Bayly\ Thomas Waynflett otherwise Pyper holdethe frelye serten londe medow and pastor, lately belongynge to the mesuage now in the occupation <called> of \the colledge/ <John Grene>, called Parckers, containing by estimation 9 acres and a half which londes dothe abutt upon the queen's hyghewaye ledynge from Monks Eleigh (*Monckesillye*) Tye to the chyrche in parte and upon the tenement of Robert Goodalle in parte called Lytell Parckers towardes the northe, and upon the londe of Henrye Scynner gentleman called Great Indrebyes towardes the sowthe, 2s. 6d.   2s. 6d.

Bullers /Bayly\ The sayd Thomas holdethe frelye his now mancion howse called Bullers, with 2 acres and a half of pastor by estimation to the same apperteynynge and abutting upon Monks Eleigh (*Monckes Illye*) Streate towardes the sowthe, and upon the londe of <James> \Alyce/ Hobard <gentleman> \widdow/ called the Tyes towardes the northe, 4d.   4d.

[*Fol. 15v*] Brownes. Ralfe Wryghte holdethe frelye his now mancion howse with an ortecharde and a gardeyne therto adjoynynge, with serten other parselles of londe and pastor lyckewyse adjoynynge, that is, one pese callede Hamondes, Backehowsefylde, 3 pytelles nowe severall called the Mersche, and 2 pytelles called Warens, containing by estimation togider 18 acres all which abutt upon the queen's hyghewaye ledynge from Lindsey (*Lenseye*) to Milden towardes the sowthe, and upon the londe of Symon Blomfylde towardes the northe, 3s. <6d.> 5d.   3s. 5d.

Moore the same Ralfe holdethe lyckwyse frelye 4 parselles of londe, medow and pastor, wherof the fyrste is called Walnut Cloose, the nexte Great Blackes, the 3rd Mydle Backes [*sic*], the laste called Lytell Blackes, with a grove to the same adjoynynge called Blackes Grove, all which adjoynethe togider, and abut upon the queen's hyghewaye ledynge from Lindsey (*Lenseye*) to Milden (*Myldynge*) towardes the northe este, and upon the londe apperteynynge to the maner of Castelens in parte, upon Broockewoode in parte, and upon Chappell Londe apperteynynge to Lindsey in parte, towardes the sowthe and containing togider by estimation 37 acres and rent, 6s.   6s.

242

[*Fol. 16r*] Ketlebaston

Darbyes. Edwarde Wyttypoll \George Waldgrave/ gentleman holdethe frelye one mesuage called Darbyes with the yarde and serten erable londes \in 3 fieldes/ therto adjoynynge containing by estimation 18 \20/ acres abutting upon the londes of the sayd Edwarde Wyttypoll towardes the sowthe este and upon the Chyrche Grene in Kettlebaston (*Ketlebarston*) towardes the northe weste and rent for the half year, 2s. 9d.   2s. 9d.

Let it be remembered for the quantyte of acres I specke but by supposall.[131]

Whyghtes. James Chaplen holdethe frelye one tenement decayed called Whyghtes with one pastor containing by estimation 1 acre and 2 erable closes containing togider 6 acres, and one medow adjoynynge at the nether end of the sayd 2 closes containing 1 acre and a half, all which parselles adjoynethe and abutt upon the demaynes of Kettlebaston (*Ketlebarston*) Hall called Blowfylde towardes the northe weste, and upon the queen's hyghewaye ledynge from Stowmarket (*Stow Marckett*) to Lavenham towerdes the sowthe este, and rent, 2s. 9d.   2s. 9d.

Wages /John Parker\ Roger Cabow holdethe frelye one mesuage wheryn he now dwellethe called Wages, with a yarde and a pytell therto adjoynynge containing by estimation 1 acre and a roode abutting upon the londe of Edwarde Wyttypoll gentleman towardes the sowthe este, and upon the queen's hyghewaye ledynge from Stowmarket (*Stowmarckett*) to Sudbury (*Sudburye*) towardes the northe weste, 2½d.
                                                                                                              2½d.

\G. Waldgrave, Wyttipoll./ More, he holdethe frelye one tenement decayed and yet a berne [*barn*] remaynynge ther, with a yarde therto adjoynynge containing 1 roode by estimation, abutting upon the bonde londe of Kettlebaston (*Ketlebarston*) Hall in the tenure of the said Roger towardes the sowthe este, and upon the forsayd hyghewaye towardes the northe weste and rent, 1½d.   1½d.

[*Fol. 16v*] Towne Medo. The towne of Kettlebaston (*Ketlebaston*) holdethe frelye one parsell of medow called the Towne Medow containing by estimation 1 acre, abutting upon the demaynes of Kettlebaston (*Ketlebarston*) Hall in the tenure of <Thomas Scherman> \Robert Wryghte/ towardes the sowthe este, and upon the glybe [*glebe*] londe of Kettlebaston (*Ketlebarston*) parsonage in parte, and the londe of Edwarde Wyttypoll gentleman in parte, and the londe of the maner of Kettlebaston (*Ketleberston*) in parte towardes the northe, and rent, 3d.   3d.

Cabows /Daniel Kempster the younger (*junior*) now 99 [*sic*]\ Robert Branston holdethe frelye one mesuage with one acre and a half of londe adjoynynge, the nether ende therof abutting upon Whyghtes Medo towardes the northe weste, the other hed abutting upon the hyghewaye ledynge from Stowmarket (*Stowmarckett*) to Lavenham towardes the sowthe este, and one longe sponge[132] of pastor containing one acre by estimation abutting upon the Chyrche Grene towardes the northe, and upon the glybe londe[133] of Kettlebaston (*Ketlebaston*) parsonage towardes the sowthe \Robert Smythe/ And one pytell of erable londe \called Springes Close/[134] containing by estimation 3 acres abutting upon the demaynes of Kettlebaston (*Ketlebarston*) in the tenure of Thomas Scherman[135] \now of William Apleton, gentleman/ in parte, and upon the londe of Edwarde Wyttypoll gentleman \G. Waldgrave/ in

---

[131] In other words, the compiler, Robert Ryce, has not actually measured this land.

[132] In left margin here is 'Edward Whitipoll, 1½d' and in the right margin, 'G.Waldegrave esquire'.

[133] In left margin here is 'Daniel Kempster, 3d.'

[134] In left margin here is 'Robert Smythe, 4d.'

[135] In left margin here is 'D. Kembolde, 1½d.'

parte towardes the sowthe, and upon the sayd pease of glybe towardes the northe, and \L. Kembolde/ also one acre of erable londe lyenge in a pytell called Lytell Hedge, abutting upon the bonde londe of Kettlebaston (*Ketlebarston*) Hall in the tenour of Robert <Branston> \R. Wryghte/ lyenge in the same fylde towerdes the sowthe, and upon the demaynes of the maner of Kettlebaston (*Ketlebarston*) Hall called Lytell Hedge, towardes the northe weste, the nether ende, and also the upper ende, abutting upon the bonde londe of Kettlebaston (*Ketleberston*) Hall in the tenure of Robert <Symson> \Wrighte/ towardes the este and weste, that is, the nether ende towardes the este, and the upper ende towardes the weste, and rent for the half year, <8d.> 10d.   10d.

[*Fol. 17r*] Blockes. George Waldgrave gentleman holdethe frelye one pease of pastor sumtymes bylded called \Stebbinges synce/ Blockes and now called Mertens, abutting upon the bonde londe of Kettlebaston (*Ketlebarston*) Hall in the tenure of Roger Cabow, towardes the sowthe este, and upon the queen's hyghewaye ledynge from Stowmarket (*Stowmarckett*) towardes Lavenham towardes the northe west, ½d.   ½d.

Scherefyld. More ye same George holdethe frelye one pease of erable londe lyenge in Scherefylde containing by estimation 4 acres abutting upon the queen's hyghewaye ledynge from Stowmarket (*Stow Marckett*) to Kettlebaston (*Ketlebarston*) towards the sowthe este and upon the londe of the same George, and parte of the sayde Scherefylde towerdes the northe weste, 6d.   6d.

Hatches. Robert Symson, holdethe frelye 5 sundrye peces of londe and pastour, wherof one lyethe in a fylde called the Five Acre Fylde, on the sowtheweste syde on the same fylde, lycke a harpe, containing 1 acre, 2 peces lyenge <called> \in/ the Eight Acre Fylde, almooste in the mydes [*midst*] of the same fylde, 1 of them containing 1 acre, the other, half a roode, which 2 peces dothe so lye as theye joyne at one corner, one other pece lyenge in Sedcotfylde, containing 1 acre, which pece joynethe and lyethe under the Five Acre Hedge, the last pese of pastor containing 1 acre half a rood by estimation, abutting upon Kedielles Crofte towardes the sowthe, and upon the bonde londe of the sayd Robert Symson, called the Hoome Pytelles towerdes the northe, and rent for the half year, 8d.   8d.

Hitcham (*Hytcham*)

Loose Hall. Nycolas Sprynge gentleman holdethe frelye all that his capytall mesuage called Loose Hall with 13 score [*260*] acres \by estimation/ of londe, medow and pastour therunto adjoynynge, abutting upon the lond of John Grymwad latelye parsell of the sayd Loose Hall [*fol. 17v*] Loosehall Medow bowght from the same towerdes the sowthe este and upon the quenes wood called Oxlewoode in parte, and upon the londe of this maner called Illyefyldes in parte, upon Coockes Londe in parte, Thomas Rusche in parte, and upon the londes of John Lever and Thomas Lever in parte towardes the northeweste and rent, 9s. 8d.   9s. 8d.

Loose Hall. John Grymwade holdethe frelye serten parselles of londe, medow and pastor, that is, one fylde called Eastefylde, one medow called Broocke Medow, one medow called Walow Medow, one fylde called [*?*]ocks \Cockes/ Londe, one pease of Great Goldewoodefylde, one pease of londe called Monckes Londe, and one other pease called Puntockes, containing in the hoole [*whole*] by estimation 80 acres adjoynynge all to gider, latelye bowght owght of Loose Hall of ye forsayd Nycolas Sprynge gentleman, abutting upon the londes of the sayd Nycolas Sprynge gentleman as apperteynenge to Loose Hall towardes the weste and upon the londe of John Awoode in parte, upon the queen's hyghewaye ledynge from Wattisham

(*Watsham*) to Hitcham (*Hytcham*) in parte, and upon the londe of Robert Wryght in parte towardes the este, 1s. 4d.   1s. 4d.

Illyewood Pastor. Thomas Bantofte holdethe for terme of yeres, one close now devyded into 3 parselles called Illye Woode Pastor containing by estimation 20 acres abutting upon the queen's wood called Oxleyewood towardes the northe, and upon the londe of Nycolas Sprynge gentleman, apperteynyng to Loosehall towardes the sowthe weste, for the half year, 5s. 4d.   5s. 4d.

[*Fol. 18r*] Rusches. Thomas Rusche holdethe frelye one mesuage with an orchard and serten other londes therto apperteynynge containing by estimation [*blank*] acres, this londe as yett can not be sertenly knowen and therfor can not be butteled,[136] but rent, 1s. 6d.   1s. 6d.

[*Blank space left on centre third of page*]

Barrettes. Thomas Wynyffe, and now G. Walgrave gentleman holdethe frelye serten londes called <Barrettes> Berrardes containing by estimation 5 score [*100*] acres sumtyme Sir Thomas Jernens lyenge in Kettlebaston (*Ketlebarston*) and as it apperethe scholde rent to this maner everye half year 2s. 4d. and more of Myhell Flegg for Crowes for the half year, 4d., bothe which ben deceyed, and as it semethe hathe ben ever sence the londes wer solde from Sir Thomas Jermen to Mr Walgrave, and Wynyffe, which is as it is supposed 27 yere past, \2s. 7d./

[*below, in another hand*] for the half year, £17 9s. 4½d.

for the year, £34 18s. 9d.

[*Fol. 18v*] This half year rentall of Monks Eleigh (*Monckesillyghe*) rentes is renewed this 24 of June in the 25 yere of the reygne of our sovereyne ladye Quene Elisabethe [*1583*].[137]

A.

Wylliam Adken for the Almes Tenement by Melcroft	1d.

B.

Symon Blomfylde for Priors	15s. 7d.
for parsell of Priors	1s. 6d.
for Croxsalles	1s. 7d.
for parsell of Croxsalles	1s. 7d.
for parcel of Brownes	1s. 7d.
for parsell of Brownes	1s. 6½d.
for Corboldes	1s. 1d.
for Chaplens Medow	3s.
for Porters	3s. 10d.
for Stertops	3d.
for Abbottes	2s. 6d.
for the Bull	1s. ½d.
the same for \Petytes/ <Boores>	10d. 7d.
[*Sub-total for Blomfylde*]	3s. <11d.> 8d.

---

[136] That is, the abuttals (bordering lands) are unknown because the exact location of this land cannot be ascertained.

[137] This section of the rental has almost certainly been compiled as a rent collection list, with annotations in the left margin similar to, but more ambiguous to, those in Rental 5 (1580/81). Robert Ryce's symbols here cannot be clearly interpreted, so the transcription of the number of half-years' rents for each tenant has not been attempted.

C

John Chaplen for Kemps[138]	2s. 2d.
Wylliam Hobartes	3s. 7d.
for Parckers	5½¼d.
Boyton Holl	13s. 4d.
Pygges crofte	2s. 1½d.
The Tufte	7d.
[*Sub-total for John Chaplen*]	£1 2s. 3½d.
Robert Chaplen for Coboldes Myll	2s.
Mell Medow	2s.
Mell Fylde	3s.
Walsehams Medow	1s.
Turnors	1s. 1d.
[*Sub-total for Robert Chaplen*]	9s. 3½d.
[*Fol. 19r*] Catren Chaplen wydow for the Harp Downe	5d.
Andrew Chaplen for Struttes	8d.
Rycharde Chaplen for Rychard Struttes	10d.
John Clopton gentleman for Thorps[139]	10s. 4d.
for Benstedes	2s. 6d.
for Lytle Tylepettes	4d.
Hyghefylde[140]	2s. 6d.
Gawes Londe	1s.
[*Sub-total for Clopton*]	16s.8d.
Francis Clopton gentleman for Stansebyes	1½d.
Rycharde Clementes for Topschops	2d.
Clocke Medow	3d.
Robert Cutler gentleman for Wyncolles	7d.
for Bowers	14s. 3½d.
for Fens	4s. <3d.> 4d.
for parsell of the Tyegate Yarde	2d.
[*Sub-total for Cutler*]	£1 5s.9½d.

D

Edward Doyle gentleman for Thalmes [*The Alms*] Tenementes	2s. 6½d.
John Dyxson for Stansebyes	3s. 7d.
more for the Teyenter Yarde	3d.
<Mistress M Danyell> \John Danyell <esquire>/ wydow for Illyghe Crofte[141]	
	1s. 6d.

G [*sic*]

Joone Golderd for Cutlers	3d.
Robert Goodale for Parckers	2d.
John Grene for Parckers	1s. 5d. 1s. 4d.

---

[138] In the left margin next to this entry is written '17s. 6d.'

[139] In the right margin, bracketed against this and the following two entries, is written '16s. 8d. of [?Mr] Clopton to please them both'.

[140] In the left margin, bracketed against this entry and the one below, is written 'Rec' Myhell 1586 Francis', and in the right margin bracketed against the same two entries, 'Myhell 1586 3s. 6d. rec' of Francis Clopton 1586'.

[141] In the left margin next to this entry is written, 'Margaret', presumably Mistress Danyell's first name.

John Grene of *Chelseforde*[142] for Parckefyld	7s. 6d.
[*Sub-total for page*] [In a different hand and ink]	<u>17s. 2½d.</u>

[*H*] (*E*)

[*Fol. 19v*] Stephen Hobart for Fosters	£1 5s. 8d.
for Byrches	4d.
Ponde Medow	12s.
Alen Downe Fylde	3s. 6d.
parsell of Parckefylde	2s. 6d.
for Vynsentes	1s. 6d.
Caves Crofte	2s.
\more for Webbes Crofte \Wylliam Broocke/	1s. 5½d./
[*Sub-total for Stephen Hobart*]	<£1 16s. 6d.> £1 17s. 11d.
James Hobart gentleman for Mondams	5d.
Winter Burtons	11d.
<del>Webbes Crofte \Wylliam Broocke of Hadleigh (*Hadleye*) G Hoberd/</del>[143]	
	<del>1s. 5½d.</del>
Walter Hobartes	£1 2s. 7½d.
Humblebanckes	2d.
Aylewerdes	3s. 10d.
Burtons[144]	1s. 7d.
Brondes	2s.
[*Sub-total for Hobart*]	£1 11s. 7d.[145]
/thys half year moste be payd backe, becawse of the season\	
Nycolas Hobart gentleman for Huntes	9d.
for Pages	11s. for the half year.
John Heywarde for Jentlemans	6d.
Alyngtons or Stertes	13½d.
[*Sub-total for Heywarde*]	<u>19½d.</u>
Wylliam Heywarde for Leyes[146]	2s. 6d.
\more for the Swan	1s. 5d./
Nycolas Heywarde for Bryckottes	2s. 5d.
Domynyckes Medow	1s. 6d.
Domynyckes Garden	6d.
[*Sub-total for Nycholas Heywarde*]	<u>4s. 5d.</u>
John Havell for Olyvers 1½d.	

J

Sir Robert Jermen Knyghte for Lytell Prestow	1s. 4d.

L

<del>Thomas Laman the younger for the Swan</del>	<del>1s. 5d.</del>
John Lorde for Em Randes	1s. 2d.
Thomas Lawdam for Gardyners	6d.
[*blank*] Lamys for Boores \<4s. 6½d.>/	<11d.> 10d.

---

[142] Probably Chelsworth, less likely, Chillesford.

[143] In the left margin next to this entry is written 'Mr Hobardes parte for the half year <4s. 9d.> 3s. 9d.'

[144] In the left margin next to this entry is written 'Phylpes £1 6s. 10d.'

[145] In the right margin next to this rather scrappy entry, which has numerous crossings out, is written 'Phylyps £1 6s. 10d.'

[146] In the right margin, bracketed against this and the next entry, is written '3s. 11d.'

M

[*Fol. 20r*] Robert Monynge gentleman for Hyglens	10s. 2½d.
Davyes Gronde	6d.
Hogfen	½d.
[*Sub-total for Monynge*]	10s.9d.
James Man for Marye Crofte	6½d.
Robert Man of Kerseye for Davyes Yarde	1½¼d.

N

John Nut for Schelynges	6½¼d.
Robert Nytyngale for Heywardes	8d.

R

Maryan Ranson widow for Barrettes	10d.
[*In a different hand*]	2s. 9d.
Robert Ryce for Mascalles	15s.
Chaplens	4s. 2d.
Reyners	1s. 1d.
Scypps Medow	4s.
Woodefylde	1s. 3d.
[*Sub-total for Ryce*]	£1 5s.6d.

S

<del>Thomas Sterne</del> \John Daye/ for the \<del>the [*illeg.*] of</del>/ of Bendysches[147]	
[*many crossings out*] \	1s. 3d./
The Medow	1s.
<del>Petytes</del> \Goodman Blomfyld/	7d.
Dowtes[148]	8d. Daye
Godden Londe \Daye/	6d. Daye
<del>John Daye parsell of Bendysches	4d.</del> Daye
4s. Daye. 3s.5d.	
<del>Henrye Scynner</del> \Lucke Melton/ gentleman for Ruschebroockes	1½d.
Cow Fen[149]	2s. 6d.
Teynter Yarde	6d.
Scottes Crofte	<del>1s. 3¼d.</del>
Cages	2d.
Galettes Medows	2s. 3d.
Kinges Crofte	2s. 1d.
Hys mancon called the Maner	7s. 10d.
Kinges or Hobart[150]	12s. 10d.
Scherps	2s.6d.
Indrebyes	3s.
[*Sub-total for Scynner/Melton*]	£1 15s. ½¼d.

---

[147] In the right margin, bracketed against this and the following two lines, is written '2s. [*?d*]'. It should be 2s. 10d., but the number of the pennies begins with the Roman numeral 'v' (*ijs. v … d.*) and disappears into the central spine stitching.

[148] In the right margin, bracketed against this and the following two lines, is written '1s. 6d.'

[149] In the right margin, bracketed against this and the following two lines, is written 'Luke Melton, <del>5s. 6d.</del> 6s. 9½d'.

[150] In the right margin next to this entry is written '£1 8s. 3d. Mr Scynner. [*A sum of money crossed through*]. Fyne 5s.'

[*Fol. 20v*] Wylliam Smythe for Tylors 2d.

T

Wylliam Teylor, clerke, for Ruschebroockes 67d.
John Turnour for Newlonde Hall 2s.

W

John Whyttell, clerke, for Byxbyes[151] 3s.8d.
  more for the Cherche Yarde Tenement[152] 2d.
Thomas Waynflett for Parckers 2s. <7d.> 8d.
  more for Bulles 4d.
Ralfe Wryght for Brownes 9s. 6d.
[*In another hand*] 18s.11d.

Kettlebaston (*Ketlebarston*)

Edward Wyttypoll gentleman for Darbys 2s. 9d.
James Chaplen for Whyghtes 2s. 9d.
Roger Cabow for Wages 4d.
Towne Medow 3d.
\<Smythe [*illeg.*] 1½d. 1s. 2d.> Kembold \3d./ 1½d. Smythe \7d./ <[*illeg.*]>/
Robert Branson for Cabows 10d.
George Walgrave gentleman for Blockes ½d.
  more for Scherefylde 6d.
Robert Symson for Hatches 8d.
Kemster hoole [*whole*] yere, 3d.
[*In another hand*] 8s. 1½d.

Hitcham (*Hytcham*)

Nycolas Sprynge gentleman for Loose Hall 9s. 8d.
John Grymwade for parsell of Loose Hall 1s. 4d.
Thomas Bantofte for Illyghewoode Pastor 5s. 4d.
Thomas Rusche 1s. 6d.
[*In another hand*] 17s.10d.

October 1587. Smythe enformeth me that he payethe:
for the half year 4d. – 3 acres
Kemster 3d. – 1 acre and a half.
Deteyned:
Thomas Wynyffe for Barrerdes, 2s. 4d.
Myhell Flegg for Crows, 3d.
Kembold 1½d. – 1 acre.
Mr Wytipoll 1½d. – 1 acre.
[*Added in another hand*]

Sum for the half year £17 6s. 10½¼d.   for the half year £17 10s. 2½d.

Sum for the year £34 13s. 9½d.   for the year £35 0s. 5d.

---

[151] In the right margin next to this entry is written 'W'.
[152] In the right margin next to this entry is written 'not payd 2d.'

[*Fol. 21r*] [*List of tenants, in two columns, as follows:*]

Dam Elysabeth Rytche

Sir Roberte Jermen, knyght

Edward Wyttypoll, gentleman

Robert Cutler, Portman of Ipswich

Thomas Sprynge gentleman

George Walgrave gentleman

Nycolas Hobart gentleman

John Clopton gentleman

Robert Monynge gentleman

Francis Clopton gentleman

Henrye Scynner gentleman

James Hobart gentleman

Edward Doyle gentleman

Sir Wylliam Teylor clerke

Sir John Whyttell clerke

Symon Blomfylde

Stephen Hobart

John Chaplen

Robert Chaplen

James Chaplen

Andrew Chaplen

Rycharde Chaplen

Ralffe Wryghte

Edwarde Coocke

Robert Symson

John Grene of Chelseford[153]

John Grene of Brent Eleigh (*Brentillye*)

John Havell

Thomas Waynflett

Thomas Lawdam

John Lorde

John Dyxson

Wylliam Heywarde

John Heywarde

Nycolas Heywarde

John Nut

Nycolas \Leonardus/ Kembolde

Roger Carbow

Thomas Laman

Robert Powlynge

Wylliam Smythe

Robert Smythe

Joone Golderde wydo

Cateren Chaplen wydo

Robert Goodale

James Man

Leonerde Rusche

John Herte

£1 8d.

£6 14s.

£4 9s. 3½d.

£2 8s. 5d.

£3 1s. 3d.

£17 13s. 5½d.

---

[153] The spelling is Chillesford (near Orford), but Chelsworth, adjacent to Monks Eleigh, is the more likely.

Rental 7. (26 June 1599)[154]

[*p. 1*] Monks Eleigh (*Monkes Elighe*). This halfe yeeres rentall made and renewed att the coorte there howlden this 26th daye of June, 1599. And in the 41st yeere of the reigne of our sovereigne Lady Elizabeth by the grace of god of England, France and Irelande, Queene, defender of the faythe etc.

The Almes tenemente. The overseers of the poore and churchwardens of Monks Eleigh (*Monkes Elighe*) for the tyme beinge doe holde by coppye one cottage lately burned and nowe newly buylte called the Almes Howse, with a garden thereto adjoynynge lyenge by Mellcrofte Gate, late in the tenure of Wylliam Adkyn, abuttinge upon the demaynes of this mannor called Mellcrofte towardes the sowthe and upon the towne streete towardes the northe, And renteth at the halfe yeere   1d.

Clickett Cottage. The inhabitantes and overseers for the poore of Monks Eleigh (*Monkes Elighe*), do holde freelye to them and to there successors, one cottage latelye a shoppe and parcell of the tenement sometyme called the Clickett, with one litle yarde as it is nowe enclosed, lately by them purchased of Wylliam Hye, clarke, and nowe used for an almes howse, all which abutteth upon the messuage late decayed of the sayd Wylliam Hie called the Clickett otherwise Abbottes sometymes Allexanders toward the sowthe and upon the towne streete towardes the northe, and contains by estimacon fower perches and renteth at the halfe yeere.   ¼d.

Clocke Meadowe. The churchwardens of Monks Eleigh (*Monkes Ellighe*) holde freelye one close of pastor called the Clocke Meadowe containing by estimation one acre and a halfe, abutting on the Waggarde Brydge towardes the sowthe and upon Oxepastor towardes the northe, and upon the Queen's highe waye on both the other sydes and renteth at the halfe yeere   3d.

[*p. 2*] A

Barretts: Cuttbert Attkynson holdeth by coppye one tenemente called Barrettes with an ortcharde and garden thereto appertayninge containing by estimation one acre, abuttinge upon the towne streete towardes the sowthe, and upon the bonde londe of this mannor called Vyncentes towardes the northe and renteth at the halfe yeere   10d.

B

Pryors: Symon Blondevylle holdeth freelye one messuage called Pryors, late Springes which certen lande, meadowe and pastor thereto appurteyninge contayninge by estimation in all 90 acres, abutting upon Stackewoode Streete towardes the easte in parte and upon the lande of John Mendham, gentleman, in parte, of the lande of Francis Danyell in parte, of the lande of George Hubberde in parte, and of the lande parcell of Brownes nowe in the tenure of the said Symon in parte towardes the weste And uppon the lande of Ralfe Wrighte sometymes Roger Martyns, gentleman, called Brownes, towardes the sowthe and upon the Queenes Highe waye leadynge from Stackewoode towardes Swyngledon in parte, upon Newelande Hall in parte,

---

[154] CCA-U63/70455/2, former reference CCA-U63/70455/2/53. A paper booklet comprising several gatherings. The first recto page of the booklet contains three doodles of what appear to be designs for quartered circular mazes or labyrinths resembling the turf maze at Wing, Rutland, and elsewhere. At the end of this rental are copies, in the hand of Robert Ryece, of a petition requesting care in the appointment of a new steward and of an agreement about a piece of glebe land in Monks Eleigh, both dated 1611. There are two other copies of this 1599 rental at CCA-U63/70455/3–4.

and upon the lande of Robert Cutler, gentleman, in parte towardes the northe, and renteth at the half yeere   18s. 7d.[155]

Parcell of Pryors: The same Symon lykewyse holdeth freelye one other errable close as parcell of Pryors late Sprynges with a grove contayninge 8 acres by estimation, abuttinge upon the waye called the Lye Lane towardes the sowthe and upon Pryors Grove towardes the weste and renteth at the halfe yeere   18½d.[156]

Croxsalls: The same Symon lykewyse holdeth freelye one other peece of lande called Croxsalls [p. 3] parcell of Sprynges containing by estimation 5 acres abutting upon the Queenes highe waye leadinge from Stackwoode to Monks Eleigh (*Monkes Ellighe*) towardes the northe and upon the Lord's woodde called Mannye Woodde towardes the sowthe and renteth at the halfe yeere   1s. 7d.

Parcell of Croxsalls: The same Symon lykewyse holdeth freelye one other parcell of lande and parcell of the said Croxsalls containing by estimation 5 acres, abutting upon the Queenes highe waye leadinge from Milden (*Myldinge*) to Swyngledon Greene towardes the weste, and upon the lande of Thomas Coe, gentleman, towardes the easte and renteth   1s. 7d. 1s. 7d.

Brownes. The same Symon lykewyse holdeth freelye certen lande, meadowe and pastor lyenge in 2 peeces, called Sadlers and Partibles and containing by estimation 20 acres sometymes Roger Martyns, gentleman, and beinge parcell of Browns abutting upon the firste said landes called Pryors nowe beinge the lande of the said Symon towardes the easte, and upon the grove of George Hubbert in parte and upon the lande of Thomas Appleton, gentleman, in parte towardes the weste and renteth
                                                                                          1s. 7d.

Parcell of Brownes: The same Symon lykewyse holdeth freelye 3 peeces of lande, meadowe and pastor called Wheate Close, the Shrubbe, and Maydes Greene, beynge lykewyse parcell of Brownes, containing by estimation 20 acres, sometymes Roger Martyns, gentleman, abutting upon the fyrste said parcell of Pryors Lande nowe the lande of the said Symon towardes the weste, and upon the lande of John Stephens toward the easteth [*sic*] and renteth   1s. 3½d.

Corboldes. The same Symon lykewyse holdeth freelye one messuage beinge now his mansion howse with the appurtenances, containing by estimation 1 acre and a half called by the names of Gaytes Whooddes and Paddocke Hall, all late Corboldes adjoyninge to the ryver by Gedforde Brydge [p. 4] towardes the sowthe and the Queen's highe waye leadinge from Chelsworth (*Chelleswoorthe*) to Lavenham towards the northe. Let it be remembered, there is also one ortchyarde or ponde yarde containing by estimation one roode parcell of the premysses abuttinge upon the Lord's ryver towards the northe and adjoinynge to the said Gedforde Brydge, this peece is nowe in the occupation of Stephen Hubbert and so thay rente all together   1s. 1d.

Porters. The same Symon lykewyse holdeth freelye one messuage called Porters otherwise Sprynges with 18 acres of lande by estimation in 2 partes, whereof the howse and one of the said partes abutt upon the Lord's Ryver towardes the northe and upon the Queen's highe waye leadynge from Gedforde Brydge to Hadleigh (*Hadley*) toward the sowthe and the other parte abutt upon the Queen's highe waye leadinge from Gedforde Brydge to Boyton Hall toward the easte and upon the lande

---

[155] Given in Roman numerals, this sum looks as if it were first written as 15s. 7d. (*xvs. vijd.*), but then, in another ink and hand, another '*iii*' has been added after the '*xv.*', making the initial 15s. into 18s.

[156] The ½d. is added in a different hand.

of John Daye in parte and of Stephen Hobert in parte toward the weste and rente togither   3s. 10½d.[157]

Stertopes. The same Symon lykewyse holdeth freelye one tenemente called Stertops with a yarde containing by estimation 3 roodes abutting upon the Lord's ryver towardes the sowthe and upon the towne streete towardes the northe and renteth 3d.

Davyesyarde. The same Symon holdeth freelye one pightell of pastor called Davyes Yarde containing one roode and a halfe, abuttinge upon Stackewoode Streete towardes the weste and upon the lande nowe of Thomas Coe, gentleman, in 3 partes, that is, sowthe, easte and northe and renteth   1½¼d.

Pettyttes. The same Symon lykewyse holdeth freelye one close of pastor called Pettyttes containing by estimation 5 acres abutting upon the highe waye leadinge from Gedforde Brydge to Boyton Hall towardes the weste and upon the bonde lande [p. 5] of Anthony Cage, gentleman, pertaynynge to his mannor of Beaumonds (*Beamondes*) in Lindsey (*Lynsey*), now called Powlinges, towardes the easte and renteth at the half yeere   7d.

Mell Meadow Fyve Acres. The same Symon holdeth freely 5 acres of meadowe by estimation, late Robert Chaplyns parcell of Cobboldes Mylle, abuttynge upon the ryver towardes the sowthe easte and the Queenes highe waye Leadynge from Bildeston (*Byldeson*) to Lavenham towardes the northe and renteth   3s.

Mell Meadow Two Acres. The same Symon holdeth lykewyse freelye one other parcell of meadowe late Robert Chaplyns containing 2 acres 28 poles as it is nowe measured abuttynge upon Turners Yarde in parte and upon parcell of the meadowe belongynge to Cobboldes Mylle towardes the northe and upon the lord's ryver towards the sowthe easte and lyeth betweene the meadowe laste above sayd called Fyve Acres towardes the northe easte and the meadowe goenge to the mell damme towardes the sowthe weaste and renteth   1s. 1d.

Kempes. The same Symon holdeth lykewyse freelye one messuage called Kempes lyenge at Stackewoode, with 3 sondrye parcells of grownde devyded, containing to gyther [*together*] by estimation 7 acres, whereof the one parcell abutteth upon Stackewoode Streete towardes the weste and upon the lande nowe of the said Symon called Cattes Crofte towardes the easte – The seconde peece called the Olde Yarde contains by estimation 1 acre and a half and abutts upon the highe waye leadinge from Stackewoode Streete to Swyngledon Greene towardes the weste and upon Reades towardes the easte and lyeth betweene Ashewoldes towardes the northe and Stackewoode Greene towardes the sowthe – The third peece called Stackewoode Fielde otherwise Kempes [p. 6] contains by estimation 4 acres and abutteth upon the hie waye leadinge from Stackwoode Greene to Gedforde Brydge towardes the northe weste and upon the hie waye leadinge to Mannye Woodde in parte and the Tufte in parte towardes the sowthe and renteth   2s. 2d.

Catts Crofte and Reades: The same Symon holdeth lykewyse freelye 2 peeces of grownde late John Chaplyns, clarke, lyenge devyded, whereof the one peece called Cattes Crofte contains by estimation 3 acres lyenge betwene Mannye Woodde towardes the sowthe easte and upon the landes of the same Symon sometymes Roberte Man in parte, and also the tenement called Kempes in parte towardes the northe weste, one heade abutting upon a lane leadinge from Stackwoode Greene to Manny Woode towardes the sowthe weaste and upon the customary lande of the mannor of Beaumonds (*Beamondes*) in Lindsey towardes the northe easte. –

---

[157] The ½d. is added in a different hand.

The 2 peece called Reades contains by estimation 4 acres lyenge betweene the hie waye leadinge from Gedforde Brydge to Stackwoode Streete towardes the sowthe, and the customarye lande of the mannor of Beaumonds called Ashewalldes on the northe easte, bothe which peeces were sometymes James Hubbertes, gentleman, and supposed parcell of his messuage Burtons and renteth to gyther   1s. 1d.
Let it be remembered that James Hobert, gentleman, after a lease which he made to one Phillippes of his grownde at Stackewoode, solde to olde John Chaplen of those landes 10 acres and unto John Whittell, clarke, of the same landes 7 acres, ratynge Chaplen to paye to the lorde for rente by the yeere for the same 3s. 4d. and ratinge Mr Whittell for his landes 2s. 4d., these landes were supposed to be parcell of Walter Hobertes which was mystaken for that Walter Hubbertes is a messuage styll entyer consystinge of 50 acres undevyded lyenge togither with the Queen's hie waye rownde abowte yt. But [p. 7] by reason the sames [sic] James Hobert had a messuage decayed at Stackewoode called Burtons, which albeit he was uncerten where it dyd lye, yett he dyd assewredly beleeve it dyd lye at Stackewoode, and holdinge this freely dyd paye rente for the same at the halfe yeere, 1s. 7d. Therefore it is probablye supposed, that these 2 parcells supposed solde to Mr Whittell and John Chaplen were parcells of this Burtons synce this John Chaplyn his soonne, clarke, solde of these 10 acres unto Symon Blondevyll 7 acres as Cattes Crofte and Reades payenge therefore at the halfe yeere 1s. 1d., and unto Thomas Coe, gentleman, he solde the other peece beinge a grove and parcell of Brookes containing 3 acres and rentynge for the same at the halfe yeere 7d. Nowe yf these landes be of thes Burtons which dyd rente at the whole yeere but 3s. 2d., And Mr Hubert dyd rate these landes to paye 5s. 8d., there is yett 2s. 6d. to be deducted owte of Walter Hobertes whole yeeres rente which then was £2 5s. 3d. and the halfe yeere £1 2s. 7½d. And so Walter Hobertes rente wylbe yett at the halfe yeere

£1 1s. 4½d.

Abbottes Parke Meadow. The same Symon lykewyse holdeth freelye one lyttle meadowe with a lane that goeth unto yt, parcell of the messuage sometymes called Abbottes late Allexanders and nowe comonly called Parke Meadowe containing 3 roods by estimation lyenge betwene Chelsworth (*Chelswoorthe*) Parke towards the easte and upon the customary meadowe of John Greene of Chelsworth (*Chellesworthe*) called Parke Filde Meadowe towardes the weste and abutting on the Lord's ryver towardes the northe and the Queen's hie waye leadynge from Gedforde Brydge to Hadleigh (*Hadly*) towards the sowthe and renteth   1s. 3d.
Let it be remembered he complayneth that this is to moche rented and hopeth the nexte coorte to be somewhat eased bycawse where the messuage was is more grownde farre and there hathe more benefytte bynne made by pullinge downe and sellinge the howses which were there many and fayer   1s. 3d.
[p. 8] Stansebyes. Alyce Brighte of Bury St Edmunds (*Burye*), wydowe, holdeth by coppye one messuage called Stansebyes with certen ponde yardes thereto adjoinynge and appurtaynynge with a meadowe adjoinynge unto the same yarde containing to gether by estimation 3 acres, the said meadowe abuttes upon the lord's ryver towardes the sowthe and the said messuage upon the towne streete towardes the northe   3s. 7d.
Teinteryarde. The same Alyce lykwyse holdeth by coppye one peece of pastor called the Teynteryarde abutting upon the said towne streete towardes the sowthe and upon the deameanes of this mannor towardes the northe, containing by estimation one roode and a halfe and renteth 3d.

254

C

William Hobbertes. Katheryn Chaplyn wydowe howldeth freelye one messuage called Wylliam Hobertes at Swyngledon with certen landes, meadowe and pastor lyenge in 2 partes containing by estimation 16 acres which messuage, with 4 acres of the aforesaid growndes abutting upon Swyngeldon Greene towardes the weste, and upon the lande of Thomas Nutte in parte, and upon the lande of Robert Cutler, gentleman, in part towardes the easte, and the reste of the foresaid lande by estimation 12 acres meadow and pastor called Dulls lyeth in 4 severall peeces and parcells adjoyninge with a severall waye thereto belonginge and renteth at the halfe yeere
3s. 7d.

Parkers. Stephen Chaplyn holdeth by coppye one tenement called Parkers with a yarde containing one roode by estimation abutting upon the towne streete towardes the sowthe and upon the demeanes of this mannor beynge the hall yarde towardes the northe and renteth   4½¼d.

Coboldes Myll. Roberte Chaplyn holdeth freelye the water myll called Cobboldes Mylle with 3 acres of pastor by estimation, abutting upon the ryver towards the sowthe and upon the Queen's highe waye leadinge [p. 9] from Lavenham to Bildeston (Byldeston) towardes the northe and 3 acres by estimation of lande and meadow abutting upon the said lord's ryver and mell damme towardes the northe and upon the Queen's highe waye leadinge from Gedforde Brydge to Hadleigh (Hadlye) towards the sowthe and upon the lande of Symon Blondevyll called Porters towardes the weste and renteth at the halfe yeere   2s.

Mell Meadow. The same Robert holdeth freelye one other lytle peece of meadowe lyenge betwene Turners Garden on the northe and the meadowe of the said Symon Blondevyll called 2 acres towardes the sowthe containing by estimation one acre and renteth   11d.

Turnors. The same Robert holdeth lykewyse freelye one orchyarde or garden called Turnors sometymes Henry Monynges, containing by estimation one acre, abutting upon the said highe waye leadynge from Lavenham to Bildeston (Byldeston) towardes the northe and upon the laste abovesaid meadow called Mell Meadowe towardes the sowthe and renteth   1s. 1d.

Topshopes. Richard Clementes holdeth freelye one tenement latelye decayed, and nowe newly re-edyfyed beinge Smythes Forge, called Topshoppes neere Gedforde Brydge abutting upon the Queen's highe waye rownde abowte and renteth   2d.

Haywardes. Edwarde Coocke holdeth by coppye one tenement called Haywardes late Robert Nityngales with a garden and ortchyarde containing by estimation one roode used sometymes for an alehowse and abutteth upon the lord's demeanes called Byfolde towardes the weste and upon the Church Streete toward the easte   8d.

Mondames. John Coppyn in righte of his wyfe holdeth freelye there mancion howse called Mondams with the yarde and lytle crofte, containing by estimation 5 acres, abutting upon the towne streete towardes the sowthe and upon the lande called Higlens now Robert Munnynges, gentleman, towardes the northe and renteth
5d.

[p. 10] Winter Burtons. The same John Coppin in righte of his wyfe holdeth freelye 2 peeces of londe sometymes a grove called Parsonage Crofte otherwise Wynter Burtons containing by estimation 15 acres abutting upon the Queen's highe waye leadinge from Monks Eleigh (Monkes Ellighe) to Preston towardes the easte and upon the demaynes of this mannor called the Bayllyves Grove towardes the weste and renteth   11d.

Brondes. The same John Coppyn in his wyves righte holdeth lykewyse freelye by coppie of coorte rowle one tenement called Brondes with his appurtenances containing by estimation one roode and abutting upon the Queen's highe waye called Fennes Streete Lane towardes the sowthe and upon Gange Brydge Meadowe towardes the northe and renteth 2s.
Let it be remembered the tenante supposeth that heere he payeth to moche rente.

Wincolls. Robert Cutler, marchante, and one of the portemen of the towne of Ipswich (*Ipswyche*) dothe acknowledge to holde freelye all that his tenement or messuage called Wyncolls, lyenge upon Swyngeldone Hyll, with all the landes meadowes and pastors to the same belonginge containing by estimation 50 acres whereof the moste parte abutts upon the comon waye leadinge from Swyngledon to Stackewodde towardes the weste and upon the lande of the wydowe Chaplyns called Dulles towards the easte, one erable fielde thereof called the Downe Fielde containing by estimation 11 acres, abutting upon the tenement of Thomas Nutte in parte and upon the Downe Pytell in parte in the tenure of the said Thomas Nutte towardes the northe, and upon a certen severall waye leadynge to Lyttle Dulles and Webbes Crofte towardes the sowthe, and one meadowe containing 2 acres and a half by estimation, lyenge by the foote cawsey [*causeway*] leadynge from Swyngeldon towardes the lord's mylle, and also 3 parcells of meadowe called the Hoppers, containing by estimation one acre [*p. 11*] one roode abuttynge all upon the ryver of the lorde towardes the northe, all which sometymes were Richarde Le[*e*], esquire's and latelye Sir Wylliam Sprynges, knight and renteth 7s.

Bowers. Richard [?]Swinford. The same Robert Cutler lykewyse holdeth freelye, dyvers parcells of lande, meadowe and pastor called Bowers or Bowers Grove containing by estimation 7 score [*140*] acres, whereof one filde called Blenfielde abutts upon the said comon waye leadynge from Swyngledon to Stackewoode towardes the easte and dyvers meadowes and pastures of bothe sydes of the ryver of the lorde runnynge from Brent Eleigh (*Brentellie*) to Scypps Crosse Brydge, and also one erable close called Pyrelynge Hyll containing by estimation 5 acres abutting upon the Queen's hie waye leadinge from Monks Eleigh (*Monkes Ellighe*) to Brent Eleigh (*Brentellighe*) towardes the sowthe and upon the lande of Wylliam Hubberte gentleman called Ballonde towardes the northe, all which were sometymes the said Richard Le[*e*], esquire's and latelye Sir Wylliam Sprynges, knyght and renteth 14s. 3½d.

Fennes. More the same Robert Cuttler holdeth lykewyse freelye, one tenement called Fennes in Swyngeldon with all the meadowes, landes and pasturs to the same appurtayninge, containing by estimation 22 acres, whereof the greatest parte abutteth upon the ryver of the lord towardes the northe and upon Swyngeldon Greene in parte and certen tenements there in parte towardes the sowthe, and one peece of errable lande containing by estimation 5 acres nowe called Foordes Close abutting upon the lande of the said Robert Cutler towardes the sowthe and upon the Queen's hie waye leadynge from Swyngldon to Little Waldingfield (*Lytle Waldingefilde*) towards the northe, lately Sir Wylliam Sprynges, knight before that, Cysely Fastolphe, before that Agnes Tymperle[*y*] and fyrste John Porters 4s. 4d.

[*p. 12*] Ty Gate Yarde: The same Roberte Cutler lykewyse holdeth freelye one parcell of one garden sometymes of the said Richarde Le[*e*], esquire's, and lately the said Sir Wylliam Sprynges, knighte, lyenge at Monks Eleigh (*Monkes Ellighe*) Tyegate, abutting upon the tenemente of John Parker called Stansebyes towardes the weste and upon the Queen's highe waye leadynge from Monks Eleigh (*Monkes Elighe*) Tye to Preston towardes the easte and renteth 2d.

Humble bankes. Thomas Coe, gentleman, holdeth freelye one peece of lande called Humblebankes lyenge at Stackewoode, containing by estimation 3 roodes abutting upon the Queen's highe waye leadynge to Leye Lane towardes the sowthe and upon the lande of the sayd Thomas called Walter Hobertes towardes the northe and renteth   2d.

Aylewardes. The same Thomas holdeth freelye one Messuage called Aylewardes with certen lande, meadowe and pastor containing by estimation 25 acres abutting upon the Holmes by Mannye Woode towardes the easte and upon the greene leadinge to Ley Lane towardes the weste and renteth   3s. 10½d.

Brookes Grove. The same Thomas holdeth freelye 3 acres of lande by estimation late John Chaplyns, clarke, called the Grove and percell sometymes of Brookes lyenge betweene the customarye landes of the mannor of Beaumonds (*Beamondes*) [*in Lindsey*] called the Holmes towardes the northe and upon a close called Gressy Cangles towardes the sowthe and one heade abutteth upon a fielde called Osleye towardes the weste and the other hedd abutts upon parte of a meadowe called Cangles Meadowe towardes the easte, all which was sometymes James Hubbertes, gentleman, and deemed parcell of his messuage called Burtons and renteth at the halfe yeere   7d.

[*p. 13*] Walter Hoberts: The same Thomas holdeth freelye one messuage at Stackewoode called Walter Hobbertes with dyvers percells of londe, meadowe and pastor containing by estimation 50 acres adjoyninge to gether and abuttynge upon the Queen's highe waye rownde abowte on every syde and renteth at the half year
£1 1s. 4½d.

D

The Almes Tenimentes. Edwarde Doylye, gentleman, holdeth by coppye 4 tenementes in Church Streete Rowe adjoyninge, abutting upon the same Church Streete towardes the easte and upon the demaynes of this mannor called Byfolde towardes the northeweste and rent,   2s. 6½d.
Let it be remembered that the 2 uppermoste of thes tenementes be the almose howses by the guyfte of Thomas Hobbert, gentleman, deceassed.

Illighe Crofte. Francys Danyell, esquire, holdeth freelye one parcell of pastor beinge a bushye pastor called Illighe Crofte, containing by estimation 4 acres and abutting upon the lande of the sayd Francis towardes the weste, and upon the lande of Symon Blondevyll towardes the easte, northe and sowthe syde and renteth 1s. 6d.

Bendishes. John Daye holdeth freelye one capytall messuage called Bendishes, with one peece of pastor adjoyninge containing by estimation 3 acres abutting upon the towne streete towardes the northe and upon the severall runnynge water of the sayd John in parte and upon the lordes ryver in parte towardes the sowthe and renteth   1s. 3d.

Bendishes meadowe. The same John Daye lykewyse holdeth freelye one meadowe containing by estimation 2 acres belonginge to the sayd messuage and abuttinge upon the sayd severall runnynge water of the sayd John Daye towardes the northe and upon the lordes ryver nowe almoste landed[158] and decayed towardes the sowthe easte and renteth at the halfe yeere   1s.

[*p. 14*] Dowtyes. The same John Daye holdeth lykewyse freelye one close of errable lande called Dowghties containing by estimation 6 acres, and abutting upon

---

[158] See p. 240, footnote 130 for this messuage in the Rental 6 (1583). The river, or this channel of it, is presumably so silted up that it is becoming land at this time.

the hie waye leadinge from Gedforde Brydge to Boyton Hall towardes the weste and upon the lande of Symon Blondevyll in parte and upon the lande of <del>Dedacre called></del> Boyton Hall called Dedacre in parte towardes the easte and renteth 8d.

Godden Lande. The same John holdeth lykewyse freelye one other severall close of errable lande called Goddon Lande containing by estimation 5 acres, abutting upon the lande of Symon Blondevyll, parcell of Porters, towardes the easte and upon the lande of Stephen Hoberte apperteyninge to Fostars towardes the weste and renteth at the halfe yeere 6d.

Rushebrooks. John Darbye,[159] gentleman, holdeth freelye one messuage sometymes Rushebrookes, with an ortchyarde and a garden thereto adjoinynge, conteynynge by estimation halfe an acre, abutting upon the bonde lande of this mannor in the tenure of the said John called Cowefenne towardes the sowthe and upon the towne streete towardes the northe and renteth 1½d.

Cowefenne. The same John Darby holdeth by coppye one meadow called Cowefenne containing by estimation 4 acres abutting upon the lord's ryver towardes the sowthe and upon the said messuage called Rushebroockes towardes the northe and rent at the halfe yeere 2s. 6d.

Teinter Yarde: The same John Darby holdeth lykewyse by coppie one peece of pastor late parcell of Burtons, sometymes Schoppes, nowe called the Taynteryarde, containing one acre by estimacion, abutting upon the bonde lande of this mannor in the tenure of Stephen Hobert called Vyncentes towardes the northe and upon the towne streete towardes the sowthe 6d.

[p. 15] Scottes Crofte. The same John Darbye holdeth freelye one peece of errable lande containing by estimation 5 acres called Scottes Crofte abutting upon the lande of Boyton Hall called Dedacre towardes the easte and upon the Queen's hie waye leadinge from Monkes Ellighe to Boyton Hall towardes the weste and renteth 1s. 3¼d.

Galletts Meadows. The same John Darby holdeth by coppye certen ruschey meadowes called Gallettes Meadowes containing by estimation 5 acres abutting upon the lord's ryver towardes the sowthe and upon the Queen's highe waye leadinge from Monkes Illighe to Lavenham towardes the northe and renteth 2s. 3d.

Alyce Cages \[illeg. annotation]/. The same John Darby holdeth lykewyse by coppie one messuage with a curtelage late percell of Lurcockes and sometymes Cages abutting upon the bonde londe of this mannor called Cowefenne in the tenure of the sayd John towardes the sowthe and upon the towne streete towardes the northe and renteth 2d.

G

Cutlers. Ralph Golderde holdeth by coppye one tenemente called Cutlers with a garden abutting upon towne streete towardes the sowthe and upon the bonde garden of John Sheader parcell of the Swanne towardes the northe and renteth 3d.

Parkers. Robert Goodale holdeth freelye one tenemente or cottage called Parkers with a garden and ortchyarde thereto appurtayninge containing by estimation 3

---

[159] John Darby was a surveyor and map-maker who was resident in Bramford by the 1590s. His surviving maps, notable for their portrayal of animals, people undertaking their country occupations and borrowings from Netherlandish artists, are held by Suffolk Archives, Norfolk Record Office, TNA and the British Library. He is currently the subject of a PhD study by Vivienne Aldous (with publications forthcoming). For an illustration of this entry and others on the same page in the rental, see Plate 12. For one of Weller's characteristic 'genealogies' of tenements based on Rushbrooks, see Plate 13.

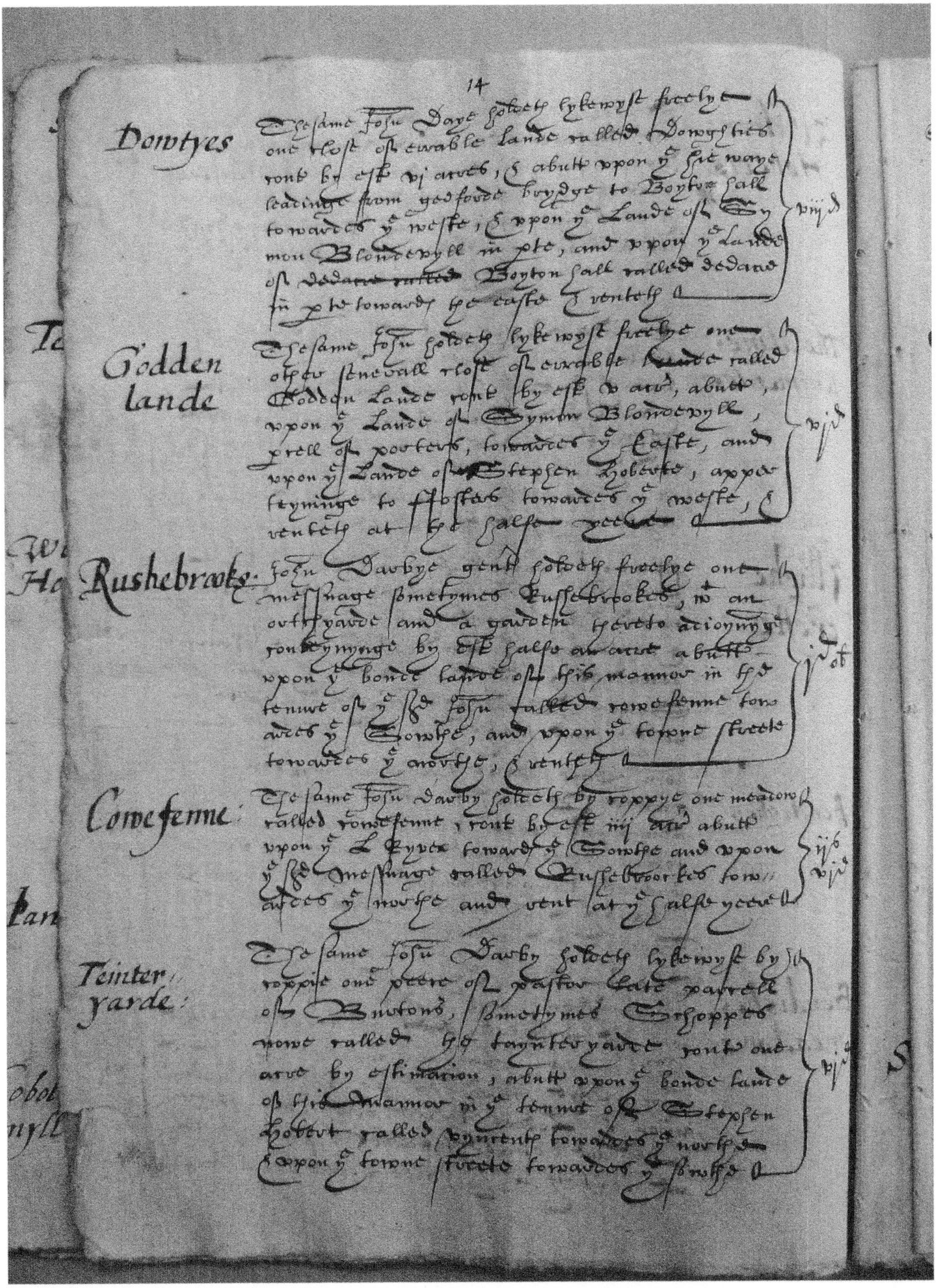

Dowtyes

Godden
lande

Rushebrooke

Comefenne

Teinter
yarde

Plate 12. Rental 7 (1599): entry showing the tenement of the Rushbrooks, then held by John Darby. (CCA-U63/70455/2, p. 14). Photo: Vivienne Aldous. Reproduced courtesy of the Chapter of Canterbury

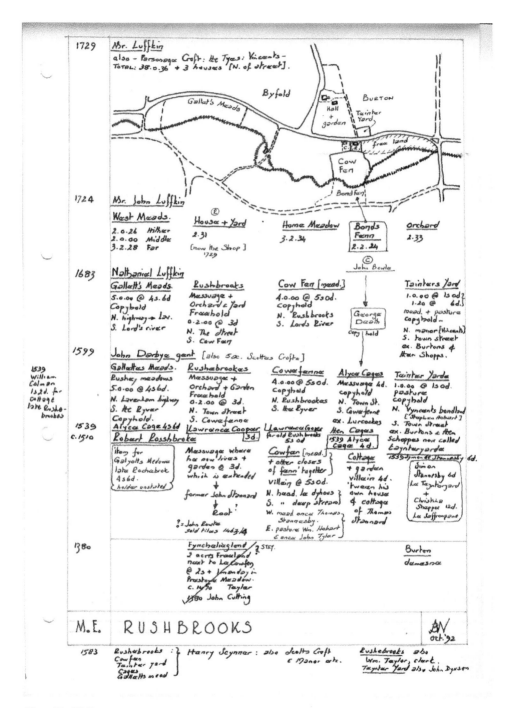

Plate 13. Weller's notes on the successive tenants of the land-holding Rushbrooks, c.1510–1729. Weller was fascinated by such 'genealogies' of land-holdings and made such notes for many of the identifiable holdings on the manor (Weller Archive, file 'Monks Eleigh: Analysis').

roodes and abutting upon the Queen's highe waye leadinge from the Tye to the churche towardes the northe and upon the lande of Thomas Waynefleete late parcell of Parkers towardes the sowthe and renteth 2d.

[*p. 16*] Parkefilde. \Edward Salter./ John Greene of Chelsworth (*Chelleswoorthe*) holdeth by coppye one fylde called Parkefielde now devyded into 2 partes containing by estimation 12 acres abutting upon the bonde lande of the mannor of Beaumonds (*Beamondes*) [*in Lindsey*] in the tenure of Stephen Hobert in parte and upon the lande of Boyton Hall in parte called Dedacre towardes the weste and upon the Queen's hiegh waye leadinge from Monks Eleigh (*Monkes Ellighe*) to Hadleigh (*Hadley*) towardes the easte with one meadowe called Parkefilde Meadow containing by estimation one acre 3 roodes and abutting upon the lord's ryver towardes the northe and upon the laste said hie waye towardes the sowthe and renteth 7s. 6d.

Scherpes. \R. Munings./ Wylliam Goodwyn holdeth freelye one tenemente of olde called Scherpes lyenge at Monks Eleigh (*Monkes Elighe*) Tye with the yarde and one longe sponge thereto adjoinynge containing by estimation 2 acres and abutting upon the Tye Greene towardes the northe and the lande of Wylliam Hoberde, gentleman, called Pages towardes the sowtheweste 1s. 3d.

Mannor. George Gardyner holdeth freelye his cappitall message where he nowe dwelleth called the Mannor with 30 acres of lande and pastor by estimation thereunto adjoyninge and abutting upon the lande of Roberte Ryece called Thyssely Fielde in parte and Mascalls in parte towardes the northe and upon the Queen's hie waye leadynge from Monks Eleigh (*Monkes Ellighe*) Tye to the churche there towardes the sowthe and renteth 7s. 10d.

Kinges Crofte. The same George Gardiner holdeth by coppy one peece of errable lande late Rysbyes called Kynges Crofte containing by estimation 8 acres abutting upon the demeanes of this mannor called Sextens Fielde towardes the sowthe and upon the lande of Wylliam Hobert, gentleman, called called [*sic*] Ravens Crofte or Ravens Crofte Meadowe towardes the northe and renteth 2s. 1d.

[*p. 17*] Parcell of Scherpes. The same George Gardiner holdeth freelye one peece of pastor parcell of Scherpes nowe called Hasells Pightell or 5 acres containing by estimation 5 acres and lyeth betwene the Queenes hie waye leadynge from Monkes Ellighe Tye to Brent Eleigh (*Brentellighe*) on the northe and the lande of William Hobert, gentleman, called Pages on the sowthe weaste and renteth 1s. 3d.

Inderbyes. The same George holdeth freelye one tenement called Inderbyes with 11 acres by estimation of lande, meadowe and pastor thereto belonginge abutting upon the lande of Wylliam Hoberte, gentleman, called Ravens Crofte towardes the weste and upon the Queen's hie waye leadinge from the Mannor Hyll at the Three Waye Leete to Sckyppes Crosse Bridge and to Swyngledon towardes the easte and renteth 4s.

Kinges or Hubberdes. The same George holdeth freelye one decayed messuage of olde called Kynges and after Hoberdes lyenge at Monks Eleigh (*Monkes Ellighe*) Tye Gate with 45 acres by estimation of lande, meadowe and pastor thereto adjoyninge, abutting upon the bonde lande of this mannor in the tenure of John Parker in parte called Lytle Hieghe Fielde and upon the deameanes of this mannor called Highefilde in parte and upon the bonde lande of this mannor called Sussells in parte towardes the northe and upon the greene called Monks Eleigh (*Monkes Ellighe*) Tye in parte and upon the lande of Mistress Ryece, wydowe, in parte called Reynors and upon the land of Robert Ryece, gentleman, called Northefylde and Thyselye Fylde towardes the sowthe and renteth 12s. 7d.

Sussells. The same George holdeth by coppye one errable close with a meadowe thereto appertayninge called Sussells, containing by estimation 20 acres and abutting upon the Queen's hie waye leadinge from Monks Eleigh (*Monkes Ellighe*) Tye to Preston towardes the weste and upon the landes of the sayd George tow [*sic*] [*p. 18*] towardes the easte and renteth at the halfe yeere   10s.
Let it be remembered that this is no parte of the Baylyves collection or charge.

H

Parkers Colledge. Wylliam Hubbert holdeth freelye one messuage called of olde Parkers, but nowe the Colledge, for the sondrye tenantes there dwellinge, with one litle yarde thereto belonginge abutting upon the Queen's hye waye leadynge from Monks Eleigh (*Monkes Ellighe*) Tye towards the churche and the fielde called Kynges Crofte sometymes pertayninge to the said messuage towardes the sowthe
                                                                    1s. 4d.

Allingtons and Asleses. Andrewe Hubert holdeth freelye 2 tenementes whereof one is called Allingtons the other Asleses adjoyninge to gether, and abutting upon the lande called Byrches in the tenure of Stephen Hubert in parte and upon parcell of the ortcharde of the bonde lande of Hughe Woode called Jentlemans in parte towardes the northe and upon the towne streete towardes the sowthe and renteth for Alington, 9½d and for Asleses, 4d.   1s. 1½d.

Layes. \to gether./ The same Andrewe Huberte holdeth by coppie one tenemente with his appurtenances called Leyes with one meadowe and hoppeyarde thereto belonginge containing by estimation 2 acres, abutting upon the towne streete righte agaynste the church streete or greene towardes the northe and upon the lord's ryver towardes the sowthe   2s. 6d.

Brickotts. George Huberte holdeth by coppie one tenement, garden and ortchyarde called Bryckottes containing by estimation halfe an acre and abutting upon the Queen's highe waye leadinge from Lavenham to Bildeston (*Byldeston*) towardes the northe and upon the demeanes of this mannor called Halle Crofte nowe Mell Crofte Pastor towardes the sowthe   2s. 5d.

Dominickes Meadowe. The same George holdeth by coppie one meadowe called Domynyckes Meadowe containing by estimation 2 acres and abutting upon the laste said hie waye towardes the northe and upon the lordes ryver neere the myll dame towardes the sowthe   1s. 6d.

[*p. 19*] Dominickes Garden. The same George holdeth by coppie one garden or meadowe beinge an ortcheyarde, containing by estimation halfe an acre, called Dominickes Garden and abutting upon the said highe waye towardes the northe and upon the comon ryver of the lordes towardes the sowthe and Renteth   6d.

Parcell of the Swanne. John Haywarde holdeth by coppye one cottage late parcell of the Swanne abutting upon the <chur> towne street towardes the sowthe and upon the hed howse or tenemente of John Sheader called the Swanne towardes the weste and renteth at the halfe yeere   5d.

Tylors. Wylliam Hye, clarke, holdeth freelye one tenemente called Tylers with a garden and ortcheyarde containing by estimation one roode and a halfe abutting upon the lord's ryver towardes the sowthe and upon the towne streete towardes the northe, more there is a roode of grownde occupied heerewith which dothe belonge to the Clickett as parcell sometymes of the same   2d.

Abbotts. The same Wylliam Hye holdeth freely one peece of grownde wheron was sometymes a principall capitall messuage nowe utterly decayed called the Clickett, otherwise Abbottes, late Alexanders, containing by estimation one acre and a roode abutting upon the lordes ryver towardes the sowthe and upon the towne streete towardes the northe   1s. 3d.

Fosters. Stephen Huberde holdeth freelye all that his mancion howse called Fosters with all the landes thereto appurtayninge containing by estimation 100 acres, lyenge and for the moste parte adjoinynge unto his said mansion howse and renteth
£1 5s. 8d.

Byrches. The same Stephen Hubberde lykewyse holdeth freelye one messuage called Byrches with the appurtenances containing by estimation halfe an acre abutting upon Monks Eleigh (*Monkes Ellighe*) towne streete towardes the sowthe and upon the bonde lande of this mannor in the tenure of the said Symon [*sic*] called Calves Crofte towardes the northe and renteth   4d.

[*p. 20*] Ponde Meadowe. The same Stephen holdeth by coppie one meadowe called Ponde Meadowe containing by estimation 3 acres abutting upon the lord's ryver towarde the northe and upon the lande of Fosters towardes the sowthe and renteth   1s.

Allen Downe. The same Stephen holdeth by coppye one filde called Allen Downe Fielde containing by estimation 18 acres, abutting upon the hie waye leadinge from Gedforde Brydge to Swyngledon towardes the northe and upon the lande parcell of Fosters towardes the sowthe and renteth   3s. 6d.

Parkefielde. The same Stephen holdeth by coppye one parcell of Parke Fielde containing by estimation 5 acres abutting upon Great Parke Fielde towardes the sowthe and upon the bonde lande of the mannor of Beamondes in the tenure of the same Stephen called the Greendle or Slade towardes the weste   2s. 6d.

Vincentes. The same Stephen holdeth by coppye one Messuage called Vyncentes with a pyghtell of lande containing by estimation 2 acres abutting upon the towne streete towardes the sowthe and upon the demeanes of this manner called Burton towardes the northe   1s. 6d.

Caves Crofte. The same Stephen holdeth by coppie one peece of lande called Caves Crofte containing by estimation 4 acres abutting upon Byrches aforesayde towarde the sowthe and the lande of John Coppin in righte of his wyfe called Parsonage Crofte towardes the northe and renteth at the halfe yeere   2s.

Webbes Crofte. The same Stephen holdeth freelye one peece of lande called Webbes Crofte containing by estimation 8 acres abutting upon the lande of Katherin Chaplyn, wydowe, called Dulles Meadowe towardes the sowthe and upon the bonde lande of this mannor called Allendowne Fielde in the tenure of the sayd Stephen Hobert towardes the northe and renteth   1s. 5½d.

[*p. 21*] Huntes. Wylliam Hubbert, gentleman, holdeth freelye one messuage called Huntes with a crofte of lande, and one pightell of pastor containing by estimation in all 3 acres abutting upon the greene comonly called Monks Eleigh (*Monkes Ellighe*) Tye towardes the northe and upon the lande of the same Wylliam Hubert called Ravens Crofte towardes the sowthe and renteth   9d.

Pages. The same Wylliam holdeth freelye certen lande, meadowe and pastor called Pages whereof one filde is called Pages Fielde containing by estimation 18 acres, one yarde called Pages Yarde containing one acre, one pightell of pastor adjoyinge called Pages Pightell containing halfe an acre, one pastor called Longe Pastor containing 4 acres, one erable filde called Ballande containing 12 acres, one erable close called Ravens Crofte with a parcell of meadowe contaynynge togyther 18 acres, one meadowe called Skyps Crosse Meadowe containing 1 acre and a half, one meadowe called Grygges Meadowe containing 2 acres and one lytle meadowe called Litle Prestowe Meadowe containing 1 acre and a half. Summe together 58 acres all which do rente at the halfe yeere   11s.

Lytle Prestowe. Sir Roberte Jermyn knighte holdeth by coppye one peece of meadowe containing by estimation halfe an acre, lyeinge in the corner of the meadowe of the said Sir Roberte called the Lordes Meadowe appurtayninge to his mannor of Shelton Hall or Brent Eleigh (*Brentelye*) Hall and abuttynge upon the comon ryver there towardes the sowthe, and upon the said meadowe called the Lordes Meadowe in parte and upon the meadowe of the sayd Sir Roberte called the Checker Meadowe in parte towardes the northe and renteth at the halfe yeere 1s. 4d.

[*p. 22*] L

Eme Randes. Robert Lenton, gentleman, holdeth freelye one messuage called Eme Randes with a crofte of lande and pastor thereto adjoinynge containing by estimation 3 acres and abutting upon the Queen's hie waye leadynge from Monks Eleigh (*Monkes Ellighe*) Tye to the churche there towardes the northe and upon the lande of Wylliam Hubert, gentleman, called Huntes towardes the sowthe weste and renteth
1s. 2d.

M

Higlens. Robert Monnynge, gentleman, holdeth freelye one messuage called Higlens sometymes Lawrence Martens with an ortcheyarde and garden thereto adjoyninge containing by estimation 2 acres with one erable fielde called Litle Higlens containing by estimation 8 acres adjoyninge unto the said messuage, one othere erable close nowe called Doove Howse Close containing by estimation 7 acres adjoyninge on the sowthe syde of the said messuage, 2 severall meadowes containing eche of them 2 acres abutting upon Walsehams Ryver, 2 parcells of coorse meadowe or pastor adjoyninge called the Slades abutting upon the said Walshames Ryver containing to gether by estimation 3 acres, one other errable close called Bull Close containing by estimation 9 acres, one other errable close now lately devyded into 2 partes called the Mellfieldes containing together by esti-mation 24 acres, one other erable close called Longe Crofte containing by estima-tion 10 acres with a meadowe to the ende of the said crofte adjoynynge containing by estimation 2 acres, all which together make 70 acres, and rente at the halfe yeere 10s. 2½d, but it is supposte by the owner that this rente shoolde not be so muche every halfe yeere, by 1s. as he can easelye prove by sondrye verye anciente rentalls of this mannor   10s. 2½d.

[*p. 23*] Davyes. The same Robert lykewyse holdeth freelye one pastor or grove, with one erable close thereto adjoyninge containing by estimation in the whole 10 acres called Davyes Pastor, abutting upon the demeanes of this mannor called the Highe Fieldes towardes the northe, and upon the said demeanes called Illighe Fielde towardes the sowthe and renteth   6d.

Hogge Fenne. The same Robert lykewyse holdeth freelye one pastor or grove meadowe called Hogge Fenne containing 2 acres abutting upon parcel of the said Higlens called Doovehowse Close towardes the weste, and upon one of the foresayd 2 meadowes appurtaynynge to the sayde Higlens towardes the easte   ½d.

Mellfielde. The same Robert holdeth lykweyse freelye one peece of errable grownde nowe devyded called Mellfielde containing by estimation 16 acres abut-ting upon the Queen's highe waye leadinge from Lavenham to Bildeston towardes the southe and upon lande parcell of Higlens towardes the northe, and upon a litle meadowe sometymes Sir Wylliam Springes, knighte, called Walsehames Meadowe towardes the easte and upon the lande parcell of the sayd Higlens towardes the weste and renteth 3s.

Walesehams Meadowe. The same Robert lykewyse holdeth freelye one longe meadowe containing by estimation 3 roodes abutting upon the ryver called Walsehames towardes the easte and upon the aforesayde Mellfielde towardes the weste and renteth 1s.

Marycrofte. James Man holdeth freelye one peece of errable lande called Marye Crofte containing by estimation 1 acre and a half abutting upon the highe waye leadinge from Monks Eleigh (*Monkes Ellige*) to Boxford (*Boxeforde*) towardes the easte and upon the lande of Roberte Cutler, gentleman, towardes the weste and renteth 6½d.

Struttes. Barthelemewe Marchante holdeth by coppye one tenemente late Struttes with a garden thereto appurtayninge abutting upon the bonde lande of this Mannor in the tenure of John Whittell, clarke, [*p. 24*] towardes the sowthe, and upon the towne streete towardes the northe and the said tenemente renteth at the half yeere, 6d., and the said garden, 2d., in all 8d.

The Bull. Robert Northefielde holdeth by coppye one tenemente called the Bull with the appurtenances abutting upon the church streete towardes the weste and upon the howse and garden of John Sheder in parte towardes the sowthe este and upon the demeanes of this mannor towardes the northe and renteth 1s. ½d.

O

Harpe Downe. Robert Offewoode holdeth freelye one crofte of errable lande in manner of a harpe containing by estimation 2 acres and a half called the Downe and abutting upon the bonde lande of this manner called Allen Downe Fielde towardes the sowthe and upon the Queen's hie waye leadinge called Fenne Streete towardes the northe and renteth 5d.

Richarde Struttes. John Offewoode holdeth by coppie one tenemente late Richarde Strutes with a certen waye and garden to the same adjoyninge, abutting upon the bonde lande of this mannor in the tenure of John Whittell, clarke, towardes the sowthe and upon the towne streete towardes the northe 10d.

P

Olivers. Ellice Pettycane holdeth by coppie one tenemente in Stackewoode Streete called Olyvers with an ortcharde thereto adjoyninge containing by estimation halfe an acre abutting upon the lande of Thomas Coe called Rayners towardes the weste and upon Stackewoode Streete towardes the easte 1½d.

Thorpes. John Parker holdeth freelye his mansion howse called Thorpes with dyvers landes meadowes and pastures thereto adjoyninge, that is, one pightell and one errable close called Gate Crofte containing 8 acres, 3 pightells thereto adjoynynge called Dedemans Layes with a lytle grove on the easte syde on the same fielde and an other litle grove on the weste syde of the same fielde nexte Langley Woode containing 9 acres, one meadowe [*p. 25*] called Lytle Valley containing 3 roodes and 2 fieldes called Langley Fieldes adjoyninge to Langley Woode containing 10 acres – in all 20 acres and rente 10s. 4d.

Benstedes. The same John holdeth also freelye Benstedes Yardes containing one acre, 3 pictells called Bensteades Croftes containing 8 acres, one other close called Water Forowe adjoyninge to the sayd pightells containing 8 acres and one harde londe meadowe called the Bigger Valleye containing by estimation 3 acres in all 20 acres and renteth 2s. 6d.

Lyttle Tylepetts. The same John holdeth freelye one litle errable pightell called Litle Tyle Pettes adjoyninge to the aforesayd Langelye Fieldes towardes the sowthe and upon the lande of Sir Roberte Jermyn, knighte, called Great Tyle Pettes towardes the northe containing by estimation one acre and renteth   4d.

Highefielde. The same John Parker holdeth by coppye one erable filde called Lytle Hieghfielde containing by estimation 15 acres and abutting upon the Queen's highe waye leadinge from Lavenham to Kettlebaston (*Ketlebarston*) towardes the northe and upon the lande meadowe of sayd John called the Valley Meadowe towardes the sowthe and renteth   2s. 6d.

Gaweslande or Stubbye. The same John Parker holdeth by coppie one erable fielde called Gaweslande or Stubbye Fielde containing by estimation 5 acres and abutting upon the said Highe Fielde towardes the easte and upon the lande of the said John called Langle Leyes towardes the weste and renteth   1s.

Stansbyes. The same John holdeth freelye one tenemente called Stansebyes with a garden of lande thereto appurtayninge containing by estimation one roode and abutting upon the greene called Monks Eleigh (*Monkes Ellighe*) Tye towardes the sowthe and upon the lande of the sayd John called Benstedes Yardes towardes the weste and upon the hiewaye called the Tye Lane towardes the easte and rent 1½d.

[*p. 26*] R

Boores and Barrawayes. Thomas Rafe holdeth by coppy 2 tenementes with the appurtenances called Boores and Barrawayes beinge adjoyned together and abutting upon the church streete towardes the easte and upon the demeanes of the lord called Byfolde towardes the northeweste and upon the Queen's hie waye leadinge from Bildeston (*Byldeston*) to Lavenham towardes the sowthe and renteth   10d.

Mascalls. Robert Ryece holdeth freelye one messuage sometyme buylded called Mascalls with these parcells of lande, meadowe pastor and woode heere followenege and thereto belonging, as one filde called Mascalls Fielde containing by estimation 9 acres, Mascalls Grove 4 acres, Mascalls Yarde 1 acre and a half, Mascalls Pightell 2 acres, Northefielde 7 acres, Thisleyfielde 12 acres, Waggardefielde 5 acres, Stubbey Fielde 5 acres, Sonde Pett Fielde 2 acres and a half and 2 peeces at in one places [*sic*] adjoyninge, in Lytlewoode Fielde, 2 acres by estimation, all to gether 50 acres and rente at the half yeere   15s.

Chaplens. The same Robert lykewyse holdeth freelye one capitall messuage called Chaplens with the yarde and one pastor thereto adjoyninge containing by estimation 6 acres and one erable fielde called Homayne Crofte containing by estimation 7 acres and abutting upon the tye greene towardes the weste and upon the lande of the sayd Roberte called Reynors in parte and upon Mascalls in parte towardes the easte and renteth   4s. 2d.

Reynors. The same Robert lykewyse holdeth freelye one tenemente called Raynors now uste [*used*] for a backehowse adjoyninge to the messuage called Chaplens with one peece of pasture called the Backehowse Yarde containing 1 acre and a half and one fielde or close of pastor called the Backehowse Yarde Raynors Pightells containing by estimation 6 acres, and abutting upon the foresayd greene called Monks Eleigh (*Monkes Ellighe*) Tye towardes the weste and upon the lande sometymes Rysbyes, and lately Henry Skynners, gentleman, [*?unkle*] and nowe Mistress Florence Ryece, wydowe, called Raynors towardes the easte and rente   1s. 1d.

[*p. 27*] Skippes Meadowe. The same Robert Ryece holdeth by coppye one meadowe called Sckyypes Crosse Meadowe containing by estimation 4 acres sometymes devyded in twoe partes lyenge upon the Queen's hie waye leadinge from Brent Eleigh (*Brentellighe*) to Monks Eleigh (*Monkes Illighe*) towardes the northe and upon the comon ryver towardes the sowthe and renteth at the halfe yeere   4s.

Woodfylde. The same Robert Ryece holdeth lykewyse by coppye one peece of errable lande in Lytle Woode Fielde containing by estimation 5 acres and abutting upon the free lande of the sayd Robert called Mascalls Harpe in parte and upon the hie waye in parte towardes the weste and upon the demeanes of the lorde called Higlens Fielde towardes the easte upon the demeanes of the lorde called Greate Woodefielde towardes the sowthe and upon the free lande of the said Robert called Mascalls Ponde Peece in the same fielde towardes the northe and renteth   1s. 3d.

Raynors Kinges. Mistress Ryece, wydowe, holdeth freelye 2 pightells adjoyninge called Rayners Pightells with a lane or \severall/ waye leadynge thereunto containing by estimation 6 acres wherof the one peece lyeth betweene the lande of the sayd Robert Ryece on the sowthe and the lande of George Gardiner on the northe parte and abutts at one heade upon the lande of the sayd Roberte Ryece called Raynors Yarde towardes the weste. And the other pightell lieth betweene the landes of the said Robert Ryece on the easte and weste parts and abutts upon the lande of the said Roberte towardes the sowthe and upon the said other pightell towardes the northe and rente at the halfe yeere   3d.

S

Parcell of Parkers. \[illeg.] [?]Flegg/ Roberte Snape holdeth by coppye one peece of grownde containing by estimation 3 pole in lengthe and 2 pole in bredthe with a poore cottage newlye thereon erected, parcell sometyme of the tenemente called Parkers abutting upon the towne streete towardes the sowthe and the demeanes of the mannor beinge the hall yarde towardes the northe and renteth at the half year 1d.

[*p. 28*] The Swanne. John Sheader holdeth by coppie one tenemente called the Swanne with a garden and ortcheyarde thereto belonginge containing by estimation halfe an acre abutting upon the churche streete towardes the weste and upon the towne streete towardes the sowthe and the sayd ortcheyarde and yardes upon the Bull in parte and upon the hall bearne in parte towardes the northe and renteth   1s.

T

Newelande Hall. John Toorner the yonger holdeth freelye one messuage called Newlande Hall with 3 acres of lande by estimation and abutting upon the Queen's highe waye leadinge from Stackwoode to Milden (*Myldinge*) Greene towardes the northeweste and upon the lande of Roberte Cutler, gentleman, towardes the weste and upon the lande of Symon Blondevylle towardes the sowthe and renteth   2s.

Rushebrookes. Wylliam Tayler, clarke, holdeth by coppie one tenemente with a garden called Rushebrookes some tymes Chaplyns and abutting upon the towne streete towards the northe and upon the bonde lande meadowe of this mannor in the tenure of John Darbye toward the sowthe and renteth   7d.

W

Bullers. Thomas Waynefleete otherwise Pyper holdeth freelye his nowe mancion howse called Bullers with 2 acres and a half of pastor by estimation to the same appurtaynynge and abutting upon the towne streete towardes the sowthe and upon the lande of John Coppin in righte of his wyfe called Tyes towardes the northe and renteth   4d.

Parkers or Sedges. The same Thomas holdeth freelye certen lande, meadowe and pastor latelye belongenge to the messuage called the Colledge otherwyse Parkers containing by estimation 9 acres and a half abutting upon the Queenes [*p. 29*] highe waye leadynge from Monks Eleigh (*Monkes Illighe*) Tye to the church in parte and upon the tenemente of Robert Goodalle in parte called Litle Parkers towardes the northe and upon the lande of George Gardiner called Great Inderbyes towardes the sowthe and renteth   2s. 6d.

Brownes 18 Acres. Ralfe Wrighte holdeth freelye one mancion howse with an ortcheyarde and a garden thereto adjoynynge with certen other parcells of lande and pastor lykewyse adjoynynge, that is, one peece called Hamondes Backehowse Fielde, 3 severall pightells called the Merishe and 2 pightells called Warens containing together by estimation 18 acres all which abutte upon the Queenes hie waye leadynge from Lindsey (*Lynsey*) to Milden (*Myldinge*) towardes the sowthe and upon the lande of Symon Blondevyll towardes the northe and renteth   3s. 5d.

Brownes 37 Acres. More, the same Ralfe Wrighte lykewyse holdeth freelye 4 parcells of lande, meadowe and pastor whereof the firste is called Wallnutt Close, the nexte Great Blakes, with a grove to the same adjoynynge called Blackes Grove, all which adjoyninge to gether do abutte upon the Queenes highe waye leadinge from Lindsey (*Lynsey*) to Milden (*Myldinge*) towardes the northe easte and upon the lande appurtayninge to the mannor of Castlelens[160] in parte and upon Brooke Woode in parte and upon Chappell Lande appurtayninge to Lindsey (*Lynsey*) in parte towardes the sowthe and contain to gether by estimation 37 acres and renteth
6s.

Bixebyes. John Whittell, clarke, holdeth by coppye one tenemente late Byxbyes with a garden and a meadowe thereto adjoyninge containing by estimation 2 acres and a halfe and abutteth upon Monks Eleigh (*Monkes Ellighe*) towne streete towardes the northe and upon the ryver of the lorde towardes the sowthe   3s. 8d.

[*p. 30*] Churche Yarde Tenemente. The same John Whittell, clarke, holdeth lykewyse by coppie one tenemente with a garden and a certen footewaye thereto adjoyninge, abuttinge upon the churcheyarde towardes the weste and upon the demaynes of this mannor called Burton Crofte toward the easte and renteth   2d.

Longe Hayes and Shorte Hayes. The same John Whittell, clarke, holdeth freely 2 peeces of pastor with a tenemente thereon newlye buylte called Longe Hayes and Shorte Hayes, parcell of a tenemente sometymes called Dulles containing by estimation 7 acres and a half parcell some tymes of Burtons as is supposed and late James Hubberdes, gentleman, liyenge betweene the landes of Roberte Cutler called Peretreefielde on the northe parte and the lande of Symon Blondevyll called Illgiers in parte and Dulles Meadowe or Bottome in parte on the sowthe parte, the one heade thereof abutteth upon the kynges [*sic*] hie waye leadynge from Wyncolls Hall to Stackewood Streete towardes the weste and upon the landes of Katheryn Chaplen Wydowe called Lytle Dulles towardes the easte and renteth at the halfe yeere
1s. 2d.

Jentlemans. \[*illeg. annotation*]/. Hughe Woode holdeth by coppie one cottage with a garden containing one roode late Jentlemans, abutting upon the bonde lande of this mannor in the tenure of Nicholas Yonge towardes the northe and upon the towne streete towardes the sowthe. More he lykewyse holdeth by copye one peece of an ortcheyarde containing halfe a roode, abutting upon Byrtches in the tenure of Stephen Hobert towardes the northe and upon the free tenemente of Andrewe

---

[160] Probably the manor of Castelins or Castelyns in Groton or Thorpe Morieux (see Copinger, *Manors of Suffolk* 1 (1905), pp. 113–15 and 3 (1908), p. 207).

Hobert sometymes John Tylers towardes the sowthe and renteth at the halfe yeere
6d.

[*p. 31*] Boytonhall. Josuah Warde holdeth freelye the mannor and capitall messuage called Boyton Hall with dyvers landes, meadowes and pastors, containing by estimation 7 score [*140*] acres, abutting upon the lordes woode called Manneywoode in parte towardes the sowthe and upon the lande called Fosters towardes the northe and upon a close called Kempes in parte and upon the Queenes highe waye leadinge from Gedford Brydge to Stackewoode in parte towardes the weste and upon the waye leadinge from Monks Eleigh (*Monkes Ellighe*) to *Hadleigh* (*Hadley*) towardes the easte   13s. 4d.

Piggescrofte. The same Josuah Warde holdeth freelye one close called Pigges Crofte nowe Raynors containing by estimation 10 acres abutting upon the Queen's highe waye leadinge from Gedforde Brydge to Stackewoode towardes the easte and upon the lande called Fosters towards the weste   2s. 1½d.

The Tufte. The same Josuah Warde holdeth freelye one peece of lande under Mannye Woode called the Tuffte containing by estimation 4 acres and abutting upon the sayd Mannye Woode towardes the sowthe and upon the landes of Boyton Hall toward the northe   7d.

Y

Gardiners. Nicholas Yonge, clarke, holdeth by coppie one tenemente late Gardiners with halfe an acre of lande abutting upon the towne streete towardes the sowthe and upon the bonde lande of this mannor called Barrettes Ortcheyarde in parte and upon Caves Crofte in parte toward the northe   6d.

Schellinges. Roberte Yonge holdeth by copye one tenemente called Schellinges with his appurtenances abutting upon the bonde lande of this mannor called Vyncentes towardes the northe [*p. 32*] and upon Monks Eleigh (*Monkes Ellighe*) towne streete towardes the sowthe and rentethe at the halfe yeere   6½¼d.

Kettlebaston (*Ketlebarston*)

Towne Meadowe. The towne of Kettlebaston (*Ketlebarston*) holdeth freelye one parcell of meadowe called the Towne Meadowe containing by estimation one acre, abutting upon the demeanes of Kettlebaston (*Ketlebarston*) Hall in the tenure of Roberte Wrighte towardes the sowthe easte and upon the gleebe lande of Kettlebaston (*Ketlebarston*) parsonage in parte, and the lande of George Waldegrave, esquire, in parte and the lande of the mannor of Kettlebaston (*Ketlebarston*) Hall in parte towardes the northe and renteth   3d.

Hatches. Roberte Sympson holdeth freelye 5 sondry peeces of lande and pastor whereof one lyeth in a field called the 5 Acre Fielde on the sowtheweste syde of the same fielde lyke a harpe containing one acre, 2 peeces lyenge in the 8 Acre Fielde almoste in the myddeste of the same fielde whereof one contayneth one acre, the other halfe a roode, which 2 peeces doe so lye as thaye joyne at one corner, one other peece lyeth in Sedcott Fielde containing 1 acre, which peece joyneth and lyeth under the 5 Acre Hedge, the laste peece of pastor containing by estimation one acre and halfe a roode by estimation abutting upon Kediells Crofte towardes the sowthe and upon the bonde lande of the said Roberte Sympson called the Home Pightells towardes the northe and renteth at the half year   8d.

Parcell of Cabbowes. Roberte Smythe holdeth freelye one pightell of errable lande parcell of Cabbowes called Springes Close containing by estimation 3 acres abutting upon the demeanes of Kettlebaston (*Ketlebarston*) nowe in the tenure of

269

Wylliam Appleton, gentleman, in parte and upon the lande of George Waldegrave, esquier, [*p. 33*] in parte towardes the sowthe and upon the lande of Kettlebaston (*Ketlebarston*) Gleebe towardes the northe and renteth at the halfe yeere   4d.

Blockes. George Waldegrave, esquier, holdeth freelye one peece of pastor some-tymes buylded called Stebbinges synce Blockes and nowe called Martyns, abutting upon the bonde lande of Kattlebaston (*Ketlebarston*) Hall in the tenure of John Parker toward the sowthe easte and upon the Queenes highe waye leadinge from Stowmarket (*Stowe market*) to <~~Kettlebaston (*Ketlebarston*)~~> Lavenham towardes the northe weste   ½d.

Shearefilde. More the same George holdeth freelye one peece of errable lande lyenge in Shearefilde containing by estimation 4 acres, abutting upon the Queen's highe waye leadinge from Stowmarket (*Stowe markett*) to Lavenham towardes the sowthe easte and upon the lande of the same George and parte of the said Shiere-fielde towardes the northe weste   6d.

Darbyes. The same George lykewyse holdeth freelye one messuage called Darbyes with the yarde and certen errable landes in 3 fieldes thereto adjoyninge containing by estimation 20 acres abutting upon the landes of the sayd George toward the sowtheaste and upon the Churche Greene in Kettlebaston (*Ketlebarston*) towardes the northe weaste and renteth   2s. 9d.

Parcell of Wages. The same George lykewyse holdeth freelye one tenemente decayed, and yett a bearne remaynynge theare with a yarde thereto adjoinynge, containing by estimation 1 roode and abutting upon the bonde lande of Kettlebaston (*Ketlebarston*) Hall in the tenure of John Parker towardes the sowthe easte and upon the Queenes highe waye leadinge from Stowmarket (*Stowe markett*) to Sudbury (*Sudburye*) towardes the northe weaste and renteth at the halfe yeere   1½d.

[*p. 34*] Parcell of Cabbowes. The same George lykwyse holdeth freelye one longe sponge [*spong*] of pastor, parcell of Cabbowes containing by estimation one acre, abutting upon the Churche Greene towardes the northe and upon the gleebe lande of Kettlebaston (*Ketelbarston*) parsonage towardes the sowthe and renteth at the halfe yeere   1½d.

Whightes. James Chaplen holdeth freelye one tenemente decayed called Whites with one pastor containing by estimation 1 acre and 2 erable closes containing 4 acres and one meadowe adjoyninge at the nether ende of the sayd closes containing 1 acre and a half abutting upon the demeanes of Kettlebaston (*Ketlebarston*) Halle called Blowe Filde towardes the northeweste and upon the Queenes highe waye leadinge from Stowmarket (*Stowe markett*) to Lavenham towardes the sowthe easte and renteth   2s. 1d.

Parcell of Whightes. Danyell Kempster the soonne of John Kempester nowe 12 years of age, holdeth freelye one peece of erable grownde, parcell of Whightes, late James Chaplens, called Adams containing by estimation 2 acres abutting upon the tenemente of John Prycke, clarke, in parte, and upon the lande of James Chaplen called Whites in parte toward the sowthe easte and upon the meadowe of the sayd James Chaplen towardes the northweste and lyeth betwene the lande of the sayd Dannyell Kempster called Cabbowes towardes the sowtheweste and the lande of the sayd James called Whightes towardes the northe easte   7d.

Parcell of Cabbowes. The same Danyell Kempster holdeth lykewyse freelye one messuage with one acre and a halfe of lande adjoynynge, the nether ende wherof abutteth upon Whites Meadowe towardes the northeweste and the other hed abutteth upon the highe waye leadinge from Stowmarket (*Stowe markett*) to Lavenham towardes the sowthe easte   4d.

[*p. 35*] Wages. John Parker holdeth freelye one messuage called Wages with a yarde and a pightell thereto adjoinynge containing by estimation one acre and a roode abutting upon the lande of George Waldegrave, esquier, towardes the sowthe easte and upon the Queenes highe waye leadynge from Stowmarket (*Stowe market*) to Sudbury towardes the northe weste and renteth 2½d.

Parcell of Cabbowes. Robert Kembolde holdeth freelye one acre of errable lande lyenge in a pightell called Lytle Hedge abutting upon the bonde lande of Kettlebaston (*Ketlebarston*) <lande> Hall called Lytle Hedge towardes the northe weaste, the nether ende and upper ende whereof abutt upon the bonde lande of Kettlebaston (*Ketlebarston*) Hall in the tenure of Robert Wrighte towardes the easte and weste, that is, the nether ende towardes the easte and the upper ende towardes the weste and renteth at the half yeere 2½d.

Prickes Parke. John Pricke, clarke, and nowe mynister of Kettlebaston (*Ketlebarston*) holdeth freelye one peece of pasture with a tenemente nowe thereon newlye buylte containing by estimation one roode \late/ parcell of Whightes and nowe comonlye called Pryckes Parke all which was bowghte latelye of James Chaplen lyenge betweene the messuage of Dannyell Kempester called Cabbowes towardes the sowthe weaste and the lande of James Chaplen called Whites towardes the northeaste and abutting upon the highe waye leadynge from Stowmarket (*Stowe markett*) to Lavenham (*Lannam*) towardes the sowthe easte and upon the lande of the sayd Danyell Kempster called Whites and nowe Adams towardes the northeweaste and renteth at the halfe yeere 1d.

[*p. 36*] Hitcham

Loosehall. Thomas Springe gentleman holdeth freelye all that his capitall messuage called Loose Hall with 13 score [*260*] acres of by estimation of lande meadowe and pastor thereunto adjoyninge abutting upon the lande of John Grymwoode lately parcell of the sayd Loose Hall toward the sowthe easte and upon the Queenes woodde called Oxelewoode in parte and upon the lande of this manner called Illighfielde in parte, upon Cockes Lande in parte, Thomas Rushe in parte and upon the landes of John Lever and Thomas Lever in parte towardes the northeweste and renteth

9s. 8d.

Parcel of Loosehall. John Grymwoode holdeth freelye certen parcells of lande meadowe and pastor that is one fielde called Eastefielde, one meadowe called Brooke Meadowe, one meadowe called Wallowe Meadowe, one fielde called Cockes Lande, one peece of Great Goolde Woode Fylde, one peese of lande called Monkes Lande, and one other peece called Puntockes containing to gether in the whole by estimation 80 acres adjoyninge all to gether lately bowghte owte of Loose Hall of Nicholas Springe, gentleman, abutting upon the landes of the sayd Thomas Springe as appurtayninge to Loosehall towardes the weste and upon the lande of John a Woode in parte upon the Queenes highewaye leadinge from Wattisham (*Watsham*) to Hitcham (*Hytcham*) in parte and upon the lande of Roberte Wrighte in parte towardes the easte and renteth 1s. 4d.

[*p. 37*] Ellighe Woodepastor. Thomas Bantofte holdeth for terme of yeeres one close nowe devyded into 3 parcells called Illighe Woodde Pastor containing by estimation 20 acres, abutting upon the Queenes woodd called Oxelewoodde towardes the northe and upon the lande of Thomas Springe, gentleman, appurtayninge to Loosehall towardes the sowthe weste and renteth at the halfe yeere, 5s. 4d. 5s. 4d.

Rushes. Thomas Rushe holdeth freelye one messuage with an ortcheyarde, and certen other landes thereto appurtayninge containing by estimation [*blank*] acres

271

this is lande as yett can not be certenly knowen, and therefore can not be butteled
but renteth at the halfe yeere   1s. 6d.

Rentes Detayned

Barrardes. George Wynnyffe and nowe George Waldegrave, esquier, doe holde
freelye serten landes called Barrardes containing by estimation 5 score [*100*] acres,
sometymes Sir Thomas Jermyns, knighte, lyenge in Kettlebaston (*Ketlebarston*),
and as it appereth shoolde rente to this mannor every halfe yeere   2s. 4d.

Crowes. And more of Mihell Flegge for Crowes which lykewyse shoolde rente
to this manner at the halfe yere   3d.
Bothe which parcells be detayned, and as it seemeth have beene ever synce the
mannor of Barrardes was solde from Sir Thomas Jermyn unto Mr Waldegrave and
Mr Wynnyffe which was, as is thowghte, abowte the raigne of [*blank*].

[*p. 38 blank, p. 39*] Monks Eleigh (*Monkes Illighe*). Let it be remembered, at the
Coorte there holden the 29 of Apryll 1600, in the 42nd year of [*Queen*] Elizabeth,
came Symon Blomfilde and Mr Hye, betweene whom after there was great variance
for the unequall proportion of there rentes of the Clickett, it was then ordered that
Symon Blomfilde shoolde paye for his Clyckett Meadow, 1s. 6d. a year and Mr Hye
shoolde paye for the Clyckett,   1s. 9d. a year.

More complaynte was then made by R Monnynges, gentleman, by his attorney
R.R. [*?Robert Ryece*] that his messuage called Higlens was overcharged in rente by
2s. a year and upon certen ancient rentalls then shewed, the receiver Mr Wynter and
the stewarde called Roberte Grove who came with the receyver discharged the sayd
rente of 2s. as by the entery in the coorte appereth, the coppy wherof remayneth
with my cosen Monynges. [*Remaining half page blank.*]

Copy of a petition to the dean and chapter of Christ Church, Canterbury, from the
tenants (named) of the manor of Monks Eleigh respecting the appointment of a
steward, 27 January 1611[/12], [*written in the hand of Robert Ryece*]

[*p. 40*] Right Woo[*rshipfu*]ll. Understandinge the great desyer which some of late
have had, to farme the royalties of this your mannor of Monks Eleigh (*Monkes
Illighe*), in which they spare not to speake that thay have allredy accomplished the
same: Wee, whose names arre here underwritten, tennantes to your mannor, and
in the name and behalfe of the reste not here mentioned, coolde [*could*] not but
for divers good considerations entreate you even with the uttermost of our affections, to so good Lordes, to vowtesafe [*vouchsafe*] a staye for a while heerein, yf
any suche have solicited therein. Wee well knowe of your contynewall advisednes,
and uprightnes, in all your other courses, so have wee not the leaste cawse, to
inspecte any of your proceedinges heerein. The matter which wee wolde be bowlde
to laye before you, is, ever since this mannor hathe bynne in your lands, with your
predicessors as to the ch[*?urch*] both our auncestors with our selves, shoolde be
to[*o*] ingratefull yf wee should not acknowledge a most moderate wyse and lovinge
dealinge with us, even such as wee arre not now to expecte any longer, the same
commynge into the handes of farmors of inferior regarde, and unlymyted affection. The experience of the woorlde at this day enformeth us how many there be,
that desyer to employe there whole estates to holde, depende and lyve under the
ch[*?urch*], but especially under this your seigniory, where allienations arre observed
to befalle more often to the greater benefyte of the lorde, then in the mannor of any
lay lord as encoraged by the ever conscionable, and moderate dealinges in the one
and deterred by the unbownded ever exactinge desyres of the other. So can wee not,

but acknowledge also wee have had a plentiful taske, and experience of your often compassionate and most wyse determynation, of sondry differences have amonge your tenantes, at your comynge amonge us; where the very awe of your presences, uppon the manyfolde proofe of your uprighte judgementes (to the great encrease of your estimation) hathe geven a redy ende to all such variaunces, utterly to be bereaved, by the farmors monopoly of thes your royalties wee desyer not heerein the leaste parte of your losses, but whatsoever shall arise due as accustomed, with all cheerefull wyllyngnes to yeelde the same, to so good lordes, yea with muche more contente, then unto a farmor, whose steppes wee feare wyll gyve some diminution and mercifull dealinge. The laste motyve which with not lesse liberty and [illeg.] affection, wee woold entreate, we may commende unto your worshippes is; that it woolde please you to be very carefull and respective in the choyce of your nexte stewarde, whereupon dependeth a great parte of your estimation here. Thankes be to the lorde by your good providence and oversightes, wee have hitherto so lyved in the sunne shine of your favour [*p. 41*] that wee have no cawse to complayne. But yf wee shalbe exposed to your mercenary stewarde of an unlimited farmour, especially when the awefull regarde of your wonted presences shall not be at hande, to overwaye and contayne hym in his fytt courses, we have juste cause of apprehension and feare. it hathe pleased his most excellent majestye, by a publique lawe to bownde and lymytt the exorbitante stewardes of his courtes; May not therefore his poore caveat with this our ernest entreatye be the more regarded? Wee desyer not any mans losse, much lesse to abridge the leaste mighte of wonted dewe, that which wee woolde entreate is, to have suche a wyse, and understandinge stewarde, which may respecte especiallye the brightnes of your estimation, which for justice and mercye hathe shyned here with all emynencye, farre above \all/ the courtes of thes partes, that your rytes and customes maye be inviolablye preserved, all buysynes of your courte may be with a wyse moderation handled; juditiously entered and fayerly enrowled, to the encreasinge of the number of your tenantes, seenge all things managed and distributed with so wyse and comely a proportion. Yf wee have spoken heerein owghte to any offence, it was no parte of our desyers: yf wee have fallen upon some things worthie of due consideration, we beseech the everlyvinge thay may receyve such a lyvelye impression in your thowghtes that thay may produce all honorable effects. So shall wee as wee \have/ ever juste cawse, styll entreate the everlyvinge for your preservation and longe contynewances, in all true honor and happynes. Monkes Illighe this 27 of January 1611.

Your worships tennantes in all good affection and redines to be commanded.

Robert Ryece [*signature, but the following names are copied in the same hand, probably Ryece's*].

Edwarde Salter	Robert Downes
Robert Munninge	Josua Warde
William Hubert	John Parker
Symonde Blomfylde	John Hubert
Stephen Hubert	George Gardiner

To the Right woorshipfull our very good maysters the Deane, Receavour, Prebendes and all the reste of that woorshipfull societye and chapter of Christes Churche in Canterbury

Yeve[161] these

[*In Latin, italic script*] Agrees with the original (*Concordat cum Originali*).

[*p. 42*] Copy of an agreement between Mr Edward Salter, parson of Monks Eleigh and his tenant Josua Warde respecting part of the parish glebe, 3–8 March 1611/12 [*in the handwriting of Robert Ryece*]

Whereas there hathe byn late question and difference between Master Edwarde Salter, bachelor of dyvinitye and now parson of Monks Eleigh (*Monkes Illighe*) in the cownty of Suffolk on the one partie and Josua Warde of the sayd towne and cowntye, yeoman, on the other partie, concernynge one pasture, peece of gleabe, late errable, lyenge there in a close nowe comonly called Bearne Crofte, and nowe farmed amonge others by the sayd Josua Warde of the sayd Master Edward Salter, which sayd peece of gleabe lande resteth ambiguous and dowbtefull howe farre it should extende, bycawse the sayd Master Salter affirmeth it dothe abutte upon the comon waye there towardes the sowthe, whereunto he is moved by the scite of the place, probabyllyties and other good testimonyes. And the sayd Josua Warde averreth that the sayd peece of gleabe goeth no farther then the plowed landes endes, as thay do now lye, beinge heere unto induced by the probable testimony of awncient persons knowenge and occupienge the same.

Now for that it appeereth playnely that the sayd Josua Warde with his predicessors occupiers of the farme called Boyton Hall have tyme owte of mynde (beyond that which no memory of man can remember) farmed of the parsons of Monks Eleigh (*Monkes Illighe*), and occupied the sayd parcell of gleabe, but with what lymyttes uncertayne. And so howsoever it may be certenly supposed that this peece of gleebe with sondry others now lyenge intermised in those partes, lyenge so inconveniently and remote from the parsonage of Monks Eleigh (*Monkes Illighe*), gave the parson incumbentes of those tymes (more enclyned to devotion and holye lyfe then to care of secular proffitt) firste occasion to accept of a yeerely consideration for the same accordinge to the full vallewe, as every age dyd affourde, which course ever synce by the successors have byn contynewed.

And for that the sayd Master Salter moved only with a desyer to understande, preserve and mayntayne the rightes of his church (whereunto by canonical oathe he is bownde) hathe entered into this clayme and demande, wherein notwithstandinge so farre forthe as it concerneth hym, and the dutye of his church, he is most wyllinge to submytte hym selfe to the order and arbitrating of us his neighbouris and pareshioners heere under named, whose uprightnes, experience and longe [*p. 43*] knowledge of these parcells geveth \hym/ good hope that wee wyll applye our best endeavours so farre as so dowtefull a cawse wyll require, to setle some good corse, most pleasinge to god, with the leaste detrimente to the church yf only and to the comon peace of the towne heere amonge us.

And for that the sayd Josua Warde, with no sinister intente or meaninge, hathe and dothe keepe his righte and present possession dyvolved unto hym by acquisition and purchase from suche his predicessors, occupiers of the lande, whom he ever fyndeth in quiett possession of the same, with owte the leaste interruption for owhte that every he coulde any ways see or heere. Notwithstandinge that it shall not appeere that he hathe any lytigious humor or corrupted desyer to clogge his conscience, with any such supposed injuste gayness. But rather as one studious of all peace, desyrous

---

[161] *Yeven*, to give freely, voluntarily or generously, especially in response to a request (see *MED*), in other words, 'Please comply with our request in this petition.'

by all good meanes to enertayne all unfayned amytye wth the sayd Master Salter his very reverende and loving pastor. Yea rather to adde to that church that which might be to the good quiett thereof. That it mighte be more evydente to the woorlde, howe farre he is from detractinge ennythinge from the rightes, fee and demeasnes of holye church. And so well knowenge how precious a thinge godly peace is, hathe most willingly submitted hym selfe, to be ordered herein, but us his neighbours and pareshioners of this sayd towne heere undernamed.

So that wee, Robert Munnynge, gentleman, Robert Downes, gentleman, John Parker, Thomas Gosselyn, George Gardiner, Charles Sterne, Wylliam Raffe, George Chaplyn and Henry Munnynge, all pareshioners of the towne of Munkes Illighe by vertue of the sayd refermente and submission, do hereupon mediate, deeme, order and entreate, that considering all the testimonye which hathe byn produced, and the uttermost of our owne longe knowledges, or of any other that can saye any thinge in the cawse the matter resteth yett bothe ambiguous, difficulte and dowbtefull, that an upright desire can fynde no suer grownde [p. 44] which ways in every poynte safely to enclyne it woolde please the sayd Master Salter and Josua Warde for a fynall ende of all this difference thus to be ordered.

Firstly, that the sayd gleabe as it is heere followenge described and contayned may styll as in former tymes be lett and demised to farme by the sayd Master Salter and his successors to the sayd Josua Warde his successors and assignes, upon suche yeerely rente as thay can beste agree upon.

And concerning the greene or mere lyenge betweene the landes endes of the sayd gleabe and the comon waye there, bycawse to any understanding judgement, it can not be, but to evydente that when the charitable affections of memorable antiquytie fyrste dedicated this peece of gleabe unto the holye church, whither it then laye as in a champion filde as some ingeniouslye have deemed, or whither it was at the fyrste from all antiuytie enclosed, as the olde and awnciente trees, [?]stantyves and monuments do no lesse expresse, as other with more probabyllytie have conjectured, yett it can not be any ways intended, but that this peece of gleabe had bothe a certen and neere waye leading unto yt, otherwise suche guyfte [gift] had byn bothe fruteles and ridiculous. And therefore considering that this green, mere or hedlonde which lyethe between the landes endes of the gleabe and the comon waye there contayninge in bredthe scarce one pole and three quarters, can not to any meane [?intendiment and caparitie] well wayenge and observing the same, but be reputed as a parcell true parcel and member of the gleabe. Wee deeme it therefore expedient and doe hereby mediate, entreate, order and arbitrate that from henceforthe the sayd greene hedlonde or mere, with all the ditche thereto adjoyninge nexte to the comon waye, maye be may and shall essentially be accepted, and undowbtedly allowed as a parte of the other intended gleabe. And so the whole peece of gleabe besides the dytche thereto adjoyninge nexte the comon waye, now measured not circularly or in bowenge[?] manner as the lande lyeth and trendeth, but in righte lyne [p. 45] to extende, and contayne from the top of the dytche banke or stantyve next to the comon waye upon the sowthe unto the other ende towardes the northe, thyrtye syxe pole in lengthe and no more. And for the bredthe of it as it there lyeth, betweene the meeres at the nether ende and in the myddest it contayneth eyghte pole, and at the upper ende next the comon waye, it contayneth somewhat more then eyghte pole.

Moreover, bycawse this peece being so overgrowen with the lengthe of tyme in a settled possession of longe prescription that the true discussinge and naturall decydinge hereof as otherwise it mighte be required may seeme to exceede our abyllyties, not for the wante of good wylles but of sownde evidence to enforme us in the same. And so that which hetherto wee have sayd for repayre of supposed wronge done to holy church can not, but by some be deemed, a manifest wronge to the sayd Josua Warde and his successors. For the avoydinge therefore, of all suche clamours, complayntes and future exceptions: wee do heereby also mediate, intreate, order and arbitrate that the sayd Josua Warde, his assignes and successors, even as tyme \owte/ of mynde beyonge the which memory of man can remember, thay have quietly used, occupied and possessed there passage and dryfte over the sayd mere at the upper ende nexte the sayd comon waye shall styll at all tymes from henceforthe and heere-after, have, holde, use and enjoye his and theire quiet passage and repassage which dryfte to and froe, over the sayd peece or gleabe upon the greene mere or hedlonde at the upper ende nexte the comon waye with owte any interruption, impeachement or molestation of the sayde Master Salter or his assignes or of his successors parsons and propriietors of Monkes Illighe aforesayd.

Provyded allwayes that yf it shall at any tyme heereafter falle owte that the sayd Josua Warde, his assignes or successors shalbe by the sayd Master [*p. 46*] Salter, his assignes or successors, withstoode, stopped, molested, impeached or any ways hyndered in his or there ordinary waye dryfte and due passage over the sayd gleabe, at the upper ende nexte the comon waye as is heretofore more fully mencioned and declared, that then this present order, mediation and arbytrament, and every clawse and article mencioned in the same shall in all poytnes stande and be utterly voyde, frustrate and of none effecte and the sayd Josua Ward his assignes and successors shall every waye stande and abyde in his and there full libertye, power and freedome in all ample manner as ever he or thay did before the making of this sayd order, mediation or arbytrament or any parte thereof.

In wytnes whereof, wee have unto bothe partes of these indentures sett our handes and seales this thirde daye of Marche in the yeere of the reigne of our sovereign lord James, by the grace of God, kynge of Englande, Scottlande, Fraunce and Irelande, defendor of the faythe etc. that is to saye of Englande, Fraunce and Irelande, the 9th and of Scotland the 45th and in the yeere of oure lorde God, 1611[*/12*].

And the sayd Master Edwarde Salter and Josua Warde in signification of there good approbation, consente, lykinge and wyllinge agreement, to this our mediation, order and arbytrament, have heereunto sett their handes and seales the daye and yeere laste above written in the presence of others heere undernamed wyttessinge [*sic*] the same. Sealed and subscribed the 8 day of Marche 1611[*/12*].

Edwarde Salter	Robert Munninges	John Parker	George Gardiner
Josua Warde	Robert Downes	Thomas Goslyn	Charles Sterne
	William Rafe	George Chaplyn	Henry Munning

Wittesses [*sic*] Thomas Munnynge

Rental 8. (11 September 1683)[162]

[*p. 1*] Monks Eleigh (*Monkes Illeigh*). A yearly rentall made and renewed at a court there holden the eleaventh day of September in the 35th yeare of the reigne of King Charles the second and in the year of the Lord 1683 by the consent of the homage upon the viewe of an ancient Rentall made att a Court holden for the said Mannour,

---

[162] CCA-U63/70455/17, former CCA document number 'CCA-U63/70455/17/53' endorsed, together with '1684 [*sic*] Rental' and 'A Rental of Monkes Illeigh made at a Court of Survey held there September 11th, 1684 [*sic*]'. The 1684 date is incorrect. The date of 11 September 35 Chas.II given in the heading is 1683.

26th of June in the 41th[163] yeare of the reigne of Queen Elizabeth [*1599*] and by the perusal of other rentals rolls and records of the said mannour and other evidence as followeth

The Almes Tenement. The churchwardens and overseers of the poore of Monks Eleigh (*Monks Illeigh*) do holde by copy one cottage called the Almes House with a garden thereunto adjoyning lying by Mellcrofte Gate, abutting upon the demesnes of the mannor called Mell Crofte towards the south and upon the town street towards the north, rent   2d.

Clickett Cottage: The same do holde freely one cottage latelye parcell of the tenement called the Clickett with a little yard abutting upon an orchard whereupon a messuage sometime stood called the Clickett, otherwise Abbotts, sometime of William Hye and before Allexanders and now in the occupacon of Job Merchant towards the north containing by estimation foure perches, rent   1d.

Clockmeadowe: The churchwardens of Monks Eleigh (*Monks Illeigh*) hold freely one close of pasture called the Clockmeadowe containing by estimacon one acre and an halfe abutting upon the Waggarde Bridge towards the south and Oxpasture towards the north and upon the king's high way on both the other sydes, rent 6d.

Barretts. George Chaplin holdeth by copy one tenement called Barretts with an orchard and garden thereunto belonging, containing by estimation one acre abutting upon the town street towards the south and upon the bond lands of this mannour called Vincents towardes the north, rent   1s. 8d.

[*p. 2*] Pryors. George Warren, gentleman, holdeth freely one messuage called Pryors, late Springs, with certain lands, meadowes and pastures thereunto belonging containing by estimation 74 acres or thereabouts abutting upon Stackewood in part towards the east, and upon the lands somtime of John Mendham in part and of the lands formerly of William Daniell and now of William Bassett, esquire, in part and of the lands heretofore of George Hubberd and now of Jolliffe Stone in part and of the lands parcell of Brownes now in the tenure of Thomas Sorrell, gentleman, in parte towards the west and upon other lands parcell of Brownes formerly of Ralph Wright and after of Roger Martyn and now of Robert Sewell, gentleman, towards the south and upon the kings highway leading from Stackwood towards Swingledon in part upon Newland Hall in part and upon a parcel of Pryors lately sold to John Green towards the north, rent   £1 15s. 2d.

Parte of Pryors. John Greene holdeth freely one close of land containing by estimation 6 acres late parcell of Pryors abutting upon the said lands called Pryors in the tenure of George Warrant towards the east, west and south, and upon the lands formerly of Robert Cutler and now of the said John Green towards the north, the whole rent of Pryors aforemenconed was £1 17s. 2d., so the proporcon thereof to be paid by Green is   2s.

Parcel of Pryors. The said George Warren holdeth also by free deed one other close of land parcell also of Pryors with a grove containing 8 acres by estimation abutting upon the waye called Lye Lane towards the south and upon Pryors grove towards the west, rent   3s. 1d.

[*p. 3*] Davyes Yard. The said George Warren holdeth freely one pightle of land or pasture containing one rood and an halfe abutting upon Stackwood Street towards

---

[163] '41th' represents the common parlance of the period, i.e. 'the one and fortieth'.

the weste and upon the lands heretofore of Thomas Coe and now of Mr Stone towards the east, north and south   3½d.

Kemps. [Blank] Prentice, gentleman, holdeth freely one messuage called Kemps lying att Stackwood with 3 closes containing togeather 7 acres or thereabouts, whereof the one piece abutteth upon Stackwood Street towards the west and upon Catts Croft towards the east, the 2d. piece called the Old Yard containing by esti-macon 1 acre and an halfe abutting upon the highway leading from Stackwood Street to Swingledon Green towards the west and upon Reads towards the east and lyeth between Ashwolds towards the north and Stackwood Green towards the south, the 3d. piece called Stackwood Field otherwise Kemps containing by estimation 4 acres abutteth upon the highway leading from Stackwood Green to Gedford Bridge towards the north west and upon the highway leading to Mannywood in part and the Tuft in part towards the south, rent   4s. 4d.

Croxalls. The same holdeth freely one parcell of land called Croxalls, parcell of Springs, containing by estimation 5 acres abutting upon the highwaye leading from Stackwood to Monks Eleigh (Monks Illeigh) towards the north and upon Manny-wood towards the south rent   3s. 2d.

Parcell of Croxalls. The same holdeth freely an other parcell of Croxalls containing by estimation 5 acres abutting upon the highway leadinge from Milden (Milding) to Swingledon Greens [sic] towards the west and upon the lands formerly of Thomas Coe and now of Mr Stone towards the east,   3s. 2d.

[p. 4] Cats Crofte. Reades. The same holdeth freely two peices of ground some-time John Chaplins whereof the one called Catts Croft contains by estimation 3 acres lying between Mannywoode towards the south east and upon the lands some-time of Robert Mann in parte and the said tenement called Kemps in parte towardes the northweste, one head abutting upon a lane leading from Stackwood Green to Manny Wood towards the southwest and upon the customary land of the mannour of Beaumonds (Beamonds) [in Lindsey] towardes the northeast. The other piece called Reads contains by estimation 4 acres lying between the highway leading from Gedford Bridge to Stackwood Streete towards the south and the customary lands of the mannour of Beamonds called Ashewoldes on the northeast rent   2s. 2d.

Brownes. Thomas Sorrell, gentleman, holdeth freely certaine lands called Sadlers containing by estimation 7 acres parcel of Browns which with an other parcel of Brownes called Partibles, containing 13 acres now belonging to the said George Warran, are abutting upon the first said lands called Pryors towards the east and upon the grove heretofore of John Hubberd in part and the lands of Thomas Appleton, gentleman, in part towards the west, rent for both is paid by the said Thomas Sorrell in lieu thereof Mr Warren payeth the rent of certaine woods in Mr Sorrells tenure, rent is   3s. 2d.

Parcell of Brownes. The same holdeth freely 3 peices of land, meadow and pasture called Wheat Close, the Strubbe and Maids Greene likewise parcell of Brownes, containing by estimation 20 acres abutting upon the firste said parcell of Pryors land towards the west and upon the lands sometimes of John Stephens toward the east, rent   3s. 1d.

[p. 5] Corboldes. John Marchant holdeth freely one messuage with the appur-tenances containing by estimation 1 acre and halfe called by the names of Gaytes Woods and Padlock Hall late Corbolds adjoining to a river by Gedforde Bridge towards the south and the highway leading from Chelsworth to Lavenham toward the north, rent   2s. 2d.

Porters. Ann Canham, widow, holdeth freely a messuage called Porters otherwise Spriggs with 18 acres of land by estimation, lying in two parts whereof the house and one of the said parts abutt upon the lords river towards the north and upon the highway leading from Gedford Bridge to Hadleigh toward the south and the other part abutteth upon the highway leading from Gedford Bridge to Boyton Hall towards the east and upon the lands sometimes of John Day and now of Mrs Caly in part and the lands sometimes of Stephen Hubberd and now of Robert Coleman, gentleman, in part towards the west, rent   7s. 9d.

Pettytts. The same holdeth freely one close of pasture called Pettytts containing by estimation 5 acres abutting upon the high way leading from Gedford Bridge to Boyton Hall towardes the west and upon the lands called Powling now belonging to the said Mrs Canham towards the east, rent   1s. 2d.

Abbotts Park Meadow. The same holdeth freely one meadow with a lane containing 3 roods lying between Chelsworth Park towards the east and Chelworth part [sic] feild meadow sometime of John Greene and now of George Salter, gentleman, towards the west and abutteth upon the lords river towards the north and the high way leading from Gedford Bridge to Hadleigh towards the south Rent
       2s. 6d.

[p. 6] Mell Meadow. The same holdeth freely 5 acres of meadow by estimation sometime Robert Chaplins parcell of Cobbolds Mill abutting upon the river towards the south and the highway leading from Bildeston (*Biddleston*) to Lavenham towards the north, rent   6s. 0d.

Mell Meadow 2 acres. The same holdeth likewise freely one other parcell of meadow sometime Robert Chaplins containing 2 acres 28 pole lying between the said Mell Meadow toward the north east and a meadow going to the mill dam belonging to Cobbolds Mill now in the tenure of Edmund Clarke towards the south west, rent   2s. 2d.

Stertopes. Samuel Baker holdeth freely one tenement called Stertops with a yarde containing by estimation 3 roods abutting upon the lords river towards the south and upon the town street towards north, rent   6d.

Topshopps. The same holdeth freely a tenement sometimes a smith's forge called Toppshopps near Geddford Bridge now in the possession of Michaell Kitchen abutting upon the kings high way round about, rent   4d.

Stanesbyes. Susan Dare, widow, holdeth by copy a messuage called Stanesbyes with certain yards, a pond thereto belonging, together with a meadow adjoining unto the said yard containing together by estimation 3 acres the said meadow abutteth upon the lord's river towards the south and the town street towards the north, rent
       7s. 2d.

William Hobbertes. Ann Chaplin, widow, howldeth freely one messuage called Wylliam Hobbards at Swingledon with certaine lands, meadowes and pastures lying in 2 parts, the said messuage and 4 acres of the lands [p. 7] abutt upon Swingledon Green towards the west and upon the lands formerly of Thomas Nutt and now of Miles Bucket, gentleman, in part and the lands sometime of Robert Cutler now belonging to Mr Hale in part toward the east, and the rest of the said lands containing 12 acres by estimation lye in 4 severall parcells adjoining with a way thereunto belonging   7s. 2d.

Parkers. Robert Addams holdeth by copy one tenement called Parkers with a yard containing about 1 rood abutting upon the town street towards the south and upon the demeasnes of the mannour being the hall yard toward the north, rent   9½d.

Cobbolds Mill. Edmund Clarke holdeth freely the watermill called Cobbolds with 3 acres of pasture abutting the river towards the south and upon the highway leading from Lavenham to Bildeston (*Biddleston*) towards the north together with 3 acres of land and meadow abutting upon the said river and mill damm towards the north and upon the highway leading from Gedford Bridge to Hadleigh towards the south and upon the lands aforemenconed called Porters towards the west, rent
4s. 0d.

Mell Meadow. The same likewise holdeth freely a little piece of meadow containing by estimation one acre lying between Turners Garden on the north and the said meadow of the said Anne Canham aforemenconed called 2 acres toward the south, rent
1s. 10d.

Turnors Yard. The same likewise holdeth freely one yard or garden called Turnors sometime Henry Monnings containing by estimation 1 acre abutting upon the said highway leading from Lavenham to Bildeston towards the north and upon the said meadow called Millmeadow towards the south, rent
2s. 2d.

[*p. 8*] Haywards. George Leppingwell holdeth by copy 1 tenement called Haywards with a garden and an orcharde containing by estimation one rood abutting upon the lord's lands called Byfold towards the west and upon the Church Streete towards the east, rent
1s. 4d.

Mondames. Robert White of Boxford, gentleman, holdeth freely 1 croft containing by estimation 5 acres whereupon 3 tenements called Mondames heretofore stood abutting upon the towne street towards the south and upon the lande called Higlens formerly Mr Mounings and now Mr Richard Coleman towards the north. Rent
10d.

Brondes. The same holdeth by copy one croft whereupon a tenement formerly stood called Brondes containing by estimation 1 rood and abutteth upon the highway called Fenns Street Lane towards the south and upon Gangbridge Meadow towards the north and now layd into the said meadow. Rent
4s.

Eme Rands. The same holdeth freely a messuage called Eme Rands and a crofte of land and pasture thereunto adjoining containing by estimation 3 acres abutting upon the high way leading from Monks Eleigh (*Monks Illeigh*) Tye to the churche there towards the north and upon the lands called Hunts heretofore of William Hobert, gentleman, and now of Hunt towards the south west. Rent 2s.   4d.

Mascales. The same holdeth freely one messuage called Maskales with one field called Maskales Field containing by estimation 9 acres, Maskales Grove 4 acres, Maskales Yarde 1 acre and halfe, Maskales Pightle 2 acres, North Fielde 7 acres, Thisley Feilde 12 acres, Waggard Feilde 5 acres, Stubbyfielde 5 acres, Sandpit Field 2 acres and an half and 2 peices in one place adjoyning in Littlewood Feild 2 acres by estimation. All together 50 acres, rent
£1 10s. 0d.

[*p. 9*] Chaplins. The same holdeth freely a toft called Chaplens with the yard and one close of pasture thereunto adjoyning containing by estimation 6 acres and one other close of land called Homaine Croft containing by estimation 7 acres and abutting upon the Tye Green towards the west and upon the lands next hereafter menconed called Raynes in part and upon Maskales aforesaid in parte towards the east. Rent
8s. 4d.

Rayners. The same holdeth freely a toft called Rayners with a piece of pasture called the Blackhouse Yard containing one acre and an halfe and one field or close of pasture called Reynors Pightle containing by estimation 6 acres abutting upon the green called Monks Eleigh (*Monks Illeigh*) Tye towards the west upon the lands here next menconed called Raynors Kings towards the east and renteth   2s. 2d.

Raynors Kings. The same holdeth freely two pightles called Reyners with a lane or severall wayes leading thereunto containing by estimation 6 acres lying between the land sometime of Robert Rice on the south and the land sometime of George Gardner on the north parte and abutteth one head upon the land of the said Robert Rice called Rayners Yard towards the west and south. Rent   6d.

Woodsells \otherwise Woodfielde/. The same holdeth by copy 1 piece of land in Little Woodfield containing by estimation 5 acres and abutteth upon Maskales aforesaid in parte and upon the highway in parte towards the west and upon the lord's lands called Higlens Feilds towards the east and upon the lords lands called Woodefields towards the south and upon the lands called Maskales Pond Peice in the same field towards the north. Rent   2s. 6d.

[*p. 10*] Winter Burtons. George Salter, gentleman, holdeth freely two peices of land sometime a grove called Parsonage Croft otherwise Winter Bourtons containing by estimation 15 acres abutting upon the highway leading from Monks Eleigh (*Monks Illeigh*) to Preston towards the east and upon the demeasnes of the mannor antiently called Baylives Grove towards the west, rent   1s. 10d.

Scotcroft. The same holdeth freely one peice of land containing by estimation 5 acres called Scotts Croft abutting upon the land Dedacres sometime belonging to Boyton Hall on the east and upon the high way leading from Monks Eleigh (*Monks Illeigh*) to Boyton Hall towards the west, rent   2s. 6d.

Parkfield. The same holdeth by copy a field called Parkfield now divided into two parts containing by estimation 12 acres abutting upon the bond lands of the mannor of Beaumonds (*Bemonds*) formerly in the tenure of Stephen Hobart and now of Robert Colman, gentleman, in parte and upon Boyton Hall lands called Dedacres in part towards the west and upon the highway leading from Monks Eleigh (*Monks Illeigh*) to Hadleigh towards the east with one meadow called Parkfeild Meadow containing by estimation 1 acre 3 roods abutting upon the lords river towards the north and upon the said highway towards the south. Rent   15s.

Layes. The same holdeth by copy one tenement with the appurtenances called Layes with one meadow and hop ground thereunto belonging containing by estimation 2 acres abutting upon the towne street right against the church street or green towards the south. Rent   5s.

Dedacres. The same holdeth freely 2 closes called Great Dedacres and Little Dedacres with a peice of pasture called the Lodge Peice containing together 20 acres and were sometime parcel of Boyton Hall herein after mencioned, rent   4s.

[*p. 11*] Wyncolls. Henry Hale, gentleman, holdeth freely a messuage or tenement called Wyncolls lying upon Swyngeldon Green Hyll and divers lands herein after mencioned: that is the Wash Meadow and the Long Meadow containing 6 acres, <del>Peartree Feild and the Lay adjoining</del> and halfe, the Downfield containing 11 acres, the Holmfield containing 12 acres, Whiteland containing 10 acres and two parcells of meadow called the Hoppers containing 1 acre, Barnecroft containing 6 acres, Pearetree Field and the Lay adjoining containing 25 acres, the said lands belonging to Wyncolls in the tenure of the said Henry Hale abbutting upon the common way leading from Swyngledon to Stackwood towards the west and upon the lands of the said \Widdow/ Chaplyn called Dulls towards the east and the said parcells called Whiteland and Barncroft upon Bowers herein after mencioned towards the west and upon the said highway leading to Stackwood towards the east. Rent for this \by agreement/   18s. 3d.

An other part of Wyncolls. Myles Buckett [*sic*] holdeth freely an other parte of the lands belonging to Wyncolls, that is, one meadow containing two acres and an

281

halfe lying by the foot cawsey leading from Swyngledon towards the lords mill. And alsoe one parcel of meadow called the Hopper containing one rood abutting upon the lord's river towards the north, his rent not aporconed.

The lands parcel of Bowers following ly in Milden (*Milding*)

[*p. 12*] Bowers in Milden (*Milding*). William Wyles holdeth freely a messuage or tenement called Bowers and divers lands thereunto belonging herein particularized, that is to say, Bowers Garden containing 4 acres and halfe, a field called 4 Acres, a field called Sandpitts containing 5 acres abutting upon the highway, one meadow containing 2 acres and halfe abutting upon the river and upon Combes Hill, one field called 2 Acres lying between the gleab, a field called Little Blendfield containing 10 acres, one field called Great Blendfield containing 15 acres and two pightles of pasture containing 3 acres which said lands abutt upon the lands of Wyncolls aforesaid towards the east and the lands now of the heires of Henry Gyver towards the west, rent by agreement   8s.

Other parcel of Bowers. Henry Havers, clerk, holdeth freely one messuage called Waterfurrows lately erected and certain lands formerly parcel of Bowers containing 30 acres, that is to say, one field called Water Furrow containing 6 acres, the Homefield containing 5 acres, the Lay 4 acres, 2 pightles called the Bottom and the New Break together with a field called the Pasture Lay containing together 11 acres, Barne Croft containing 4 acres abutting upon the highway on the east west and north and abutting upon the gleab lands of Milden (*Milding*) on the south, rent 6s.

Other part of Bowers. John Green holdeth freely a messuage lately erected and 4 closes of land and pasture parcell of Bowers containing about 20 acres and abutting upon the gleab land of Milden (*Milding*) and a lane leading thereunto of the one parte and the kings high way leading from Monks Eleigh (*Monks Illeigh*) to Boxford and on the other parte, rent by agreement   2s.

[*p. 13*] Other part of Bowers. Roger Green holdeth freely a tenement lately erected called Collars wth divers parcells of land containing about 15 acres and 1 grove containing 2 acres abutting upon the highway leading to Milden (*Milding*) Parsonage towards the east and upon the lands of the Lord Allington an on Collards Grove towards the west, rent   2s. 6d.

Other part of Bowers. The heires of Henry Eyver, gentleman, hold freely 2 fields called Combs Hills parcel of Bowers containing 15 acres abutting upon the highway leading from Monks Eleigh (*Monks Illeigh*) to Waldingfield and upon the lords rivers [*sic*] and the lands of Wells Hall towards the west, rent   1s.

Other part of Bowers. The Lady Reeves holdeth freely one grove called Collards Grove containing 12 acres. Rent   1s.

Other part of Bowers. [*Blank*] Preston, esquire, holdeth freely 2 woods, parcell of Bowers or Wyncolls, the one called Reeves Wood and the other Bulls Wood together with a parcell of land called Reeves Bottom, rent   3s.

Let it be remembered, after the Cutlers sold Wyncolls and Bowers to Mr Chaplin, the said Mr Chaplin sold the same in parcells and aportioned the rent at his pleasure and parte of the lands belonging to \Wincolls were sold together with some of the lands belonging to/ Bowers, so it is difficult to reduce them exactly to the said rental made in the 41th yeare of the Queen [*Elizabeth I, i.e. 1599*] wherein the yearely rent of Wincolls was 14s., the rent of Bowers was £1 8s. 7d. and the particulars as now a portioned are thereabouts.

Here end the lands of Bowers which lye in Milden (*Milding*), these following ly in Monks Eleigh (*Monks Illeigh*).

[*p. 14*] Fenne. Robert Kerrington, gentleman, holdeth freely one tenement called Fenns in Swingeldon with the meadows landes and pastures thereunto belonging containing by estimation 22 acres whereof the greatest parts abutt upon the Lords river towards the north and upon Swingeldon Green in parte and certain tenements there in parte towards the south, and he likewise holds one peice of land containing by estimation 5 acres called Foordes Close abutting upon the lands of Henry Hale aforesaid towards the south and upon the highway leading from Swingledon to Little Waldingfeild towards the north sometime of Robert Cutler, rent   £0 7s. 8d.

Part of Fenne. [*blank*] in right of his wife, daughter of [*blank*] Knock holdeth freely one tenement with a hop yard parcell of Fenns now in the occupacon of Robert Biggsby lying att Swingledon Green, rent   £0 1s. 0d.

Humble bancks. [*blank*] Stone, gentleman, holdeth freely a peice of land called Humble bancks lying att Stackewood containing by estimation 3 roods abutting on the highway leading to Ley lane towards the south and upon the lands of the said Stone called Walter Hubberts towards the north, rent   £0 0s. 4d.

Aylewards. The same holdeth freely a Toft with certaine lands meadowes and pastures called Aylewards containing by estimation 25 acres abutting upon the Holmes by Mannywoode towards the east and upon the greene leading to Ley Lane towards the west and rent   £0 7s. 9d.

[*p. 15*] Bucksgrove. The same holdeth freely 3 acres of land by estimation sometime of Thomas Coe called the grove formerly parcell sometime of Brooks lying betweene the customarye lands of the Mannour of Beaumonds called the Holms towards the north and upon a close called Gressey Cangles towards the south, one heade abutts upon a feilde called Ossley towards the west and the other head upon parte of a meadow called Cangles towards the east, rent   £0 1s. 2d.

Walter Hobarts. The same holdeth freely one messuage att Stackewood called Walter Hobarts with divers parcells of land meadow and pasture containing by estimation 50 acres abutting upon the Kings highway on every syde. Rent £2 2s. 9d.

The Alms tenement. They are held by copy by some Trustees of the parish of Monks Eleigh (*Monks Illeigh*), are now 2 tenements formerly 4 tenements, they abut upon church streete towards the east and upon the demesnes of the Mannour towards the northwest, rent   £0 5s. 1d.

Illeighe Croft. William Bassett holds freely one parcell of pasture called Illeighe Croft containing by estimation 4 acres abutting on the lands of the said Bassett towards the west and upon the lands of the aforesaid George Warren towards the east north and south, rent   £0 2s. 6d.

Bendishes. Abraham Caly in right of his wife, the daughter of John Day, holds freely a Capitall messuage called Bendishes with a peice of pasture adjoining containing by estimation 3 acres abutting upon the streete towards the north and upon the severall running waters of the said Abraham in parte and upon the Lords river in parte towards the south, rent   £0 2s. 6d.

[*p. 16*] Bendishes meadow. The same holdeth freely one meadow containing by estimation 2 acres belonging to the aforesaid messuage and abutting upon the said severall runnings of the sayd Abraham towards the north and upon the Lord's river now almost landed towards the south east   £0 2s. 0d.

Dowtyes. The same holdeth freely one close of land called Dowtyes containing by estimation 6 acres and abutt upon the highway leading from Gedford bridge to Boyton Hall towards the west and upon the lands of Mrs Canham in parte and upon Dedacre in parte towards the east, rent   £0 1s. 4d.

Goddenland. The same holdeth freely one close of land called Goddon lands containing by estimation 5 acres abutting upon the lands of Mr Canham parcell of porters towards the east and upon the land of Robert Coleman gentleman, perteyning to Fosters towards the west, rent £0 1s. 0d.

Rushbrooks. Nathaniell Lufkin holdeth freely one messuage somtime Rushbrooks with an orchard and yards containing halfe an acre abutting upon the bond lands of this mannor in the tenure of the said Nathaniel called Cow Fenn towards the south and upon the town street towards the north, rent £0 0s. 3d.

Cow Fenn. The same holdeth by copy one Meadow called Cow Fenn containing by estimation 4 acres abutting upon the Lords river towards the south and upon Rushbrooks towards the north, rent £0 5s. 0d.

[p. 17] Tainter yard. The same holdeth by Coppy one peice of pasture sometimes parcell of Burtons after Scoppes and now the Tainter yard containing 1 acre abutting on the bond land of this mannor called Vincents towards the north and upon the towne streete towards the south. Rent £0 1s. 0d.

Galletts meadows. The same holdeth by copy certaine meadowes called Galletts Meadow containing 5 acres abutting upon the Lords river towards the south and upon the highway leading from Monks Eleigh (*Monks Illeighe*) to Lavenham (*Lanham*) towards the north [*deleted*] £0 4s. 6d.

Tainter yard. The same holdeth by copy one peice of pasture called the Tainter yard abutting upon the street towards the south and upon the demeasnes of this Mannour towards the north containing by estimation 1 rood and an halfe, rent
£0 0s. 6d.

Alice Cages. The same holdeth by copy one messuage with a Curtilage late parcell of Lurcocks sometime Cages abutting upon Cow fenn aforesaid towards the south and upon the streete towards the north. Rent £0 0s. 4d.

Cutlers. Thomas Ruse, gentleman, holdeth by copy one tenement with a garden called Cutlers abutting upon the streete towards the south and upon a Garden parcell of the Swan towards the north, rent £0 0s. 6d.

Parcell of Parkers. The same holdeth by copy one peice of ground containing by estimation 3 pole in length and 2 pole in breadth with a cottage erected parcell of the tenement called Parkers abutting upon the streete towards the south and upon the Hall yard towards the north, rent £0 0s. 2d.

[p. 18] Parkers. Alice King holdeth freely one tenement with an orchard and garden called Parkers containing by estimation 3 roods abutting upon the high way leading from the Tye to Church towards the north and upon the land of Mr Thomas Newman towards the south, rent £0 0s. 4d.

Sharps. Mr Munnings holdeth freely one tenement called Sharpes lying at Monks Eleigh (*Monks Illeigh*) Tye with a yard and one long spong (*sponge*) of ground adjoining containing about 2 acres abutting upon the Tye green towards the north and upon the land of Mr Hunt in right of his wife called Pages towards the southwest, rent £0 2s. 6d.

The mannor. Mr Thomas Neman holdeth freely one messuage called the mannor sometime George Garners with 30 acres of land and pasture thereunto adjoining abutting upon Roberte Wrights called Thystley feilde in part and Maskalls in part towards the north and upon the Highway leading from Monks Eleigh (*Monks Illeigh*) Tye towards the church towards the south, rent £0 15s. 8d.

Kings Croft. The same holdeth by copy one peice of arable land somtime Risbyes called Kings Croft containing by estimation 8 acres abutting upon the demesnes

284

called Stephen Hungates feild towards the south and upon the land of Ravens Croft towards the north, rent £0 4s. 2d.

Parcell of Sharpes. The same holdeth freely one parcell of land or pasture parcell of Sharpes called Hasells Pightells containing 5 acres and lyeth between the Highway leading from Monks Eleigh (*Monks Illeigh*) Tye to Brent Eleigh (*Burnt Illeigh*) on the north and the land called Pages on the south west, rent £0 2s. 6d.

[*p. 19*] Inderbyes. The same holdeth freely 11 acres by estimation of lande meadow and pasture called Inderbyes abutting upon the lands called Ravens Croft now of Mister Barlow towards the west and upon the Highway leading from the mannor hill to the three waye Leet to Scrips croft bridge towards the east, rent

£0 7s. 2d.

Colledge otherwise Parkins. The same holdeth freely part of certaine lands some-times belonging to a messuage called the Colledge otherwise Parkers containing by estimation 9 acres and an halfe abutting upon the Highway leading from Monks Eleigh (*Monks Illeigh*) Tye to the church in part and upon the tenement now of Alice King in part called little Parkers towards the north and upon the lands formerly of George Garners called Great Inderbyes towards the south, The other parte of the premises is held by Hunt the whole rent is 5s. Mrs Newmans proportion is

£0 1s. 8d.

Tenement Inderbyes. Mathew Brett holdeth freely the tenement of Inderbyes abutting upon the said lands called Inderbyes belonging to the said Mr Newman and upon the said high way leading from the Tye to Church and from the house to Scrips croft. Rent £0 0s. 10d.
This Rent with the rent for Inderbys makes 8s. which was the Old rent.

Kings or Hoberts. Bartholomew Canham, gentleman, holdeth freely one decayed messuage of old called Kings after Hobarts sometime George Garners lying at Monks Eleigh (*Monks Illeigh*) Tye gate with 45 acres by estimation of land meadow and pasture abutting upon the Bond lande of Mr Harte formerly of John Parker called little high feild in part and upon the bond land called Sussells in part towards the north and upon Monks Eleigh (*Monks Illeigh*) Tye in part and upon the lands of Mr White formerly [*p. 20*] of Mr Rice in part called Reyners and upon the land called northfeild and Thistly field towards the south. Rent [*blank*]

Sussells. The same holdeth by copy one Close of land with a meadow thereto belonging called Sussells containing by estimation 20 acres abutting upon the Highway leading from Monks Eleigh (*Monks Illeigh*) Tye to Preston towards the west upon the lands of the said Bartholomew towards the east, renteth £20 but not in charge to the Bayliffe to collect it

Parkers Colledge. John French holdeth freely one messuage anciently called Parkers now the Colledge formerly divers tenements with one little yard abutting on the high way from Monks Eleigh (*Monks Illeigh*) Tye to the church and field called Kings Croft towards the south, rent £0 2s. 8d.

Allingtons. Alice Clark widow holdeth freely one tenement Allingtons abutting upon the land called Birches now John Beaumonts in parte and upon parcell of the orchard of the bond land called Tentemaines in part towards the north and upon the street towards the south, rent £0 1s. 9d.

Asleses. Edward Sympson holdeth freely one tenement called Asleses with a little yard abutting upon Birches towards the north and east and on the street towards the south, and upon the said tenement called Allingtons towards the west, renteth In ancient Rentalls these 2 last tenements and laid in one intire rent of 2s. 5d.

£0 0s. 8d.

[*p. 21*] Bricketts. Mr Hindes holdeth by copy one tenement orchard and garden called Bricketts containing by estimation halfe an acre abutting upon the highway leading from Lavenham (*Lanham*) to Bildeston (*Bilson*) towards the north and upon the demesnes called mell Crofte towards the south, rent £0 4s. 10d.

Dominicks meadow. William Baker, Clerke holdeth by copy one meadow called Dominicks containing by estimation 2 acres abutting upon the high way last menconed towards the north and upon the Lords river near the Mill damm towards the south, rent £0 3s. 0d.

Dominicks garden. The same holdeth by copy one Garden or meadow containing by estimation halfe an acre called Dominicks garden abutting upon the last menconed high way towards the north and the said River towards the south, rent £0 1s. 0d.

Parcell of the Swan. [*blank*] Bird holdeth by copy one cottage late Heywards and parcell of the Swan abutting upon the street towards the south and upon the Swan towards the west £0 0s. 10d.

Tylers. John Markant holdeth freely one tenement called Tylers formerly of William Hy, clerke with an orchard and garden containing by estimation 1 rood and half abutting upon the said river towards the south and upon the streete towards the north with a <garden> rood of ground occupied therewith parcell of the Clickett rent £0. 0s.4d.

Abbotts. The same holdeth freely one peice of ground whereon formerly was a messuage called the Clicketts [*otherwise*] Abbotts sometime Alexanders containing by estimation 1 acre and 1 rood abutting upon the said River towards the south and upon the street towards the north, rent £0 2s. 6d.

[*p. 22*] Birches. John Beaumont junior gentleman, holdeth freely one messuage called Birches containing by estimation halfe an acre abutting upon the street towards the south and upon the bond land of this mannor called Calves croft towards the north, rent £0 0s. 8d.

Calvs croft. The same holdeth by copy one peice of land called Calvs croft containing by estimation 4 acres abutting upon Birches aforesaid towards the south and upon Parsonage Croft towards the north, rent £0 4s. 0s.

Vincents. John Beaumont senior, gentleman, holdeth by copy one messuage called Vincents with a pightell of land containing by estimation 2 acres abutting upon the streete towards the south and upon the Burtons towards the north, rent £0 3. 0d.

Mary croft. John Beaumont junior holdeth freely one peice of land called Mary croft formerly of James Man containing by estimation 1 acre and halfe abutting upon the highway from Monks Eleigh (*Monks Illeigh*) to Boxford towards the east and upon the land of Harry Havers formerly Cutlers towards the west, rent £0 1s. 1d.

Fosters. Robert Colman, gentleman, holdeth freely All that Capitall messuage called Fosters with all the lands thereunto belonging containing by estimation 100 acres lying near and for the most part adjoining to the said messuage, renteth £2 11s. 4d.

Pond meadow. The same holdeth by copy 1 meadow called Pond meadow containing by estimation 3 acres abutting upon the Lords river towards the north and upon Fosters towards the south, rent £0 2s. 0d.

[*p. 23*] Allen down. The same holdeth by copy one feild called Allen down feilde containing by estimation 18 acres, abutting upon the high way leading from Gedford bridge to Swyngledon towards the north and upon parcell of Fosters towards the south, rent £0 7s. 0d.

Parkfeild. The same holdeth by copy 1 parcell of Parkfeild containing by estimation 5 acres abutting upon great Parkfeild towards the south and upon the bond land of the mannor of Beamonts in the tenure of the said Robert called the Grindell of Slade towards the west, rent   £0 5s. 0d.

Webbs croft. The same holdeth freely one peice of land so called containing by estimation 8 acres abutting upon the lands of widdow Chaplin called Dulls meadow towards the south and upon Allen downe field aforesaid formerly Stephen Hobarts towards the north, rent   £0 2s. 11d.

Hunts Pages. [*blank*] Hunt in right of his wife, widdow of Richard Bruning holdeth freely one messuage called Hunts with a crofte of land and a pightle of pasture containing 3 acres abutting upon the green called Monks Eleigh (*Monks Illeigh*) Tye towards the north and upon lands called Ravens Croft towards the south And one feild and certain parcells of land formerly of William Hobart called Pages containing by estimation 18 acres and one yard containing 1 acre called Pages yard, 1 pightell called Pages Pightell containing halfe an acre, one pasture called Long pasture containing 4 acres, and other land containing the the whole 50 acres be the same more or less and part of the lands afore-[*p. 24*]-menconed called Colledge [*otherwise*] Parkes whereof Mr Thomas Newman hath the other part, which said lands for the most part abutting on the lands of Thomas Newman belonging to a messuage called the mannor in part and upon Ravens croft in part and upon the lands of Mr Richard Coleman belonging to Stonecroft.   Rent £0 16s. 10s.
The whole Rent of Hunts is 1s. 6d. and the rent of Pages in the Rentall of 41 Eliz: [*1599*] includeing Ravenscroft is £1 2s. 0d. in all £1 3s. 6d. whereof the heires of Mr William Hobart payes 10s. yearly as is hereafter sett forth, and Mr Hunt payes 13s. 6d. to which is added 3s. 4d. yearly for Hunts part of land called Colledg otherwise Parkers.

William Hobarts land. The Heires of Mr William Hobart or Mrs Barlore his widow holds freely one field containing 12 acres called Balland, 1 close called Ravens croft with a parcell of meadow containing [blank] acres, one meadow called Scrips cross meadow containing 1 acre and halfe and 1 meadow called Guys meadow containing 1 acre and halfe. These in the Rentall of 41 Eliz [*1599*] are included in the litle pages Rent   £0 10s. 0d.

Little Preston. Mr Richard Colman of Brent Eleigh (*Burnt Ileigh*) holdeth by copy one peice of meadow containing by estimation halfe an acre lyeinge in the Corner of his meadow called the Lords meadow belonging to Shelton [*p. 25*] Hall [otherwise] Brent Eleigh (*Burnt Ileigh*) Hall abutting upon the common River there towards the south and upon the said meadow called the Lords meadow and upon the Chequer meadow in part towards the north, rent   £0 2s. 8d.

Higlens. Edmund Colman of Bury St Edmunds esquire holdeth freely one messuage called Higlens sometime Robert Monings with an orchard and garden thereto belonging containing 2 acres, one feilde called little Higlens containing by estimation 8 acres, one other close called Dove house close containing by estimation 7 acres adjoining to the south side of the said messuage, 2 severall meadowes containing each of them 2 acres abutting upon Walshams river, 2 parcells of meadow or pasture adjoining called the Slades abutting upon the said river containing together by estimation 3 acres, one close called Bules containing by estimation 9 acres, one close divided into two parcells called the mell feild containing by estimation 24 acres, one close called Longs croft containing by estimation 10 acres with a meadow to the end of the said croft containing by estimation 2 acres, all which together make 67 acres, Rent   £1 0s. 5d.

Davyes. The same likewise holdeth freely one field of pasture or grove with a close of land containing together by estimation 10 acres called Davyes pasture, abutting upon the demesnes of the mannor called High feilds towards the north, and upon the said demesnes called Ileigh feilde towards south renteth   £0 1s. 0d.

Hogg Fenn. The same holdeth freely 1 meadow called Hogg Fenn containing 2 acres abutting upon parcell of the said Higlens called Dove House Close towards the west, and upon one of the said two meadows belonging to Higlens towards the east, Rent   £0 0s. 1d.

[*p. 26*]. Mellfeild. The same holdeth likewise freely one peice of arrable land heretofore divided called Melfield containing by estimation 16 acres abutting upon the highway leading from Lavenham (*Lanham*) to Bildeston (*Bidleston*) towards the South and upon parcell of Higlens towards the north and upon a little meadow called washams towards the east and upon other lands parcell of Higlens towards the west, renteth   £0 6s. 0d.

Walsham Meadow. The same holdeth freely 1 long meadow containing by estimation 3 roods abutting upon the River called Walshams towards the east and upon Mellfeild aforesaid towards the west, renteth   £0 2s. 0d.

Strutts. John Marchant holdeth by copy one tenement late Strutts with a Garden abutting upon the land of this Manour towards the south, and upon the street towards north   £0 1s. 4d.

The Bull. Bridget How holdeth by copy one tenement called the Bull abutting upon the street towards the west and upon the lands of this mannor in part towards the north, renteth   £0 2s. 1d.

Harpe Downe. John Wordly holdeth freely one croft of land in manner of an Harp containing by estimation 2 acres [*and a half*] called the Down abutting upon the bond land of this mannor called Allen down feilde towards the south and the highway called Fenns street towards north, rent   £0 0s. 10d.

Richard Strutts. John Syer in right of his wife holdeth by copy 1 tenemente somtime Richard Strutts with a certain way and garden thereto belonging abutting upon the bondland of this Mannour towards the south and upon the town street towards north, rent   £0 1s. 8d.

[*p. 27*] Olivers. John Sparrow holdeth by copy 1 tenement in Stackwoods street called Olivers with an orchard containing by estimation 2 roods abutting upon the lands called Reyners towards west and upon Stackwood street towards east, renteth   £0 0s. 3d.

Thorpe. [*blank*] Parker, gentleman, holdeth freely his Mansion house called Thorpe with divers lands, meadows and pasture thereunto neer or adjoininge [*that is*] 1 pightle and 1 close called gatecroft containing 8 acres, 3 pightells called dedmans layes with a little grove on the east side on the same and an other little croft on the west side thereof next Langly wood containing 9 acres, one meadow called Kiltle containing 3 roodes and 2 feildes called Langly feilds adjoining to Langly wood containing 10 acres   £1 0s. 8d.

Benstedes. The same likewise holdeth freely Benstedes yards containing 1 acre 3 pightells called Benstedes crofts containing 8 acres, one other close called Water Furrow adjoininge to the said pightells containing 8 acres and one hardelonde meadow called the Bigger Vally containing by estimation 3 acres, in all 20 acres, renteth   £0 5s. 0d.

Little Tylepitts. The same holdeth freely one litle pightle called Little Tyle pitts adjoininge to Langly feilds aforesaid towards south and upon the lands somtime of

Sir Robert Jermyn called Great Tyle Pitts towards north containing by estimation one acre, rent £0 0s. 8d.

[*p. 28*] Highfeilds. The same holdeth by copy one feilde called Little High Feild containing by estimation 15 acres and abutting upon the High way leading from Lavenham (*Lanham*) to Kettlebaston (*Kittlebarton*) towards north and upon the vally meadow aforesaid towards south, rent £0 5s. 0d.

Gawesland or Stubby. The same holdeth by copy one feilde called Gawes lande or Stubby containing by estimation 5 acres and abutting upon Highefeild aforemenconed towards the east and upon the said Langly layes towards the west, renteth £0 2s. od.

Stansbyes. The same holdeth freely one tenement called Stansbyes with a garden containing by estimation one rood abutting upon the green called Monks Eleigh (*Monks Ileigh*) Tye towards south and upon the said lands called Bensteds towards the west and upon the Highway called the Tye lane towards the east, renteth £0 0s. 3d.

Tygate yard. The same holdeth freely part of one garden sometime of Sir William Spring at Monks Eleigh (*Monks Ileigh*) Tygate abutting upon the tenement called Stansbyes towards west and upon the Highway leading from Monks Eleigh (*Monks Ileigh*) Ty to Preston towards east, renteth £0 0s. 4d.

Boores and Barrawaies. Michael Nyce holdeth by copy of the the said tenementes called Boores, the rent of both tenements being 1s. 8d. per [*sic*] and there is paid for Boores by Agreement £0 1s. 3d.

Mary Weeden holdeth by copy the other of the said tenements called Barrawaies. The said tenements joine together and abut upon the church street towards east and upon the Lord's demesnes called [*p. 29*] Byfold towards northwest and upon the High way leading from Bildeston (*Bidleston*) to Lavenham (*Lanham*) towards the south and rent apportioned £0 0s. 5d.

Skips meadow. Dorothy Goslin, widdow holdeth by copy one meadow called Skipps Cross meadow containing by estimation 4 acres lying upon the high way leading from Brent Eleigh (*Brent Ileigh*) to Monks Eleigh (*Monks Ileigh*) towards the south and upon the comon river there, rent £0 8s. 0d.

The Swann. Richard Duke esquire, Lessee of the said mannor and profits except the rents hath lately seized into his hands for some forfeiture the said tenement called the Swan held by copy with a garden and orchard thereunto belonginge containing by estimation halfe an acre abutting upon church street towards the south and upon the Bull in part and the Hall barn in part towards north, renteth £0 2s. 0d.

Newlandehall. The overseers of Monks Eleigh (*Monks Ileigh*) hold freely a messuage called Newland Hall: The rent of this and the 3 acres of land next mentioned is 4s. the rent apportioned for the said messuage is £0 1s. 8d.

John Green holdeth freely the said 3 acres of land formerly belonging to Newlande Hall aforesaid the said messuage and lands abut upon the high way leading from Stackwood to Milden (*Milding*) Green towards the northwest and upon the lands sometime of Robert Cutlers yard toward the west and upon the lands somtime of Simon Blondevile toward the south, rent apportioned for the said 3 acres £0 2s. 4d.

[*p. 30*] Rushbrookes. [*blank*] holdeth by copy one tenement with a garden called Rushbrookes sometime Chaplins and after William Taylors and abutting upon the town street towards north and upon the bond land meadow of this Mannour sometime of John Darby towards south, rent £0 1s. 2d.

Bullers. [*blank*] holdeth freely a messuage called Bullers with two acres and halfe of pasture by estimation thereto belonging abutting upon the towne street towards south and upon certain lands called Tyes towards the north, renteth
£0 0s. 8d.

Brownes 18 acres. [*blank*] Sewel, gentleman, holdeth freely a mansion house with an orchard and garden thereunto adjoininge and about 8 acres of the said 18 acres [*that is*] one pightell called Hammonds back housefeild and two pightells called Marens, the antient rent of these was 6s. 10d. the antient rent of Brownes 37 acres 12s. Mr Sewells rent apportioned for the said messuage and 8 acres and for part of Brownes 37 acres is £0 9s. 10d.

Beniamin Green holdeth the residue of Brownes 18 acres [*that is*] 3 pightells called the Mershe containing 10 acres or thereabouts with a tenement thereupon now [*illeg.*], his rent apportioned at £0 3s. 0d.

The said messuage and 18 acres called Brownes 18 acres abut upon the high way leading from Lindsey to Milden (*Milding*) towards the south and upon the lands somtime of Simon [*p. 31*] <upon the lands> Blondervill herein before menconed towards north.

Brownes 37 acres. The said Mr Sewell holdeth freely about 13 acres of the said 37 acres rent apportioned as before.

[*blank*] Freborne, gentleman, holdeth freely about 24 acres residue of the said 37 acres in the tenure of Beare, his rent apportioned £0 6s. 0d.

The said 37 containe these parcells, one closed called Wallnutt close, an other called Blacks grove and 2 closes more all which are abutting upon the High way leading from Lindsey to Milden (*Mulding*) toward north east and upon the lands belonging to the Mannour of Castlelens in part, upon Brookwood in part and upon Chappel land apperteining to Lindsey in part towards the south and contain together 37 acres

Bixbyes. Michael Nice holdeth by copy one tenement sometime Bixbyes with a garden and a meadow thereunto adjoining containing by estimation 2 acres and halfe abutting upon Monks Eleigh (*Monks Ileigh*) street towards north and upon the river towards south, rent £0 7s. 4d.

Polling Hill parcel of Bowers. The same holdeth freely a small close parcel of Bowers aforemenconed called Pollinghill rent apportioned £0 0s. 6d.

Churchyard tenement. Myles Buckett, gentleman, holdeth by copy one tenement with a Garden and a certaine footway thereunto adjoining abutting upon the church yard towards west, and upon Burton Croft towards east: rent £0 0s. 4d.

[*p. 32*] Long Hayes and Short Hayes. John Brownsmith holdeth freely 2 peices of pasture with a tenement thereupon built called long Hayes and short Hayes, parcell of certain lands called Dulls containing by estimation 7 acres and halfe, lying between the lands called Peartree feild on the north and certain lands called Illyers in parte and dull meadow or bottome in part on the south, one head abutting upon the high way leading from Wincolls to Stackwood street towards west and upon the lands called Little Dulls towards east: rent £0 2s. 4d.

Fritlemans [*sic*] otherwise Jentlemans.[164] John Marchant holdeth by copy one cottage with a Garden containing one rood somtime Jitlemans abutting upon the lands of this Mannour towards north and upon the town street towards the south;

---

[164] Fritlemans is clearly written but found nowhere else, an unlikely miscopying from Rental 7 (1599).

And hee holdeth by copy one peice of an orchard abutting upon Byrtihes towards north and the free tenement sometime of Andrewe Hobart towards south: rent

£0 1s. 0d.

Boyton hall. Robert Kenington, gentleman, holdeth freely the mannor and Capitall messuage called Boyton hall with diverse lands meadows and pastures containing by estimation 120 acres abutting upon the Manney wood in parte towards south and upon the lands called Fosters towards north and upon the lands called Kemps in parte and upon the high way leading from Gedford bridge to Stackwood in part towards west and upon the way leading from Monks Eleigh (*Monks Ileigh*) to Hadleigh towards east: the ancient rent of the whole was £1 6s. 8d. but Mr George Salter hath the 2 dedacres and pays 4s. [*yearly*] so the rent remaining is £1 2s. 8d.

[*p. 33*] The Tufte. The same holdeth freely one peice of land under Manny wood called the Tufte containing by estimation 4 acres and abutting upon the said wood towards the south and on the lands of Boyton Hall toward north rent £0 1s. 2d.

Piggs Croft. Michael Nice holdeth freely one Close called Piggs croft somtime Raynors containing by estimation 10 acres abutting upon the high way leading from Gedford bridge to Stackwood towards east and upon the lands called Fosters towards west: rent £0 4s. 3d.

Gardiners. [*blank*] holdeth by copy one tenement called Gardiners with halfe an acre of land abutting upon the street towards south and upon the bond land of this mannor called Barretts towards north , rent £0 1s. 0d.

Shellings. Nathaniel Lufkin holdeth by copy one tenement called Schellings with the appurtenances abutting upon the bond land of this mannor called Vincents towards north and upon the street towards south rent £0 1s. 1½d.

Kettlebaston (*Ketlebarston*)

Town Meadow. The Trustees for the said town of Kettlebaston holdeth freely one parcell of meadow upon the demesnes of Kettlebarston Hall towards south east and upon the gleab land of the Parsonage there in part and the lands somtime George Waldegrave esquire in part and the lands of Kettlebarston Hall in part towards the north, rent £0 0s. 6d.

[*p. 34*] Hatches. William Wright holdeth freely 5 peices of land and pasture whereof one lyeth in a field called the 5 acres feild on the south west syde thereof lyke an harp containing one acre, 2 peices lying in the eight acre feild almost in the middle thereof, whereof one contains 1 acre and the other halfe a rood which peices joine at one corner, one other peice lyeth in Sedcott feild containing by estimation one acre \which peice thereof it joyneth and lyeth under the 5 acres hedge the last peice containing 1 acre/ and halfe a rood abutting upon Rediells croft towards south and upon the bond land somtime of Robert Simpson called the pightells towards north £0 1s. 4d.

Parcell of Cabbowes. Nathaniel Gynn in right of his wife, the widow of [*blank*] Death, holdeth freely one peice of land parcell of Cabbows called Springs close containing by estimation 3 acres abutting upon the demesnes of Kettlebaston Hall in part and upon the lands sometime of the said George Waldegrave in part towards the south upon the lande of Kettlebaston Glebe towards north £0 0s. 8d.

Blocks. Isaac Bennet holdeth freely one peice of pasture formerly a tenement thereon called Stebbings since Blocks and after Martins, abutting upon the bond land of Kettlebaston Hall somtime in the tenure of John Parker toward south east and upon the high way leading from Stowemarket to Lavenham (*Lanham*) north, rent £0 0s. 1d.

Shearefeilde. Sir George Winniffe, knight holdeth freely one peice of lande lying in Shearefeilde containing by estimation 4 acres abutting upon the high way leading from Stowmarket (*Stow market*) to Lavenham (*Lanham*) towards south east upon the lands of the said Sir George part of Shearefeild towards the north west £0 1s. 0d.

[*p. 35*] Darbyes. Joseph Beaumont, Doctor of Divinity holdeth freely one messuage called Darbyes with the yards and certain lands in 3 feildes thereto adjoininge containing by estimation 20 acres abutting upon the lands of the said Joseph toward the south east and upon the church green in Kettlebaston (*K\ettle Barston/*) towards the north west renteth £0 1s. 0d.

Parcel of wages. The said Sir G Winniffe holdeth freely one tenement decayed and part of a barn remaineing with the yards thereunto adjoining containing by estimation one rood abutting upon the bond land of Kettlebaston Hall somtime in the tenure of John Parker towards south east and upon the high way leading from Stowmarket (*Stow market*) to Sudbury (*Sudburye*) towards the north west renteth £0 0s. 3d.

Parcel of Cadbowes. John Prick holdeth freely one long sponge of pasture parcell of Cadbowes containing by estimation 1 acre abutting upon the church green towards north and upon the gleab land of Kettlebaston towards south £0 0s. 3d.

Whightes. Mrs Gooday holdeth freely one tenement decayed which one peice of past contained by estimation 1 acre and 2 closes of land containing 4 acres and one meadow adjoininge at the nether end of the said closes containing one acre and a half abutting upon the demesnes of Kettlebaston Hall called Blowfeild towards northwest and upon the high way leading from Stowmarket (*Stow market*) to Lavenham (*Lanham*) towards south east £0 4s. 2d.

Parcell of Whights. The same holdeth freely one peice of land parcell of whights somtimes James Chaplins called Adams containing by estimation 2 acres abutting upon the tenement somtime of John Bick, clerk in part [*p. 36*] and the said lands called Whights in part towards south east and upon a meadow sometimes of James Chaplin towards northwest between the lands called Cabbows towards southwest and the lands somtime of the said James White towards north east renteth

£0 1s. 2d.

Parcell of Cabbowes. [*blank*] holdeth freely 1 messuage with an acre and half adjoyninge the nether end whereof abutt upon whites meadow towards northwest and the other head abutt upon the high way leading from Stowmarket (*Stowe market*) to Lavenham (*Lanham*) towards south east, renteth £0 0s. 9d.

Wages. Isaac Bennet holdeth freely one messuage called wages with a yard and a pightle thereto adjoininge containing by estimation 1 acre and a rood abutting upon the lands somtime of George Waldegrave Equire towards south east and upon the high way leading from Stowmarket (*Stow market*) to Sudbury towards north west renteth £0 0s. 5d.

Parcel of Cabbowes. Richard Murrells holdeth freely one acre of land in a pightell called little Hedg lately belonging to Stephen Bosly abutting upon the bond land of Kettlebaston Hall called littlehedge towards north west, the nether end and upper end whereof abutt upon the bond land of Kettlebaston Hall somtime in the tenure of Robert Wright towards east and west [*that is*] the upper end towards west and the nether end towards the east rent £0 0s. 3d.

Pricks parke. John Prick holdeth freely 1 peice of pasture with a tenement thereupon erected containing by estimation one rood late parcell of Whites and called Pricks park lying between a messuage called formerly Whites and now Addams towards the north west £0 0s. 2d.

[*p. 37*] Hitcham

Loose Hall. William, Lord Allington holdeth freely All that Capitall messuage called Loose Hall with 160 acres of land meadow and pasture by estimation thereunto adjoininge abutting upon the lands sometime of John Grimwood somtime parcell of Loose Hall towards the south east and upon the wood called Oxele wood in part and upon the lands of this mannor called Illeighfeild in part upon Cooks land in part upon the lands somtime of Thomas Rush in part upon the lands somtime of John Lever and Thomas Lever in part towards northwest rent   £0 19s. 4d.

Parcell of Loose Hall. John Grimwood holdeth freely certain lands meadow and pasture [*that is*] one feild called eastfeild, one meadow called Brook meadow, one meadow called wallowe meadow, one feild called Cocks land, one peice against the goldwood feild, one peice of land called Monks, and one other peice called Puntockes lying altogether containing in the whole by estimation 80 acres late parcell of Loose hall and abutting upon the lands belonging to Loose hall towards west and upon the lands somtime of John Awood in part upon the High way leading from Wattisham (*Watsham*) to Hitcham in part and upon the land somtime of Robert Wright in part towards east rent   £0 2s. 8d.

[*p. 38*] Ileigh wood Pasture. /query Why this put into the Rental since Mr Duke holds it by Lease.\ Richard Duke esquire holdeth for Terme of yeares one close divided into 3 parcels called Ileigh wood pasture containing by estimation 20 acres abutting upon the wood called Oxelewood towards the north and upon the lands belonging to Loose Hall towards the south west renteth   £0 10s. 8d.

Bushes. Mathew Isaac holdeth freely one messuage with an orchard, and certain lands thereunto belonging, these lands lately were the lands of French and contain by estimation [*blank*] acres   £0 3s. 0d.

VII

PETITION AND LEGAL DOCUMENTS
RELATING TO A RIOT IN 1481[1]

This affray took place in the month of August and the year must be 1481, the twenty-first regnal year of Edward IV and the final year of Adam Turnour's lease of the manor of Monks Eleigh. He was lessee, or farmer, of the manor between 1460/61 (at the latest) and 1479/80. Turnour, as lessee (and the victim of kidnap amidst the disorder) and his landlord and lord of the manor, the prior of Christ Church, Canterbury (whose manorial stock had been purloined), took the matter to one of the royal courts, although it is not clear which. The documents suggest it went to court as an equity case: the records transcribed here are all in English and comprise paper copies of an equity procedure, comprising the petition (with draft) of the plaintiffs (the prior and Turnour), which formed the bill of complaint to open the case, the answer of the defendants (William Hobart, his sons and servants) and the plaintiffs' replication (responding to the answer). The result is unknown, although it is notable that Andrew Vyncent, not Adam Turnour, was the lessee of the manor in the farmer's accounts for 1481–82 (CCA-DCc/MA/6, fol. 138v, not included in this volume).

In this set of documents, which are far more narrative than the other more formulaic ones in this volume, the original spelling has been retained to reflect Middle English usage, so that the rest of the volume's standard rules of modernising do not apply here.

Copy Petition to the King by the Plaintiffs[2]

To the Kynge o[*ur sover*]eigne lorde
Shewen unto youre highnesse your full humble oratoure and bedeman the priour of your monastery of Christchirche in Caunterbery and youre humble subiecte and true liegeman Adam Turnour fermour unto your seid Oratour of his maner of Monkes Illegh in the Counte of Suffolk piteously complaynyng and every of theym severally compleyneth howe that the 6 day of Auguste in the 21st (*xxjth*)[3] yere of your most noble reigne William Hobert[4] thelder of Monkes Illegh foresaid, clothmaker,

---

1. See Introduction, p. li.
2. CCA-DCc-MSSB/C/215, one sheet of paper, rolled, crumpled, dirty and damaged in places. English. A damaged draft of this petition also exists at CCA-DCc-MSSB/C/216. Any differences between that draft and this petition have been footnoted within this transcript of the petition.
3. The 'one and twentieth' year, but the king is not named (see above as to date).
4. The draft [CCA-DCc-MSSB/C/216] survives from this point onwards (its earlier part being damaged). William Hobert was William Hobert of Layham (eldest brother of Sir James Hobart (d. 1517), judge and attorney-general to Henry VII), who had two sons called Thomas (the elder) and Nicholas [W.C. Metcalfe (ed.), *The Visitations of Suffolk Made by Hervey, Clarenceux, 1561; Cooke,*

Thomas Hobert and Nicholas Hobert his sones beyng with hym daily in housold and William Clerk,[5] Thomas Ayleward, Henry Stannard and William Stannard servantez of the seid William Hobert with other evyll disposed persones, their adherents assembled and arrayed in riotouse wise and in maner of werre [*war*] with force and armes[6] that is to sey, swerdes, gleyves, bowes, arrowes and other abilymentes of werre defensibly arrayed came unto the seid maner. And than and there riotously and ayenst your peas forcibly entred the seid maner and there withoute eny warante, auctorite or cause reasonable toke the seid Adam Turnour[7] and from thens lad [*led*] hym ayenst his will to the house of the seid William Hobart in Monkes Illegh foresaid and there hym enprisoned and in prisone kept contynuelly by the space [*of*] 6 houres[8] and put hym in grete feere and ynvard[9] of his life. And in the meane tyme[10] riot[*ously*] with the seid force [*?and arms*] toke and droufe oute of the demene londes of the seid maner a bole [*bull*], 16 kene[11] and 60 sheep of the store of the seid maner leten to the seid fermour by the seid priour your oratour and there kept the seid catell in the close yerde of the seid William Hobert by the space of 10 dayes and more.[12] Wherethorowe the seid catell was like to bee enfamished and lost [*?*]through[13] grete hurte and damage of either of your seid suppliauntez.[14] Wheruppon the seed Adam gave knowelege to oon Thomas Kabyll[15] gentilman then servaunt <of> and of counseill with the seid priour and beyng his surveyoure of the seid maner.[16] Wherfore the seid Thomas Kebyll the 12 day of the seid moneth of Auguste next folowyng came[17] to the seid William Hobert, his seid 2 sones, William Clerk, Thomas Ayleward, Henry Stannard and William Stannard[18] to undrestonde of theym the cause of the seid entree unto the seid maner and of the seid taking and

---

Clarenceux, 1577 and Raven, Richmond Herald, 1612, with Notes and an Appendix of Additional Suffolk Pedigrees (Exeter, 1882), p. 145 (Hobart of Monk's Illeigh); John B. Weller, 'The Wives of Sir James Hobart (1440–1517), Attorney-General 1486–1507', *The Ricardian* 12, issue 152 (March 2001), pp. 218–48. William Hobert's son Thomas of Layham (d. 1515) may have been the compiler of Rental 2 and inherited his father's lands in Monks Eleigh and elsewhere (see p. 203, footnote 27).

5 Draft has '<oon> William Clerk <of Illeigh>'.
6 Draft has just 'riotous wise with force and armes'.
7 Draft adds here 'son of the seid fermoure'.
8 Draft says 'by the space of half a day or therabout and in the meane time'.
9 Or possibly 'inbard' (this scribe writes 'b' and 'v' virtually identically). The word is very clearly written, but obscure. The draft has 'despair', so perhaps it is a version of 'inward', a rare verb meaning 'to make inward or subjective' (*OED*), hinting perhaps at a despairing state of mind.
10 Draft has 'and besides that, while they so kept him in prison'.
11 'Kene', kine, cows, cattle. One bull and seventeen cows are amongst the various animals listed as the store of the manor's livestock attached to Accounts 2 (1310–11), so the numbers of animals forming the manorial stock had not changed much in 160 years.
12 Draft has 'by the space of 10 or 12 dayes'.
13 Draft has 'was enfamisshed like to be lost'.
14 Draft has 'hurt and damage of your seid Oratour and his seid fermoure'.
15 Thomas Kebell (1439–1500) of Humberstone, Leicestershire, a leading common lawyer and attorney to Lord Hastings (E.W. Ives, 'Thomas Kebell (*c.* 1439–1500)', *ODNB* (2004); E.W. Ives, *The Common Lawyers of Pre-Reformation England: Thomas Kebell, a Case Study* (New York, 1983)). In reviewing Ives' book, Anne Sutton describes Kebell as 'assertive, confident, impudent and loved to hear the sound of his own voice', so he was probably more than a match for William Hobart (A.F. Sutton, 'Book Review: *The Common Lawyers of Pre-Reformation England*', *The Ricardian* 6 (March 1984), p. 312).
16 Draft has 'gave knoweleche to your seid Oratour of the seid ryott so doon in his seid maner'.
17 Draft has 'And upon that, your seid Oratour gave in commaundement to oon Thomas Kebell his servant, and of his counseill to go.'
18 Draft omits Thomas Ayleward, Henry Stannard and William Stannard here.

enprisonyng of the seid Adam[19] and of the dryvyng awey of the catell aboveseid in the fourme aforeseid.[20] And than and there the seid Thomas Kabyll in reasible and curteys wise movid them and desired to undrestonde of theym for what cause and why they had soo straungely delt with youre seid oratour and his fermoure shewyng forthwith unto theym that the seid catell was by the seid priour [leten[21]] to his seid fermour as parcel of the store of his seid maner. The which William Hobart, his 2 sones, William Clerke, Thomas Aylward, Henry Stannard and William Stannard[22] made their answer severally to the seid Thomas Kebyll forthwith in this wise 'Thowe nor thy lorde nor noone of his churlish monkes gete noo catell here'. And forthwith the seid William Hobart, his 2 sones, William Clerk, Thomas Aylward, Henry Stannard and William Stannard with dyvers other evyll disposed persones[23] their adherentez myschevously disposed and sete in riote withoute any grounde or cause yeven to theym on the partie [sic] of the seid Thomas Kebyll or of the seid Adam or any other riotously[24] theer made assaute and affray upon the seyd Thomas Kebyll and Adam Turnour and[25] theym bette, woundid and evill entreted soe that they were in dispayre of their lyves contrarie to the ordre of your lawes and of your peas and not withstondyng that grete assaute and affray soo made and doon upon the seid Thomas Kebyll and Adam,[26] yit the seid William Hobert, his 2 sones, William Clerk, Thomas Aylward, Henry Stannard and William Stannard[27] and their adherentez nat cessyng but <del>continued</del> contynuyng stille their seid malice[28] daily and hourely manassed [menaced], [?]seyen and thretened theym the seid priour or eny of his come unto his seid manor for to see eny directon to bee taken in the seid matiere or in eny other concerning the seid prioure his fermoure or servauntez or yf eny persone theer woll receyve hym or eny of his, or yeve eny comfort to hym or to to eny of his the seid riotouse persones woll bette and slee theym. And in token of accomplishment of their seid maliciouse purpose the seid riotouse persones daily and hourely goo in harneys with wepons as swerdes, gleyves, bowes and arrowes and other wepons as well to the parish chirche theere as into all other places. Where-through noon officer dare[29] take uppon hym for drede of his life to execute eny warant accordyng to your lawes ayenst them or eny of theym ne the seid priour ne eny of his dare come to the seid maner to take the issues and profites therof unto the right grievous hurte and damage of either of your seid suppliauntez and a full hevy ensample unto other evill disposed persones of semblable doyng of lesse than a covenable remedie there ayenst by your habundant grace the rather bee purveyed.

---

[19] Draft has 'the cause of the seid emprisonement of the seid Adam' and omits the entry into the manor here.

[20] Draft inserts here 'Upon the whiche comaundement so geven and in performyng of the same / the seid Thomas Kebell cam to the seid William Hobert withynne the precinct of the seid maner on the xij[the] day of the seid moneth of August the seid two sones of the seid William Hobert and William Clerk and other evill disposed persones their adherentz thame there beying present with hym.'

[21] Supplied from draft.

[22] Draft omits Thomas Ayleward, Henry Stannard and William Stannard here.

[23] Draft has 'the seid William Hobert his seid two sonnes the seid William Clerk \and their seid adherentz/'.

[24] Draft has 'or eny other othe servantz of your seid orator with the seid Thomas Kebell thanne beyng there in goddes pease and yours <del>Ryottes</del> Ryottously'.

[25] Draft has 'and other the servantz of your seid orator'.

[26] Draft has 'the seid Thomas Kebell and his seid feliship'.

[27] Draft omits Thomas Aylward, Henry Stannard and William Stannard.

[28] Draft inserts here 'ageyns your seid Oratour his seid fermoure and servantz'.

[29] Draft has 'noon officer of yours ne dare'.

That it may please your highnesse of your bounteuous and benygne grace the prem-
issez tenderly considered for to graunte your gratyous letters of privie seale to bee
directed to the seid William Hobert chargyng hym by the same upon a grevous
payne theryn to bee conteyned for to appere afore your moste roiall persone and
the lords of your counseill[30] at a place and tyme by your noble grace theryn to be
lymyted and also to brynge thider with hym his seid 2 sones, William Clerk, Thomas
Aylward, Henry Stannard and William Stannard there to answere to the premisses
and over that to doo and receyve that by your highnesse by thadvyse of your seid
lords shall bee awarded. And your seid suppliauntez shall pray to almighty god and
to Seynt Thomas for the preservacon of your moost roiall persone and excellent
astate all the dayes of their lyves.

This is the answere of Willam Hobart, Thomas Hobert, Nicholas Hobert and
Henry Stannard to the bille of complaint putte ayenst theym by the prioure of
Cristes churche of Caunterbery and Adam Turnour.[31]

The seid William, Thomas, Nicholas and Henry Stannard seyen that the matier
conteyned in the seid bille is ymagyned and fayned and also determinable atte
commune lawe. And moreover they seyen to all maner coming with force and
<arne> armes, riotous entrees, with force unlaufull, assembles, affrays, manasses
[*menaces*], thretes, emprisonamentez ayenst youre peas and lawes, using, weryng
or beryng eny maner harneys, armour or wepons or eny other thyng supposed to
bee doon ayenst your peas and lawes as is comprised in the seid bille, they nor eny
of theym bee therof nothing gilty. And furthermore for the declaracon of the trouth
and for their answere for all the <remenaunt> remanent of the matiers comprised
in the seid bille, they sey that the seid Adam Turnour was endetted to the seid
William Hobert in the summe of £15 for the paiement wherof the seid Adam and
oon John Boore and William Clerk[32] were bounden by 2 severall obligacons eche
of theym in £5 payable atte severall days, wherof the dayes were passed. And for
the non-payment therof the same William Hobert sued an action of dette of the seid
£15 aye[*nst*] the seid Adam and had a capias awarded ayenst hym and for favour
love and neighburughod eneschewyng of [*damaged*] trouble, vexation and coste
that might have comen unto the seid Adam by reason of the seid processe. The seid
Thomas Hobert by the commaundement of the seid William Hobert his fader sent
for the seid John Boore and William Clerk, the which were bounden for the seid
Adam, desiring theym and also for their indempnite to goo, moeve, cause and stere
the seid Adam to pay and content the seid £15 unto the seid William Hobert or ellys
the same William Hobert wolde take suche remedie as the lawe wolde yeve hym.
Where uppon the seid John Boore and William Clerk yede [*went*] unto the seid
Adam, than beyng atte seid maner, and shewed hym all the premisses and desired
hym to pay and content the seid William Hobert the seid £15. Whereuppon the seid
Adam came to the seid William Hobert to his owen dwelling place atte Munksilly
aforeseid and than and there seied unto the seid William Hobert, for that hee had
not the seid £15 redy to <pay> bee paied in hande, desired the seid William Hobert
to take of hym for parte of contentacon of the seid £15 suche catell as hee might
by lawe and good conscience sell hym saying unto the seid William Hobert in this

---

[30] The draft, badly damaged, ends here.
[31] Another answer is given below: court process allowed several answers and replications, so it is possible that some are missing between the two answers.
[32] Boore and Clerk were tenants of the manor. See Rental 2 (*c.* 1503–*c.* 1513) above, p. 203.

wise, he hadde 60 shepe which they eche of theym saie in dede that they were nat parte of the store of the seid maner. And as for other grete beestez he had a bole and 16 kyne with other grete bestez which were the store of the seid maner under this fourme and condicon [*damaged*] might selle theym and eschaunge theym at his wille. And saied that hee and other were bounden by endenture of [*most of next line damaged*] the price of [*damaged to end of line and page*].

Defendants' Answer and Plaintiffs' Replication[33]

[Another Answer[34] by the plaintiffs (William Hobert, Thomas Hobert, Nicholas Hobert and Henry Stannard) to the plaintiffs' petition.]
[*Damaged*] indeed that under that fourme and condicon the seid bole [*?*]and [*damaged*] [*one line illeg.*] [*damaged*] bole, 16 kene and 60 sheep [*damaged and two lines illeg.*] than and there the seid Adam desired the seid William [*rest of line illeg. and damaged*] bole, 16 kene and 60 sheep were [*damaged, and several lines illeg.*] came to the felde where as the seid bole, 16 kene [*damaged*] seid catall to the use and behoufe of the seid William Hobert] [*damaged*] which the seid William Hobert, Thomas Hobert [*damaged*] seid William Hobert the which bee the seid bole, 16 kyne and 60 [*sheep*] [*damaged*] to be taken awey oute of the seid maner withoute that that the [*damaged*] [*Nich*]olas and Henry or eny of theym entreed the seid maner or eny parcel of hit in [*damaged*] [*?*]supposed by the seid bille. And afterward the 12 daye of Auguste last past the seid [*damaged*] Adam, Andrewe Vyncent, John Ranson, William Sparwe, Thomas Stanesby, John [*damaged*] and Richard Cobold and came to the parish churche of Monkes Illegh aforeseid [*damaged*] [*?*]William Hobert, Thomas Hobert Nicholas and Henry in goddes peas and yours in [*damaged*] and whan evesonge was doon the seid Thomas Kebyll with all the other [*damaged*] unto the seid William Hobert hym assaulted and reviled hym and called him foole [*damaged*] [*?*]unfitting langage without eny manassas and thretes ayenst your lawe and [*section 2*] peas [*damaged*] Hobert, Thomas Hobert, Nicholas and Henry departed oute of the Churche <del>entyn</del> entendyng to goo home to their [*damaged*] reasible maner and withoute eny maner vexacon except oonly the seid Thomas Hobard and Henry had [*damaged*] a short dagger as they daily yede [*went about*] with, and the seid William Hobert and Nicholas having noo maner of [*damaged*] uppon theym [*damaged*] evyll there and than came the seid Thomas Kebyll, Adam, Andrew, John Ranson, [*damaged*] William [*damaged*], John Breton, Thomas Breton and Richard Cobold with stones in their hands and [*damaged*] daggers and made assaute uppon the seid William Hobert, Thomas Hobert, Nicholas and [*damaged*] Hobert howe hee had taken the seid cattall contrarie to the lawe and therfore hee shuld [*damaged*] assaute upon all the defendauntz with force and armes ayenst your peas. And fourthwith threw stones atte theym and toke the seid William Hobart on the visage and sore wounded hym and the seid John Ranson toke the seid Henry Stannard uppon the hede with a grete staff and fellid hym to the grounde and fouly wounded hym. And overmore also the seid Thomas Kebyll, Adam, Andrewe, John Ranson, William

---

33   CCA-DCc-ChAnt/I/227B, four sheets of paper stitched head to tail (originally a roll), damaged. Head very rubbed, worn and stained. Areas of damage caused by damp spots from when it was rolled give large stained circles, some of which have worn through, leaving holes. Some mutilation around edges. The answer and replication procedurally follow the opening petition or bill of complaint (CCA-DCc/ MSSB/C/215–16) above.

34   This answer is different from the one above.

Sparwe, Thomas Stanesby, John Breton, Thomas Breton and Richard Cobold with grete force and armes ayenst your peas and lawes made [*damaged*] seid William Hobert, Thomas Hobert, Nicholas and Henry and uppon all other the defendauntez [*damaged*] them there and than sore bete and wounded ayenst your peas and lawes. And they and [*damaged*] the harme that the seid Thomas Kebill, [*Adam*], Andrewe, John Ranson, William Sparwe, Thomas Sta[*nesby, John Breton, Thomas*] Breton and Richard Cobold hadde was in thair assaute and in the defense of the seid William Hobert, Thomas Hobert, Nicholas and Henry and the other the defendauntez. And afterward all the seid bestes and shepe by the commaundement of my lord Howard were delivered to the seid Adam to kepe unto tyme the matiers and varian[*ces*] betweene theym were parfitely examyned withoute that the seid William Hobert, Thomas Hobert, Nicholas and Henry or eny of theym imprisoned the seid Adam by the space of 6 houres or eny part therof and withoute that they the seid William Hobert, Thomas Hobert, Nicholas and Henry or eny of theym seied or moeved eny such uncurteis words or langage that [*damaged*] Kebyll or his lorde the priour nor eny of his churlish monkes shulde have noo catall there as is supposed [*damaged*] [*wit*]houte that that they or eny of them manassed or threted the seid priour, Thomas Kebyll, Adam or [*damaged*] before rehersed and named or any of his servauntes, frendes, coumforters or welwillors yf they came to the seid maner to take any issues and profites of the seid maner to kyll theym and slee theym or any of theym or threted any man that comforted the seid priour or any of his to bete and slee theym or any of theym in maner and fourme as is supposed in the seid bill. And without that that [*sic*] the seid William Hobert, Thomas Hobert, Nicholas and Henry or any of theym usen weepen [*weapon*] and bere daily or hourely to the churche or eny other places any maner of harneys or wepen or owe to bere eny malyce or grugge ayenst the seid priour or any of his, but according to youre lawes and peas or any [*damaged*] doon or seied ayenst your peas and lawes as is supposed by the seid bille. All which matiers the seid William [*Thomas*], Nicholas and Henry and every of theym bee redy to prove as this Court woll awarde and asken Jugement and prayen to bee restored unto the seid catall and also their damages for their wrongfull vexacon in this behalf.

This is the replicacon of William, priour of Cristechurch
of Caunterbery and Adam Turnour to the answere of William
Hobert, Thomas <Hohe> Hobert, Nicholas Hobert and Henry Stannard
[*Section 3*] The seid prioure and Adam Turnour severally seyen that the seid William, Thomas, Nicholas and Henry Stannard been gilty and everyche of theym is gilty of the seid <riote> coming with force and armes, riotes, entrees with force, unlaufull assemblez, affrays, manasses, thretes, improsonamentes, using and beryng defensible arraye and weepens ayens your peas and lawes as is supposed by the seid bill of compleynt. And moreover the seid priour and Adam severally seyen that the seid William Hobert, Thomas Hobart, Nicholas and Henry Stannard imprisoned the seid Adam by the space of 6 houres and seied and moved uncourteys wordes and langage as is supposed by the seid bille of compleynt. And as to the matier by the seid William Hobert, Thomas Hobart, Nicholas and Henry Stannard allegged in their seid answere for their declaracon of the taking of the seid bole, 16 kyne and 60 shepe, the seid priour and Adam and either of theym seyen that the seid 60 shepe atte \seid/ tyme of takyng of theym was parcel of the store of the seid maner as is allegged in the seid bille of compleynt. And that the seid bole and 16 kyne atte seid tyme of takyng of theym were also part of the store of the seid maner. The same bole

300

and 16 kyne or the price of theym to bee delivered to the seid priour atte ende of the seid terme atte his electon.[35] Withoute that that the seid bole and 16 kyne or eny of theym were parcel of the store of the seid maner undre suche fourme and condicon as the seid William Hobert, Thomas Hobart, Nicholas and Henry Stannard have surmised in their seid answere or that the seid Adam seied that the seid bole and 16 kene or eny of theym were store of the seid maner under such fourme or condicon as is allegged in the seid answere. And withoute that that the seid Adam desired the seid William Hobert to take of hym for part of the contentacon of the seid £15 such catell as he might by lawe and conscience sell to hym or that hee seied that the seid 60 shepe were nat part of the store of the seid maner or that the seid William Hobert bought of the seid Adam the seid bole, kene and shepe or that hee desired the seid William Hobert to come into the demene londes of the seid maner to have delivere of the same bole, kyne and shepe as the seid William Hobert, Thomas Hobart, Nicholas and Henry Stannard have supposed by their seid answere. And as to the matier allegged by the seid William Hobert, Thomas Hobart, Nicholas and Henry Stannard for answere to the seid assaute, betyng, wounding and evill entretyng of the seid Thomas Kebill and Adam Turnour, the seid priour and Adam and either of theym seyen that that the seid William Hobert, Thomas Hobart, Nicholas and Henry Stannard to geder with the seid William Clerk, Thomas Aylward and William Stannard with divers other evill disposed persons riotously of their owen wrong and withoute eny suche cause as the seid William Hobert, Thomas Hobart, Nicholas and Henry Stannard have allegged in their seid answere made assaute uppon the seid Thomas Kebyll and Adam Turnour and them bette, wounded and evill entreted as is supposed by the seid bill of compleynt. And as to eny mysrule or mysbehavyng surmysed by the seid answere to bee doon by the seid Thomas Kebyll and Adam Turnour hit is but matier fayned of malice and evill will and nat of trouthe. And as for eny offence or myshaver [?*misbehaviour*] surmysed in the seid answere to bee doon by the seid Andrewe Vyncent, Thomas Stanesby, John Breton, Thomas Breton, and Richard Cobold, the seid priour and Adame and either of theym seyen the seid Andrewe Vyncent, Thomas Stanesby, John Breton, Thomas Breton and Richard Cobold been sadde[36] men, thryftie, discrete and of good disposicon and were present atte seid riote, assaute, affray and other offences specified in the said bille of compleynt doon the seid 12 day of Auguste, coming by soden chaunce fro evynsonge oute of the parish chirche of Monkes Illegh aforeseid not called nor desired by eny of the seid parties. And of their good [*section 4*] disposicon putte theym self in devour and diligence in appesyng of the same riote, affray and other offences. And yf their presens and diligence hadde not been meny, other grete inconvenyences shuld have followed of the same riote, affray, assaute and other offences. And to thentent [*the intent*] and by cause the seid Andrewe Vyncent, Thomas Stanesby, John Breton, Thomas Breton and Richard Cobold shuld not bee admitted as indifferent persones to testifie the trouthe of such thynges as they knowe in the premises, the seid matier supposed ayenst theym in the seid answere is by craft ymagened, feyned and contrived and is noo matier of trouthe. And where knoulegge came to the kynges highnesse of the seid riote, assaute, affray and other offencez comprised in the seid bille of compleynt, it plesid his seid highnesse by his letterz under his privie signet to comaunde his servaunt Robert Brent on[*e*] his yomen of the corowne

---

[35] 'At his electon', that is, at his choice (price or animals).
[36] That is, grave, serious, dignified (*OED*).

to goo to Monkes Illegh foresaid to undrestonde the cause and maner of the same riote, assaute, affray and other offences and to make therof report ayen to his seid highnesse. And when the seid Robert Brent came thider to execute that commaundement, the seid John Breton and other by thassent and atte desire of the seid Thomas Hobart were admytted as true, trusty and indifferent persones to report and enfourme the seid Robert Brent what persones were causers and begynners of the same riote, affray and other offences. Which John Breton and other then and there rehersyng the maner of delyng in that behalf shewed to the seid Robert Brent that the seid Thomas Hobart and his company were causers of the same riote, assaute, affray and other offences. All which matiers the seid prioure and Adam Turnour and either of them bee redy to prove as this Court will awarde and prayen that the seid Robert Brent emong other may bee examined of his delyng and what hee can sey in the premises.

GLOSSARY

Annunciation of the Blessed Virgin Mary	25 March (New Year, and a quarter day)
Christmas	25 December (a quarter day)
Invention of the Holy Cross	3 May
Lady Day	25 March (as above)
Lammas Day	1 August
Palm Sunday	Sixth Sunday in Lent, the Sunday before Easter
Pentecost	Seventh Sunday after Easter Day (Whit Sunday)
Purification of the Blessed Virgin Mary	2 February
St Ambrose	4 April
St Andrew the apostle	30 November
St Barnabas the apostle	11 June
St Edmund the king	20 November
St Faith the virgin	6 October
St John the Baptist, beheading of	24 June (a quarter day)
St John before the Latin Gate	6 May
St Katherine	25 November
St Michael (Michaelmas)	29 September (a quarter day)
St Osyth the virgin	7 October
St Oswald the bishop	28 February
St Paul, conversion of	25 January
St Peter and St Paul the apostles	29 June
St Peter in chains (*ad vincula*)	1 August
St Philip and St James the apostles	1 May
St Thomas the apostle, translation of	3 July
St Thomas, archbishop and martyr, translation of	7 July

Vocabulary

Affeerors: assessors (usually two) of **amercements** in manorial court proceedings

Akyrwar: a measurement of **warland**

Ale-taster: a manorial official responsible for ensuring compliance with the assize of ale

Amercement: a financial penalty imposed by a court

Assize rents: fixed or certain rents

Assize of bread and ale: a procedure in the manorial court's leet jurisdiction for the statutory regulation of the price and quality of bread and ale sold

Attachment: the arrest or seizure of a person by order of the court; a person might attach him- or herself by binding themselves with pledges or sureties to appear in court

Attorn: to transfer oneself from the homage and allegiance of one lord to another, to agree to be the tenant of a new landlord

Bailiff: the manorial official (a freeman, sometimes an outsider brought in for a wage) responsible for the day-to-day running of the manor (see also **reeve**; **serjeant**). The term is also used in the earlier period of demesne management for an official supervising a number of manors for a particular lord, in the case of Canterbury, below the steward but above the day-to-day bailiff.

Bedrip: a day's service of boon-reaping by a tenant for their manorial lord

Benerthe: a day's service of boon-ploughing by a tenant for their manorial lord

Boon-work: a service performed by a manorial tenant for their lord, theoretically as a willing response to a boon (a request or entreaty) or as a favour; see also *bedrip, benerthe*

Borchtruminge: another, possibly Kentish, English word meaning a view of **frankpledge** (and see p. 33, footnote 16 and Plate 7)

Bordloggys: probably similar to *bordclog*, 'a piece of rough timber, block from which boards are made' (*MED*)

Bordstokkys: a piece of cut timber or a block of wood from which boards could be cut (*MED, stok* n.1)

Bullimong: a mixture of various crops (such as oats, peas, vetches) sown together for fodder

Cantle: a piece, part or portion; an allowance for difference between razed and heaped measure. 'Measured by cantle' a measurement of volume by heaped measure

Capon: a castrated cockerel

Cart-clut, **cart-clout**: see *clut*

Chaff: the husks of threshed or winnowed grain; inferior corn

Clove gillyflower: the clove-pink flower (*Dianthus caryophyllus*), the scent and dried buds of which resemble clove spice, often used to represent a purely nominal payment, similar to rose or peppercorn rents. Such nominal rents gave the grantor a residual interest (before 1290, as a technical feudal lord of the grantee) in the property being conveyed.

Clut, **clout**: a metal patch or plate to prevent excessive wear or to reinforce woodwork on a plough or cart (e.g. *cart-clut, rest-clut, stredelclute*)

Copy, copyhold tenure: a customary tenure of unfree land, the proof of title to which was a copy of the manorial court roll entry recording the tenant's admission to the tenancy

Cotys (le): a peasant's cottage; a shelter or coop for livestock

Demesne: that part of a manor retained by the lord for his own use and maintenance

Deye (le): dairymaid or dairyman

Distraint: the confiscation of goods to enforce a court order or judgement

Doggis, **dogs**: 'a heavy metal clamp or brace of some kind' (*MED*)

Dower: a widow's right to a portion (customarily one third) of her deceased husband's lands for her lifetime, for her, and any children's, maintenance

Dredge, drage: mixed corn, usually barley and oats, sown together

Ebdomada: the term applied to the system of sourcing weekly **food-farms** or supplies from Canterbury's estates to feed the monks in Canterbury (from the Latin (*h*)*ebdomada* 'seven days'). See Introduction, **pp. 000–000.**

Encroachment: the unauthorised extension of land boundaries (e.g. by ploughing over a boundary, or enclosing a piece of someone else's land)

Essoin: an excuse for not attending court. A suitor was allowed three such excusals before incurring a fine for non-attendance

Escheat: the reversion of a land-holding to the lord on failure of heirs or outlawry of the tenant; land that has escheated to the lord

Estreat: extract or copy of a record of a court

Evysbord: eavesboard(s), wooden boards forming the eaves of a building

Famulus, plural *famuli*: servants, especially house servants, attendants; staff employed by the lord to work the demesne of the manor

Fan: a winnowing fan or basket; a flail

Farm: the technical legal term for a lease; a fixed sum paid for a lease

Farmer: lessee

Ffate (le): vat, a large vessel

Fealty: the oath of fidelity sworn by a new tenant to a lord

Fine: a money payment to the lord for a particular concession

Fine, common: a payment made to the lord each year at the leet by members of the frankpledge (also known as hundred-penny, cert-money or tithing-penny)

Food-farms: see **ebdomada**

Four-penny nails, *iiij penynail*: nails of a size to be originally worth 4d. per 100

Five-penny nails, *fyvepenynail*: nails of a size to be originally worth 5d. per 100

Forestaller: a person who purchases goods before they reach market and re-sells them at a higher price later in the day (and see **regrator**)

Frankpledge: the system of law-enforcement within the manor, under which a group of men (usually ten in number and known as a **tithing**) were bound to one another by mutual surety to ensure good conduct and investigation of civil and criminal wrongs

Frankpledge, view of: the procedure of ensuring that the frankpledge did its duty and each tithing was up to strength, undertaken by the leet

Free bench: a widow's rights, by custom, in her deceased husband's land, analogous to dower rights

Garderobe: see **wardrobe**

Gavel, gafol: (Latin, *gabulum*) rent or payment of tribute to a feudal superior, often used in compound words, e.g. **gavelearth, landgavel** (see Introduction, p. xxxvii) (*MED*)

Gavelearth: a service of ploughing and sowing in lieu of rent (*MED*)

Gersum(a): the fine or relief payable by a new tenant to the lord on admission to a land-holding

Gimmer: a ewe between its first and second shearing

Gleyve, or **glaive**: some kind of bladed weapon, possibly a lance, bill or kind of sword (*OED*)

Groundselling: the act of laying the foundations of a building, particularly one with a wooden frame; laying the foundation timber beams or groundsels

Hames, hamys: parts of the collar of a cart-horse; or hooks (with eyes, as fastenings for gates)

Hamsoken: assaulting a person in their own house; forceable house-breaking

Hall-mote: manorial court, court baron, held by custom in the manorial hall

Hayward: manorial officer responsible for maintaining hedges and enclosures, protecting grain from trespass and theft, and especially supervising the grain harvest as a kind of overseer under the bailiff (also known in the last capacity as a *messor* or **reap-reeve**)

Herbage: herbaceous growth or vegetation, especially grass or hay; the right of pasturage or payment for pasturage, depending on the context

Heriot: an unfree tenant's best beast, payable to the lord on the tenant's death

Hogget: a sheep in its second year; a yearling sheep

Hue and cry: the process of raising the alarm and pursuing, with horn and voice, for apprehending felons and people who have made assaults

Hurter: 'the shoulder of an axle, against which the nave of the wheel strikes; also a strengthening piece on the shoulder of an axle' (*OED*)

Increment: the amount of grain covered by the difference between heaped and razed measure

Issue, of issue: crops or livestock newly produced or born in the period covered by the current accounting year

Landgavel: see **Gavel**

Lathnayll: lath-nails, for attaching tiles to the laths on a roof

Leyrwite: a fine paid to the lord when a villein woman fornicated

Lind(e): linden or lime tree (*Tilia europaea*), or the wood of the lime

Lins, lyns: a linchpin

Lute: clay mixed with other components used to create a seal between two surfaces

Manupastus: a member of the household, literally 'one fed by hand' (*DMLBS*)

Maslin: a mixture of different kinds of grain, especially rye and wheat

Merchet: a fine payable to the lord when a villein's daughter married, usually higher if she married outwith the manor

Messor: a reaper; the **reap-reeve** (or **hayward**) in charge of the harvest

Metecorn: an allowance of grain as food for servants (*MED*)

Mondaylands: land-holdings (particularly in East Anglia), the labour services for which were originally done on Mondays

Multure, mill multure: a payment, usually in kind, made to a lord in return for grinding corn

Murrain: a general term for any illness of livestock

Neethows, (le), **neat-house**: cow-shed

Neif: a hereditary serf or unfree peasant, a villein by blood

Osmund, osmond: a type of wrought iron made in Sweden and other parts of the Baltic from bog iron ore. In the medieval period, it was 'imported in small bars and used for the manufacture of arrowheads, fish hooks etc. and for hardening the edges of tools and weapons' (*MED, OED, DMLBS*)

Pale: fence

Pannage: the right to graze pigs in woodland

Perquisites: profits, especially of the manorial court

Pittance: food or drink, or money in lieu of the same, provided to members of a religious community in return for the performance of a spiritual service or office, usually as a charitable bequest

Prigge, prignail: a type of small nail, similar to a brad-nail

Purpresture: an illegal encroachment, or enclosure of another person's land

Reap-reeve: the manorial official in charge of the harvest, the **hayward** or *messor* (*DMLBS*)

Recruits: young livestock that are transferred into classes of older animals as they age (e.g. calves recruited into the cows, piglets into the pigs etc.) in manorial accounting terminology

Rector: the person or institution entitled to the parish's **tithes**. In Monks Eleigh, the priory of Christ Church, Canterbury, was rector and appointed a **vicar** to serve as parson of the parish church.

Reeve: the manorial official (an unfree tenant of the manor) responsible for the day-to-day running of the manor (see also **bailiff**; **serjeant**). The term (Latin, *praepositus, prepositus*) can also be used to describe otherwise unspecified officials of various kinds

Regrator, regratrix: a person buying goods in a market to sell later in the day for a higher price (and see **forestaller**)

Relief: the fine payable by a new free tenant on admission to a land-holding

Remainders, of the remainders: livestock already in existence before the beginning of the current accounting year; that which remains as the stock of the manor at the end of it

Rest-clut, **rest-clout**: a metal plate on share-beam of a plough (and see *clut*)

Seam: (Latin, *summa, salma*) a measure of volume of dry commodities such as grain, beans, salt, fish or similar. In Monks Eleigh in the thirteenth century it was equivalent to a quarter (8 bushels), although the volume of a seam could vary according to time, place and commodity. The word can also mean a pack-saddle, and therefore by extension, a load carried on a pack-saddle or pack-horse, or more generally a load (*DMLBS*)

Seisin: possession of land

Serjeant: the manorial official (either free or unfree) responsible for the day-to-day running of the manor (see also **bailiff**; **reeve**). Its Latin *serviens* can also be used to mean servant, official or unfree tenant

S(s)epcot, **shep-cot**: sheep-cot, sheep house or sheep-shed (*MED*)

Spekynges: spike-nails, large iron nails (*MED*)

Stok, le stok: possibly a Suffolk dialect word for the place at the back of the fireplace, or immediately above it (E. Moor, *Suffolk Words and Phrases* (1823), p. 400)

Stot: a small, cheap horse, perhaps of an inferior kind or a young castrated ox used as a draught animal (*OED*)

Strake: an iron strip or tyre connecting the felloes on the outer rim of a wheel

Stredelclute, **straddle-clout**: 'a metal plate used as reinforcement on part of cart or plough' (see also **clut**)

Stues, **stews**: a pond or tank to keep fish until needed for the table (*OED*)

Suit of court: the obligation of a tenant to attend the manorial court

Tally: a receipt for payment, originally kept by notching a stick and splitting it, giving vendor and purchaser a matching physical receipt

Tielpynnes, **tile-pins**: pegs used to fasten roof-tiles to the laths (*OED*)

Tithes: one tenth part of the produce of the land, payable by parishioners to the **rector** of the parish church

Tithing: see **frankpledge**

Trendle, trundle: a circular or cylindrical component of a mechanical device, a wheel, drum of cylinder, especially in a mill. See also **trundle staves**.

Trundle staves: (Latin, *trendstavum,* ME *trendel+staf*) the spindle of the trundle wheel in a mill, the 'bar, rod or spindle of trundle wheel' (*OED* 'trundle' n. 2)

Undirframe, (le): under-frame or principal wooden foundation framework for a building

Villein: an unfree tenant or serf, tied to the land of the lord

Vicar: a delegate or deputy; an incumbent of a parish church who is not the **rector**

Virgult': (Latin, *virgultura* or *virgultum*) an enclosed plantation of shrubs or small trees, copse, grove, orchard or coppice (*DMLBS*)

Wardrobe, *garderobe*: clothes store, a privy or a store-room for valuables

Warland, *le War*: land that carried obligations to the state such as military service and especially the payment of tax or *geld*. The unit of measurement of warland (*akyrwar*) used for working out the liability for geld (*le war*) was variable in area, being based on the ability of the land in question to pay geld (see Introduction, **pp. 000–000**).

Wether: castrated one- or two-year-old sheep

Woodward: manorial officer responsible for woodland

Yede: to go, walk about or travel (*MED*)

BIBLIOGRAPHY

MANUSCRIPT SOURCES

Charters (and see footnotes to individual charters for details and enrolments)

CCA-DCc-ChAnt/H/122–23 (in folder 'H' as Monks Eleigh, is called Hellega therein)

CCA-DCc-ChAnt/I/215–27D (in folder 'I' for Illeigh/Ylleigh)

CCA-DCc-ChAnt/M/418–19 (in folder 'M' for Monks Eleigh)

CCA-DCc-ChAnt/Z/178 (folder Z, an artificial collection of miscellaneous documents)

CCA-DCc/Register/B, fols 143r–146v (enrolled copies of twenty-seven of the above charters)

CCA-DCc/Register/E, fols 385r–387v (enrolled copies of nineteen of the above charters)

SA(I), HD 1538/307/1–5 (feoffments relating to property in Monks Eleigh, thirteenth century)

Extents and Custumals (and see footnotes to individual extents for details and enrolments)

CCA-DCc-RE/87, Assize rents (probably *c.* 1250–1260)

CCA-DCc-RE/105, Extent (probably *c.* 1250)

CCA-DCc/Register/B, fols 147r–149r, Various copies of extents and lists of services and customs (between *c.* 1260 and 1330)

CCA-DCc/Register/H, fol. 160v, Valuation (*c.* 1260–*c.* 1270)

CCA-DCc/Register/J, pp. 108–13, Various copies of extents and lists of services and customs (between *c.* 1260 and 1330)

CCA-DCc/Register/K, fol. 108r, Works and customs (between 1285/86 and 1310/11)

CCA-DCc/Register/O, fols 64r–v, fols 91r–v, Works and customs (between 1285/86 and 1310/11)

CCA/DCc/Register/P, fols 119r–120r, Valuation (*c.* 1260–*c.* 1270)

CCA-DCc-Rental/38 (part), Deteriorations (*c.* 1213)

TNA, E 142/46, Extent of lands and stock in the manor of Monks Eleigh (1210–11)

Accounts (and see footnotes to individual accounts for details and enrolments)

CCA-DCc-BR/Illeigh/1, Serjeant's accounts (1285–86)

CCA-DCc-BR/Illeigh/2, Serjeant's accounts (1310–11)

CCA-DCc-BR/Illeigh/8, Reeve's account (1329–30)

CCA-DCc-BR/Illeigh/19 (building accounts only), Serjeant's account (1343–44)

CCA-DCc-BR/Illeigh/20 (building accounts only), Serjeant's account (1345–46)

CCA-DCc-BR/Illeigh/21, Serjeant's account (1358–59)

CCA-DCc-BR/Illeigh/22 (building accounts only), Serjeant's account (1359–60)

CCA-DCc-BR/Illeigh/23 (building accounts only), Serjeant's account (1365–66)

CCA-DCc-BR/Illeigh/24 (building accounts only), Serjeant's account (1366–67)

CCA-DCc-BR/Illeigh/25 (building accounts only), Serjeant's account (1367–68)
CCA-DCc-BR/Illeigh/26 (building accounts only), Serjeant's account (1368–69)
CCA-DCc-BR/Illeigh/27 (building accounts only), Serjeant's account (1370–71)
CCA-DCc-BR/Illeigh/28 (building accounts only), Serjeant's account (1371–72)
CCA-DCc-BR/Illeigh/29 (building accounts only), Serjeant's account (1372–73)
CCA-DCc-BR/Illeigh/30 (building accounts only), Serjeant's account (1375–76)
CCA-DCc-BR/Illeigh/31 (building accounts only), Serjeant's account (1377–78)
CCA-DCc-BR/Illeigh/32 Serjeant's account (1379–80)
CCA-DCc-BR/Illeigh/33 (building accounts only), Farmer's view (1400–1)
CCA-DCc-BR/Illeigh/34 (building accounts only), Farmer's view (1406–7)
CCA-DCc-MA/133, r.4 (building accounts only), Farmer's view (1429–30)
CCA DCc/MA 134 r.2d (building accounts only), Farmer's view (1430–31)
CCA DCc/MA 136 r.5 (building accounts only), Farmer's view (1432–33)
CCA DCc/MA 138 r.2 (building accounts only), Farmer's view (1434–35)
CCA-DCc-BR/Illeigh/35 (building accounts only), Farmer's view (1437–38)
CCA DCc/MA 144 r.1 (building accounts only), Farmer's view (1449–50)
CCA DCc/MA 148 (part) (building accounts only), Farmer's view (1454–55)
CCA DCc/MA 149, (part) (building accounts only), Farmer's view (1455–56)
CCA DCc/MA 150 r.1 (building accounts only), Farmer's view (1460–61)
CCA DCc/MA 6, fol. 47v–48v, Farmer's account (1478–1480)
CCA DCc/MA 6, fol. 138v–139r, Farmer's account (1481–82)

Court Rolls (and see footnotes to individual court rolls for details and enrolments):
CCA-U15/14/18 (1305–1305/6)
CCA-U15/12/19 (*?c.* 1349–50)
CCA-U15/14/20 (*c.*1350/51–1350/51)
CCA-U15/15/12 (*?c.*1350/51–1351/52)
CCA-U15/15/1 (1351/52)
CCA-U15/15/2 (1359)
CCA-U15/15/3 (1361)
CCA-U15/15/4 (1361–1361/62)
CCA-U15/15/5 (1363)
CCA-U15/15/13 (1363 or 1364)
CCA-U15/15/7 (1364)
CCA-U15/15/6 (1364)
CCA-U15/14/19 (1365 or 1366)
CCA-U15/15/8 (1366/67–1367)
CCA-U15/15/9 (1368–69)
CCA-U15/15/10 (1371/72–1372)
CCA-U15/15/11 (1373/74)
CCA-U15/15/14, part 1 (1413)
CCA-DCc-ChAnt/I/259 (1414)
CCA-U15/15/15 (1415)
CCA-U15/15/14, part 2 (1419)
CCA-U15/15/16 (1420–1422)
CCA-U15/15/17, fols 23r–24r (1545)
CCA-U15/15/17, fols 46r–48r, Estreats only (1586–1590)

Maps

SA(B), FL 607/1/3, 'A Map of the Town and Parish of Monks Eleigh' by John Miller, surveyor, 1724

Selection from J.B. Weller's own drawings in the J.B. Weller Archive (UoS)

Rentals (and see footnotes to individual rentals for details and enrolments)

CCA-DCc/Register/B, fols 149v–157r, Rental (1379–80)

CCA-DCc/MA 33, fols 43v–50v, Rental (*c.* 1503–*c.* 1513)

CCA-U63/70455/1, Rental (*c.* 1525)

CCA-U15/15/17, fols 48v–50r, Rental (*c.* 1525)

CCA-U15/15/17, fols 50r–51v, Rental (*c.* 1544–45)

CCA-U15/15/17, fols 56v–55v (in back of volume, reversed), Rental (1580/81)

CCA-U15/15/17, fols 2r–21r, Rental (1583)

CCA-U63/70455/2, Rental (1599)

CCA-U63/70455/17, Rental (1683)

Petition and Legal Documents

CCA-DCc-MSSB/C/215 (the petition) & CCA-DCc-MSSB/C/216 (draft), Copy plaintiffs' petition and draft to king commencing the legal suit (1481)

CCA-DCc-ChAnt/I/227B, Defendants' answer and plaintiffs' replication (1481)

Wills

TNA, PROB 11/14/325, PCC will of William Foorth of Hadleigh, made 2 August 1504, proved 25 October 1504

TNA, PROB 11/18/224, PCC will of Thomas Hobbart of Leyham, Suffolk, made 14 March 1513/14, proved 3 November 1515

TNA, PROB 11/21/478, PCC will of Thomas Arundell Erle of Arundell, proved 29 November 1524

TNA, PROB 11/22/549, PCC will (nuncupative) of William Bendisshe or Bendish of Leyham, made 4 July 1528, proved 9 July 1528

PRINTED PRIMARY SOURCES

Bailey, M. (ed.), *The English Manor c. 1200–c. 1500* (Manchester, 2002)

Bishop, T.A.M., *Scriptores Regis* (Oxford, 1961)

HMC, *Fifth Report of the Royal Commission on Historical Manuscripts* (London, 1876)

Davis, R.H.C. (ed.), *Kalendar of Abbot Samson of Bury St. Edmunds* (London, 1954)

Flower, C., M.C.B. Dawes and A.C. Wood (eds), *Calendar of Inquisitions Post Mortem, Henry VII*, volume III (London, 1955)

Gallagher, E. (ed.), rev. Summerson, H., *The Crown Pleas of the Suffolk Eyre of 1240*, SRS 64 (2021)

Greenway, D.E. (ed.), *Fasti Ecclesiae Anglicanae 1066–1300: Volume 2, Monastic Cathedrals (Northern and Southern Provinces)* (London, 1971), including 'Canterbury: Archbishops' (pp. 3–8) and 'Priors of Canterbury' (pp. 8–12).

Hardy, W. (ed.), 'Calendar of Patent Rolls for 2 Edw. I (1273–74),' being Appendix I, no. 4 in *Forty-Third Annual Report of the Deputy Keeper of the Public Records* (London, 1882)

Harper-Bill, C. and R. Mortimer (eds), *Stoke-by-Clare Cartulary*, SRS Charters Series 5, part 2 (1983)

Harvey, P.D.A. (ed.), *Manorial Records of Cuxham, Oxfordshire, A.D. 1200–1359* (London, 1976)

Lock, R. (ed.), *The Court Rolls of Walsham Le Willows, 1351–1399*, SRS 45 (2002)

Lyte, H.C. Maxwell (ed.), *Calendar of Patent Rolls, Edward I: Volume 4, 1301–1307* (London, 1898)

— (ed.), *Calendar of Close Rolls, Edward I: Volume 1, 1272–1279* (London, 1900)

Lyte, H.C. Maxwell, J.G. Black and R.H. Brodie (eds), *Calendar of Patent Rolls, 1485–94* (London, 1914)

Nichols, J.F., 'Milton Hall, Essex: The Extent of 1309', *Transactions of the Southend-on-Sea and District Antiquarian and Historical Society* 2, no. 1 (1929), pp. 1–35

Nichols, J.F., 'An Early Fourteenth-Century Petition', *EcHR* 2, no. 2 (January 1930), pp. 300–7

Pigot, H., 'Extenta Manerii de Hadleghe', *PSIAH* 3 (1863), pp. 229–52, translated in Hervey, J., 'Extent of Hadleigh Manor', *PSIAH* 11, no. 2 (1902), pp. 152–72

Searle, W.G. (ed.), *Christ Church Canterbury: I. The Chronicle of John Stone; II Lists of the Deans, Priors and Monks of Christ Church, Canterbury* (Cambridge, 1902)

SECONDARY SOURCES

Adams, M., 'The Development of Roof-Tiling and Tile-Making on Some mid-Kent Manors of Christ Church Priory in the Thirteenth and Fourteenth Centuries', *Archaeologia Cantiana* 116 (1996), pp. 35–59

Abels, R., 'Byrhtnoth [Brihtnoth] (d. 991)', *ODNB* (2004)

Amor, N.R., *From Wool to Cloth: The Triumph of the Suffolk Clothier* (Bungay, 2016)

— *Keeping the Peace in Medieval Suffolk* (Stanningfield, 2021)

Andrews, S. and R. Hoppitt, 'Helming Leget, Royal Servant and a Possible Designed Landscape at Pond Hall, Hadleigh', *PSIAH* 42, no. 3 (2011), pp. 300–24

Bailey, M., *Medieval Suffolk: An Economic and Social History, 1200–1500* (Woodbridge, 2007)

— 'Villeinage in England: A Regional Case Study, *c.* 1250–*c.* 1349', *EcHR* New Series 62, no. 2 (May 2009), pp. 430–57

— 'The Transformation of Customary Tenures in Southern England, *c.* 1350 to *c.* 1500', *AgHR* 62, no. 2 (2014), pp. 210–30

— *After the Black Death: Economy, Society and the Law in Fourteenth-Century England* (Oxford, 2021)

Beaven, A.B., *The Aldermen of the City of London Temp. Henry III – 1912* (London, 2 vols, 1908, 1912)

Bell, A.R., C. Brooks and H. Killick, 'Medieval Property Investors, *c.* 1300–1500', *Enterprise and Society* 20, no. 3 (September 2019), pp. 575–612

Bell, A.R., C. Brooks and H. Killick, 'A Reappraisal of the Freehold Property Market in Late Medieval England', *Continuity and Change* 34, no. 3 (December 2019), pp. 287–313

Briggs, K. and K. Kilpatrick, *A Dictionary of Suffolk Place-Names*, English Place-Name Society (Nottingham, 2016)

Britnell, R.H., '*Advantagium mercatoris*: A Custom in Medieval English Trade', *Nottingham Medieval Studies* 24 (1980), pp. 37–50

Burrow, C., 'Sir Thomas Wyatt (*c.* 1503–1542), Poet and Ambassador', with a subsection on Sir Henry Wyatt (*c.* 1460–1536), *ODNB* (2004)

Copinger, W.A., *The Manors of Suffolk: Notes on Their History and Devolution; Volume 1, The Hundreds of Babergh and Blackbourn* (London, 1905); *Volume 3, The Hundreds of Carlford and Colneis, Cosford and Hartismere* (Manchester, 1909)

Coss, P., 'Neifs and Villeins in Later Medieval England', *Reading Medieval Studies* 40 (2014), pp. 192–202

Croot, P., *The World of the Small Farmer: Tenure, Profit and Politics in the Early Modern Somerset Levels* (Hatfield, 2017)

Drew, J.S., 'Manorial Accounts of St Swithun's Priory, Winchester', *EHR* 62 (January 1947), pp. 20–41 (reprinted in E.M. Carus-Wilson (ed.), *Essays in Economic History* 2 (London, 1962), pp. 12–30

Du Boulay, F.R.H., *The Lordship of Canterbury: An Essay on Medieval Society* (London, 1966)

Dyer, C., 'Changes in Diet in the Late Middle Ages: The Case of Harvest Workers', *AgHR* 36 (1988), pp. 21–37

— 'Sheepcotes: Evidence for Medieval Sheepfarming', *Medieval Archaeology* 39, no. 1 (1995), pp. 136–64

Faith, R., *The English Peasantry and the Growth of Lordship* (London and Washington, 1997)

— 'Social Theory and Agrarian Practice in Early Medieval England: The Land without *Polyptyques*', *Revue belge de philologie et d'histoire* 90, no. 2 (2012), pp. 299–314

Firth, C. H. and R.S. Rait (eds), *Acts and Ordinances of the Interregnum, 1642–1660* (London, 1911)

Goult, W., *A Survey of Suffolk Parish History* (Ipswich, 1990)

Harlow, C.G., 'Robert Ryece of Preston, 1555–1638', *PSIAH* 32, no. 1 (1970), pp. 43–69

Harvey, P.D.A., 'The Pipe Rolls and the Adoption of Demesne Farming in England', *EcHR* 2nd Series, 27 (1974), pp. 345–59

— 'Manorial Records', in M. Faull (ed.), P.D.A. Harvey and S. Thomas, *Medieval Manorial Records* (Leeds, 1983)

— *Manorial Records*, British Records Association Series Archives and the User no. 5 (London, 1984, revised 1999)

Hearnshaw, F.J.C., *Leet Jurisdiction in England Especially as Illustrated by the Records of the Court Leet of Southampton* (Southampton, 1908)

Hervey, Lord F. (ed.), *Suffolk in the XVIIth Century: The Breviary of Suffolk by Robert Reyce, 1618* (London, 1902)

Hervey, S.H.A. (ed.), *Suffolk in 1524, Being the Return for a Subsidy Granted in 1523, with Map of Suffolk in Hundreds* (Suffolk Green Books 10, 1910)

Hone, N.J., *The Manor and Manorial Records* (London, 1912)

Horrox, R, 'Pole, John de la, Earl of Lincoln (*c.* 1460–1487)', *ODNB* (2004)

Hudson, W. (ed.), *Leet Jurisdiction in the City of Norwich during the XIIIth and XIVth Centuries with a Short Notice of Its Later History and Decline from the Rolls in the Possession of the Corporation* (London, Selden Society Vol. 5, 1892)

Ives, E.W., *The Common Lawyers of Pre-Reformation England: Thomas Kebell, a Case Study* (New York, 1983)

313

— 'Thomas Kebell (*c*. 1439–1500)', *ODNB* (2004)

— 'Hobart, Sir James (d. 1517)', *ODNB* (2004)

Keynes, S. 'Æthelred II [Ethelred; Known as Ethelred the Unready] (*c*. 966–8–1016)', *ODNB* (2004)

Lamond, E. (ed.), *Walter of Henley's Husbandry, together with an Anonymous Husbandry Seneschaucie and Robert Grosseteste's Rules*, with an introduction by W. Cunningham (London, 1890)

Langdon, J., 'The Economics of Horses and Oxen in Medieval England', *AgHR* 30, no. 1 (1982), pp. 31–40

— *Horses, Oxen and Technological Innovation: The Use of Draught Animals in English Farming from 1066 to 1500* (New York and Cambridge, 1986)

Maitland, F.W., *Domesday Book and Beyond: Three Essays in the Early History of England* (Cambridge, 1907)

Mate, M., 'The Farming Out of Manors: A New Look at the Evidence from Canterbury Cathedral Priory', *Journal of Medieval History* 9, no. 4 (1983), pp. 331–43

Metcalfe, W.C. (ed.), *Visitations of Essex Made by Hawley, 1552; Hervey, 1558; Cooke, 1570; Raven, 1612 and Owen and Lilly, 1634* (London, 1878)

— (ed.), *The Visitations of Suffolk Made by Hervey, Clarenceux, 1561; Cooke, Clarenceux, 1577 and Raven, Richmond Herald, 1612, with Notes and an Appendix of Additional Suffolk Pedigrees* (Exeter, 1882)

Mills, A.D., *Suffolk Place-Names: Their Origins and Meanings* (Monks Eleigh, 2014)

Moor, E., *Suffolk Words and Phrases* (Woodbridge, 1823)

Neilson, N., 'Customary Rents', no. IV in Paul Vinogradoff (ed.), *Oxford Studies in Social and Legal History* 2 (Oxford, 1910)

Nichols, J.F., '*Custodia Essexae*: A Study of the Conventual Property Held by the Priory of Christ Church, Canterbury in the Counties of Essex, Suffolk and Norfolk' (London University PhD Thesis, 1930)

Northcote, A.F., *Notes on the History of Monks' Eleigh* (Ipswich, 1930)

Oschinsky, O. (ed.), *Walter of Henley and other Treatises on Estate Management and Accountancy* (Oxford, 1971)

Page, M., 'The Technology of Medieval Sheep Farming: Some Evidence from Crawley, Hampshire, 1208–1349', *AgHR* 51, no. 2 (2003), pp. 137–54

Page, W. (ed.), *Victoria History of the County of Suffolk: Volume 2* (London, 1907, reprinted 1975 and see websites below)

— (ed.), *Victoria History of the County of Kent: Volume 2* (London, 1926 and see websites below)

Pratt, D., 'Demesne Exemption from Royal Taxation in Anglo-Saxon and Anglo-Norman England', *EHR* 128, no. 530 (February 2013)

Tilahun, G., A. Feuerverger and M. Gervers, 'Dating Medieval English Charters', *The Annals of Applied Statistics* 6, no. 4 (2012), pp. 1615–40

Reaney, P.H., 'Early Essex Clergy', *Essex Review* 49 (1940)

— 'Lafham', *PSIAH* 28, no. 1 (1958), p. 101

Redstone, V.B., 'Calendar of Pre-Reformation Wills, Testaments, Probates, Administrations, Registered at the Probate Office, Bury St Edmunds', *PSIAH* 12, no. 3 (1906)

Reynolds, S., 'Tenure and Property in Medieval England', *Historical Research* 88, no. 242 (November 2015), pp. 563–76

Robertson, J.C., *Materials for the Life of Thomas Becket* (London, 1875)

Saltman, A., *Theobald, Archbishop of Canterbury* (London, 1956)

Segui, S., 'The Hue and Cry in Medieval English Towns', *Historical Research* 87, no. 236 (May 2014), pp. 179–93

Slavin, P., 'Goose Management and Rearing in Late Medieval Eastern England, *c.* 1250–1400', *AgHR* 58, no. 1 (2010), pp. 1–29

Smith, R.A.L., *Canterbury Cathedral Priory: A Study in Monastic Administration* (Cambridge, 1943)

Stone, E., 'Profit-and-Loss Accountancy at Norwich Cathedral Priory', *Transactions of the Royal Historical Society* 5th Series, 12 (1962), pp. 25–48

Summerson, H., 'Robert of Thornham [Turnham] (d. 1211)', *ODNB* (2004)

Sutton, A., 'Book Review: E.W. Ives, *The Common Lawyers of Pre-Reformation England*', *The Ricardian* 6 (March 1984), pp. 311–13

Weller, J.B., *Medieval Investment: Demesne Buildings within Christ Church Priory, Canterbury, 1285–1322; Fixed Equipment and Agricultural Productivity; based on Prior Henry of Eastry's Memorandum: Nova Opera Henrici Prioris* (Bildeston, 1986)

— 'The Wives of Sir James Hobart (1440–1517), Attorney-General 1486–1507', *The Ricardian* 12 (March 2001), pp. 218–48

— 'The Manor of Eleigh Monachorum (Monks Eleigh, Suffolk): Lease of Demesne 21 November 1400', *Suffolk Review*, New Series 45 (Autumn 2005), pp. 2–15; transcript of the 1400 lease of the manor in J.B. Weller, 'Appendix A: Lease of Manor, 21 November 1400', *Suffolk Review*, New Series 46 (Spring 2006), pp. 42–44

Witney, K.P., 'Kentish Land Measurements of the Thirteenth Century', *Archaeologia Cantiana* 109 (1991), pp. 29–40

Woods, M., *Medieval Hadleigh: The Chief Manor and the Town* (Layham, 2018)

WEBSITES

AgHR online via https://www.bahs.org.uk/AGHRvolumes.html

Aldous, Vivienne, Suffolk Records Society online list of Monks Eleigh manorial documents, most of which are held at Canterbury Cathedral Archives, https://suffolkrecordssociety.com

Anglo-American Legal Tradition (AALT), http://aalt.law.uh.edu/AALT.html, includes digital images of specific Suffolk feet of fines referred to in the text in respect of Charter 3 (1191–1213), online at http://aalt.law.uh.edu/AALT7/CP25(1)/CP25_1_213_7-18/IMG_0208.htm and http://aalt.law.uh.edu/AALT7/CP25(1)/CP25_1_213_7-18/IMG_0371.htm

Bell, A.R., C. Brooks and H. Killick, 'The First Real Estate Bubble? Land Prices and Rents in Medieval England *c.* 1300-1500' (ICMA Centre, published online 26 March 2018 via https://www.icmacentre.ac.uk/research/projects/land-prices-rents-medieval-england

British History Online, https://www.british-history.ac.uk includes the text of *VCH Kent 2*; *VCH Suffolk 2*; A.B. Beaven, *The Aldermen of the City of London Temp. Henry III – 1912* (London, 1908, 1912); C.H. Firth and R.S. Rait (eds), *Acts and Ordinances of the Interregnum, 1642–1660* (London, 1911); H.C. Maxwell Lyte (ed.), *Calendar of Close Rolls, Edward I: Volume 1, 1272–1279* (London, 1900); H.C. Maxwell Lyte (ed.), *Calendar of Patent Rolls, Edward I: Volume 4, 1301–1307* (London, 1898); C. Flower, M.C.B. Dawes and A.C. Wood (eds), *Calendar of Inquisitions Post Mortem, Henry VII*, volume III (London, 1955)

British Library catalogues online via https://www.bl.uk/

Canterbury Cathedral Archives online catalogue via https://archives.canterbury-cathedral.org/CalmView/Default.aspx

Canterbury Cathedral Library and Archives Image Gallery online via https://ims.canterbury-cathedral.org/viewcontainer.tlx?containerid=13959251850

DEEDS (Documents of Early England Data Set) Research Project, the University of Toronto's database of medieval charters and other property deeds, online at https://deeds.library.utoronto.ca/

Dictionary of Medieval Latin from British Sources online via the Logeion website at https://logeion.uchicago.edu/lexidium

Fawcett, C., 'A Clove of Gillyflower at Christmas', University of Nottingham Special Collections blog post at http://blogs.nottingham.ac.uk/manuscripts/2011/12/20/a-clove-of-gillyflower-at-christmas/

Googlebooks via https://books.google.co.uk/, which includes W. Hardy (ed.), 'Calendar of Patent Rolls for 2 Edward I (1273–74)', being Appendix I, no. 4 in *Forty-Third Annual Report of the Deputy Keeper of the Public Records* (London, 1882)

Goult, W., *A Survey of Suffolk Parish History* (Ipswich, 1990), digital copy online via Suffolk Heritage Explorer website at https://heritage.suffolk.gov.uk/parish-histories

The Internet Archive via https://archive.org/ includes a great many digital texts of out-of-copyright published works

Middle English Dictionary (*MED*) online at https://quod.lib.umich.edu/m/middle-english-dictionary/dictionary

ODNB online at https://www.oxforddnb.com/

PSIAH online via https://www.suffolkinstitute.org.uk/

Records of London's Livery Companies Online: Apprentices and Freemen 1400–1900 website at https://www.londonroll.org/

Suffolk Archives online catalogue via https://www.suffolkarchives.co.uk/ (many Suffolk Archives entries also in TNA's online catalogue, below)

TNA online catalogue at http://discovery.nationalarchives.gov.uk/

INDEX OF PEOPLE AND PLACES

Spelling was completely unstandardised for the whole period of the documents in this volume and many names are spelt in various different ways (some of them in very many ways) even within the same document, presenting obvious difficulties for the indexer. Because both original and modern spellings of place–names have been given throughout the main text, place-names have been gathered together in the index under their modern spelling, which should make them easy to find in the text. For surnames, however, this index tries to standardise surnames according to the commonest spelling in the documents, which is not always the modern standard (e.g. Marescall in preference to the modern Marshall), giving alternatives afterwards and with cross-references from any obvious modern equivalent which might apply. This should allow people mentioned in this volume to be matched up with those in other contemporary original documents or older published works which refer to them in their original form, such as Anselm de Ylleg' in the Feet of Fines (p. 4 n. 10) for example.

Toponyms are very often not spelt in the form of the modern place-name. Where the spelling of a toponym *never* appears the same as the modern place-name spelling, the commonest historical usage from the documents has been used, and cross-referenced from the modern place-name and any variants. Many early personal names are single names without surnames, although some give relationships such as parents, spouses or siblings and context can supply other connections. I have tried to group these sensibly so that the user will find them in their particular contexts, so there are lists under the most common toponyms as well as under 'Canterbury, Christ Church Priory monks and officials' and 'Monks Eleigh: tenants with only one name' (the majority of such single names being under the last of these). These contextualised groupings have not been cross-referenced for most names, although if there are particular people who cross over between them, a cross-reference is given (e.g. Hugh the hayward, whose occupation gradually becomes a surname for his descendants, almost universally spelt 'Heyward' in the documents).

Another large sub-group relates to sub-place-names, mostly within the manor and parish of Monks Eleigh (which is where they appear in the index), but some are also in the parishes Milden, Lindsey, Hitcham and Kettlebaston. Sub-place-names link tenants to their holdings in a personal and often long-standing way, so to help make sense of the inter-relationship and development of holdings (which could be split or joined together over time) I make no apology for including them.

Page numbers in **bold** type refer to illustrations and their captions.

Parkerysweye in Hitcham 194
Peperispyghtyl, at the gate of
Parkerysweye 194
Puntockes 244, 271, 293
Rushes or Bushes [*recte Rushes*] 228,
245, 271, 293
Wallowe, Walowe, Meadow 244, 271,
293
Hobard(e), Hobart(e), Hob(b)erd(e), Hob(b)
ert(e), Hub(b)ard(e), Hu(b)berd(e),
Hu(b)bert(e), Haberd 176
Alyce [*?wife of John Coppin*] 235–6,
242
Alyce, widow 180
Andrew 237, 262, 268–9, 291
Dorothy, daughter of Thomas, wife of
Rauffe Bendyshe 217 n.56
Geoffrey 83, 157, 159, 161–2, 165,
169–1, 173, 176, 199, 217, 219, 223
George 237, 247, 251–2, 262, 277
James, gentleman 177, 223, 226, 229,
230, 233, 235, 236, 237, 238, 242,
247, 250, 254, 257, 268
Sir James, judge and attorney-general to
Henry VII li, 179, 201, 203 n.27,
208 n.30, 210, 212–13, 215–16, 219,
295, n.4
John 102, 109, 113, 156, 159, 161–3,
165–6, 170–6, 190–1, 195, 198,
206–8, 210–1, 219, 278
John, brother of Thomas 119
John the elder 206–7
John of Kettlebaston 101
John, son of John 117, 158
John, son of William 205
Nicholas 177, 206, 208, 211, 214
Nicholas, gentleman 180, 217, 222, 226,
233, 236, 238, 241, 247, 250
Nicholas, son of William of Monks
Eleigh, clothmaker 206–7, 295–6,
298–302
Nicholas, the younger 179
Richard 177, 179, 202, 211, 223
Richard, of Stackwood 203
S 235
Stephen 225, 229, 231, 234–5, 237, 240,
247, 250, 252–3, 258, 261–3, 268,
273, 279, 281, 286
Thomas 126, 129, 130–1, 159, 161, 163,
166, 169–70, 172–4, 176, 179, 189,

191, 201, 209, 211, 214–16, 218,
228–9, 237
Thomas, brother of John 119
Thomas the elder, son of William of
Monks Eleigh, clothmaker 295–6,
298–302
Thomas, esquire, gentleman, of Leyham,
nephew of Sir James 201, 203 and
n.27, 209–11, 213, 217 n.56
his bequest of almshouses 203 n.27,
234, 257
his daughter Dorothy, wife of Rauffe
Bendyshe 217 n.56
Thomas, father of William 206–7
Thomas, of Fen Street, Monks
Eleigh 201 n.22, 207, 211
Thomas, of Milden 180
Thomas, of Preston 133
Thomas, the younger 175–6
Walter, son of William 210
William 177, 186–90, 197–8, 203, 209,
211
William, eldest brother of Sir James li
William, father of Nicholas and son of
Thomas 206–7
William, father of Walter 210
William, of Gedeford 203
William, gentleman, the elder of Monks
Eleigh, clothmaker li–iii, 217, 219,
223–4, 236, 256, 261–4, 273, 280,
287, 295–301
heirs of Mr 287
his widow, Mrs Barlore 287
William, of Stakwod 202
William of Swyngildon 211
William, the younger 209
Hodman, Simon 153
Hog, William 13
Hogoun, Seman, clerk 147, 148, 150
Holdayn, Symon 149
Holdeyn 169
Holle, John 107
Holemere, John de 109
Holeton, – de 10 n.42
Holm, John 161, 168, 173
Holmes, John 170, 218 n.70, 223
Holton St Mary 10 n.42
Honeman, *see* Huneman
Hony, John 164
Honynges, Mr 226

345

INDEX OF SUBJECTS

Page numbers in **bold** type refer to illustrations and their captions.

359

361

THE SUFFOLK RECORDS SOCIETY

For over sixty years, the Suffolk Records Society has added to the knowledge of Suffolk's history by issuing an annual volume of previously unpublished manuscripts, each throwing light on some new aspect of the history of the county.

Covering 700 years and embracing letters, diaries, maps, accounts and other archives, many of them previously little known or neglected, these books have together made a major contribution to historical studies.

At the heart of this achievement lie the Society's members, all of whom share a passion for Suffolk and its history and whose support, subscriptions and donations make possible the opening up of the landscape of historical research in the area.

In exchange for this tangible support, members receive a new volume each year at a considerable saving on the retail price at which the books are then offered for sale.

Members are also welcomed to the launch of the new volume, held each year in a different and appropriate setting within the county and giving them a chance to meet and listen to some of the leading historians in their fields talking about their latest work.

For anyone with a love of history, a desire to build a library on Suffolk themes at modest cost and a wish to see historical research continue to thrive and bring new sources to the public eye in decades to come, a subscription to the Suffolk Records Society is the ideal way to make a contribution and join the company of those who give Suffolk history a future.

THE CHARTERS SERIES

To supplement the annual volumes and serve the needs of medieval historians, the Charters Series was launched in 1979 with the challenge of publishing the transcribed texts of all the surviving monastic charters for the county. Since then, nineteen volumes have been published as an occasional series, the latest in 2018.

The Charter Series is financed by a separate annual subscription leading to receipt of each volume on publication.

CURRENT PROJECTS

Volumes approved by the Council of the Society for future publication include *The Records of Medieval Newmarket*, edited by James Davis and Joanne Sear, and *The Incorporated Hundreds of Suffolk*, edited by John Shaw; and in the Charters Series, *Bury St Edmunds Town Charters*, edited by Vivien Brown, and *Rumburgh Priory Charters*, edited by Nicholas Karn. The order in which these and other volumes appear in print will depend on the dates of completion of editorial work.

MEMBERSHIP

Membership enquiries should be addressed to Mrs Tanya Christian, 8 Orchid Way, Needham Market, IP6 8JQ; e-mail: suffolkrecordssociety@gmail.com

The Suffolk Records Society is a registered charity, no. 1084279.